# understanding human communication

# understanding
# human
# communication TWELFTH EDITION

**Ronald B. Adler**

SANTA BARBARA CITY COLLEGE, EMERITUS

**George Rodman**

BROOKLYN COLLEGE
CITY UNIVERSITY OF NEW YORK

**Athena du Pré**

UNIVERSITY OF WEST FLORIDA

NEW YORK   OXFORD
OXFORD UNIVERSITY PRESS

Oxford University Press is a department of the University of Oxford.
It furthers the University's objective of excellence in research,
scholarship, and education by publishing worldwide.

Oxford   New York
Auckland   Cape Town   Dar es Salaam   Hong Kong   Karachi
Kuala Lumpur   Madrid   Melbourne   Mexico City   Nairobi
New Delhi   Shanghai   Taipei   Toronto

With offices in
Argentina   Austria   Brazil   Chile   Czech Republic   France   Greece
Guatemala   Hungary   Italy   Japan   Poland   Portugal   Singapore
South Korea   Switzerland   Thailand   Turkey   Ukraine   Vietnam

For titles covered by Section 112 of the US Higher Education
Opportunity Act, please visit www.oup.com/us/he for the
latest information about pricing and alternate formats.

Published by Oxford University Press
198 Madison Avenue, New York, New York 10016
http://www.oup.com

**Library of Congress Cataloging-in-Publication Data**

Adler, Ronald B. (Ronald Brian), 1946–
   Understanding human communication / Ronald B. Adler, Santa Barbara City
College; George Rodman, Brooklyn College, City University of New York; Athena
du Pré, University of West Florida. — Twelfth Edition.
      pages cm
   Includes bibliographical references and index.
   1. Communication. 2. Interpersonal communication. I. Rodman, George R.,
1948– II. du Pré, Athena. III. Title.
   P90.A32 2014
   302.2—dc23
                                                      2013031831

Printing number: 9 8 7 6 5 4 3 2

Printed in the United States of America
on acid-free paper

# Brief Contents

# Contents

**CHAPTER 3**    **Communication and Culture**  75

## PART TWO: COMMUNICATION ELEMENTS

**CHAPTER 4**    **Language**  101

---

**CHAPTER 5** Listening 133

---

**CHAPTER 6** Nonverbal Communication 167

## PART THREE: INTERPERSONAL COMMUNICATION

### CHAPTER 7  Understanding Interpersonal Communication  197

### CHAPTER 8  Improving Interpersonal Relationships  237

## PART FOUR: COMMUNICATION IN GROUPS

### CHAPTER 9  Communicating in Groups and Teams  267

---

**CHAPTER 10   Solving Problems in Groups and Teams** 297

---

PART FIVE: **PUBLIC COMMUNICATION**

**CHAPTER 11   Preparing and Presenting Your Speech** 325

## CHAPTER 12  Organization and Support  353

## CHAPTER 13  Informative Speaking  379

**ALSO AVAILABLE:**

Two **bonus chapters** on **Mass Communication** and on **Communication and Service Learning** for download at www.oup.com/us/adler. Instructors: Contact your OUP sales representative or call (800) 280-0280 to order print copies.

# Preface

For some time we have noted that the title of this book, *Understanding Human Communication,* is misleading in two ways.

On one hand, the title promises too little. Helping readers *understand* the nature of human communication is certainly one goal of this book. But beyond comprehension, we hope students will learn ways to *apply* their newfound knowledge, thereby becoming more skillful communicators in their everyday lives.

On the other hand, this book's title promises too much. It's unrealistic to expect that any introduction will give readers a comprehensive understanding of such a complex subject. For that reason, we've come to realize that a more accurate title would be *Beginning to Understand Human Communication.* One measure of success is the degree to which students leave the introductory course wanting to learn more about this fascinating and important subject.

After 12 editions, it's too late to change the book's title. Nonetheless, a quick look at the contents should make our goal clear: to provide an engaging, comprehensive, useful introduction to the academic study of human communication as it is practiced in the 21st century.

We remain convinced that the best test of this book's success in achieving this goal is to ask three questions: Is its content important? Is the material clear? Is it useful? These three questions allow us to develop a comprehensive exploration of human communication that will be truly meaningful to students. You are the best judge of how well we have succeeded.

## Approach

This 12th edition builds on the approach that has served well over half a million students and their professors. Rather than take sides in the theory vs. skills debate that often rages in our discipline, *Understanding Human Communication* treats scholarship and skill development as mutually reinforcing. Its reader-friendly approach strives to present material clearly without being overly simplistic. Examples on virtually every page make concepts clear and interesting. An elegant, contemporary design makes the material inviting, as do amusing and instructive cartoons and photos that link concepts in the text to today's world.

## New to This Edition

Beyond its engaging appearance and user-friendly voice, this edition reflects both the growth of scholarship and changing trends in the academic marketplace. Long-time users will discover not only a more contemporary look and feel but expanded coverage of key concepts and a wealth of new learning tools.

### New Content

- **Expanded coverage of social media** plus new and updated "Understanding Communication Technology" boxes highlight the increasingly important role of technology in human communication. New examples throughout the text include discussions of how communication in today's world differs from that of previous eras (Chapter 1); how to shape and manage online identities (Chapter 2); how close relationships can develop online, even before people have met in person (Chapter 7); how to manage conflict in mediated relationships (Chapter 8); and how to work in virtual teams (Chapter 9). In addition to material in the main narrative covering social media, new "Understanding Communication Technology" boxes highlight notable topics, including technology as culture (Chapter 3), the unique language of Twitter (Chapter 4), the nature of "listening" in social media (Chapter 5), and developing trust in long-distance communication (Chapter 10).

- Chapter 3 is now devoted entirely to **communication and culture**, and new and updated "Understanding Diversity" boxes throughout the book further explore cultural influences on communication. A major portion of Chapter 3 focuses on cocultural factors that students are likely to encounter close to home every day. Dimensions addressed include ethnicity, regional differences, gender/sexual orientation, religion, physical abilities, age/generation, and socioeconomic status. The discussion of culture extends throughout the book, most visibly in "Understanding Diversity" boxes. New boxes in this edition explore the validity of "gaydar" in detecting sexual orientation (Chapter 6), the nature of communication in opposite-sex friendships (Chapter 7), cultural differences in managing conflict (Chapter 8), and the value of multicultural membership in task-oriented groups (Chapter 10).

- We have strengthened and updated coverage of **communication strategies for career success** in an expanded career appendix and "@Work" boxes throughout the text. Topics in the main text include the role of effective listening in leadership (Chapter 5), the pros and cons of independence versus working in teams (Chapter 9), and the role of "followership" (Chapter 10). The appendix, "Communicating for Career Success," contains advice on how to communicate professionally in seeking employment and once on the job.

- **Revised and expanded discussions of gender, gender roles, and sexual orientation** (particularly in Chapter 4) highlight the evolving relationship between gender and communication.

- **Expanded coverage of communication apprehension** features tips, exercises, and activities to help students become more confident speakers.

- We have incorporated **new scholarship** throughout this edition. For example, Chapter 2 discusses biological factors that shape the self-concept and clarifies the differences between biological sex and gender as they apply to communication. Chapter 4 offers updated coverage of gender and language use. Chapter 5 introduces a new research-tested typology of listening styles. The coverage of nonverbal communication in Chapter 6 contains substantially updated discussions of deception cues, gender, and power. Chapter 7 explores personal preferences for expressing intimacy, and Chapter 8 explores the link between close relationships and physical health. Chapters 11 through 14 all contain new sample speeches on a variety of interesting and timely topics, each with detailed commentary illustrating how principles of effective speaking work in real life.

## New Learning Tools

- **Self-assessments** in every chapter invite students to evaluate and improve their communication skills and to consider their identities as communicators.

- **Chapter-opening profiles** of real people highlight real communication challenges and are woven into the fabric of the chapter content. Questions at the end of the communicator profiles prompt students to connect the material to their own lives.

- **"On Your Feet"** prompts get students speaking in class, even before the public speaking unit, to give them the practice they need to be confident, effective speakers.

- **Checklists** in the public speaking chapters are handy reference tools to help students build their skill sets and internalize what they have learned.

- **"Check Your Understanding"** questions at the end of each chapter echo the learning objectives in the chapter opener. These not only test comprehension but also help students apply the material to their everyday lives.

- Provocative **marginal questions** throughout the book encourage students to link the material to their own experiences, such as how they communicate through social media.

- **New captioned photos** capture the role of communication in everyday life by shining a spotlight on popular films and television programming as well as public figures and popular themes.

## Support for Teaching and Learning

An **enhanced support package** for every chapter (described in detail below) includes video links, pre- and post-reading quizzes, activities, discussion topics, examples, tools for recording and uploading student speeches for assessment, an online gradebook, and more.

# Hallmark Features

Although we have developed many new features for this edition, we have retained and fine-tuned hallmark features to support student success.

- **"Understanding Communication Technology"** boxes focus on topics such as how social media can meet a variety of communication needs, the etiquette of revealing what you've learned about others online, and the dangers of being overly connected via the Internet.

- **"Understanding Diversity"** boxes address subjects such as managing identity during the process of "coming out," the potential for misunderstandings during translation from one language to another, and how lessons from other cultures can enhance listening skills.

- **"@Work"** boxes show students how key concepts from the text operate in the workplace. Topics include how multitasking can interfere with face-to-face interaction, building social capital for career enhancement, and dealing with sexual harassment.

- **"Ethical Challenge"** boxes engage students in debates such as whether honesty is always the best policy, the acceptability of presenting multiple identities, and how to deal effectively with difficult group members.

- **Short selected readings** show how elements of communication operate in contemporary society.

- Marginal **cultural idioms** not only highlight the use of idioms in communication but also help nonnative English speakers understand expressions and colloquialisms.

- Each chapter includes an outline, learning objectives, a list of the boldfaced key terms and their definitions, and a wealth of activities. A glossary is included at the back of the text.

## Optional Chapters

Along with the topics included in the text itself, custom chapters are available on **Mass Communication** and on **Communication and Service Learning**. Ask your Oxford University Press representative for details, or see the *Understanding Human Communication* website at **www.oup.com/us/adler.**

## Ancillary Package

This edition of *Understanding Human Communication* contains a results-oriented package of ancillary materials that will make teaching more efficient and learning more effective. As the world has changed, so has the need for learning materials that support this textbook. Adopters of *Understanding Human Communication*, 12th Edition, will be pleased to find a complete suite of supplements—online and print—for students and instructors.

### Online Learning

This edition of *Understanding Human Communication* offers new options for online learning:

- **Dashboard** *(access code required)*: The Dashboard platform by Oxford University Press delivers high-quality content, tools, and assessments to track student progress in an intuitive, Web-based learning environment.
  - Dashboard gives instructors the ability to manage digital content from *Understanding Human Communication*, 12th Edition, and its supplements in order to make assignments, administer tests, and track student progress.
    Assessments are designed to accompany this text and are automatically graded so that instructors can easily check students' progress as they complete their assignments. The color-coded gradebook illustrates at a glance where students are succeeding and where they can improve.
  - With Dashboard, students have access to a variety of interactive study tools designed to enhance their learning experience, including critical thinking activities and questions; multiple choice pre- and posttests to accompany each chapter; a frequently updated YouTube channel with clips from films, television shows, ads, and Internet videos that illustrate key communication concepts and theories; and sample speeches.
  - Dashboard is engineered to be simple, informative, and mobile. All Dashboard content is engineered to work on mobile devices, including iOS platforms.

- **Course cartridges:** As an alternative to Dashboard, instructors may order course cartridges by contacting their Oxford University Press sales representative.

- **Companion website** *(free)*: An open-access student website at **www.oup .com/us/adler** offers practice quizzes, flashcards, and other study tools. This companion site is perfect for students who are looking for a little extra study material online. For instructors, a password-protected part of this site includes the Instructor's Manual, with PowerPoint lecture slides and Prezi presentations.

Contact your OUP sales representative or call **(800) 280-0280** for more information on these options for online learning.

## For Instructors

- The **Instructor's Manual and Test Bank** (print) provides the largest, most comprehensive support package of any text for this course. The Instructor's Manual includes teaching tips and course information for multiple course formats (including face-to-face, hybrid, and online courses), chapter-by-chapter overviews, objectives, critical thinking and classroom activities, speaking opportunities, short in-class quizzes, premade handouts, and suggested online readings. The comprehensive Test Bank includes 60 exam questions per chapter in multiple-choice, short-answer, and essay formats. The questions have been extensively revised for this edition, are labeled according to difficulty, and include the page reference and chapter section where the answers may be found.

- The **Instructor's CD and Computerized Test Bank** includes the full Instructor's Manual, a computerized test bank, and prebuilt, editable PowerPoint-based and Prezi lecture presentations to accompany each chapter of the main book.

- Instructors wishing to access either the **password-protected section of the companion website at www.oup.com/us/adler** or Dashboard (described above) should contact their OUP sales representative or call **(800) 280-0280**.

- *Now Playing*, **Instructor's Edition** (print) includes an introduction on how to incorporate film and television clips in class, as well as even more film examples, viewing guides and assignments, a complete set of sample responses to the discussion questions in the student edition, a full list of references, and an index by subject for ease of use. *Now Playing* also has an accompanying companion website at **www.oup.com/us/nowplaying**, which features descriptions of films from previous editions and selected film clips. A Netflix subscription is available to adopters of the *Understanding Human Communication/Now Playing* package—instructors should contact their OUP sales representative or call **(800) 280-0280** for access.

- **Companion website**: A password-protected section of the website at **www .oup.com/us/adler** offers instructors access to the Instructor's Manual, including both PowerPoint-based and Prezi slides for every chapter. These visual aids do more than summarize chapter content. They take the work out of class preparation by presenting ready-to-go lessons complete with live video links, learning activities, discussion prompts, and more. Contact your OUP sales representative or call **(800) 280-0280** for access.

## For Students

- *Now Playing* (print), available free in a package with a new copy of the book, looks at contemporary films and television shows through the lens of communication principles. Originally conceived and written by Russell F. Proctor II of Northern Kentucky University and updated yearly by Darin Garard of Santa Barbara City College, *Now Playing* illustrates how communication concepts play out in a variety of situations, using a mass medium that is interactive, familiar, and easily accessible to students. *Now Playing* also has an accompanying companion website at **www.oup.com/us/nowplaying**, which features descriptions of films and selected film clips.

- The **Student Success Manual** (print) is packed with tips that will guide students to mastering the course material. It includes a primer on effective study habits as well as chapter-specific information such as outlines, key terms, review questions, and critical thinking exercises. It is available free in a package with a new copy of the book.

- A free **companion website** at **www.oup.com/us/adler** offers access to activities, quizzes, tutorials, flashcards, speech ideas, and more.

## E-Book

An e-version of this book is available through CourseSmart.

## Acknowledgments

Anyone involved with creating a textbook knows that success isn't possible without the contributions of many people.

We owe a debt to our colleagues whose reviews helped shape the edition you are holding. In particular, we wish to thank **Leeva Chung** of the University of San Diego for her insightful comments on Chapter 3, along with the following reviewers commissioned by Oxford University Press:

**Deanna Armentrout**
West Virginia University

**Miki Bacino-Thiessen**
Rock Valley College

**Marie Baker-Ohler**
Northern Arizona University

**Kimberly Batty-Herbert**
South Florida Community College

**Mark Bergmooser**
Monroe County Community College

**Shepherd Bliss**
Sonoma State University

**Cheryl Chambers**
Mississippi State University

**Kelly Crue**
Saint Cloud Technical & Community College

**Amber Davies-Sloan**
Yavapai College

**Sarah Fogle**
Embry-Riddle Aeronautical University

**Cole Franklin**
East Texas Baptist University

**Betsy Gordon**
McKendree University

**Sharon Grice**
Kirkwood Community College–Cedar Rapids

**Deborah Hill**
Sauk Valley Community College

**Brittany Hochstaetter**
Wake Technical Community College

**Kimberly Kline**
University of Texas at San Antonio

**Carol Knudson**
Gateway Tech College–Kenosha

**Kara Laskowski**
Shippensburg University

**Natashia Lopez-Gomez**
Notre Dame De Namur University

**Jennifer McCullough**
Kent State University

**Brenda Meyer**
Anoka Ramsey Community College–Cambridge

**Randy Mueller**
Gateway Technical College, Kenosha

**Gregg Nelson**
Chippewa Valley Technical College, River Falls

**Stacey A. Peterson**
Notre Dame of Maryland University

**Robert Pucci**
SUNY Ulster

**Terry Quinn**
Gateway Technical College, Kenosha

**Dan Rogers**
Cedar Valley College

**Karen Solliday**
Gateway Technical College

**Don Taylor**
Blue Ridge Community College

**Cornelius Tyson**
Central Connecticut State University

**Kathy Wenell-Nesbit**
Chippewa Valley Technical College

**Shawnalee Whitney**
University of Alaska, Anchorage

**Jason Ziebart**
Central Carolina Community College

We also continue to be grateful to the many professors whose reviews of previous editions continue to bring value to this book: **Pete Bicak**, SUNY Rockland; **Brett N. Billman**, Bowling Green State University; **Beth Bryant**, Northern Virginia Community College, Loudoun; **Jo-Anne Bryant**, Troy State University–Montgomery; **Ironda Joyce Campbell**, Pierpont Community and Technical College; **Patricia Carr Connell**, Gadsden State Community College; **Dee Ann Curry**, McMurry University; **Heather Dorsey**, University of Minnesota; **Rebecca A. Ellison**, Jefferson College; **Gary G. Fallon**, Broward Community College and Miami International University of Art and Design; **Amber N. Finn**, Texas Christian University; **Mikako Garard**, Santa Barbara City College; **Samantha Gonzalez**, University of Hartford; **Lisa Katrina Hill**, Harrisburg Area Community College–Gettysburg Campus; **Emily Holler**, Kennesaw State University; **Maria Jaskot-Inclan**, Wilbur Wright College; **Kara Laskowski**, Shippensburg University of Pennsylvania; **Jennifer Lehtinen**, State University of New York at Orange; **Kurt Lindemann**, San Diego State University; **Judy Litterst**, St. Cloud State College; **Bruce C. McKinney**, University of North Carolina–Wilmington; **Jim Mignerey**, St. Petersburg College; **Kimberly M. Myers**, Manchester College and Indiana University–Purdue University Fort Wayne; **Catriona O'Curry**, Bellevue Community College; **Emily Osbun-Bermes**, Indiana University–Purdue University at Fort Wayne; **Doug Parry**, University of Alaska at Anchorage; **Daniel M. Paulnock**, Saint Paul College; **Cheryl Pawlowski**, University of Northern Colorado; **Kelly Aikin Petkus**, Austin Community College–Cypress Creek; **Russell F. Proctor**, Northern Kentucky University; **Shannon Proctor**, Highline Community College; **Elizabeth Ribarsky**, University of Illinois at Springfield; **Dan Robinette**, Eastern Kentucky University; **B. Hannah Rockwell**, Loyola University Chicago; **Theresa Rogers**, Baltimore City Community College, Liberty; **Michele Russell**, Northern Virginia Community College; **Gerald Gregory Scanlon**, Colorado Mountain College; **David Schneider**, Saginaw Valley State University; **Cady Short-Thompson**, Northern Kentucky University; **Patricia Spence**, Richland Community College; **Sarah Stout**, Kellogg Community College; **Curt VanGeison**, St. Charles Community College; **Robert W. Wawee**, The University of Houston–Downtown; **Princess Williams**, Suffolk County Community College; and **Rebecca Wolniewicz**, Southwestern College.

Many thanks are due to colleagues who developed and refined the package of ancillary materials that will help instructors teach more effectively and students succeed in mastering the material in this text. **Kimberly Batty-Herbert** of South Florida State College thoroughly updated and revised the Instructor's Manual, making it a useful and efficient teaching tool for instructors. This edition's Test Bank owes its content to the efforts of **Beth Gillis** of the College of DuPage, **Jesse Harver** of Virginia Polytechnic Institute and State University, **John James** of the University of West Florida, **Derrick Long** of Old Dominion University, **Jacki Brucher Moore** of Kirkwood Community College, and **Charlotte Toguchi** of Kapi'olani Community College. **Tanika Smith** of Prince George's Community College and **John James** of the University of West Florida created the array of online activities for both Dashboard and the open-access companion website, whereas **Jacki Brucher Moore** and **Beth Gillis** created the online tests and quizzes for both Dashboard and the companion website, providing excellent study guidance and learning assessment for students. **Dan Rogers** of Cedar Valley College authored the Student Success Manual, which contains major content updates and additions. This edition features newly designed and revised PowerPoint presentations for each chapter. **John James** worked with us to create slides that offer excellent visual guidance for both in-class and online settings. In addition to PowerPoint-based slides, James helped us create a set of Prezi presentations—Web-based, interactive presentations that provide a new and engaging learning experience for students. **Darin Garard** of Santa Barbara City College has continued to craft useful content for the annual *Now Playing* film and television supplement with a keen eye for movies, television shows, and scenes that offer relevant commentary for students in communication courses.

In an age when publishing is becoming increasingly corporate, impersonal, and sales driven, we continue to be grateful for the privilege and pleasure of working with the professionals at the venerable Oxford University Press. They blend the best old-school practices with cutting-edge thinking.

Our hardworking Editor, Mark T. Haynes, has invested more time and energy into this edition than any we've ever worked with. Development Editor Lauren Mine has been a true partner in developing this edition, and it's a far better product thanks to her input. A case could be made for including both Mark and Lauren as coauthors. Associate Editor Caitlin Kaufman has helped make this edition more useful for both instructors and students and took the lead on producing our new suite of ancillary materials, and Editorial Assistant Grace Ross has skillfully managed countless details. Senior Production Editor Barbara Mathieu's steady hand and Art Director Michele Laseau's design talents have transformed this project from a caterpillar-like manuscript into a butterfly. We are also grateful to the hardworking and talented Lisa Grzan, Managing Editor; to the eagle-eyed Laura Wilmot and Leslie Anglin for reviewing this manuscript; and to Susan Monahan for her indexing talents. We are especially thankful to Josh Hawkins for his suggestions about photos from feature films and television shows that appear throughout this book.

Finally, as always, we thank our families for their understanding and support while we've worked on this edition for more than a year. When it comes to communication, they are the best judges of whether we practice what we preach.

Ron Adler

George Rodman

Athena du Pré

# About the Authors

**Ronald B. Adler** is Professor of Communication, Emeritus, at Santa Barbara City College. He is coauthor of *Interplay: The Process of Interpersonal Communication*, Twelfth Edition (OUP, 2013), *Looking Out, Looking In* (2014), and *Communicating at Work: Principles and Practices for Business and the Professions* (2013).

**George Rodman** is Professor in the Department of Television and Radio at Brooklyn College, City University of New York, where he founded the graduate media studies program. He is the author of *Mass Media in a Changing World*, Fourth Edition (2012), *Making Sense of Media* (2001), and several books on public speaking.

**Athena du Pré** is Professor of Communication at the University of West Florida. She is the author of *Communicating About Health: Current Issues and Perspectives*, Fourth Edition (OUP, 2014), as well as other books, journal articles, and chapters on communicating effectively in modern organizations.

# understanding
# human
# communication

# Communication: What and Why

## Chapter Outline

## LEARNING OBJECTIVES

1 Apply the communication model described on pages 10–11 to a specific incident, explaining how that exchange is part of a relational, symbolic process.

2 Explain the ways in which communication technologies have changed over time.

3 Describe the similarities and differences between mediated and face-to-face communication.

4 Give examples of the various uses and gratifications of social media.

5 List and explain the key needs you and others attempt to satisfy by communicating.

6 Assess the degree to which communication in a specific situation is competent, and suggest ways of increasing the competence level.

7 Identify how misconceptions about communication can create problems, and suggest how a more accurate analysis of the situations can lead to better outcomes.

**As a child, Quint Studer** had hearing aids and a speech impediment. He struggled in school, and his slight build made him a target for bullies and ill equipped to fulfill his dream of becoming a major league baseball player. "My first two years of high school, I just tried not to get stuffed into my locker by the bigger guys," he says.

Today, Studer is one of the nation's most lauded public speakers, authors, and business leaders. He regularly makes the 100 Most Powerful People in Healthcare list,[1] and the consulting firm he founded has hundreds of clients. Studer didn't make it to the majors in baseball, but he and his wife, Rishy, now own a minor league team.

What catapults a shy child with the odds against him into a powerful and eloquent business leader? According to Studer, it has a great deal to do with communication: "The most important thing I learned was how to listen—really listen—to people. When people know you're going to listen and that you care about them, then, to-gether, you can make some amazing things happen."

Studer also knows how to reach an audience. He has been called "one of the world's most charismatic public speakers."[2] He regularly addresses groups of 1,000 or more, who pay upwards of $1,000 each to attend his talks. Studer says there are still words he can't pronounce. But audiences would never guess that. "Sometimes people think I'm pausing for effect," he says, laughing, "but I'm actually trying to find the right word—one that I can say."

In this chapter, we'll consider Studer's remarkable story as we explore the meaning of communication, key principles in communicating effectively, different types of communication, how communication affects our lives, and the impact of communication technology.

*Quint Studer wasn't voted "most likely to succeed" as a young man. Yet few people have accomplished as much as he has. You can use Studer's story as a springboard to envisioning your future.*

- What do you want your life to look like in 10 years? In what ways might communication skills help you reach your life goals?

- What communication strengths do you already possess that you can build on?

- What communication skills would you most like to improve?

Quint Studer's story makes a strong case for the importance of communication. But perhaps the strongest argument for studying this subject is its central role in our lives. The amount of time we spend communicating is staggering. In one study, researchers measured the amount of time a sample group of college students spent on various activities.[3] They found that the subjects spent an average of more than 61 percent of their waking hours engaged in some form of communication. Whatever one's occupation, the results of such a study wouldn't be too different. Most of us are surrounded by others, trying to understand them and hoping that they under-stand us: family, friends, coworkers, teachers, and strangers.

# Communication Defined

The term *communication* isn't as simple as it might seem. People use it in a variety of ways that are only vaguely related:

- A dog scratches at the back door, signaling its desire to be let out of the house.

- Data flows from one computer database to another in a cascade of electronic impulses.

- Strangers who live thousands of miles apart spot each other's postings on a social networking website, and they become friends through conversations via e-mail, text messaging, and instant messaging.

- Locals approach a group of confused-looking people who seem to be from out of town and ask if they can help.

- In her sermon, a religious leader encourages the congregation to get more involved in the community.

There is clearly some relationship among uses of the term such as these, but we need to narrow our focus before going on. A look at the table of contents of this book shows that it obviously doesn't deal with animals. Neither is it about Holy Communion, the bestowing of a material thing, or many of the other subjects mentioned in the *Oxford English Dictionary*'s 1,200-word definition of *communication*.

What, then, are we talking about when we use the term *communication*? As the reading on page 6 shows, there is no single, universally accepted usage. This isn't the place to explore the differences between these conceptions or to defend one against the others. What we need is a working definition that will help us in our study.

## Characteristics of Communication

As its title suggests, this is a book about understanding human communication—so we'll start by explaining what it means to study communication that is unique to members of our species. For our purposes we'll define human **communication** as *the process of creating meaning through symbolic interaction*. Examining this definition reveals some important insights.

**Communication Is a Process**   We often think about communication as if it occurs in discrete, individual acts such as one person's utterance or a conversation. But in fact, communication is a continuous, ongoing process. There are probably people in your life who have changed your outlook through their words and actions. This change typically occurs over time, not instantly.

For Quint Studer, that person was his high school soccer coach. "I loved the sport," Studer recalls, "but, at first, I'd go running for the ball, kick with everything I had, and miss it entirely." Instead of sidelining the boy, however, his coach offered praise. "Coach King kept me from feeling like a loser," Studer says.[4] "He'd say, 'Great hustle!' Then he'd kindly throw in, 'Next time, try to get a foot on it.'"

Even what appears to be an isolated message is often part of a much larger process. Consider, for example, a friend's compliment about your appearance. Your interpretation of those words will depend on a long series of experiences stretching far back in time: How have others judged your appearance? How do you feel

# The Many Meanings of *Communication*

Few words have as many meanings as *communication*. The term can refer to everything from messages on T-shirts to presidential speeches, from computer code to chimpanzee behavior. Brent Ruben explores the many reasons for this diversity of meaning.

**Interdisciplinary Heritage** Communication has captured the interest of scholars from a wide range of fields. Ever since classical times, philosophers have studied the meaning and significance of messages. In the 20th century, social scientists joined the field: Psychologists examine the causes and effects of communication as it relates to individuals. Sociologists and anthropologists examine how communication operates within and among societies and cultures. Political scientists explore the ways communication influences governmental affairs. Engineers devise methods of conveying messages electronically. Zoologists focus on communication between animals. With this kind of diversity, it's no surprise that *communication* is a broad and sometimes confusing term.

**Field and Activity** Sometimes the word *communication* refers to a field of study (of nonverbal messages or effects of televised violence on children, for example). In other cases it denotes an activity that people do. This confusion doesn't exist in most disciplines. People may study history or sociology, but they don't "historicate" or "sociologize." Having only one word that refers to both the field of study and the activity that it examines leads to confusion.

**Humanity and Social Science** Unlike most disciplines, communication straddles two very different academic domains. It has one foot firmly planted in the humanities, where it shares concerns with disciplines like English and philosophy. At the same time, other scholars in the field take an approach like their colleagues in the social sciences, such as psychology, sociology, and anthropology. And to confuse matters even further, communication is sometimes associated with the performing arts, especially in the area of oral interpretation of literature.

**Natural and Professional Communication** This is a natural activity that we all engage in unconsciously. At the same time, there are professional communication experts whose specialized duties require training and skill. Careers such as marketing, public relations, broadcasting, speechmaking, counseling, journalism, and management all call for talent that goes far beyond what is required for everyday speaking and listening.

**Communication and Communications** Even the name of the field is confusing. Traditionally, *communications* (with an *s*) has been used when referring to activities involving technology and the mass media. *Communication* is typically used to describe face-to-face and written messages, as well as the field as a whole. With the growth of communication technology, the two terms are being used interchangeably more often.

*Brent Ruben*

---

Think of a single "act" of communication in a relationship that is familiar to you. Now explore how that event is part of a relational process by imagining it as a scene in a movie telling the story of this relationship. How was the meaning of this scene shaped by what came before? How is what happened here likely to shape future exchanges?

about your looks? How honest has your friend been in the past? How have you been feeling about each other recently? All this history will help shape your response to the friend's remark. In turn, the words you speak and the way you say them will shape the way your friend behaves toward you and others—both in this situation and in the future.

This simple example shows that it's inaccurate to talk about "acts" of communication as if they occur in isolation. To put it differently, communication isn't a series of incidents pasted together like photographs in a scrapbook; instead, it is more like a motion picture in which the meaning comes from the unfolding of an interrelated series of images. The fact that communication is a process is reflected in the transactional model introduced later in this chapter.

**Communication Is Relational, Not Individual** Communication isn't something we do *to* others; rather, it is something we do *with* them. Like many types of dancing, communication depends on the involvement of a partner. A great dancer who doesn't consider and adapt to the skill level of his or her partner can make both people look bad. In communication and in dancing, even two highly skilled partners must work at adaptation and coordination. Finally, relational communication—like dancing—is a unique creation that arises out of the way in which the partners interact: It varies with different partners.

Psychologist Kenneth Gergen captures the relational nature of communication well when he points out how our success depends on interaction with others. As he says, "one cannot be 'attractive' without others who are attracted, a 'leader' without others willing to follow, or a 'loving person' without others to affirm with appreciation."[5]

Because communication is relational, or transactional, it's often a mistake to suggest that just one person is responsible for a relationship. It's easy to blame each other for a disappointing outcome, but that's often fruitless and counterproductive. It's usually far better to ask, "How did we handle this situation poorly, and what can we do to make it better?"

The transactional nature of communication shows up in school, where teachers and students influence one another's behavior. For example, teachers who regard some students negatively may treat them with subtle or overt disfavor. As a result, these students are likely to react to their teachers' behavior negatively, which reinforces the teachers' original attitudes and expectations.[6]

**Communication Is Symbolic**  **Symbols** are used to represent things, processes, ideas, or events in ways that make communication possible. Chapter 4 discusses the nature of symbols in more detail, but this idea is so important that it needs an introduction now.

Along with individual skill, contestants on shows like *So You Think You Can Dance* must work smoothly together in order to succeed. How well is your communication synchronized with others in important relationships?

The most significant feature of symbols is their arbitrary nature. For example, there's no logical reason why the letters in the word *book* should stand for the object you're reading now. Speakers of Spanish call it a *libro*, and Germans call it a *Buch*. Even in English, another term would work just as well as long as everyone agreed to use it in the same way. We overcome the arbitrary nature of symbols by linguistic rules and customs. Effective communication depends on agreement among people about these rules. This is easiest to see when we observe people who don't follow linguistic conventions. For example, recall how unusual the speech of children and nonnative speakers of a language often sounds.

Animals don't use symbols in the varied and complex ways that we do. There's nothing symbolic about a dog scratching at the door to be let out; there is a natural connection between the door and the dog's goal. By contrast, the significance of a word or action is only arbitrarily related to the meaning we give it.

Illustrating the symbolic nature of communication, Quint Studer recalls an experience from his days as a teacher, when he helped a developmentally disabled student land a coveted job at a local fast food restaurant.

> She would wear her McDonald's uniform on days when she had to work after school. Then one day I looked at the schedule and I realized she was wearing her uniform, but she didn't work that day. I was about to explain that she didn't have to wear it every day. Then it dawned on me: She *wanted* to wear it, because it made her feel worthwhile.[7]

Besides reflecting our identity, symbolic communication allows people to think or talk about the past (whereas cats have no concept of their ancestors from a century ago), explain the present (a trout can't warn its companions about its close call with a fishing hook), and speculate about the future (a crow has no awareness of the year 2025, let alone tomorrow).

## Modeling Communication

So far we have introduced a basic definition of communication and considered its characteristics. This information is useful, but it only begins to describe the process we will be examining throughout this book. One way to understand more about what it means to communicate is to look at some models that describe what happens when two or more people interact. As you will see, over the years, scholars have developed an increasingly accurate and sophisticated view of this process.

**A Linear Model**   Until about 50 years ago, researchers viewed communication as something that one person "does" to another.[8] In this **linear communication model**, communication is like giving an injection: A **sender encodes** ideas and feelings into some sort of **message** and then conveys them to a **receiver**, who **decodes** them (Figure 1-1).

One important element of the linear model is the communication **channel**—the method by which a message is conveyed between people. For most people, face-to-face contact is the most familiar and obvious channel. Writing is another channel. In addition to these long-used forms, **mediated communication** channels include telephone, e-mail, instant messaging, faxes, voice mail, and even videoconferencing. (The word *mediated* reflects the fact that these messages are conveyed through some sort of communication medium.) The self-assessment below will help you appreciate how the channel you choose can help determine the success of your messages.

---

## SELF-ASSESSMENT

## Your Communication Choices

Consider which communication channel(s) you would use in each situation described below. Be prepared to explain the reasoning behind your choices.

| Scenario | Your Communication Choice | | | | |
|---|---|---|---|---|---|
| | Face-to-Face | Phone | E-mail | Text | Social Media |
| **1.** You have been concerned about a friend. The last time you were together, you asked, "Is anything wrong?" Your friend replied, "I'm fine." Now it's been several weeks since you have heard from your friend, and you're worried. Which channel do you think is best for gauging your friend's true emotions? | | | | | |
| **2.** You're extremely angry and frustrated with a professor and need to deal with this concern before the problem gets worse. Which communication choice offers you the best opportunity to address the problem? | | | | | |
| **3.** On Thursday your boss tells you it's okay to come in late Monday morning. You're worried he will forget that he gave you permission. What channel(s) can you use to make sure he remembers? | | | | | |
| **4.** You're applying for a job when a friend says, "You won't believe the photo I took of you at that party last weekend!" How would you like your friend to share the photo with you? | | | | | |
| **5.** You just had a once-in-a-lifetime encounter with a celebrity, and you can't wait to show your friends the pictures. How would you do that most quickly and effectively? | | | | | |

The channel you choose can make a big difference in the effect of a message. For example, a typewritten love letter probably wouldn't have the same effect as a hand-written note or card. Likewise, saying "I love you" for the first time via text message would make a very different statement than saying the words in person.

The linear model also introduces the concept of **noise**—a term social scientists use to describe any forces that interfere with effective communication. Noise can occur at every stage of the communication process. Three types of noise can disrupt communication—external, physiological, and psychological.

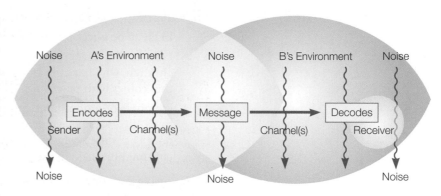

**FIGURE 1-1  Linear Communication Model**

*External noise* (also called "physical" noise) includes those factors outside the receiver that make hearing difficult, as well as many other kinds of distractions. For instance, too much cigarette smoke in a crowded room might make it hard for you to pay attention to another person, and sitting in the rear of an auditorium might make a speaker's remarks unclear. External noise can disrupt communication almost anywhere in our model—in the sender, channel, message, or receiver. *Physiological noise* involves biological factors in the receiver or sender that interfere with accurate reception: illness, fatigue, and so on. *Psychological noise* refers to forces within a communicator that interfere with the ability to express or understand a message accurately. For instance, an outdoors person might exaggerate the size and number of the fish he caught in order to convince himself and others of his talents. In the same way, you might be so upset to learn you failed a test that you would be unable (perhaps unwilling) to understand clearly where you went wrong.

A linear model shows that communicators often occupy different **environments**—fields of experience that help them understand others' behavior. In communication terminology, *environment* refers not only to a physical location but also to the personal experiences and cultural backgrounds that participants bring to a conversation.

Consider just some of the factors that might contribute to different environments:

- A might belong to one ethnic group and B to another.
- A might be rich and B poor.
- A might be in a rush and B have nowhere to go.
- A might have lived a long, eventful life, and B might be young and inexperienced.
- A might be passionately concerned with the subject and B indifferent to it.

Notice how the model in Figure 1-1 shows that the environments of A and B overlap. This area represents the background that the communicators must have in common. As the shared environment becomes smaller, communication becomes more difficult. Consider a few examples in which different perspectives can make understanding difficult:

- Bosses who have trouble understanding the perspective of their employees will be less effective managers, and

Communicators in today's connected world are challenged by a flood of text messages, photos, tweets, pings, and e-mails that distract receivers from the situation at hand. How successfully do you juggle the competing demands of face-to-face conversation and electronic messages? How could you do better?

workers who do not appreciate the challenges of being a boss are more likely to be uncooperative (and probably less suitable for advancement).

- Parents who have trouble recalling their youth are likely to clash with their children, who have never known and may not appreciate the responsibility that comes with parenting.

- Members of a dominant culture who have never experienced how it feels to be "different" may not appreciate the concerns of people from nondominant cocultures, whose own perspectives make it hard to understand the cultural blindness of the majority.

Differing environments make understanding others challenging but certainly not impossible. Hard work and many of the skills described in this book provide ways to bridge the gap that separates all of us to a greater or lesser degree. For now, recognizing the challenge that comes from dissimilar environments is a good start. You can't solve a problem until you recognize that it exists.

**A Transactional Model**   Because of its simplicity, the linear model doesn't do a very good job of representing the way most communication operates. The transactional communication model in Figure 1-2 presents a more accurate picture in several respects.

Most notably, the **transactional model** shows that both sending and receiving are simultaneous. Although some types of mass communication do flow in a one-way, linear manner, most types of personal communication are two-way exchanges.[9] The roles of sender and receiver that seemed separate in the linear model are now superimposed and redefined as those of "communicators." This new term reflects the fact that at a given moment we are capable of receiving, decoding, and responding to another person's behavior, while at the same time that other person is receiving and responding to ours.

Consider, for instance, the significance of a friend's yawn as you describe your romantic problems. Or imagine the blush you may see as you tell one of your raunchier jokes to a new acquaintance. Nonverbal behaviors like these show that most face-to-face communication is a two-way affair. The discernible response of a receiver to a sender's message is called **feedback**. Not all feedback is nonverbal, of course. Sometimes it is oral, as when you ask an instructor questions about an upcoming test or volunteer your opinion of a friend's new haircut. In other cases it is written, as when you answer the questions on a midterm exam or respond to a letter from a friend. Figure 1-2 makes the importance of feedback clear. It shows that most communication is, indeed, a two-way affair.

Some forms of mediated communication like e-mail and text messaging don't appear to be simultaneous. Even here, though, the process is more complicated than the linear model suggests. For example, if you've ever waited impatiently for the response to a text message or instant message, you understand that even a nonresponse can have symbolic meaning. Is the unresponsive recipient busy? Thoughtful? Offended? Indifferent? Whether or not your interpretation is accurate, the silence is a form of communication.

Another weakness of the traditional linear model is the questionable assumption that all communication involves **encoding**, putting thoughts into a symbolic form such

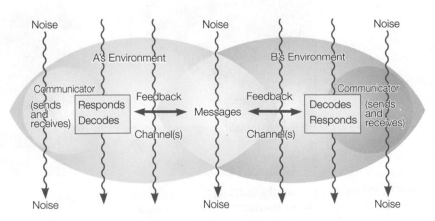

**FIGURE 1-2 Transactional Communication Model**

as words. We certainly do choose symbols to convey most verbal messages. But what about the many nonverbal cues that occur whether or not people speak: facial expressions, gestures, postures, vocal tones, and so on? Cues like these clearly do offer information about others, although they are often unconscious and thus don't involve encoding. For this reason, the transactional model replaces the term *encodes* with the broader term *responds*, because it describes both intentional and unintentional actions that can be observed and interpreted.[10]

# Types of Communication

Within the domain of human interaction, there are several types of communication. Each occurs in a different context. Despite the features they all share, each has its own characteristics.

## Intrapersonal Communication

By definition, **intrapersonal communication** means "communicating with oneself."[11] One way that each of us communicates internally is by listening to the little voice that lives in our mind. Take a moment and listen to what it is saying. Try it now, before reading on. Did you hear it? It may have been saying something like "What little voice? I don't have any little voice!" This voice is the "sound" of your thinking.

Quint Studer says his inner voice has sometimes held him back. "I used to assume other people were smarter than me," he recalls. "No one wants to look stupid, so I played it safe. I set my expectations too low." He reached a turning point, however, when he realized that feeling overwhelmed is a natural part of learning.

The way we mentally process information influences our interaction with others. Even though intrapersonal communication doesn't include other people directly and may not be apparent, it does affect almost every type of interaction. You can understand the role of intrapersonal communication by imagining your thoughts in each of the following situations:

More than 5 million people have viewed Tanya Davis's YouTube video "How to Be Alone," in which she suggests that life is enriched by listening attentively to our own thoughts. How can intrapersonal communication (communicating with yourself) help you relate more effectively to others?

- You are planning to approach a stranger whom you would like to get to know better.

- You pause a minute and look at the audience before beginning a 10-minute speech.

- The boss yawns while you are asking for a raise.

- A friend seems irritated lately, and you're not sure whether you are responsible.

The way you handle all of these situations would depend on the intrapersonal communication that precedes or accompanies your overt behavior. Much of Chapter 2 deals with the perception process in everyday situations, and part of Chapter 13 focuses on the intrapersonal communication that can minimize anxiety when you deliver a speech.

## Dyadic/Interpersonal Communication

Social scientists call two persons interacting a **dyad**, and they often use the term **dyadic communication** to describe this type of communication. Dyadic communication can occur in person or via mediated channels that include telephone, e-mail, text messaging, instant messaging, and social networking websites.

Dyadic relationships—with friends, romantic partners, and even strangers—can be among the most rewarding types of communication. How are your most important dyadic relationships maintained through communication?

Dyadic is the most common type of personal communication. One study revealed that college students spend almost half of their total communication time interacting with one other person.[12] Observation in a variety of settings ranging from playgrounds to train stations and shopping malls shows that most communication is dyadic in nature.[13] Even communication within larger groups (think of classrooms, parties, and families as examples) consists of multiple, often shifting dyadic encounters.

Relating one to one with another person can be a powerful experience, as Quint Studer found when he began working with teens striving to overcome substance abuse. The process led to many strong relationships, both with teens and with health and social service providers. "No matter what you're doing, it all comes down to relationships," he says.

Dyadic interaction is sometimes considered identical to **interpersonal communication**, but as Chapter 7 explains, not all two-person interaction can be considered interpersonal in the fullest sense of the word. In fact, you will learn that the qualities that characterize interpersonal communication aren't limited to twosomes. They can be present in threesomes or even in small groups.

## Small Group Communication

In **small group communication** every person can participate actively with the other members. Small groups are a common fixture of everyday life. Your family is a group. So are an athletic team, a group of coworkers in several time zones connected online, and several students working on a class project.

Whether small groups meet in person or via mediated channels, they possess characteristics that are not present in a dyad. For instance, in a group, the majority of members can put pressure on those in the minority to conform, either consciously or unconsciously, but in a dyad no such pressures exist. Conformity pressures can also be comforting, leading group members to take risks that they would not dare to take if they were alone or in a dyad. With their greater size, groups also have the ability to be more creative than dyads. Finally, communication in groups is affected strongly by the type of leader who is in a position of authority. Groups are such an important communication setting that Chapters 9 and 10 focus exclusively on them.

Which communication contexts are the most important in your current life? Are other contexts likely to become more important in the future?

## Organizational Communication

Larger, more permanent collections of people engage in **organizational communication** when they collectively work to achieve goals. Organizations operate for a variety of reasons: commercial (like a corporation), nonprofit (like a charity or religious group), political (a government or political action group), health-related (a hospital or doctor's office), and even recreational (a YMCA or sports league).

Regardless of the context, organizational communication possesses some characteristics that make it worth studying as a unique context. For example, specific roles (sales associate, general manager, corporate trainer) shape what people communicate about and their relationship to one another. Also, the complicated nature of interaction in organizations makes the study of communication networks important. As you'll read in Chapter 3, each organization develops its own culture, and analyzing the traditions and customs of organizations is a useful field of study.

The appendix in this book offers some useful tips about communicating in organizations.

## Public Communication

**Public communication** occurs when a group becomes too large for all members to contribute. One characteristic of public communication is an unequal amount of speaking. One or more people are likely to deliver their remarks to the remaining members, who act as an audience. This leads to a second characteristic of public settings: limited verbal feedback. The audiences aren't able to talk back in a two-way conversation the way they might in a dyadic or small group setting. This doesn't mean that speakers operate in a vacuum when delivering their remarks. Audiences often have a chance to ask questions and offer brief comments, and their nonverbal reactions offer a wide range of clues about their reception of the speaker's remarks.

Public speakers usually have a greater chance to plan and structure their remarks than do communicators in smaller settings. For this reason, several chapters of this book describe the steps you can take to prepare and deliver an effective speech.

> cultural idiom

**operate in a vacuum:**
operate independently of outside influences

## Mass Communication

**Mass communication** consists of messages that are transmitted to large, widespread audiences via electronic and print media: newspapers, magazines, television, radio, blogs, websites, and so on. As you can see in the Mass Communication section of this book's companion website (oup.com/us/uhc12), mass communication differs from the interpersonal, small group and organizational, and public varieties in several ways.

- First, most mass messages are aimed at a large audience without any personal contact between sender and receivers.

- Second, many of the messages sent via mass communication channels are developed, or at least financed, by large organizations. In this sense, mass communication is far less personal and more of a product than the other types we have examined so far.

- Finally, mass communication is often controlled by many gatekeepers, who determine what messages will be delivered to consumers, how they will be constructed, and when they will be delivered. Sponsors (whether corporate or governmental), editors, producers, reporters, and executives all have the power to influence mass messages in ways that don't affect most other types. Although blogs have given ordinary people the chance to reach enormous audiences, the bulk of mass messages are still controlled by corporate and governmental sources.

Because of these and other unique characteristics, the study of mass communication raises special issues and deserves special treatment.

After doctors told Randy Pausch he had less than 6 months to live, the 47-year-old professor and Disney Imagineer delivered a "Last Lecture" at Carnegie Mellon University. He chose the topic "Really Achieving Your Childhood Dreams."
    You can view this powerful talk by searching for "Randy Pausch Last Lecture" on YouTube. As you watch Pausch's speech, ask yourself what you would talk about if you had the microphone and an attentive audience.

## Communication in a Changing World

Over the past several decades, the nature of communication has changed dramatically. Today we are equipped with a range of communication technologies that, even two decades ago, would have been the stuff of fantasy and science fiction.

Yet along with the technological opportunities in today's world, communication challenges abound. How do we use the newest tools of communication in ways that make life richer and more satisfying instead of harried and confounding? How can we deal with people whose communication practices differ dramatically from our own, often in ways that are frustrating but hard to pin down? This section will provide some tools to help answer these questions.

### Changing Technology

Figure 1-3 shows that communication technology is changing more rapidly than ever before. For most of human history, face-to-face speech was the primary form of communication. Writing developed approximately 5,000 years ago; but until the last few centuries the vast majority of people were illiterate. In most societies only a small elite class mastered the arts of reading and writing. Books were scarce, and the amount of information available was small. Speaking and listening were the predominant communication "technologies."

By the mid-18th century, literacy grew in industrial societies, giving ordinary people access to ideas that had been available only to the most privileged. By the end of the 19th century, affordable rail travel increased mobility, and the telegraph made possible transmission of both news and personal messages over vast distances.

The first half of the 20th century introduced a burst of communication technology. The invention of the telephone extended the reach of both personal and business relationships. Radio and, later, television gave mass audiences a taste of the wider world. Information was no longer a privilege of the elite class.

By the dawn of the 21st century, cellular technologies and the Internet broadened the ability to communicate even further, beyond the dreams of earlier generations. Pocket-sized telephones made it cheap and easy to talk, send data, and exchange images with people around the globe. Now, new fiber-optic technology allows for more than 150 million phone calls every second.[14] Videoconferencing is another channel for remote connection, allowing us to see

---

**Into the Future**
Analysts predict we may one day communicate via lifelike holographs, wear augmented-reality glasses, and send messages via brainwaves.

**Phones, Radio, and Television**
Telephones shrank distance, expanding the reach of both personal relationships and commerce. Radio and later television gave mass audiences a taste of the wider world. Information was no longer a privilege of the elite class.

**1963:** First communication satelite
**1936:** Regular TV broadcasts (London)
**1920:** First radio broadcast
**1876:** First telephone demonstrated
**1843:** Long-distance telegraph

**Literate Populations**
By the mid-18th century, literacy grew in industrial societies, giving ordinary people access to ideas that had been available only to the most privileged.

**Face-to-Face Communication**
For most of human history, face-to-face speech was the primary form of communication. Speaking and listening were the predominant communication "technologies."

**2000s**

**Computer Age**
By the dawn of the 21st century, communication technology expanded beyond the dreams of earlier generations.

**2010:** iPad enhances mobile computing
**2009:** Smartphone sales top 170 million
**2006:** Twitter launched
**2005:** YouTube.com appears online
**1997:** First social network (SixDegrees.com)
**1996:** Instant messaging developed
**1994:** Personal blogging begins
**1992:** First text message sent
**1991:** World Wide Web begins
**1981:** IBM markets first personal computer
**1975:** First microcomputer, the Altair 8800
**1973:** First cell phone call
**1972:** First e-mail with "@" in address
**1969:** ARPANET (forerunner to Internet)

**1900s**

**1800s**

**Trains, Telegraphs, and Mail Service**
By the end of the 19th century, affordable rail travel increased mobility, and the telegraph made possible transmission of both news and personal messages over vast distances.

**1700s**

**Writing**
Writing developed approximately 5,000 years ago; but until the last few centuries the vast majority of people were illiterate, and books were scarce.

**3000+ BC**

**1620:** Sign language (Spain)
**1605:** First newspaper (Germany)
**1450:** First movable type printing press
**868:** First surviving book printed (China)
**AD  105:** Paper invented (China)
**BC**

**300:** World's first library (Egypt)
**776:** Carrier pigeons (Greece)
**900:** First postal service (China)
**3000+:** Writing invented

**FIGURE 1-3  The Accelerating Pace of Communication Technology**

one another's facial cues, body movements, and gestures almost as if we were face-to-face.

The accelerating pace of innovations in communication technology is astonishing: It took 38 years for radio to reach 50 million listeners. It took television only 13 years to capture the same number of viewers. It took less than 4 years for the Internet to attract 50 million users. Facebook added 100 million users in less than 9 months.[15]

### Changing Discipline

The study of communication has evolved to reflect the changing world. The first systematic analysis of how to communicate effectively was Aristotle's *Rhetoric*, written 2,500 years ago.[16] The ancient philosopher set forth specific criteria for effective speaking (called the "Canons of Rhetoric"), which still can be used to judge effective public communication. In various forms, rhetoric has been part of a classical liberal arts education since Aristotle's era. Today it is commonly taught in public speaking courses that are offered in most colleges and universities.

In the early 20th century, the study of communication expanded from the liberal arts, where it had been housed for more than 2,000 years, and began to capture the attention of social scientists. As persuasive messages began to reach large numbers of people via print, film, and broadcasting, scholars began to study how the media shaped attitudes and behaviors. During and after World War II, the effectiveness of government propaganda was an important focus of research.[17] Since then, media effects has become one of the most widely studied areas in the field of communication.

In the 1950s, researchers began asking questions about human relationships in family and work settings, marking the beginning of research on small group communication.[18] The analysis of decision making and other small group communication processes emerged as a major area of study in the field and continues today.

In the 1960s, social scientists expanded their focus to study how communication operates in personal relationships.[19] Since then, scholars have studied a wide range of phenomena, including how relationships develop, the nature of social support, the role of emotions, how honesty and deception operate, and how new technologies affect interpersonal relationships. Other branches of the discipline examine communication in organizations, the influence of gender on interaction, and how people from different backgrounds communicate with one another. The list on page 6 suggests the scope of topics studied in the discipline, showing that the focus of the field has expanded far beyond its rhetorical roots.

The 1930s cartoon detective Dick Tracy communicated with a two-way wristwatch radio. Such a device seemed like science fiction to earlier generations, but similar technologies (think smartphones) are commonplace today. Think about the communication technologies you use. How would your life be different without them?

# Understanding Social Media

Until recently, when people heard the word *media*, they most likely thought of television, radio, and other forms of mass communication. But today, not all media are aimed at mass audiences. The term **Web 2.0** is often used to describe how the Internet has evolved from a one-way medium (rather like old-style publishers and broadcasters) into what one scholar called a *masspersonal* phenomenon[20] in which individual users interact in a host of ways that include social networking sites, video- and photo-sharing services, and blogs. If you blog, tweet, post photos on a website such as Tumblr, or maintain a page on Facebook or some other social networking site, you have experience with Web 2.0. You're not only a consumer of mediated messages but a creator of them.

As the name suggests, people use **social media** for personal reasons, often to reach small groups of receivers. You're using social media when you exchange text messages, e-mails, and instant messages; and when you use social networking

*"Anyone following me on Twitter already knows what I did this past summer."*

Source: Alex Gregory / The New Yorker Collection / www.cartoonbank.com

websites like Facebook and Google+. As mentioned earlier, the number of social media technologies has exploded in the past few decades, giving communicators today an array of choices that would have amazed someone from a previous era.

Social media are different from the mass variety in some important ways. Most obvious is the *variable size of the target audience.* Whereas the mass media are aimed at large audiences, the intended audience in social media can vary. On one hand, you typically address e-mails, text messages, and IMs to a single, or maybe a few, receivers. In fact, you'd probably be embarrassed to have some of your personal messages circulate more widely. On the other hand, blogs, tweets, and other postings are often aimed at much larger groups of receivers.

Unlike mass media, social media are *interactive*: The recipients of your messages can—and usually do—talk back. For example, nearly 9 in 10 teens who post photos online say that people comment at least sometimes on the images they post.[21] This figure reflects the difference between traditional print media, in which communication is essentially one way, and far more interactive web-based social media.

Unlike traditional forms of mass communication, social media are also distinguished by *user-generated content.* You decide what goes on your Facebook page and what topics are covered on your blog. There aren't any market researchers to tell you what the audience wants. No staff writers, editors, designers, or marketers craft your message. It's all you.

Despite these characteristics, the boundary between mass and interpersonal communication isn't as clear as it might first seem. Consider, for example, You-Tube and other streaming video websites. They provide a way for individuals to publish their own content (your graduation, baby's first birthday party) for a limited number of interested viewers. On the other hand, some videos go "viral," receiving thousands, or even millions, of hits. (Since first appearing in 2006, the exploits of "lonelygirl15" have been viewed more than 100 million times.)

Twitter is another example of the fuzzy boundary between personal and mass media. Many people broadcast updates to a rather small group of interested parties. ("I'm at the concert—Great seats!") On the other hand, millions of fans follow the tweets of favorite celebrities. Twitter offers an interesting blend of messages from real friends and celebrities, "strangely intimate and at the same time celebrity-obsessed," as one observer put it. "You glance at your Twitter feed over that first cup of coffee, and in a few seconds you find out that your nephew got into med school and Shaquille O'Neal just finished a cardio workout in Phoenix."[22]

Blogs also straddle the categories of mass and social media. Some are highly personal: You can set one up and share your opinions with anybody who cares to read them. Others (like the Huffington Post, Gizmodo, or Daily Kos) are much closer to traditional mass media, published regularly and reaching audiences numbering in the hundreds of thousands.

## Mediated Versus Face-to-Face Communication

Think back to the "Communication Choices" self-assessment on page 8. Did you notice that, aside from face-to-face communication, all the choices are technology mediated? What does face-to-face communication have in common with the mediated options? How is it different?

In some ways, mediated and face-to-face communication are quite similar. Both include the same elements described on pages 8–11: senders, receivers, channels, feedback, and so on. Both are used to satisfy physical, identity, social, and practical needs, as we discuss in the next section. Despite these similarities, the two forms of communication are different in some important ways.

**Message Richness**    Social scientists use the term **richness** to describe the abundance of nonverbal cues that add clarity to a verbal message. As Chapter 6 explains in detail, face-to-face communication is rich because it abounds with nonverbal messages that give communicators cues about the meanings of one another's words and offer hints about their feelings.[23] By comparison, most mediated communication is a much leaner channel for conveying information.

**Synchronicity**    **Synchronous communication** occurs in real time. In-person communication is synchronous. So are phone conversations. By contrast, **asynchronous communication** occurs when there's a time gap between when a message is sent and when it's received. Voice mail messages are asynchronous. So are "snail mail" letters, e-mails, and Twitter postings. Asynchronous messages give you the chance to mull over different wording, or even ask others for advice about what to say, so they're a good option when you want to avoid saying the wrong thing in the heat of the moment. You might even choose not to respond at all. You can ignore most problematic text messages without much fallout. That isn't a good option if the person who wants an answer gets you on the phone or confronts you in person.

**Permanence**    What happens in a face-to-face conversation is transitory. By contrast, the text and video you send via hard copy or mediated channels can be stored indefinitely and forwarded to others. Sometimes permanence is useful. For example, you might want a record documenting your boss's permission for time off work. In other cases, though, permanence can be problematic. You probably wish you could delete an e-mail sent in anger or embarrassing photos posted online.

## How People Use Social Media

In the mid-20th century, researchers began to study the question "What do media do to people?" They sought answers by measuring the effects of print and broadcast media on users. Did programming influence viewers' use of physical violence? Did it affect academic success? What about family communication patterns?

In following decades, researchers began to explore a different question: "What do people do *with* media?"[24] (For an example, see Figure 1-4.) This branch of study became known as *uses and gratifications* theory. In the digital age, researchers continue to explore how we use both social media and face-to-face communication. Table 1-1 shows the findings of one study.

Mediated communication can sometimes—but not always—be as rewarding as face-to-face interaction. How does the amount and nature of your mediated communication affect your in-person relationships?

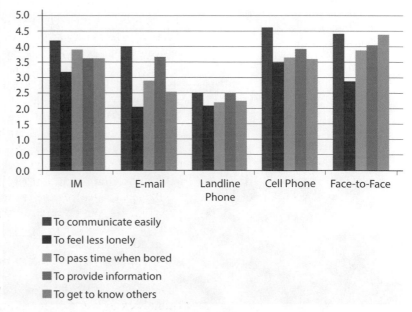

**FIGURE 1-4 Satisfaction Scores for Selected Communication Media**

*Source:* Adapted from A. J. Flanagan. (2005). IM online: Instant messaging use among college students. *Communication Research Reports, 22,* 173–187.

The uses listed there fall into four broad categories:[25]

(1) **Information**: What do people think of a new film or musical group? Can anybody trade work hours this weekend? Is there a good Honda mechanic nearby? Can your network provide leads on getting your dream job?

(2) **Personal relationships**: Seeing what your friends are up to, tracking down old classmates, announcing changes in your life to the people in your personal networks, and finding a romantic partner.

(3) **Personal identity**: Observing others as models to help you become more effective, getting insights about yourself from trusted others, and asserting your personal values and getting feedback from others.

(4) **Entertainment**: Gaming online with a friend, sharing your music playlists with others, joining the fan base of your favorite star, and finding interest or activity groups to join.

## Communicating Competently with Social Media

Perhaps you've found yourself in situations like these:

- You want to bring up a delicate issue with a friend or family member or at work. You aren't sure whether to do so in person, on the phone, or via some mediated channel like texting or e-mail.

- You're enjoying a film at the theater—until another moviegoer starts a cell phone conversation.

- A friend posts a picture of you online that you would rather not be seen by others.

- Someone you care about is spending too much time online, crowding out real-life encounters.

- Reading a text message while you rush to an appointment, you bump into another pedestrian.

- Even though you know it's a bad idea, you read a text message while driving and nearly hit a cyclist.

- You are copied on an e-mail or text message that was obviously not meant for your eyes.

- You receive so many e-mail messages that you have trouble meeting school and work deadlines.

None of these situations would have existed a generation ago. They highlight the need for a set of social agreements that go beyond the general rules of communicative competence outlined in this chapter. The following pages offer some guidelines that have evolved in recent years. Although they won't cover every situation involving mediated communication, they can help you avoid some problems and deal most effectively with others that are bound to arise.

**Choose the Best Medium**  Sometimes the choice of a medium is a no-brainer. If a friend says, "Call me while I'm on the road," you know what to do. If your boss or professor

Facebook, cofounded by Mark Zuckerberg, became one of the fastest-growing communication technologies in recent history. How important are social media to your daily life, and how would your communication be different without them?

Table 1-1     Choosing a Communication Channel

**Choosing the best communication channel can make the difference between success and failure on the job. This table offers guidelines for choosing the channel that is best suited for a particular situation.**

| | SYNCHRONICITY | RICHNESS OF INFORMATION CONVEYED | SENDER'S CONTROL OVER MESSAGE | CONTROL OVER RECEIVER'S ATTENTION | EFFECTIVENESS FOR DETAILED MESSAGES |
|---|---|---|---|---|---|
| **FACE-TO-FACE** | Synchronous | High | Moderate | Highest | Weak |
| **TELEPHONE, TELE-CONFERENCING, AND VIDEOCONFERENCING** | Synchronous | Moderate | Moderate | Moderate | Weak |
| **VOICE MAIL** | Asynchronous | Moderate | High | Low | Weak |
| **E-MAIL** | Asynchronous | Low | High | Low | High |
| **INSTANT MESSAGING** | Almost synchronous | Low | High | Varies | Weak |
| **TEXT MESSAGING AND TWITTER** | Varies | Low | High (given brief-ness of message) | Low | Good for brief messages |
| **HARD COPY (E.G., HANDWRITTEN OR TYPED MESSAGE)** | Asynchronous | Low | High | Low | High |

*Source:* Adapted from R. B. Adler, J. M. Elmhorst, & K. Lucas. (2003). *Communicating at work: Strategies for success in business and the professions* (11th ed.). New York: McGraw-Hill, p. 14.

only responds to e-mails, then it would be foolish to use any other approach. But in many other situations, you have several options available. Table 1-1 outlines the advantages and drawbacks of the most common ones. Choosing the best channel can make a real difference in your success. In one survey, managers who were identified as most "media sensitive" were almost twice as likely as their less-savvy peers to receive top ratings in performance reviews.[26]

Choosing the right medium is just as important in personal relationships. Anyone who has been dumped via text message knows that it only adds insult to injury. Just because there is an option that allows you to avoid a difficult conversation doesn't mean you should take the easy way out. Many difficult conversations are better when conducted face-to-face. These types of conversations include, but aren't limited to, sharing really bad news, ending a relationship, and trying to resolve a conflict.

In situations like these, a useful guideline is what's been called the "platinum rule": treating others as *they* would like to be treated. Ask yourself how the recipient of your message would prefer to receive it, and act accordingly, even though it's difficult.

**Be Careful What You Post**     Most of us cringe at the sight of old yearbook photos, hardly believing that we are the same person as the adolescent looking out from those glossy pages. Older adults can safely assume that most of their questionable, odd, and rebellious behavior is tucked away in those dusty yearbooks, never to be seen by their current friends and coworkers. This isn't the case for modern teens and young adults, however, who may be forever haunted by adolescent mistakes in the form of digital text and photos posted online.

As a cautionary tale about how your digital goofs can haunt you, consider the case of Jean-Sun Hannah Ahn. A few days after being crowned Miss Seattle

After an embarrassing tweet went viral, Miss Seattle, Jean-Sun Hannah Ahn, learned that anything posted on the Web can reach a broad audience, with unintended consequences. Have you ever sent a message that could later embarrass you?

in 2012, she tweeted to her friends back in Arizona: "Ew, I'm seriously hating Seattle right now . . . Take me back to az! Ugh can't stand cold rainy Seattle and the annoying people." The message made news in the town where she had just been honored. After she publicly apologized, Ahn vowed that, in the future, "I will call my friends or text them if I'm feeling down or want to complain about something."[27] Her experience is a reminder that, once sent, electronic messages often have a life of their own.

Some incautious posts can go beyond being simply amusing. Consider the phenomenon of "sexting." One survey revealed that 10 percent of young adults between the ages of 14 and 24 have texted or e-mailed a nude or partially nude image of themselves to someone else, and 15 percent have received such pictures or videos of someone else they know.[28] Perhaps even more disturbing, 8 percent reported that they had been forwarded nude or partially nude images of someone they knew.[29] When minors are involved, authorities can make arrests for manufacturing, disseminating, or even possessing child pornography. Far worse, some teens have committed suicide when explicit photos were posted online.[30] Even without such dire consequences, it's not hard to imagine the unpleasant consequences of a private photo or text going public.

**Be Considerate**   Mediated communication calls for its own rules of etiquette. Here are a few.

**Respect Others' Need for Undivided Attention**   It might be hard to realize that some people are insulted when you divide your attention between your in-person conversational partner and distant contacts. As one observer put it, "While a quick log-on may seem, to the user, a harmless break, others in the room receive it as a silent dismissal. It announces: 'I'm not interested.'"[31]

Chapter 5 has plenty to say about the challenges of listening effectively when you are multitasking. Even if you think you can understand others while dealing with communication media, it's important to realize that they may perceive you as being rude.

**Keep Your Tone Civil**   If you've ever shot back a nasty reply to a text or instant message, posted a mean comment on a blog, or forwarded an embarrassing e-mail, you know that it's easier to behave badly when the recipient of your message isn't right in front of you.

The tendency to transmit messages without considering their consequences is called **disinhibition**, and research shows it is more likely in mediated channels than in face-to-face contact.[32] Sometimes communicators take disinhibition to the extreme, blasting off angry—even vicious—e-mails, text messages, and website postings. The common term for these outbursts is **flaming**. Flames are problematic because of their emotional and irreversible nature. Once you've calmed down, the aggressive message can continue to cause pain.

Flaming isn't the only type of mediated harassment. Ongoing "cyberbullying" has become a widespread phenomenon, often with dire consequences. More than 4 in 10 teens report being the target of online harassment. Recipients of cyberbullying often feel helpless and scared, to such a degree that one report found they are eight times more likely to carry a weapon to school than other students. There are at least 41 reported cases in which victims of cyberbullying committed suicide in the United States, Canada, Great Britain, and Australia,[33] a sobering statistic in light of reports that 81 percent of cyberbullies admit their only reason for bullying is because "it's funny."[34]

One way to behave better in asynchronous situations is to ask yourself a simple question before you send, post, or broadcast: Would you deliver the same message to the recipient in person? If your answer is no, then you might want to think before hitting the "enter" key.

**Respect Privacy Boundaries**     Sooner or later you're bound to run across information about others that you suspect they would find embarrassing. If your relationship is close enough, you might consider sending out a for-your-information alert. In other cases, you may intentionally run a search about someone. Even if you uncover plenty of interesting information, it can be smart to avoid mentioning what you've discovered to the object of your searching.

**Be Mindful of Bystanders**     If you spend even a little time in most public spaces, you're likely to encounter communicators whose use of technology interferes with others: Restaurant patrons whose phone voices intrude on your conversation, pedestrians who are more focused on their handheld device than on avoiding others, or people in line who are trying to pay the cashier and talk on their cell phone at the same time. If you aren't bothered by this sort of behavior, it can be hard to feel sympathetic with others who are offended by it. Nonetheless, this is another situation in which the platinum rule applies: Consider treating others the way *they* would like to be treated.

**Balance Mediated and Face Time**     It's easy to make a case that many relationships are better because of social media. And as you've already read in this chapter, research supports this position. With all the benefits of communication technology, it's worth asking whether there is such a thing as *too much* mediated socializing.

Indeed, there is a link between heavy reliance on mediated communication and conditions including depression, loneliness, and social anxiety.[35] People who spend excessive time on the Internet may begin to experience problems at school or work and withdraw further from their offline relationships.[36] Many people who pursue exclusively online social contacts do so because they have social anxiety or low social skills to begin with. For these people, retreating further from offline relationships may diminish their already low social skills.

Researchers have been especially interested in determining when cyber communication crosses the bridge from normal to excessive.[37] How many of the following points describe you?

- I find it difficult to avoid the urge to go online (e.g., to check Facebook on my phone).
- I spend more and more time online.
- I often spend more time online than I anticipated or intended.
- I have tried to reduce my Internet use, but I have not been successful at cutting back.
- My Internet use causes me to do poorly at work, home, or school.
- I engage in social or recreational activities less than I should because of the Internet.

All harassment causes damage. In what ways might cyberbullying be worse than traditional physical bullying?

**"I need a more interactive you."**

*Source:* Mick Stevens / www.cartoonbank.com

Although experts disagree about whether Internet addiction disorder (IAD) is a certifiable addiction or just a symptom of another issue, they suggest several strategies for reining in excessive Internet use. Unlike other addictions, such as those to drugs and alcohol, treatment for Internet addiction focuses on moderation and controlled use of the Internet rather than abstinence.[38] If you are worried about your Internet use:

- Keep track of the amount of time you spend online so you can accurately assess whether it is too much.
- Insert planned Internet time into your daily schedule and see if you can stick to it.
- Make a list of problems in your life that may have occurred because of your time spent online.
- If you do not feel able to change your behavior on your own, seek the help of a counselor or therapist.

**Be Safe**   As more and more people spend time online, Internet safety has become a major issue. Predators used to be people who burglarized your home or approached you in a dark alley. Now, thieves and con artists don't have to find us, because we find them. Many people fail to realize the hazards of posting certain information in public forums, and other people don't even realize that what they are posting is public. You may post your "on vacation" status in Facebook, assuming that only your friends can see your message. But if a friend uses a public computer or lets another friend see your page, unintended recipients are viewing your information.[39]

As a rule, don't disclose information in a public-access medium that you would not tell a stranger on the street. Even personal e-mails present a problem: They can be forwarded, and accounts can even be hacked. The safest bet is to assume that mediated messages can be seen by unintended recipients, some of whom you may not know or trust.

Careless use of social media can damage more than your reputation. Talking on a cell phone while driving is just as dangerous as driving under the influence of alcohol or drugs. Cell phone use while driving (handheld or hands-free) lengthens a driver's reaction time as much as having a blood alcohol concentration at the legal limit of .08 percent.[40] In the United States alone, drivers distracted by cell phones cause about 5,474 deaths and 448,000 injuries every year.[41] Even a hands-free device doesn't eliminate the risks. Drivers carrying on phone conversations are 18 percent slower to react to brake lights. They also take 17 percent longer to regain the speed they lost when they braked.[42]

Text messaging poses even a greater hazard on the road than conversing. In 2007, before a large-scale campaign to discourage the practice, one-fifth of experienced adult drivers in the United States sent text messages while driving.[43] Studies have found that texting while driving causes a 400 percent increase in time spent with eyes off the road. Drivers who are sending or reading a text message spend about 5 seconds looking at their devices before a crash or near crash, allowing them to travel more than 100 yards at typical highway speeds with their eyes off the road.[44]

# Functions of Communication

So why do we speak, listen, read, write, and text so much? There's a good reason: Communication satisfies many of our needs.

## Physical Needs

Communication is so important that it is necessary for physical health. In fact, evidence suggests that an absence of satisfying communication can even jeopardize life itself. Medical researchers have identified a wide range of hazards that result from a lack of close relationships.[45] For instance:

- People who lack strong relationships have 2 to 3 times the risk of early death, regardless of whether they smoke, drink alcoholic beverages, or exercise regularly.

- Terminal cancer strikes socially isolated people more often than those who have close personal relationships.

- Divorced, separated, and widowed people are 5 to 10 times more likely to need hospitalization for mental problems than their married counterparts.

- Pregnant women under stress and without supportive relationships have 3 times more complications than pregnant women who suffer from the same stress but have strong social support.

- Socially isolated people are 4 times more susceptible to the common cold than those who have active social networks.[46]

Studies indicate that social isolation is a major risk factor contributing to coronary disease, comparable to physiological factors such as diet, cigarette smoking, obesity, and lack of physical activity.[47]

Research like this demonstrates the importance of having satisfying personal relationships. Remember: Not everyone needs the same amount of contact, and the quality of communication is almost certainly as important as the quantity. The important point here is that personal communication is essential for our well-being. To paraphrase an old song, "people who need people" aren't "the luckiest people in the world," they're the *only* people!

> In the last day, how have you communicated to satisfy your physical, identity, social, and practical needs?

## Identity Needs

Communication does more than enable us to survive. It is the way—indeed, the only way—we learn who we are. As you'll read in Chapter 2, our sense of identity comes from the way we interact with other people. Are we smart or stupid, attractive or ugly, skillful or inept? The answers to these questions don't come from looking in the mirror. We decide who we are based on how others react to us.

Deprived of communication with others, we would have no sense of identity. This fact is illustrated by the case of the famous "Wild Boy of Aveyron," who spent his early childhood without any apparent human contact. The boy was discovered in 1800 while digging for vegetables in a French village garden.[48] He showed no behaviors one would expect in a social human. The boy could not speak but uttered only weird cries. More significant than this absence of social skills was his lack of any identity as a human being. As author Roger Shattuck put it, "the boy had no human sense of being in the world. He had no sense of himself as a person related to other persons."[49] Only after the influence of a loving "mother" did the boy begin to behave—and, we can imagine, think of himself as a human. Contemporary stories support the essential role that communication plays in shaping identity. In 1970, authorities discovered a 12-year-old girl (whom they called Genie) who had spent virtually all her life in an otherwise empty, darkened bedroom with almost no human contact. The child could not speak and had no sense of herself as a person until she was removed from her family and "nourished" by a team of caregivers.[50]

## Understanding Communication Technology

## Social Media Meet Communication Needs

As handheld devices become more powerful, communication technology can help address your needs wherever there's a Wi-Fi or phone signal. Together, Apple and Google offer more than 1.5 million inexpensive or free applications. Here are just a few.

### Physical Needs

- *Global SOS:* Look up telephone emergency phone numbers in more than 150 countries.
- *Life Biorhythm:* Track your biological patterns to schedule critical encounters when at your best physically, emotionally, and intellectually.
- *iTriage:* Research symptoms, find doctors, and locate emergency facilities.

### Identity Needs

- *Photo Makeover:* Adjust photos to improve appearance, including enlarging eyes and tweaking face shape.
- *CLIPish:* Customize messages with millions of images: animations, emoticons, clip art, wallpapers, symbols, and more.

### Social Needs

- *Loopt Mix:* Connect with nearby strangers whose interests match yours.
- *Friend Mapper:* Display the geographic location of nearby friends.

### Practical Needs

- *Translate:* Translate words and phrases between many popular languages.
- *Career Builder:* Search for a job from any location.
- *Mint:* Balance your budget, track expenses, and check balances in multiple accounts. ●

Like Genie and the boy of Aveyron, each of us enters the world with little or no sense of identity. We gain an idea of who we are from the ways others define us. As Chapter 3 explains, the messages we receive in early childhood are the strongest, but the influence of others continues throughout life. Chapter 3 also explains how we use communication to manage the way others view us.

## Social Needs

Besides helping to define who we are, communication provides a vital link with others. Researchers and theorists have identified a range of social needs we satisfy by communicating: pleasure (e.g., "because it's fun," "to have a good time"); affection (e.g., "to help others," "to let others know I care"); inclusion (e.g., "because I need someone to talk to or be with," "because it makes me less lonely"); escape (e.g., "to put off doing something I should be doing"); relaxation (e.g., "because it allows me to unwind"); and control (e.g., "because I want someone to do something for me," "to get something I don't have").[51]

As you look at this list of social needs for communicating, imagine how empty your life would be if these needs weren't satisfied. Then notice that it would be impossible to fulfill them without communicating with others. Because relationships with others are so vital, some theorists have gone as far as to argue that communication is the primary goal of human existence. Anthropologist Walter Goldschmidt terms the drive for meeting social needs as the "human career."[52]

### Practical Needs

We shouldn't overlook the everyday, important functions that communication serves. Communication is the tool that lets us tell the hair stylist to take just a little off the sides, direct the doctor to where it hurts, and inform the plumber that the broken pipe needs attention *now*!

Beyond these obvious needs, a wealth of research demonstrates that communication is an important key to effectiveness in a variety of everyday settings. For example, a survey of more than 400 employers identified "communication skills" as the top characteristic that employers seek in job candidates.[53] It was rated as more important than technical competence, work experience, or academic background. In another survey, more than 90 percent of the personnel officials at 500 U.S. businesses stated that increased communication skills are needed for success in the 21st century.[54]

Communication is just as important outside of work. College roommates who are both willing and able to communicate effectively report higher satisfaction with one another than do those who lack these characteristics.[55] Married couples who were identified as effective communicators reported happier relationships than did less skillful husbands and wives.[56] In school, the grade point averages of college students were related positively to their communication competence.[57] In "getting acquainted" situations, communication competence played a major role in whether a person was judged physically attractive, socially desirable, and good at the task of getting acquainted.[58]

In the movie *Beginners*, Oliver Fields (Ewan McGregor) is so hungry for companionship after the death of his father that he begins imagining he's communicating with his father's Jack Russell terrier, Arthur. Many people say talking to their pets makes them feel good. What needs do you think are fulfilled by such behavior?

## Communication Competence: What Makes an Effective Communicator?

It's easy to recognize good communicators, and even easier to spot poor ones. But what are the characteristics that distinguish effective communicators from their less successful counterparts? Answering this question has been one of the leading challenges for communication scholars.[59] Although all the answers aren't yet in, research has identified a great deal of important and useful information about communication competence.

We've been talking about Quint Studer throughout the chapter. His career segued from teaching to health care administration, where he used his listening and leadership skills to help two failing hospitals rise to the 99th percentile in the nation and stay there. Studer's track record has been so extraordinary that businesses around the country seek his advice. In addition to headlining his own consulting firm, Studer is the author of six books and the recipient of numerous national leadership awards. Perhaps now you have an idea how outstanding communication skills helped a small, shy boy become one of the country's leading executives.

### Communication Competence Defined

Although scholars are still working to clarify the nature of **communication competence**, most would agree that effective communication involves achieving one's goals in a manner that, ideally, maintains or enhances the relationship in which it

## SELF-ASSESSMENT

### Your Communication Strengths and Goals

**INSTRUCTIONS:**

You can complete this assessment in two ways:

**1.** Rate yourself on each of the items below.

**2.** Invite people who know you well to rate you.

| | Rarely | Sometimes | Often | Almost Always |
|---|---|---|---|---|
| **1.** Well informed and prepared for meetings | | | | |
| **2.** Clear and confident when expressing ideas | | | | |
| **3.** Impatient with others | | | | |
| **4.** Confident speaking before an audience | | | | |
| **5.** Good at helping people understand complex information | | | | |
| **6.** Apt to spend more time talking than listening | | | | |
| **7.** Known to text or talk on the phone during class, meetings, or personal conversations | | | | |
| **8.** Fascinated by different customs and worldviews | | | | |
| **9.** Well organized and good at meeting deadlines | | | | |
| **10.** Instrumental in helping others reach agreement | | | | |
| **11.** In contact with a wide range of people | | | | |
| **12.** Inclined to say things in the heat of the moment and then regret it later | | | | |
| **13.** Open to new ideas and ways of thinking | | | | |
| **14.** Attentive to implied meanings and what people convey through body language and tone of voice | | | | |
| **15.** Intended meaning frequently misunderstood by others | | | | |
| **16.** Inclined to avoid discussing matters that involve conflict or sensitive issues | | | | |
| **17.** Apt to interrupt others to challenge what they are saying | | | | |

**EVALUATING YOUR RESPONSES**

Most of us are better at some forms of communication than others. Evaluate your scores in light of the information below to see where you are already strong and where you might strengthen your communication skills.

**Listening**

Three of the most common barriers to listening are impatience, inattentiveness, and eagerness to defend one's point of view. If you scored "rarely" on items 3, 6, 7, and 17, give yourself a pat on the back. If not, consider how you might build your listening skills.

**Interpersonal Communication**

Interpersonal communication involves a complicated array of skills. If you scored "rarely" on items 3 and 15 and 17, you are probably effective at expressing yourself and taking time to negotiate meaning with others. Likewise, if you scored "often" or "almost always" on item 14, you are probably tuned in to messages that are implied but not spoken aloud, concepts we'll discuss in Chapters 6 and 7. If you scored "rarely" on item 2, you probably have a good grip on your emotional reactions. However, if you scored "often" or "almost always" on item 16, you may be bottling up your emotions rather than engaging in open communication.

**Diversity Awareness**

If you scored "often" or "almost always" on items 8, 11, and 13, you have what it takes to be interculturally competent. Curiosity and open-mindedness are assets.

**Group and Team Skills**

If you scored high ("often" or "almost always") on items 1, 2, 9, and 10, you have many of the qualities valued in team members—preparedness, confidence, patience, and diplomacy. But if you scored high on items 3 or 6, you may come off as intimidating or indifferent at times, which can hamper effective teamwork.

**Public Speaking Skills**

If you scored "often" or "almost always" on items 2, 4, and 5, you have an edge when it comes to public speaking. The measure of a great speaker is not absence of nerves but the ability to process information and summon the confidence to present it clearly and powerfully to others. ●

---

occurs.[60] This definition suggests several important characteristics of communication competence. To take a closer look at the ways you communicate well and how you might improve, fill out the "Strengths and Goals" self-assessment on page 26 and/or ask a friend to rate you on the communication dimensions listed. As you think about the results, notice how they reflect the following principles.

**There Is No "Ideal" Way to Communicate**    Your own experience shows that a variety of communication styles can be effective. Some very successful people are serious, whereas others use humor; some are gregarious, whereas others are quiet; and some are straightforward, whereas others hint diplomatically. Just as there are many kinds of beautiful music and art, there are many kinds of competent communication.

The type of communication that succeeds in one situation might be a colossal blunder in another. The joking insults you routinely trade with a friend might be insensitive and discouraging if he or she had just suffered a personal setback. The language you use with your peers might offend a family member, and last Saturday night's romantic approach would probably be out of place at work on Monday morning. For this reason, being a competent communicator requires flexibility in understanding what approach is likely to work best in a given situation.[61]

**Competence Is Situational**    Because competent behavior varies so much from one situation and person to another, it's a mistake to think that communication competence is a trait that a person either possesses or lacks. It's more accurate to talk about *degrees* or *areas* of competence.[62] You and the people you know are probably quite competent in some areas and less so in others. You might deal quite skillfully with peers, for example, but feel clumsy interacting with people much older or younger, wealthier or poorer, or more or less attractive than yourself. In fact, your competence with one person may vary from one situation to another. This means that it's an overgeneralization to say, in a moment of distress, "I'm a terrible communicator!" It would be more accurate to say, "I didn't handle this situation very well, even though I'm better in others."

**Competence Is Relational**    Because communication is transactional, something we do with others rather than to them, behavior that is competent in one relationship isn't necessarily competent in others.

A fascinating study on relational satisfaction illustrates that what constitutes satisfying communication varies from one relationship to another.[63] Researchers Brent Burleson and Wendy Sampter hypothesized that people with sophisticated communication skills (such as managing conflict well, giving ego-support to others, and providing comfort to relational partners) would be better at maintaining friendships than would be less skilled communicators. To their surprise, the results did not support this hypothesis. In fact, friendships were most satisfying when partners possessed matching skill levels. Apparently, relational satisfaction arises in part when our style matches those of the people with whom we interact.

> cultural idiom

**keeping closer tabs on:**
paying closer attention to

The same principle holds true in the case of jealousy. Researchers have uncovered a variety of ways by which people deal with jealousy in their relationships.[64] The ways included keeping closer tabs on the partner, acting indifferent, decreasing affection, talking the matter over, and acting angry. The researchers found that no type of behavior was effective or ineffective in every relationship. They concluded that approaches that work with some people would be harmful to others. Findings like these demonstrate that competence arises out of developing ways of interacting that work for you and for the other people involved.[65]

**Competence Can Be Learned**   To some degree, biology is destiny when it comes to communication style.[66] Studies of identical and fraternal twins suggest that traits including sociability, anger, and relaxation seem to be partially a function of our genetic makeup. Fortunately, biology isn't the only factor that shapes how we communicate: Communication is a set of skills that anyone can learn. As children grow, their ability to communicate effectively develops. For example, older children can produce more sophisticated persuasive attempts than can younger ones.[67] Along with maturity, systematic education (such as the class in which you are now enrolled) can boost communicative competence. Even a modest amount of training can produce dramatic results. After only 30 minutes of instruction, one group of observers became significantly more effective in detecting deception in interviews.[68] One study revealed that college students' communication competence increases over their undergraduate studies.[69] Even without systematic training, it's possible to develop communication skills through the processes of trial and error and observation. We learn from our own successes and failures, as well as from observing other models—both positive and negative.

## Characteristics of Competent Communicators

Although competent communication varies from one situation to another, scholars have identified several common denominators that characterize effective communication in most contexts.

> cultural idiom

**common denominators:**
features common to several instances

**A Wide Range of Behaviors**   Effective communicators are able to choose their actions from a wide range of behaviors. To understand the importance of having a large communication repertoire, imagine that someone you know repeatedly tells jokes—perhaps discriminatory ones—that you find offensive. You could respond to these jokes in a number of ways. You could:

> cultural idiom

**counting on:**
depending on

**soften the blow:**
ease the effect

- Say nothing, figuring that the risks of bringing the subject up would be greater than the benefits.
- Ask a third party to say something to the joke teller about the offensiveness of the jokes.
- Hint at your discomfort, hoping that your friend would get the point.
- Joke about your friend's insensitivity, counting on humor to soften the blow of your criticism.
- Express your discomfort in a straightforward way, asking your friend to stop telling the offensive jokes, at least around you.
- Simply demand that your friend stop.

With this choice of responses at your disposal (and you can probably think of others as well), you could pick the one that had the best chance of success. But if you were able to use only one or two of these responses when raising a delicate issue—always keeping quiet or always hinting, for example—your chances of success would be much smaller. Indeed, many poor communicators are easy to spot by their limited range of responses. Some are chronic jokers. Others are always belligerent. Still others are quiet in almost every situation. Like a piano player who knows only one tune or a chef who can prepare only a few dishes, these people are forced to rely on a small range of responses again and again, whether or not they are successful.

**Ability to Choose the Most Appropriate Behavior**    Simply possessing a large array of communication skills isn't a guarantee of effectiveness. It's also necessary to know which of these skills will work best in a particular situation. Choosing the best way to send a message is rather like choosing a gift: What is appropriate for one person won't be appropriate for another one at all. This ability to choose the best approach is essential because a response that works well in one setting would flop miserably in another one.

Although it's impossible to say precisely how to act in every situation, there are at least three factors to consider when you are deciding which response to choose: the context, your goal, and the other person.

**Skill at Performing Behaviors**    After you have chosen the most appropriate way to communicate, it's still necessary to perform the required skills effectively. There is a big difference between knowing about a skill and being able to put it into practice. Simply being aware of alternatives isn't much help, unless you can skillfully put these alternatives to work.

Just reading about communication skills in the following chapters won't guarantee that you can start using them flawlessly. As with any other skills—playing a musical instrument or learning a sport, for example—the road to competence in communication is not a short one. You can expect that your first efforts at communicating differently will be awkward. After some practice you will become more skillful, although you will still have to think about the new way of speaking or listening. Finally, after repeating the new skill again and again, you will find you can perform it without conscious thought.

> Think of someone you consider a competent communicator. How does he or she match the characteristics described in this section?

**Empathy/Perspective Taking**    People have the best chance of developing an effective message when they understand the other person's point of view. And because others aren't always good at expressing their thoughts and feelings clearly, the ability to imagine how an issue might look from the other's point of view is an important skill. The value of taking the other's perspective suggests one reason why listening is so important. Not only does it help us understand others, it also gives us information to develop strategies about how to best influence them. Because empathy is such an important element of communicative competence, much of Chapters 2 and 5 are devoted to this topic.

**Cognitive Complexity**    Cognitive complexity is the ability to construct a variety of frameworks for viewing an issue. Cognitive complexity is an ingredient of communication competence because it allows us to make sense of people using a variety of perspectives. For instance, imagine that a longtime friend seems to be angry with you. One possible explanation is that your friend is offended by something you've done. Another possibility is that something upsetting has happened in another part of your friend's life. Or perhaps nothing at all is wrong, and you're just being overly sensitive. Researchers have found that the ability to analyze the behavior of others in a variety of ways leads to greater "conversational sensitivity," increasing the chances of acting in ways that will produce satisfying results.[70]

**Self-Monitoring**    Psychologists use the term *self-monitoring* to describe the process of paying close attention to one's behavior and using these observations to shape

## Call Centers and Culture

In a sleek new office building, two dozen young Indians are studying the customs of a place none of them has ever seen. One by one, the students present their conclusions about this fabled land.

"Americans eat a lot of junk food. Table manners are very casual," says Ritu Khanna.

"People are quite self-centered. The average American has thirteen credit cards," says Nerissa Dcosta.

"Seventy-six percent of the people mistrust the government. In the near future, this figure is expected to go up to 100 percent," says Sunny Trama.

The Indians, who range in age from twenty to twenty-seven, have been hired to take calls from cranky or distraught Americans whose computers have gone haywire. To do this, they need to communicate in a language that is familiar but a culture that is foreign.

"We're not saying India is better or America is better," says their trainer, Alefiya Rangwala. "We just want to be culturally sensitive so there's no disconnect when someone phones for tech support."

Call centers took root here during the 2001 recession, when U.S. companies were struggling to control expenses. By firing American customer service workers and hiring Indians, the firms slashed their labor costs by 75 percent.

At first, training was simple. The centers gave employees names that were acceptable to American ears, with Arjun becoming Aaron and Sangita becoming Susan. The new hires were instructed to watch *Friends* and *Ally McBeal* to get an idea of American folkways.

But whether Aaron and Susan were repairing computers, selling long-distance service, or fulfilling orders for diet tapes, problems immediately cropped up. The American callers often wanted a better deal or an impossibly swift resolution and were aggressive and sometimes abrasive about saying so.

The Indians responded according to their own deepest natures: They were silent when they didn't understand, and they often committed to more than their employers could deliver. They would tell the Americans that someone would get back to them tomorrow to check on their problems, and no one would.

Customer satisfaction plummeted. The U.S. clients grew alarmed. Some even returned their business to U.S. call centers.

Realizing that a new multibillion-dollar industry with 150,000 employees was at risk, Indian call centers have recently embarked on much more comprehensive training. New hires are taught how to express empathy, strategies to successfully open and close conversations, and above all how to be assertive, however unnatural it might feel.

"We like to please," says Aparajita Ajit, whose title is "head of talent transformation" for the call-center firm Mphasis. "It's very difficult for us to say no."

Originally, the ever-agreeable Indian agents had a hard time getting people to pay bills that were six months overdue. Too often, says trainer Deepa Nagraj, the calls would go like this:

"Hi," the Indian would say. "I'd like to set up a payment to get your account current. Can I help you do that?"

"No," the American responds.

"OK, let me know if you change your mind," the Indian says and hangs up.

Now, says Nagraj, the agents take no excuses. ●

David Streitfeld

---

It's easy to understand how knowledge of a different culture is essential for satisfying communication. If possible, interview someone who came to this country from another one where the rules for communication are different. What practices did your informant find different and surprising? What would you need to know to communicate competently in that person's home culture?

the way one behaves. Unlike Calvin in the cartoon on this page, high self-monitors are able to separate a part of their consciousness and observe their behavior from a detached viewpoint, making observations such as

*"I'm making a fool out of myself."*

*"I'd better speak up now."*

*"This approach is working well. I'll keep it up."*

Chapter 2 explains how too much self-monitoring can be problematic. Still, people who are aware of their

# Calvin and Hobbes

## by Bill Watterson

Source: CALVIN and HOBBES © 1994 Watterson. Distributed by UNIVERSAL PRESS SYNDICATE. Reprinted with permission. All Rights Reserved.

behavior and the impression it makes are more skillful communicators than people who are low self-monitors.[71] For example, they are more accurate in judging others' emotional states, better at remembering information about others, less shy, and more assertive. By contrast, low self-monitors aren't even able to recognize their incompetence. (Calvin, in the nearby cartoon, does a nice job of illustrating this problem.) One study revealed that poor communicators were blissfully ignorant of their shortcomings and more likely to overestimate their skill than were better communicators.[72] For example, experimental subjects who scored in the lowest quartile on joke-telling skill were more likely than their funnier counterparts to grossly overestimate their sense of humor.

**Commitment to the Relationship**    One feature that distinguishes effective communication in almost any context is commitment. People who seem to care about the relationship communicate better than those who don't.[73] This concern shows up in commitment to the other person and to the message you are expressing.

# Clarifying Misconceptions About Communication

Having spent time talking about what communication is, we ought to also identify some things it is not.[74] Recognizing some misconceptions is important, not only because they ought to be avoided by anyone knowledgeable about the subject, but also because following them can get you into trouble.

## Communication Does Not Always Require Complete Understanding

Most people operate on the implicit but flawed assumption that the goal of all communication is to maximize understanding between communicators. Although some understanding is necessary for us to comprehend one another's thoughts, there are some types of communication in which understanding as we usually conceive it isn't the primary goal.[75] Consider, for example, the following:

- *Social rituals.* "How's it going?" you ask. "Great," the other person replies. The primary goal in exchanges like these is mutual acknowledgment: There's obviously no serious attempt to exchange information.

- *Many attempts to influence others.* A quick analysis of most television commercials shows that they are aimed at persuading viewers to buy products, not to understand the content of the commercial. In the same way, many of our attempts at persuading another to act as we want don't involve a desire to get the other person to understand what we want—just to comply with our wishes.

- *Deliberate ambiguity and deception.* When you decline an unwanted invitation by saying, "I can't make it," you probably want to create the impression that the decision is really beyond your control. (If your goal was to be perfectly clear, you might say, "I don't want to get together. In fact, I'd rather do almost anything than accept your invitation.") As Chapters 4 and 7 explain in detail, we often equivocate precisely because we want to obscure our true thoughts and feelings.

- *Coordinated action.* Examples are conversations in which satisfaction doesn't depend on full understanding. The term **coordination** has been used to describe situations in which participants interact smoothly, with a high degree of satisfaction but without necessarily understanding one another well.[76] Coordination without understanding can be satisfying in far more important situations. Consider the words "I love you." This is a phrase that can have many meanings: Among other things, it can mean "I admire you," "I feel great affection for you," "I desire you," "I am grateful to you," "I feel guilty," "I want you to be faithful to me," or even "I hope *you* love *me*."[77] It's not hard to picture a situation in which partners gain great satisfaction—even over a lifetime—without completely understanding that the mutual love they profess actually is quite different for each of them. "You mean you mostly love me because I've been there for you? Hey, a *dog* is there for you!"

## Communication Will Not Solve All Problems

"If I could just communicate better . . ." is the sad refrain of many unhappy people who believe that if they could just express themselves better, their relationships would improve. Though this is sometimes true, it's an exaggeration to say that communicating—even communicating clearly—is a guaranteed panacea. Here's a reminder guide about the limits of communication.

---

Ethical Challenge

## To Communicate or Not to Communicate?

The explanations on pages 31–34 make it clear that communication is not a panacea. Explaining yourself and understanding others will not solve all problems; in fact, sometimes more communication leads to more problems. Think of an occasion (real or hypothetical) in which more interaction would make matters worse. Imagine that the other person (or people) involved in this situation is (are) urging you to keep the channels of communication open. You know that if you do communicate more, the situation will deteriorate, yet you don't want to appear uncooperative. What should you do?

---

## Communication Isn't Always a Good Thing

In truth, communication is neither good nor bad in itself. Rather, its value comes from the way it is used. Communication can be a tool for expressing warm feelings and useful facts, but under different circumstances the same words and actions can cause both physical and emotional pain.

## Meanings Rest in People, Not Words

It's a mistake to think that, just because you use a word in one way, others will do so, too.[78] Sometimes differing interpretations of symbols are easily caught, as when we might first take the statement "He's loaded" to mean the subject has had too much to drink, only to find out that he is quite wealthy. In other cases, however, the ambiguity of words and nonverbal behaviors isn't so apparent and thus has more far-reaching consequences. Remember, for instance, a time when someone said to you, "I'll be honest," and only later did you learn that those words hid precisely the opposite fact. In Chapter 4 you'll read a great deal more about the problems that come from mistakenly assuming that meanings rest in words.

## Communication Is Not Simple

Most people assume that communication is an aptitude that people develop without the need for training—rather like breathing. After all, we've been swapping ideas with one another since early childhood, and there are lots of people who communicate pretty well without ever having had a class on the subject. Though this picture of communication as a natural ability seems accurate, it's actually a gross oversimplification.[79]

Many people do learn to communicate skillfully because they have been exposed to models of such behavior by those around them. This principle of modeling explains why children who grow up in homes with stable relationships between family members have a greater chance of developing such relationships themselves. But even the best communicators aren't perfect: They often suffer the frustration of being unable to get a message across effectively, and they frequently misunderstand others. Furthermore, even the most successful people you know probably can identify ways in which their relationships could profit from better communication. These facts show that communication skills are rather like athletic ability: Even the most inept of us can learn to be more effective with training and practice, and those who are talented can always become better.

## More Communication Isn't Always Better

Although it's certainly true that not communicating enough is a mistake, there are also situations when *too much* communication is a mistake. The "@Work" box below illustrates how technology contributes to information overload. Sometimes excessive communication simply is unproductive, as when we "talk a problem to death," going over the same ground again and again without making any headway. And there are times when communicating too much can actually aggravate a problem. We've all had the experience of "talking ourselves into a hole"—making a bad situation worse

 **ON YOUR FEET**

*A Mistaken Assumption*
Briefly describe an incident that illustrates one of the misconceptions described in this section. What were the mistaken assumptions? What were the consequences of this incident? How could the communicators involved have handled this situation more effectively?

---

### @Work

## Can You Be *Too* Connected?

Communication technology has led to a dramatic growth in teleworking—flexible work arrangements in which people can work nearly anywhere. Along with their benefits, the technologies that keep us connected have a downside. When your boss, colleagues, and customers can reach you at any time, you can become too distracted to be productive.

Communication researchers Paul Leonardi, Jeffrey Treem, and Michele Jackson discovered that remote workers developed two strategies to reduce contact and thereby increase their efficiency.[80] The first simply involved *disconnecting* from time to time: logging off the computer, forwarding the phone call to voice mail, or simply ignoring incoming messages. The researchers labeled the second strategy *dissimulation*. Teleworkers disguise their activities to discourage contact: changing their instant message status to "in a meeting" or posting a fake "out of the office" message online.

It's important to note that these strategies were typically used not to avoid work but to get more done. These findings show that too much connectivity is like many other parts of life: More isn't always better.

*For more on increasing your efficiency and productivity at work, see the appendix, Communicating for Career Success.* ●

by pursuing it too far. As two noted communication scholars put it, "more and more negative communication merely leads to more and more negative results."[81]

There are even times when *no* communication is the best course. Any good salesperson will tell you that it's often best to stop talking and let the customer think about the product. And when two people are angry and hurt, they may say things they don't mean and will later regret. At times like these it's probably best to spend a little time cooling off, thinking about what to say and how to say it.

## Summary

This chapter began by defining communication as it will be examined in *Understanding Human Communication*: the process of creating meaning through symbolic interaction.

We presented a linear and a transactional communication model, demonstrating the superiority of the transactional model in representing the process-oriented nature of human interaction.

We introduced several communication contexts that will be covered in the rest of the book: intrapersonal, dyadic, small group, public, and mass.

The nature of human communication has changed more rapidly in the last century than at any time in history, partly because of new technologies. Over the past century, the academic discipline of communication has evolved to reflect those changes. New communication technologies have expanded the options for how to communicate. Because every communication channel possesses unique characteristics, the increased number of methods for communicating presents both opportunities and challenges.

We described the characteristics of various communication media, described how they are used in contemporary society, and offered guidelines for using social media competently.

Communication satisfies several types of needs: physical, identity, social, and practical.

Communication competence is situational and relational in nature, and it can be learned. Competent communicators are able to choose and perform appropriately from a wide range of behaviors, as well as being cognitively complex self-monitors who can take the perspective of others and who are committed to important relationships.

We concluded by discussing what communication is *not* by refuting several common misconceptions. Communication doesn't always require complete understanding. It is not always a good thing that will solve every problem, and more communication is not always better. Meanings are in people, not in words. Communication is neither simple nor easy.

## Key Terms

**asynchronous communication** Communication that occurs when there's a time gap between when a message is sent and when it is received. *p. 17*

**channel** The medium through which a message passes from sender to receiver. *p. 8*

**communication** The process of creating meaning through symbolic interaction. *p. 5*

**communication competence** The ability to maintain a relationship on terms acceptable to all parties. *p. 25*

**coordination** Interaction in which participants interact smoothly, with a high degree of satisfaction but without necessarily understanding one another well. *p. 32*

**decoding** The process in which a receiver attaches meaning to a message. *p. 10*

**disinhibition** The tendency to transmit messages without considering their consequences. See also *Flaming*. *p. 20*

**dyad** A two-person unit. *p. 11*

**dyadic communication** Two-person communication. *p. 11*

**encoding** The process of putting thoughts into symbols, most commonly words. *p. 10*

**environment** Both the physical setting in which communication occurs and the personal perspectives of the parties involved. *p. 9*

**feedback** The discernible response of a receiver to a sender's message. *p. 10*

**flaming** Sending angry and/or insulting e-mails, text messages, and website postings. *p. 20*

**interpersonal communication** Communication in which the parties consider one another as unique individuals rather than as objects. It is characterized by minimal use of stereotyped labels; unique, idiosyncratic social rules; and a high degree of information exchange. *p. 12*

**intrapersonal communication** Communication that occurs within a single person. *p. 11*

**linear communication model** A characterization of communication as a one-way event in which a message flows from sender to receiver. *p. 8*

**mass communication** The transmission of messages to large, usually widespread audiences via broadcast means (such as radio and television), print (such as newspapers, magazines, and books), multimedia (such as CD-ROM, DVD, and the World Wide Web), and other forms of media such as recordings and movies. *p. 13*

**mediated communication** Communication sent via a medium other than face-to-face interaction, e.g., telephone, e-mail, and instant messaging. It can be both mass and personal. *p. 8*

**message** A sender's planned and unplanned words and nonverbal behaviors. *p. 8*

**noise** External, physiological, and psychological distractions that interfere with the accurate transmission and reception of a message. *p. 9*

**organizational communication** Communication that occurs among a structured collection of people in order to meet a need or pursue a goal. *p. 12*

**public communication** Communication that occurs when a group becomes too large for all members to contribute. It is characterized by an unequal amount of speaking and by limited verbal feedback. *p. 13*

**receiver** One who notices and attends to a message. *p. 8*

**richness** A term used to describe the abundance of nonverbal cues that add clarity to a verbal message. *p. 17*

**sender** The originator of a message. *p. 8*

**small group communication** Communication within a group of a size such that every member can participate actively with the other members. *p. 12*

**social media** Digital communication channels used primarily for personal reasons, often to reach small groups of receivers. *p. 15*

**symbol** An arbitrary sign used to represent a thing, person, idea, event, or relationship in ways that make communication possible. *p. 7*

**synchronous communication** Communication that occurs in real time. *p. 17*

**transactional communication model** A characterization of communication as the simultaneous sending and receiving of messages in an ongoing, irreversible process. *p. 10*

**Web 2.0** A term used to describe how the Internet has evolved from a one-way medium into a "masspersonal" phenomenon. *p. 15*

## Check Your Understanding

1. Use the transactional model and explanation on pages 10–11 to analyze the success or failure of communication in a specific incident.

2. Think about your communication over the past week. How would it have been different if you were transported back in time 25 years? 50 years? A century?

3. List the most significant times you have communicated via social media. How would these exchanges have been different if you had communicated in person? Which type of communication would have been most effective?

4. Apply the uses and gratifications categories on pages 17–19 to analyze the ways you use social media.

5. Using the categories on pages 23–25, describe the key needs you attempt to satisfy by communicating.

6. Use the criteria in this chapter to identify the degree to which your communication is less than fully competent, and suggest ways of increasing your competence level.

7. What misconceptions about communication have caused the greatest problems in your life? How could you approach similar situations more constructively in the future?

## Activities

1. **Analyzing Your Communication Behavior** Prove for yourself that communication is both frequent and important by observing your interactions for a one-day period. Record every occasion in which you are involved in some sort of human communication as it is defined on page 5. Based on your findings, answer the following questions:

   1. What percentage of your waking day is involved in communication?

   2. What percentage of time do you spend communicating in the following contexts: intrapersonal, dyadic, small group, and public?

   3. What percentage of your communication is devoted to satisfying each of the following types of needs: physical, identity, social, and practical? (Note that you might try to satisfy more than one type at a time.)

   Based on your analysis, describe 5 to 10 ways you would like to communicate more effectively. For each item on your list of goals, describe who is involved (e.g., "my boss," "people I meet at parties") and how you would like to communicate differently (e.g., "act less defensively when criticized," "speak up more instead of waiting for them to approach me"). Use this list to focus your studies as you read the remainder of this book.

2. **Choosing the Most Effective Communication Channel** Decide which communication channel would be most

effective in each of the following situations. Be prepared to explain your answer.

1. In class, an instructor criticizes you for copying work from other sources, but the work really was your own. You are furious, and you don't intend to accept the attack without responding. Which approach(es) would be best for you to use?

   a. Send your instructor an e-mail or write a letter explaining your objections.

   b. Telephone your instructor and explain your position.

   c. Schedule a personal meeting with your instructor.

2. You want to see whether the members of your extended family are able to view the photos you've posted on your family website. How can you find out how easily they can access the website?

   a. Demonstrate the website at an upcoming family get-together.

   b. Send them a link to the website as part of an e-mail.

   c. Phone family members and ask them about their ability to access websites.

3. You want to be sure the members of your office team are able to use the new voice mail system. Should you

   a. Send each employee an instruction manual for the system?

   b. Ask employees to send you e-mails or memos with any questions about the system?

   c. Conduct one or more training sessions in which employees can try out the system and you can clear up any questions?

4. You've just been given two free tickets to tomorrow night's concert. How can you best find out whether your friend can go with you?

   a. Send her an e-mail and ask for a quick reply.

   b. Leave a message on your friend's voice mail asking her to phone you back.

   c. Send an instant message via your computer.

3. **Increasing Your Communicative Competence** Prove for yourself that communication competence can be increased by following these steps.

   1. Identify a situation in which you are dissatisfied with your present communication skill.

   2. Identify at least three distinct, potentially successful approaches you might take in this situation that are different from the one you have taken in the past. If you are at a loss for alternatives, consider how other people you have observed (both real people and fictional characters) have handled similar situations.

   3. From these three alternatives, choose the one you think would work best for you.

   4. Consider how you could become more skillful at performing your chosen approach. For example, you might rehearse it alone or with friends, or you might gain pointers from watching others.

   5. Consider how to get feedback on how well you perform your new approach. For instance, you might ask friends to watch you. In some cases, you might even be able to ask the people involved how you did.

   This systematic approach to increasing your communicative competence isn't the only way to change, but it is one way to take the initiative in communicating more effectively.

4. **Medium and Message Effectiveness** Send the same message to four friends, but use a different medium for each person. For example, ask the question "How's it going?" Use the following media:

   - E-mail
   - Instant message
   - Text message
   - Telephone

   Notice how each response differs and what that may say about the nature of the medium.

5. **Social Media Analysis** Construct a diary of the ways you use social media in a three-day period. For each instance when you use social media (e-mail, a social networking website, phone, Twitter, etc.), describe

   1. The kind(s) of social media you use

   2. The nature of the communication (e.g., "Wrote on friend's Facebook wall," "Reminded roommate to pick up dinner on the way home")

   3. The type of need you are trying to satisfy (information, relational, identity, entertainment)

   Based on your observations, describe the types of media you use most often and the importance of social media in satisfying your communication needs.

6. **Media Fast** Gain insight about the role of mediated communication in your life by going on a "media fast." For a 24-hour period, restrict your communication to only face-to-face interaction. Avoid all print and electronic channels: telephone, TV and radio, the Internet. Then explore the impact of mediated communication

by describing both the negative and positive effects of life without media. Consider how you could modify your everyday life to enhance its quality by modifying the ways you use media.

## For Further Exploration

**For more resources about the nature of communication, see the *Understanding Human Communication* website at www.oup.com/us/adler.** There you will find a variety of resources: "Media Room" clips from popular films and television shows to further illustrate important concepts, a list of relevant books and articles, links to descriptions of feature films and television shows at the *Now Playing* website, study aids, and a self-test to check your understanding of the material in this chapter.

CHAPTER 2

# The Self, Perception, and Communication

## Chapter Outline

### LEARNING OBJECTIVES

1. Understand the communicative influences that shape the self-concept.

2. Explain how self-fulfilling prophecies influence behavior.

3. Describe the perceptual tendencies and situational factors that influence perception.

4. Explain the importance of empathy in communication and how the skill of perception checking can enhance your ability to take another's perspective.

5. Explain how the process of identity management can result in the presentation of multiple selves.

6. Explain the ethical dimensions of identity management.

**Susan Cain** is a former Wall Street attorney, consultant, and trainer, with clients including JP Morgan and General Electric. She graduated from Princeton University and Harvard Law School. "From all this you might guess that I'm a hardcore, wonderfully self-confident, pound-the-table kind of person," she says, "when in fact I'm just the opposite."[1]

Cain identifies herself as an introvert—a personality type that she argues is undervalued in a world that prizes extroversion. "I prefer listening to talking, reading to socializing, and cozy chats to group settings. I like to think before I speak (softly)."

Cain describes the many messages that can cause introverts to feel inadequate, inferior, and ashamed. "Why are you being so mellow?" she recalls being asked by the most popular girl at summer camp. "We should all work very hard to be outgoing," a counselor told her. Cain explains the insidious effect of messages like these that bash introversion. "We all internalize it from a very early age without even having a language for what we're doing."

Like many introverts, Cain recalls faking extroversion to gain approval. "I became a Wall Street lawyer, of all things, instead of the writer that I had always longed to be. . . . And I was always going off to crowded bars when I really would have preferred to just have a nice dinner with friends. And I made these self-negating choices so reflexively that I wasn't even aware I was making them."

In her book *Quiet: The Power of Introverts in a World That Can't Stop Talking,*[2] Cain argues that the world needs introverts. She cites research showing that soft-spoken leaders often deliver better outcomes than extroverts. She offers examples of introverted heroes, including Rosa Parks, Charles Darwin, and Gandhi. Cain also explains how solitude is a necessary ingredient of creativity, and how quiet reflecton can help solve problems.

Despite the merits of introversion, Cain recognizes the value of stretching beyond one's comfort zone. "When the cause is right, I'm willing to make a little noise." In what she calls her "Year of Speaking Dangerously," Cain undertook an ambitious tour of lectures and media appearances. She was interviewed dozens of times and spoke on stage before crowds of 1,000 or more. Despite her accomplishments, she confides, "I've never given a speech without being terrified first."

Cain takes nothing away from more vocal types, whom she honors for different gifts: "I actually love extroverts, including my beloved husband." In her own marriage and beyond, Cain recognizes that the two styles can be complementary: "We need more of a yin and yang between these two types," she says.

### As you reflect on Susan Cain's story, think about the following questions:

- How does your personality shape the way you communicate?

- What factors helped shape the way you relate to others? How would you like to change the way you view yourself and how you communicate?

- How accurate are your perceptions of others, and how do those peceptions shape the nature of your relationships with them?

Susan Cain's story demonstrates the central themes of this chapter:

- The messages people send—consciously or not—can shape others' self-concepts and thus influence their communication.
- The beliefs each of us hold about ourselves have a powerful effect on our own communication behav̶...
- The image we present to the world varies from one situation to another.
- People often perceive the world in radically different ways, which presents major challenges for successful communicating.

These simple truths play a role in virtually all the important messages we send and receive. The goal of this chapter is to show how the ways in which we perceive ourselves and others shape our communication.

# Communication and the Self

Nothing is more fundamental to understanding how we communicate than our sense of self. For that reason, the following pages introduce the notion of self-concept and explain how the way we view ourselves shapes our interaction with others.

## Self-Concept Defined

The **self-concept** is a set of relatively stable perceptions that each of us holds about ourselves. The self-concept includes our conception of what is unique about us and what makes us both similar to and different from others. To put it differently, the self-concept is rather like a mental mirror that reflects how we view ourselves: not only physical features but also emotional states, talents, likes and dislikes, values, and roles.

We will have more to say about the nature of the self-concept shortly, but first you will find it valuable to gain a personal understanding of how this theoretical construct applies to you. You can do so by answering a simple question: "Who are you?"

A man or woman? What is your age? Your religion? Occupation?

There are many ways of identifying yourself. Take a few more minutes and list as many ways as you can to identify who you are. You'll need this list later in this chapter, so be sure to complete it now. Try to include all the characteristics that describe you, including:

- Your moods or feelings
- Your appearance and physical condition
- Your social traits
- Talents you possess or lack
- Your intellectual capacity
- Your belief systems (religion, philosophy)
- Your strong beliefs
- Your social roles

> How do you identify yourself? Consider all the dimensions in this list.

Even a list of 20 or 30 terms would be only a partial description. To make this written self-portrait complete, your list would have to be hundreds—or even thousands—of words long.

Of course, not all items on such a list would be equally important. For example, the most significant part of one person's self-concept might consist of social roles, whereas for another it might consist of physical appearance, health, friendships, accomplishments, or skills.

An important element of the self-concept is **self-esteem**: our evaluations of self-worth. One person's self-concept might include being religious, tall, or athletic. That person's self-esteem would be shaped by how he or she felt about these qualities: "I'm glad that I am athletic," or "I am embarrassed about being so tall," for example.

> How would you describe your level of self-esteem? How is it affected by messages you receive in face-to-face exchanges and via social media?

Self-esteem has a powerful effect on the way we communicate.[3] People with high self-esteem are more willing to communicate than people with low self-esteem. They are more likely to think highly of others and expect to be accepted by others. They aren't afraid of others' reactions and perform well when others are watching them. They work harder for people who demand high standards of performance, and they are comfortable with others whom they view as superior in some way. When confronted with critical comments, they are comfortable defending themselves. By contrast, people with low self-esteem are likely to be critical of others and expect rejection from them. They are also critical of their own performances. They are sensitive to possible disapproval of others and perform poorly when being watched. They work harder for undemanding, less critical people. They feel threatened by people they view as superior in some way and have difficulty defending themselves against others' negative comments. Take the self-assessment on page 43 to reflect on your own level of self-esteem.

Despite its obvious benefits, self-esteem doesn't guarantee success in personal and professional relationships.[4] People with an exaggerated sense of self-worth may *think* they make better impressions on others, but neither impartial observers nor objective tests verify these beliefs. It's easy to see how people with an inflated sense of self-worth could irritate others by coming across as condescending know-it-alls, especially when their self-worth is challenged.[5]

## Biology, Personality, and the Self

Take another look at the list of terms you used to describe yourself on page 41. You'll almost certainly find some that reflect your **personality**—characteristic ways that you think and behave across a variety of situations. Personality tends to be stable throughout life: Research suggests that our temperament at age 3 is highly predictive of how we will behave as adults.[6]

People around the world embody many of the same personality traits. For example, languages as diverse as Hungarian, Dutch, English, Italian, and Korean have words to describe people who are extroverted, patient, emotional, honest, humble, and imaginative.[7]

These traits may be universal because personality is determined partly by genetics. Scientists have found genes that predispose people to be novelty seekers, shy, or emotional.[8] Some studies show that biology accounts for as much as half of communication-related personality traits such as extroversion,[9] shyness,[10] assertiveness,[11] verbal aggression,[12] and overall willingness to communicate.[13] As further evidence, identical twins, who have the same DNA, have more similar personalities than fraternal twins, whose DNA is different.[14] In other words, to some degree, we come programmed to communicate in characteristic ways.

Even though you may have a disposition toward traits like shyness or aggressiveness, you can do a great deal to control how you actually communicate.[15] Even shy people can learn how to reach out to others, and those with aggressive tendencies can learn to communicate in more sociable ways. One author put it this way: "Experiences can silence genes or activate them. Even shyness is like Silly Putty

## SELF-ASSESSMENT

# Communication and Your Self-Esteem

| | Mostly True | Mostly False |
|---|---|---|
| **1.** People enjoy talking to me. | | |
| **2.** If someone criticizes my work, I feel horrible. | | |
| **3.** When I face a difficult communication challenge, I know I can succeed if I work at it. | | |
| **4.** When people tell me they love me, I have a hard time believing it. | | |
| **5.** I am comfortable admitting when I am wrong. | | |
| **6.** People would like me more if I were better looking or more successful. | | |
| **7.** I feel confident making big decisions about my relationships. | | |
| **8.** I frequently let people down. | | |
| **9.** It is more important that I am comfortable with myself than that others like me. | | |
| **10.** I am frequently afraid of saying the wrong thing or looking stupid. | | |

### EVALUATING YOUR RESPONSES

Give yourself one point for every odd-numbered question you answered Mostly True and one point for every even-numbered question you answered Mostly False. Add the two together and look for your score below. Then ask yourself how your self-esteem shapes the way you communicate.

### SCORES

**8 to 10**—You have very high self-esteem.

**5 to 7**—You have relatively high self-esteem.

**3 to 6**—You have relatively low self-esteem.

**0 to 2**—You have very low self-esteem. ●

once life gets hold of it."[16] Throughout this book you will learn about communication skills that, with practice, you can build into your repertoire.

We inherit a portion of our personality, but as you will see next, that isn't the only factor that influences our communication.

## Communication and Development of the Self

So far we've talked about what the self-concept is, but at this point you may be asking what it has to do with the study of human communication. We can begin to answer this question by looking at how you came to possess your own self-concept.

Our identity comes almost exclusively from communication with others. The term **reflected appraisal** metaphorically describes how we develop an image of ourselves from the way we think others view us. As we learn to speak and understand language, verbal messages—both positive and negative—contribute to the developing self-concept. These messages continue later in life, especially when they come from what social scientists term **significant others**—people whose opinions we especially value. A teacher from long ago, a special friend or relative, or perhaps a barely known acquaintance whom you respected can all leave an imprint on how you view yourself. To see the importance of significant others, ask yourself how you arrived at your opinion of you as a student, as a potential

In *The Perks of Being a Wallflower*, Charlie (Nicolas Lerman) is resigned to being cast as a friendless loser by his high school classmates. His fortunes change when he's befriended by eccentric senior Patrick (Ezra Miller) and Patrick's stepsister Sam (Emma Watson). Being seen as an interesting guy changes Charlie's self-concept. How has your self-perception changed for better or worse due to the evaluations of significant others?

 ON YOUR FEET

**Your Significant Others**

Think of a significant other—someone who has profoundly influenced your life. What did this person say or do that made a difference? Share how those messages helped shape your self-concept.

romantic partner, as a competent worker, and so on, and you will see that these self-evaluations were probably influenced by the way others regarded you.

As we grow older, the influence of significant others is less powerful.[17] The evaluations of others still influence beliefs about the self in some areas, such as physical attractiveness and popularity. For example, TV makeover shows, with their underlying message of "you must improve your appearance," can lead viewers to feel worse about themselves.[18] In other areas, however, the looking glass of the self-concept has become distorted, so that it shapes the input of others to make it conform with our existing beliefs. For example, if your self-concept includes the element "poor student," you might respond to a high grade by thinking, "I was just lucky" or "The professor must be an easy grader."

You might argue that not every part of one's self-concept is shaped by others, insisting there are certain objective facts that are recognizable by self-observation. After all, nobody needs to tell you that you are taller than others, speak with an accent, can run quickly, and so on. These facts are obvious.

Though it's true that some features of the self are immediately apparent, the *significance* we attach to them—the rank we assign them in the hierarchy of our list and the interpretation we give them—depends greatly on the social environment. The interpretation of characteristics such as weight depends on the way people important to us regard them. Being anything less than trim and muscular is generally regarded as undesirable because others tell us that slenderness is an ideal. In the United States, young women frequently exposed to media images are more likely than other women to feel they are overweight and to have eating disorders.[19] By contrast, in cultures and societies where greater weight is considered beautiful, a Western supermodel would be considered unattractive. In the same way, the fact that one is single or married, solitary or sociable, aggressive or passive takes on meaning depending on the interpretation that society attaches to those traits. Thus, the importance of a given characteristic in your self-concept has as much to do with the significance that you and others attach to it as with the existence of the characteristic.

## Culture and the Self-Concept

Cultures affect the self-concept in both obvious and subtle ways. As you'll read in Chapter 3, most Western cultures are highly individualistic, whereas other cultures—most Asian ones, for example—are traditionally much more collective. When asked to identify themselves, Americans, Canadians, Australians, and Europeans would probably respond by giving their first name, surname, street, town, and country. Many Asians do it the other way around.[20] If you ask Hindus for their identity, they will give you their caste and village as well as their name. The Sanskrit formula for identifying oneself begins with lineage and goes on to family and house and ends with one's personal name.[21]

These conventions for naming aren't just cultural curiosities: They reflect a very different way of viewing oneself.[22] In collective cultures a person gains identity by belonging to a group. This means that the degree of interdependence among members of the society and its subgroups is much higher. Feelings of pride and self-worth are likely to be shaped not only by what the individual does but also by the behavior of other members of the community. This linkage to

## Ethical Challenge

### Is Honesty the Best Policy?

By now it should be clear that each of us has the power to influence others' self-concepts. Even with the best of intentions, there are cases when an honest message is likely to reduce another person's self-esteem. Consider a few examples:

- Your friend, an aspiring artist, asks, "What do you think of my latest painting?" You think it's terrible.

- After a long, hard week you are looking forward to spending the evening at home. A somewhat insecure friend who just broke off a long romantic relationship calls to ask if you want to get to-gether. You don't.

- A good friend asks to use your name as a reference for a potential employer. You can't honestly tell the employer that your friend is qualified for the job.

In situations like these, how do you reconcile the desire to avoid diminishing another person's self-esteem with the need to be honest? Based on your conclusions, is it possible to always be both honest and supportive?

others explains the traditional Asian denial of self-importance—a strong contrast to the self-promotion that is common in individualistic Western cultures. In Chinese written language, for example, the pronoun *I* looks very similar to the word for *selfish*.[23]

## The Self-Concept and Communication with Others

So far we've focused on how the self-concept has been shaped by our interpretations of messages from our cultural environment and influential others. Now we will explore how the self-concept shapes the way we communicate *with* other people.

Figure 2-1 pictures the relationship between the self-concept and behavior. It illustrates how the self-concept both shapes much of our communication behavior and is shaped by it. For example, self-concept has been shown as the single greatest factor in determining whether people who are being teased interpret the teaser's motives as friendly or hostile, and whether they respond with comfort or defensiveness.[24] Children who have a low opinion of themselves are more likely to see themselves as victims of bullying, both in their classrooms and online.[25]

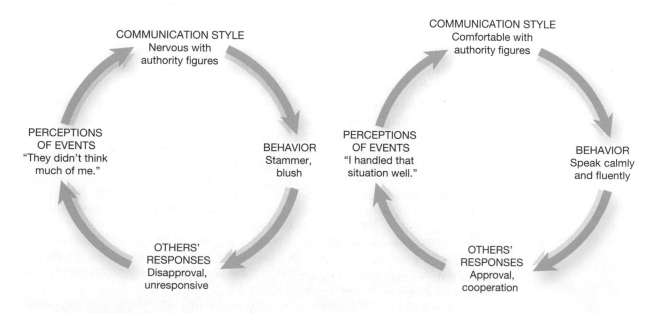

**FIGURE 2-1  The Relationship Between the Self-Concept and Behavior**

In the movie *Precious*, a young woman (Gabourey Sidibe) believes what the abusive people in her life have told her: She is a failure who is stupid, fat, ugly, and unworthy of love. Messages from a teacher and social worker help create self-fulfilling prophecies that give Precious the strength to leave her abusive household and start a new life. What self-fulfilling prophecies (constructive or damaging) have shaped the way you communicate?

We can begin to examine the process by considering the self-concept you bring to an event. Suppose, for example, that one element of your self-concept is "nervous with authority figures." That image probably comes from the evaluations of significant others in the past—perhaps teachers or former employers. If you view yourself as nervous with authority figures like these, you will probably behave in nervous ways when you encounter them in the future—in a teacher-student conference or a job interview. That nervous behavior is likely to influence how others view your personality, which in turn will shape how they respond to you—probably in ways that reinforce the self-concept you brought to the event. Finally, the responses of others will affect the way you interpret future events: other job interviews, meetings with professors, and so on. This cycle illustrates how the chicken-and-egg nature of the self-concept, which is shaped by significant others in the past, helps to govern your present behavior and influences the way others view you.

## The Self-Fulfilling Prophecy and Communication

The self-concept is such a powerful force that it can influence our future behavior and that of others. A **self-fulfilling prophecy** occurs when a person's expectation of an outcome, and subsequent behavior, makes the outcome more likely to occur than it would otherwise have been. This happens all the time. For example, think of the following instances, which you may have experienced:

- You expected to become nervous during a job interview, and your anxiety caused you to answer questions poorly.
- You anticipated having a good (or terrible) time at a party, and your expectations led you to act in ways that shaped the outcome to fit your prediction.
- A teacher or boss explained a new task to you, saying that you probably wouldn't do well at first. You took these comments to heart, and as a result you didn't do well.
- A friend described someone you were about to meet, saying that you wouldn't like the person. Due in part to the prediction, you looked for—and found—reasons to dislike the new acquaintance.

In each of these cases, the outcome happened at least in part because of the expectation that it would happen.

There are two types of self-fulfilling prophecies. The first type occurs when your own expectations influence your own behavior. In sports you have probably psyched yourself into playing either better or worse than usual. The same principle operates for nervous public speakers: Communicators who feel anxious about facing an audience often create self-fulfilling prophecies about doing poorly that cause them to perform less effectively.[26] (Chapter 11 offers advice on overcoming this kind of communication apprehension.)

Research has demonstrated the power of this first type of self-fulfilling prophecy. In one study, communicators who predicted that conflict episodes would be

> cultural idiom
>
> **psyched yourself:**
> boosted confidence by thinking
> positively

intense were likely to be highly emotional during them and to engage in personal attacks.[27] On the bright side, people who expect that others will be friendly and accepting usually act friendlier and more outgoing themselves.[28] As you might expect, they find a warmer reception than people who are fearful of rejection. As the cartoon on this page suggests, self-fulfilling prophecies can be physiologically induced: Researchers have found that putting a smile on your face, even if you're not in a good mood, can lead to a more positive disposition.[29]

A second category of self-fulfilling prophecies occurs when one person's expectations govern another's actions.[30] This principle was demonstrated in a classic experiment.[31] Researchers told teachers that 20 percent of the children in a certain elementary school showed unusual potential for intellectual growth. The names of the 20 percent were drawn by means of a table of random numbers—much as if they were drawn out of a hat. Eight months later these unusual or "magic" children showed significantly greater gains in IQ than did the remaining children, who had not been singled out for the teachers' attention. The change in the teachers' behavior toward these allegedly "special" children led to changes in the intellectual performance of these randomly selected children.

To put this phenomenon in context with the self-concept, we can say that when a teacher communicates to students the message "I think you're bright," they accept that evaluation and change their self-concepts to include that evaluation. Unfortunately, we can assume that the same principle holds for those students whose teachers send the message "I think you're stupid."

This type of self-fulfilling prophecy has been shown to help shape the self-concept and thus the behavior of people in a wide range of settings outside of schools. In medicine, for example, patients who unknowingly receive placebos—substances such as injections of sterile water or doses of sugar pills that have no curative value—often respond just as favorably to treatment as do people who actually receive a drug. The patients believe they have taken a substance that will help them feel better, and this belief actually brings about a "cure." The self-fulfilling prophecy operates in families as well. If parents tell their children long enough that they can't do anything right, the children's self-concepts will soon incorporate this idea, and they will fail at many or most of the tasks they attempt. On the other hand, if children are told they are capable or lovable or kind persons, there is a much greater chance of their behaving accordingly.[32]

The self-fulfilling prophecy is an important force in communication, but it doesn't explain all behavior. There are certainly times when the expectation of an event's outcome won't bring about that outcome. Your hope of drawing an ace in a card game won't in any way affect the chance of that card turning up in an already-shuffled deck, and your belief that good weather is coming won't stop the rain from falling. In the same way, believing you'll do well in a job interview when you're clearly not qualified for the position is unrealistic. Similarly, there will probably be people you don't like and occasions you won't enjoy, no matter what your attitude. To connect the self-fulfilling prophecy with the "power of positive thinking" is an oversimplification.

In other cases, your expectations will be borne out because you are a good predictor and not because of the self-fulfilling prophecy. For example, children are not equally well equipped to do well in school, and in such cases it would be

*"I don't sing because I am happy.
I am happy because I sing."*

wrong to say that a child's performance was shaped by a parent or teacher even though the behavior did match what was expected. In the same way, some workers excel and others fail, some patients recover and others don't—all according to our predictions but not because of them.

As we keep these qualifications in mind, it's important to recognize the tremendous influence that self-fulfilling prophecies play in our lives. To a great extent we are what we believe we are. In this sense we and those around us constantly create our self-concepts and thus ourselves.

## Perceiving Others

The first part of this chapter explored how our self-perceptions affect the way we communicate. The following pages examine how the ways we perceive others shape our interaction with them.

### Steps in the Perception Process

In 1890 the psychologist William James described an infant's world as "one great blooming, buzzing confusion."[33] Babies—all humans, in fact—need some mechanisms to sort out the avalanche of stimuli that bombard us every moment. As you will read in the following pages, many of these stimuli involve others' behavior, and how we deal with those stimuli shapes our communication.

We sort out and make sense of others' behavior in three steps: selection, organization, and interpretation.

**Selection**   Because we're exposed to more input than we can possibly manage, the first step in perception is the **selection** of which data we will attend to.

Some external factors help shape what we notice about others. For example, stimuli that are *intense* often attract our attention. Something that is louder, larger, or brighter stands out. This explains why—other things being equal—we're more likely to remember extremely tall or short people and why someone who laughs or talks loudly at a party attracts more attention (not always favorable) than quieter guests.

We also pay attention to *contrast* or *change* in stimulation. Put differently, unchanging people or things become less noticeable. This principle offers an explanation (excuse?) for why we take consistently wonderful people for granted when we interact with them frequently. It's only when they stop being so wonderful or go away that we appreciate them.

Along with external factors like intensity and contrast, *internal factors* shape how we make sense of others. For example, our *motives* often determine how we perceive people. Someone on the lookout for a romantic adventure will be especially aware of attractive potential partners, whereas the same person in an emergency might be oblivious to anyone but police or medical personnel.

Our *emotional state* also shapes what we select. Consider mood: There is some evidence that the attitude/expectation we bring to a situation shapes our level of happiness or unhappiness.[34] Once started, this process can create a spiral. If you're happy about your relationship, you will be more likely to interpret your partner's behavior in a charitable way. This, in turn, can lead to greater

How do we select, organize, and interpret our perceptions of others?

happiness. Of course, the same process can work in the opposite direction. One study revealed that, when spouses who felt uncertain about the status of their marriage saw their partners conversing with strangers, they were likely to perceive the conversations as relational threats, even though the conversations seemed quite ordinary to outsiders.[35]

**Organization**   After selecting information from the environment, we must arrange it in some meaningful way in order to make sense of the world. We call this stage **organization**.

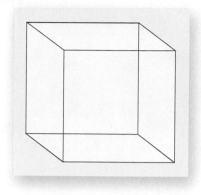

**FIGURE 2-2 Shape-Shifting Cube**

The raw sense data we perceive can be organized in more than one way. The cube in Figure 2-2 illustrates this principle. If you look at the drawing long enough, you'll find that the faces of the cube change places. From one perspective you are looking down on the figure from above, but if you shift your point of view you will see it from beneath.

We organize our perceptions of other people using *perceptual schema*, cognitive frameworks that allow us to give order to the information we have selected.[36] Four types of schema help us classify others:

1. *Physical constructs* classify people according to their appearance: beautiful or ugly, fat or thin, young or old, etc.

2. *Role constructs* use social position: student, attorney, wife, etc.

3. *Interaction constructs* focus on social behavior: friendly, helpful, aloof, sarcastic, etc.

4. *Psychological constructs* refer to internal states of mind and dispositions: confident, insecure, happy, neurotic, etc.

The kinds of constructs we use strongly affect the way we relate to others. For example, boys between 8 and 11 years old tend to categorize peers according to their achievements, what they like and dislike, and personality, whereas girls in the same age range tend to perceive them according to their background and family.[37]

In online environments in which few nonverbal cues exist, it's harder to categorize people we haven't met in person. In text-based situations, strangers often rely on text-based cues to form impressions of others. In one study, for example, students relied on screen names to form impressions of strangers.[38] Experimenters asked college students to form impressions of fictional characters with names like "packerfan4" and "stinkybug." Using just the screen names, most of the respondents assigned attributes including biological sex, ethnicity, and age to the supposed owners of these names.

What constructs do you use to classify the people you encounter in your life? Consider how your relationships might change if you used different schema.

Once we have an organizing scheme to classify people, we use that scheme to make generalizations about members of the groups who fit our categories. For example, if you are especially aware of a person's sex, you might be alert to the differences between the way men and women behave or the way they are treated. If religion plays an important part in your life, you might think of members of your faith differently than you do others. If ethnicity is an important issue for you, you probably tune in to the differences between members of various ethnic groups. There's nothing wrong with generalizations about groups as long as they are accurate. In fact, it would be impossible to get through life without them. But faulty overgeneralizations can lead to problems of stereotyping, which you'll read about a few pages later.

**Interpretation**   Once we have selected and organized our perceptions, we interpret them in a way that makes some sort of sense. **Interpretation** plays a role in virtually every type of communication. Is the person who smiles at you across a crowded room interested in romance or simply being polite? Is a friend's kidding a sign of affection or irritation? Should you take an invitation to "drop by any time" literally or not?

There are several factors that cause us to interpret a person's behavior in one way or another. The first is our *degree of involvement* with the person. For example, research suggests that we tend to view people with whom we have or seek a relationship more favorably than those whom we observe from a detached perspective.[39]

*Relational satisfaction* is a second factor that influences our interpretation. The behavior that seems positive when you are happy with a partner might seem completely different when the relationship isn't satisfying. For example, if our feelings are hurt by a friend or romantic partner, we are more likely to forgive and forget if we are generally happy in the relationship than if we are dissatisfied with it, in which case we tend to be more upset, blame more, and harbor hurt feelings longer.[40]

> cultural idiom
**gouged by:**
charged an excessive amount

A third factor that influences interpretations is *personal experience*. What meanings have similar events held? For instance, if you've been gouged by landlords in the past, you might be skeptical about an apartment manager's assurances that careful housekeeping will ensure the refund of your cleaning deposit.

*Assumptions about human behavior* also influence interpretations. Do you assume people are lazy, dislike work, avoid responsibility, and must be coerced to do things, or do you believe people exercise self-direction and self-control, possess creativity, and seek responsibility? Imagine the differences in a boss who assumes workers fit the first description versus one who assumes they fit the second.

*Expectations* are another factor that shapes our interpretations. When we anticipate people will behave in certain ways, our expectations color the way we interpret their behavior. For instance, if you go into a conversation expecting a hostile attitude, you're likely to hear a negative tone in the other person's voice—even if that tone isn't there. We'll talk more about how expectations affect perception later in this chapter.

> cultural idiom
**jilted:**
rejected

*Knowledge of others* affects the way we interpret their actions. For instance, if you know a friend has just been jilted by a lover or fired from a job, you'll interpret his or her aloof behavior differently than if you were unaware of what happened. If you know an instructor is rude to all students, then you won't be likely to take his or her remarks personally.

Although we have talked about selection, organization, and interpretation separately, the three phases of perception can occur in differing sequences. For example, a parent's or babysitter's past interpretation (such as "Jason is a troublemaker") can influence future selections (his behavior becomes especially noticeable) and the organization of events (when there's a fight, the assumption is that Jason started it). As with all communication, perception is an ongoing process in which it is hard to pin down beginnings and endings.

## Influences on Perception

How we select, organize, and interpret data about others is influenced by a variety of factors. Some of our perceptual judgments are affected by physiology, others by cultural and social factors.

**Physiological Influences**   Some communication problems come from ignoring physiological (bodily) differences in how each of us experiences the world.[41] Consider a few examples:

"Turn down that radio! It's going to make me go deaf."
"It's not too loud. If I turn it down, it will be impossible to hear it."

"It's freezing in here."
"Are you kidding? We'll suffocate if you turn up the heat!"

"Why don't you pass that truck? The highway is clear for half a mile."
"I can't see that far, and I'm not going to get us killed."

The range of physiological influences is broad. For example, *age* can shape perceptions. Until they approach the age of 7, children aren't able to take another person's point of view. This fact helps explain why youngsters often seem egocentric, selfish, and uncooperative. A parent's exasperated "Can't you see I'm too tired to play?" just won't make sense to a 4-year-old full of energy, who imagines that everyone else must feel the same.

*Health and nutrition* also influence the way we interact. When you're ill or have been working long hours or studying late for an exam, the world can seem quite different than when you are well rested. People who are sleep deprived, for example, perceive time intervals as longer than they really are. So the 5 minutes you're waiting for a friend to show up may seem longer, leaving you feeling more impatient than you otherwise would be.[42] Your own experience probably confirms that nutrition shapes communication. Being hungry (and getting grumpy) or having overeaten (and getting tired) affects how we interact with others. One study found that teenagers who reported that their family did not get enough food to eat were almost three times as likely as other teens to have been suspended from school, almost twice as likely to have difficulty getting along with others, and four times as likely to have no friends.[43]

*Biological cycles* also affect perception and communication. Each of us has a daily cycle in which all sorts of changes constantly occur, including variations in body temperature, sexual drive, alertness, tolerance to stress, and mood.[44] These cycles can affect the way we relate toward one another. Researchers in one study found that men had more negative views of their partners after a night in which they didn't sleep well. For women, it was the other way around: Their sleep patterns were disrupted when they perceived problems in the relationship. The researchers observe that sleep, mood, and interpersonal communication are mutually influential.[45]

Some differences in perception are rooted in *neurology*. For instance, people with ADHD (attention deficit hyperactivity disorder) are easily distracted from tasks and have difficulty delaying gratification.[46] It's easy to imagine how those with ADHD might find a long lecture boring and tedious, while other audience members are fascinated by it.[47] Also, young women with ADHD are more likely to have conflicts with their mothers and have fewer romantic relationships than those without ADHD.[48] People with bipolar disorder experience significant mood swings in which their perceptions of events, friends, and even family members shift dramatically. The National Institute of Mental Health estimates that between 5 million and 7 million Americans are affected by these two disorders alone[49]—and there are many other psychological conditions that influence people's perceptions.

**Cultural Influences**   As we will discuss in depth in Chapter 3, culture provides a perceptual filter that influences the way we interpret even the simplest

In the film *Temple Grandin*, Claire Danes dramatizes the true story of a woman whose world is shaped by autism. Despite the prejudices and ignorance of the 1960s, Grandin earned a Ph.D. in animal science. She claims that her professional success is due in part to her hypersensitivity to the behavior and emotions of animals. In what ways do you experience the world differently than the people around you? How does this influence your communication?

events. This filter extends to sex and gender roles, occupational roles, and relational roles, to name a few.

**Sex and Gender Roles**   Social expectations about masculine and feminine behavior have a powerful influence on our identity and how we communicate. Consider a few examples:

- A mother says to her daughter, "Don't act that way. It isn't ladylike."

- A same sex-couple you know is frustrated when people assume that one of them plays a more masculine role and one a more feminine role in the relationship.

- You overhear a work colleague call your female supervisor "a bitch." You realize that term is never used to describe men.

For most people, gendered expectations began the moment they were born—or even before, with the selection of clothing, blankets, toys, and nursery décor. Yet we don't often question the assumptions that underlie cultural expectations about gender.

Let's start with a few misconceptions. One is that people are either male or female. Actually, hormone levels and other factors make biological sex a more complicated formula than you might think. The feelings and actions of both men and women are shaped by a mixture of estrogen and testosterone.

A second misconception is that "sex" and "gender" are the same. In fact, **sex** is a biological category (male, female, intersexed, and so on), whereas **gender** is a socially constructed set of expectations about what it means to be "masculine" or "feminine." A statement about a man's long hair looking girlish reveals a particular cultural assumption. In many cultures, long hair is considered masculine. Thus, it is possible, even necessary, for a woman to embody some attributes associated with masculine gender, and vice versa for men. Indeed, as you will soon see, there are advantages to embodying both "masculine" and "feminine" qualities.

A third misconception is that masculine and feminine behaviors occur at opposite poles on a single continuum. Early theorizing suggested that stereotypical masculine and feminine behaviors are not opposites but rather two separate sets of behavior.[50] One alternative to the masculine-feminine dichotomy is the idea of four *psychological sex types*, including masculine, feminine, **androgynous** (combining masculine and feminine traits), and undifferentiated (neither masculine nor feminine). These days, we use the term *gender* instead of the phrase "psychological sex type." Thus, whether people are male or female, they might be masculine, feminine, androgynous, or undifferentiated, based on society's definitions. Although there are women and men who fit into all of the categories, in general, people see themselves as either sex typed (masculine male/feminine female) or androgynous.[51]

Although the differences between men and women's behavior are not as great as many people think, evidence points to some differences at the extremes. For example, especially masculine males tend to see their interpersonal relationships as opportunities for competitive interaction, as opportunities to win something. Especially feminine females typically see their interpersonal relationships as opportunities to be nurturing, to express their feelings and emotions.[52] Androgynous individuals tend to see their relationships as opportunities to behave in a variety of ways, depending on the nature of the relationship, the context in which it takes place,

*"How is it gendered?"*

Source: Edward Koren / The New Yorker Collection / www.cartoonbank.com

and the myriad other variables affecting what might constitute appropriate behavior. These variables are usually ignored by the sex-typed masculine males and feminine females, who have a smaller repertoire of behaviors.

Women and men often judge the same behaviors quite differently. Men tend to rate verbal and nonverbal behaviors as more flirtatious and seductive than do women.[53] Women react differently depending on their age and marital status.[54] Some types of behavior men find innocuous have been judged as being harassing by women.[55] Not surprisingly, much of the difference comes from experience: Women who report having been harassed are more likely to find harassment in subsequent interactions.[56] Experience isn't the only factor, though: Younger women are more likely to perceive harassment than older ones, who, presumably, have a different set of expectations about what kinds of communication are and aren't appropriate. Also, attitudes play a role: People who disapprove of socializing and dating between coworkers are more likely to perceive harassment than those who accept this sort of relationship.[57]

**Occupational Roles**   The kind of work we do also governs our view of the world. Imagine five people taking a walk through a park. One, a botanist, is fascinated by the variety of trees and plants. The zoologist is on the lookout for interesting animals. The third, a meteorologist, keeps an eye on the sky, noticing changes in the weather. The fourth, a psychologist, is totally unaware of the goings-on of nature, concentrating instead on the interaction among the people in the park. The fifth, a pickpocket, quickly takes advantage of the others' absorption to collect their wallets. There are two lessons in this little story: The first, of course, is to watch your wallet carefully. The second is that our occupational roles frequently govern our perceptions.

Perhaps the most dramatic illustration of how occupational roles shape perception occurred in the early 1970s. Stanford psychologist Philip Zimbardo recruited a group of well-educated middle-class young men.[58] He randomly chose 11 to serve as "guards" in a mock prison set up in the basement of Stanford's psychology building. He issued the guards uniforms, handcuffs, whistles, and billy clubs. The remaining 10 participants became "prisoners" and were placed in rooms with metal bars, bucket toilets, and cots.

Zimbardo let the "guards" establish their own rules for the experiment. The rules were tough: no talking during meals and rest periods and after lights-out. Troublemakers received short rations.

Faced with these conditions, the "prisoners" began to resist. The guards reacted to the rebellion by clamping down hard on protesters, and what had been an experiment suddenly became very real. Some guards turned sadistic, physically and verbally abusing the prisoners. The experiment was scheduled to go on for 2 weeks, but after 6 days Zimbardo had to call it off. It seems that *what* we are is determined largely by society's designation of *who* we are.

**Relational Roles**   Think back to the "Who am I?" list you made earlier in this chapter. It's likely your list included roles you play in relation to others: daughter, roommate, spouse, friend, and so on. Roles like these don't just define who you are—they also affect your perception.

Take, for example, the role of parent. As most new mothers and fathers will attest, having a child alters the way they see the world. They might perceive their crying baby as a helpless soul in need of comfort, whereas nearby strangers have a less charitable appraisal. As the child grows, parents often pay more attention to the messages in the child's environment. One father we know said he never noticed how much football fans curse and swear until he took his 6-year-old to a game with him. In other words, his role as father affected what he heard and how he interpreted it.

The roles involved in romantic love can also dramatically affect perception. These roles have many labels: partner, spouse, boyfriend/girlfriend, sweetheart, and so on. There are times when your affinity biases the way you perceive the object of your affection. You may see your sweetheart as more attractive than other people do, and perhaps you overlook some faults that others notice.[59] Your romantic role can also change the way you view others. One study found that when people are in love, they view other romantic candidates as less attractive than they normally would.[60]

Perhaps the most telltale sign of the effect of "love goggles" is when they come off. Many people have experienced breaking up with a romantic partner and wondering later, "What did I ever see in that person?" The answer—at least in part—is that you saw what your relational role led you to see.

## Narratives, Perception, and Communication

We all have our own story of the world, and often our story is quite different from those of others. A family member or roommate might think your sense of humor is inappropriate, whereas you think you're quite clever. You might blame an unsatisfying class on the professor, who you think is a long-winded bore. On the other hand, the professor might characterize the students as superficial and lazy and blame the class environment on them. (The discussion of emotive language in Chapter 4 will talk about the sort of name-calling embedded in the previous sentences.)

> cultural idiom
> **long-winded:**
> speaking for a long time

Social scientists call the personal stories that we and others create to make sense of our personal world **narratives**.[61] In a few pages we will look at how a tool called "perception checking" can help bridge the gap between different narratives. For now, though, the important point is that differing narratives can lead to problematic communication.

After they take hold, narratives offer a framework for explaining behavior and shaping future communication. One study of sense making in organizations illustrates how the process operates on the job.[62] Researchers located employees who had participated in office discussions about cases in which a fellow worker had received "differential treatment" from management about matters such as time off, pay, or work assignments. The researchers then analyzed the conversations that employees held with fellow workers about the differential treatment. The analysis revealed that these conversations were the occasion in which workers created and reinforced the meaning of the employee's behavior and management's response. For example, consider the way workers made sense of Jane Doe's habit of taking late lunches. As Jane's coworkers discuss her behaviors, they might decide that her late lunches aren't fair—or they might agree that late lunches aren't a big deal. Either way, the coworkers' narrative of office events *defines* those events. Once they are defined, coworkers tend to seek reinforcement for their perceptions by keeping a mental scorecard rating their fellow employees and management. ("Did you notice that Bob came in late again today?" "Did you notice that the boss chose Jane to go on that trip to New York?") Although most of us like to think we make judgments about others on our own, this research suggests that sense making is an *interactive* process. In other words, reality in the workplace and elsewhere isn't "out there"; rather, we create it with others through communication.

> What's one narrative about yourself you have constructed on the Internet? How conscious were you in crafting this narrative? How accurate is it?

Research on long-term happy marriages demonstrates that shared narratives don't have to be accurate to be powerful.[63] Couples who report being happily married after 50 or more years seem to collude in a relational narrative that doesn't always jibe with the facts. They agree that they rarely have conflict, although objective analysis reveals that they have had their share of disagreements and challenges. Without overtly agreeing to do so, they choose to blame outside forces or unusual

> cultural idiom
> **jibe with:**
> agree with

circumstances for problems instead of attributing responsibility to each other. They offer the most charitable interpretations of each other's behavior, believing that the spouse acts with good intentions when things don't go well. They seem willing to forgive, or even forget, transgressions. Examining this research, one scholar concludes:

> Should we conclude that happy couples have a poor grip on reality? Perhaps they do, but is the reality of one's marriage better known by outside onlookers than by the players themselves? The conclusion is evident. One key to a long happy marriage is to tell yourself and others that you have one and then to behave as though you do![64]

## Common Perceptual Tendencies

Shared narratives may be desirable, but they can be hard to achieve. Some of the biggest problems that interfere with understanding and agreement arise from errors in what psychologists call **attribution**—the process of attaching meaning to behavior. We attribute meaning to both our own actions and the actions of others, but we often use different yardsticks. Research has uncovered several perceptual errors that can lead to inaccurate attributions—and to troublesome communication.[65] By becoming aware of these errors, we can guard against them and avoid unnecessary conflicts.

> **cultural idiom**
> **yardsticks:**
> standards of comparison

**We Make Snap Judgments**   Our ancestors often had to make quick judgments about whether strangers were likely to be dangerous, and there are still times when this ability can be a survival skill.[66] But there are many cases when judging others without enough knowledge or information can get us into trouble. If you've ever been written off by a potential employer in the first few minutes of an interview or have been unfairly rebuffed by someone you just met, then you know the feeling. Snap judgments become particularly problematic when they are based on **stereotyping**—exaggerated beliefs associated with a categorizing system. Stereotypes based on "primitive categories" like race, sex, and age may be founded on a kernel of truth, but they go beyond the facts at hand and make claims that usually have no valid basis.[67]

Three characteristics distinguish stereotypes from reasonable generalizations:

1. *Categorizing others on the basis of easily recognized but not necessarily significant characteristics.* For example, perhaps the first thing you notice about a person is his or her skin color—but that may not be nearly as significant as the person's intelligence or achievements.

2. *Ascribing a set of characteristics to most or all members of a group.* For example, you might unfairly assume that all older people are doddering or that all men are insensitive to women's concerns.

3. *Applying the generalization to a particular person.* Once you believe all old people are geezers and all men are jerks, it's a short step to considering a particular senior citizen as senile, or a particular man as a chauvinist pig.

By adulthood, we tend to engage in stereotyping frequently, effortlessly, and often unconsciously.[68] Once we create and hold stereotypes, we seek out isolated behaviors that support our inaccurate beliefs. For example, men and women in conflict with each other often remember only behaviors of the opposite sex that fit their stereotypes.[69] They then point to these behaviors—which might not be representative of how the other

In the sci-fi thriller *Inception*, evil corporations invade people's minds to learn their secrets and distort their perceptions. The film brings home the idea that what we perceive as true is sometimes an illusion. Can you think of a time when you radically changed your perception of a situation or a person?

person typically behaves—as "evidence" to suit their stereotypical and inaccurate claims: "Look! There you go criticizing me again. Typical for a woman!"

Stereotypes can plague interracial communication.[70] For example, surveys of college student attitudes show that many blacks characterize whites as "demanding" and "manipulative," whereas many whites describe blacks as "loud" and "ostentatious." Many African American women report having been raised with stereotypical characterizations of whites (e.g., "Most whites cannot be trusted"). These ideas are often perpetuated in the media. Video games tend to depict minority male characters as excessively violent thugs and athletes.[71]

However, there is some evidence that attitudes can change.[72] Participants in one study initially rated white managers to be more competent, achievement-oriented, and manipulative than black managers and black managers to be more interpersonally skilled and less polished than their white counterparts. However, those judgments largely disappeared when the participants were told that all of the managers were successful.

One way to avoid the kinds of communication problems that come from excessive stereotyping is to "decategorize" others, giving yourself a chance to treat people as individuals instead of assuming that they possess the same characteristics as every other member of the group to which you assign them.

**We Often Judge Ourselves More Charitably Than We Judge Others**   In an attempt to convince ourselves and others that the positive face we show to the world is true, we tend to judge ourselves in the most generous terms possible. Social scientists have labeled this tendency the **self-serving bias**.[73] When others suffer, we often blame the problem on their personal qualities. On the other hand, when we suffer, we find explanations outside ourselves. Consider a few examples:

- When they botch a job, we might think they weren't listening well or trying hard enough; when we botch a job, the problem was unclear directions or not enough time.
- When he lashes out angrily, we say he's being moody or too sensitive; when we blow off steam, it's because of the pressure we've been under.
- When she gets caught speeding, we say she should have been more careful; when we get caught, we deny we were driving too fast, or we say, "Everybody does it."

The egocentric tendency to rate ourselves more favorably than others see us has been demonstrated experimentally.[74] In one study, members of a random sample of men were asked to rank themselves on their ability to get along with others.[75] Defying mathematical laws, all subjects—every last one—put themselves in the top half of the population. Sixty percent rated themselves in the top 10 percent of the population, and an amazing 25 percent believed they were in the top 1 percent. In the same study, 70 percent of the men ranked their leadership in the top 25 percent of the population, whereas only 2 percent thought they were below average. Sixty percent said they were in the top 25 percent in athletic abilities, whereas only 6 percent viewed themselves as below average.

Evidence like this suggests how uncharitable attitudes toward others can affect communication. Your harsh opinions of others can lead to judgmental messages, and self-serving defenses of your own actions can result in a defensive response when others question your behavior.

**We Pay More Attention to Negative Impressions Than Positive Ones**   What do you think about Harvey? He's handsome, hardworking, intelligent, and honest. He's also very conceited.

> cultural idiom

**botch:**
carry out (a task) badly

**lashes out:**
attacks verbally

**blow off steam:**
release excess energy or anger

Did the last quality mentioned make a difference in your evaluation? If it did, you're not alone. Research shows that when people are aware of both the positive and negative traits of another, they tend to be more influenced by the negative traits. In one study, for example, researchers found that job interviewers were likely to reject candidates who revealed negative information, even when the total amount of information was highly positive.[76]

Sometimes this attitude makes sense. If the negative quality clearly outweighs any positive ones, you'd be foolish to ignore it. A surgeon with shaky hands and a teacher who hates children, for example, would be unsuitable for their jobs whatever their other virtues. But much of the time it's a bad idea to pay excessive attention to negative qualities and overlook positive ones. This is the mistake some people make when screening potential friends or dates. They find some who are too outgoing or too reserved, others who aren't intelligent enough, and still others who have the wrong sense of humor. Of course, it's important to find people you truly enjoy, but expecting perfection can lead to much unnecessary loneliness.

**We Are Influenced by What Is Most Obvious**  Every time we encounter another person, we are bombarded with more information than we can possibly manage. You can appreciate this by spending 2 or 3 minutes just reporting on what you can observe about another person through your five senses. ("Now I see you blinking your eyes. . . . Now I notice you smiling. . . . Now I hear you laugh and then sigh. . . . Now I notice you're wearing a red shirt. . . .") You will find that the list seems almost endless and that every time you seem to near the end, a new observation presents itself.

Faced with this tidal wave of sense data, we need to whittle down the amount of information we will use to make sense of others. There are three factors that cause us to notice some messages and ignore others. For example, we pay attention to stimuli that are *intense* (loud music, brightly dressed people), *repetitious* (dripping faucets, persistent people), or *contrastive* (a normally happy person who acts grumpy or vice versa). *Motives* also determine what information we select from our environment. If you're anxious about being late for a date, you'll notice whatever clocks may be around you; if you're hungry, you'll become aware of any restaurants, markets, and billboards advertising food in your path. Motives also determine how we perceive people.

If intense, repetitious, or contrastive information were the most important thing to know about others, there would be no problem. But the most noticeable behavior of others isn't always the most important. For example:

- When two children (or adults, for that matter) fight, it may be a mistake to blame the one who lashes out first. Perhaps the other one was at least equally responsible, by teasing or refusing to cooperate.

- You might complain about an acquaintance whose malicious gossiping or arguing has become a bother, forgetting that, by previously tolerating that kind of behavior, you have been at least partially responsible.

- You might blame an unhappy working situation on the boss, overlooking other factors beyond her control such as a change in the economy, the policy of higher management, or demands of customers or other workers.

**We Cling to First Impressions, Even If Wrong**  Labeling people according to our first impressions is an inevitable part of the perception process. These labels are a way of making interpretations. "She seems cheerful." "He seems sincere." "They sound awfully conceited."

If they're accurate, impressions like these can be useful ways of deciding how to respond best to people in the future. Problems arise, however, when the labels we attach are inaccurate, because after we form an opinion of someone, we tend to hang on to it and make any conflicting information fit our image.

Suppose, for instance, you mention the name of your new neighbor to a friend. "Oh, I know him," your friend replies. "He seems nice at first, but it's all an act." Perhaps this appraisal is off base. The neighbor may have changed since your friend knew him, or perhaps your friend's judgment is simply unfair. Whether or not the judgment is accurate, after you accept your friend's evaluation, it will probably influence the way you respond to the neighbor. You'll look for examples of the insincerity you've heard about—and you'll probably find them. Even if the neighbor were a saint, you would be likely to interpret his behavior in ways that fit your expectations. "Sure he *seems* nice," you might think, "but it's probably just a front." As you read earlier in this chapter, this sort of suspicion can create a self-fulfilling prophecy, transforming a genuinely nice person into someone who truly becomes an undesirable neighbor as he reacts to your suspicious behavior.

The power of first impressions is important in personal relationships. A study of college roommates found that those who had positive initial impressions of each other were likely to have positive subsequent interactions, manage their conflicts constructively, and continue living together.[77] The converse was also true: Roommates who got off to a bad start tended to spiral negatively. This reinforces the wisdom and importance of the old adage, "You never get a second chance to make a first impression."

Given the almost unavoidable tendency to form first impressions, the best advice we can offer is to keep an open mind and be willing to change your opinion as events prove that the first impressions were mistaken.

**We Tend to Assume That Others Are Similar to Us**   People commonly imagine that others possess the same attitudes and motives that they do. For example, research shows that people with low self-esteem imagine that others view them unfavorably, whereas people who like themselves imagine that others like them, too.[78] The frequently mistaken assumption that others' views are similar to our own applies in a wide range of situations. For example:

- You've heard an off-color joke that you found funny. You might assume that it won't offend a friend. It does.

- You've been bothered by an instructor's tendency to get off the subject during lectures. If you were a professor, you'd want to know if anything you were doing was creating problems for your students, so you decide that your instructor will probably be grateful for some constructive criticism. Unfortunately, you're wrong.

- You lost your temper with a friend a week ago and said some things you regret. In fact, if someone said those things to you, you would consider the relationship finished. Imagining that your friend feels the same way, you avoid making contact. In fact, your friend feels that he was partly responsible and has avoided you because he thinks you're the one who wants to end things.

Examples like these show that others don't always think or feel the way we do and that assuming that similarities exist can lead to problems. For example, men are more likely than women to think that flirting indicates an interest in having sex.[79]

> cultural idiom

**front:**
pretense

In the Oscar-winning film *Silver Linings Playbook*, Pat (Bradley Cooper) and Tiffany (Jennifer Lawrence) form understandably negative first impressions of each other. Have you ever clung to mistaken first impressions?

How can you find out the other person's real position? Sometimes by asking directly, sometimes by checking with others, and sometimes by making an educated guess after you've thought the matter out. All these alternatives are better than simply assuming that everyone would react the way you do.

Don't misunderstand: We don't always commit the kind of perceptual errors described in this section. Sometimes, for instance, people are responsible for their misfortunes, and sometimes our problems are not our fault. Likewise, the most obvious interpretation of a situation may be the correct one. Nonetheless, a large amount of research has proved again and again that our perceptions of others are often distorted in the ways listed here. The moral, then, is clear: Don't assume that your first judgment of a person is accurate.

## Perception in Mediated Communication

As the cartoon on this page suggests, mediated communication offers fewer cues about others than you get in face-to-face interaction. The ability to edit a message before posting makes it easy to craft an identity that doesn't match what you would encounter in person.

Despite the apparent barriers to accurate perception in mediated channels, people can form accurate impressions of one another over mediated channels—though not in the same ways as when they communicate in person.[80] Early in relationships, people who meet in person have more accurate impressions of one another than those who have met online.[81] But over time, people can get to know each other well online and may even share information about themselves that they would be reluctant to disclose in person.[82]

In text-based channels, receivers depend more heavily on the writing style[83] and symbols (e.g., smiley-faced emoticons)[84] to get a sense of the sender. Once you know how to spot them, other cues abound. For example, spelling errors create impressions about the writer.[85] The time it takes to get a response to your message also shapes perceptions.[86] A quick reply to your invitation suggests different things than does a long delay.

## Empathy, Perception, and Communication

By now it's clear that differing perceptions present a major challenge to communicators. One solution is to increase the ability to empathize. **Empathy** is the ability to re-create another person's perspective, to experience the world from the other's point of view.

**Dimensions of Empathy**   As we'll use the term here, **empathy** has three dimensions.[87] On one level, empathy involves *perspective taking*—the ability to take on the viewpoint of another person. This understanding requires a suspension of judgment, so that for the moment you set aside your own opinions and take on those of the other person. Besides cognitive understanding, empathy also has an *emotional* dimension that allows us to experience the feelings that others have. We know their fear, joy, sadness, and so on. When we combine the perspective-taking and emotional dimensions, we see that empathizing allows us to experience the other's perception—in effect, to become that person temporarily. A third dimension of empathy is a genuine *concern* for the welfare of the other person. When we empathize, we go beyond just thinking and feeling as others do and genuinely care about their well-being.

It is easy to confuse empathy with **sympathy**, but the concepts are different in two important ways. First, sympathy means you feel compassion for another person's predicament, whereas empathy

*"On the Internet, nobody knows you're a dog."*

means you have a personal sense of what that predicament is like. Consider the difference between sympathizing with an unwed mother or a homeless person and empathizing with them—imagining what it would be like to be in their position. Despite your concern, sympathy lacks the degree of identification that empathy entails. When you sympathize, it is the other's confusion, joy, or pain. When you empathize, the experience becomes your own, at least for the moment. Both perspectives are important ones, but empathy is clearly the more complete of the two.

Empathy is different from sympathy in a second way. We only sympathize when we accept the reasons for another's pain as valid, whereas it's possible to empathize without feeling sympathy. You can empathize with a difficult relative, a rude stranger, or even a criminal without feeling much sympathy for that person. Empathizing allows you to understand another person's motives without requiring you to agree with them. After empathizing, you will almost certainly understand a person better, but sympathy won't always follow.

The ability to empathize seems to exist in a rudimentary form in even the youngest children.[88] Virtually from birth, infants become visibly upset when they hear another infant crying, and children who are a few months old cry when they observe another child crying. Young children have trouble distinguishing others' distress from their own. If, for example, one child hurts his finger, another child might put her own finger in her mouth as if she were feeling pain. Researchers report cases in which children who see their parents crying wipe their own eyes, even though they are not crying.

Although infants and toddlers may have a basic capacity to empathize, studies with twins suggest that the degree to which we are born with the ability to sense how others are feeling varies according to genetic factors. Although some people may have an inborn edge, environmental experiences are the key to developing the ability to understand others. Specifically, the way in which parents communicate with their children seems to affect their ability to understand others' emotional states. When parents point out to children the distress that others feel from their misbehavior ("Look how sad Jessica is because you took her toy. Wouldn't you be sad if someone took away your toys?"), those children gain a greater appreciation that their acts have emotional consequences than they do when parents simply label behavior as inappropriate ("That was a mean thing to do!").

There is no consistent evidence that suggests that the ability to empathize is greater for one sex or the other.[89] Some people, however, seem to have a hereditary capacity for greater empathizing than do others.[90] Studies of identical and fraternal twins indicate that identical female twins are more similar to one another in their ability to empathize than are fraternal twins. Interestingly, there seems to be no difference between males. Although empathy may have a biological basis, environment can still play an important role. For example, parents who are sensitive to their children's feelings tend to have children who reach out to others.[91]

Total empathy is impossible to achieve. Completely understanding another person's point of view is simply too difficult a task for humans with different backgrounds and limited communication skills. Nonetheless, it is possible to get a strong sense of what the world looks like through another person's eyes.

A willingness to empathize can make a difference in everyday disputes. For example, communication researchers have spelled out how understanding opposing views can

*"How would you feel if the mouse did that to you?"*

increase understanding and constructive problem solving in conflicts between environmentalists who want to preserve native species and landowners who want to earn a profit. After the parties begin to see each other's point of view, they can discover ways of protecting native species *and* allow landowners to carry on their enterprises.[92]

**Perception Checking**     Good intentions and a strong effort to empathize are one way to understand others. Along with a positive attitude, however, there is a simple tool that can help you interpret the behavior of others more accurately. To see how this tool operates, consider how often others jump to mistaken conclusions about your thoughts, feelings, and motives:

*"Why are you mad at me?" (Who said you were?)*

*"What's the matter with you?" (Who said anything was the matter?)*

*"Come on now. Tell the truth." (Who said you were lying?)*

As you'll learn in Chapter 7, even if your interpretation is correct, a dogmatic, mind-reading statement is likely to generate defensiveness. The skill of **perception checking** provides a better way to handle your interpretations. A complete perception check has three parts:

1. A description of the behavior you noticed
2. At least two possible interpretations of the behavior
3. A request for clarification about how to interpret the behavior

Perception checks for the preceding three examples would look like this:

*"When you stomped out of the room and slammed the door* [behavior], *I wasn't sure whether you were mad at me* [first interpretation] *or just in a hurry* [second interpretation]. *How did you feel* [request for clarification]?*"*

*"You haven't laughed much in the last couple of days* [behavior]. *I wonder whether something's bothering you* [first interpretation] *or whether you're just feeling quiet* [second interpretation]. *What's up* [request for clarification]?*"*

*"You said you really liked the job I did* [behavior], *but there was something about your voice that made me think you may not like it* [first interpretation]. *Maybe it's just my imagination, though* [second interpretation]. *How do you really feel* [request for clarification]?*"*

Perception checking is a tool for helping us understand others accurately instead of assuming that our first interpretation is correct. Because its goal is mutual understanding, perception checking is a cooperative approach to communication. Besides leading to more accurate perceptions, it minimizes defensiveness. Instead of saying in effect, "I know what you're thinking . . . ," a perception check takes the more respectful approach that states or implies, "I know I'm not qualified to judge you without some help."

Sometimes a perception check won't need all of the parts listed earlier to be effective:

*"You haven't dropped by lately. Is anything the matter* [single interpretation combined with request for clarification]?*"*

*"I can't tell whether you're kidding me about being cheap or if you're serious* [behavior combined with interpretations]. *Are you mad at me?"*

*"Are you sure you don't mind driving? I can use a ride if it's no trouble, but I don't want to take you out of your way* [no need to describe behavior]."*

> cultural idiom

**dropped by:**
made an unplanned visit

Of course, a perception check can succeed only if your nonverbal behavior reflects the open-mindedness of your words. An accusing tone of voice or a hostile glare will contradict the sincerely worded request for clarification, suggesting that you have already made up your mind about the other person's intentions.

# Communication and Identity Management

> cultural idiom

**turn the tables:**
reverse an existing situation

So far we have described how communication shapes the way communicators view themselves and others. In the remainder of this chapter we turn the tables and focus on **identity management**—the communication strategies people use to influence how others view them. In the following pages you will see that many of our messages aim at creating desired impressions.

## Public and Private Selves

To understand why identity management exists, we have to discuss the notion of self in more detail. So far we have referred to the "self" as if each of us had only one identity. In truth, each of us possesses several selves, some private and others public. Often these selves are quite different.

The **perceived self** is a reflection of the self-concept. Your perceived self is the person you believe yourself to be in moments of honest self-examination. We can call the perceived self "private" because you are unlikely to reveal all of it to another person. You can verify the private nature of the perceived self by reviewing the self-concept list you developed while reading page 41. You'll probably find some elements of yourself there that you would not disclose to many people, and some that you would not share with anyone. You might, for example, be reluctant to share some feelings about your appearance ("I think I'm rather unattractive"), your intelligence ("I'm not as smart as I wish I were"), your goals ("the most important thing to me is becoming rich"), or your motives ("I care more about myself than about others").

In contrast to the perceived self, the **presenting self** is a public image—the way we want to appear to others. In most cases the presenting self we seek to create is a socially approved image: diligent student, loving partner, conscientious worker, loyal friend, and so on. Social norms often create a gap between the perceived and presenting selves. For instance, Table 2-1 shows that the self-concepts of the members of one group of male and female college students were quite similar, but that their public selves were different in several respects from both their private selves and the public selves of the opposite sex.[93]

Sociologist Erving Goffman used the word **face** to describe the presenting self, and he coined the term **facework** to describe the verbal and nonverbal ways we act to maintain our own presenting image and the images of others.[94] He argued that each of us can be viewed as a kind of playwright, who creates roles that we want others to believe, as well as the performer who acts out those roles.

Facework involves two tasks: managing our own identity and communicating in ways that reinforce the identities that others are trying to present.[95] You can see how these two goals operate by recalling a time when you've used self-deprecating humor to defuse a potentially unpleasant situation. Suppose, for example, that a friend gave you confusing directions to a party that caused you

For years, superstar Whitney Houston's public image of glamour and sophistication masked a personal life that was far more complicated and painful. How closely do your public and private selves match?

Table 2-1    Self-Selected Adjectives Describing Perceived and Presenting Selves of College Students

| PERCEIVED SELF | | PRESENTING SELF | |
|---|---|---|---|
| **MEN** | **WOMEN** | **MEN** | **WOMEN** |
| 1. Friendly | 1. Friendly | 1. Wild | 1. Active |
| 2. Active | 2. Responsible | 2. Able | 2. Responsible |
| 3. Responsible | 3. Independent | 3. Active | 3. Able |
| 4. Independent | 4. Capable | 4. Strong | 4. Bright |
| 5. Capable | 5. Sensible | 5. Proud | 5. Warm |
| 6. Polite | 6. Active | 6. Smart | 6. Funny |
| 7. Attractive | 7. Happy | 7. Brave | 7. Independent |
| 8. Smart | 8. Curious | 8. Capable | 8. Proud |
| 9. Happy | 9. Faithful | 9. Responsible | 9. Sensible |
| 10. Funny | 10. Attractive | 10. Rough | 10. Smart |

*Source:* Adapted from C. M. Shaw & R. Edwards. Self-concepts and self-presentations of males and females: Similarities and differences. *Communication Reports, 10*, 55–62.

to be late. "Sorry I got lost," you might have said. "I'm a terrible navigator." This sort of mild self-put-down accomplishes two things at once: It preserves the other person's face by implicitly saying, "It's not your fault." At the same time, your mild self-debasement shows that you're a nice person who doesn't find faults in others or make a big issue out of small problems.[96]

## Characteristics of Identity Management

Now that you have a sense of what identity management is, we can look at some characteristics of this process.

**We Have Multiple Identities**    In the course of even a single day, most people play a variety of roles: respectful student, joking friend, friendly neighbor, and helpful worker, to suggest just a few. We even play a variety of roles with the same person. As you grew up, you almost certainly changed characters as you interacted with your parents. In one context you acted as the responsible adult ("You can trust me with the car!"), and in another context you were the helpless child ("I can't find my socks!"). At some times—perhaps on birthdays or holidays—you were a dedicated family member, and at other times you may have played the role of rebel. Likewise, in romantic relationships we switch among many ways of behaving, depending on the context: friend, lover, business partner, scolding critic, apologetic child, and so on.

The ability to construct multiple identities is one element of communication competence. For example, the style of speaking or even the language itself can reflect a choice about how to construct one's identity. We recall an African American colleague who was also minister of a Southern Baptist congregation consisting mostly of black members. On campus his manner of speaking was typically professorial, but a visit to hear him preach one Sunday revealed a speaker whose style was much more animated and theatrical, reflecting his identity in that context. Likewise, one scholar pointed out that bilingual Latinos in the United States often

Angus T. Jones, who played Jake on TV's *Two and a Half Men*, denounced the show as "filth" and urged people to stop watching. Speculation is that the show's racy content clashed with Jones's newfound identity as a born-again Christian. Have you ever tried to change your identity? Did you find it difficult to persuade others to regard you in a new way?

choose whether to use English or Spanish depending on the kind of identity they are seeking in a given conversation.[97]

**Identity Management Is Collaborative**   As we perform like actors trying to create a front, our "audience" is made up of other actors who are trying to create their own characters. Identity-related communication is a kind of process theater in which we collaborate with other actors to improvise scenes in which our characters mesh.

You can appreciate the collaborative nature of identity management by thinking about how you might handle a gripe with a friend or family member who has failed to pass along a phone message that arrived while you were away from home. Suppose that you decide to raise the issue tactfully in an effort to avoid seeming like a nag (desired role for yourself: "nice person") and also to save the other person from the embarrassment of being confronted (hoping to avoid suggesting that the other person's role is "screw-up"). If your tactful bid is accepted, the dialogue might sound like this:

**You:**    " . . . By the way, Jenny told me she came by yesterday. If you wrote a note, I guess I missed seeing it."

**Other:**   "Oh . . . sorry. I meant to write a note, but as soon as she left, my phone rang, and then I had to run off to class."

**You:**    *(in friendly tone of voice)* "That's okay. I sure would appreciate from now on if you'd leave me a note."

**Other:**   "No problem."

In this upbeat conversation, both you and the other person accepted one another's bids for identity as basically thoughtful people. As a result, the conversation ran smoothly. Imagine, though, how different the outcome would be if the other person didn't accept your role as "nice person":

**You:**    " . . . By the way, Jenny told me she came by yesterday. If you wrote a note, I guess I missed seeing it."

**Other:**   (defensively) "Okay, so I forgot. It's not that big a deal. You're not perfect yourself, you know!"

At this point you have the choice of persisting in trying to play the original role: "Hey, I'm not mad at you, and I know I'm not perfect!" Or, you might switch to the new role of "unjustly accused person," responding with aggravation, "I never said I was perfect. But we're not talking about me here . . ."

As this example illustrates, *collaboration* doesn't mean the same thing as *agreement*.[98] The small issue of the forgotten note might mushroom into a fight in which you and the other person both adopt the role of combatants. The point here is that virtually all conversations provide an arena in which communicators construct their identities in response to the behavior of others. As you read in Chapter 1, communication isn't made up of discrete events that can be separated from one another. Instead, what happens at one moment is influenced by what each party brings to the interaction and by what happened in their relationship up to that point.

**Identity Management Can Be Conscious or Unconscious**   At this point you might object to the notion of strategic identity management, claiming that most of your communication is spontaneous and not a deliberate attempt to present yourself in a certain way. However, you might acknowledge that some of your communication involves a conscious attempt to manage impressions.

## Understanding Diversity

## Managing Identity and Coming Out

I grew up in a mid-size town in Mexico. My siblings and I were taught to never do anything to "dishonor" the name of our family.

From a very early age I sensed I was not a boy who liked girls. My father was very involved in Mexican rodeo, and he expected me to ride a horse, rope, and deal with cattle. I quit when I was twelve. My dad never understood why.

Middle school was hard. I coped with bullies by being funny and making fun of others before they could make fun of me. I had a girlfriend for a year. It was all pretend but it helped ease the harassment. By high school I knew was gay and wanted to live openly. But my religious upbringing, peer group, and family's reputation were all in the way of me coming out.

I started living a double life during college. Guilt became the main emotion I felt. I became very cold and distant with everyone in my family. To cover up my identity, I had a girlfriend for three years. After college I met the first openly gay men who were comfortable and happy. I fell in love with one of them, and he helped me understand that I needed to have the courage to accept who I am and to stop hiding this from my family.

It took three more years for me to come out to my siblings. Those were the hardest conversations I have ever endured. My siblings urged me to not tell my parents, who they said would be upset and saddened. Unfortunately I followed their suggestion, and my mom passed without me ever sharing this part of myself. Still, I am sure she knew the truth. I have never told my dad directly that I am gay. When we talk, he always asks me how I am doing and how John (my partner) is doing. That is his way of letting me know he knows.

I can sleep much better at night since I came out sixteen years ago. Since then, I have stopped worrying what others think about me. There is no guilt and I feel complete. I know I am happy. ●

J. C. Rivas

There's no doubt that sometimes we are highly aware of managing our identities. Most job interviews and first dates are clear examples of conscious identity management. But in other cases we unconsciously act in ways that are really small public performances.[99] For example, experimental subjects expressed facial disgust in reaction to eating sandwiches laced with a supersaturated saltwater solution only when there was another person present: When they were alone, they made no faces when eating the same sandwiches.[100] Another study showed that communicators engage in facial mimicry (such as smiling or looking sympathetic in response to another's message) in face-to-face settings only when their expressions can be seen by the other person. When they are speaking over the phone and their reactions cannot be seen, they do not make the same expressions.[101] Studies like these suggest that most of our behavior is aimed at sending messages to others—in other words, identity management.

The experimental subjects described in the last paragraph didn't consciously think, "Somebody is watching me eat this salty sandwich, so I'll make a face," or, "Since I'm in a face-to-face conversation I'll show I'm sympathetic by mimicking the facial expressions of my conversational partner." Reactions like these are often instantaneous and outside of our conscious awareness.

In the same way, many of our choices about how to act in the array of daily interactions aren't deliberate, strategic decisions. Rather, they rely on "scripts" that we have developed over time. You probably have a variety of roles for managing your identity from which to choose in familiar situations such as dealing with strangers, treating customers at work, interacting with family members, and so on. When you find yourself in familiar situations like these, you probably slip into these roles quite often. Only when those roles don't seem quite right

> cultural idiom

**"scripts":**
reflexive responses

do you deliberately construct an approach that reflects how you want the scene to play out.

Despite the claims of some theorists, it seems like an exaggeration to suggest that all behavior is aimed at managing identities. Young children certainly aren't strategic communicators. A baby spontaneously laughs when pleased and cries when sad or uncomfortable, without any notion of creating an impression in others. Likewise, there are almost certainly times when we, as adults, act spontaneously. But when a significant other questions the self we try to present, the likelihood of acting to prop it up increases. This process isn't always conscious: At a nonconscious level of awareness we monitor others' reactions and swing into action when our face is threatened—especially by significant others.[102]

**People Differ in Their Degree of Identity Management**   Some people are much more aware of their identity management behavior than others. These high self-monitors have the ability to pay attention to their own behavior and others' reactions, adjusting their communication to create the desired impression. By contrast, low self-monitors express what they are thinking and feeling without much attention to the impression their behavior creates.[103]

There are certainly advantages to being a high self-monitor.[104] People who pay attention to themselves are generally good actors who can create the impression they want, acting interested when bored, or friendly when they really feel quite the opposite. This allows them to handle social situations smoothly, often putting others at ease. They are also good "people-readers" who can adjust their behavior to get the desired reaction from others. Along with these advantages, there are some potential disadvantages to being an extremely high self-monitor. The analytical nature of high self-monitors may prevent them from experiencing events completely, because a portion of their attention will always be viewing the situation from a detached position. High self-monitors' ability to act means that it is difficult to tell how they are really feeling. In fact, because high self-monitors change roles often, they may have a hard time knowing themselves how they really feel.

People who score low on the self-monitoring scale live life quite differently from their more self-conscious counterparts. They have a simpler, more focused idea of who they are and who they want to be. Low self-monitors are likely to have a narrower repertoire of behaviors, so that they can be expected to act in more or less the same way regardless of the situation. This means that low self-monitors are easy to read. "What you see is what you get" might be their motto. Although this lack of flexibility may make their social interaction less smooth in many situations, low self-monitors can be counted on to be straightforward communicators.

By now it should be clear that neither extremely high nor low self-monitoring is the ideal. There are some situations in which paying attention to yourself and adapting your behavior can be useful, but there are other situations in which reacting without considering the effect on others is a better approach. This need for a range of behaviors demonstrates again the notion of communicative competence outlined in Chapter 1: Flexibility is the key to successful relationships.

## Why Manage Identities?

Why bother trying to shape others' opinions? Sometimes we create and maintain a front to follow social rules. As children we learn to act polite, even when bored. Likewise, part of growing up consists of developing a set of manners for various occasions: meeting strangers, attending school, going to religious services, and so on. Young children who haven't learned all the do's and don'ts of polite society often embarrass their parents by behaving inappropriately ("Mommy, why is that

## Identity Management in the Workplace

Some advisors encourage workers to "just be yourself" on the job. But there are times when disclosing certain information about your personal life can damage your chances for success.[105] This is especially true for people with "invisible stigmas"—traits that run the risk of being viewed unfavorably.[106]

Many parts of a worker's identity have the potential to be invisible stigmas: religion (evangelical Christian, Muslim), sexual orientation (gay, lesbian, bisexual), health (bipolar, HIV positive). What counts as a stigma to some people (politically progressive, conservative) might be favored in another organization.[107]

As you consider how to manage your identity at work, consider the following:

- *Proceed with caution.* In an ideal world, everyone would be free to reveal themselves without hesitation. But in real life, total candor can have consequences, so it can be best to move slowly.

- *Assess the organization's culture.* If your workplace seems supportive of differences—and especially if it appears to welcome people like you—then revealing more of yourself may be safe.

- *Consider the consequences of not opening up.* Keeping an important part of your identity secret can also take an emotional toll.[108] If keeping quiet is truly necessary, you may be better off finding a more welcoming place to work.

- *Test the waters.* If you have a trusted colleague or manager, think about revealing yourself to that person and asking advice about whether and how to go further. But realize that even close secrets can leak, so be sure the person you approach can keep confidences. ●

man so fat?"), but by the time they enter school, behavior that might have been excusable or even amusing just isn't acceptable. Good manners are often aimed at making others more comfortable. For example, able-bodied people often mask their discomfort on encountering someone with a disability by acting nonchalant or stressing similarities between themselves and the other person.[109]

Social rules govern our behavior in a variety of settings. It would be impossible to keep a job, for example, without meeting certain expectations. Salespeople are obliged to treat customers with courtesy. Employees need to appear reasonably respectful when talking to the boss. Some forms of clothing would be considered outrageous at work. By agreeing to take on a job, you are signing an unwritten contract that you will present a certain face at work, whether or not that face reflects the way you might be feeling at a particular moment.

Even when social roles don't dictate the proper way to behave, we often manage identities for a second reason: to accomplish personal goals. You might, for example, dress up for a visit to traffic court in the hope that your front (responsible citizen) will convince the judge to treat you sympathetically. You might act sociable to your neighbors so they will agree to your request that they keep their dog off your lawn. We also try to create a desired impression to achieve one or more of the social needs described in Chapter 1: affection, inclusion, control, and so on. For instance, you might act more friendly and lively than you feel on meeting a new person, so that you will appear likable. You could sigh and roll your eyes when arguing politics with a classmate to gain an advantage in an argument. You might smile and preen to show the attractive stranger at a party that you would like to get better acquainted. In situations like these you aren't being deceptive as much as putting your best foot forward.

All these examples show that it is difficult—even impossible—not to create impressions. After all, you have to send some sort of message. If you don't act friendly when meeting a stranger, you have to act aloof, indifferent, hostile, or in

> cultural idiom

**putting your best foot forward:**
making the best appearance possible

some other manner. If you don't act businesslike, you have to behave in an alternative way: casual, goofy, or whatever. Often the question isn't whether or not to present a face to others; the question is only which face to present.

## Identity Management in Mediated Communication

At first glance, computer-mediated communication (CMC) seems to have limited potential for identity management. As you read in Chapter 1, text-based messages lack the "richness" of other channels. They don't convey the postures, gestures, or facial expressions that are an important part of face-to-face communication. They even lack the vocal information available in telephone messages. These limitations might seem to make it harder to create and manage an identity when communicating via computer.

Recently, though, communication scholars have begun to recognize that what is missing in CMC can actually be an advantage for communicators who want to manage the impressions they make. For example, research shows that teens tend to strategically post photos that make them appear attractive and socially engaged with others.[110] E-mail authors can edit their messages until they create just the desired impression.[111] They can choose the desired level of clarity or ambiguity, seriousness or humor, logic or emotion. Unlike face-to-face communication, electronic correspondence allows a sender to say difficult things without forcing the receiver to respond immediately, and it permits the receiver to ignore a message rather than give an unpleasant response. Options like these show that CMC can serve as a tool for impression management at least as well as face-to-face communication.

CMC generally gives us more control over managing identities than we have in face-to-face communication. Asynchronous forms of CMC like e-mail, blogs, and web pages allow you to edit your messages until you convey the right impression. With e-mail (and, to a lesser degree, with texting and instant messaging) you can compose difficult messages without forcing the receiver to respond immediately, and ignore others' messages rather than give an unpleasant response. Perhaps most important, with CMC you don't have to worry about stammering or blushing, apparel or appearance, or any other unseen factor that might detract from the impression you want to create.

CMC allows strangers to change their age, history, personality, appearance, and other matters that would be impossible to hide in person.[112] A quarter of teens have pretended to be a different person online, and a third confess to having given false information about themselves while e-mailing and instant messaging. A survey of one online dating site's participants found that 86 percent felt others misrepresented their physical appearance in their posted descriptions.[113]

Like the one-to-one and small group channels of e-mail and instant messaging, "broadcasting" on the media is also a tool for managing one's identity. Blogs, personal web pages, and profiles on social networking websites all provide opportunities for communicators to construct an identity.[114] See the "Understanding Communication Technology" box for a look at virtual identity management.

## Identity Management and Honesty

After reading this far, you might think that identity management sounds like an academic label for manipulation or phoniness. If the perceived self is the "real" you, it might seem that any behavior that contradicts it would be dishonest.

There certainly are situations in which identity management is dishonest. A manipulative date who pretends to be affectionate in order to gain sexual favors is clearly unethical and deceitful. So are job applicants who lie about academic

> cultural idiom
> **"richness":**
> completeness

How closely does your identity on social media match the way you present yourself in person?

**Understanding Communication Technology**

## Avatars Offer New Virtual Identities

"Want to become a blue-skinned troll or a pink-haired elf? Want a perfect body without setting foot in the gym? You've got it! Want to partake in a love story filled with knights and damsels in distress? Go for it!," says Shannon Symonds, blogger and electronic games historian.[115] Symonds is a fan of social networking environments such as *Second Life* in which people communicate with one another in settings and situations they create themselves. It's the ultimate in identity management, complete with 3D technology and sound effects.

Virtual communication might take place within an enchanted forest, a sci-fi spaceship, or under the ocean. As virtual worlds become more sophisticated, avatars can take nearly any form the user likes. One full-time mom, who describes herself as short with a "squeaky little voice" that commands no respect, swaggers through the virtual world as Stygion Physic, whom she describes as "the biggest, blackest" avatar imaginable. In that guise, she says, "everyone listens to me. . . . I say, 'OK, everybody follow me!' And they do. No questions asked."[116]

Via their avatars, inhabitants of virtual worlds can set out on adventures, travel to exotic places, attend concerts, engage in conversations, and even have sex and give birth—all in digital format. Particularly for people with limited mobility, virtual worlds provide a means of social interaction they wouldn't have otherwise. Jason Rowe interacts in the virtual world via a massive, armored avatar. Although muscular dystrophy has made it impossible for Rowe to use more than his thumbs, online, he can slay dragons and ride mountain bikes on equal footing with others, he says.[117]

Although the options for establishing a new identity seem limitless, communication scholars have found that people manage their online identities in much the same way they

Jason Rowe and his avatar, Rurouni Kenshin.

*Maxim* magazine named a Second Life avatar, pictured here, one of its "Top 100 Women" of the year.

do in person, by forming social circles and striving to maintain face.[118] And, just as in real life, people tend to gravitate toward avatars with whom they have something in common and who seem trustworthy. According to one study, it may be fun to masquerade as a monster or robot, but if you want your avatar to have a lot of friends, nothing beats a human form.[119] (For a sampling, search for "Second Life" at YouTube.com.) ●

records to get hired or salespeople who pretend to be dedicated to customer service when their real goal is to make a quick buck. But managing identities doesn't necessarily make you a liar. In fact, it is almost impossible to imagine how we could communicate effectively without making decisions about which front to present in one situation or another. It would be ludicrous for you to act the same way with strangers as you do with close friends, and nobody would show the same face to a 2-year-old as to an adult.

Each of us has a repertoire of faces—a cast of characters—and part of being a competent communicator is choosing the best role for the situation. Consider a few examples:

> cultural idiom

**to make a quick buck:**
to earn money with little effort

**Ethical Challenge**

## Honesty and Multiple Identities

Presenting different identities to the world isn't inherently dishonest. Nonetheless, there are certainly cases when it is deceitful to construct an identity that doesn't match your private self.

You can explore the ethics of multiple identities by identifying two situations from your life:

1. A time when you presented a public identity that didn't match your private self in a manner that wasn't unethical.

2. A situation (real or hypothetical) in which you have presented or could present a dishonest identity.

Based on the situations you and your classmates present, develop a code of ethics that identifies the boundary between ethical and unethical identity management.

- You have been communicating online for several weeks with someone you just met, and the relationship is starting to turn romantic. You have a physical trait that you haven't mentioned yet.

- You offer to teach a friend a new skill: playing the guitar, operating a computer program, or sharpening a tennis backhand. Your friend is making slow progress with the skill, and you find yourself growing impatient.

- At a party with a companion, you meet someone you find very attractive, and you are pretty sure that the feeling is mutual. You feel an obligation to spend most of your time with the person with whom you came, but the opportunity here is very appealing.

- At work you face a belligerent customer. You don't believe that anyone has the right to treat you this way.

- A friend or family member makes a joke about your appearance that hurts your feelings. You aren't sure whether to make an issue of the remark or pretend that it doesn't bother you.

In each of these situations—and in countless others every day—you have a choice about how to act. It is an oversimplification to say that there is only one honest way to behave in each circumstance and that every other response would be insincere and dishonest. Instead, impression management involves deciding which face—which part of yourself—to reveal. For example, when teaching a new skill, you can choose to display the patient instead of the impatient side of yourself. In the same way, at work you have the option of acting hostile or nondefensive in difficult situations. With strangers, friends, or family you can choose whether or not to disclose your feelings. Which face to show to others is an important decision, but in any case you are sharing a real part of yourself. You may not be revealing everything—but, as you will learn in Chapter 7, complete self-disclosure is rarely appropriate.

It's also worth noting that not all misrepresentations are intentional. Researchers have used the term "foggy mirror" to describe the gap between participants' self-perceptions and a more objective assessment. An online dater who describes himself or herself as being "average" in weight might be engaging in wishful thinking rather than telling an outright lie.[120]

## Summary

Perceptions play a key role in how think about ourselves and others, and hence how we communicate. Perceptions of oneself are just as subjective as perceptions of others, and they influence communication at least as much. Although individuals are born with some innate personality characteristics, the self-concept is shaped dramatically by communication with others, as well as by cultural factors. Once established, the self-concept can lead us to create self-fulfilling prophecies that determine how we behave and how others respond to us.

Perceptual errors can affect the way we view and communicate with others. Along with universal psychological influences, cultural factors affect perceptions. We often incorporate our perceptions into personal narratives. These narratives not only tell a story but suggest a particular interpretation that others may accept or challenge.

Increased empathy is a valuable tool for increasing understanding of others and hence communicating more effectively with them. Perception checking is one tool for increasing the accuracy of perceptions and for increasing empathy.

Identity management consists of strategic communication designed to influence others' perceptions of an individual. Identity management operates when we seek, consciously or unconsciously, to present one or more public faces to others. These faces may be different from the private, spontaneous behavior that occurs outside of others' presence. Identity management is usually collaborative: Communication goes most smoothly when we communicate in ways that support others' faces, and they support ours. Some communicators are high self-monitors who are intensely conscious of their own behavior, whereas others are low self-monitors who are less aware of how their words and actions affect others.

Identity management occurs for two reasons. In many cases it aims at following social rules and conventions. In other cases it aims at achieving a variety of content and relational goals. In either case, communicators engage in creating impressions by managing their manner, appearance, and the settings in which they interact with others. Although identity management might seem manipulative, it can be an authentic form of communication. Because each person has a variety of faces that he or she can present, choosing which one to present need not be dishonest.

## Key Terms

**androgynous** Combining both masculine and feminine traits. *p. 52*

**attribution** The process of attaching meaning. *p. 55*

**empathy** The ability to project oneself into another person's point of view, so as to experience the other's thoughts and feelings. *p. 59*

**face** The socially approved identity that a communicator tries to present. *p. 62*

**facework** Verbal and nonverbal behavior designed to create and maintain a communicator's face and the face of others. *p. 62*

**gender** Socially constructed roles, behaviors, activities, and attributes that a society considers appropriate for men and/or women. *p. 52*

**identity management** Strategies used by communicators to influence the way others view them. *p. 62*

**interpretation** The perceptual process of attaching meaning to stimuli that have previously been selected and organized. *p. 49*

**narrative** The stories people create and use to make sense of their personal worlds. *p. 54*

**organization** The perceptual process of organizing stimuli into patterns. *p. 49*

**perceived self** The person we believe ourselves to be in moments of candor. It may be identical to or different from the presenting and ideal selves. *p. 62*

**perception checking** A three-part method for verifying the accuracy of interpretations, including a description of the sense data, two possible interpretations, and a request for confirmation of the interpretations. *p. 61*

**personality** The set of enduring characteristics that define a person's temperament, thought processes, and social behavior. *p. 42*

**presenting self** The image a person presents to others. It may be identical to or different from the perceived and ideal selves. See also *Face*. *p. 62*

**reflected appraisal** The influence of others on one's self-concept. *p. 43*

**selection** The perceptual act of attending to some stimuli in the environment and ignoring others. *p. 48*

**self-concept** The relatively stable set of perceptions each individual holds of himself or herself. *p. 41*

**self-esteem** The part of the self-concept that involves evaluations of self-worth. *p. 42*

**self-fulfilling prophecy** A prediction or expectation of an event that makes the outcome more likely to occur than would otherwise have been the case. *p. 46*

**self-serving bias** The tendency to interpret and explain information in a way that casts the perceiver in the most favorable manner. *p. 56*

**sex** A biological category such as male, female, or inter-sexed *p. 52*

**significant other** A person whose opinion is important enough to affect one's self-concept strongly. *p. 43*

**stereotyping** The perceptual process of applying exaggerated beliefs associated with a categorizing system. *p. 55*

**sympathy** Compassion for another's situation. See also *Empathy. p. 59*

## Check Your Understanding

1. Identify your messages that influence the self-concepts of others, and the messages from significant others that influence your self-concept.

2. Describe the communication-related self-fulfilling prophecies that you have imposed on yourself, that others have imposed on you, and that you have imposed on others.

3. Explain how the perceptual tendencies described in this chapter have led you to develop distorted perceptions of yourself and others.

4. Use perception checking to view a situation from another person's perspective, and describe how increased empathy can affect your relationship with that person.

5. Describe the various identities you attempt to create, the communication strategies you use to do so, how successful you are, and the ethical merit of your identity management strategies.

## Activities

1. **Exploring Narratives** Think about a situation in which relational harmony is due to you and the other people involved sharing the same narrative. Then think about another situation in which you and the other person use different narratives to describe the same situation. What are the consequences of having different narratives in this situation?

2. **Experiencing Another Culture** Spend at least an hour in a culture that is unfamiliar to you and in which you are a minority. Visit an area where another cultural, age, or ethnic group is the majority. Attend a meeting or patronize an establishment where you are in the minority. Observe how communication practices differ from those of your own culture. Based on your experience, discuss what you can do to facilitate communication with people from other cultural backgrounds whom you may encounter in your everyday life. (As you develop a list of ideas, realize that what you might consider helpful behavior could make communicators from different cultures even more uncomfortable.)

3. **Empathy Exercise** Choose a disagreement you presently have with another person or group. The disagreement might be a personal one—such as an argument about how to settle a financial problem or who is to blame for a present state of affairs—or it might be a dispute over a contemporary public issue, such as the right of women to obtain abortions on demand or the value of capital punishment.

   1. In 300 words or so, describe your side of the issue. State why you believe as you do, just as if you were presenting your position to an important jury.

   2. Now take 300 words or so to describe in the first-person singular the other person's perspective on the same issue. For instance, if you are a religious person, write this section as if you were an atheist: For a short while get in touch with how the other person feels and thinks.

   3. Now show the description you wrote to your "opponent," the person whose beliefs are different from yours. Have that person read your account and correct any statements that don't reflect his or her position accurately. Remember: You're doing this so that you can more clearly understand how the issue looks to the other person.

   4. Make any necessary corrections in the account you wrote, and again show it to your partner. When your partner agrees that you understand his or her position, have your partner sign your paper to indicate this.

   5. Now record your conclusions to this experiment. Has this perceptual shift made any difference in how you view the issue or how you feel about your partner?

4. **Perception-Checking Practice** Practice your perception-checking ability by developing three-part verifications for the following situations:

   1. You made what you thought was an excellent suggestion to an instructor. The instructor looked uninterested but said she would check on the matter right away. Three weeks have passed, and nothing has changed.

   2. A neighbor and good friend has not responded to your "Good morning" for 3 days in a row. This person is usually friendly.

3. You haven't received the usual weekly phone call from the folks back home in more than a month. The last time you spoke, you had an argument about where to spend the holidays.

4. An old friend with whom you have shared the problems of your love life for years has recently changed when around you: The formerly casual hugs and kisses have become longer and stronger, and the occasions in which you "accidentally" brush up against one another have become more frequent.

5. **Identifying Your Identities** Keep a 1-day log listing the identities you create in different situations: at school and at work, and with strangers, various family members, and different friends. For each identity,

1. Describe the persona you are trying to project (e.g., "responsible son or daughter," "laid-back friend," "attentive student").

2. Explain how you communicate to promote this identity. What kinds of things do you say (or not say)? How do you act?

## For Further Exploration

**For more resources about the self and perception, see the *Understanding Human Communication* website at www.oup .com/us/adler.** There you will find a variety of resources: "Media Room" clips from popular films and television shows to further illustrate important concepts, a list of books and articles, links to descriptions of feature films and television shows at the *Now Playing* website, study aids, and a self-test to check your understanding of the material in this chapter.

CHAPTER 3

# Communication and Culture

## Chapter Outline

## LEARNING OBJECTIVES

**1** Identify how cultures and cocultures play a significant role in your own sphere, and in society at large.

**2** Give examples illustrating when cultural and cocultural factors do and don't play a role in communication.

**3** Distinguish between overgeneralizations and actual cultural and cocultural differences in communication.

**4** Explain and give examples of cultural values, norms, and cultural/cocultural codes that shape and affect communication.

**5** Use the criteria in this chapter to assess your intercultural and cocultural communication competence, and describe how you could communicate more competently.

## "How are you?"

The question seems simple, but it can be tricky to answer, as Bin "Robin" Luo, an exchange student from China, has learned. In China, people seldom talk to strangers, says Luo. By contrast, many Americans seem especially outgoing. But when people in China speak together, they tend to focus intently on each other. Americans don't always do that.

"I still consider 'How are you?' as more than just a 'Hello,'" Luo says, after 5 months in the United States. "I want to stop and explain my feelings. But sometimes Americans just ask and then walk past you without waiting for your answer."

Luo, an engineering student from Guangdong Province in southern China, says he was eager to study in the United States because the country and its educational system are highly respected. He thought it would be fascinating to learn about cultural ways so different from his own. Luo's interest in living abroad isn't unique: Around the world, one in seven foreign exchange students are from China, and about half of them choose the United States.[1] Indeed, the United States hosts more students from China than from any other country.

Adapting to cultural differences isn't always easy. Americans may be surprised to hear that many foreigners find the United States a hard place to make friends. Luo says this is partly because, without knowing the culture well, it's hard to tell when Americans are genuinely interested in friendship and when they are just being polite.

"When I have talked to someone more than 15 minutes, I would think we can go further as friends," Luo says. "But Americans may consider it a casual conversation, and they may say, 'Let's get together' or 'I'll call you' but not follow through." He says he generally admires the optimistic attitude and forthrightness he has encountered, but he is puzzled by some of the communication patterns of his fellow students.

*Robin Luo's story shows that even a simple statement such as "How are you?" can be interpreted many different ways. Take a moment to think about your own experiences involving culture and communication.*

- Have you ever interacted with people from a culture significantly different from your own? If so, did they communicate in ways that surprised or puzzled you? How?

- Have you ever felt like a cultural stranger or minority, even in your home community? If so, how did it affect your communication with others?

- What could you do to communicate more successfully with people from cultural backgrounds different from your own?

Robin Luo's experiences as an exchange student shed light on how culture influences communication. But you don't have to be a world traveler to encounter people from different places and cultures in today's global village. Without leaving home, we are more connected with people from different backgrounds than at any time in history. That's partly because travel is easier than ever before, and the Internet makes communicating around the world as easy as communicating around town. It's also because society is more diverse than ever—in terms of culture, age, ethnicity, physical ability, personal identity, family background, and more.

As you'll see in this chapter, this diversity presents both obvious benefits and unique communication challenges. We will explore both. The main themes in this chapter include

- When culture does—and when it doesn't—affect communication
- The mostly hidden values and norms that can shape interaction between people from different backgrounds
- How diversity within our own culture shapes communication
- Some ways that sending and receiving messages are shaped and affected by culture
- How to become more competent in communicating with people from different backgrounds

## Understanding Cultures and Cocultures

Defining **culture** isn't an easy task. One early survey of scholarly literature revealed 500 definitions, phrasings, and uses of the concept.[2] For our purposes, here is a clear and comprehensive definition of *culture*: "the language, values, beliefs, traditions, and customs people share and learn."[3]

When you think of cultures, you may think of different nationalities. But *within* a society, differences also exist. Social scientists use the term **coculture** to describe the perception of membership in a group that is part of an encompassing culture. The sons and daughters of immigrants, for example, might be immersed in mainstream American culture while still identifying with the customs of their parents' homeland. Members of cocultures often develop unique patterns of communication. The academic term that describes interaction among members of different cocultures is **intergroup communication**.

Cocultures in today's society include, for example,

- Age (e.g., teen, senior citizen)
- Race/ethnicity (e.g., African American, Latino, white)
- Sexual orientation (e.g., LGBTQ)
- Physical disability (e.g., wheelchair users, deaf persons)
- Language (e.g., native and nonnative speakers)
- Religion (e.g., Mormon, Muslim)
- Activity (e.g., biker, gamer)

Membership in cocultures can be a source of identity, enrichment, and pride. But when the group is stigmatized by others, being identified as a member isn't always so fulfilling. Some research suggests that recognizable members of underrepresented groups are disadvantaged in employment interviews and social settings, in which the rules are established by the dominant culture.[4] Studies of Jamaican[5] and Latino[6] children indicate that skin

Despite living in Brooklyn, one of the most culturally diverse spots in the United States, the friends on HBO's *Girls* spend much of their time with people who look and speak like them. Creator and star Lena Dunham has been criticized for the show's culturally homogeneous characters. How closely does your circle of acquaintances match the diversity of today's society?

color influences self-identification and self-esteem. Other research focuses on reactions to people with disabilities. Although almost all of U.S. high school students polled in one survey said they would greet a classmate with a physical disability and would gladly lend the person a pen or pencil, more than a third were reluctant to spend time with the same classmate outside of school, mostly because they felt awkward and they assumed they wouldn't have much in common.[7]

The odds of overturning stereotypes may seem insurmountable. But the news isn't all bad: People who interact daily with people from different cultural backgrounds are less likely to be prejudiced than those who do not.[8] (We'll talk more about this later in the chapter.) Positive media images also have an influence. For example, the popularity of U.S. First Lady Michelle Obama has helped support the idea that dark skin is beautiful, not only in the United States but around the world.[9]

Membership in a coculture can shape the nature of communication. Sometimes the influence is obvious. For example, it's no surprise that members of the millennial generation rely more on social media to communiate than their grandparents, or even their parents.[10] Children who are native language speakers will have a very different experience in school than nonnative speakers, and gay men and lesbians can find it awkward to discuss their romantic relationships with some heterosexual people.

> With what cocultures do you identify? Which ones are most fundamental to your identity? Compare your answers to those of your classmates. How diverse is your group?

In other cases, though, cocultural communication practices aren't so obvious. For example, ethnic background can influence what people consider the most important qualities in a friendship. One study found that Latinos were highly likely to value relational support and bonding with friends. By contrast, Asian Americans (as a group, of course) placed a greater value on helping one another achieve personal goals. For African Americans in the study, the most important quality in a friend was respect for and acceptance of the individual. European Americans reported that they valued friends who met their task-related needs, offered advice, shared information, and had common interests.[11]

## Intercultural and Intergroup Communication: A Matter of Salience

Intercultural and intergroup communication—at least as we'll use the terms here—don't always occur when people from different backgrounds interact. Those backgrounds must have a significant impact on the exchange before we can say that culture has made a difference. Social scientists use the term **salience** to describe how much weight we attach to cultural characteristics. Consider a few examples in which culture has little or no salience:

- A group of preschool children is playing together in a park. These 3-year-olds don't recognize that their parents may come from different countries, or even that they don't speak the same language. At this point we wouldn't say that intercultural or intergroup communication is taking place. Only when cultural factors (diet, sharing, or parental discipline, for example) become salient do the children begin to think of one another as different.

- Members of a school athletic team—some Asian American, some African American, some Latino, and some white—are intent on winning the league championship. During a game, cultural distinctions aren't salient. There's plenty of communication, but it isn't fundamentally intercultural or intergroup. Away from their games, the players are friendly when they encounter one another, but they rarely socialize. If they did, they might notice some fundamental differences in the way members of each group communicate.

- A husband and wife were raised in different religious traditions. Most of the time their religious heritage makes little difference, and the partners view themselves as a unified couple. Every so often, however—perhaps during the holidays or when meeting members of each other's family—the different backgrounds are more salient. At those times we can imagine the partners feeling quite different from each other—thinking of themselves as members of separate cultures.

These examples show that in order to view ourselves as a member of a culture or coculture, there has to be some distinction between "us" and "them." Social scientists use the label **in-groups** to describe groups with which we identify and are emotionally connected and **out-groups** to label those we view as different and with whom we have no sense of affiliation.[12]

The characters in the TV sitcom *Modern Family* reflect the diversity of today's society. Gay and straight, native-born and immigrant, and young and older family members all are bound by a love and affection that's far more salient than their differences. What are the most salient factors in your relationships?

## Cultural Differences Are Generalizations

It's important not to overstate the influence of culture on communication. There are sometimes greater differences *within* cultures than *between* them. Consider the matter of formality as an example: By most measures, U.S. culture, broadly, is far more casual than many others. But Figure 3-1 shows that there may be more common ground between a formal American and a casual member of a formal culture than there is between two Americans with vastly differing levels of formality.

Furthermore, within every culture, members display a wide range of communication styles. For instance, although most Asian cultures tend to be collectivistic, many members of those cultures identify themselves as individualists. It's important to remember that generalizations—even when accurate and helpful—don't apply to every member of a group.

# Cultural Values and Norms Shape Communication

Some cultural influences on communication are obvious. You don't have to be a scholar or researcher to appreciate how different languages or customs can make communication between groups both interesting and challenging.

Along with the obvious differences, far less visible values and norms shape how members of cultures think and act.[13] This section will look at several of these subtle yet vitally important values and norms that shape the way members of a culture communicate. Unless communicators are aware of these differences, they may see people from other cultures as unusual—or even

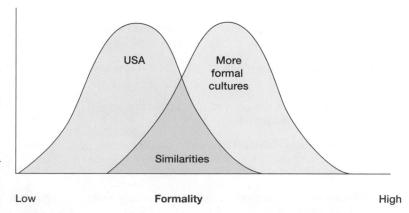

**FIGURE 3-1** **Differences and Similarities Within and Between Cultures**

*Source:* Adapted from F. Trompenaars. (2012). *Riding the waves of culture*, 3rd ed. New York: McGraw-Hill, p. 67.

offensive—without realizing that their apparently odd behavior comes from fol-lowing a different set of beliefs and unwritten rules about the "proper" way to communicate.

## Individualism and Collectivism

Some cultures value the individual more than the group, whereas others place greater emphasis on the group. Members of **individualistic cultures** view their pri-mary responsibility as helping themselves, whereas communicators in **collectivistic cultures** feel loyalties and obligations to an in-group: one's extended family, com-munity, or even the organization one works for.[14]

The way names are treated offers an insight into the difference between in-dividualism and collectivism. When asked to identify themselves, individualistic Americans, Canadians, Australians, and Europeans would probably respond by giving their first name, surname, street, town, and country. But collectivistic South Asians do it the other way around. If you ask Hindus for their identity, they will give you their caste and village and then their family name, and finally their given name.[15] Chinese naming conventions also reflect that culture's collectivist roots. The student profiled at the beginning of this chapter writes his name Luo Bin in China, putting his family name first. But in the United States, where individualism is prized, he follows the convention of putting his surname last: Bin (Robin) Luo.

The differences between individualist and collectivist orientations extend be-yond naming and are reflected in the very structure of some languages. As men-tioned in Chapter 2, the Chinese pronoun *I* looks very similar to the word for *selfish*.[16] The Japanese language has no equivalent to the English pronoun *I*. Instead, different words are used to refer to one's self depending on the social situation, age, gender, and other social characteristics.[17] Individualistic and collectivistic cultures have very different approaches to communication. For example, individualistic cultures are relatively tolerant of conflicts, using a direct, solution-oriented ap-proach. By contrast, members of collectivistic cultures are less direct, often placing a greater emphasis on harmony.[18] Individualistic cultures are also characterized by self-reliance and competition, whereas collectivistic cultures are more attentive to and concerned with the opinions of significant others.[19] Table 3-1 illustrates some of the main differences between individualistic and collectivistic cultures.

Table 3-1    The Self in Individualistic and Collectivistic Cultures

| INDIVIDUALISTIC CULTURES | COLLECTIVISTIC CULTURES |
| --- | --- |
| Self is separate, unique individual; should be independent, self-sufficient. | People belong to extended families or in-groups; "we" or group orientation. |
| Individual should take care of himself or herself and immediate family. | Person should take care of extended family before self. |
| There are many flexible group memberships; friends are based on shared interests and activities. | Emphasis is placed on belonging to a very few permanent in-groups, which have a strong influence over the person. |
| There are rewards for individual achievement and initiative; individual decision is encouraged; individual credit and blame are assigned. | There are rewards for contribution to group goals and well-being; cooperation with in-group members is encouraged; group decisions are valued; credit and blame are shared. |
| High value is placed on autonomy, change, youth, individual security, equality. | High value is placed on duty, order, tradition, age, group secu-rity, status, and hierarchy. |

*Source:* Adapted by Sandra Sudweeks from H. C. Triandis. (1990). Cross-cultural studies of individualism and collectivism. In J. Berman (Ed.), *Nebraska symposium on motivation* (pp. 41–133). Lincoln: University of Nebraska Press; and E. T. Hall. (1976). *Beyond culture.* New York: Doubleday.

Collectivistic societies produce team players, whereas individualistic ones are far more likely to produce and reward superstars. Some research suggests that collectivist groups have a higher sense of teamwork and are more productive than groups of individualistic members.[20]

Members of collectivist societies are typically less publicly egotistical, because touting personal accomplishments would put the individual ahead of the group. "Chinese tend to describe themselves a little bit lower than what they actually are," exchange student Robin Luo explains. "Chinese will say they are so-so even if they are very good." Americans, he has noticed, express themselves differently. As members of an individualistic culture, they are comfortable talking about their own accomplishments or even saying they are really good or the best at something. This sort of cultural difference can lead to misunderstandings in the classroom, a job interview, and other scenes in which Americans may mistakenly assume that people who are humble lack confidence or achievements.

Cultural differences can also affect the level of comfort or anxiety that people feel when communicating. In societies in which the need to conform is great, there is a higher degree of communication apprehension. For example, South Koreans exhibit more conflict avoidance and more apprehension about speaking in front of people than members of individualistic cultures such as the United States.[21] It's important to realize that different levels of communication apprehension don't mean that shyness is a "problem" in some cultures. In fact, just the just the opposite is true: In these cultures, reticence is valued. When the goal is to avoid being the nail that sticks out, it's logical to feel nervous when you make yourself appear different by calling attention to yourself. A self-concept that includes "assertive" might make a Westerner feel proud, but in much of Asia people may speak forthrightly to members of their in-group but consider it inappropriate or shameful to do so with out-group members.

Culture plays an important role in our ability to understand the perspectives of others. Research shows that people raised in individualist cultures, which value independence, are often less adept at seeing others' point of view than those from collectivist cultures. In one study, Chinese and American players were paired together in a game that required them to take on the perspective of their partners.[22] By all measures, the collectivist Chinese had greater success in perspective taking than did their American counterparts.

The difference between individualism and collectivism shows up in everyday interaction. Communication researcher Stella Ting-Toomey has developed a theory that explains cultural differences in important norms, such as honesty and directness.[23] She suggests that in individualistic Western cultures where there is a strong "I" orientation, the low-context norm of speaking directly is honored, whereas in collectivistic cultures where the main desire is to build connections between the self and others, high-context, indirect approaches that maintain harmony are considered more desirable. "I gotta be me" could be the motto of a Westerner, but "If I hurt you, I hurt myself" is closer to the Asian way of thinking.

## High and Low Context

Social scientists have identified two distinct ways that members of various cultures deliver messages.[24] The first deals with context, the set of circumstances that surround a situation and give it meaning. A **low-context culture** uses language primarily to express thoughts, feelings, and ideas as directly as possible. By contrast, a **high-context culture** relies heavily on subtle, often nonverbal cues to maintain social harmony. Rather than upsetting others by speaking directly, communicators in these societies learn to discover meaning from the context in which a message is delivered: the nonverbal behaviors of the speaker, the history of the relationship, and the general social rules that govern interaction between people.

Research shows that Americans are likely to state their concerns or complaints up front, whereas people raised in high-context cultures usually hint at them.[25] Luo, the Chinese exchange student profiled on page 76, gives an example:

> Suppose a guy feels bad about his roommate eating his snacks. If he is Chinese, he may try to hide his food secretly or choose a certain time to say, "My snacks run out so fast, I think I need to buy more next time." Before this, he also may think about whether his roommate would hate him if he says something wrong. But Americans may point out directly that someone has been eating their food.

It's easy to see the potential for misunderstanding in situations like this. The roommate from China may feel it is obvious, based on the situation and his indirect statement, that he is upset about his roommate eating his food. But the American—who may expect his friend to say outright if he is upset—may miss the point entirely. Table 3-2 summarizes some key differences in how people from low- and high-context cultures use language.

Mainstream culture in the United States, Canada, northern Europe, and Israel falls toward the low-context end of the scale. Longtime residents generally value straight talk and grow impatient with "beating around the bush." By contrast, most Asian and Middle Eastern cultures fit the high-context pattern. For them, maintaining harmony is important, so communicators avoid speaking directly if that threatens another person's "face," or dignity.

High- and low-context differences also operate within domestic cocultures. For example, researchers presented European Americans and people of color—Asian American, African American, and Latino—with examples of racist messages.[26] Some of these messages were direct and blatantly offensive, whereas others were indirect and less overtly racist. Researcher Laura Leets found that European American participants judged the directly racist messages as more hurtful, whereas Asian American respondents rated the indirectly racist comments as more damaging. The researcher concluded that the traditional Asian tendency to favor high-context messages explains why Asian Americans were more offended by indirectly racist speech.

It's easy to see how the clash between directness and indirectness can present challenges. To members of high-context cultures, communicators with a low-context style can appear overly talkative, lacking in subtlety, and redundant. On the other hand, to people from low-context backgrounds, high-context communicators often seem evasive, or even dishonest.

American celebrities like Kanye West aren't bashful about expressing their feelings forcefully in social media and on television. Where on the high- to low-context spectrum would your style of emotional expression fit?

## Table 3-2    High- and Low-Context Communication Styles

| LOW CONTEXT | HIGH CONTEXT |
| --- | --- |
| Majority of information carried in explicit verbal messages, with less focus on the situational context. | Important information carried in contextual cues such as time, place, relationship, situation. Less reliance on explicit verbal messages. |
| Self-expression valued. Communicators state opinions and desires directly and strive to persuade others to accept their viewpoint. | Relational harmony valued and maintained by indirect expression of options. Communicators abstain from saying "no" directly. |
| Clear, eloquent speech considered praiseworthy. Verbal fluency admired. | Communicators talk "around" the point, allowing others to fill in the missing pieces. Ambiguity and use of silence admired. |

## Uncertainty Avoidance

Uncertainty may be universal, but cultures have different ways of coping with an unpredictable future. The term **uncertainty avoidance** is used to reflect the degree to which members of a culture feel threatened by ambiguous situations and how much they try to avoid them.[27] As a group, residents of some countries (including Singapore, Great Britain, Denmark, Sweden, Hong Kong, and the United States) are relatively unthreatened by change, whereas others (such as natives of Belgium, Greece, Japan, and Portugal) find new or ambiguous situations discomforting.

A culture's degree of uncertainty avoidance is reflected in the way its members communicate. In countries that avoid uncertainty, deviant people and ideas are considered dangerous, and intolerance is high. People in these cultures are especially concerned with security, so they have a strong need for clearly defined rules and regulations. It's easy to imagine how most relationships in cultures with a low tolerance for uncertainty—family, work, friendships, and romance—are likely to fit a predictable pattern. By contrast, people in a culture that is less threatened by the new and unexpected are more likely to tolerate—or even welcome—people who don't fit the norm.

After growing up in China in a culture that has relatively high uncertainty avoidance, Robin Luo says Americans often seem relatively fearless to him. "They are seldom afraid of making mistakes," he marvels. By contrast, "in China, when we face a problem, we may be quiet and consider a lot about its consequences before taking actions, even if not much is likely to happen." He explains that Americans speak in ways that make them sound and feel confident, and they are willing to make decisions, if when they know only "about 70 percent" of the details about a situation. As you might imagine, either of these approaches can be effective, depending on the situation.

## Power Distance

**Power distance** refers to the extent of the gap between social groups who possess resources and influence and those who don't. Cultures with low power distance believe in minimizing the difference between various social classes. Rich and poor, educated and uneducated groups may still exist, but there's a pervasive belief in low-power-difference cultures that one person is as good as another regardless of his or her station in life.

Austria, Denmark, Israel, and New Zealand are the most egalitarian countries. At the other end of the spectrum are countries with a high degree of power distance: Philippines, Mexico, Venezuela, India, and Singapore.[28] Anyone familiar with communication in the United States and Canada knows that those cultures value equality, even if it's not perfectly enacted. For example, they might call their bosses by their first names and challenge the opinions of people in higher-status positions.

By contrast, in cultures with high power distance it may seem rude to treat everyone the same way. In the Japanese workplace, for example, new acquaintances exchange business cards immediately, which helps establish everyone's relative status. The oldest or highest-ranking person receives the deepest bows from others, the best seat, the most deferential treatment, and so on. This treatment isn't regarded as elitist or disrespectful. Indeed, treating a high-status person the same as everyone else would seem rude.

As an exchange student from China, Robin Luo has observed that Americans often interact informally with their bosses and professors, even to the extent of calling them by their first names. That would not happen in China, he says.

> Where would you rate your communication on a low-high context spectrum? Is there any difference between the directness of your face-to-face communication and messages you express in social media? How would your relationships be affected if your communication were more direct? Less direct?

## Power Distance and Culture in the Workplace

On-the-job communication is different in low- and high-power-distance societies.[29] In countries with higher degrees of power distance, employees have much less input into the way they perform their work. In fact, workers from these cultures are likely to feel uncomfortable when given freedom to make their own decisions or when a more egalitarian boss asks for their opinion: They prefer to view their bosses as benevolent decision makers. The reverse is true when management from a culture with an egalitarian tradition tries to do business in a country whose workers are used to high power distance. They can be surprised to find that employees do not expect much say in decisions and do not feel unappreciated when they aren't consulted. They may regard dutiful,

submissive, respectful employees as lacking initiative and creativity—traits that helped them gain promotions back home. Given these differences, it's easy to understand why multinational companies need to consider fundamental differences in communication values and behavior when they set up shop in a new country. ●

Do you work with people from cultures with beliefs about power distance that differ from yours? How do those differences show up when you work together? Can you think of ways to manage these differences that will improve both personal relationships and workplace effectiveness?

There, students may call an engineering professor Wang Doctor, Wang Professor, or Wang Engineer (they put a person's name before his or her title). If a student develops a close relationship with the professor, he or she may address him or her as "Professor" or "Engineer." But it would be considered disrespectful to omit the title or to use a first name. This is even true among students of different ranks. Classmates address a senior or a club president formally, by last name and title, unless he or she is a very close friend.

### Beliefs About Talk and Silence

Beliefs about the very value of talk differ from one culture to another.[30] Western cultures tend to view talk as desirable and use it for social purposes as well as to perform tasks. Silence has a negative value in these cultures. It is likely to be interpreted as lack of interest, unwillingness to communicate, hostility, anxiety, shyness, or a sign of interpersonal incompatibility. Westerners are typically uncomfortable with silence, which they find embarrassing and awkward.

On the other hand, Asian cultures tend to perceive talk quite differently. For thousands of years, Asian cultures have discouraged the expression of thoughts and feelings. Silence is valued, as Taoist sayings indicate: "In much talk there is great weariness" or "One who speaks does not know; one who knows does not speak." Unlike Westerners, who tend to be uncomfortable with silence, Japanese and Chinese people more often believe that remaining quiet is the proper state when there is nothing to be said. To Asians, a talkative person is often considered a show-off or a fake.

Members of some Native American communities also honor silence. For example, traditional members of western Apache tribes maintain silence when others lose their temper. As one member explained, "When someone gets mad at you and starts yelling, then just don't do anything to make him get worse."[31] Apache also consider that silence has a comforting value. The idea is that words are often unnecessary in periods of grief, and it is comforting to have loved ones present without the pressure to maintain conversations with them.

It's easy to see how these different views of speech and silence can lead to communication problems when people from different cultures meet. Both the "talkative" Westerner and the "silent" Asian and Native American are behaving in ways they believe are proper, yet each may view the other with disapproval and mistrust. Only when they recognize the different standards of behavior can they adapt to one another, or at least understand and respect their differences.

## Competitive and Cooperative Cultures

Cultures are a bit like people in that they fall somewhere on a spectrum between competitive and cooperative (or, as Geert Hofstede described them, masculine and feminine).[32] For example, competitive (or masculine) qualities such as independence, competitiveness, and assertiveness are highly valued in Japan, Italy, Nigeria, and Great Britain. In these cultures, women are often expected to take care of home and family life, whereas men are expected to shoulder most of the financial responsibilities.

Gender roles are less differentiated in cooperative cultures—which makes sense when you consider that they emphasize equality, relationships, cooperation, and consensus building.[33] In Iceland, the Netherlands, and Norway, both men and women tend to consider harmony and cooperation to be more important than competition. Cultural orientations influence how people communicate with one another and what motivates them. Male leaders in competitive cultures tend to focus more on employees' achievements than on their unique qualities and relationships, whereas the opposite is true of leaders in cooperative cultures.[34]

Some countries, such as Taiwan, fall near the midpoint on this scale because natives of those cultures place relatively equal value on competitive and cooperative qualities.[35] The United States has long been considered a moderately competitive culture, but some people feel it's moving closer to the middle of the spectrum. In fact, there is speculation that the world is becoming more balanced overall.[36] This is partly because women have entered the workplace in record numbers and partly because technology now exposes people to a world of new ideas, fashions, and outlooks that go beyond traditional gender roles.

# Cocultures and Communication

Much of how we view ourselves and how we relate to others grows from our cultural and cocultural identity—the groups with which we identify. Where do you come from? What's your ethnicity? Your religion? Your sexual orientation? Your age?

In the following pages we will look at some—though by no means all—of the factors that help shape our cultural identity, and hence the way we perceive and communicate with others.

## Ethnicity and Race

**Race** is a social construct originally created to explain differences between people whose ancestors originated in different regions of the world—Africa, Asia, Europe, and so on. Modern scientists acknowledge that, although there are some genetic differences between people with different heritage, they mostly involve superficial qualities such as hair color and texture, skin color, and the size and shape of facial features. As one analyst puts it:

> There is less to race than meets the eye. . . . The genes influencing skin color have nothing to do with the genes influencing hair form, eye shape, blood type, musical talent, athletic ability or forms of intelligence. Knowing someone's skin color doesn't necessarily tell you anything else about him or her.[37]

There are several reasons why race has little use in explaining individual differences. Most obviously, racial features are often misinterpreted. A well-traveled

CNN news anchor Soledad O'Brien considers herself black as well as Latina. Do you find that people make judgments about your background based on your appearance? If so, does that influence how they interact with you?

friend of ours from Latin America says that she is often mistaken as Italian, Indian, Spanish, or Native American.

More important, there is more genetic variation within races than between them. Some people with Asian ancestry are short, but others are tall. Some have sunny dispositions, and others are more dour. Some are terrific athletes, and others were born clumsy. The same applies to people from every background. Even within a physically recognizable population, personal experience plays a far greater role than superficial characteristics like skin color.[38] As you read in Chapter 2, stereotyping is usually a mistake.

Rather than thinking about race, it's more fruitful to think in terms of **ethnicity**, which is a social rather than a biological construct. Ethnicity refers to the degree to which a person identifies with a particular group, usually on the basis of nationality, culture, religion, or some other unifying perspective.[39] This goes beyond physical indicators. For example, a person may have physical characteristics that appear Asian but be more ethnically working class or Mormon.

Even ethnicity can be problematic, because it is usually simplistic to think of people as members of a single category. Consider U.S. president Barack Obama. He is generally recognized as the country's first African American president, despite the fact that his mother was white. Obama experienced a variety of cultures while living in Indonesia, Hawaii, California, New York, Chicago, and Washington, DC. A single term can't describe such a culturally complex background.

Being identified as belonging to more than one group can be challenging. Consider someone like Heather Greenwood, who is biracial. Strangers inquire how her children can be fair skinned, because she is dark. Others ask if she is the children's nanny or joke that the kids must have been "switched in the hospital" when they were born. The implication, Greenwood says, is that a legitimate family is either one color or another. She hears comments such as these nearly every day. "Each time is like a little paper cut, and you think, 'Well, that's not a big deal.' But imagine a lifetime of that. It hurts," she says.[40]

Along with the challenges, multiple-group membership can be a bonus. Like President Obama, many people say they are more open minded and respectful of others as a result of coming from culturally rich backgrounds. Research indicates they are also more comfortable establishing relationships with a diverse array of people, which increases their options for friendships, romantic partners, and professional colleagues.[41]

## Regional Differences

Where you come from can shape feelings of belonging, and how others regard you. Accent is a case in point. Speakers of standard ("newscaster") English are viewed as more competent and self-confident than others, and the content of their messages gets higher ratings.[42] In one experiment, researchers asked human resource professionals to rate the intelligence, initiative, and personality of job applicants after listening to a brief recording of their voices. The speakers with recognizable regional accents—from the southern United States or New Jersey, for example—were tagged for lower-level jobs, whereas those with less pronounced speech styles were recommended for higher-level jobs that involved more public contact.[43]

The effect of nonnative accents is even stronger. In one study, jurors in the United States found testimony less believable when delivered by witnesses speaking with Mexican, German, or Middle Eastern accents.[44] Not surprisingly, other research shows that speakers with nonnative accents feel stigmatized by the bias against them, often leading to a lower sense of belonging and more communication problems.[45]

Accent isn't the only way that regional differences can be significant. Sociolinguist Deborah Tannen recorded the conversation at her Thanksgiving Day dinner and found that what counted as interruptions varied depending on where one was raised.[46] The guests included two Christians who grew up in California, three Jewish people from New York, and a British woman. Tannen found that the New York Jewish guests spoke with what she called a "high-involvement" style that worked well with their companions from the same background but was regarded differently by the Englishwoman and the Californians:

> At times the Californians felt interrupted when their Jewish friends mistook a pause for breath as a turn-relinquishing one. At other times, exclamations like "Wow!" or "That's impossible!" which were intended to encourage the conversation, stopped it instead. The New Yorkers in my study assumed that a speaker who wasn't finished wouldn't stop just because someone else started.[47]

*"Anything you say with an accent may be used against you."*

Source: Paul Noth / The New Yorker Collection / www.cartoonbank.com

Even facial expressions have a regional basis. In the United States unwritten rules about smiling vary from one part of the country to another. People from southern and border states smile the most, and Midwesterners smile more than New Englanders.[48] Given these differences, it's easy to imagine how a college freshman from North Carolina might regard a new roommate from Massachusetts as unfriendly, and how the New Englander might view the southerner as overly expressive.

A fascinating series of studies revealed that climate and geographic latitude were remarkably accurate predictors of communication predispositions.[49] People living in southern latitudes of the United States are more socially isolated, less tolerant of ambiguity, higher in self-esteem, more likely to touch others, and more likely to verbalize their thoughts and feelings. This sort of finding helps explain why communicators who travel from one part of a country to another find that their old patterns of communicating don't work as well in their new location. A southerner whose relatively talkative, high-touch style seemed completely normal at home might be viewed as pushy and aggressive in a new northern home.

## Sexual Orientation and Gender Identity

"NOBODY KNOWS I'M GAY." That witty saying is emblazoned on thousands of T-shirts sold by former comedian Skyler Thomas, a champion of the LGBTQ movement. *LGBTQ* stands for lesbian, gay, bisexual, transgender, and queer—a collection of adjectives that describes people with diverse sexual orientations and gender identities.

Not all LGBTQ individuals are gay. Transgender individuals don't feel that their biological sex is a good description of who they are. For example, some people who were born boys identify more with a feminine identity, and vice versa. And people typically describe themselves as queer if they don't feel that other gender adjectives describe them well or if they dislike the idea of gender categorizations in general. The Q sometimes stands for "questioning" as well, underlining the idea that gender is not always a fixed or static construct.[50]

The "NOBODY KNOWS I'M GAY" shirts point to a communication dilemma facing many LGBTQ individuals. On the one hand, being open about their gender identity has advantages—including a sense of being authentic with others and belonging to a supportive coculture. On the other hand, the disclosure can be risky. People may be shocked or judgmental. They may ridicule LGBTQ individuals, discriminate against them, or even attack them. On average, one in five hate crimes in the United States targets people on the basis of their sexual orientation.[51]

CNN host Anderson Cooper didn't tell the public he was gay for years because he considered it private information, he felt it might put him and others in danger, and he thought he could do a better job as a journalist if he "blended in."[52] However, Cooper says his silence sometimes felt disingenuous. "I have given some the mistaken impression that I am trying to hide something," he says. He also felt that he was missing an opportunity to dispel some of the fear and prejudice that surround the issue. "The tide of history only advances when people make themselves fully visible," Cooper said, in a public statement in 2012. "The fact is, I'm gay, always have been, and I couldn't be more happy, comfortable with myself, and proud."

For people whose "coming out" announcements make headlines, going public happens all at once. However, that is not the case for most LGBTQ individuals. "Coming out is a process that never ends," reflects Jennifer Potter, a physician who is gay. "Every time I meet someone new I must decide if, how, and when I will reveal my sexual orientation."[53] She says it's often easy to "pass" as heterosexual, but then she experiences the awkwardness of people assuming she has a boyfriend or husband, and it saddens her when she cannot openly refer to her partner or invite her to take part in social gatherings.

Although they acknowledge the communication dilemma they face, most LGBTQ individuals don't want the public to see them in tragic terms. Aside from issues of social acceptance, their lives are just as "happy and productive" as other people's.

The social climate has become more receptive to LGBTQ individuals than in the past, at least in most of the developed world. As one report put it,

> Most LGBT people who are now adults can recall feeling that they were "the only one" and fearing complete rejection by their families, friends, and associates should their identity become known. Yet today, in this era of GSAs [gay-straight alliances] . . . openly gay politicians and civil unions; debates about same-sex marriage, gay adoption, and gays in the military; and a plethora of websites aimed specifically at LGBT youth, it is hard to imagine many youths who would believe they are alone in their feelings.[54]

Among those websites is ItGetsBetter.org, at which people can post messages to encourage LGBTQ youth that any harassment they may be experiencing is not their fault and that people care about making it better. Since Dan Savage and Terry Miller launched the It Gets Better Project in 2010, people have posted more than 50,000 videos, which have been viewed more than 50 million times.[55] Savage says it shows what can happen when communication technology and good intentions combine.[56]

## ON YOUR FEET

### Cultural Membership

What are some of the cultural groups you identify with? Which of them has played the greatest role in shaping your communication style and expectations? How? In what ways is it helpful or necessary to adapt your communication to fit different cocultural groups?

## Religion

In some cultures, religion is the defining factor in shaping in- and out-groups. Whether you belong to the Shia or Sunni sects is enormously important in many parts of the Islamic world. Within recent memory, Protestants and Catholics in Northern Ireland fought to the death to defend their view of Christianity.

In less extreme but still profound ways, religion shapes how and with whom many people communicate. For example, members of the orthodox Jewish community consider it important to marry within the faith. In one study, some of the young Jewish women interviewed said a man's religious preference is as important or more important than his personality.[57] They also described a cultural gap between dating solely to find a suitable spouse and the "American style" of dating, in which couples may spend time together, and even have sex, although they don't plan to marry. Dating within the orthodox faith is communication centered and focused, a bit like a job interview. As one woman in the study put it: "When you're not touching the person . . . you're more professional, you take decisions much more seriously."

Other research suggests that, in general, teens who believe that only one religion has merit date less frequently than other teens, perhaps because their pool of acceptable partners is smaller.[58] However, religious teens who respect the viewpoints of multiple religions typically date more frequently than their nonreligious peers.[59] And the odds are good for interfaith relationships. Studies show that, if they communicate openly and respectfully about matters of faith, interfaith couples are just as likely as other couples to stay together.[60]

Religious beliefs affect family life as well. Members of evangelical churches are likely to view parents as family decision makers and honor children for following their advice without question.[61] Religious activities such as reading scripture at home are most common among Jehovah's Witnesses and members of the Church of Jesus Christ of Latter Day Saints (Mormons), evangelical churches, and historically black churches.[62] These congregations are also the most likely to believe there is only one true religion.

U.S. president John F. Kennedy said, "Tolerance implies no lack of commitment to one's own beliefs. Rather it condemns the oppression or persecution of others." Using this standard, how tolerant are you in everyday conversation and on social media?

## Physical Ability/Disability

Whereas identities like ethnicity or nationality require years of immersion, disability is "a club anyone can join, anytime. It's very easy. Have a stroke and be paralyzed. . . . Be in a car wreck and never walk again."[63]

Although able-bodied people might view disability as an unfortunate condition, many people with disabilities find that belonging to a community of similar people can be rewarding. Deaf culture is a good example: The shared experiences of deafness can create strong bonds. Most notably, distinct languages build a shared worldview and solidarity. There are Deaf schools, Deaf competitions (e.g., Miss Deaf America), Deaf performing arts (including Deaf comedians), and other organizations that bring deaf people together.

In the independent film *Arranged*, Rochel and Nasira—an Orthodox Jew and a Muslim, respectively—meet as new teachers at a Brooklyn school. Colleagues and students expect friction, but the women become close friends as they discover they have much in common. Think about others whom you might reflexively regard as different. What might you discover that you have in common if you learned more about them?

*Murderball* documents the hard-core determination and physicality of wheelchair rugby players. Competitors like those in this film help dispel the stereotypical notion that people with disabilities seek or welcome sympathy. Have you ever been inspired to think differently about people after you have seen what they can accomplish?

Despite stereotypes, "different than" doesn't have to mean "less than." One former airline pilot who lost his hearing described his trip to China:

> Though we used different signed languages, these Chinese Deaf people and I could make ourselves understood; and though we came from different countries, our mutual Deaf culture held us together. . . . *You* couldn't do that in China. . . . Who's disabled then?[64]

Regardless of the specific physical condition, it's important to treat a disability as one feature, not as a defining characteristic of others. Describing someone as "a person who is blind" is both more accurate and less constricting than calling her a "blind person." This difference might seem subtle—until you imagine which label you would prefer if you lost your sight.

## Age/Generation

Imagine how odd it would seem to hear an 8-year-old or a senior citizen talking, dressing, or otherwise acting like a 20-something. We tend to think of getting older as a purely physical process. But age-related communication reflects culture at least as much as biology. In many ways, we learn how to "do" being various ages—how to dress, how to talk, and what not to say and do—in the same way we learn how to play other roles in our lives.

Relationships between older and younger people are shaped by cultural assumptions that change over time. At some points in history, older adults have been

---

### Understanding Diversity

## Communicating with People Who Have Disabilities

Research has revealed some clear guidelines for interacting with people who have disabilities.[65] They include:

1. Speak directly to people with disabilities, rather than looking at and talking to their companions.

2. If you volunteer assistance, wait until your offer is accepted before proceeding. Then listen to or ask for instructions.

3. Treat adults as such. For example, don't address people who have disabilities by their first names unless you're doing so with others.

4. When you're introduced to a person with a disability, offer to shake hands. (People with limited hand use or who wear an artificial limb can usually shake hands.)

5. When meeting a person who is visually impaired, identify yourself and others who may be with you.

6. When speaking with someone who uses a wheelchair, place yourself at eye level in front of the person.

Remember: A wheelchair is part of the user's personal body space, so don't touch or lean on it without permission.

7. When you're talking with a person who has difficulty speaking, be patient and wait for him or her to finish. Ask short questions that require a nod, shake of the head, or brief answers. Never pretend to understand if you are having difficulty doing so.

8. With a person who is deaf, speak clearly, slowly, and expressively to determine whether the person can read your lips. (Not all people who are deaf can read lips.)

9. Don't be embarrassed if you happen to use common expressions such as "See you later" or "Did you hear about that?" that seem to relate to a person's disability.

10. Relax. Don't be afraid to ask questions when you're unsure of what to do. ●

regarded as wise, accomplished, and even magical.[66] At others, they have been treated as "dead weight" and uncomfortable reminders of mortality and decline.[67]

Today, for the most part, Western cultures honor youth, and attitudes about aging are more negative than positive. On balance, people over age 40 are still twice as likely as younger ones to be depicted in the media as unattractive, bored, and in declining health.[68] And people over age 60, especially women, are still under-represented in the media. However, the data present a different story. Studies show that, overall, people in their 60s are just as happy as people in their 20s.[69]

Unfavorable attitudes about aging can show up in interpersonal relationships. Even though gray or thinning hair and wrinkles don't necessarily signify diminished capacity, they may be interpreted that way—with powerful consequences. People who believe older adults have trouble communicating are less likely to interact with them. When they do, they tend to use the mannerisms listed Table 3-3.[70] Even when these speech styles are well intentioned, they can have harmful effects. Older adults who are treated as less capable than their peers tend to perceive *themselves* as older and less capable.[71] And challenging ageist treatment presents seniors with a dilemma: Speaking up can be taken as a sign of being cranky or bitter, reinforcing the stereotype that those seniors are curmudgeons.[72]

Youth doesn't always live up to its glamorous image. Teens and young adults typically experience intense pressure, both internally and from people around them, to establish their identity and prove themselves.[73] At the same time, adolescents typically experience what psychologists call a personal fable (the sense that they are different than everybody else) and an imaginary audience (a heightened self-consciousness that makes it seem as if people are always observing and judging them).[74] These characterize a natural stage of development, but they lead to some classic communication challenges. For one, teens often feel that their parents and other people can't understand them because their situations are different and unique. Couple this with the sense that others are being overly attentive and critical and you have a good recipe for conflict and frustration. Parents may be baffled that their "extensive experience" and "good advice" are summarily rejected. And young people may wonder why people butt into their affairs with "overly critical judgments" and "irrelevant advice."

## Table 3-3    Patronizing Speech Directed at Seniors

| ELEMENT | DEFINITION AND EXAMPLE |
|---|---|
| Simplified grammar | Use of short sentences without multiple clauses. "Here's your food. You can eat it. It is good." |
| Simplified vocabulary | Use of short words rather than longer equivalents. Saying *dog* instead of *Dalmation*, or *big* instead of *enormous*. |
| Endearing terms | Calling someone "sweetie" or "love." |
| Increased volume, reduced rate | Talking LOUDER and s-l-o-w-e-r! |
| High and variable pitch | Using a slightly squeaky voice style, and exaggerating the pitch variation in speech (a "sing-song" type speech style). |
| Use of repetition | Saying things over and over again. Repeating. Redundancy. Over and over again. The same thing. Repeated. Again. And again . . . |
| Use of baby-ish terms | Using words like *doggie* or *choo-choo* instead of *dog* or *train*: "Oh look at the cute little doggie, isn't he a coochie-coochie-coo!" |

*Source:* J. Harwood. (2007). *Understanding communication and aging: Developing knowledge and awareness.* Newbury Park, CA: Sage, p. 76.

Communication challenges also can arise when members of different generations work together. For example, millennials (those born between 1980 and 2000) tend to have a much stronger need for affirming feedback than previous generations.[75] Because of their strong desire for achievement, they want clear guidance on how to do a job correctly—but do not want to be micromanaged when they do it. After finishing the task, they have an equally strong desire for praise. To a baby boomer boss, that type of guidance and feedback may feel more like a nuisance. In the boss's experience, "no news is good news," and not being told that you screwed up should be praise enough. Neither perspective is wrong. But when members of these cocultures have different expectations, miscommunication can occur.

## Socioeconomic Status

Social class can have a major impact on how people communicate. Research shows that people in the United States typically identify themselves as belonging to the working class, middle class, or upper class, and that they feel a sense of solidarity with people in the same social strata.[76] This is especially true for working-class people, who tend to feel that they are united both by hardship and by their commitment to hard, physical work. One working-class college student put it this way:

> I know that when all is said and done, I'm a stronger and better person than they [members of the upper class] are. That's probably a horrible thing to say and it makes me sound very egotistical, but . . . it makes me more glad that I've been through what I've been through, because at the end of the day, I know I had to bust my a** to be where I want, and that makes me feel really good.[77]

These communication styles can have consequences later in life. College professors often find that working-class and first-generation college students who are raised not to challenge authority can have a difficult time speaking up, thinking critically, and arguing persuasively.[78] The effects of social class continue into the workplace, where skills like assertiveness and persuasiveness are career enhancers. People who come from working-class families and attain middle- or upper-class careers face special challenges. New speech and language, clothing, and nonverbal patterns often are necessary to gain acceptance.[79] Many of these individuals also must cope with emotional ambivalences related to their career success.[80] See the "@Work" box in this section for more about workplace cultures.

Even within the same family, educational level can create intercultural challenges. First-generation college (FCG) students feel the intercultural strain of "trying to live simultaneously in two vastly different worlds" of school and home. Communication researchers Mark Orbe and Christopher Groscurth discovered that many FGC students alter their communication patterns dramatically between their two worlds.[81]

Because no one in their family has attended college, FGC students often cope with an unfamiliar environment by trying to assimilate—going out of their way to fit in on campus. Sometimes assimilating requires self-censorship, as FGC students avoid discussions that might reveal their educational or socioeconomic backgrounds. In addition, some FGC students say they overcompensate by studying harder and getting more involved on campus than their non-FGC classmates, just to prove they belong in the college culture.

In *Beasts of the Southern Wild*, 6-year-old Hushpuppy (Quvenzhané Wallis) and her father, Wink (Dwight Henry), live in an impoverished but tight-knit bayou community called the Bathtub. When a hurricane forces them to evacuate, the culture clash with well-meaning aid workers from outside is too much to bear. Do socioeconomic differences present communication challenges for you?

At home, FGC students also engage in self-censorship, but for different reasons. They are cautious when talking about college life for fear of threatening and alienating their families. The only exception is that some feel a need to model their new educational status to younger family members so "they can see that it can be done."[82]

At the other end of the socioeconomic spectrum, gangs fit the definition of a coculture. Members have a well-defined identity, both among themselves and according to the outside world. This sense of belonging is often reflected in distinctive language and nonverbal markers such as clothing, tattoos, and hand signals. Gangs provide people who are marginalized by society a sense of identity and security in an often dangerous and hostile world. But the benefits come at considerable cost. When compared to similar youths, gang members have higher rates of delinquency and drug use. They commit more violent offenses and have higher arrest rates.[83]

## @Work

### Organizations Are Cultures, Too

A man stopped by a Nordstrom department store in Oregon to buy an Armani tuxedo for his daughter's wedding. The next day he received a call saying the tux was ready and waiting. He picked it up and left a happy customer.

The kicker is that Nordstrom doesn't sell Armani tuxedos. The salesperson had one overnighted from another supplier and then altered to fit the customer perfectly.[84] It didn't matter that Nordstrom didn't make a penny off the sale. Doing whatever it takes to please customers is part of the company's corporate culture.

As this story illustrates, organizations have cultures that can be just as distinctive as those of larger societies. **Organizational culture** reflects a relatively stable, shared set of rules about how to behave and a set of values about what is important. In everyday language, culture is the insiders' view of "the way things are around here."

Not all the rules and values of an organization are written down. And some of them that are written down aren't actually followed. Perhaps the workday officially ends at 5 p.m., but you quickly notice that most people stay until at least 6:30. That says something about the culture. Or, even though it doesn't say so in the employee handbook, employees in some companies consider one another as extended family, taking personal interest in the lives of coworkers. That's culture, too.

Because you're likely to spend as much time at work as you do in personal relationships, selecting the right organization is as important as choosing a best friend. Research shows that we are likely to enjoy our jobs and do them well if we believe that the organization's values reflect our own and that its values are consistently and fairly applied.[85] For example, Nordstrom rewards team members for offering great customer service without exception. On the other hand, a boss who talks about customer service but violates those principles cultivates a culture of cynicism and dissatisfaction.

Ask yourself these questions when considering whether a specific organization's culture is a good fit for you. (Notice how important communication is in each case.)

- How does the organization present itself online and on the telephone?
- Is the tone welcoming and inviting?
- Are customers happy with the service and quality provided?
- Do members of the organization have the resources and authority to do a good job?
- Do employees have fun? Are they encouraged to be creative?
- Is there a spirit of cooperation or competition among team members?
- What criteria are used to evaluate employee performance?
- What happens during meetings? Is communication open or highly scripted?
- How often do people leave their jobs to work somewhere else?
- Do leaders make a point of listening, respecting, and collaborating with employees?
- Do people use their time productively or are they bogged down with inefficient procedures or office politics?

Research suggests that communication is the vehicle through which we both create and embody culture. At a personal and organizational level, effective, consistent, value-based communication is essential to success. ●

Tolerance for gay and lesbian people has grown as their visibility has increased in mainstream media. Talk show host and comedian Ellen DeGeneres has been a trailblazer by presenting television audiences with a humorous, positive face of someone with a different sexual orientation. How have media portrayals affected your attitudes toward historically marginalized groups?

# Developing Intercultural Communication Competence

What distinguishes competent and incompetent intercultural communicators? Before we answer this question, take a moment to complete the self-assessment on page 95 to evaluate your intercultural communication sensitivity.

To a great degree, interacting successfully with strangers calls for the same ingredients of general communicative competence outlined in Chapter 1. It's important to have a wide range of behaviors and to be skillful at choosing and performing the most appropriate ones in a given situation. A genuine concern for others plays an important role. Cognitive complexity and the ability to empathize also help. Finally, self-monitoring is important, because it is often necessary to make midcourse corrections in your approach when dealing with strangers.

But beyond these basic qualities, communication researchers have worked long and hard to identify qualities that are unique, or at least especially important, ingredients of intercultural communicative competence.[86]

## Increased Contact

More than a half century of research confirms that, under the right circumstances, spending time with people from different backgrounds leads to a host of positive outcomes: reduced prejudice, greater productivity, and better relationships.[87] The link between exposure and positive attitudes, called the *contact hypothesis*, has been demonstrated in a wide range of contacts: between gays and straights, people from different cultures and cocultures, and people with and without disabilities.[88]

By itself, exposure isn't enough. In order to make contacts successful, some other conditions are important. The first is a genuine desire to know and understand others. People who are willing to communicate with others from different backgrounds report a greater number of diverse friends than those who are less willing to reach out.[89] Other conditions also contribute to positive relationships: They include equal status; a low-stress, cooperative climate; and the chance to disconfirm stereotypes.

Along with face-to-face contacts, the Internet offers a useful way to enhance contact with people from different backgrounds.[90] Online venues make it relatively easy to connect with people you might never meet in person. The asynchronous nature of these contacts reduces the potential for stress and confusion that can easily come in person. It also makes status differences less important: When you're online, gaps in material wealth or physical appearance are much less apparent.

## Tolerance for Ambiguity

When we encounter communicators from different cultures, the level of uncertainty is especially high. Consider the basic challenge of communicating in an unfamiliar language. Pico Iyer captures the ambiguity that arises from a lack of fluency when he describes his growing friendship with Sachiko, a Japanese woman he met in Kyoto:

> I was also beginning to realize how treacherous it was to venture into a foreign language if one could not measure the shadows of the words one used. When I had told her, in Asuka, *"Jennifer Beals ga suki-desu. Anata mo"* ("I like Jennifer Beals—and I like you"), I had been pleased to find a way of conveying affection, and yet, I thought, a perfect distance. But later I looked up *suki* and found that I had delivered an almost naked protestation of love. . . .

⊽ ON YOUR FEET

Share an example of intercultural or cocultural *in*competence you have witnessed, either in person or in social media, such as Facebook or Twitter. What mistakes were made? How could the communicator(s) involved have handled the situation more competently?

## What Is Your Intercultural Sensitivity?

Below is a series of statements concerning intercultural communication. There are no right or wrong answers. Imagine yourself interacting with people from a wide variety of cultural groups, not just one or two. Record your first impression to each statement by indicating the degree to which you agree or disagree, using the following scale.

**5** = strongly agree     **4** = agree     **3** = uncertain     **2** = disagree     **1** = strongly disagree

_____ **1.** I enjoy interacting with people from different cultures.

_____ **2.** I think people from other cultures are narrow minded.

_____ **3.** I am pretty sure of myself in interacting with people from different cultures.

_____ **4.** I find it very hard to talk in front of people from different cultures.

_____ **5.** I always know what to say when interacting with people from different cultures.

_____ **6.** I can be as sociable as I want to be when interacting with people from different cultures.

_____ **7.** I don't like to be with people from different cultures.

_____ **8.** I respect the values of people from different cultures.

_____ **9.** I get upset easily when interacting with people from different cultures.

_____ **10.** I feel confident when interacting with people from different cultures.

_____ **11.** I tend to wait before forming an impression of culturally distinct counterparts.

_____ **12.** I often get discouraged when I am with people from different cultures.

_____ **13.** I am open minded to people from different cultures.

_____ **14.** I am very observant when interacting with people from different cultures.

_____ **15.** I often feel useless when interacting with people from different cultures.

_____ **16.** I respect the ways people from different cultures behave.

_____ **17.** I try to obtain as much information as I can when interacting with people from different cultures.

_____ **18.** I would not accept the opinions of people from different cultures.

_____ **19.** I am sensitive to my culturally distinct counterpart's subtle meanings during our interaction.

_____ **20.** I think my culture is better than other cultures.

_____ **21.** I often give positive responses to my culturally different counterpart during our interaction.

_____ **22.** I avoid those situations in which I will have to deal with culturally distinct persons.

_____ **23.** I often show my culturally distinct counterpart my understanding through verbal or nonverbal cues.

_____ **24.** I have a feeling of enjoyment toward differences between my culturally distinct counterpart and me.

To determine your score, begin by reverse-coding items 2, 4, 7, 9, 12, 15, 18, 20, and 22 (if you indicated 5, reverse-code to 1; if you indicated 4, reverse-code to 2; and so on). Higher scores on the total instrument and each of the five subscales indicate a greater probability of intercultural communication competence.

Sum items 1, 11, 13, 21, 22, 23, and 24 ☐ Interaction Engagement (range is 7–35)

Sum items 2, 7, 8, 16, 18, and 20 ☐ Respect for Cultural Differences (6–30)

Sum items 3, 4, 5, 6, and 10 ☐ Interaction Confidence (5–25)

Sum items 9, 12, and 15 ☐ Interaction Enjoyment (3–15)

Sum items 14, 17, and 19 ☐ Interaction Attentiveness (3–15)

Sum of all the items ☐ (24–120, with a midpoint of 48)

Permission to use courtesy of Guo-Ming Chen. Chen, G. M., & Sarosta, W. J. (2000). The development and validation of the intercultural sensitivity scale. *Human Communication, 3,* 1–14.

Meanwhile, of course, nearly all her shadings were lost to me. . . . Once, when I had to leave her house ten minutes early, she said, "I very sad," and another time, when I simply called her up, she said, "I very happy"—and I began to think her unusually sensitive, or else prone to bold and violent extremes, when really she was reflecting nothing but the paucity of her English vocabulary. . . . Talking in a language not one's own was like walking on one leg; when two people did it together, it was like a three-legged waltz.[91]

Competent intercultural communicators accept—even welcome—this kind of ambiguity. Iyer describes the way the mutual confusion he shared with Sachiko actually helped their relationship develop:

Yet in the end, the fact that we were both speaking in this pared-down diction made us both, I felt, somewhat gentler, more courteous, and more vulnerable than we would have been otherwise, returning us to a state of innocence.[92]

Without a tolerance for ambiguity, the mass of often confusing and sometimes downright incomprehensible messages that impact intercultural interactions would be impossible to manage. Some people seem to come equipped with this sort of tolerance, whereas others have to cultivate it. One way or the other, that ability to live with uncertainty is an essential ingredient of intercultural communication competence.

## Open-Mindedness

Being comfortable with ambiguity is important, but without an open-minded attitude a communicator will have trouble interacting competently with people from different backgrounds. To understand open-mindedness, it's helpful to consider three traits that are incompatible with it. **Ethnocentrism** is an attitude that one's own culture is superior to others. An ethnocentric person thinks—either privately or openly—that anyone who does not belong to his or her in-group is somehow strange, wrong, or even inferior. Travel writer Rick Steves describes how an ethnocentric point of view can interfere with respect for other cultural practices:

We [Americans] consider ourselves very clean and commonly criticize other cultures as dirty. In the bathtub we soak, clean, and rinse, all in the same water. (We would never wash our dishes that way.) A Japanese visitor, who uses clean water for each step, might find our way of bathing strange or even disgusting. Many cultures spit in public and blow their nose right onto the street. They couldn't imagine doing that into a small cloth, called a hanky, and storing that in their pocket to be used again and again.

Too often we think of the world in terms of a pyramid of "civilized" (us) on the top and "primitive" groups on the bottom. If we measured things differently (maybe according to stress, loneliness, heart attacks, hours spent in traffic jams, or family togetherness) things stack up differently.[93]

Ethnocentrism leads to an attitude of **prejudice**—an unfairly biased and intolerant attitude toward others who belong to an out-group. (Note that the root term

---

| Ethical Challenge | Most people acknowledge the importance of treating others from different cultural backgrounds with respect. But what communication obligations do you have when another person's cultural values are different from yours on fundamental matters, such as abortion or gender equity? |
| :--- | :--- |
| Civility When Values Clash | Either on your own or with a group, craft a set of guidelines that cover communication in cases like these. How should you behave when confronted with views you find shocking or abhorrent? |

in *prejudice* is "pre-judge.") An important element of prejudice is **stereotyping**—exaggerated generalizations about a group. Stereotypical prejudices include the obvious exaggerations that all women are emotional, all men are sex-crazed and insensitive goons, all older people are out of touch with reality, and all immigrants are welfare parasites.

## Knowledge and Skill

Attitude alone isn't enough to guarantee success in intercultural encounters. Communicators need to possess enough knowledge of other cultures to know what approaches are appropriate. The rules and customs that work with one group might be quite different from those that succeed with another. The ability to "shift gears" and adapt one's style to the norms of another culture or coculture is an essential ingredient of communication competence.[94]

How can a communicator acquire the culture-specific information that leads to competence? Scholarship suggests three strategies for moving toward a more mindful, competent style of intercultural communication.[95] *Passive observation* involves noticing what behaviors members of a different culture use and applying these insights to communicate in ways that are most effective. *Active strategies* include reading, watching films, and asking experts and members of the other culture how to behave, as well as taking academic courses related to intercultural communication and diversity.[96] The third strategy, *self-disclosure*, involves volunteering personal information to people from the other culture with whom you want to communicate. One type of self-disclosure is to confess your cultural ignorance: "This is very new to me. What's the right thing to do in this situation?" This approach is the riskiest of the three described here, because some cultures may not value candor and self-disclosure as much as others. Nevertheless, most people are pleased when strangers attempt to learn the practices of their culture, and they are usually more than willing to offer information and assistance.

## Patience and Perseverance

Becoming comfortable and competent in a new culture or coculture may be ultimately rewarding, but the process isn't easy. After a "honeymoon" phase, it's typical to feel confused, disenchanted, lonesome, and homesick.[97] To top it off, you may feel disappointed in yourself for not adapting as easily as you expected. This stage—which typically feels like a crisis—has acquired the labels *culture shock* or *adjustment shock*.[98]

You wouldn't be the first person to be blindsided by culture shock. Barbara Bruhwiler, who was born in Switzerland and has lived in South Africa for five years, says she loves her new home but still experiences moments of confusion and distress.[99] Likewise, when Lynn Chih-Ning Chang came to the United States from Taiwan for graduate school, she cried every day on the way home from class.[100] All her life, she had been taught that it was respectful and ladylike to sit quietly and listen, so she was shocked that American students spoke aloud without raising their hands, interrupted one another, addressed the teacher by first name, and ate food in the classroom. What's more, Chang's classmates answered so quickly that, by the time she was ready to say something, they were already on a new topic. The same behavior that made her "a smart and patient lady in Taiwan," she says, made her seem like a "slow learner" in the United States.

Communication theorist Young Yum Kim has studied cultural adaptation extensively. She says it's natural to feel a sense of push and pull between the familiar and the novel.[101] Kim encourages sojourners to regard stress as a good sign. It means they have the potential to adapt and grow. With patience, the sense of crisis begins to wane, and once again, there's energy and enthusiasm to learn more.

> cultural idiom
**out of touch:**
lacking understanding

> cultural idiom
**shift gears:**
change what one is doing

Communication can be a challenge while you're learning how to operate in new cultures, but it can also be a solution.[102] Chang, the Taiwanese student adapting to life in America, learned this firsthand. At first, she says, she was reluctant to approach American students, and they were reluctant to approach her. Gradually, she got up the courage to initiate conversations, and she found that her classmates were friendly and receptive. Eventually, she made friends, began to fit in, and successfully completed her degree.

The transition from culture shock to adaptation and growth is usually successful, but it isn't a smooth, linear process. Instead, people tend to take two steps forward and one step back, and to repeat that patterns many times. Kim[103] calls this a "draw back and leap" pattern. Above all, she says, if people are patient and they keep trying, the rewards are worth it.

For his part, our profiled student, Robin Luo, says he is learning a lot more than engineering during his time as an exchange student in the United States. "Americans are friendly, passionate, and inspiring," he says. "They teach me to hold an optimistic attitude against whatever I encounter in life."

## Summary

Communicating with people from different backgrounds is more common today than ever before. Some encounters involve people from different cultures, whereas others involve communicating with people from different cocultures within a given society. Although cultural characteristics are real and important, they are generalizations that don't apply equally to every member of a group. Furthermore, cultural differences aren't a salient factor in every intergroup encounter.

Many of the values and norms that shape intercultural communication aren't immediately apparent. Members of some cultures value autonomy and individual expression, whereas others are more collectivistic. Some pay close attention to subtle, contextual cues, whereas others pay more attention to the words people use. Cultures differ on other dimensions as well. They include uncertainty avoidance, power distance, and beliefs about talk and silence.

A variety of cocultures exist within our society. They are defined by factors including ethnicity, regional differences, religion, physical abilities/disabilities, age, and socioeconomic status. Each coculture has its own communication norms. Understanding and adapting to these can make intergroup communication more effective and satisfying.

There are several dimensions to becoming a more competent communicator in intercultural and cocultural encounters. They include increased exposure, tolerance for ambiguity, open-mindedness, knowledge of differences, skill in conforming to the other's communication style, and patience and perseverance.

## Key Terms

**coculture** The perception of membership in a group that is part of an encompassing culture. *p. 77*

**collectivistic culture** A culture in which members focus on the welfare of the group as a whole, rather than a concern by individuals for their own success. See also *Individualistic culture*. *p. 80*

**culture** The language, values, beliefs, traditions, and customs people share and learn. *p. 77*

**ethnicity** A social construct that refers to the degree to which a person identifies with a particular group, usually on the basis of nationality, culture, religion, or some other unifying perspective. *p. 86*

**ethnocentrism** The attitude that one's own culture is superior to others'. *p. 96*

**high-context culture** A culture that relies heavily on subtle, often nonverbal cues to maintain social harmony. *p. 81*

**in-groups** Groups with which we identify. See also *Out-groups*. *p. 79*

**individualistic culture** A culture in which members focus on the value and welfare of individual members, as opposed to a concern for the group as a whole. *p. 80*

**intergroup communication** The interaction between members of different cocultures. *p. 77*

**low-context culture** A culture that uses language primarily to express thoughts, feelings, and ideas as directly as possible. *p. 81*

**organizational culture** A relatively stable, shared set of rules about how to behave and a set of values about what is important. *p. 93*

**out-groups** Groups of people that we view as different from us. See also *In-groups*. *p. 79*

**power distance** The degree to which members of a group are willing to accept a difference in power and status. *p. 83*

**prejudice** An unfairly biased and intolerant attitude toward others who belong to an out-group. *p. 96*

**race** A social construct originally created to explain differences between people whose ancestors originated in different regions of the world—Africa, Asia, Europe, and so on. *p. 85*

**salience** How much weight we attach to a particular person or phenomenon. *p. 78*

**stereotyping** The perceptual process of applying exaggerated beliefs associated with a categorizing system. *p. 97*

**uncertainty avoidance** The cultural tendency to seek stability and honor tradition instead of welcoming risk, uncertainty, and change. *p. 83*

## Check Your Understanding

1. What cultures and cocultures do you encounter in your own life?

2. Describe situations when cultural and coculture factors have played a factor in the success of your communication with others from different backgrounds. Are there other situations when different backgrounds were *not* a salient factor in your communication?

3. Describe cases you have experienced or observed that illustrate the inaccuracy of stereotyping people from different cultures and/or cocultures.

4. Which of the cultural values and norms described on pages 79–85 play the biggest role in your experiences communicating with people from different cultural or coculture backgrounds?

5. Evaluate your competence in communicating in intercultural and coculture encounters. How could you communicate more effectively in these sorts of encounters?

## Activities

1. **About the Americans** Imagine you were commissioned to write a book or craft a video titled *About the Americans*, aimed at people from other parts of the world ready to visit the United States for the first time. What communication-related topics would you include? What advice would you give?

2. **Coculture Tree** Using the model format below, create a diagram resembling a family tree that shows your various cultural and coculture identities. Describe how your communication with others is shaped by various dimensions of your identity.

3. **Minimizing Cultural Problems** Describe two interesting cases when coculture differences in communication have led to problems. Based on your studies, explain how the problematic communication might have been prevented, minimized, or overcome.

## 🛜 For Further Exploration

**For more resources about the nature of communication, see the *Understanding Human Communication* website at www.oup.com/us/adler.** There you will find a variety of resources: "Media Room" clips from popular films and television shows to further illustrate important concepts, a list of books and articles, links to descriptions of feature films and television shows at the *Now Playing* website, study aids, and a self-test to check your understanding of the material in this chapter.

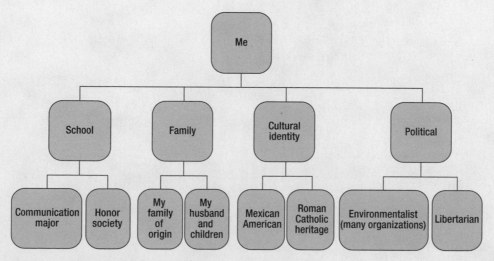

**Coculture Tree** (See activity 2)

**CHAPTER 4**

# Language

**4**

## Chapter Outline

## LEARNING OBJECTIVES

**1** Describe the symbolic, person-centered, rule-governed nature of language.

**2** Explain how language both shapes and reflects attitudes.

**3** Explain how the types of troublesome language described on pages 114–123 can create problems, and how better use of language could have prevented those problems.

**4** Explain how gender and nongender variables described on pages 124–126 affect communication.

**French is known as the language of love.** But for Meiga Loho-Noya, who spent most of her childhood in Paris, it's also the language of mathematics.

"It's funny to hear her," says her husband, Zac Hughes. "She'll be computing in French, then pop out with an answer to the problem in English." With a puzzled shrug, Loho-Noya explains, "I don't know why. I just think about math more easily in French."

Loho-Noya speaks French, English, and Spanish fluently. She was born in Venezuela to a Spanish mother and a French father. As a young girl she moved with her family to Paris, where she learned French. In the sixth grade Loho-Noya began learning English, both in school and by studying the lyrics to American pop songs. She was excited to master what she calls "the language of business" and travel the world.

Hughes's linguistic and cultural background couldn't be more different. He was born in the southern United States and has lived in the same town since he was 4 years old. He attended private schools that emphasized traditional social roles. Despite a couple of Spanish classes in high school, Hughes considers himself basically monolingual. "I remember almost nothing from school," Hughes says. "When traveling abroad, my wife spends probably half of her time translating for me. She is very patient."

Loho-Noya's travels have made her aware that language involves not only words, but how people use them. For example, she has noticed that people in Anglo and Latin cultures express emotions differently. In Latin cultures, people use more body language and less personal distance, whereas Anglos seem to rely more on words to express how they feel.

With such different backgrounds, you might think communication between Loho-Noya and Hughes would be difficult. However, they feel they communicate very well. For one thing, they have a lot in common. Both grew up in close-knit, extended families. Hughes's family maintains an Italian tradition of large meals and family gatherings, which are familiar to Loho-Noya as well. He enjoys traveling through Europe with her, and they have started a tradition called "Spanish Sundays" in which they try to communicate in that language all day. Loho-Noya teases that she may add "French Fridays" to the mix. Hughes can now speak a bit of Spanish, and he hopes to be fluent by the time they have children. Just as importantly, they get along well because they enjoy learning from their differences. "Being with someone so different from yourself—it's like you add another dimension to your life," Hughes says.

*Loho-Noya and Hughes's relationship illustrates many challenges and rewards of using language. Consider situations in which language either hindered you or helped you establish a satisfying connection with someone.*

- When learning to use a new language, what challenges beyond grammar and vocabulary have you encountered?

- When listening to someone who is learning your first language, what cues did you notice that distinguished that person from a native speaker?

- Think about a misunderstanding involving you and another person fluent in your language. What was the source of the problem?

- If you were orienting a nonnative speaker to using your first language in everyday conversation, what rules would you point out that aren't in a dictionary or grammar book?

- If you're proficient in using more than one language, what differences do you notice between the ones you speak? Are some languages better than others for expressing certain messages?

We will describe Hughes and Loho-Noya's experiences in the following pages as we explore the nature of linguistic communication. By the time you have finished reading this chapter, you will better appreciate the complexity of language, its power to shape our perceptions of people and events, and its potential for incomplete and inaccurate communication. Perhaps more important, you will be better equipped to use the tool of language more skillfully to improve your everyday interaction.

# The Nature of Language

Humans speak about 10,000 dialects.[1] Although most of these sound different from one another, all possess the same characteristics of **language**: a collection of symbols governed by rules and used to convey messages between individuals. A closer look at this definition can explain how language operates and suggest how we can use it more effectively.

## Language Is Symbolic

There's nothing natural about calling your loyal, four-footed companion a "dog" or the object you're reading right now a "book." These words, like virtually all language, are **symbols**—arbitrary constructions that represent a communicator's thoughts. Not all linguistic symbols are spoken or written words. Sign language, as "spoken" by most deaf people, is symbolic in nature and not the pantomime it might seem to nonsigners. There are literally hundreds of different sign languages spoken around the world that represent the same ideas differently.[2] These distinct languages include American Sign Language, British Sign Language, French Sign Language, Danish Sign Language, Chinese Sign Language—even Australian Aboriginal and Mayan sign languages.

Symbols are more than just labels: They are the way we experience the world. You can prove this by trying a simple experiment.[3] Work up some saliva in your mouth, and then spit it into a glass. Take a good look, and then drink it up. Most people find this process mildly disgusting. But ask yourself why this is so. After all, we swallow our own saliva all the time. The answer arises out of the symbolic labels we use. After the saliva is in the glass, we call it *spit* and think of it in a different way. In other words, our reaction is to the name, not the thing.

The naming process operates in virtually every situation. How you react to a stranger will depend on the symbols you use to categorize him or her: gay (or straight), religious (or not), attractive (or unattractive), and so on.

## Meanings Are in People, Not Words

Ask a dozen people what the same symbol means, and you are likely to get 12 different answers. Does an American flag bring up associations of patriots giving their lives for their country? Fourth of July parades? Cultural imperialism? How about a cross: What does it represent? The message of Jesus Christ? Firelit rallies of Ku Klux Klansmen? Your childhood Sunday school? The necklace your sister always wears?

As with physical symbols, the place to look for meaning in language isn't in the words themselves but rather in the way people make sense of them. One unfortunate example of this fact occurred in Washington, DC, when the newly appointed city ombudsman used the word *niggardly* to describe an approach to budgeting.[4] Some African American critics accused him of uttering an unforgivable racial slur. His defenders pointed out that the word, which means "miserly," is derived from Scandinavian languages and that it has no link to the racial slur it resembles. Even though the criticisms eventually died away, they illustrate that, correct or not, the

On his satirical TV program, Steven Colbert indirectly mocks politically conservative pundits. A viewer who took Colbert's words literally would completely miss the point of his reporting. What role does irony play in your communication?

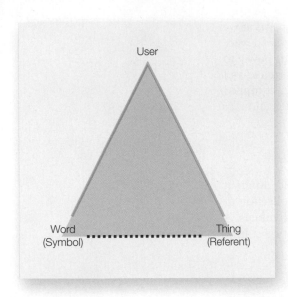

FIGURE 4-1 **Ogden and Richards's Triangle of Meaning**

meanings people associate with words have far more significance than do their dictionary definitions.

Linguistic theorists C. K. Ogden and I. A. Richards illustrated the fact that meanings are social constructions in their well-known "triangle of meaning" (Figure 4-1).[5] This model shows that there is only an indirect relationship—indicated by a broken line—between a word and the thing it claims to represent. Some of these "things" or referents do not exist in the physical world. For instance, some referents are mythical (such as unicorns), some are no longer tangible (such as Elvis, if he really is dead), and others are abstract ideas (such as "love").

Problems arise when people mistakenly assume that others use words in the same way they do. It's possible to have an argument about *feminism* without ever realizing that you and the other person are using the word to represent entirely different things. The same goes for *environmentalism, Republicans, rock music,* and thousands upon thousands of other symbols. Words don't mean; people do—and often in widely different ways. Loho-Noya, whom we introduced at the beginning of the chapter, says that some idioms still throw her, although she has been speaking English for years. "The other day Zac's sister said, 'My husband has been such a ham lately,' and I just stared at her," she says. "I had no idea what that meant."

Despite the potential for linguistic problems, the situation isn't hopeless. We do, after all, communicate with one another reasonably well most of the time. And with enough effort, we can clear up most of the misunderstandings that occur. The key to more accurate use of language is to avoid assuming that others interpret words the same way we do. In truth, successful communication occurs when we negotiate the meaning of a statement.[6] As one French proverb puts it: The spoken word belongs half to the one who speaks it and half to the one who hears.

## Language Is Rule Governed

Languages contain several types of rules. **Phonological rules** govern how words sound when pronounced. For instance, the words *champagne, double,* and *occasion* are spelled identically in French and English, but all are pronounced differently. Nonnative speakers learning English are plagued by inconsistent phonological rules, as a few examples illustrate:

He could lead if he would get the lead out.

A farm can produce produce.

The dump was so full it had to refuse refuse.

The present is a good time to present the present.

I did not object to the object.

The bandage was wound around the wound.

I shed a tear when I saw the tear in my clothes.

Phonological rules aren't the only ones that govern the way we use language to communicate. **Syntactic rules** govern the structure of language—the way symbols can be arranged. For example, correct English syntax requires that every word contain at least one vowel and prohibits sentences such as "Have you the cookies brought?" which is a perfectly acceptable word order in German. Although most of us aren't able to describe the syntactic rules that govern our language, it's easy to recognize their existence by noting how odd a statement that violates them appears.

Technology has spawned versions of English with their own syntactic rules.[7] For example, people have devised a streamlined version of English for instant messages, texts, and tweets that speeds up typing in real-time communication (although it probably makes teachers of composition grind their teeth in anguish):

**A:** Hey

**B:** r u @ home?

**A:** ys

**B:** k I'm getting offline now

**A:** y

**B:** cuz i need to study for finals u can call me tho bye

**A:** TTYL

**Semantic rules** deal with the meaning of specific words. Semantic rules are what make it possible for us to agree that "bikes" are for riding and "books" are for reading; they also help us to know whom we will and won't encounter when we open doors marked "men" or "women." Without semantic rules, communication would be impossible, because each of us would use symbols in unique ways, unintelligible to one another.

Semantic misunderstandings occur when words can be interpreted in more than one way, as the following humorous notices prove:

> The peacemaking meeting scheduled for today has been canceled due to a conflict.

> For those of you who have children and don't know it, we have a nursery downstairs.

> The ladies of the Church have cast off clothing of every kind. They may be seen in the basement on Friday afternoon.

> Sunday's sermon topic will be "What Is Hell?" Come early and listen to our choir practice.

**Pragmatic rules** govern how people use language in everyday interaction, which communication theorists have characterized as a series of *speech acts*.[8] Consider the example of a male boss saying, "You look very pretty today" to a female employee. It's easy to imagine how the subordinate might be offended by a comment that her boss considered an innocent remark. Scholars of language have pointed out several levels at which the rules each person uses can differ. You can understand these levels by imagining how they would operate in our example:

**EACH PERSON'S SELF-CONCEPT**

Boss: Views himself as a nice guy.

Subordinate: Determined to succeed on her own merits, and not her appearance.

**THE EPISODE IN WHICH THE COMMENT OCCURS**

Boss: Casual remark at the start of the workday.

Employee: A possible come-on?

The TV series *Switched at Birth* features many deaf or hearing-impaired characters. Though they cannot hear or speak, the characters communicate fluently using American Sign Language (ASL)—a language with its own syntactic, semantic, and pragmatic rules.

# What the *@#$!?

How do you react when someone unexpectedly uses profanity during normal conversation? Are you offended? Surprised? Intrigued? Like all verbal messages, swearwords speak volumes beyond their literal meaning.

A semantic analysis doesn't reveal much about the meaning of swearwords and phrases like "damn it" or "s—t." A closer look at when and how people curse reveals that the use and interpretation of profanity are governed by pragmatic rules. People who swear are more likely to do so in the company of others they know and trust, because doing so often indicates a level of comfort and acceptance of the other: "It's great to see you, you old S.O.B.!" Cursing can also define relational boundaries, showing who is a member of one's in-group. For example, some African Americans use the "n" word to describe close in-group members, whereas the same word would be unacceptable from an out-group member. Swearing can also be a way to enhance solidarity between people. For example, research suggests that the swearing patterns of bosses and coworkers can help people feel connected on the job. Looking at the pragmatic rules governing profanity helps explain why some people are offended by language that others consider benign.

*What pragmatic rules govern the use of swearwords in the language communities you belong to? Have you ever violated those rules? If so, what were the consequences? Could you adjust your use of language to better match the prevailing pragmatic rules?*

**PERCEIVED RELATIONSHIP**

Boss: Views employees like members of the family.

Employee: Depends on boss's goodwill for advancement.

**CULTURAL BACKGROUND**

Boss: Member of generation in which comments about appearance were common.

Employee: Member of generation sensitive to sexual harassment.

As this example shows, pragmatic rules don't involve semantic issues, because the words themselves are usually understood well by almost everybody. Instead, they involve how those words are understood and used. Hughes says he learned this lesson when he visited Europe with Loho-Noya. Finding words to communicate was fairly easy, but using them appropriately was a different matter. For example, while attempting to make conversation with a woman in Paris, he asked, "How long have you been here? What do you do?" The woman was taken aback. Loho-Noya explained that he had violated a pragmatic rule. French people consider that asking about someone's occupation is akin to asking about their income. "If you do that in Paris," Hughes realized, "it's like you're *way* into their business."

## The Power of Language

On the most obvious level, language allows us to satisfy basic functions such as describing ideas, making requests, and solving problems. But beyond these functions, the way we use language also influences others and reflects our attitudes in more subtle ways, which we will examine now.

### Language Shapes Attitudes

The power of language to shape ideas has been recognized throughout history. The first chapters of the Bible report that Adam's dominion over animals was demonstrated by his being given the power to give them names.[9] As we will now see, our speech—sometimes consciously and sometimes not—shapes others' values, attitudes, and beliefs in a variety of ways.

**Naming**    "What's in a name?" Juliet asked rhetorically. If Romeo had been a social scientist, he would have answered, "A great deal." Research has demonstrated that names are more than just a simple means of identification: They shape the way others think of us, the way we view ourselves, and the way we act.

At the most fundamental level, some research suggests that even the phonetic sound of a person's name affects the way we regard him or her, at least when we don't have other information available. One study revealed that reasonably accurate predictions about who will win an election can be made on the basis of some phonetic features of the candidates' surnames.[10] Names that were simple, easily pronounced, and rhythmic were judged more favorably than ones that lack these qualities. For example, in one series of local elections, the winning candidates had names that resonated with voters: Sanders beat Pekelis, Rielly defeated Dellwo, Grady outpolled Schumacher, Combs trounced Bernsdorf, and Golden prevailed over Nuffer. Names don't guarantee victory, but in 78 elections, 48 outcomes supported the value of having an appealing name.

Names are one way to shape and reinforce a child's personal identity. Naming a baby after a family member (e.g., "Junior" or "Trey") can create a connection between the youngster and his or her namesake. Name choice can also be a powerful way to make a statement about cultural identity. For example, in recent decades a large percentage of names given to African American babies have been distinctively black.[11] In California, more than 40 percent of black girls born in a single

---

## @Work

### What's in a Name?

When it comes to career success, names matter more than you might imagine.

Research suggests that many people pass judgment on prospective workers simply on the basis of their first name. In one study, prospective employers rated applicants with common first names more highly than those with unique or unusual ones.[14] This bias presents challenges for people with unique names, and for those from cultures with different naming practices.

Sometimes naming biases reflect stereotypes about gender. People predict career success based on how closely a person's name matches the gender associated with his or her job.[15] When college students were asked how people with various names were likely to do in their careers, they predicted that women with feminine names like Emma or Marta were more likely to be successful in traditionally female occupations like nursing. By contrast, they estimated that men with masculine names like Hank or Bruno would do better in traditionally male jobs like plumbing.

Findings like this are worth noting if you hope to succeed in a field in which your identity doesn't match traditional expectations. For example, if you are a woman thinking about the field of law, research suggests that your chances of success are greatest if your parents had the foresight to give you a traditionally male name. Researchers examined the relationship between the perceived masculinity of a person's name and his or her success in the field of law.[16] They found that a woman named "Cameron" is roughly three times more likely to become a judge than one named "Sue." A female "Bruce" is five times more likely.

Most people aren't willing to change their name to further career goals. But it is possible to choose variants on a name that have a professional advantage. For example, Marie Celeste Smith might consider identifying herself on job application documents as M. C. Smith, and Christina Jones might encourage people to use her nickname, Chris. Someone with a hard-to-pronounce name might choose a nickname for work purposes. For example, it's a custom in China for businesspeople and students of English to choose a Western name that complements the one they were born with: Guanghiui goes by Arthur and Junyuan is called Joanna. In a competitive job market, little differences can mean a great deal. ●

_Based on the research described here, do you think your name may affect your career? Have others' names ever shaped your perceptions?_

year had names that not a single white baby born in the entire state was given. Researchers suggest that distinctive names like these are a symbol of solidarity with the African American community. Conversely, choosing a less distinctive name can be a way of integrating the baby into the majority culture. Whether common or unusual, the impact of names recedes after communicators become more familiar with one another.[12]

Choosing a newborn's name can be especially challenging for people from nondominant cultures with different languages. One writer from India describes the problem he and his wife faced when considering names for their first child:

> How will the child's foreign name sound to American ears? (That test ruled out Shiva, my family deity; a Jewish friend put her foot down.) Will it provoke bullies to beat him up on the school playground? (That was the end of Karan, the name of a warrior from the Mahabharata, the Hindu epic. A boy called "Karen" wouldn't stand a chance.) Will it be as euphonic in New York as it is in New Delhi? (That was how Sameer failed to get off the ground. "Like a bagel with a schmear!" said one ruthless well-wisher.)[13]

First names aren't the only linguistic elements that may shape attitudes about men and women.

**Credibility**   Scholarly speaking is a good example of how speech style influences perception. We refer to what has been called the Dr. Fox hypothesis.[17] "An apparently legitimate speaker who utters an unintelligible message will be judged competent by an audience in the speaker's area of apparent expertise." The Dr. Fox hypothesis got its name from one Dr. Myron L. Fox, who delivered a talk followed by a half-hour discussion on "Mathematical Game Theory as Applied to Physical Education." The audience included psychiatrists, psychologists, social workers, and educators. Questionnaires collected after the session revealed that these educated listeners found the lecture clear and stimulating.

Despite his warm reception by this learned audience, Fox was a complete fraud. He was a professional actor whom researchers had coached to deliver a lecture of double-talk—a patchwork of information from a *Scientific American* article mixed with jokes, non sequiturs, contradictory statements, and meaningless references to unrelated topics. When wrapped in a linguistic package of high-level professional jargon, however, the meaningless gobbledygook was judged as important information. In other words, Fox's audience reaction was based more on the credibility that arose from his use of impressive-sounding language than on the ideas he expressed.

The same principle seems to hold for academic writing.[18] A group of 32 management professors rated material according to its complexity rather than its content. When a message about consumer behavior was loaded with unnecessary words and long, complex sentences, the professors rated it highly. When the same message was translated into more readable English, with shorter words and clearer sentences, the professors judged the same research as less competent.

**Status**   In the classic musical *My Fair Lady*, Professor Henry Higgins transformed Eliza Doolittle from a lowly flower girl into a high-society woman by replacing her cockney accent with an upper-crust speaking style. Decades of research have demonstrated that the power of speech to influence status is a fact.[19] Several factors combine to create positive or negative impressions: accent, choice of words, speech rate, and even the apparent age of a speaker. In most cases, speakers of standard dialect are rated higher than nonstandard speakers in a variety of ways: They are viewed as more competent and more self-confident, and the content of their messages is rated more favorably. The unwillingness or inability of a communicator to use the standard dialect fluently can have serious consequences. For instance, speakers of Black English, a distinctive dialect with its own accent, grammar, syntax, and semantic rules, are rated as less intelligent, professional, capable, socially acceptable, and employable by speakers of standard English.[20]

**Sexism and Racism**    By now it should be clear that the power of language to shape attitudes goes beyond individual cases and influences how we perceive entire groups of people. For example, Casey Miller and Kate Swift argue that incorrect use of the pronoun *he* to refer to both men and women can have damaging results.

> On the television screen, a teacher of first-graders who has just won a national award is describing her way of teaching. "You take each child where you find him," she says. "You watch to see what he's interested in, and then you build on his interests."
>
> A five-year-old looking at the program asks her mother, "Do only boys go to that school?"
>
> "No," her mother begins, "she's talking about girls too, but—" But what? The teacher being interviewed on television is speaking correct English. What can the mother tell her daughter about why a child, in any generalization, is always he rather than she? How does a five-year-old comprehend the generic personal pronoun?[21]

It's usually easy to use nonsexist language. For example, the term *mankind* may be replaced by *humanity, human beings, human race,* or *people; man-made* may be replaced by *artificial, manufactured,* and *synthetic; manpower* may be replaced by *human power, workers,* and *workforce;* and *manhood* may be replaced by *adulthood.*

The use of labels for racist purposes has a long and ugly past. Names have been used throughout history to stigmatize groups that other groups have disapproved of.[22] By using derogatory terms to label some people, the out-group is set apart and pictured in an unfavorable light. Diane Mader provides several examples of this:

> We can see the process of stigmatization in Nazi Germany when Jewish people became vermin, in the United States when African Americans became "niggers" and chattel, in the military when the Vietnam-era enemy became "gooks."[23]

The power of racist language to shape attitudes is difficult to avoid, even when it is obviously offensive. In one study, experimental subjects who heard a derogatory label used against a member of a minority group expressed annoyance at this sort of slur, but despite their disapproval, the negative emotional terms did have an impact.[24] Not only did the unwitting subjects rate the minority individual's competence lower when that person performed poorly, but also they found fault with others who associated socially with the minority person—even members of the subject's own ethnic group.

In *Django Unchained*, a freed slave rescues his wife from a cruel plantation owner. The characters—both black and white—make liberal use of the "n" word. Despite its being set in the antebellum South, where such language was common, many viewers feel the film's language goes too far. Are there ever times when it's appropriate and acceptable to use language that might offend others?

Ethical Challenge

## Sexist and Racist Language

One of the most treasured civil liberties is freedom of speech. At the same time, most people would agree that some forms of racist and sexist speech are hateful and demeaning to their targets. As you have read in these pages, language shapes the attitudes of those who hear it.

How do you reconcile the principle of free speech and the need to minimize hateful and discriminatory messages? Do you think laws and policies can and should be made that limit certain types of communication? If so, how should those limits be drafted to protect civil liberties? If not, can you justify the necessary protection of even sexist and racist language?

## Language Reflects Attitudes

Besides shaping the way we view ourselves and others, language reflects our attitudes. Feelings of control, attraction, commitment, responsibility—all these and more are reflected in the way we use language.

**Power**   Communication researchers have identified a number of language patterns that add to, or detract from, a speaker's ability to influence others, as well as reflecting how a speaker feels about his or her degree of control over a situation.[25] Table 4-1 summarizes some of these findings by listing several types of "powerless" language.

You can see the difference between powerful language and powerless language by comparing the following statements:

"Excuse me, sir, I hate to say this, but I . . . uh . . . I guess I won't be able to turn in the assignment on time. I had a personal emergency and . . . well . . . it was just impossible to finish it by today. I'll have it in your mailbox on Monday, okay?"

"I won't be able to turn in the assignment on time. I had a personal emergency, and it was impossible to finish it by today. I'll have it in your mailbox on Monday."

Even a single type of "powerless" speech mannerism, such as hedges, appears to make a person appear less authoritative or socially attractive.[26] By contrast,

## Table 4-1    Powerless Language

| TYPE OF USAGE | EXAMPLE |
|---|---|
| Hedges | "I'm kinda disappointed . . ."<br>"I think we should . . ."<br>"I guess I'd like to . . ." |
| Hesitations | "Uh, can I have a minute of your time?"<br>"Well, we could try this idea . . ."<br>"I wish you would—er—try to be on time." |
| Intensifiers | "So that's how I feel . . ."<br>"I'm not very hungry." |
| Polite forms | "Excuse me, sir . . ." |
| Tag questions | "It's about time we got started, isn't it?"<br>"Don't you think we should give it another try?" |
| Disclaimers | "I probably shouldn't say this, but . . ."<br>"I'm not really sure, but . . ." |

speakers whose talk is free of such mannerisms are typically rated as more competent, dynamic, and attractive.[27] In employment interviews, powerful speech results in more positive attributions of competence and employability than speech perceived to be powerless.[28]

It's important to realize that power isn't the only goal in most relationships. Even if the goal is to gain influence, research shows that a little less power can produce better results. In one study, women who used tentative speech were more successful at changing men's attitudes about social issues than women who communicated more assertively.[29] In the same study, women judged somewhat tentative men to be more trustworthy than more assertive men. In both cases, the less assertive speakers seemed friendlier and less coercive. This may reflect our tendency to believe and trust people who build supportive, friendly relationships with us.[30] Ultimately, because most power is shared with others, people who invest in relationships may not seem powerful in traditional or obvious ways, but they may have a great deal of influence in the long run. Our student-teacher example illustrates how this combination of powerless mannerisms and powerful mannerisms can help the student get what he wants while staying on good terms with the professor:

> "Excuse me, Professor Rodman. I want you to know that I won't be able to turn in the assignment on time. I had a personal emergency, and it was impossible to finish it by today. I'll definitely have it in your mailbox on Monday."

Whether or not the professor finds the excuse acceptable, it's clear that this last statement combines the best features of powerful speech and powerless speech: a combination of self-assurance and goodwill.

Simply counting the number of powerful or powerless statements won't always reveal who has the most control in a relationship. Social rules often mask the real distribution of power. Sociolinguist Deborah Tannen describes how politeness can be a face-saving way of delivering an order:

> I hear myself giving instructions to my assistants without actually issuing orders: "Maybe it would be a good idea to . . . ;" "It would be great if you could . . ." all the while knowing that I expect them to do what I've asked right away. . . . This rarely creates problems, though, because the people who work for me know that there is only one reason I mention tasks—because I want them done. I *like* giving instructions in this way; it appeals to my sense of what it means to be a good person . . . taking others' feelings into account.[31]

As this quote suggests, high-status speakers often realize that politeness is an effective way to get their needs met while protecting the face of the less powerful person. The importance of achieving both content goals and relational goals helps explain why a mixture of powerful speech and polite speech is usually most effective.[32] Of course, if the other person misinterprets politeness for weakness, it may be necessary to shift to a more powerful speaking style.

Powerful speech that gets the desired results in mainstream North American and European culture doesn't succeed everywhere with everyone.[33] In Japan, saving face for others is an important goal, so communicators there tend to speak in ambiguous terms and use hedge words and qualifiers. In most Japanese sentences the verb comes at the end of the sentence so the "action" part of the statement can be postponed. Traditional Mexican culture, with its strong emphasis on cooperation, makes a priority of using language to create harmony in interpersonal relationships, rather than taking a firm or oppositional stance, in order to make others feel more at ease. Korean culture represents yet another group of people that prefer "indirect" (for example, "perhaps," "could be") to "direct" speech.

> cultural idiom
> **saving face:**
> protecting one's dignity

## Language and Worldview

For almost 150 years, some theorists have put forth the notion of **linguistic relativism**: the notion that the worldview of a culture is shaped and reflected by the language its members speak.[34] (The best-known declaration of linguistic relativism is the *Sapir-Whorf hypothesis*.[35]) The most famous example of linguistic relativism is the notion that the Inuit of Alaska and Canada have a large number of words (estimated from 17 to 100) for what most of us simply call "snow." The need to survive in an Arctic environment led the Inuit to make distinctions that would be unimportant to residents of warmer environments, and after the language makes these distinctions, speakers are more likely to see the world in ways that match the broader vocabulary.

Even though there is some doubt that the Inuit really do have 100 words for snow,[36] other examples seem to support the principle of linguistic relativism.[37] For instance, bilingual speakers seem to think differently when they change languages. In one study, French Americans were asked to interpret a series of pictures. When they spoke in French, their descriptions were far more romantic and emotional than when they used English to describe the same kind of pictures. Likewise, when students in Hong Kong were asked to complete a values test, they expressed more traditional Chinese values when they answered in Cantonese than when they answered in English. In Israel, both Arab and Jewish students saw bigger distinctions between their group and "outsiders" when using their native language than when they used English, a neutral language. Examples like these show the power of language to shape cultural identity—sometimes for better and sometimes for worse.

The power of linguist relativism has been debated by social scientists for decades.[38] Although the academic jury may still be out, many multilingual speakers vouch for the power of language to shape thoughts. ●

*"You'll have to phrase it another way. They have no word for 'fetch.'"*

*Source:* Drew Dernavich / The New Yorker Collection / www.cartoonbank.com

**Affiliation**    Power isn't the only way language reflects the status of relationships. Language can also be a way of building and demonstrating solidarity with others. An impressive body of research has demonstrated that communicators who want to show affiliation with one another adapt their speech in a variety of ways, including their choice of vocabulary, rate of talking, number and placement of pauses, and level of politeness.[39] On an individual level, close friends and lovers often develop special terms that serve as a way of signifying their relationship.[40] Using the same vocabulary sets these people apart from others, reminding themselves and the rest of the world of their relationship. The same process works among members of larger groups, ranging from street gangs to military personnel. Communication researchers call this linguistic accommodation **convergence**.

Communicators can experience convergence online as well as in face-to-face interactions. Members of online communities often develop a shared language and conversational style, and their affiliation with one another can be seen in increased uses of the pronoun "we."[41] On a larger scale, IM and e-mail users create and use shortcuts that mark them as Internet-savvy. If you know what ROTF,

IMHO, and JK mean, you're probably part of that group. (For the un-initiated, those acronyms mean "rolling on the floor laughing," "in my humble opinion," and "just kidding.") Interestingly, instant-messagers may find that their cyber language creeps into everyday conversations.[42] (Have you ever said "LOL" instead of the words "laughing out loud"—or instead of actually laughing out loud?)

When two or more people feel equally positive about one another, their linguistic convergence will be mutual. But when communicators want or need the approval of others, they often adapt their speech to suit the others' style, trying to say the "right thing" or speak in a way that will help them fit in. We see this process when immigrants who want to gain the rewards of material success in a new culture strive to master the prevalent language. Likewise, employees who seek advancement tend to speak more like their superiors: Supervisors adopt the speech style of managers, and managers converge toward their bosses.

The principle of speech accommodation works in reverse, too. Communicators who want to set themselves apart from others adopt the strategy of **divergence**, speaking in a way that emphasizes their difference from others. For example, members of an ethnic group, even though fluent in the dominant language, might use their own dialect as a way of showing solidarity with one another—a sort of "us against them" strategy. Divergence also operates in other settings. A physician or attorney, for example, who wants to establish credibility with his or her client might speak formally and use professional jargon to create a sense of distance. The implicit message here is "I'm different (and more knowledgeable) than you."

Convergence and divergence aren't the only ways to express affiliation. **Linguistic intergroup bias** reflects whether or not we regard others as part of our in-group. Researchers have discovered a tendency to describe the *positive* behaviors of others with whom we identify as personality traits.[43] A positive bias leads us to describe in-group members in favorable terms and out-group members negatively. For example, if an in-group member gives money to a homeless person, we are likely to describe her behavior as a positive personality trait: "Sue is a generous person." If an out-group member (someone with whom we don't identify) gives the same homeless person some money, we are likely to describe her behavior as a discrete behavior: "Sue gave away money." The same in-group preferences are revealed when we describe undesirable behaviors. If an in-group member behaves poorly, we are likely to describe the behavior using a concrete descriptive action verb, such as "John cheated in the game." In contrast, if the person we are describing is an out-group member, we are more likely to use general disposition adjectives such as "John is a cheater." These selective language choices are so subtle and subconscious that when asked, people being studied report that there were no differences in the way they described in-group versus out-group members' behavior. We tend to believe we are less biased than we are, but our language reveals the truth about our preferences.

**Attraction and Interest**   Social customs discourage us from expressing like or dislike in many situations. Only a careless person would respond to the question "What do you think of the cake I baked for you?" by saying, "It's terrible." Bashful or cautious suitors might not admit their attraction to a potential partner. Even when people are reluctant to speak candidly, the language they use can suggest their degree of interest and

> Recall a time when you adapted your language to accommodate to the norms of a speech community in which you wanted to become more engaged. How much did you change your former style of speech and/or writing? How successful was your attempt at linguistic convergence?

On the television show *Homeland*, CIA agent Carrie Mathison (Claire Danes) uses powerful language with suspected terrorist Nicholas Brody (Damian Lewis). Sometimes she tries to intimidate and frighten him, while at other times, she adapts her speech to gain his trust, solidarity, and attraction. How do you adapt your language as you manage your relationships?

attraction toward a person, object, or idea. Morton Weiner and Albert Mehrabian outline a number of linguistic clues that reveal these attitudes.[44]

- **Demonstrative pronoun choice.** *These* people want our help (positive) versus *Those* people want our help (less positive).

- **Negation.** It's *good* (positive) versus It's *not bad* (less positive).

- **Sequential placement.** Dick and Jane (Dick is more important) versus Jane and Dick (Jane is more important). However, sequential placement isn't always significant. You may put "toilet bowl cleaner" at the top of your shopping list simply because it's closer to the market door than is champagne.

**Responsibility**   In addition to suggesting liking and importance, language can reveal the speaker's willingness to accept responsibility for a message.

- **"It" versus "I" statements.** *It's* not finished (less responsible) versus *I* didn't finish it (more responsible).

- **"You" versus "I" statements.** Sometimes *you* make me angry (less responsible) versus Sometimes *I* get angry when you do that (more responsible). "I" statements are more likely to generate positive reactions from others as compared to accusatory ones.[45]

- **"But" statements.** It's a good idea, *but* it won't work. You're really terrific, *but* I think we ought to spend less time together. (*But* cancels everything that went before the word.)

- **Questions versus statements.** Do you think we ought to do that? (less responsible) versus I don't think we ought to do that (more responsible).

## Troublesome Language

Besides being a blessing that enables us to live together, language can be something of a curse. We have all known the frustration of being misunderstood, and most of us have been baffled by another person's overreaction to an innocent comment. In the following pages we will look at several kinds of troublesome language, with the goal of helping you communicate in a way that makes matters better instead of worse.

### The Language of Misunderstandings

The most obvious kind of language problems are semantic: We simply don't understand others completely or accurately. Most misunderstandings arise from some common problems that are easily remedied—after you recognize them.

**Equivocal Language**   **Equivocal words** have more than one correct dictionary definition. Some equivocal misunderstandings are simple, at least after they are exposed. A nurse once told her patient that he "wouldn't be needing" the materials he requested from home. He interpreted the statement to mean he was near death, when the nurse meant he would be going home soon. A colleague of ours mistakenly sent some confidential materials to the wrong person after his boss told him to "send them to Richard," without specifying which Richard. Some equivocal misunderstandings can be embarrassing, as one woman recalls:

No doubt this sign draws a laugh from many who see it. Can you think of other words that have multiple meanings?

In the fourth grade the teacher asked the class what a period was. I raised my hand and shared everything I had learned about girls getting their period. But he was talking about the dot at the end of a sentence. Oops![46]

> cultural idiom
**a period:**
occurrence of menstruation

Some equivocal statements arise from cultural or cocultural differences. While teaching in Ireland, an American friend of ours asked a male colleague if he would give her a ride to the pub. After a few chuckles, he said, "you mean a lift." Our friend was surprised to learn that the word "ride" has sexual connotations in Ireland.

Equivocal misunderstandings can have serious consequences. Equivocation at least partially explains why men may sometimes persist in attempts to become physically intimate when women have expressed unwillingness to do so.[47] Interviews and focus groups with college students revealed that women often use ambiguous phrases to say "no" to a man's sexual advances: "I'm confused about this." "I'm not sure that we're ready for this yet." "Are you sure you want to do this?" "Let's be friends" and even, "That tickles." (The researchers found that women were most likely to use less direct phrases when they hoped to see or date the man again. When they wanted to cut off the relationship, they were more likely to give a direct response.) Whereas women viewed indirect statements as equivalent to saying "no," men were more likely to interpret them as less clear-cut requests to stop. As the researchers put it, "male/female misunderstandings are not so much a matter of males hearing resistance messages as 'go,' but rather their not hearing them as 'stop.'" Under the law, "no" means precisely that, and anyone who argues otherwise can be in for serious legal problems.

**Relative Words**   **Relative words** gain their meaning by comparison. For example, is the school you attend large or small? This depends on what you compare it to: Alongside a campus like UCLA, with an enrollment of more than 30,000 students, it probably looks small, but compared to a smaller institution, it might seem quite large. In the same way, relative words like *fast* and *slow*, *smart* and *stupid*, *short* and *long* depend for their meaning on what they're compared to. (The "large" size can of olives is the smallest you can buy; the larger ones are "giant," "colossal," and "supercolossal.")

Some relative words are so common that we mistakenly assume that they have a clear meaning. For instance, if a new acquaintance says, "I'll call you soon," when can you expect to hear from him or her? In one study, graduate students were asked to assign numerical values to terms such as *doubtful, toss-up, likely, probable, good chance*, and *unlikely*.[48] There was a tremendous variation in the meaning of most of these terms. For example, the responses for *possible* ranged from 0 to 99 percent. *Good chance* meant between 35 and 90 percent, whereas *unlikely* fell between 0 and 40 percent.

Using relative words without explaining them can lead to communication problems. Have you ever responded to someone's question about the weather by saying it was warm, only to find out that what was warm to you was cold to the other person? Or have you followed a friend's advice and gone to a "cheap" restaurant, only to find that it was twice as expensive as you expected? Have you been disappointed to learn that classes you've heard were "easy" turned out to be hard, that journeys you were told would be "short" were long, that "unusual" ideas were really quite ordinary? The problem in each case came from failing to anchor the relative word used to a more precisely measurable word.

**Slang and Jargon**   **Slang** is language used by a group of people whose members belong to a similar coculture or other group. Some slang is related to specialized interests and activities. For instance, cyclists who talk about "bonking" are referring to running out of energy. Rapsters know that "bling" refers to jewelry and a "whip" is a nice-looking car.

Other slang consists of *regionalisms*—terms that are understood by people who live in one geographic area but that are incomprehensible to outsiders. This sort of use illustrates how slang defines insiders and outsiders, creating a sense of identity and solidarity.[49] Residents of the largest U.S. state know that when a fellow Alaskan says, "I'm going outside," he or she is leaving the state. In the East End of London, cockney dialect uses rhyming words as substitutes for everyday expressions: "bacon and eggs" for "legs," and "Barney Rubble" for "trouble." This sort of use also illustrates how slang can be used to identify insiders and outsiders: With enough shared rhyming, slang users could talk about outsiders without the clueless outsiders knowing that they were the subject of conversation ("Lovely set of bacons, eh?" "Stay away from him. He's Barney.").

Slang can also be age related. Most college students know that drinkers wearing "beer goggles" have consumed enough alcohol that they find almost everyone of the opposite—or sometimes the same—sex attractive. At some schools, a "monkey" is the "other" woman or man in a boyfriend's or girlfriend's life: "I've heard Mitch is cheating on me. When I find his monkey, I'm gonna do her up!"[50]

> With your classmates, compile a list of slang or jargon that's part of each person's culture, coculture, or job. What terms are widely understood? Which ones are more obscure? How do slang and jargon create feelings of belonging and exclusion?

Almost everyone uses some sort of **jargon**: the specialized vocabulary that functions as a kind of shorthand for people with common backgrounds and experience. Skateboarders have their own language to describe maneuvers: "ollie," "grind," and "shove it." Some jargon consists of *acronyms*—initials of terms that are combined to form a word. Stock traders refer to the NASDAQ (pronounced "naz-dak") securities index, and military people label failure to serve at one's post as being AWOL (absent without leave). The digital age has spawned its own vocabulary of jargon. For instance, computer users know that "viruses" are malicious programs that migrate from one computer to another, wreaking havoc. Likewise, "cookies" are tiny files that remote observers can use to monitor a user's computer habits. Some jargon goes beyond being descriptive and conveys attitudes. For example, cynics in the high-tech world sometimes refer to being fired from a job as being "uninstalled." They talk dismissively about the nonvirtual world as the "carbon community" and of books and newspapers as "treeware." Some technical support staffers talk of "banana problems," meaning those problems that could be figured out by monkeys, as in "This is a two-banana problem at worst."[51]

Jargon can be a valuable kind of shorthand for people who understand its use. The trauma team in a hospital emergency room can save time, and possibly lives, by speaking in shorthand, referring to "GSWs" (gunshot wounds), "chem 7" lab tests, and so on, but the same specialized vocabulary that works so well among insiders can mystify and confuse family members of the patient, who don't understand the jargon. The same sort of misunderstandings can arise in less critical settings when insiders use their own language with people who don't share the same vocabulary. Jeffrey Katzman of the William Morris Agency's Hollywood office experienced this sort of problem when he met with members of a Silicon Valley computer firm to discuss a joint project.

> cultural idiom

**techies:**
computer experts

When he used the phrase "in development," he meant a project that was as yet merely an idea. When the techies used it, on the other hand, they meant designing a specific game or program. Ultimately, says Katzman, he had to bring in a blackboard and literally define his terms. "It was like when the Japanese first came to Hollywood," he recalls. "They had to use interpreters, and we did too."[52]

### Understanding Communication Technology

## Twitter Lingo Incites Controversy

Actor Ralph Fiennes pushed a powerful button when he proclaimed that Twitter is dumbing down the English language.[53] He isn't the first to suggest such a notion. People have weighed in with millions of online posts, some condemning and others applauding the truncated language some call *Twenglish*.

On one side of the debate are people who argue that English reduced to abreves and acronyms loses its luster and intelligence. One professor, for example, bemoans the influx of college admission essays with sentences that lack verbs and are speckled with shorthand symbols such as *4* and *U*.[54]

Proponents of Twitterspeak argue that language is an art form that is meant to be used creatively. People invent and repurpose words because it's fun, because speaking the same language is a sign of group membership, and because we want to talk about phenomena that don't yet have names.[55] *Forbes* writer Alex Knapp says he was a nonbeliever until he became an avid tweeter. Now he admires the artistry and discipline of expressing ideas in only a couple dozen words or so. "The 140 character restraint not only forces efficiency, but it also lends itself to some really, really fun wordplay," he says.[56]

Because Twenglish changes so rapidly, using it skillfully is both interesting and challenging.[57] New terms arise to describe emerging technologies, and others disappear. By the time parents figured out that "totes jelly" means totally jealous, many Twitter users were onto something new. That means the parents of the baby reportedly named Hashtag[58] may soon regret their decision!

Would Shakespeare be aghast if he knew how drastically language has changed? Maybe not. The Bard was fond of wordplay himself. Words such as *advertising*, *gossip*, and *swagger* (among about 1,700 others) didn't exist until he invented them.[59]

Will formal English morph to be more Twitter-like? As one blogger puts it, we'll just have to W8 N C. ●

**Overly Abstract Language**   Most objects, events, and ideas can be described with varying degrees of specificity. Consider the material you are reading. You could call it:

A book

A textbook

A communication textbook

*Understanding Human Communication*

Chapter 4 of *Understanding Human Communication*

Page 117 of Chapter 4 of *Understanding Human Communication*

In each case your description would be more and more specific. Semanticist S. I. Hayakawa created an **abstraction ladder** to describe this process.[60] This ladder consists of a number of descriptions of the same thing. Lower items focus specifically on the person, object, or event, whereas higher terms are generalizations that include the subject as a member of a larger class. To talk about "college," for example, is more abstract than to talk about a particular school. Likewise, referring to "women" is more abstract than referring to "feminists," or more specifically naming feminist organizations or even specific members who belong to them.

Higher-level abstractions are a useful tool, because without them language would be too cumbersome to be useful. It's faster, easier, and more useful to talk about *Europe* than to list all of the countries on that continent. In the same way, using relatively abstract terms like *friendly* or *smart* can make it easier to describe people than listing their specific actions.

**Abstract language**—speech that refers to events or objects only vaguely—serves a second, less obvious function. At times it allows us to avoid confrontations by deliberately being unclear.[61] Suppose, for example, your boss is enthusiastic about a new approach to doing business that you think is a terrible idea. Telling the truth might seem too risky, but lying—saying, "I think it's a great idea"—wouldn't feel right either. In situations like this an abstract answer can hint at your true belief without a direct confrontation: "I don't know. . . . It's sure unusual. . . . It *might* work." The same sort of abstract language can help you avoid embarrassing friends who ask for your opinion with questions like, "What do you think of my new haircut?" An abstract response like, "It's really different!" may be easier for you to deliver—and for your friend to receive—than the clear, brutal truth: "It's really ugly!" We will have more to say about this linguistic strategy of equivocation later in this chapter.

Although vagueness does have its uses, highly abstract language can cause several types of problems. The first is *stereotyping*. Consider claims like, "All whites are bigots," "Men don't care about relationships," "The police are a bunch of pigs," or "Professors around here care more about their research than they do about students." Each of these claims ignores the very important fact that abstract descriptions are almost always too general, that they say more than we really mean.

Besides creating stereotypical attitudes, abstract language can lead to the problem of *confusing others*. Imagine the lack of understanding that results from imprecise language in situations like this:

**A:** We never do anything that's fun anymore.

**B:** What do you mean?

**A:** We used to do lots of unusual things, but now it's the same old stuff, over and over.

**B:** But last week we went on that camping trip, and tomorrow we're going to that party where we'll meet all sorts of new people. Those are new things.

**A:** That's not what I mean. I'm talking about really unusual stuff.

**B:** *(becoming confused and a little impatient)* Like what? Taking hard drugs or going over Niagara Falls in a barrel?

**A:** Don't be stupid. All I'm saying is that we're in a rut. We should be living more exciting lives.

**B:** Well, I don't know what you want.

The best way to avoid this sort of overly abstract language is to use **behavioral descriptions** instead. (See Table 4-2.) Behavioral descriptions move down the abstraction ladder to identify the specific, observable phenomenon being discussed. A thorough description should answer three questions:

1. **Who is involved?** Are you speaking for just yourself or for others as well? Are you talking about a group of people ("the neighbors," "women") or specific individuals ("the people next door with the barking dog," "Lola and Lizzie")?

2. **In what circumstances does the behavior occur?** Where does it occur: everywhere or in specific places (at parties, at work, in public)? When does it occur: when you're tired or when a certain subject comes up? The behavior you are describing probably doesn't occur all the time. In order to be understood, you need to pin down what circumstances set this situation apart from other ones.

**ON YOUR FEET**

*Understanding Misunderstandings*

Share a memorable incident when you misunderstood someone else or when others misunderstood you. What was the basis of the misunderstanding? What were the consequences? How could you have used the information in these pages to prevent future understandings like the one you've described?

> cultural idiom

**in a rut:**
having fixed and monotonous routines and habits

Table 4-2    **Abstract and Behavioral Descriptions**

| | ABSTRACT DESCRIPTION | BEHAVIORAL DESCRIPTION | | | |
|---|---|---|---|---|---|
| | | WHO IS INVOLVED | IN WHAT CIRCUMSTANCES | SPECIFIC BEHAVIORS | REMARKS |
| **PROBLEM** | I talk too much. | People I find intimidating | When I want them to like me | I talk (mostly about myself) instead of giving them a chance to speak or asking about their lives. | Behavioral description more clearly identifies behaviors to change. |
| **GOAL** | I want to be more constructive. | My roommate | When we talk about household duties | Instead of finding fault with her ideas, suggest alternatives that might work. | Behavioral description clearly outlines how to act; abstract description doesn't. |
| **APPRECIATION** | "You've really been helpful lately." | (Deliver to fellow workers) | When I've had to take time off work because of personal problems | "You took my shifts without complaining." | Give both abstract and behavioral descriptions for best results. |
| **REQUEST** | "Clean up your act!" | (Deliver to target person) | When we're around my family | "Please don't tell jokes that involve sex." | Behavioral description specifies desired behavior. |

(3) **What behaviors are involved?** Though terms such as *more cooperative* and *helpful* might sound like concrete descriptions of behavior, they are usually too vague to do a clear job of explaining what's on your mind. Behaviors must be *observable*, ideally both to you and to others. For instance, moving down the abstraction ladder from the relatively vague term *helpful*, you might come to behaviors such as *does the dishes every other day*, *volunteers to help me with my studies*, or *fixes dinner once or twice a week without being asked*. It's easy to see that terms like these are easier for both you and others to understand than are more vague abstractions.

Behavioral descriptions can improve communication in a wide range of situations, as Table 4-2 illustrates. Research also supports the value of specific language. One study found that well-adjusted couples had just as many conflicts as poorly adjusted couples, but the way the well-adjusted couples handled their problems was significantly different. Instead of blaming one another, the well-adjusted couples expressed their complaints in behavioral terms.[62] For instance, instead of saying, "You're a slob," an enlightened partner might say, "I wish you wouldn't leave your dishes in the sink."

## Disruptive Language

Not all linguistic problems come from misunderstandings. Sometimes people understand one another perfectly and still end up in conflict. Of course, not all disagreements can, or should, be avoided. But eliminating three bad

The women on the *Real Housewives* series often use disruptive language with one another, which leads to disagreements and confrontations. How could the women on these shows change their language to communicate better with one another? Would viewers still want to watch the shows without such displays of disruptive communication?

linguistic habits from your communication repertoire can minimize the kind of clashes that don't need to happen, allowing you to save your energy for the unavoidable and important struggles.

**Confusing Facts and Opinions**   **Factual statements** are claims that can be verified as true or false. By contrast, **opinion statements** are based on the speaker's beliefs. Unlike matters of fact, they can never be proved or disproved. Consider a few examples of the difference between factual statements and opinion statements:

| FACT | OPINION |
|---|---|
| It rains more in Seattle than in Portland. | The climate in Portland is better than in Seattle. |
| Kareem Abdul Jabbar is the all-time leading scorer in the National Basketball Association. | Kareem is the greatest basketball player in the history of the game. |
| Per capita income in the United States is higher than in several other countries. | The United States is not the best model of economic success in the world. |

When factual statements and opinion statements are set side by side like this, the difference between them is clear. In everyday conversation, we often present our opinions as if they were facts, and in doing so we invite an unnecessary argument. For example:

"That was a dumb thing to say!"

"Spending that much on [ ] is a waste of money!"

"You can't get a fair shake in this country unless you're a white male."

Notice how much less antagonistic each statement would be if it were prefaced by a qualifier like "In my opinion . . ." or "It seems to me . . . ."

**Confusing Facts and Inferences**   Labeling your opinions can go a long way toward relational harmony, but developing this habit won't solve all linguistic problems. Difficulties also arise when we confuse factual statements with **inferential statements**—conclusions arrived at from an interpretation of evidence. Consider a few examples:

| FACT | INFERENCE |
|---|---|
| He hit a lamppost while driving down the street. | He was daydreaming when he hit the lamppost. |
| You interrupted me before I finished what I was saying. | You don't care about what I have to say. |
| You haven't paid your share of the rent on time for the past 3 months. | You're trying to weasel out of your responsibilities. |
| I haven't gotten a raise in almost a year. | The boss is exploiting me. |

There's nothing wrong with making inferences as long as you identify them as such: "She stomped out and slammed the door. It looked to me as if she were furious." The danger comes when we confuse inferences with facts and make them sound like the absolute truth.

One way to avoid fact-inference confusion is to use the perception-checking skill described in Chapter 2 to test the accuracy of your inferences. Recall that a perception check has three parts: a description of the behavior being discussed,

> cultural idiom
> **a fair shake:**
> honest treatment

> cultural idiom
> **to weasel out of:**
> to get out of doing something

your interpretation of that behavior, and a request for verification. For instance, instead of saying, "Why are you laughing at me?" you could say, "When you laugh like that *[description of behavior]*, I get the idea you think something I did was stupid *[interpretation]*. Are you laughing at me *[question]*?"

**Emotive Language** Emotive **language** contains words that sound as if they're describing something when they are really announcing the speaker's attitude toward something. Do you like that old picture frame? If so, you would probably call it "an antique," but if you think it's ugly, you would likely describe it as "a piece of junk." Emotive words may sound like statements of fact but are always opinions.

Barbra Streisand pointed out how some people use emotive language to stigmatize behavior in women that they admire in men:

> A man is commanding—a woman is demanding.
>
> A man is forceful—a woman is pushy.
>
> A man is uncompromising—a woman is a ball-breaker.
>
> A man is a perfectionist—a woman's a pain in the ass.
>
> He's assertive—she's aggressive.
>
> He strategizes—she manipulates.
>
> He shows leadership—she's controlling.
>
> He's committed—she's obsessed.
>
> He's persevering—she's relentless.
>
> He sticks to his guns—she's stubborn.
>
> If a man wants to get it right, he's looked up to and respected.
>
> If a woman wants to get it right, she's difficult and impossible.[63]

When feelings run strong, it's easy to use emotive language instead of more objective speech. Recall a time when you used emotive language. What were the consequences?

Problems occur when people use emotive words without labeling them as such. You might, for instance, have a long and bitter argument with a friend about whether a third person was "assertive" or "obnoxious," when a more accurate and peaceable way to handle the issue would be to acknowledge that one of you approves of the behavior and the other doesn't.

## Evasive Language

None of the troublesome language habits we have described so far is a deliberate strategy to mislead or antagonize others. Now, however, we'll consider euphemisms and equivocations, two types of language that speakers use by design to avoid communicating clearly. Although both of these have some very legitimate uses, they also can lead to frustration and confusion.

**Euphemisms** A **euphemism** (from the Greek word meaning "to use words of good omen") is a pleasant term substituted for a more direct but potentially less pleasant one. We are using euphemisms when we say "restroom" instead of "toilet" or "full-figured" instead of "overweight." There certainly are cases in which the euphemistic pulling of linguistic punches can be face saving. It's probably

*"Be honest with me Roger. By 'mid-course correction' you mean divorce, don't you."*

## Your Use of Language

Circle the number in each continuum that best represents you.

**1.** I often pause to think carefully about the words I use. ⟷ I like fast-paced conversations in which I don't have to weigh every word.

   1       2       3       4       5

**2.** I am precise and factual when I tell a story. ⟷ I tend to exaggerate to get a laugh or make a point.

   1       2       3       4       5

**3.** I am careful not to offend anyone when I speak. ⟷ I regularly use curse words and like to tell an off-color joke now and then.

   1       2       3       4       5

**4.** When I am upset, I delay talking until I calm down. ⟷ I am upfront about how I feel, even when I'm upset.

   1       2       3       4       5

**5.** I am careful to use gender-neutral language. ⟷ I see no harm in words such as "policeman" and "salesman."

   1       2       3       4       5

**6.** I pride myself on speaking proper English. ⟷ I enjoy using up-to-date slang and jargon.

   1       2       3       4       5

**7.** I'm careful to ask others what they mean rather than assuming I understand their ideas and motives. ⟷ I'm pretty good at understanding what's on others' minds without needing to ask for a lot of clarification.

   1       2       3       4       5

**8.** In sensitive situations I try to use diplomatic language. ⟷ I am honest, even when it's not what people want to hear.

   1       2       3       4       5

### INTERPRETING YOUR RESPONSES

If you circled mostly 1s, 2s, and 3s, you tend to be a mindful communicator who regards language as a powerful and precise tool. Low scores on items 1, 2, and 4 suggest that you typically avoid emotive language and exaggerations. Low scores on items 3 and 5 indicate that you are cautious about using language that might be considered offensive. A low score on item 7 shows that you recognize the potential for misunderstandings, even in apparently clear statements. A low score on item 8 suggests that you are tactful, but your language may seem euphemistic or equivocal at times.

If you circled mostly 3s, 4s, and 5s, you tend to use language in artistic and spontaneous ways, but you may sometimes go too far. High scores on items 1 and 8 suggest that you value open communication and a good debate, but keep in mind that your spontaneity may lead you to risky inferences. High scores on items 2 and 6 indicate you value colorful language and are probably an engaging storyteller, but you may confuse people who aren't familiar with your style or vocabulary. If you scored high on item 4, you probably confront issues head-on, but be careful that your language doesn't become overly emotive, which can escalate an argument. High scores on items 3 and 5 indicate that you don't take words too seriously, but bear in mind that others may. Your statements may cause offense. ●

more constructive to question a possible "statistical misrepresentation" than to call someone a liar, for example. Likewise, it may be less disquieting to some to refer to people as "senior citizens" rather than as "old."

Like many businesses, the airline industry uses euphemisms to avoid upsetting already nervous flyers.[64] For example, rather than saying "turbulence," pilots and flight attendants use the less frightening term "bumpy air." Likewise, they refer to thunderstorms as "rain showers," and fog as "mist" or "haze." And savvy flight personnel never use the words "your final destination."

Despite their occasional advantages, many euphemisms are not worth the effort it takes to create them. Some are pretentious and confusing, such as a middle school's labeling of hallways as "behavior transition corridors." Other euphemisms are downright deceptive, such as the U.S. Senate's labeling of a $23,200 pay raise as a "pay equalization concept."

**Equivocation**    It's 8:15 p.m., and you are already a half-hour late for your dinner reservation at the fanciest restaurant in town. Your partner has finally finished dressing and confronts you with the question, "How do I look?" To tell the truth, you hate your partner's outfit. You don't want to lie, but on the other hand you don't want to be hurtful. Just as important, you don't want to lose your table by waiting around for your date to choose something else to wear. You think for a moment and then reply, "You look amazing. I've never seen an outfit like that before. Where did you get it?"

Your response in this situation was an **equivocation**—a deliberately vague statement that can be interpreted in more than one way. Earlier in this chapter we talked about how *unintentional* equivocation can lead to misunderstandings. But our discussion here focuses on *intentionally ambiguous speech* that is used to avoid lying on one hand and telling a painful truth on the other. Equivocations have several advantages.[65] They spare the receiver from the embarrassment that might come from a completely truthful answer, and it can be easier for the sender to equivocate than to suffer the discomfort of being honest.

As with euphemisms, high-level abstractions, and many other types of communication, it's impossible to say that equivocation is always helpful or harmful. As you learned in Chapter 1, competent communication behavior is situational. Your success in relating to others will depend on your ability to analyze yourself, the other person, and the situation when deciding whether to be equivocal or direct.

> cultural idiom
> **beating around the bush:**
> approaching something in an indirect way

---

Ethical Challenge

## Euphemisms and Equivocations

For most people, "telling it like it is" is usually considered a virtue and "beating around the bush" is a minor sin. You can test the function of indirect speech by following these directions:

1. Identify five examples of euphemisms and equivocations in everyday interaction.

2. Imagine how matters would have been different if the speakers or writers had used direct language in each situation.

3. Based on your observations, discuss whether equivocation and euphemisms have any place in face-to-face communication.

---

# Gender and Language

So far we have mostly discussed language use as if it were identical for men and women. Some theorists and researchers, though, have argued that there are significant differences between the way men and women speak, whereas others have argued that any differences are not significant.[66] As we explore the results of research on gender differences in communication, keep in mind that findings describe general characteristics for men and women. As an individual, your behavior may not match the findings in every respect.

## Language Similarities and Differences by Gender

Before reading further, make two lists: one consisting of the similarities between how men and women communicate, and one noting the differences. Now see how well your observations match the wealth of research on the subject.

**Content**    The first research on the influence of gender on conversational topics was conducted more than 70 years ago. Despite the changes in male and female roles since then, some gender-linked patterns remain remarkably similar.[67] For example, both men and women still talk frequently about work, movies, and television. The differences between men and women are more striking than the similarities, however. Female friends spend more time discussing relational issues such as family, friends, and emotions. Men, on the other hand, are more likely to discuss recreational topics such as sports, technology use, and nightlife.

These differences can lead to frustration when men and women try to converse with one another. Researchers report that *trivial* is the word often used by both sexes to describe topics discussed by the opposite sex.

**Reasons for Communicating**    Research shows that the notion that men and women communicate in dramatically different ways is exaggerated. Both men and women, at least in the dominant cultures of the United States and Canada, use language to build and maintain social relationships.[68] How men and women accomplish these goals is often different, though. Although most communicators try to make their interaction enjoyable, men are more likely than women to emphasize making conversation fun. Their discussions involve a greater amount of joking and good-natured teasing. By contrast, women's conversations focus more frequently on feelings, relationships, and personal problems. In fact, communication researcher Julia Wood flatly states that "for women, talk is the essence of relationships."[69] When a group of women was surveyed to find out what kinds of satisfaction they gained from talking with their friends, the most common theme mentioned was a feeling of empathy— "to know you're not alone," as some put it.[70] Whereas men commonly described same-sex conversations as something they liked, women characterized their woman-to-woman talks as a kind of contact they needed. The greater frequency of female conversations reflects their importance. Nearly 50 percent of the women surveyed said they called friends at least once a week just to talk, whereas less than half as many men did so. In fact, 40 percent of the men surveyed reported that they never called another man just to talk.

Because women use conversation to pursue social needs, female speech typically contains statements showing support for the other person, demonstrations of equality, and efforts to keep the conversation going. With these goals, it's not surprising that traditionally female speech often contains statements of sympathy and empathy: "I've felt just like that myself," "The same thing happened to me!" Women are also inclined to ask lots of questions that invite the other person to share information: "How did you feel about that?" "What did you do next?" The importance of nurturing a relationship also explains why female speech is often somewhat powerless and tentative. Saying, "This is just my opinion . . ." is less likely to put off a conversational partner than a more definite "Here's what I think . . . ."

Men's speech is often driven by quite different goals than women's. Men are more likely to use language to accomplish the job at hand than to nourish relationships. This explains why men are less likely than women to disclose their vulnerabilities, which might be considered a sign of weakness. When someone else is sharing a problem, instead of empathizing, men are prone to offer advice:

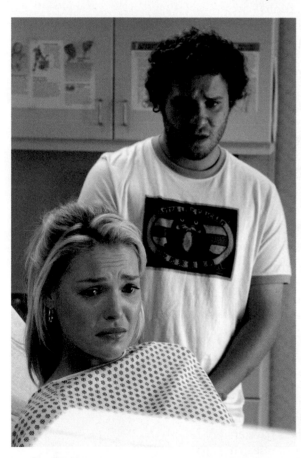

In *Knocked Up*, Alison (Katherine Heigl) and Ben (Seth Rogen) attempt to start a relationship after a one-night stand leads to an unintended pregnancy. As they get to know each other, they demonstrate different communication styles that have been influenced by gender. Do you find that there are many language differences in your relationships with members of the other sex? If so, how do you compromise and bridge these differences?

"That's nothing to worry about . . ." or "Here's what you need to do . . . ." Besides taking care of business, men are more likely than women to use conversations to exert control, preserve their independence, and enhance their status. This explains why men are more prone to dominate conversations and one-up their partners. Men interrupt their conversational partners to assert their own experiences or point of view. (Women interrupt too, but they usually do so to offer support: quite a different goal.) Just because male talk is competitive doesn't mean it's not enjoyable. Men often regard talk as a kind of game: When researchers asked men what they liked best about their all-male talk, the most frequent answer was its ease.[71] Another common theme was appreciation of the practical value of conversation: new ways to solve problems. Men also mentioned enjoying the humor and rapid pace that characterized their all-male conversations.

**Conversational Style**    Some scholarship shows little difference between the ways men and women converse. For example, the popular myth that women are more talkative than men may not be accurate. Researchers found that men and women speak roughly the same number of words per day.[72]

How closely does your speech match the stereotypically male or female styles described in these pages?

On the other hand, there are ways in which women do behave differently in conversations than do men.[73] For example, women ask more questions in mixed-sex conversations than do men—nearly three times as many, according to one study. Other research has revealed that in mixed-sex conversations, men interrupt women far more than the other way around. Some theorists have argued that differences like these result in women's speech that is less powerful and more emotional than men's. Research has supported these theories—at least in some cases. Even when clues about the speakers' sex were edited out, raters found clear differences between transcripts of male speech and female speech. In one study women's talk was judged more aesthetic, whereas men's talk was seen as more dynamic, aggressive, and strong. In another, male job applicants were rated more fluent, active, confident, and effective than female applicants.

Some gender differences also exist in mediated communication. For example, instant messages written by women tend to be more expressive than ones composed by men.[74] They are more likely to contain laughter ("hehe") emoticons (smiley faces), emphasis (italics, boldface, repeated letters), and adjectives. However, there are no significant gender differences in a number of other variables—such as questions, words per turn, and hedges.

Given these differences, it's easy to wonder how men and women manage to communicate with one another at all. One reason why cross-sex conversations do run smoothly is because women accommodate to the topics men raise. Both men and women regard topics introduced by women as tentative, whereas topics that men introduce are more likely to be pursued. Thus, women seem to grease the wheels of conversation by doing more work than men in maintaining conversations. A complementary difference between men and women also promotes cross-sex conversations: Men are more likely to talk about themselves with women than with other men, and because women are willing to adapt to this topic, conversations are likely to run smoothly, if one-sidedly.

An accommodating style isn't always a disadvantage for women. One study revealed that women who spoke tentatively were actually more influential with men than those who used more powerful speech.[75] On the other hand, this tentative style was less effective in persuading women. (Language use had no effect on men's persuasiveness.) This research suggests that women who are willing and able to be flexible in their approach can persuade both other women and men—as long as they are not dealing with a mixed-sex audience.

> cultural idiom
> **to grease the wheels:**
> to facilitate

**Nongender Variables** Despite the differences in the ways men and women speak, the link between gender and language use isn't as clear-cut as it might seem. Research reviews have found that the ways women and men communicate are much more similar than different. For example, one analysis of more than 1,200 research studies found that only 1 percent of variance in communication behavior resulted from sex difference.[76] There is no significant difference between male speech and female speech in areas such as use of profanity, use of qualifiers such as "I guess" or "This is just my opinion," tag questions, and vocal fluency.[77] Some on-the-job research shows that male and female supervisors in similar positions behave the same way and are equally effective. In light of the considerable similarities between the sexes and the relatively minor differences, some communication scholars suggest that the "men are from Mars, women are from Venus" claim should be replaced by the metaphor that "men are from North Dakota, women are from South Dakota."[78]

A growing body of research explains some of the apparent contradictions between the similarities and differences between male speech and female speech. They have revealed other factors that influence language use as much as or more than does gender. For example, social philosophy plays a role. Feminist wives talk longer than their partners, whereas nonfeminist wives speak less than their husbands. Orientation toward problem solving also plays a role in conversational style. The cooperative or competitive orientations of speakers have more influence on how they interact than does their gender.

The speaker's occupation and social role also influence speaking style. For example, male day-care teachers' speech to their students resembles the language of female teachers more closely than it resembles the language of fathers at home. Overall, doctors interrupt their patients more often than the reverse, although male patients do interrupt female physicians more often than their male counterparts. At work, task differences exert more powerful effects on whether speakers use gender-inclusive language (such as "he or she" instead of just "he") than does biological sex.[79] A close study of trial transcripts showed that the speaker's experience on the witness stand and occupation had more to do with language use than did gender. If women generally use "powerless" language, this may possibly reflect their historical social role in society at large. As the balance of power grows more equal between men and women, we can expect many linguistic differences to shrink.

Another powerful force that influences the way individual men and women speak is their **sex role**—the social orientation that governs behavior—rather than their biological gender. Researchers have identified three sex roles: masculine, feminine, and androgynous. These sex roles don't always line up neatly with gender. There are "masculine" females, "feminine" males, and androgynous communicators who combine traditionally masculine and feminine characteristics.

Research shows that linguistic differences are often a function of these sex roles more than the speaker's biological sex. Masculine sex-role communicators—whether male or female—use more dominant language than either feminine or androgynous speakers. Feminine speakers have the most submissive speaking style, whereas androgynous speakers fall between these extremes. When two masculine communicators are in a conversation, they often engage in a one-up battle for dominance, responding to the other's bid for control with a counter attempt to dominate the relationship. Feminine sex-role speakers are less predictable. They use dominance, submission, and equivalent behavior in an almost random fashion. Androgynous individuals are more predictable: They most frequently meet another's bid for dominance with a symmetrical attempt at control but then move quickly toward an equivalent relationship.

> cultural idiom

**one-up:**
to respond in order to maintain one's superiority

## Understanding Gender Differences in Language Use

By now you've gained an appreciation for the complicated relationship between gender and language use. Now, let's look at what's behind those patterns.

**Biological Factors**    Although gender is socially constructed, it is related to sex, which is biological. Our behavior is driven partly by sex hormones—primarily estrogen and testosterone. Both women's and men's bodies make the same hormones, but the amounts they produce differ. And within each sex, hormone production varies. For this reason it's more accurate to talk about the link between hormone level and behavior than to make gross generalizations based on biological sex.[80] For example, men with high testosterone levels are more competitive than those with lower levels of the hormone, and they respond more emotionally when faced with setbacks.[81] Research also suggests that men with higher levels of testosterone are less likely than others to engage in emotional, socially connecting language.[82] By contrast, estrogen is associated with heightened emotional experiences and expression of emotion.[83]

Despite these differences, it's overly simplistic to regard testosterone as an antisocial substance and estrogen as an emotional one. In some conditions, testosterone can motivate behaviors that are highly altruistic, especially in individuals holding socially protective positions, such as firefighters, police officers, and soldiers.[84] And despite the common belief that women are moody because of cyclic changes in estrogen, only 3 to 8 percent of women experience hormonal moods swings beyond the range of everyday emotions.[85] All in all, hormones are one factor, but not usually the most important factor, in how we interact with others.[86]

**Social Factors**    Along with biology, social norms shape the way men and women communicate. In contemporary society, power and material success have been widely regarded as measures of success and sources of prestige. In many, if not most, societies, males have been expected to serve as the providers in this regard. By contrast, women have historically had less overt power and occupied more nurturing roles.

Given these facts it's not surprising that men have been associated with the task-focused *instrumental* style of communication described in the previous pages, and that women have historically adopted *affective* styles of speech that promote smoothly functioning relationships.

Both instrumental and affective communication styles have obvious advantages. An instrumental focus is clear and decisive. Because it's associated with traditionally powerful roles, this approach to speaking is a way to gain and keep control. But along with these advantages, characteristically male speech has some downsides. It can be regarded as confrontational and off-putting. And although a no-nonsense approach might be efficient, it isn't ideally suited to keeping personal relationships running smoothly and happily. The flip side is also true: An affective style that works well in personal relationships can lead to a lack of recognition and respect in task-oriented environments. Even in personal relationships, being exclusively focused on nurturing can make it hard to stand up to intimidation.

## Transcending Gender Boundaries

By now it's probably clear that neither stereotypically male or female styles of speech meet all communication needs. You can improve your linguistic competence by switching and combining styles. If you reflexively take an instrumental approach that focuses on the content of others' remarks, consider paying more attention to the unstated relational messages behind their words. If you generally focus on the unexpressed-feelings part of a message, consider being more task oriented. If your first instinct is to be supportive, consider the value of offering advice; and if advice is your reflexive way of responding, think about whether offering support and understanding might sometimes be more helpful. Research confirms what common sense suggests: A "mixed-gender strategy" that balances the traditionally masculine, task-oriented approach with the characteristically feminine, relationship-oriented approach is rated most highly by both male and female respondents.[87] Choosing the approach that is right for the other communicator and the situation can create satisfaction far greater than that which comes from using a single stereotypical style.

This chapter began with the story of Loho-Noya and Hughes, who have bridged language differences to build a long-term relationship. They have experienced the challenges of coming from different linguistic traditions and have found their life is enriched by cultural and linguistic diversity. Even close to home, all of us face challenges of using language to understand and get along with others. Although language is an imperfect method of connecting, the tools in this chapter can help you bridge barriers in ways that can make communication more successful and satisfying.

Barney Stinson—played by Neil Patrick Harris in the show *How I Met Your Mother*—regularly brags about his exploits as a womanizer. Barney's behavior is recognizable as satire partly because, in real life, Harris is openly gay. What social roles shape your use of language?

## Summary

Language is both one of humanity's greatest assets and the source of many problems. This chapter highlighted the characteristics that distinguish language and suggested methods of using it more effectively.

Any language is a collection of symbols governed by a variety of rules and used to convey messages between people. Because of its symbolic nature, language is not a precise tool: Meanings rest in people, not in words themselves. In order for effective communication to occur, it is necessary to negotiate meanings for ambiguous statements.

Language not only describes people, ideas, processes, and events; it also shapes our perceptions of them in areas such as status, credibility, and attitudes about gender and ethnicity. Along with influencing our attitudes, language reflects them. The words we use and our manner of speech reflect power, responsibility, affiliation, attraction, and interest.

Many types of language have the potential to create misunderstandings. Other types of language can result in unnecessary conflicts. In other cases, speech and writing can be evasive, avoiding expression of unwelcome messages.

The relationship between gender and language is complex. Although there are differences in the ways men and women speak, not all differences in language use can be accounted for by the speaker's gender. Occupation, social philosophy, and orientation toward problem solving also influence the use of language, and psychological sex role can be more of an influence than biological sex.

## Key Terms

**abstract language** Language that lacks specificity or does not refer to observable behavior or other sensory data. See also *Behavioral description. p. 118*

**abstraction ladder** A range of more- to less-abstract terms describing an event or object. *p. 117*

**behavioral description** An account that refers only to observable phenomena. *p. 118*

**convergence** Accommodating one's speaking style to another person, who usually is desirable or has higher status. *p. 112*

**divergence** A linguistic strategy in which speakers emphasize differences between their communicative style and others' in order to create distance. *p. 113*

**emotive language** Language that conveys the sender's attitude rather than simply offering an objective description. *p. 121*

**equivocal words** Words that have more than one dictionary definition. *p. 114*

**equivocation** A vague statement that can be interpreted in more than one way. *p. 123*

**euphemism** A pleasant-sounding term used in place of a more direct but less pleasant one. *p. 121*

**factual statement** A statement that can be verified as being true or false. See also *Inferential statement; Opinion statement. p. 120*

**inferential statement** A conclusion arrived at from an interpretation of evidence. See also *Factual statement. p. 120*

**jargon** The specialized vocabulary that is used as a kind of shorthand by people with common backgrounds and experience. *p. 116*

**language** A collection of symbols, governed by rules and used to convey messages *between individuals. p. 103*

**linguistic intergroup bias** The tendency to label people and behaviors in terms that reflect their in-group or out-group status. *p. 113*

**linguistic relativism** A moderate form of linguistic determinism that argues that language exerts a strong influence on the perceptions of the people who speak it. *p. 112*

**opinion statement** A statement based on the speaker's beliefs. See also *Factual statement. p. 120*

**phonological rules** Linguistic rules governing how sounds are combined to form words. *p. 104*

**pragmatic rules** Rules that govern how people use language in everyday interaction. *p. 105*

**relative words** Words that gain their meaning by comparison. *p. 115*

**semantic rules** Rules that govern the meaning of language as opposed to its structure. See also *Syntactic rules. p. 105*

**sex role** The social orientation that governs behavior, in contrast to a person's biological gender. *p. 127*

**slang** Language used by a group of people whose members belong to a similar coculture or other group. *p. 115*

**symbols** Arbitrary constructions that represent a communicator's thoughts. *p. 103*

**syntactic rules** Rules that govern the ways in which symbols can be arranged as opposed to the meanings of those symbols. See also *Semantic rules. p. 104*

## Check Your Understanding

1. Analyze a specific incident that illustrates the symbolic, person-centered, rule-governed nature of language.

2. Recall incidents when (a) language shaped attitudes and (b) the choice of words reflected a communicator's attitudes.

3. Explain how the types of troublesome language described on pages 114–123 have caused problems in a situation you experienced or observed. How could better use of language have avoided those problems?

4. Describe how the gender and nongender variables described on pages 123–128 affect the communication in your life.

## Activities

1. **Powerful Speech and Polite Speech** Increase your ability to achieve an optimal balance between powerful speech and polite speech by rehearsing one of the following scenarios:

   1. Describing your qualifications to a potential employer for a job that interests you

   2. Requesting an extension on a deadline from one of your professors

   3. Explaining to a merchant why you want a cash refund on an unsatisfactory piece of merchandise when the store's policy is to issue credit vouchers

   4. Asking your boss for 3 days off so you can attend a friend's out-of-town wedding

   5. Approaching your neighbors whose dog barks while they are away from home

   Your statement should gain its power by avoiding the types of powerless language listed in Table 4-1 on page 110. You should not become abusive or threatening, and your statement should be completely honest.

6. **Slang and Jargon** Find a classmate, neighbor, coworker, or other person whose background differs significantly from yours. In an interview, ask this person to identify the slang and jargon terms that you take for granted but that he or she has found confusing. Explore the following types of potentially confusing terms:

   1. Regionalisms

   2. Age-related terms

   3. Technical jargon

   4. Acronyms

3. **Low-Level Abstractions** You can develop your ability to use low-level abstractions by following these steps:

   1. Use your own experience to write each of the following:

      a. A complaint or gripe

      b. One way you would like someone with whom you interact to change

      c. One reason why you appreciate a person with whom you interact

   2. Now translate each of the statements you have written into a low-level abstraction by including:

      a. The person or people involved

      b. The circumstances in which the behavior occurs

      c. The specific behaviors to which you are referring

   3. Compare the statements you have written in Steps 1 and 2. How might the lower-level abstractions in Step 2 improve the chances of having your message understood and accepted?

4. **Gender and Language**

   1. Note differences in the language use of three men and three women you know. Include yourself in the analysis. Your analysis will be most accurate if you record the speech of each person you analyze. Consider the following categories:

      a. Conversational content

      b. Conversational style

      c. Reasons for communicating

      d. Use of powerful/powerless speech

2. Based on your observations, answer the following questions:

   a. How much does gender influence speech?

   b. What role do other variables play? Consider occupational or social status, cultural background, social philosophy, competitive-cooperative orientation, and other factors in your analysis.

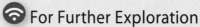 ## For Further Exploration

**For more resources about language, see the *Understanding Human Communication* website at www.oup.com/us/ adler.** There you will find a variety of resources: "Media Room" clips from popular films and television shows to further illustrate important concepts, a list of books and articles, links to descriptions of feature films and television shows at the *Now Playing* website, study aids, and a self-test to check your understanding of the material in this chapter.

**CHAPTER 5**

# Listening

## Chapter Outline

## LEARNING OBJECTIVES

1 Understand the most common misconceptions about listening, and assess how successfully you avoid them.

2 Appreciate and manage the challenges that make effective listening difficult.

3 Diagnose which faulty behaviors characterize your listening.

4 Understand the reasons for poor listening, and devise strategies for coping with them.

5 Know when and how to listen to accomplish a task, enhance relationships, analyze a message, and critically evaluate another's remarks.

6 Use the skills introduced on pages 155–161 to offer social support when presented with another person's problem.

**David Isay remembers** his grandmother as a small whirlwind. She raised her four younger sisters after their parents died when she was 13. She later earned a Ph.D. in psychology, worked for the United Nations, helped finance Broadway plays, and was the first advice columnist for the *New York Post*.[1] And she was wise. She once counseled readers of her column that "'honesty' without compassion and understanding is not honesty, but subtle hostility."[2]

Even as young man, Isay (pronounced eye-zay) was in awe of his grandmother's fearless spirit. Maybe that's why he grabbed a tape recorder after Thanksgiving dinner when he was 11 or 12 and asked to interview her as well as her sisters and his grandfather.[3]

"I was a lousy interviewer—butting in incessantly with goofy comments—but I captured their voices nonetheless,"[4] recalls Isay. After his grandparents and great aunts had died, Isay was dismayed when he realized that the audiotape had been lost. "I wanted to make sure no one ever made the idiotic mistake I did of losing the voice of a loved one," he says.[5]

Inspired by the idea that everyday people have a lot to say—and we have a lot to learn by listening—Isay launched a career producing radio documentaries. Then, in 2005, he went a step further by placing a recording booth in Grand Central Terminal and inviting people to share their stories. One copy of each recording went home with the storyteller and another joined a permanent collection in the Library of Congress.

The booth grew into StoryCorps, the most ambitious oral history project of all time. To date, more than 45,000 people across the United States have recorded stories.[6] Isay has won numerous awards and written several best-selling books, including *Listening Is an Act of Love*. StoryCorps interviews are broadcast on National Public Radio and are available online at npr.org.

Isay has noticed that people often cry when a loved one brings them into the booth to tell their stories. "To say, 'I care about you enough to sit here for 40 minutes and really listen to what you have to say,' is really a profound thing," he observes.[7] The booth provides an environment in which people can actively listen rather than worry about the time, take over the storyline themselves, or become distracted by the phone or television.

These days, Isay promotes the day after Thanksgiving as the National Day of Listening. He encourages others to use the holiday the way he did years ago, as an opportunity to focus on what loved ones have to say. Listening is "the least expensive but most meaningful gift you can give."[8]

*David Isay proposes that one of the most respectful things we do is give one another our undivided attention.*

- How would you rate yourself as a listener? How would others rate you?

- What makes it difficult for you to listen effectively?

- How well do significant others in your life listen to you?

David Isay has made thoughtful listening his life's work. But you don't have to be a professional listener to appreciate the importance of this vital but often overlooked communication skill. This chapter will help you become a better listener by giving you some important information about the subject. We'll talk about some common misconceptions concerning listening and show you what really happens when listening takes place. We'll discuss some poor listening habits, explain why they occur, and suggest better alternatives.

# The Importance of Listening

The need for good listening skills cannot be overemphasized. In his best-selling book, Stephen Covey identifies listening—making understanding others a top priority—as one of the "seven habits of highly effective people."[9] An impressive body of evidence backs up this claim. Leaders who are good listeners typically have more influence and stronger relationships with team members.[10] In fact, leaders' listening skills are even more influential than their talking skills.[11]

People with good listening skills are more likely than others to be hired and promoted.[12] One reason is that listening skills are a key to good service. Customers and clients prefer physicians,[13] salespeople,[14] and other service providers who listen well. This is because good listeners are judged to be both appealing and trustworthy.[15]

Listening is just as important in personal relationships. In a survey that asked respondents to rank the importance of various communication skills, listening topped the family/social list.[16] In committed relationships, listening to personal information in everyday conversations is considered an important ingredient of satisfaction[17] and relational stability.[18] And as the StoryCorps profile on page 134 shows, listening is fundamental to our humanity and sense of well-being. For this reason, some theorists have argued that effective listening is an essential ingredient in effective relational communication.[19]

Despite the importance of listening, experience shows that much of the listening we and others do is not very effective. We misunderstand others and are misunderstood in return. We become bored and feign attention while our minds wander. We engage in a battle of interruptions in which each person fights to speak without hearing the other's ideas. Some of this poor listening is inevitable, perhaps even justified. But in other cases we can be better receivers by learning a few basic listening skills.

# Misconceptions About Listening

In spite of its importance, listening is misunderstood by most people. Because these misunderstandings so greatly affect our communication, we need to take a look at four common misconceptions that many communicators hold.

## Listening and Hearing Are Not The Same Thing

**Hearing** is the process in which sound waves strike the eardrum and cause vibrations that are transmitted to the brain. **Listening** occurs when the brain reconstructs these electrochemical impulses into a representation of the original sound and then gives them meaning.

We begin hearing sounds around us even before we're born.[20] Barring illness, injury, or earplugs, hearing can't be stopped. As one neuroscientist put it, hearing . . . is easy. You and every other vertebrate that hasn't suffered some genetic, developmental or environmental accident have been doing it for hundreds of millions of years. It's your life line, your alarm system, your way to escape danger and pass on your genes.[21]

> cultural idiom
**tune out:**
not listen

Although hearing is automatic, listening is another matter. Many times we hear but do not listen. Sometimes we deliberately tune out unwanted signals: everything from a neighbor's power lawn mower or the roar of nearby traffic to a friend's boring remarks or a boss's unwanted criticism.

A closer look at listening—at least the successful variety—shows that it consists of several stages. After hearing, the next stage is **attending**—the act of paying attention to a signal. An individual's needs, wants, desires, and interests determine what is attended to, or selected, to use the term introduced in Chapter 2.

The next step in listening is **understanding**—the process of making sense of a message. Communication researchers use the term **listening fidelity** to describe the degree of congruence between what a listener understands and what the message sender was attempting to communicate.[22] Chapter 4 discussed many of the ingredients that combine to make understanding possible: a grasp of the syntax of the language being spoken, semantic decoding, and knowledge of the pragmatic rules that help you figure out a speaker's meaning from the context. In addition to these steps, understanding often depends on the ability to organize the information we hear into recognizable form. As early as 1948, Ralph Nichols related successful understanding to a large number of factors, most prominent among which were verbal ability, intelligence, and motivation.[23]

**Responding** to a message consists of giving observable feedback to the speaker. Offering feedback serves two important functions: It helps you clarify your understanding of a speaker's message, and it shows that you care about what that speaker is saying.

Listeners don't always respond visibly to a speaker—but research suggests that they should. In one study, children distinguished "good" from "bad" listeners in terms of eye contact and reacting with appropriate facial expressions.[24] Nonverbal responding is just as important in the business world. One study of 195 critical incidents in banking and medical settings showed that a major difference between effective listening and ineffective listening was the kind of feedback offered.[25] Good listeners showed that they were attentive by nonverbal behaviors such as keeping eye contact and reacting with appropriate facial expressions. Their verbal behavior—answering questions and exchanging ideas, for example—also

*Source:* King Feature Syndicate.

demonstrated their attention. It's easy to imagine how other responses would signal less effective listening. A slumped posture, bored expression, and yawning send a clear message that you are not tuned in to the speaker.

Adding responsiveness to our listening model demonstrates the fact, discussed in Chapter 1, that communication is transactional in nature. Listening isn't just a passive activity. As listeners we are active participants in a communication transaction. At the same time that we receive messages we also send them.

The final step in the listening process is **remembering**.[26] Research has revealed that people remember only about half of what they hear *immediately after* hearing it.[27] This is true even if people work hard at listening. This situation would probably not be too bad if we remembered the half we retain, but we don't. Within 2 months half of the half is forgotten, bringing what we remember down to about 25 percent of the original message. This loss, however, doesn't take 2 months: People start forgetting immediately (within 8 hours the 50 percent remembered drops to about 35 percent). Of course, these amounts vary from person to person and depend on the importance of the information being recalled.[28] Given the amount of information we process every day—from instructors, friends, the radio, TV, and other sources—the **residual message** (what we remember) is a small fraction of what we hear.

## Listening Is Not A Natural Process

Another common myth is that listening is like breathing: a natural activity that people do well. The truth is that listening is a skill much like speaking: Everybody does it, though few people do it well.

One study illustrates this point: 144 managers in a study were asked to rate their listening skills. Astonishingly, not one of the managers described himself or herself as a "poor" or "very poor" listener, whereas 94 percent rated themselves as "good" or "very good."[29] The favorable self-ratings contrasted sharply with the perceptions of the managers' subordinates, many of whom said their boss's listening skills were weak. As we have already discussed, some poor listening is inevitable. The good news is that listening can be improved through instruction and training.[30] Despite this fact, the amount of time devoted to teaching listening is far less than that devoted to other types of communication. Table 5-1 reflects this upside-down arrangement.

## All Listeners Do Not Receive the Same Message

When two or more people are listening to a speaker, we tend to assume that they all are hearing and understanding the same message. In fact, such uniform comprehension isn't the case. Recall the discussion of perception in Chapter 3, in which we pointed out the many factors that cause each of us to perceive an event differently. Physiological factors, social roles, cultural background, personal interests, and needs all shape and distort the raw data we hear into uniquely different messages.

> cultural idiom
> **tuned in:**
> focused, paying attention

### Table 5-1    Comparison of Communication Activities

|  | LISTENING | SPEAKING | READING | WRITING |
|---|---|---|---|---|
| **LEARNED** | First | Second | Third | Fourth |
| **USED** | Most | Next to most | Next to least | Least |
| **TAUGHT** | Least | Next to least | Next to most | Most |

# Overcoming Challenges to Effective Listening

Despite the importance of good listening, people seem to get worse at the skill as they grow up. In a classic study, teachers at various grade levels were asked to stop their lectures periodically and ask students what they were talking about. Ninety percent of first-grade children could repeat what the teacher had been saying, and 80 percent of the second-graders could do so, but when the experiment was repeated with teenagers, the results were much less impressive. Only 44 percent of junior high school students and 28 percent of senior high school students could repeat their teachers' remarks.[31]

Why does listening ability decline with age? One theory is that young children rely almost solely on auditory communication until they learn to read.[32] After that, visual input is a distraction, making listening more difficult. But there are ways to preserve and strengthen listening skills. Evidence suggests that reading aloud to children boosts not only the children's reading skills but their listening skills as well.[33] That's an advantage, because students spend about two-thirds of their time in the classroom listening.[34]

Listening poses a challenge in relationships, too. One experiment found that adults listened more attentively and courteously to strangers than to their spouses. When faced with decision-making tasks, couples interrupted each other more frequently and were generally less polite than they were to strangers.[35]

What kinds of poor listening habits plague communication? To find out, read on.

## Mindful Listening Requires Effort

Most people assume that listening is fundamentally a passive activity in which the receiver absorbs a speaker's ideas like a sponge absorbs water. It's true that some listening is basically passive. Social scientists use the term **mindless listening** to describe this sort of activity.[36] The term "mindless" may sound negative, but given the number of messages to which we're exposed, it's impractical to listen carefully and thoughtfully 100 percent of the time. Furthermore, this sort of low-level information processing can free us to focus on messages that do require more careful attention.[37] By contrast, **mindful listening** is hard work. The physical changes that occur during careful listening show the effort it takes: Heart rate quickens, respiration increases, and body temperature rises.[38] Notice that these changes are similar to the body's reaction to physical effort. This is no coincidence, because mindful listening can be just as taxing as more obvious efforts.

## Faulty Listening Behaviors

Although we can't listen effectively all the time, most people possess one or more habits that keep them from understanding truly important messages.

**Pseudolistening**  Pseudolistening is an imitation of the real thing. Pseudolisteners give the appearance of being attentive: They look you in the eye, nod and smile at the right times,

The character of Miranda Priestly (played by Meryl Streep) in *The Devil Wears Prada* could be a case study titled "Don't Let This Happen to You." She regularly ignores people (especially her assistant), demonstrates defensive habits, interrupts, and hogs the stage for herself. Which faulty listening behaviors do you think you possess? How could you be a more mindful listener?

*Source:* © Scott Adams/Dist. by United Feature Syndicate, Inc.

and may even answer you occasionally. That appearance of interest, however, is a polite facade to mask thoughts that have nothing to do with what the speaker is saying.

**Selective Listening**    **Selective listeners** respond only to the parts of a speaker's remarks that interest them. All of us are selective listeners from time to time, such as when we start paying attention to what a friend is saying only when the conversation turns to our favorite topic.

**Defensive Listening**    **Defensive listeners** take innocent comments as personal attacks. Examples include teenagers who perceive parental questions about friends and activities as distrustful snooping, insecure breadwinners who explode when their mates mention money, and touchy parents who view any questioning as a threat to their authority and parental wisdom. Many defensive listeners are suffering from shaky public images and avoid admitting this by projecting their insecurities onto others.

> cultural idiom
>
> **breadwinners:**
> those who support their families with their earnings

**Ambushing**    **Ambushers** listen carefully, but only because they are collecting information to attack what you have to say. The cross-examining prosecution attorney is a good example of an ambusher. Using this kind of strategy will justifiably initiate defensiveness on the other's part.

**Insulated Listening**    **Insulated listeners** are almost the opposite of their selective-listening cousins. Instead of looking for something specific, these people avoid certain topics. Whenever a subject arises they'd rather not deal with, insulated listeners simply fail to hear it or, rather, to acknowledge it.

**Insensitive Listening**    **Insensitive listeners** are the final example of people who don't receive another person's messages clearly. People often don't express their thoughts or feelings openly but instead communicate them through subtle and unconscious choice of words or nonverbal clues or both. Insensitive listeners aren't able to look beyond the words and behavior to understand their hidden meanings. Instead, they take a speaker's remarks at face value.

In one of your most important relationships, which faulty listening behaviors do you find most annoying? What would the other person say about *your* most annoying listening faults?

> cultural idiom
>
> **at face value:**
> literally

**Stage Hogging**    **Stage hogs** (sometimes called "conversational narcissists") try to turn the topic of conversations to themselves instead of showing interest in the speaker.[39] Interruptions are a hallmark of stage hogging. Besides preventing the listener from learning potentially valuable information, stage hogging can damage the relationship between the interrupter and the speaker. For example, applicants who interrupt the questions of an employment interviewer are likely to be rated less favorably than job seekers who wait until the interviewer has finished speaking before they respond.[40]

## Reasons for Poor Listening

What causes people to listen poorly? There are several reasons, some of which can be avoided or overcome and others that are sad but inescapable facts of life.

**Message Overload**   The amount of speech most of us encounter every day makes careful listening to everything we hear impossible. Along with the deluge of face-to-face messages, we are bombarded by phone calls, e-mails, tweets, texts, and instant messages. Besides those personal messages, we're awash in programming from the mass media. This deluge of communication has made the challenge of attending tougher than at any time in human history.[41] Background noise typically reduces our listening ability and our ability to concentrate on cognitive tasks.[42] The "@Work" box on this page highlights the dangers of multitasking and argues that managing information overload can lead to better results.

**Rapid Thought**   Listening carefully is also difficult for a physiological reason. Although we are capable of understanding speech at rates up to 600 words per minute, the average person speaks between 100 and 140 words per minute.[46] Thus, we have a great deal of mental "spare time" to spend while someone is talking. And the temptation is to use this time in ways that don't relate to the speaker's ideas, such as thinking about personal interests, daydreaming, planning a rebuttal, and so on. The trick is to use this spare time to understand the speaker's ideas better rather than to let your attention wander. Try to rephrase the speaker's ideas in your own words. Ask yourself how the ideas might be useful to you. Consider other angles that the speaker might not have mentioned.

**Psychological Noise**   Another reason why we don't always listen carefully is that we're often wrapped up in personal concerns that are of more immediate importance to us than the messages others are sending. It's hard to pay attention to someone else when you're anticipating an upcoming test or thinking about the wonderful time you had last night with good friends. Yet we still feel we have to "listen" politely to others, and so we continue with our charade. It usually takes a conscious effort to set aside your personal concerns if you expect to give others' messages the attention they deserve.

> cultural idiom

**charade:**
pretense

---

### @Work

## Multitasking: A Recipe for Inattention

Multitasking may be a fact of life on the job, but research suggests that dividing your attention has its costs. In one widely reported study, volunteers tried to carry out various problem-solving tasks while being deluged with phone calls and e-mails.[43] Even though experimenters told the subjects to ignore these distractions, the average performance drop was equivalent to a 10-point decline in IQ. In other words, trying to work on one task while listening to messages about a different matter can make you more stupid.

You might expect that greater exposure to multiple messages would improve multitasking performance, but just the opposite seems to be the case. Heavy media multitaskers perform worse on task switching than light media multitaskers.[44] Although chronic multitaskers believe they are competent at processing information, in fact they're worse than those who focus more on a single medium.[45]

You may not be able to escape multiple demands at work, but don't hold any illusions about the cost of information overload. When the matter at hand is truly important, the most effective approach may be to turn off the phone and close down the e-mail program or Web browser and devote your attention to the single task before you. ●

Figure 5-1 illustrates four ways in which preoccupied listeners lose focus when distracted by psychological noise. Everyone's mind wanders at one time or another, but excessive preoccupation is both a reason for and a sign of poor listening.

**Physical Noise** The world in which we live often presents distractions that make it hard to pay attention to others. The sound of traffic, music, others' speech, and the like interfere with our ability to hear well. Also, fatigue or other forms of discomfort can distract us from paying attention to a speaker's remarks. Consider, for example, how the efficiency of your listening decreases when you are seated in a crowded, hot, stuffy room that is surrounded by traffic and other noises. In such circumstances even the best intentions aren't enough to ensure clear understanding. You can often listen better by insulating yourself from outside distractions. This may involve removing the sources of noise: turning off the television, shutting the book you were reading, closing the window, and so on. In some cases, you and the speaker may need to find a more hospitable place to speak in order to make listening work.

**Hearing Problems** Sometimes a person's listening ability suffers from a hearing problem—the most obvious sort of physiological noise, as defined in Chapter 1. One survey explored the feelings of adults who have spouses with hearing loss. Nearly two-thirds of the respondents said they feel annoyed when their partner can't hear them clearly. Almost a quarter said that beyond just being annoyed, they felt ignored, hurt, or sad. Many of the respondents believe their spouses are in denial about their condition, which makes the problem even more frustrating.[47]

After a hearing problem has been diagnosed, it's often possible to treat it. The real tragedy occurs when a hearing loss goes undetected. In such cases, both the person with the defect and others can become frustrated and annoyed at the ineffective communication that results. If you suspect that you or someone you know suffers from a hearing loss, it's wise to have a physician or audiologist perform an examination.

**Faulty Assumptions** We often give others a mental brush-off because we assume their remarks don't have much value. When one business consultant asked some of her clients why they interrupted colleagues, she received the following responses:

My idea is better than theirs.

If I don't interrupt them, I'll never get to say my idea.

I know what they are about to say.

They don't need to finish their thoughts since mine are better.

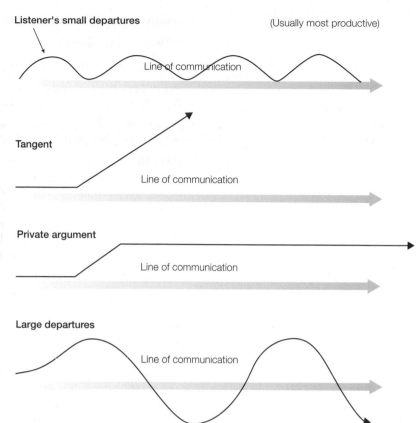

Listener's small departures (Usually most productive)

Line of communication

Tangent

Line of communication

Private argument

Line of communication

Large departures

Line of communication

**FIGURE 5-1: Four Thought Patterns.** It's common for attention to stray when listening. Serious problems arise when we begin thinking about unrelated topics or constructing rebuttals.

> cultural idiom

**give . . . brush-off:**
to dismiss or not pay attention to

Nothing about their idea will improve with further development.

It is more important for me to get recognized than it is to hear their idea.

I'm more important than they are.[48]

The egotism behind these comments is stunning. Dismissing others' ideas before considering them may be justified sometimes, but it's obviously a mistake to rule out so much of what others say . . . especially when you consider how you would feel if other people dismissed your comments without hearing you out.

**Talking Has More Apparent Advantages**    It often appears that we have more to gain by speaking than by listening. Whatever the goal—to have a prospective boss hire you, to convince others to vote for the candidate of your choice, or to describe the way you want your hair cut—the key to success seems to be the ability to speak well. Another apparent advantage of speaking is the chance it provides to gain the admiration, respect, or liking of others—or so you may think. Tell jokes, and everyone may think you're a real wit. Offer advice, and they might be grateful for your help. Tell them all you know, and they could be impressed by your wisdom.

Although speaking at the right time can lead people to appreciate you, talking too much can result in the kind of stage hogging described on page 139. Not all interruptions are attempts at stage hogging. Men typically interrupt conversations more than women and for different reasons. Men's goal in interrupting is more often to control the discussion, whereas women's is to communicate agreement, to elaborate on the speaker's idea, or to participate in the topic of conversation.[49] These sorts of responses are more likely to be welcomed as a contribution to the conversation and not as attempts to grab the stage.

If you find yourself hogging the conversation, try a simple experiment. Limit the frequency and length of your responses to a fraction of their usual amount. If you were speaking 50 percent of the time, cut back to 25 percent—or even less. If you interrupt the speaker every 15 seconds, try to let him or her talk for closer to a minute. You are likely to discover that you're learning more—and probably gaining the appreciation of the other person.

**Cultural Differences**    The behaviors that define a good listener vary by culture. Americans are most impressed by listeners who ask questions and make supportive statements.[50] By contrast, Iranians tend to judge people's listening skills based on more subtle indicators such as their posture and eye contact. This is probably because the Iranian culture relies more on context.[51] (As you may remember from Chapter 3, members of high-context cultures are particularly attentive and sensitive to nonverbal cues.) Germans are most likely to think someone a good listener if he or she shows continuous attention to the speaker.[52] One lesson is that, whereas people in some cultures may overlook a quick glance at a cell phone or TV screen, others may interpret that behavior as rudely inattentive.

**Media Influences**    A final challenge to serious listening is the influence of contemporary mass media, especially television and radio. A growing amount of programming consists of short segments: news items, commercials, music videos, and so on.

> cultural idiom

**rule out:**
fail to consider

> cultural idiom

**grab the stage:**
gain attention

# Calvin and Hobbes

**by Bill Watterson**

(Think of *Sesame Street* and MTV.) In the same vein, news stories (e.g., *USA Today* and the television news) consist of brief stories with a declining portion of text and a growing amount of graphical information. These trends discourage the kind of focused attention that is necessary for careful listening, especially to complicated ideas and feelings.

# Types of Listening

By now you can see that listening well isn't easy. As you'll read in the following pages, there are a number of reasons people invest the effort to listen carefully. To see which of these goals are important to you, take the Self-Assessment on pages 144–145 before reading further.

Each category in the instrument reflets a distinct reason for listening. What did you learn about your own goals for listening from your scores?

## Task-Oriented Listening

**Task-oriented listening** aims to secure information necessary to get a job done. The situations that call for task-oriented listening are endless and varied: following an instructor's comments in class, hearing a description of a new piece of merchandise or software that you're thinking about buying, getting tips from a coach on how to improve your athletic skill, taking directions from your boss—the list goes on and on.

Task-oriented listening is most concerned with efficiency. Task-oriented listeners view time as a scarce and valuable commodity, and they can grow impatient when they think others are wasting it.

A task orientation can be an asset when deadlines and other pressures demand fast action. It's most appropriate when taking care of business is the primary concern: Such listeners keep a focus on the job at hand and encourage others to be organized and concise.

> ## cultural idiom
>
> **put off:**
> displease
>
> **put you off:**
> cause one displeasure
>
> **long-winded:**
> speaking for a long time

Despite its advantages, a task orientation can put off others when it seems to disregard their feelings. A no-nonsense task-oriented approach isn't always appreciated by speakers who—by virtue of culture or temperament—lack the skill or inclination to be clear and direct. Also, an excessive focus on getting things done quickly can hamper the kind of thoughtful deliberation that some jobs require. Finally, task-oriented listeners seem to minimize emotional issues and concerns, which may be an important part of business and personal transactions.

You can become more effective as an informational listener by approaching others with a constructive attitude and by using some simple but effective skills.

When task-oriented listening is appropriate, the following guidelines will help you be more effective.

**Look for Key Ideas**   It's easy to lose patience with long-winded speakers who never seem to get to the point—or to have a point, for that matter. Nonetheless, most people do have a central idea in what they say, or what we will call a "thesis" in Chapter 11. By using your

Like the contestants on shows like *Top Chef*, your success depends on listening carefully to the people who can shape your career. How well do you listen to instructions and feedback?

## Your Listening Styles

To discover your listening tendencies, fill in the survey below. Use 1 as "strongly disagree" and 7 as "strongly agree." The section(s) where you mark higher numbers (5, 6, or 7) suggests types of listening that you value the most.

| | Strongly Disagree | | | | | | Strongly Agree |
|---|---|---|---|---|---|---|---|
| **Relational Listening** | | | | | | | |
| When listening to others, it is important to understand the feelings of the speaker. | 1 | 2 | 3 | 4 | 5 | 6 | 7 |
| When listening to others, I am mainly concerned with how they are feeling. | 1 | 2 | 3 | 4 | 5 | 6 | 7 |
| I listen to understand the emotions and mood of the speaker. | 1 | 2 | 3 | 4 | 5 | 6 | 7 |
| I listen primarily to build and maintain relationships with others. | 1 | 2 | 3 | 4 | 5 | 6 | 7 |
| I enjoy listening to others because it allows me to connect with them. | 1 | 2 | 3 | 4 | 5 | 6 | 7 |
| When listening to others, I focus on understanding the feelings behind words. | 1 | 2 | 3 | 4 | 5 | 6 | 7 |
| **Analytical Listening** | | | | | | | |
| I wait until all the facts are presented before forming judgments and opinions. | 1 | 2 | 3 | 4 | 5 | 6 | 7 |
| I tend to withhold judgment about others' ideas until I have heard everything they have to say. | 1 | 2 | 3 | 4 | 5 | 6 | 7 |
| When listening to others, I attempt to withhold making an opinion until I've heard their entire message. | 1 | 2 | 3 | 4 | 5 | 6 | 7 |
| When listening to others, I consider all sides of the issue before responding. | 1 | 2 | 3 | 4 | 5 | 6 | 7 |
| I fully listen to what a person has to say before forming any opinions. | 1 | 2 | 3 | 4 | 5 | 6 | 7 |
| To be fair to others, I fully listen to what they have to say before making judgments. | 1 | 2 | 3 | 4 | 5 | 6 | 7 |

ability to think more quickly than the speaker can talk, you may be able to extract the thesis from the surrounding mass of words you're hearing. If you can't figure out what the speaker is driving at, you can always ask in a tactful way by using the skills of questioning and paraphrasing, which we examine now.

**Ask Questions**   Questioning involves asking for additional information to clarify your idea of the sender's message. If you ask directions to a friend's house, typical questions might be, "Is your place an apartment?" or "How long does it take to get there from here?" In potentially serious emotional situations, questions could include, "Why does that bother you so much?" or "You sound upset—is there something wrong?" Notice that one key element of these questions is that they request the speaker to elaborate on information already given.

| | Strongly Disagree | | | | | | Strongly Agree |
|---|---|---|---|---|---|---|---|
| **Task-Oriented Listening** | | | | | | | |
| I am impatient with people who ramble on during conversations. | 1 | 2 | 3 | 4 | 5 | 6 | 7 |
| I get frustrated when people get off topic during a conversation. | 1 | 2 | 3 | 4 | 5 | 6 | 7 |
| When listening to others, I become impatient when they appear to be wasting time. | 1 | 2 | 3 | 4 | 5 | 6 | 7 |
| I prefer speakers who quickly get to the point. | 1 | 2 | 3 | 4 | 5 | 6 | 7 |
| I find it difficult to listen to people who take too long to get their ideas across. | 1 | 2 | 3 | 4 | 5 | 6 | 7 |
| When listening to others, I appreciate speakers who give brief, to-the-point presentations. | 1 | 2 | 3 | 4 | 5 | 6 | 7 |
| **Critical Listening** | | | | | | | |
| When listening to others, I focus on any inconsistencies and/or errors in what's being said. | 1 | 2 | 3 | 4 | 5 | 6 | 7 |
| I often catch errors in other speakers' logic. | 1 | 2 | 3 | 4 | 5 | 6 | 7 |
| I tend to naturally notice errors in what other speakers say. | 1 | 2 | 3 | 4 | 5 | 6 | 7 |
| I have a talent for catching inconsistencies in what a speaker says. | 1 | 2 | 3 | 4 | 5 | 6 | 7 |
| When listening to others, I notice contradictions in what they say. | 1 | 2 | 3 | 4 | 5 | 6 | 7 |
| Good listeners catch discrepancies in what people say. | 1 | 2 | 3 | 4 | 5 | 6 | 7 |

Adapted with the authors' permission from Bodie, G. D., Worthington, D. L., & Gearhart, C. G. (2013). The Revised Listening Styles Profile (LSP-R): Development and validation. *Communication Quarterly, 61,* 72–90.

doi: 10.1080/01463373.2012.720343.

Despite their apparent benefits, not all questions are equally helpful. Whereas **sincere questions** are aimed at understanding others, **counterfeit questions** are really disguised attempts to send a message, not receive one.

Counterfeit questions come in several varieties:

1. *Questions that make statements.* "Are you finally ready to go now?" "You can't be serious about that, right?" Comments like these are certainly not genuine requests for information. Emphasizing certain words can also turn a question into a statement: "You lent money to Tony?" We also use questions to offer advice. The person who responds with "Are you going to stand up to him and give him what he deserves?" clearly has stated an opinion about what should be done.

> cultural idiom

**to stand up to:**
to confront courageously

(2) *Questions that carry hidden agendas.* "Are you busy Friday night?" is a dangerous question to answer. If you say, "No," thinking the person has something fun in mind, you won't like hearing, "Good, because I need some help moving my piano."

(3) *Questions that seek "correct" answers.* Most of us have been victims of question-askers who want to hear only a particular response. "Which shoes do you think I should wear?" can be a sincere question—unless the asker has a pre-determined preference. When this happens, the asker isn't interested in listening to contrary opinions, and "incorrect" responses get shot down. Some of these questions may venture into delicate territory. "Honey, do you think I look ugly?" can be a request for a "correct" answer.

(4) *Questions that are based on unchecked assumptions.* "Why aren't you listening to me?" assumes the other person isn't paying attention. "What's the matter?" assumes that something is wrong. As Chapter 2 explains, perception checking is a much better way of checking out assumptions: "When you kept looking over at the TV, I thought you weren't listening to me, but maybe I was wrong. *Were* you paying attention?"

> cultural idiom
> **shot down:**
> rejected or defeated

Unlike counterfeit questions, sincere questions are genuine requests for new information that clarifies a speaker's thoughts or feelings. Although the value of sincere questioning might seem obvious, people don't use this information-seeking approach enough. Communicators are often reluctant to show their ignorance by asking for an explanation of what seems like an obvious point. At times like those it's a good idea to recall a quote attributed to Confucius: "He who asks a question is a fool for 5 minutes. He who does not ask is a fool for life."

**Paraphrase**    Questioning is often a valuable tool for increasing understanding. Sometimes, however, questions won't help you understand a speaker's ideas any more clearly. Now consider another type of feedback—one that would tell you whether you understood what had already been said before you asked additional questions. This sort of feedback, termed **paraphrasing**, involves restating in your own words the message you thought the speaker had just sent, without adding anything new.

> (*To a direction giver*) "You're telling me to drive down to the traffic light by the high school and turn toward the mountains, is that it?"

> (*To the boss*) "So you need me both this Saturday *and* next Saturday—right?"

> (*To a professor*) "When you said, 'Don't worry about the low grade on the quiz,' did you mean it won't count against my grade?"

In other cases, a paraphrase will reflect your understanding of the speaker's feelings:

> "You said 'I've had it with this relationship!' Are you angry or relieved that it's over?"

> "You said you've got a minute to talk, but I'm not sure whether it's a good time for you."

> "You said 'Forget it,' but it sounds like you're mad. Are you?"

Whether your paraphrasing reflects a speaker's thoughts or feelings, and whether it focuses on a specific comment or a general theme, the key to success is to restate the other person's comments in your own words as a way of cross-checking the information. If you simply repeat the speaker's comments verbatim, you will sound foolish—and you still might well be misunderstanding what has been said. Notice the difference between simply parroting a statement and really paraphrasing:

> cultural idiom
> **parroting:**
> repeating without understanding

| | |
|---|---|
| **Speaker:** | "I'd like to go, but I can't afford it." |
| **Parroting:** | "You'd like to go, but you can't afford it." |
| **Paraphrasing:** | "So if we could find a way to pay for you, you'd be willing to come. Is that right?" |
| **Speaker:** | "What's the matter with you?" |
| **Parroting:** | "You think there's something wrong with me?" |
| **Paraphrasing:** | "You think I'm mad at you?" |

As these examples suggest, effective paraphrasing is a skill that takes time to develop. You can make your paraphrasing sound more natural by taking any of three approaches, depending on the situation:

*Source:* © 1997 Ted Goff www.tedgoff.com.

① **Change the speaker's wording.**

| | |
|---|---|
| **Speaker:** | "Bilingual education is just another failed idea of bleeding-heart liberals." |
| **Paraphrase:** | "Let me see if I've got this right. You're mad because you think bilingual ed sounds good, but it doesn't work?" *(Reflects both the speaker's feeling and the reason for it.)* |

② **Offer an example of what you think the speaker is talking about.** When the speaker makes an abstract statement, you may suggest a specific example or two to see if your understanding is accurate.

| | |
|---|---|
| **Speaker:** | "Lee is such a jerk. I can't believe the way he acted last night." |
| **Paraphrase:** | "You think those jokes were pretty offensive, huh?" *(Reflects the listener's guess about speaker's reason for objecting to the behavior.)* |

③ **Reflect the underlying theme of the speaker's remarks.** When you want to summarize the theme that seems to have run through another person's conversation, a complete or partial perception check is appropriate:

| | |
|---|---|
| **Paraphrase:** | "You keep reminding me to be careful. It sounds like you're worried that something might happen to me. Am I right?" *(Reflects both the speaker's thoughts and feelings and explicitly seeks clarification.)* |

Learning to paraphrase isn't easy, but it can be worth the effort, because it offers two very real advantages. First, it boosts the odds that you'll accurately and fully understand what others are saying. We've already seen that using one-way listening or even asking questions may lead you to think that you've understood a speaker when, in fact, you haven't. Paraphrasing, on the other hand, serves as a way of double-checking your interpretation for accuracy. Second, paraphrasing guides you toward sincerely trying to understand another person instead of using nonlistening styles such as stage hogging, selective listening, and so on. Listeners who paraphrase to check their understanding of a conversational partner's comments are judged to be more socially attractive than listeners who do not.[53]

If you force yourself to reflect the other person's ideas in your own words, you'll spend your mental energy trying to understand that speaker instead of using less constructive listening styles. For this reason, some communication

> cultural idiom
**bleeding-heart liberals:**
persons motivated by sympathy rather than practicality

> cultural idiom
**boosts the odds:**
increases the chances of success

Imagine that you used the listening skills described in these pages in your most important relationships. How would your communication look different to the other people involved? How would these relationships be different?

experts suggest that the ratio of questioning and paraphrasing to confronting should be at least 5:1, if not more.[54]

**Take Notes**   Understanding others is crucial, of course, but comprehending their ideas doesn't guarantee that you will remember them. As you read earlier in this chapter, listeners usually forget almost two-thirds of what they hear.

Sometimes recall isn't especially important. You don't need to retain many details of the vacation adventures recounted by a neighbor or the childhood stories told by a relative. At other times, though, remembering a message—even minute details—is important. The lectures you hear in class are an obvious example. Likewise, it can be important to remember the details of plans that involve you: the time of a future appointment, the name of a phone caller whose message you took for someone else, or the orders given by your boss at work.

At times like these it's smart to take notes instead of relying on your memory. Sometimes these notes may be simple and brief: a phone number jotted on a scrap of paper or a list of things to pick up at the market. In other cases—a lecture, for example—your notes need to be much longer. When detailed notes are necessary, a few simple points will help make them effective:

① *Don't wait too long before beginning to jot down ideas.* If you don't realize that you need to take notes until 5 minutes into a conversation, you're likely to forget much of what has been said and miss out on other information as you scramble to catch up.

② *Record only key ideas.* Don't try to capture every word of long messages. If you can pin down the most important points, your notes will be easier to follow and much more useful.

③ *Develop a note-taking format.* The exact form you choose isn't important. Some people use a formal outlining scheme with headings designated by roman numerals, letters, and numbers, whereas others use simple lists. You might come up with useful symbols: boxes around key names and numbers or asterisks next to especially important information. After you develop a consistent format, your notes will not only help you remember information but also help you whip others' ideas into a shape that's useful to you.

## Relational Listening

**Relational listening** aims at emotionally connecting with others. Relationally oriented listeners are typically extroverted, attentive, and friendly. They are more focused on understanding people than trying to control them.[55]

A relational orientation has obvious strengths. But it has some less obvious drawbacks. It's easy to become overly involved with others' feelings. Relational listeners may lose their detachment and ability to assess the quality of information others are giving in an effort to be congenial and supportive.[56] Less relationally oriented communicators can view them as overly expressive, and even intrusive.

**Take Time**   The goal of task-oriented listening is efficiency, but relational listening couldn't be more different. Encouraging others to share their thoughts and feelings can take time. If you're in a hurry, it may be best to reschedule relationally focused conversation for a better time. The good news is that the gift of attention often speaks for itself, even when you don't know what to say. Medical studies show that, even when doctors cannot cure patients, patients' coping skills are positively linked to the amount of time their doctor spends listening to them.[57]

> cultural idiom

**scramble to catch up:**
to begin in a hurried fashion that which should have been started sooner

> cultural idiom

**whip into shape:**
organize quickly

**Listen for Unexpressed Thoughts and Feelings**    People don't say what's on their minds or in their hearts. There are lots of reasons why: Tact, confusion, lack of awareness, fear of being judged negatively . . . the list is a long one.

When relationship building is the goal, it can be valuable to listen for unexpressed messages. Consider a few examples:

| STATEMENT | POSSIBLE UNEXPRESSED MESSAGE |
| --- | --- |
| "Don't apologize. It's not a big deal." | "I'm angry (or hurt, disappointed) by what you did." |
| "You're going clubbing tonight? That sounds like fun! | "I'd like to come along." |
| "Check out this news story. That's my little sister!" | "I'm proud of what she did." |
| "That was quite a party you [neighbors] had last night. You were going strong at 2 A.M." | "The noise bothered me." |
| "You like gaming? I do too!" | "Perhaps we can be friends." |

There are several ways to explore unexpressed messages. You can *ask questions* using the guidelines described on pages 144–146: "How did you feel when he said that?" "Is there something I can do to help?" You can *paraphrase*, as described on pages 146–148: "Sounds like that really surprised you," or "So you aren't sure what to do next, right?" Or, as you'll read in a few pages, you can *prompt* the speaker to volunteer more information: "Really?" "Is that right?" You'll read more about listening as a form of social support later in this chapter.

When you consider exploring unexpressed feelings and thoughts, be careful not to pry. Proceed carefully, and phrase your hunches tentatively. For more advice, review the description of perception checking on pages 61–62 in Chapter 2.

**Encourage Further Comments**    Even if you don't explore unexpressed messages, you can strengthen relationships simply by encouraging others to say more. Even if you're not a stage hog, it's easy to redirect a conversation back to yourself. Instead, try a simple experiment to prove the value of focusing on the speaker. In your next conversation, focus on drawing out the other person. If you express a sincere desire to learn more, you're likely to be surprised by the positive results. The speaker may be grateful that you have helped him or her work through a problem, when all you have really done is listen and ask questions. Great teachers harness this power regularly. They know that students often learn more when they are asked questions and encouraged to work through problems than when they are given the answers up front.[58]

## Analytical Listening

Whereas relational listening aims to enhance the relationship, the goal of **analytical listening** is to understand the message. Analytical listeners explore an issue from a variety of perspectives in order to understand it as fully as possible.

Ben Stein played the droning economics teacher in the comedy classic *Ferris Bueller's Day Off*. He also appears as a comically monotonous spokesperson on numerous TV commercials. What strategies can you use to be a good listener when the information is important, but the delivery is uninspiring?

Analytical listening is the right idea when your goal is to assess the quality of ideas, and when there is value in looking at issues from a wide range of perspectives. It's especially valuable when the issues at hand are complicated. On the other hand, a thorough analytical approach can be time consuming. So when a deadline is approaching, you may not respond as quickly as the other person would like.

When you want to listen analytically, follow these steps.

**Listen for Information Before Evaluating**   The principle of listening for information before evaluating seems almost too obvious to mention, yet all of us are guilty of judging a speaker's ideas before we completely understand them. The tendency to make premature judgments is especially strong when the idea you are hearing conflicts with your own beliefs. As one writer put it,

> the right to speak is meaningless if no one will listen. . . . It is simply not enough that we reject censorship . . . we have an affirmative responsibility to hear the argument before we disagree with it.[59]

You can avoid the tendency to judge before understanding by following the simple rule of paraphrasing a speaker's ideas before responding to them. The effort required to translate the other person's ideas into your own words will keep you from arguing, and if your interpretation is mistaken, you'll know immediately.

**Separate the Message from the Speaker**   The first recorded cases of blaming the messenger for an unpleasant message occurred in ancient Greece. When messengers would arrive reporting losses in battles, their generals were known to respond to the bad news by having the messengers put to death. This sort of irrational reaction is still common (though fortunately less violent) today. Consider a few situations in which there is a tendency to get angry with a communicator bearing unpleasant news: An instructor tries to explain why you did poorly on a major paper; a friend explains what you did to make a fool of yourself at the party last Saturday night; the boss points out how you could do your job better. At times like this, becoming irritated with the bearer of unpleasant information not only can cause you to miss important information but also can harm your relationships.

There's a second way that confusing the message and the messenger can prevent you from understanding important ideas. At times you may mistakenly discount the value of a message because of the person who is presenting it. Even the most boring instructors, the most idiotic relatives, and the most demanding bosses occasionally make good points. If you write off everything a person says before you consider it, you may be cheating yourself out of some valuable information.

**Search for Value**   Even if you listen with an open mind, sooner or later you will end up hearing information that is either so unimportant or so badly delivered that you're tempted to tune out. Although making a quick escape from such tedious situations is often the best thing to do, there are times when you can profit from paying close attention to apparently worthless communication. This is especially true when you're trapped in a situation in which the only alternatives to attentiveness are pseudolistening or downright rudeness.

Once you try, you probably can find some value in even the worst situations. Consider how you might listen opportunistically when you find yourself locked in a boring conversation with someone whose ideas are worthless. Rather than torture yourself until escape is possible, you could keep yourself amused—and perhaps learn something useful—by listening carefully until you can answer the following (unspoken) questions:

"Is there anything useful in what this person is saying?"

"What led the speaker to come up with ideas like these?"

"What lessons can I learn from this person that will keep me from sounding the same way in other situations?"

Listening with a constructive attitude is important, but even the best intentions won't always help you understand others. The following skills can help you figure out messages that otherwise might be confusing, as well as help you see how those messages can make a difference in your life.

## Critical Listening

The goal of **critical listening** is go beyond trying to understand and analyze the topic at hand, and instead, try to assess its quality. At their best, critical listeners apply the tools of analytical listening to see whether an idea holds up under careful scrutiny.

Critical listening can be especially helpful when the goal is to investigate a problem. But people who are critical listeners can also frustrate others, who may think that they nit-pick everything others say.

When critical listening is appropriate, follow these guidelines.

**Examine the Speaker's Evidence and Reasoning**  Speakers usually offer some kind of support to back up their statements. A car dealer who argues that domestic cars are just as reliable as imports might cite frequency-of-repair statistics from *Consumer Reports* or refer you to satisfied customers, for example; and a professor arguing that students don't work as hard as they used to might tell stories about then and now to back up the thesis.

Chapter 12 describes several types of supporting material that can be used to prove a point: definitions, descriptions, analogies, statistics, and so on. Whatever form the support takes, you can ask several questions to determine the quality of a speaker's evidence and reasoning:[60]

1. *Is the evidence recent enough?* In many cases, ranging from trivial to important, old evidence is worthless. If the honors were earned several years ago, the cuisine from an "award-winning" restaurant may be barely edible today. The claim "Tony is a jerk" may have been true in the past, but people do change. Before you accept even the most credible evidence, be sure it isn't obsolete.

2. *Is enough evidence presented?* One or two pieces of support may be exceptions and not conclusive evidence. You might have heard this example of generalizing from limited evidence: "I never wear seat belts. I knew somebody who wasn't wearing them in an accident, and his life was saved because he was thrown clear from the car." Although not wearing seat belts might have been safer in this instance, on the average, experts agree that when you consider all vehicle accidents, the chances of avoiding serious injury are much greater if you wear seat belts.

3. *Is the evidence from a reliable source?* Even a large amount of recent evidence may be worthless if the source is weak. Your cousin, the health food fanatic, might not have the qualifications to talk about the poisonous effects of commercially farmed vegetables. On the other hand, the opinion of an impartial physician, nutritionist, or toxicologist would carry more weight.

④ *Can the evidence be interpreted in more than one way?* A piece of evidence that supports one claim might also support others. For example, you might hear someone argue that statistics showing women are underrepresented in the management of a company are part of a conspiracy to exclude them from positions of power. The same statistics, though, could have other explanations: Perhaps fewer women have been with the company long enough to be promoted, or perhaps this is a field that has not attracted large numbers of women. Alternative explanations don't necessarily mean that the one being argued is wrong, but they do raise questions that need to be answered before you accept an argument.

Besides taking a close look at the evidence a speaker presents, a critical listener will also look at how that evidence is put together to prove a point. Logicians have identified a number of logical fallacies—errors in reasoning that can lead to false conclusions. In fact, logicians have identified more than 100 fallacies.[61] Chapter 14 identifies some of the most common ones.

**Evaluate the Speaker's Credibility**   The acceptability of an idea often depends on its source. If your longtime family friend, the self-made millionaire, invited you to invest your life savings in jojoba fruit futures, you might be grateful for the tip. If your deadbeat brother-in-law made the same offer, you would probably laugh off the suggestion.

Chapter 14 discusses credibility in detail, but two questions provide a quick guideline for deciding whether or not to accept a speaker as an authority:

① *Is the speaker competent?* Does the speaker have the experience or the expertise to qualify as an authority on this subject? Note that someone who is knowledgeable in one area may not be as well qualified to comment in another area. For instance, your friend who can answer any question about computer programming might be a terrible advisor when the subject turns to romance.

② *Is the speaker impartial?* Knowledge alone isn't enough to certify a speaker's ideas as acceptable. People who have a personal stake in the outcome of a topic are more likely to be biased. The unqualified praise a commission-earning salesperson gives a product may be more suspect than the mixed review you get from a user. This doesn't mean you should disregard any comments you hear from an involved party—only that you should consider the possibility of intentional or unintentional bias.

**Examine Emotional Appeals**   Sometimes emotion alone may be enough reason to persuade you. You might lend your friend $20 just for old times' sake even though you don't expect to see the money again soon. In other cases, it's a mistake to let yourself be swayed by emotion when the logic of a point isn't sound. The excitement or fun in an ad or the lure of low monthly payments probably isn't good enough reason to buy a product you can't afford. Again, the fallacies described in Chapter 14 will help you recognize flaws in emotional appeals.

As you read about task-oriented, relational, analytical, and critical approaches to listening, you may have noted that you habitually use some more than others. Researchers are still working to determine how much we rely on different approaches—and how much we should.[62] There's no question that you can control the way you listen to and use the styles that best suit the situation at hand.

As the owner of a crisis management firm on the TV drama *Scandal*, Olivia Pope (Kerry Washington) has to be a critical listener to evaluate new clients and help them manage public images. What strategies do you use to distinguish the accuracy of messages?

> cultural idiom

**deadbeat:**
one who does not regularly pay bills

**laugh off:**
dismiss with a laugh

When your relationship with the speaker needs attention, adopt a relational approach. When clarity is the issue, be an action-oriented listener. If analysis is called for, put on that style. And when efficiency is what matters most, become a model of task-oriented orientation. You can also boost your effectiveness by assessing the listening preferences of your conversational partners and adapting your style to them.

> How could you adjust your use of the various types of listening (task-oriented, relational, analytical, critical) to become a better listener?

## Listening and Social Support

Along with task-oriented, analytical, critical, and relational listening, there's another style of listening and responding with a different focus. In **supportive listening**, the primary aim is to help the speaker deal with personal dilemmas. Sometimes the problem is a big one: "I'm not sure this marriage is going to work" or "I can't decide whether to drop out of school." At other times the problem is more modest. A friend might be trying to decide what birthday gift to buy or where to spend a vacation. Supportive listeners are typically judged to be optimistic, honest, understanding, and encouraging.[63]

There's no question about the value of receiving support when faced with personal problems. Research shows that supportive communication can reduce loneliness and stress and build self-esteem.[64] There is even evidence that people with good support networks tend to live longer than others.[65] And the benefits go both ways. People who provide social support often feel an enhanced sense of well-being themselves.[66] Indeed, social support has been shown to be among the most important communication skills a friend—or a teacher or a parent—can have.[67]

### Social Support and Mediated Communication

Until recently most social support came from personal acquaintances: friends, family, coworkers, neighbors, and so on. In the last 15 years, though, there has been an explosion of "virtual communities" in which strangers meet online to share interests and concerns, and to gain support from one another on nearly every problem. The most popular support topics include medical conditions, eating disorders, sexual orientation, divorce, shyness, addictions, and loneliness.[68]

In some aspects, online help is similar to the face-to-face variety. The goals are to gain information and emotional support. In other ways, online support differs from the kind people seek in person.[69] The most obvious difference is *anonymity:* Most members of online communities are strangers who usually have not met in person, and may not even know each other's real names. Also, online groups often focus specifically on a single issue, whereas traditional relationships cover a wide range of topics. Another difference involves the rate and amount of self-disclosure: In traditional relationships, people usually reveal personal information slowly and carefully, but with the anonymity of online support groups, they typically open up almost immediately.

It's unlikely that online support groups will ever replace face-to-face relationships, but

In the film *My Week with Marilyn*, Colin Clark (Eddie Redmayne) is a young man who provides a sincere listening ear for Marilyn Monroe (Michelle Williams), a world-famous actress in the midst of a troubled relationship and crippled with self-doubt while shooting her latest movie. Which type of listening do you think is most appropriate in such a situation?

## Understanding Communication Technology

### Who Is Listening to You Online?

During a lecture, Australian university student Jonathan Pease tweeted the following message: "Sitting in the back row at syndey uni carving 'Rooney eats it' on the desk . . . feels good to be a rebel :)." He soon discovered that his online audience included Sydney University officials, who soon posted a tweet of their own: "Defacing our desks Jonathan? ;) Hope you enjoyed your course."[70] Luckily for Pease, the authorities had a sense of humor. Their response also reinforced an important point: When you go online, your audience may include more viewers than you imagine.

University officials aren't the only ones who track people online. The practice known as "social media listening" has become a sensation among marketing professionals who want to understand consumers' preferences better and develop relationships with them. Robert Caruso realized this when he saw a commercial for Total Bib on TV and tweeted to his friends that it reminded him of a *Saturday Night Live* sketch. "A few hours later, I received a reply tweet from Total Bib thanking me for the mention and engaging me in conversation," Caruso says, "I was pretty amazed since I was not following them previously, they were simply monitoring the

stream." Not only that, but Total Bib representatives looked up Caruso online and learned that he was a single father with a toddler, so they sent him a complimentary bib. Caruso said he was touched by the personal attention.[71]

So-called listening software is now available to monitor websites, Facebook, Google searches, blogs, Twitter, and more. That means that marketing professionals monitor people's online search terms and the websites they visit, in addition to the messages and photos they post.

At its best, monitoring technology allows marketers to listen avidly to consumers. At its worst, it can be "unethical and creepy," in the words of Tom Petrocelli, a technology blogger and marketing specialist.[72] Petrocelli is a fan of media listening when it's done well, but he counts the following actions in the creepy column: spying on employees, requiring them to share their "friends" list with the marketing team, and sending out mass e-mails or tweets uninvited.

One thing is for sure: Whether you consider Internet monitoring to be an invasion of privacy or marketing genius, the odds are that, if you are online, someone is listening. ●

for hundreds of thousands of people, they provide another valuable tool for getting the help they often desperately need.

### Gender and Social Support

Researchers have found some important ways that men and women respond differently to others' problems.[73] As a group, women are more likely than men to give supportive responses when presented with another person's problem. They are also more skillful at composing supportive messages. By contrast, men tend to respond to others' problems by offering advice or by diverting the topic. In a study of helping styles in sororities and fraternities, researchers found that sorority women frequently respond with emotional support when asked to help; also, they rated their sisters as being better at listening nonjudgmentally, and at comforting and showing concern for them. Fraternity men, on the other hand, fit the stereotypical pattern of offering help by challenging their brothers to evaluate their attitudes and values.

These differences are real, but they aren't as dramatic as they might seem. For example, men are as likely as women to respond supportively when they perceive that the other person is feeling a high degree of emotional stress. Women, on the other hand, are more likely to respond supportively even when others are only moderately stressed.

A number of factors interact with gender to shape how people provide social support, including cultural background, personal goals, expressive style, and cognitive complexity. Based on these findings, it's important to respond in a way that fits with your personal style and is likely to be appreciated by the other person.

## Types of Supportive Responses

Whatever the relationship and topic, there are several styles by which you can respond supportively to another person's remarks.[74] Each of these styles has its advantages and disadvantages. As you read them, you can aim to choose the best style for the situation at hand.

**Advising**    When approached with another's problem, the most common tendency is an **advising response**: to help by offering a solution.[75] Although such a response is sometimes valuable, often it isn't as helpful as you might think.[76] In fact, researchers have discovered that advice is actually unhelpful at least as often as it is helpful.[77]

There are several reasons why advice doesn't work especially well. First, it can be hard to tell when the other person wants to hear the helper's idea of a solution.[78] Sometimes the request is clear: "What do you think I should do?" At other times, though, it isn't clear whether certain statements are requests for direct advice. Ambiguous statements include requests for opinions ("What do you think of Jeff?"), soliciting information ("Would that be an example of sexual harassment?"), and announcement of a problem ("I'm really confused . . .").

Even when someone with a problem asks for advice, offering it may not be helpful. Your suggestion may not offer the best course to follow, in which case it can even be harmful. There's often a temptation to tell others how we would behave in their place, but it's important to realize that what's right for one person may not be right for another.[79] A related consequence of advising is that it often allows others to avoid responsibility for their decisions. A partner who follows a suggestion of yours that doesn't work out can always pin the blame on you. Finally, often people simply don't want advice: They may not be ready to accept it, needing instead simply to talk out their thoughts and feelings.

Advice is most welcome when it has been requested and when the advisor seems concerned with respecting the face needs of the recipient.[80]

Before offering advice, you need to be sure that four conditions are present:[81]

> cultural idiom
> **pin the blame on:**
> claim the fault lies with

> cultural idiom
> **respecting the face needs:**
> protecting one's dignity

① *Be confident that the advice is correct.* You may be certain about some matters of fact, such as the proper way to solve a school problem or the cost of a piece of merchandise, but resist the temptation to act like an authority on matters you know little about. Furthermore, it is both unfair and risky to make suggestions when you aren't positive that they are the best choice. Realize that just because a course of action worked for you doesn't guarantee that it will work for everybody.

② *Ask yourself whether the person seeking your advice seems willing to accept it.* In this way you can avoid the frustration of making good suggestions, only to find that the person with the problem had another solution in mind all the time.

③ *Be certain that the receiver won't blame you if the advice doesn't work out.* You may be offering the suggestions, but the choice and responsibility for accepting them are up to the recipient of your advice.

④ *Deliver your advice supportively, in a face-saving manner.* Advice that is perceived as being offered constructively, in the context of a solid relationship, is much better than critical comments offered in a way that signals a lack of respect for the receiver.[82]

> cultural idiom
> **face-saving:**
> protecting one's dignity

In *The Help*, exploited and fearful African American housekeepers in the 1960s begin to share their stories when an aspiring journalist proves that she is a compassionate listener. Have you ever been willing to share personal information to a sincere listener? How can you be an effective relational listener to others?

> cultural idiom

**wake-up call:**
a warning or caution to pay attention

> cultural idiom

**a put-down:**
an insulting or degrading remark

**Judging**   A **judging response** evaluates the sender's thoughts or behaviors in some way. The judgment may be favorable—"That's a good idea" or "You're on the right track now"—or unfavorable—"An attitude like that won't get you anywhere." But in either case it implies that the person doing the judging is in some way qualified to pass judgment on the speaker's thoughts or behaviors.

Sometimes negative judgments are purely critical. How many times have you heard such responses as "Well, you asked for it!" or "I told you so!" or "You're just feeling sorry for yourself"? Although comments like these can sometimes serve as a verbal wake-up call, they usually make matters worse.

At other times negative judgments are less critical. These involve what we usually call *constructive criticism*, which is intended to help a person improve in the future. This is the sort of response given by friends about everything from the choice of clothing to jobs and to friends. Another common setting for constructive criticism occurs in school, where instructors evaluate students' work to help them master concepts and skills. But whether or not it's justified, even constructive criticism runs the risk of arousing defensiveness because it may threaten the self-concept of the person at whom it is directed.

Judgments have the best chance of being received when two conditions exist:

① *The person with the problem has requested an evaluation from you.* Occasionally an unsolicited judgment may bring someone to his or her senses, but more often this sort of uninvited evaluation will trigger a defensive response.

② *Your judgment is genuinely constructive and not designed as a put-down.* If you are tempted to use judgments as a weapon, don't fool yourself into thinking that you are being helpful. Often the statement "I'm telling you this for your own good" simply isn't true.

If you can remember to follow these two guidelines, your judgments will probably be less frequent and better received.

**Analyzing**   In an **analyzing statement**, the listener tries to help by offering an interpretation of a speaker's message. The motive here is different from the kind of analysis described on pages 149–151, in which the goal was to benefit you, the listener. In this case, the analysis is aimed at helping the other person.

Analyses like these are probably familiar to you:

"I think what's really bothering you is . . ."

"She's doing it because . . ."

"I don't think you really meant that."

"Maybe the problem started when she . . ."

Interpretations are often effective ways to help people with problems to consider alternative meanings—meanings they would have never thought of without your help. Sometimes a clear analysis will make a confusing problem suddenly clear, either suggesting a solution or at least providing an understanding of what is occurring.

At other times, an analysis can create more problems than it solves. There are two problems with analyzing. First, your interpretation may not be correct, in which case the speaker may become even more confused by accepting it. Second, even if your interpretation is correct, saying it aloud might not be useful. There's a chance that it will arouse defensiveness (because analysis implies superiority and judgment), and even if it doesn't, the person may not be able to understand your view of the problem without working it out personally.

How can you know when it's helpful to offer an analysis? There are several guidelines to follow:

1. *Offer your interpretation in a tentative way rather than as absolute fact.* There's a big difference between saying, "Maybe the reason is . . ." or "The way it looks to me . . ." and insisting, "This is the truth."

2. *Your analysis ought to have a reasonable chance of being correct.* An inaccurate interpretation—especially one that sounds plausible—can leave a person more confused than before.

3. *You ought to be sure that the other person will be receptive to your analysis.* Even if you're completely accurate, your thoughts won't help if the other person isn't ready to consider them.

4. *Be sure that your motive for offering an analysis is truly to help the other person.* It can be tempting to offer an analysis to show how brilliant you are or even to make the other person feel bad for not having thought of the right answer in the first place. Needless to say, an analysis offered under such conditions isn't helpful.

**Questioning**    A few pages ago we talked about questioning as one way to understand others better. A questioning response can also be a way to help others think about their problems and understand them more clearly.[83] For example, questioning can help a conversational partner define vague ideas more precisely. You might respond to a friend with a line of questioning: "You said Greg has been acting 'differently' toward you lately. What has he been doing?" Another example of a question that helps clarify is as follows: "You told your roommates that you wanted them to be more helpful in keeping the place clean. What would you like them to do?"

Questions can also encourage people to examine situations in more detail by talking either about what happened or about personal feelings—for example, "How did you feel when they turned you down? What did you do then?" This type of questioning is particularly helpful when you are dealing with someone who is quiet or is unwilling under the circumstances to talk about the problem very much.

Although questions have the potential to be helpful, they also run the risk of confusing or distracting the person with the problem. The best questioning follows these principles:

1. *Don't ask questions just to satisfy your own curiosity.* You might become so interested in the other person's story that you will want to hear more. "What did he say then?" you might be tempted to ask. "What happened next?" Responding to questions like these might confuse the person with the problem, or even leave him or her more agitated than before.

2. *Be sure your questions won't confuse or distract the person you're trying to help.* For instance, asking someone, "When did the problem begin?" might provide some clue about how to solve it—but it could also lead to a long digression that would only confuse matters. As with advice, it's important to be sure you're on the right track before asking questions.

3. *Don't use questions to disguise your suggestions or criticism.* We've all been questioned by parents, teachers, or other figures who seemed to be trying to trap

> cultural idiom

**turned you down:**
rejected your request or offer

us or indirectly to guide us. In this way, questioning becomes a strategy that can imply that the questioner already has some idea of what direction the discussion should take but isn't willing to tell you directly.

**Comforting**    A **comforting** response can take several forms:

| | |
|---|---|
| Agreement | "You're right—the landlord is being unfair." |
| | "Yeah, that class was tough for me, too." |
| Offers to help | "I'm here if you need me." |
| | "Let me try to explain it to him." |
| Praise | "I don't care what the boss said: I think you did a great job!" |
| | "You're a terrific person! If she doesn't recognize it, that's her problem." |
| Reassurance | "The worst part is over. It will probably get easier from here." |
| | "I know you'll do a great job." |
| Diversion | "Let's catch a movie and get your mind off this." |
| | "That reminds me of the time we . . ." |
| Acknowledgment | "I can see that really hurts." |
| | "I know how important that was to you." |
| | "It's no fun to feel unappreciated." |

These sorts of comforting words often can be just what the other person needs. In other instances, though, this kind of comment isn't helpful at all; in fact, it can even make things worse. Telling a person who is obviously upset that everything is all right, or joking about a serious matter, can trivialize the problem. People might see your comments as a put-down, leaving them feeling worse than before.

As with the other styles we'll discuss, comforting can be helpful, but only in certain circumstances.[84] For the occasions when comforting is an appropriate response, follow these guidelines:

① *Make sure your comforting remarks are sincere.* Phony agreement or encouragement is probably worse than no support at all, because it adds the insult of your dishonesty to whatever pain the other person is already feeling.

② *Be sure the other person can accept your support.* Sometimes we become so upset that we aren't ready or able to hear anything positive.

Even if your advice, judgments, and analysis are correct and your questions are sincere, and even if your support comes from the best motives, these responses often fail to help. One recent survey demonstrates how poorly such traditional responses work.[85] Mourners who had recently suffered from the death of a loved one reported that 80 percent of the statements made to them were unhelpful. Nearly half of the "helpful" statements were advice: "You've got to get out more." "Don't question God's will." Despite their frequency, these responses were helpful only 3 percent of the time. The next most frequent response was reassurance, such as "She's out of pain now." Like

Even if it doesn't solve problems, comforting responses can sometimes help others feel less troubled. What role does comforting play in your repertoire of supportive communication?

advice, this kind of support was helpful only 3 percent of the time. Far more helpful were expressions that acknowledged the mourner's feelings.

One American Red Cross grief counselor explained to survivors of the September 11, 2001, terrorist attacks on the United States that simply being present can be more helpful than trying to reassure grief-stricken family members who lost loved ones in the tragedy:

> Listen. Don't say anything. Saying "it'll be okay," or "I know how you feel" can backfire. Right now that's not what a victim wants to hear. They want to know people are there and care about them. Be there, be present, listen. The clergy refer to it as a "ministry of presence." You don't need to do anything, just be there or have them know you're available.[86]

**Prompting**    Advising, judging, analyzing, questioning, and comforting are all active approaches to helping that call for a great deal of input from the respondent. Another approach to problem solving is more passive. **Prompting** involves using silences and brief statements of encouragement to draw others out, and in so doing to help them solve their own problems. Consider this example:

**Pablo:** Julie's dad is selling a complete computer system for only $1,200, but if I want it I have to buy it now. He's got another interested buyer. It's a great deal. But buying it would wipe out my savings. At the rate I spend money, it would take me a year to save up this much again.

**Tim:** Uh huh.

**Pablo:** I wouldn't be able to take that ski trip over winter break . . . but I sure could save time with my schoolwork . . . and do a better job, too.

**Tim:** That's for sure.

**Pablo:** Do you think I should buy it?

**Tim:** I don't know. What do you think?

**Pablo:** I just can't decide.

**Tim:** *(silence)*

**Pablo:** I'm going to do it. I'll never get a deal like this again.

> cultural idiom
>
> **wipe out:**
> deplete

Prompting works especially well when you can't help others make a decision. At times like this your presence can act like a catalyst to help others find their own answers. Prompting will work best when it's done sincerely. Your nonverbal behaviors—eye contact, posture, facial expression, tone of voice—have to show that you are concerned with the other person's problem. Mechanical prompting is likely to irritate instead of help.

**Reflecting**    A few pages ago you read about the value of paraphrasing to understand others. The same approach can be used as a helping tool. We will use the term **reflecting** to describe it here, to emphasize that the goal is not as much to clarify your understanding as to help the other person hear and think about the words he or she has just spoken. When you use this approach, be sure to reflect both the *thoughts* and the *feelings* you hear being expressed. This conversation between two friends shows how reflecting can offer support and help a person find the answer to her own problem:

**Jill:** I've had the strangest feeling about my boss lately.

**Mark:** What's that? *(A simple question invites Jill to go on.)*

**Jill:** I'm starting to think maybe he has this thing about women—or maybe it's just about me.

> cultural idiom
**coming on to:**
making a sexual advance to

**Mark:** You mean he's coming on to you? *(Mark paraphrases what he thinks Jill has said.)*

**Jill:** Oh no, not at all! But it seems like he doesn't take women—or at least me—seriously. *(Jill corrects Mark's misunderstanding and explains herself.)*

**Mark:** What do you mean? *(Mark asks another simple question to get more information.)*

**Jill:** Well, whenever we're in a meeting or just talking around the office and he asks for ideas, he always seems to pick men. He gives orders to women—men, too—but he never asks the women to say what they think.

**Mark:** So you think maybe he doesn't take women seriously, is that it? *(Mark paraphrases Jill's last statement.)*

> cultural idiom
**a male chauvinist pig:**
a male who believes that men are superior to women

**Jill:** Yeah. Well, he sure doesn't seem interested in their ideas. But that doesn't mean he's a total woman-hater or a male chauvinist pig. I know he counts on some women in the office. Our accountant Teresa has been there forever, and he's always saying he couldn't live without her. And when Brenda got the new computer system up and running last month, I know he appreciated that. He gave her a day off and told everybody how she saved our lives.

**Mark:** Now you sound confused. *(Reflects her apparent feeling.)*

**Jill:** I am confused. I don't think it's just my imagination. I mean I'm a good producer, but he has never—not once—asked me for my ideas about how to improve sales or anything. And I can't remember a time when he's asked any other women. But maybe I'm overreacting.

**Mark:** You're not positive whether you're right, but I can tell that this has you concerned. *(Mark paraphrases both Jill's central theme and her feeling.)*

**Jill:** Yes. But I don't know what to do about it.

**Mark:** Maybe you should . . . *(Starts to offer advice but catches himself and decides to ask a sincere question instead.)* So what are your choices?

**Jill:** Well, I could just ask him if he's aware that he never asks women's opinions. But that might sound too aggressive and angry.

**Mark:** And you're not angry? *(Tries to clarify how Jill is feeling.)*

**Jill:** Not really. I don't know whether I should be angry because he's not taking ideas seriously, or whether he just doesn't take my ideas seriously, or whether it's nothing at all.

**Mark:** So you're mostly confused. *(Reflects Jill's apparent feeling again.)*

> cultural idiom
**where I stand with:**
how I am perceived by

**Jill:** Yes! I don't know where I stand with my boss, and not being sure is starting to get to me. I wish I knew what he thinks of me. Maybe I could just tell him I'm confused about what is going on here and ask him to clear it up. But what if it's nothing? Then I'll look insecure.

**Mark:** *(Mark thinks Jill should confront her boss, but he isn't positive that this is the best approach, so he paraphrases what Jill seems to be saying.)* And that would make you look bad.

**Jill:** I'm afraid maybe it would. I wonder if I could talk it over with anybody else in the office and get their ideas . . .

**Mark:** . . . see what they think . . .

**Jill:** Yeah. Maybe I could ask Brenda. She's easy to talk to, and I do respect her judgment. Maybe she could give me some ideas about how to handle this.

**Mark:** Sounds like you're comfortable with talking to Brenda first.

**Jill:** *(Warming to the idea.)* Yes! Then if it's nothing, I can calm down. But if I do need to talk to the boss, I'll know I'm doing the right thing.

**Mark:** Great. Let me know how it goes.

Reflecting a speaker's ideas and feelings in this way can be surprisingly help-ful.[87] First, reflecting helps the other person to sort out the problem. In the dia-logue you just read, Mark's paraphrasing helped Jill pin down the real source of her concern: what her boss thinks of her, not whether he doesn't take women seriously. The clarity that comes from this sort of perspective can make it possible to find solutions that weren't apparent before. Reflecting is also helpful because it helps the person to unload more of the concerns he or she has been carrying around, often leading to the relief that comes from catharsis. Finally, listeners who reflect the speaker's thoughts and feelings (instead of judging or analyzing, for example) show their involvement and concern.

> cultural idiom
**pin down:**
identify specifically

Reflecting can be helpful, but it is no panacea. A study by noted researcher John Gottman revealed that this approach is not an end in itself; rather, it is one way to help others by understanding them better.[88]

There are several factors to consider before you decide to paraphrase:

① *Is the problem complex enough?* Sometimes people are simply looking for in-formation and not trying to work out their feelings. At times like this, para-phrasing would be out of place.

② *Do you have the necessary time and concern?* The kind of paraphrasing we've been discussing here takes a good deal of time and can be stressful.[89] There-fore, if you're in a hurry to do something besides listen, it's wise to avoid starting a conversation you won't be able to finish. It's far better to state hon-estly that you're unable or unwilling to help than to pretend to care when you really don't.

③ *Are you genuinely interested in helping the other person?* Remember that reflect-ing is a form of helping someone else. The general obligation to reciprocate the other person's self-disclosure with information of your own isn't neces-sary when the goal is to solve a problem. Research shows that speakers who reveal highly intimate personal information don't expect, or even appreci-ate, the same kind of disclosure from a conversational partner.[90]

④ *Can you withhold judgment?* Use this style only if you can comfortably para-phrase without injecting your own judgments. It's sometimes tempting to rephrase others' comments in a way that leads them toward the solution you think is best without ever clearly stating your intentions. As you will read in Chapter 8, this kind of strategy is likely to backfire by causing defensive-ness if it's discovered. If you think the situation meets the criteria for advice described earlier in this chapter, you should offer your suggestions openly.

⑤ *Is your paraphrasing in proportion to other responses?* Although reflecting can be a very helpful way of responding to others' problems, it can become artifi-cial and annoying when it's overused.

## When and How to Help

Before committing yourself to helping another person—even someone in obvious distress—make sure your support is welcome. In one survey, some people reported occasions when social support wasn't necessary, because they felt capable of han-dling the problem by themselves.[91] Many regarded uninvited help as an intrusion, and some said it left them feeling more nervous than before. The majority of respon-dents expressed a preference for being in control of whether their distressing situa-tion should be discussed with even the most helpful friend. In general, women are more likely to seek social support from friends and family members than are men.[92]

When help is welcome, there is no single best way to provide it. Research shows that *all* styles can help others accept their situation, feel better, and have a sense of control over their problems.[93] There is enormous variability in which style will

**ON YOUR FEET**

*Helpful Listeners*

Describe an incident in which another person's listening was helpful to you. What was the challenge you were facing? Who was the listener? What did he or she do that proved most helpful?

work with a given person.[94] This fact explains why communicators who are able to use a wide variety of helping styles are usually more effective than those who rely on just one or two styles.[95]

You can boost the odds of choosing the best helping style in each situation by considering three factors.

① *The situation*: Sometimes people need your advice. At other times your encouragement and comforting will be most helpful, and at still other times your analysis or judgment may be truly useful. And, as you have seen, there are times when your prompting and reflecting can help others find their own answer.

② *The other person*: Some people are able to consider advice thoughtfully, whereas others use suggestions to avoid making their own decisions. Many communicators are extremely defensive and aren't capable of receiving analysis or judgments without lashing out. Still others aren't equipped to think through problems clearly.

③ *Your own strengths and weaknesses*: You may be best at listening quietly, offering a prompt from time to time. Or perhaps you are especially insightful and can offer a truly useful analysis of the problem. Of course, it's also possible to rely on a response style that is unhelpful. You may be overly judgmental or too eager to advise, even when your suggestions aren't invited or productive.

In most cases, the best way to help is to use a combination of responses in a way that meets the needs of the occasion and suits your personal communication style.[96]

This chapter began by introducing David Isay, the developer of StoryCorps. As we close, keep in mind Isay's conviction that listening is more than hearing. It can be a way of connecting with others and showing respect. Swedish author Henning Mankell, who lives in Mozambique, describes the rich tradition of storytelling that thrives in that part of the world. "In Africa, listening is a guiding principle," he says.[97] Storytelling is a daily means of entertainment and education. Mankell shares this example of a conversation between two men in Mozambique:

> I heard the two men talking about a third old man who had recently died. One of them said, "I was visiting him at his home. He started to tell me an amazing story about something that had happened to him when he was young. It was a long story. Night came, and we decided that I should come back the next day to hear the end. But when I arrived, he was dead."

After a few moments of reflective silence, the other man said: "That's not a good way to die—before you've told the end of your story."

## Summary

Even the best message is useless if it goes unreceived or if it is misunderstood. For this reason, listening—the process of giving meaning to an oral message—is a vitally important part of the communication process. We began our look at the subject by identifying and refuting several myths about listening. Our conclusion here was that effective listening is a skill that needs to be developed in order for us to be truly effective in understanding others.

We next took a close look at five steps in the process of listening: hearing, attending, understanding, responding, and remembering. We described some of the challenges that make effective listening so difficult. We described seven faulty listening behaviors and nine more reasons why people often listen poorly. You can become a better listener by recognizing which of these faulty behaviors and reasons characterize your communication.

This chapter also discussed several types of listening: task-oriented, relational, analytic, and critical. Effective listeners practice the techniques appropriate to each and are good at choosing listening goals that are appropriate for the circumstances.

Task-oriented listening helps people accomplish mutual goals. It involves an active approach in which people often identify key ideas, ask questions, and take notes. It may also involve either questioning or paraphrasing—restating the speaker's message in your own words.

Relational listening involves the willingness to spend time with people to better understand their feelings and perspectives. It is most effective when the listener is patient, encourages the speaker to continue, and is sensitive to underlying meanings.

Analytic listening involves the willingness to suspend judgment and consider a variety of perspectives to achieve a clear understanding. This type of listening requires people to discern between what is true and what is not.

Critical listening is appropriate when the goal is to judge the quality of an idea. A critical analysis will be most successful when the listener ensures correct understanding of a message before passing judgment, when the speaker's credibility is taken into account, when the quality of supporting evidence is examined, and when the logic of the speaker's arguments is examined carefully.

The aim of supportive listening is to help the speaker, not the receiver. Various helping responses include advising, judging, analyzing, questioning, comforting, prompting, and reflecting the speaker's thoughts and feelings. Listeners can be most helpful when they use a variety of styles, focus on the emotional dimensions of a message, and avoid being too judgmental.

## Key Terms

**advising response** Helping response in which the receiver offers suggestions about how the speaker should deal with a problem. *p. 155*

**ambushing** A style in which the receiver listens carefully to gather information to use in an attack on the speaker. *p. 139*

**analytical listening** Listening in which the primary goal is to fully understand the message, prior to any evaluation. *p. 149.*

**analyzing statement** A helping style in which the listener offers an interpretation of a speaker's message. *p. 156*

**attending** The process of focusing on certain stimuli from the environment. *p. 136*

**comforting** A response style in which a listener reassures, supports, or distracts the person seeking help. *p. 158*

**counterfeit question** A question that disguises the speaker's true motives, which do not include a genuine desire to understand the other person. *p. 145*

**critical listening** Listening in which the goal is to *evaluate* the quality or accuracy of the speaker's remarks. *p. 151*

**defensive listening** A response style in which the receiver perceives a speaker's comments as an attack. *p. 139*

**hearing** The process wherein sound waves strike the eardrum and cause vibrations that are transmitted to the brain. *p. 135*

**insensitive listening** The failure to recognize the thoughts or feelings that are not directly expressed by a speaker, and instead accepting the speaker's words at face value. *p. 139*

**insulated listening** A style in which the receiver ignores undesirable information. *p. 139*

**judging response** A reaction in which the receiver evaluates the sender's message either favorably or unfavorably. *p. 156*

**listening** The process wherein the brain reconstructs electrochemical impulses generated by hearing into representations of the original sound and gives them meaning. *p. 135*

**listening fidelity** The degree of congruence between what a listener understands and what the message sender was attempting to communicate. *p. 136*

**mindful listening** Active, high-level information processing. *p. 138*

**mindless listening** Passive, low-level information processing. *p. 138*

**paraphrasing** Feedback in which the receiver rewords the speaker's thoughts and feelings. Feedback can be used to verify understanding, demonstrate empathy, and help others solve their problems. *p. 146*

**prompting** Using silence and brief statements of encouragement to draw out a speaker. *p. 159*

**pseudolistening** An imitation of true listening in which the receiver's mind is elsewhere. *p. 138*

**questioning** A style of helping in which the receiver seeks additional information from the sender. Some questioning responses are really disguised advice. *p. 144*

**reflecting** Listening that helps the person speaking hear and think about the words just spoken. *p. 159*

**relational listening** A listening style that is driven primarily by the concern to build emotional closeness with the speaker. *p. 148*

**remembering** The act of recalling previously introduced information. Recall drops off in two phases: short term and long term. *p. 137*

**residual message** The part of a message a receiver can recall after short- and long-term memory loss. *p. 137*

**responding** Providing observable feedback to another person's behavior or speech. *p. 136*

**selective listening** A listening style in which the receiver responds only to messages that interest him or her. *p. 139*

**sincere question** A question posed with the genuine desire to learn from another person. See also *Counterfeit question. p. 145*

**stage hogging** A listening style in which the receiver is more concerned with making his or her own point than with understanding the speaker. *p. 139*

**supportive listening** The reception approach to use when others seek help for personal dilemmas. *p. 153*

**task-oriented listening** A listening style that is primarily concerned with accomplishing the task at hand. *p. 143*

**understanding** The act of interpreting a message by following syntactic, semantic, and pragmatic rules. *p. 136*

## Check Your Understanding

1. Which of the listening misconceptions listed on pages 135–137 characterize your attitudes about listening? What can you do to change your thinking and behavior?

2. Which challenges to the listening process described on pages 138–143 present the greatest challenges to your effectiveness? Develop an action plan for managing them.

3. Which of the faulty behaviors described on pages 138–140 characterize your listening? How can you overcome them?

4. Which factors described on pages 140–143 contribute most to your ineffective listening? How can you cope with them?

5. On your own or with feedback from others who know you well, assess your ability to listen for each of the following goals: to accomplish a task, enhance relationships, analyze ideas, and critically evaluate messages. Which types of listening are your strongest and weakest? Develop an action plan to improve your skill in the most critical areas.

6. What responses do you typically use when offering social support? How effective are they? How can you improve your skill at offering social support?

## Activities

1. **Recognizing Listening Misconceptions** You can see how listening misconceptions affect your life by identifying important situations when you have fallen for each of the following assumptions. In each case, describe the consequences of believing these erroneous assumptions.

   a. Thinking that because you were hearing a message you were listening to it.

   b. Believing that listening effectively is natural and effortless.

   c. Assuming that other listeners were understanding a message in the same way as you.

2. **Your L.Q. (Listening Quotient)** Explain the poor listening behaviors listed on pages 138–140 to someone who knows you well. Then ask your informant to describe which, if any, of them you use. Also explore the consequences of your listening behavior.

3. **Your Listening Preferences** Analyze your effectiveness as a listener by answering the following questions.

   1. Which of the listening styles described on pages 143–153 do you use?

   2. Does your listening style change in various situations, or do you use the same style most or all of the time?

   3. What are the consequences (beneficial and harmful) of the listening styles you use?

   4. How could you adapt your listening styles to improve your communication effectiveness?

4. **Informational Listening Practice** Listening carefully for information isn't easy. It takes hard work and concentration. You can improve your skill in this important area and convince yourself of the difference good informational listening makes by following these steps.

   1. Find a partner with whom you have an important relationship. This may be a family member, lover, friend, fellow worker, or even an "enemy" with whom you interact frequently.

   2. Invite your partner to explain his or her side of an issue that the two of you have difficulty discussing. Your job during this conversation is to understand your partner. You should not even attempt to explain your position. (If you find the prospect of trying to understand the other person distressing, consider how this attitude might interfere with your ability to listen carefully.)

   3. As your partner explains his or her point of view, use the skills outlined on pages 143–153 to help you understand. You can discover how well you are grasping your partner's position by occasionally

paraphrasing what you think he or she is saying. If your partner verifies your paraphrase as correct, go on with the conversation. If not, try to listen again and play back the message until the partner confirms your understanding.

4. After the conversation is over, ask yourself the following questions:

a. As you listened, how accurate was your first understanding of the speaker's statements?

b. How did your understanding of the speaker's position change after you used paraphrasing?

c. Did you find that the gap between your position and that of your partner narrowed as a result of your both using paraphrasing?

d. How did you feel at the end of your conversation? How does this feeling compare to your usual emotional state after discussing controversial issues with others?

e. How might your life change if you used paraphrasing at home? At work? With friends?

5. **Supportive Response Styles** This exercise will help improve your ability to listen empathically in the most successful manner. For each of the following statements:

1. Write separate responses, using each of the following styles:

a. Advising

b. Judging

c. Analyzing

d. Questioning

e. Comforting

f. Prompting

g. Reflecting

2. Discuss the pros and cons of using each response style.

3. Identify which response seems most effective, explaining your decision.

a. At a party, a guest you have just met for the first time says, "Everybody seems like they've been friends for years. I don't know anybody here. How about you?"

b. Your best friend has been quiet lately. When you ask if anything is wrong, she snaps, "No!" in an irritated tone of voice.

c. A fellow worker says, "The boss keeps making sexual remarks to me. I think it's a come-on, and I don't know what to do."

d. It's registration time at college. One of your friends asks if you think he should enroll in the communication class you've taken.

e. Someone with whom you live remarks, "It seems like this place is always a mess. We get it cleaned up, and then an hour later it's trashed."

## For Further Exploration

For more resources about listening, see the *Understanding Human Communication* website at www.oup.com/us/adler. There you will find a variety of resources: "Media Room" clips from popular films and television shows to further illustrate important concepts, a list of books and articles, links to descriptions of feature films and television shows at the *Now Playing* website, study aids, and a self-test to check your understanding of the material in this chapter.

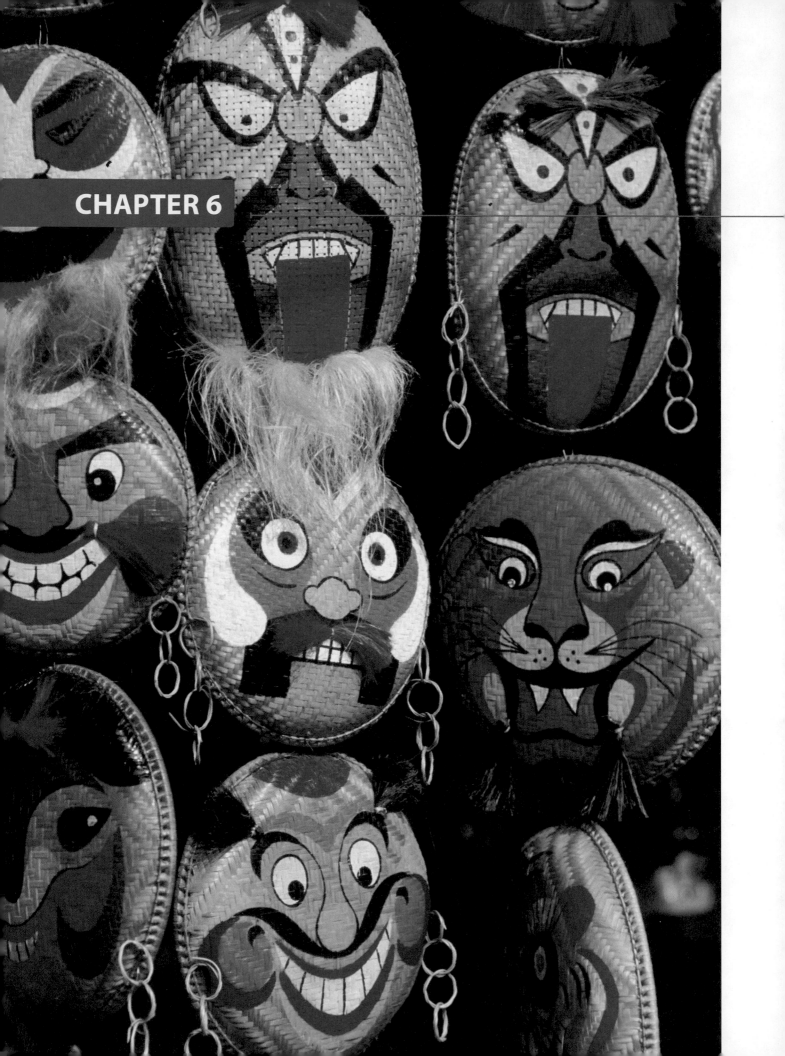

# Nonverbal
# Communication

## Chapter Outline

### LEARNING OBJECTIVES

1 Explain the characteristics of nonverbal communication, outlined on pages 169–173.

2 Describe the functions served by nonverbal communication.

3 Explain the ways in which culture and gender affect nonverbal communication.

4 Identify nonverbal behaviors in a communication exchange and assess their possible meanings.

The detective twirls a pen in his fingers. His feet are on the desk in front of him as he talks on the phone. His relaxed demeanor is in sharp contrast to the furtive movements and quick responses of the suspect on the other end of the line.

So goes a pivotal scene in the movie *Fight Club*, in which Thom Gossom Jr. (shown here) plays Detective Stern. In this scene, the way his character talks and behaves communicates as much as, or even more than, the words he uses.

Gossom says nonverbal communication is important to his success as an actor. But his appreciation for nonverbal communication doesn't end at the movie set or stage door. He uses similar skills in everyday life.

One example is a technique called playing against the scene. Gossom explains, "That's when you act the opposite of what's expected—say, calm in a tense setting or jovial in a sad one." Actors accomplish this mostly through nonverbal cues. In the *Fight Club* scene, Gossom purposefully adopted casual, slow mannerisms, even though it was an emotionally loaded situation. In real life, he says, playing against the scene can keep arguments from escalating, inspire enthusiasm when people are discouraged, and capture people's attention.

"Acting is about controlling your emotional expressions and using them in the right way," Gossom says. "That's part of life, too. Some people feel they need to scream to get their point across. But I think that when you're calm and people lean forward to hear you, you're even more powerful."

Gossom learned a lot about nonverbal communication growing up. He was raised in Birmingham, Alabama, when the city was "fiercely segregated."[1] Being a minority in the midst of racial tensions taught him to pay close attention to nonverbal cues. "Especially at first, I didn't speak as much as other people. I'd stay quiet for a time and get a feel for things first. I observed everything."

After high school, Gossom became one of the first two African American football players at Auburn University. Making the team was a dream come true, he says. But although fans cheered for him from the stands, discrimination off the field persisted. Again, he learned to be a good listener and observer to avoid trouble. Those were difficult times, he says, but the communication skills he developed have served him well. Because he pays attention to subtle cues that other people often overlook, Gossom has the capacity to "go into the depth and soul of a character" he creates as an actor or writer. He feels the same skills benefit him in everyday life.

*Thom Gossom Jr.'s experiences both on and off stage have taught him about the importance of skillful nonverbal communication. As you read this chapter, consider these questions:*

- What nonverbal cues catch your attention most? What do you tend to overlook?

- How do your nonverbal actions affect others?

- How do you play with the scene in your everyday nonverbal communication? Are there cases in which it might be better to play against the scene?

You don't have to be a trained actor to realize that there's often a gap between what people say and what they feel. An acquaintance says, "I'd like to get together again" in a way that leaves you suspecting the opposite. (But how do you know?) A speaker tries to appear confident but acts in a way that almost screams out, "I'm nervous!" (What tells you this?) You ask a friend what's wrong, and the "nothing" you get in response rings hollow. (Why does it sound untrue?)

> cultural idiom
> **rings hollow:**
> sounds insincere

Then, of course, there are times when another's message comes through even though there are no words at all. A look of irritation, a smile, a sigh—signs like these can say more than a torrent of words.

All situations like these have one element in common—the message was sent nonverbally. The goal of this chapter is to introduce you to this world of nonverbal communication. Although you have certainly recognized nonverbal messages before, the following pages should introduce you to a richness of information you have never noticed. And though your experience won't transform you into a mind reader, it will make you a far more accurate observer of others—and yourself.

We need to begin our study of *nonverbal communication* by defining this term. At first this might seem like a simple task. If *non* means "not" and *verbal* means "words," then *nonverbal communication* appears to mean "communication without words." This is a good starting point after we distinguish between vocal communication (by mouth) and verbal communication (with words). After this distinction is made, it becomes clear that some nonverbal messages are vocal, and some are not. Likewise, although many verbal messages are vocal, some aren't. Table 6-1 illustrates these differences.

What about languages that don't involve spoken words? For example, is American Sign Language considered verbal or nonverbal communication? Most scholars would say sign language is verbal,[2] which helps to narrow our working definition of **nonverbal communication**: "messages expressed through nonlinguistic means." This rules out not only sign languages but also written words, but it includes messages transmitted by vocal means that don't involve language—sighs, laughs, and other utterances we will discuss soon.

## Characteristics of Nonverbal Communication

Our brief definition only hints at the richness of nonverbal messages. You can begin to understand their prevalence by trying a simple experiment. Spend an hour or so around a group of people who are speaking a language you don't understand. Your goal is to see how much information you can learn about the people you're observing from means other than the verbal messages they transmit. This experiment will reveal several characteristics of nonverbal communication.

Table 6-1   **Types of Communication**

|  | VOCAL COMMUNICATION | NONVOCAL COMMUNICATION |
|---|---|---|
| **VERBAL COMMUNICATION** | Spoken words | Written words |
| **NONVERBAL COMMUNICATION** | Tone of voice, sighs, screams, vocal qualities (loudness, pitch, and so on) | Gestures, movement, appearance, facial expression, and so on |

*Source*: Adapted from John Stewart, J., & D'Angelo, G. (1980). *Together: Communicating interpersonally* (2nd ed.). Reading, MA: Addison-Wesley, p. 22. Copyright © 1993 by McGraw-Hill. Reprinted/adapted by permission.

## Nonverbal Behavior Has Communicative Value

It's virtually impossible not to communicate nonverbally.[3] Suppose you were instructed to avoid communicating any messages at all. What would you do? Close your eyes? Withdraw into a ball? Leave the room? As the photo on page 171 illustrates, the meaning of some nonverbal behavior can be ambiguous. You may not be able to tell exactly what is going on, but the nonverbal cues certainly have communicative value.

Of course, we don't always intend to send nonverbal messages. Unintentional nonverbal behaviors differ from intentional ones.[4] For example, we often stammer, blush, frown, and sweat without meaning to do so. Some theorists argue that unintentional behavior may provide information, but it shouldn't count as communication. Others draw the boundaries of nonverbal communication more broadly, suggesting that even unconscious and unintentional behavior conveys messages and thus is worth studying as communication.[5] We take the broad view here because, whether or not nonverbal behavior is intentional, we use it to form impressions about one another.

Although nonverbal behavior reveals information, we aren't always conscious of what we are communicating nonverbally. In one study, less than a quarter of experimental subjects who had been instructed to show increased or decreased liking of a partner could describe the nonverbal behaviors they used.[6] Furthermore, just because communicators are nonverbally expressive doesn't mean that others will tune in to the abundance of unspoken messages that are available. One study comparing the richness of e-mail to in-person communication confirmed the greater amount of information available in face-to-face conversations, but it also showed that some communicators (primarily men) failed to recognize these messages.[7]

The fact that you and everyone around you are constantly sending nonverbal clues is important because it means that you have a constant source of information available about yourself and others. If you can tune in to these signals, you will be more aware of how those around you are feeling and thinking, and you will be better able to respond to their behavior.

## Nonverbal Communication Is Primarily Relational

Some nonverbal messages serve utilitarian functions. For example, a police officer uses gestures to direct the flow of traffic, and a conductor leads members of a symphony. But nonverbal communication also serves a far more common (and more interesting) series of social functions.[8]

One important social function of nonverbal communication involves identity management. Chapter 2 discussed how we strive to create an image of ourselves as we want others to view us. Nonverbal communication plays an important role in this process—in many cases it is more important than verbal communication. Consider, for example, what happens when you attend a party where you are likely to meet strangers you would like to get to know better. Instead of projecting your image verbally ("Hi! I'm attractive, friendly, and easygoing"), you behave in ways that will present this identity. You might smile a lot and try to strike a relaxed pose. It's also likely that you will dress carefully—even if the image involves looking as if you hadn't given a lot of attention to your appearance.

Along with identity management, nonverbal communication allows us to define the kind of relationships we want to have with others. You can appreciate this fact by thinking about the wide range of ways you

The title character in the animated film *Wall-E* barely speaks. Nonetheless, this loveable robot expresses a wealth of emotions. What meanings can you deduce from the nonverbal behaviors of others? What nonverbal messages do you express?

> cultural idiom

**tune in to:**
pay attention to

Stop for a moment to observe your own nonverbal cues. What might someone deduce from your posture, your facial expression, your clothing, and other cues? Do you think those impressions would be accurate?

could behave when greeting another person. You could wave, shake hands, nod, smile, pat the other person on the back, give a hug, or avoid all contact. Even trying to *not* communicate can send a message. For example, when Thom Gossom was a college freshman, he spotted some of his teammates in biology class. "I moved in their direction, but they dropped their heads and averted their eyes," he recalls. "They didn't want me sitting with them."

Nonverbal communication performs a third valuable social function: conveying emotions that we may be unwilling or unable to express—or ones we may not even be aware of. In fact, nonverbal communication is much better suited to expressing attitudes and feelings than ideas.[9] You can prove this for yourself by imagining how you could express each item on the following list nonverbally:

- You're bored.
- You are opposed to capital punishment.
- You are attracted to another person in the group.
- You want to know if you will be tested on this material.
- You are nervous about trying this experiment.

The first, third, and fifth items in this list all involve attitudes; you could probably imagine how each could be expressed nonverbally through what social scientists call **affect displays**—facial expressions, body movements, and vocal traits described in this chapter. By contrast, the second and fourth items involve ideas, and they would be quite difficult to convey without using words. The same principle holds in everyday life: Nonverbal behavior offers many cues about the way people feel—often more than we get from their words alone.

## Nonverbal Communication Is Ambiguous

Before you get the idea that this chapter will turn you into a mind reader, it is important to realize that nonverbal communication is often difficult to interpret accurately. To appreciate the ambiguous nature of nonverbal communication, study the photo at right. What emotions do you imagine the couple is feeling: Grief? Anguish? Agony? In fact, none of these is even close. They just learned that they won $1 million in the New Jersey state lottery!

Nonverbal communication can be just as ambiguous in everyday life. For example, relying on nonverbal cues in romantic situations can lead to inaccurate guesses about a partner's interest in a sexual relationship.[10] Workers of the Safeway supermarket chain discovered firsthand the problems with nonverbal ambiguity when they tried to follow the company's new "superior customer service" policy that required them to smile and make eye contact with customers. Twelve employees filed grievances over the policy, reporting that several customers had propositioned them, misinterpreting their actions as come-ons.[11]

Although all nonverbal behavior is ambiguous, some emotions are easier to decode accurately than others. In laboratory experiments, subjects are better at identifying positive facial expressions such as happiness, love, surprise, and interest than negative ones such as fear, sadness, anger, and disgust.[12] In real life, however, spontaneous nonverbal expressions are so ambiguous that observers are able to identify the emotions they convey no more accurately than by blind guessing.[13]

Some people are more skillful than others at accurately decoding nonverbal behavior.[14] For example, those who are

> cultural idiom
> **come-ons:**
> sexual advances
> **blind guessing:**
> coming to a conclusion without any factual basis for judgment

What emotions do you imagine this couple is feeling?

better senders of nonverbal messages also are better receivers. Decoding ability also increases with age and training, although there are still differences in ability owing to personality and occupation. For instance, extroverts are relatively accurate judges of nonverbal behavior, whereas dogmatists are not. Interestingly, women seem to be better than men at decoding nonverbal messages. More than 95 percent of the studies examined in one analysis showed that women are more accurate at interpreting nonverbal signals.[15] Despite these differences, even the best nonverbal decoders do not approach 100 percent accuracy.

When you do try to make sense out of ambiguous nonverbal behavior, you need to consider several factors: the context in which the behaviors occur (e.g., smiling at a joke suggests a different feeling from what is suggested by smiling at another's misfortune); the history of your relationship with the sender (e.g., friendly, hostile); the other's mood at the time; and your feelings (when you're feeling insecure, almost anything can seem like a threat). The important idea is that when you become aware of nonverbal messages, you should think of them not as facts but rather as clues that need to be checked out.

## Nonverbal Communication Is Different from Verbal Communication

As Table 6-2 shows, nonverbal communication differs in several important ways from spoken and written language. These differences suggest some reasons why it is so valuable to focus on nonverbal behavior. For example, whereas verbal messages are almost always intentional, nonverbal cues are often unintended, and sometimes unconscious.

## Nonverbal Skills Are Important

It's hard to overemphasize the importance of effective nonverbal expression and the ability to read and respond to others' nonverbal behavior. Nonverbal encoding and decoding skills are strong predictors of popularity, attractiveness, and socio-emotional well-being.[16] Good nonverbal communicators are more persuasive than people who are less skilled, and they have a greater chance of success in settings ranging from careers to poker to romance. Nonverbal sensitivity is a major part of what some social scientists have called "emotional intelligence," and researchers have come to recognize that it is impossible to study spoken language without paying attention to its nonverbal dimensions.[17]

One way to appreciate the importance of nonverbal skills is to see the challenges faced by people who lack them. Due to a processing deficit in the right hemisphere of the brain, people born with a syndrome called nonverbal learning

Table 6-2  **Some Differences Between Verbal and Nonverbal Communication**

|  | **VERBAL COMMUNICATION** | **NONVERBAL COMMUNICATION** |
|---|---|---|
| **COMPLEXITY** | One dimension (words only) | Multiple dimensions (voice, posture, gestures, distance, etc.) |
| **FLOW** | Intermittent (speaking and silence alternate) | Continuous (it's impossible not to communicate nonverbally) |
| **CLARITY** | Less subject to misinterpretation | More ambiguous |
| **IMPACT** | Has less impact when verbal and nonverbal cues are contradictory | Has stronger impact when verbal and nonverbal cues are contradictory |
| **INTENTIONALITY** | Usually deliberate | Often unintentional |

disorder (NVLD) have trouble making sense of nonverbal cues.[18] People with NVLD often misinterpret humorous or sarcastic messages literally, because those cues are based heavily on nonverbal signals.

People with NVLD also have trouble figuring out how to behave appropriately in new social situations, so they rely on rote formulas that often don't work. For example, a child who has learned the formal way of meeting an adult for the first time by shaking hands and saying, "Pleased to meet you" might try this approach with a group of peers. The result, of course, is to be regarded as odd or nerdy. And their disability leads them to miss nonverbal cues sent by other children that this isn't the right approach.[19]

Even for those of us who don't suffer from NVLD, the nuances of nonverbal behavior can be confusing.

# Influences on Nonverbal Communication

Much nonverbal communication is universal. For example, researchers have found at least six facial expressions that humans everywhere use and understand: happiness, sadness, fear, anger, disgust, and surprise.[20] Even children who have been blind since birth reveal their feelings using these expressions. Despite these similarities, there are some important differences in the way people use and understand nonverbal behavior. We'll look at some of these differences now.

## Culture

Cultures have different nonverbal languages as well as verbal ones. Fiorello LaGuardia, legendary mayor of New York from 1933 to 1945, was fluent in English, Italian, and Yiddish. Researchers who watched films of his campaign speeches with the sound turned off found that they could tell which language he was speaking by the changes in his nonverbal behavior.[21]

The meaning of some gestures varies from one culture to another. The "okay" gesture made by joining thumb and forefinger to form a circle is a cheery affirmation to most Americans, but it has less positive meanings in other parts of the world.[22] In France and Belgium it means, "You're worth zero." In Greece and Turkey it is a vulgar sexual invitation, usually meant as an insult. Given this sort of cross-cultural ambiguity, it's easy to imagine how an innocent tourist might wind up in serious trouble.

Less obvious cross-cultural differences can damage relationships without the parties ever recognizing exactly what has gone wrong. Edward Hall points out that, whereas Americans are comfortable conducting business at a distance of roughly 4 feet, people from the Middle East stand much closer.[23]

> cultural idiom

**wind up in:**
end up being in

*Source:* DILBERT © Scott Adams/Dist. by United Feature Syndicate, Inc.

It is easy to visualize the awkward advance-and-retreat pattern that might occur when two diplomats or businesspeople from these cultures meet. The Middle Easterner would probably keep moving forward to close the gap that feels so wide, whereas the American would continually back away. Both would feel uncomfortable, probably without knowing why.

Like distance, patterns of eye contact vary around the world.[24] A direct gaze is considered appropriate for speakers in Latin America, the Arab world, and southern Europe. On the other hand, Asians, Indians, Pakistanis, and northern Europeans gaze at a listener peripherally or not at all. In either case, deviations from the norm are likely to make a listener uncomfortable.

Even within a culture, various groups can have different nonverbal rules. For example, many white teachers in the United States use quasi-questions that hint at the information they are seeking. An elementary teacher might encourage the class to speak up by making an incorrect statement that demands refutation: "So twelve divided by four is six, right?" Most white students would recognize this behavior as a way of testing their understanding. But this style of questioning is unfamiliar to many students raised in traditional black cultures, who aren't likely to respond until they are directly questioned by the teacher.[25] Given this difference, it is easy to imagine how some teachers might view minority children as unresponsive or slow, when in fact they are simply playing by a different set of rules.

Communicators become more tolerant of others after they understand that many nonverbal behaviors that seem unusual are the result of cultural differences. In one study, American adults were presented with videotaped scenes of speakers from the United States, France, and Germany.[26] When the sound was cut off, viewers judged foreigners more negatively than their fellow citizens. But when the speakers' voices were added (allowing viewers to recognize that they were from a different country), the critical ratings dropped.

Despite differences like these, many nonverbal behaviors have the same meanings around the world. Smiles and laughter are a universal signal of positive emotions, for example, whereas the same sour expressions convey displeasure in every culture.[27] Charles Darwin believed that expressions like these are the result of evolution, functioning as survival mechanisms that allowed early humans to convey emotional states before the development of language.

Although nonverbal expressions like these may be universal, the way they are used varies widely around the world. In some cultures, display rules discourage the overt demonstration of feelings like happiness or anger. In other cultures, the same feelings are perfectly appropriate. Thus, a person from Japan might appear much more controlled and placid than an Arab, when in fact their feelings might be identical.[28]

The same principle operates closer to home among cocultures. For example, observations have shown that black women in all-black groups are nonverbally more expressive and interrupt one another more than do white women in all-white groups.[29] This doesn't mean that black women always feel more intensely than their white counterparts. A more likely explanation is that the two groups follow different cultural rules. The researchers found that, in racially mixed groups, both black and white women moved closer to the others' style. This nonverbal convergence shows that skilled communicators can adapt their behavior when interacting with members of other cultures or cocultures in order to make the exchange smoother and more effective.

## Gender

It's easy to identify stereotypical differences in masculine and feminine styles of nonverbal communication. Just think about exaggerated caricatures of macho men and delicate women that appear in animated films such as *Tarzan* and *The Little*

## Understanding Diversity

### How Accurate Is Gaydar?

Many gay and lesbian people claim they can spot kindred spirits at a glance. Some evidence does suggest that it's possible to identify sexual orientation by simply looking at a person. Experimental subjects in several studies did better than chance at guessing a person's sexual orientation after seeing facial photographs for fractions of a second.[30]

Other research has provided mixed evidence about the accuracy of gaydar. For example, the intuition of gay and lesbian guessers varies widely, and the gap between them and heterosexual observers vanishes as more information becomes available.[31] The accuracy of detecting sexual orientation drops significantly when subjects try to identify people whose appearance doesn't match stereotypes.[32] This may help explain the surprised reactions many gay men and lesbians report when they "come out" and publicly declare their sexual orientation.

To the extent that gaydar does exist, it's imperfect in the same ways as most nonverbal interpretations. ●

*Mermaid*. Many humorous films and plays have been created around the results that arise when characters try to act like members of the other sex.

Although few of us behave like stereotypically masculine or feminine movie characters, there are recognizable differences in the way men and women look and act. In general, women are more nonverbally expressive than men, and women are better at recognizing others' nonverbal behavior. More specifically, research shows that, compared with men, women

- Smile more
- Use more facial expressions
- Use more head, hand, and arm gestures (but less expansive gestures)
- Touch others more
- Stand closer to others
- Are more vocally expressive
- Make more eye contact[33]

Despite these differences, men's and women's nonverbal communication patterns have a good deal in common.[34] Differences like the ones noted above are noticeable, but they are outweighed by the similar rules we follow in most dimensions of nonverbal behavior. You can prove this by imagining what it would be like to use radically different nonverbal rules: standing only an inch away from others, sniffing strangers, or tapping people's foreheads to get their attention. Moreover, according to a recent study, male-female nonverbal differences are less pronounced in conversations involving gay and lesbian participants.[35] Gender and culture certainly have an influence on nonverbal style, but the differences are often a matter of degree rather than kind.

Most communication scholars agree that social factors have more influence than biology does in shaping how men and women behave. For example, the ability to read nonverbal cues may have more to do with women's historically less powerful social status: People in subordinate work positions also have better decoding skills.[36] As women continue to gain equal status in the workplace and home, a paradoxical result may be less sensitivity at reading nonverbal cues.

All in all, although biological sex and cultural norms certainly have an influence on nonverbal style, they aren't as dramatic as the "men are from Mars, women are from Venus" thesis suggests.

 **ON YOUR FEET**

**Nonverbal Rules**

Imagine you are teaching someone about the rules of nonverbal communication in a particular group—for example, a culture, profession, neighborhood, family, or gender. Identify three rules of appropriateness concerning, for example, how people make (or avoid) eye contact, touch others, dress, show emotions, or use their voices. Explain the rules aloud in a way outsiders can understand.

# Functions of Nonverbal Communication

Although verbal and nonverbal messages differ in many ways, the two forms of communication operate together on most occasions. The following discussion explains the many functions of nonverbal communication and shows how nonverbal messages relate to verbal ones.

## Repeating

If someone asked you for directions to the nearest drugstore, you could say, "North of here about two blocks," repeating your instructions nonverbally by pointing north. This sort of repetition isn't just decorative: People remember comments accompanied by gestures more than those made with words alone.[37]

## Substituting

When a friend asks you what's new, you might shrug your shoulders instead of answering in words. Social scientists use the term **emblems** to describe deliberate nonverbal behaviors that have precise meanings known to everyone within a cultural group. For example, most Americans know that a head nod means "yes," a head shake means "no," a wave means "hello" or "good-bye," and a hand to the ear means "I can't hear you." (These same gestures mean different things in other cultures, which can cause a great deal of intercultural confusion, as you might imagine.)

Not all substituting consists of emblems, however. Sometimes substituting responses are more ambiguous and less intentional. A sigh, smile, or frown may substitute for a verbal answer to your question, "How's it going?" As this example suggests, nonverbal substituting is especially important when people are reluctant to express their feelings in words.

Thom Gossom, the actor we profiled at the beginning of the chapter, once played a role on *NYPD Blue* without speaking a single word. He portrayed a mute homeless person whom police questioned about a homicide. To prepare for the role, Gossom spent a few hours every day in public without speaking. "I ordered coffee at the coffee shop. I interacted with people," he says, "I learned what it felt like not to speak." In character, he communicated distress by wincing, tugging at his hair, nodding, and using a range of facial expressions and gestures. The episode won an Emmy. Gossom says the experience taught him that nonverbal cues can substitute for verbal communication in powerful ways.

> Try interacting with people for an hour without using words. What were you able to convey easily through nonverbal means? What was most difficult?

## Complementing

Sometimes nonverbal behaviors match the content of a verbal message. Consider, for example, a friend apologizing for forgetting an appointment with you. Your friend's sincerity would be reinforced if the verbal apology were accompanied by the appropriate nonverbal behaviors: the right tone of voice, facial expression, and so on. We often recognize the significance of complementary nonverbal behavior when it is missing. If your friend's apology were delivered with a shrug, a smirk, and a light tone of voice, you probably would doubt its sincerity, no matter how profuse the verbal explanation was.

Much complementing behavior consists of **illustrators**—nonverbal behaviors that accompany and support spoken words. Scratching the head when searching for an idea and snapping your fingers when it occurs are examples of illustrators that complement verbal messages. Research shows that North Americans use illustrators more often when they are emotionally aroused, for example, when they are furious, horrified, very agitated, distressed, or excited, and when trying to explain ideas that are difficult to put into words.[39]

## Understanding Communication Technology

# Expressiveness in Online Communication

Communication scholars have characterized face-to-face interaction as "rich" in nonverbal cues that convey feelings and attitudes. Even telephone conversations carry a fair amount of emotional information via the speakers' vocal qualities. By comparison, most text-based communication on the Internet, such as e-mail and text messaging, is relatively lean in relational information. With only words, subtlety is lost. This is why hints and jokes that might work well in person or on the phone often fail when communicated online.

Just like true facial expressions, emoticons can clarify the meaning that isn't clear from words alone.[38] For example, see how each graphic below creates a different meaning for the same statement:

- You are driving me crazy
- You are driving me crazy
- You are driving me crazy

Ever since the early days of e-mail, Internet correspondents have devised a series of "emoticons" using typed characters to convey feelings. The most common of these is the symbol :), which, of course, means that the writer is pleased or joking. Less commonly used emoticons convey other emotions. A frown is :-( and surprise is :-0, for example.

Even though you can't make your voice louder or softer or change its tone in type, you can use regular keyboard characters to convey a surprisingly large range of feelings.

**Asterisks**   Not all e-mail and instant messaging systems allow the use of italics, which are useful for emphasizing a point. Enclosing a statement in asterisks can add the same sort of light emphasis. Instead of saying

> I really want to hear from you,

you can say

> I *really* want to hear from you.

Notice how changing the placement of asterisks produces a different message:

> I really want to hear from *you.*

**Capitalization**   Capitalizing a word or phrase can also emphasize the point:

> I hate to be a pest, but I need the $20 you owe me TODAY.

Overuse of capitals can be offensive. Be sure to avoid typing messages in all uppercase letters, which creates the impression of shouting:

> HOW ARE YOU DOING? WE ARE HAVING A GREAT TIME HERE. BE SURE TO COME SEE US SOON.

**Multiple Methods of Emphasis**   When you want to emphasize a point, you can use multiple methods:

> I can't believe you told the boss that I sleep with a teddy bear! I wanted to *die* of embarrassment. Please don't *EVER* **EVER** do that kind of thing again. ●

## Accenting

Just as we use italics to emphasize an idea in print, we use nonverbal devices to emphasize oral messages. Pointing an accusing finger adds emphasis to criticism (as well as probably creating defensiveness in the receiver). Stressing certain words with the voice ("It was *your* idea!") is another way to add nonverbal accents.

## Regulating

Nonverbal behaviors can control the flow of verbal communication. For example, parties in a conversation often unconsciously send and receive turn-taking cues.[40] When you are ready to yield the floor, the unstated rule is as follows: Create a rising vocal intonation pattern, then use a falling intonation pattern, or draw out the final syllable of the clause at the end of your statement. Finally, stop speaking. If you want to maintain your turn when another speaker seems ready to cut you off, you can suppress the attempt by taking an audible breath, using a sustained intonation pattern (because rising and falling patterns suggest the end of a statement), and

> cultural idiom

**the floor:**
the right or privilege to speak

**to cut you off:**
to interrupt you in order to stop you from proceeding with your remarks

avoiding any pauses in your speech. Other nonverbal cues exist for gaining the floor and for signaling that you do not want to speak.

## Contradicting

People often simultaneously express different and even contradictory messages in their verbal and nonverbal behaviors. A common example of this sort of mixed message is the experience we've all had of hearing someone with a red face and bulging veins yelling, "Angry? No, I'm not angry!"

Even though some of the ways in which people contradict themselves are subtle, mixed messages have a strong impact. Studies suggest that when a receiver perceives an inconsistency between verbal and nonverbal messages, the nonverbal one carries more weight—more than 12.5 percent more, according to some research.[41]

Many contradictions between verbal and nonverbal messages are unintentional, revealing feelings that the person exhibiting them would rather keep under cover. But there are other times when contradicting can be strategic. One deliberate use of mixed messages is to save face by sending a nonverbal message that might be awkward if expressed verbally. For example, think of a time when you became bored with a conversation while your companion kept rambling on. At such a time the most straightforward statement would be, "I'm tired of talking to you and want you to stop talking." Although it might feel good to be so direct, this kind of honesty is impolite for anyone over 5 years of age. Instead of being blunt in situations like this, a face-saving alternative is to express your interest nonverbally. While nodding politely and murmuring "uh-huh" and "no kidding?" at the appropriate times, you can signal a desire to leave by looking around the room, turning slightly away from the speaker, or even making a point of yawning. In most cases such clues are enough to end the conversation without the awkwardness of expressing outright what's going on.

## Deceiving

Some people are better at hiding deceit than others. For example, most people become more successful liars as they grow older. Research shows that this is especially true for women.[42] High self-monitors are usually better at hiding their deception than communicators who are less self-aware, and raters judge highly expressive liars as more honest than those who are more subdued.[43] Not surprisingly, people whose jobs require them to act differently than they feel, such as actors, lawyers, diplomats, and salespeople, are more successful at deception than the general population.[44]

*Source:* DILBERT © Scott Adams/Dist. by United Feature Syndicate, Inc.

Decades of research have revealed that there are no surefire nonverbal cues that indicate deception.[45] This fact helps explain why most people have only a coin flip's chance—50 percent—of accurately identifying a liar.[46] We seem to be worse at catching deceivers when we participate actively in conversations than when we observe from the sidelines.[47] It's easiest to catch liars when they haven't had a chance to rehearse, when they feel strongly about the information being hidden, or when they feel anxious or guilty about their lies.[48] Trust (or lack of it) also plays a role in which deceptive messages are successful: People who are suspicious that a speaker may be lying pay closer attention to the speaker's nonverbal behavior (e.g., talking faster than normal, shifted posture) than do people who are not suspicious.[49] Table 6-3 lists situations in which deceptive messages are most likely to be obvious.

Some people are better than others at uncovering deception. For example, women are consistently more accurate than men at detecting lying and what the underlying truth is.[50] The same research showed that, as people become more intimate, their accuracy in detecting lies actually declines. This is a surprising fact: Intuition suggests that we ought to be better at judging honesty as we become more familiar with others. Perhaps an element of wishful thinking interferes with our accurate decoding of these messages. After all, we would hate to think that a lover would lie to us. When intimates *do* become suspicious, however, their ability to recognize deception increases.[51] Despite their overall accuracy at detecting lies, women are more inclined to fall for the deception of intimate partners than are men. No matter how skillful or inept we may be at interpreting nonverbal behavior, training can make us better.[52]

Communication scholars have studied deception detection for years. One review of decades of research on the subject revealed three findings that have been supported time and again in studies. They are as follows:

- We are accurate in detecting deception only slightly more than half the time.
- We overestimate our abilities to detect others' lies.
- We have a strong tendency to judge others' messages as truthful—in other words, we want to believe people wouldn't lie to us (which biases our ability to detect deceit).[53]

As one writer put it, "there is no unique telltale signal for a fib. Pinocchio's nose just doesn't exist, and that makes liars difficult to spot." Moreover, some popular prescriptions about liars' nonverbal behaviors simply aren't accurate.[54] For instance, conventional wisdom suggests that liars avert their gaze and fidget

> cultural idiom
> **surefire:**
> certain to succeed

## Table 6-3  Leakage of Nonverbal Clues to Deception

| DECEPTION CLUES ARE MOST LIKELY WHEN THE DECEIVER... | DECEPTION CLUES ARE LEAST LIKELY WHEN THE DECEIVER... |
| --- | --- |
| Wants to hide emotions being experienced at the moment. | Wants to hide information unrelated to his or her emotions. |
| Feels strongly about the information being hidden. | Has no strong feelings about the information being hidden. |
| Feels apprehensive about the deception. | Feels confident about the deception. |
| Feels guilty about being deceptive. | Experiences little guilt about the deception. |
| Gets little enjoyment from being deceptive. | Enjoys the deception. |
| Needs to construct the message carefully while delivering it. | Knows the deceptive message well and has rehearsed it. |

*Source*: Based on material from Ekman, P. (1981). Mistakes when deceiving. In T. A. Sebok & R. Rosenthal (Eds.), *The clever Hans phenomenon: Communication with horses, whales, apes and people* (pp. 269–278). New York: New York Academy of Sciences.

more than nonliars. Research, however, shows just the opposite: Liars often sustain *more* eye contact and fidget *less*, in part because they believe that to do otherwise might look deceitful. Popular characterizations of "scientific" lie detection aren't helpful, either. One experiment found that viewers who watched the television show *Lie to Me* (in which the lead character attempts to catch liars) were actually *worse* at detecting lies than nonviewers, in part because the show focused on nonverbal cues and ignored important verbal content.[55]

Before we finish considering how nonverbal behaviors can deceive, it's important to realize that not all deceptive communication is aimed at taking advantage of the recipient. Sometimes we use nonverbal messages as a polite way to express an idea that would be difficult to handle if expressed in words. In this sense, the ability to deliberately send nonverbal messages that contradict your words can be a kind of communication competence.

# Types of Nonverbal Communication

Now that you understand how nonverbal messages operate as a form of communication, we can look at the various forms of nonverbal behavior. The following pages explain how our bodies, artifacts (such as clothing), environments, and the way we use time all send messages.

## Body Movements

For many people, the most noticeable elements of nonverbal communication involve visible body movements. In the following pages, we will examine some of the ways both the body and face can convey meanings.

**Posture and Gesture**   Stop reading for a moment and notice how you are sitting. What does your position say nonverbally about how you feel? Are there other people near you now? What messages do you get from their posture and movements? Tune your television to any program, and without turning up the sound, see what messages are communicated by the movements and body position of the people on the screen. These simple experiments illustrate the communicative power of **kinesics**, the study of body movement, gesture, and posture.

Posture is a rich channel for conveying nonverbal information. From time to time postural messages are obvious. If you see a person drag him- or herself through the door or slump over while sitting in a chair, it's apparent that something significant is going on. But most postural cues are more subtle. For instance, the act of mirroring the posture of another person can have positive consequences. One experiment showed that career counselors who used "posture echoes" to copy the postures of clients were rated as more empathic than those who did not reflect the clients' postures.[56] Researchers have also found that partners in romantic relationships mirror one another's behaviors.[57]

Posture can communicate vulnerability in situations far more serious than mere social or business settings. One study revealed that rapists sometimes use postural clues to select victims that they believe will be easy to intimidate.[58] Easy targets are more likely to walk slowly and tentatively, stare at the ground, and move their arms and legs in short, jerky motions.

Research shows that expansive poses—hands on hips, feet propped on a desk, or hawk-like stances—are signs of power and confidence.[59] In fact, adopting these poses can actually alter how we feel about ourselves. In one study, researchers assigned 42 participants to strike and maintain either high-power or low-power poses for 2 minutes.[60] Lab tests showed that high-power posers experienced testosterone increases and lowered cortisol, both of which are linked to physiological

## How Worldly Are Your Nonverbal Communication Skills?

How well can you match the following nonverbal behaviors to their meanings in different cultures? (Note that the same behavior has multiple meanings in different cultures, so you can use it more than once.)

**a**

**The answers appear at the end of the chapter, on p. 195.**

1. Thumb and forefinger form a circle, while the other three fingers are spread out.

2. Two men hold hands in public.

3. Pinkie and pointer finger point straight up, while thumb holds the two middle fingers down.

4. Palm is held flat out toward another person.

5. Hand is in fist with thumb poking out between the forefinger and middle finger.

____ We're a couple. (United States)

____ This is worthless. (France)

____ Hook 'em horns. (United States)

____ Please give me money. (Japan)

____ We respect each other. (Arab countries)

____ OK. (United States)

____ I've got your nose! (United States)

____ I'd like to smear excrement over your face. (Greece)

____ A sign of the devil. (Italy)

____ You're an a**hole. (Latin America)

____ Please stop, or tell it to the hand. (United States)

---

empowerment. They also made bolder bets when given the chance to gamble after posing. The results suggest that a change in posture can actually improve confidence and performance in communication contexts that include job interviews, public speeches, standing up to a boss, and taking risks that can lead to success. The researchers believe people can "fake it 'til they make it" by practicing powerful poses prior to an event and letting their feelings and behaviors follow.

Gestures are a fundamental element of communication—so fundamental, in fact, that people who have been blind from birth use them.[61] One group of ambiguous gestures consists of what we usually call fidgeting—movements in which one part of the body grooms, massages, rubs, holds, fidgets, pinches, picks, or otherwise manipulates another body part. Social scientists call these behaviors **manipulators**.[62] Social rules may discourage us from performing most manipulators in public, but people still do so without noticing. For example, one study revealed that deceivers bob their heads more often than truth tellers.[63] Research confirms what common sense suggests—that increased use of manipulators is often a sign of discomfort.[64] But not all fidgeting signals uneasiness. People also are likely to use manipulators when relaxed. When they let their guard down (either alone or with friends), they will be more likely to fiddle with an earlobe, twirl a strand of hair, or clean their fingernails. Whether or not the fidgeter is hiding something, observers are likely to interpret manipulators as a signal of dishonesty. Because not all fidgeters are liars, it's important not to jump to conclusions about the meaning of manipulators.

**Face and Eyes** The face and eyes are probably the most noticed parts of the body, and their impact is powerful. For example, smiling cocktail waitresses earn larger tips than unsmiling ones, and smiling nuns collect larger donations than ones with glum expressions.[65] The influence of facial expressions and eye contact doesn't mean that their nonverbal messages are always easy to read. The

> cultural idiom

**let their guard down:**
act or speak naturally without worrying how others will react

In the film *Crazy, Stupid, Love*, romantic superstar Jacob (Ryan Gosling) coaches down-on-his-luck Cal (Steve Carrell) on how to become more appealing by undergoing a nonverbal makeover. What messages—both deliberate and unintentional—do you convey about yourself nonverbally? Could you modify your nonverbal presentation to become a more inviting version of yourself?

face is a tremendously complicated channel of expression for several reasons. One reason is the number of expressions people can produce. Another is the speed with which they can change. For example, slow-motion films have been taken that show expressions fleeting across a subject's face in as short a time as a fifth of a second. Finally, it seems that different emotions show most clearly in different parts of the face: happiness and surprise in the eyes and lower face, anger in the lower face and brows and forehead, fear and sadness in the eyes, and disgust in the lower face.

Expressions reflecting many emotions seem to be recognizable in and between members of all cultures.[66] Of course, **affect blends**—the combination of two or more expressions showing different emotions—are possible. For instance, it's easy to imagine how someone would look who is fearful and surprised or disgusted and angry.

Research indicates that people are quite accurate at judging facial expressions of these emotions.[67] Accuracy increases when judges know the "target" or have knowledge of the context in which the expression occurs or when they have seen several samples of the target's expressions.

In mainstream Euro-American culture, meeting someone's glance with your eyes is usually a sign of involvement or interest, whereas looking away signals a desire to avoid contact. Prolonged eye contact has been identified by researchers as one of the main ways people indicate attraction.[68]

Solicitors on the street—panhandlers, salespeople, petitioners—try to catch our eye because after they've managed to establish contact with a glance, it becomes harder for the approached person to draw away.

## Voice

The voice is another form of nonverbal communication. Social scientists use the term **paralanguage** to describe nonverbal, vocal messages. You can begin to understand the power of vocal cues by considering how the meaning of a simple sentence can change just by shifting the emphasis from word to word:

- *This* is a fantastic communication book.
  (Not just any book, but this one in particular.)

- This is a *fantastic* communication book.
  (This book is superior, exciting.)

- This is a fantastic *communication* book.
  The book is good as far as communication goes; it may not be so good as literature or drama.)

- This is a fantastic communication *book*.
  (It's not a play or a compact disc; it's a book.)

The impact of paralinguistic cues is strong. In fact, research shows that listeners pay more attention to the vocal messages than to the words that are spoken when asked to determine a speaker's attitudes.[69] Furthermore, when vocal factors contradict a verbal message, listeners judge the speaker's intention from the paralanguage, not from the words themselves.[70]

There are many other ways the voice communicates—through its tone, speed, pitch, volume, number and length of pauses, and **disfluencies** (such as stammering and use of "uh," "um," "er," and so on). All these factors can do a great deal to reinforce or contradict the message our words convey.

Sarcasm is one instance in which both emphasis and tone of voice help change a statement's meaning to the opposite of its verbal message. Experience this yourself with the following three statements. The first time through, say them literally, and then say them sarcastically.

- Thanks for waking me up.
- I really had a wonderful time on my blind date.
- There's nothing I like better than waking up before sunrise.

*"Wow . . . We could really fill this room with uncomfortable silences."*

Source: Alex Gregory / The New Yorker Collection / www.cartoonbank.com

Researchers have identified the communicative value of paralanguage through the use of content-free speech—ordinary speech that has been electronically manipulated so that the words are unintelligible, but the paralanguage remains unaffected. (Hearing a foreign language that you do not understand has the same effect.) Subjects who hear content-free speech can consistently recognize the emotion being expressed, as well as identifying its strength.[71]

Paralanguage can affect behavior in many ways, some of which are rather surprising. Researchers have discovered that communicators are most likely to comply with requests delivered by speakers whose speaking rates are similar to their own.[72] Besides complying with same-rate speakers, listeners also feel more positively about people who seem to talk at their own rate.

Some vocal factors influence the way a speaker is perceived by others. For example, communicators who speak loudly and without hesitations are viewed as more confident than those who pause and speak quietly.[73] People who speak more slowly are judged as having greater conversational control than fast talkers.[74] Research has also demonstrated that people with more attractive voices are rated more highly than those whose voice sounds less attractive.[75] Along with vocal qualities, accent can shape perceptions. For example, the accents of some nonnative English-speaking job seekers (e.g., those with a pronounced French accent) created favorable impressions with employers, whereas other strong accents (e.g., Japanese) had the opposite effect.[76]

## Appearance

How we appear can be just as revealing as how we sound and move. For that reason, we need to explore the communicative power of physical attractiveness and clothing.

**Physical Attractiveness**    Most people claim that looks aren't the best measure of desirability or character, but they typically prefer others whom they find attractive.[77] For example, women who are perceived as attractive have more dates,

> cultural idiom

**lighter:**
lesser in duration

**place your bet on:**
predict with confidence

receive higher grades in college, persuade males with greater ease, and receive lighter court sentences. Both men and women whom others view as attractive are rated as being more sensitive, kind, strong, sociable, and interesting than their less-fortunate brothers and sisters. Who is most likely to succeed in business? Place your bet on the attractive job applicant. More than 200 managers in one survey admitted that attractive people get preferential treatment both in hiring decisions and on the job.[78] Height is also a factor. Shorter men have more difficulty finding jobs in the first place, and men over 6 feet 2 inches receive starting salaries that average 12.4 percent higher than comparable applicants under 6 feet.[79] Based on one study of male earnings, the salary differential is about 2 percent per inch, which means that a man who is 5 feet 8 inches will earn about $300 a year more (at U.S. minimum wage) than a man who is 5 feet 7 inches, and so on.[80] Consistent with that, tall presidential candidates are historically more likely to win than short ones.

If you happen to be on the shorter side, you may find hope in new research conducted at Stanford University's Virtual Human Interaction Laboratory.[81] The research reveals that people who create a tall avatar are more persuasive in virtual reality interactions, even if they are short in real life. Furthermore, once two communicators enter back into the "real" world, the person who had the taller avatar continues to be more persuasive, regardless of real-life height.

The influence of attractiveness begins early in life. Preschoolers were shown photographs of children their own age and asked to choose potential friends and enemies. The researchers found that children as young as 3 agreed as to who was attractive ("cute") and unattractive ("homely"). Furthermore, they valued their attractive counterparts—of both the same and the other sex—more highly. Also, preschool children rated by their peers as pretty were most liked, and those identified as least pretty were least liked. Children who were interviewed rated good-looking children as having positive social characteristics ("He's friendly to other children") and unattractive children as having negative ones ("He hits other children without reason").

Teachers also are affected by students' attractiveness. Physically attractive students are usually judged more favorably—more intelligent, friendly, and popular—than their less attractive counterparts.[82] Fortunately, attractiveness is something we can control without having to call a plastic surgeon. If you aren't totally gorgeous or handsome, don't despair: Evidence suggests that, as we get to know more about people and like them, we start to regard them as better looking.[83] Moreover, we view others as beautiful or ugly on the basis of not just their "original equipment" but also how they use that equipment. Posture, gestures, facial expressions, and other behaviors can increase the attractiveness of an otherwise unremarkable person. Exercise can improve the way each of us looks. Finally, the way we dress can make a significant difference in the way others perceive us, as you'll now see.

**Clothing**   Besides protecting us from the elements, clothing is a means of nonverbal communication, providing a relatively straightforward (if sometimes expensive) method of impression management. Clothing can be used to convey, for example, economic status, educational level, social status, moral standards, athletic ability and/or interests, belief system (political, philosophical, religious), and level of sophistication.

Research shows that we do make assumptions about people based on their clothing. Communicators who wear special clothing often gain persuasiveness. For example, experimenters dressed in uniforms resembling police officers were more successful than those dressed in civilian clothing in requesting pedestrians to pick up litter and in persuading them to lend a dime for a parking meter to a motorist.[84] Likewise, solicitors wearing a sheriff's or nurse's uniform increased the level of contributions to law enforcement and health care campaigns.[85] Thom Gossom, who was profiled at the beginning of the chapter, laughs when he remembers playing a police chief once. "I had to walk from what we called base camp to where we were shooting, across the road. I noticed that, when drivers saw me, they would slow way down," he says. "I thought, 'There's power in wearing this uniform!'"

The effects of clothing operate in other contexts as well. Medical patients trust physicians dressed professionally. They were significantly more willing to share their social, sexual, and psychological problems with doctors wearing white coats or surgical scrubs than those wearing business dress or casual attire.[86] Along with uniforms, clothing style can shape others' reactions. Pedestrians are more likely to return lost coins to well-dressed people than to those dressed in low-status clothing.[87] Women who are wearing a jacket are rated as being more powerful than those wearing only a dress or skirt and blouse.[88]

As we get to know others better, the importance of clothing shrinks.[89] This fact suggests that clothing is especially important in the early stages of a relationship, when making a positive first impression is necessary, in order to encourage others to get to know us better. This advice is equally important in personal situations and in employment interviews. In both cases, your style of dress (and personal grooming) can make all the difference between the chance to progress further and outright rejection.

Awareness of the power of clothing to create impressions has spawned an entire genre of television programming. Long-running hits include the *Extreme Makeover* series, *Queer Eye for the Straight Guy*, and *What Not to Wear*. What messages do your styles of clothing convey?

## Touch

Physical touch can "speak" volumes. A supportive pat on the back, a high five, or even an inappropriate graze can be more powerful than words, eliciting a strong emotional reaction in the receiver. Social scientists use the term **haptics** when they refer to the study of touch in human behavior.

Experts argue that one reason actions speak louder than words is because touch is the first language we learn as infants.[90] Besides being the earliest means we have of making contact with others, touching is essential to healthy development. During the 19th and early 20th centuries many babies died from a disease

---

**Ethical Challenge**

## Clothing and Impression Management

Using clothing as a method of creating impressions is a fact of life. Discover for yourself how dressing can be a type of deception.

1. Identify three examples from your experience when someone dressed in a manner that disguised or misrepresented his or her true status or personal attributes. What were the consequences of this misrepresentation for you or others?

2. Now identify three occasions in which you successfully used clothing to create a favorable but inaccurate impression. What were the consequences of this deception for others?

3. Based on your conclusions, define any situations when clothing may be used as an unethical means of impression management. List both "misdemeanors," in which the consequences are not likely to cause serious harm, and "felonies," in which the deception has the potential to cause serious harm.

then called *marasmus*, which, translated from Greek, means "wasting away." In some orphanages the mortality rate was quite high, but even children in "progressive" homes, hospitals, and other institutions died regularly from the ailment. When researchers finally tracked down the causes of this disease, they found that many infants suffered from lack of physical contact with parents or nurses rather than poor nutrition, medical care, or other factors. They hadn't been touched enough, and as a result they died. From this knowledge came the practice of "mothering" children in institutions—picking babies up, carrying them around, and handling them several times each day. At one hospital that began this practice, the death rate for infants fell from between 30 and 35 percent to below 10 percent.[91]

Touch seems to increase a child's mental functioning as well as physical health. Babies who have been given plenty of physical stimulation by their mothers develop significantly higher IQs than those receiving less contact.[92] By contrast, insufficient physical contact correlates with social problems including communication apprehension and low self-disclosure.[93]

Touch also increases compliance.[100] In one study, strangers were approached by a female confederate who requested that they return a dime left in the phone booth from which they had just emerged. When the request was accompanied by a light touch on the subject's arm, the probability that the person would return the dime increased significantly.[101] In a similar experiment, people were asked by a male or female confederate to sign a petition or complete a rating scale. Again, people were more likely to cooperate when they were touched lightly on the arm. In the rating-scale variation of the study, the results were especially dramatic: 70 percent of those who were touched complied, whereas only 40 percent of the untouched people complied.[102] An additional power of touch is its on-the-job utility. One study showed that fleeting touches on the hand and shoulder resulted in larger tips for restaurant waiters.[103]

## @Work

## Touch and Career Success

The old phrase "keeping in touch" takes on new meaning once you understand the relationship between haptics and career effectiveness.

Some of the most pronounced benefits of touching occur in medicine and the health and helping professions. For example, patients are more likely to take their medicines when physicians give a slight touch while prescribing.[94] In counseling, touch increases self-disclosure and verbalization of psychiatric patients.[95]

Touch can also enhance success in sales and marketing. Touching customers in a store increases their shopping time, their evaluation of the store, and also the amount of shopping.[96] When an offer to try samples of a product is accompanied by a touch, customers are more likely to try the sample and buy the product.[97]

Touch also has an impact in school. Students are twice as likely to volunteer and speak up in class if they have received a supportive touch on the back or arm from their teacher.[98]

Even athletes benefit from touch. One study of the National Basketball Association revealed that the touchiest teams had the most successful records, whereas in the lowest-scoring teams, the team members touched one another the least.[99]

Of course, touch has to be culturally appropriate. Furthermore, touching by itself is no guarantee of success, and too much contact can be bothersome, annoying, or even downright creepy. But research confirms that appropriate contact can enhance your success. ●

## Space

There are two ways that the use of space can create nonverbal messages: the distance we put between ourselves and the territory we consider our own. We'll now look at each of these dimensions.

**Distance** The study of the way people and animals use space has been termed **proxemics**. Preferred spaces are largely a matter of cultural norms. For example, people living in hyperdense Hong Kong manage to live in crowded residential quarters that most North Americans would find intolerable.[104] Anthropologist Edward T. Hall has defined four distances used in mainstream North American culture.[105] He says that we choose a particular distance depending on how we feel toward the other person at a given time, the context of the conversation, and our personal goals.

**Intimate distance** begins with skin contact and ranges out to about 18 inches. The most obvious context for intimate distance involves interaction with people to whom we're emotionally close—and then mostly in private situations. Intimate distance between individuals also occurs in less intimate circumstances: visiting the doctor or dentist, at the hairdresser's, and during some athletic contests. Allowing someone to move into the intimate zone usually is a sign of trust.

The best time to discover the rules of personal space is when they're broken. Have you ever invaded someone's personal space? Have you ever been unexpectedly standoffish? What were the consequences?

**Personal distance** ranges from 18 inches at its closest point to 4 feet at its farthest. Its closer range is the distance at which most relational partners stand in public. We are uncomfortable if someone else "moves in" to this area without invitation. The far range of personal distance runs from about 2.5 to 4 feet. This is the zone just beyond the other person's reach—the distance at which we can keep someone "at arm's length." This term suggests the type of communication that goes on at this range: Interaction is still reasonably personal, but less so than communication that occurs a foot or so closer.

**Social distance** ranges from 4 to about 12 feet. Within it are the kinds of communication that usually occur in business situations. Its closer range, from 4 to 7 feet, is the distance at which conversations usually occur between salespeople and customers and between people who work together. We use the far range of social distance—7 to 12 feet—for more formal and impersonal situations. This is the range at which we generally sit from the boss.

**Public distance** is Hall's term for the farthest zone, running outward from 12 feet. The closer range of public distance is the one most teachers use in the classroom. In the farther range of public space—25 feet and beyond—two-way communication becomes difficult. In some cases it's necessary for speakers to use public distance owing to the size of their audience, but we can assume that anyone who voluntarily chooses to use it when he or she could be closer is not interested in having a dialogue.

Choosing the optimal distance can have a powerful effect on how we regard others and how we respond to them. For example, students are more satisfied with teachers who reduce the distance between themselves and their classes. They also are more satisfied with the course itself, and they are more likely to follow the teacher's instructions.[106] Likewise, medical patients are more satisfied with physicians who don't "keep their distance."[107]

**Territoriality**  Whereas personal space is the invisible bubble we carry around as an extension of our physical being, **territory** is fixed space. Any area, such as a room, house, neighborhood, or country, to which we assume some kind of "rights" is our territory. Not all territory is permanent. We often stake out space for ourselves in the library, at the beach, and so on by using markers such as books, clothing, or other personal possessions.

The way people use space can communicate a good deal about power and status relationships. Generally, we grant people with higher status more personal territory and greater privacy.[108] We knock before entering the boss's office, whereas a boss can usually walk into our work area without hesitating. In traditional schools, professors have offices, dining rooms, and even toilets that are private, whereas the students, who are presumably less important, have no such sanctuaries. In the military, greater space and privacy usually come with rank: Privates sleep 40 to a barracks, sergeants have their own private rooms, and generals have government-provided houses.

## Environment

The physical environment people create can both reflect and shape interaction. This principle is illustrated right at home. Researchers showed 99 students slides of the insides or outsides of 12 upper-middle-class homes and then asked them to infer the personality of the owners from their impressions.[109] The students were especially accurate after glancing at interior photos. The decorating schemes communicated accurate information about the homeowners' intellectualism, politeness, maturity, optimism, tenseness, willingness to take adventures, family orientations, and reservedness. The home exteriors also gave viewers accurate perceptions of the owners' artistic interests, graciousness, privacy, and quietness.

Besides communicating information about the designer, an environment can shape the kind of interaction that takes place in it. In one experiment, researchers found that the attractiveness of a room influenced the happiness and energy of the people working in it.[110] The experimenters set up three rooms: an "ugly" one, which resembled a janitor's closet in the basement of a campus building; an "average" room, which was a professor's office; and a "beautiful" room, which was furnished with stylish and comfortable furnishings. The subjects in the experiment were asked to rate a series of pictures as a way of measuring their energy and feelings of well-being while at work. Results of the experiment showed that while in the ugly room the subjects became tired and bored more quickly and took longer to complete their task. When they moved to the beautiful room, however, they rated the faces they were judging higher, showed a greater desire to work, and expressed feelings of importance, comfort, and enjoyment. The results teach a lesson that isn't surprising: Workers generally feel better and do a better job when they're in an attractive environment.

The design of an entire building can shape communication among its users. Architects have learned that the way housing projects are designed controls to a great extent the contact neighbors have with one another. People who live in apartments near stairways and mailboxes have many more neighbor contacts than do those living in less heavily traveled parts

> Take a fresh look at the physical environment you have created in the place where you live. What statement does it make about you? How might it affect the communication that goes on in this setting?

of the building, and tenants generally have more contacts with immediate neighbors than with people even a few doors away.[111]

So far we have talked about how designing an environment can shape communication, but there is another side to consider. Watching how people use an already existing environment can be a way of telling what kind of relationships they want. For example, Robert Sommer watched students in a college library and found that there's a definite pattern for people who want to study alone. While the library was uncrowded, students almost always chose corner seats at one of the empty rectangular tables.[112] Finally, each table was occupied by one reader. New readers would then choose a seat on the opposite side and far end of an occupied table, thus keeping the maximum distance between themselves and the other readers. One of Sommer's associates tried violating these "rules" by sitting next to, and across from, other female readers when more distant seats were available. She found that the approached women reacted defensively, either by signaling their discomfort through shifts in posture or gesturing or by eventually moving away.

## Time

Social scientists use the term **chronemics** for the study of how human beings use and structure time. The way we handle time can express both intentional and unintentional messages.[113] Social psychologist Robert Levine describes several ways that time can communicate.[114] For instance, in a culture that values time highly, like the United States, waiting can be an indicator of status. "Important" people (whose time is supposedly more valuable than that of others) may be seen by appointment only, whereas it is acceptable to intrude without notice on lesser beings. To see how this rule operates, consider how natural it is for a boss to drop in to a subordinate's office unannounced, whereas some employees would never intrude into the boss's office without an appointment. A related rule is that low-status people must never make more important people wait. It would be a serious mistake to show up late for a job interview, although the interviewer might keep you cooling your heels in the lobby. Important people are often whisked to the head of a restaurant or airport line, whereas the presumably less exalted are forced to wait their turn.

The use of time depends greatly on culture.[115] Some cultures (e.g., North American, German, and Swiss) tend to be **monochronic**, emphasizing punctuality, schedules, and completing one task at a time. Other cultures (e.g., South American, Mediterranean, and Arab) are more **polychronic**, with flexible schedules in

When singer Justin Bieber took the stage almost 2 hours late at a sold-out concert in London, his fans were outraged and took to Twitter and other social media to complain. What message did Bieber's management of time send to his fans? What messages do you send by the ways you manage time?

> cultural idiom
**cooling your heels:**
waiting impatiently

which multiple tasks are pursued at the same time. One psychologist discovered the difference between North and South American attitudes when teaching at a university in Brazil.[116] He found that some students arrived halfway through a 2-hour class and that most of them stayed put and kept asking questions when the class was scheduled to end. A half hour after the official end of the class, the professor finally closed off discussion, because there was no indication that the students intended to leave. This flexibility of time is quite different from what is common in most North American colleges!

Even within a culture, rules of time vary. Sometimes the differences are geographic. In New York City, the party invitation may say "9 P.M.," but nobody would think of showing up before 9:30. In Salt Lake City, guests are expected to show up on time, or perhaps even a bit early.[117] Even within the same geographic area, different groups establish their own rules about the use of time. Consider your own experience. In school, some instructors begin and end class punctually, whereas others are more casual. With some people you feel comfortable talking for hours in person or on the phone, whereas with others time seems to be precious and not meant to be "wasted."

<aside>
> cultural idiom

**stayed put:**
remained in place
</aside>

# Building Competence in Nonverbal Communication

By now you should appreciate the wealth of messages expressed nonverbally. You can use this information to develop your communication skills in two respects—by being more attuned to others and by becoming more aware of your own nonverbal messages.

## Tune Out Words

It's easy to overlook important nonverbal cues when you're only listening to the words being spoken. As you've already read, words sometimes hide, or even contradict, a speaker's true feelings (e.g., "I see your point," spoken with a frown). Even when spoken words accurately reflect the speaker's thoughts, nonverbal cues can reveal important information about feelings and attitudes.

You can develop skill in recognizing nonverbal cues by tuning out the content of a speaker's language. Because ignoring what your conversational partner is saying can be antagonizing, try focusing on a video or TV program in a language you don't understand. That way you can attend to vocal qualities as well as postures, gestures, facial expressions, and other cues. Once recognizing nonverbal cues has become second nature, you'll find it easier to tune in to them in your everyday conversations.

## Use Perception Checking

Because nonverbal behaviors are ambiguous, it's important to consider your interpretations as educated guesses, not absolute translations. The yawn that interrupts a story you're telling may signal boredom, but it might also be a sign that the listener is recovering from a sleepless night. Likewise, the impatient tone that greets your suggestion may be aimed at you, or it could mean that your conversational partner is having a bad day.

Perception checking (Chapter 2, pages 61–62) is one way to explore the significance of nonverbal cues. Instead of reading the other person's mind, describe the behavior you've noted, share at least two possible interpretations, and ask for clarification about how to interpret the behavior. With practice, perception checks can sound natural and reflect your genuine desire to understand:

> *To a friend:* At the party last night you said you were tired and left early (behavior). I wasn't sure whether you were bored (first interpretation) or whether something else was bothering you (second interpretation). Or maybe you *were* just tired (third interpretation). What was going on?

> *At work:* I need to ask you about something that happened at the end of yesterday's meeting. When I started to ask about the vacation schedule, you interrupted me and said we were running over time and you had to make an important phone call. I'm wondering whether the phone call was the only reason you cut me off, or whether you think I said something wrong. Can you fill me in?

Not every situation is important enough to call for a perception check, and sometimes the meaning of nonverbal cues may seem so clear that you don't need to investigate. But there will certainly be times when exploring alternate interpretations is better than jumping to conclusions.

Notice the nonverbal cues of someone around you right now. Consider at least three interpretations of the behaviors you have observed. How might you use perception checking to determine if any of them are accurate?

## Pay Attention to Your Own Nonverbal Behavior

Along with attending more carefully to the unspoken messages of others, there's value in monitoring your own nonverbal behavior.

You can get an appreciation for this fact by asking someone to record a video of you in unguarded moments. With a smartphone, this sort of recording should be easy to make without your becoming aware and self-conscious. If you're like most people, you're likely to be surprised by at least some of what you see. Research suggests that most of us have blind spots when it comes to our own communication.[118] For example, we sometimes overestimate how well we are hiding our anxiety, boredom, or eagerness from others. With this in mind, consider the following questions honestly: How does your voice sound? How closely does your appearance match what you've imagined? What messages do your posture, gestures, and face convey?

Once you have a sense of your most notable nonverbal behaviors, you can monitor them without the need for technology.

## Summary

Nonverbal communication consists of messages expressed by nonlinguistic means.

Nonverbal behavior is an integral part of virtually all communication, and nonverbal skill is a positive predictor of relational success. There are several important characteristics of nonverbal communication. First is the simple fact that it is impossible not to communicate nonverbally; humans constantly send messages about themselves that are available for others to receive. The second characteristic is that nonverbal communication is ambiguous; there are many possible interpretations for any behavior. This ambiguity makes it important for the receiver to verify any interpretation before jumping to conclusions about the meaning of a nonverbal message. Finally, nonverbal communication is different from verbal communication in complexity, flow, clarity, impact, and intentionality.

Some nonverbal communication is influenced by culture and gender. While there are some universal expressions, even the manner in which these expressions are used reflects the communicator's culture and gender. And behaviors that have special meanings in one culture may express different messages in another.

Nonverbal communication serves many functions: repeating, substituting, complementing, accenting, regulating, and contradicting verbal behavior, as well as deceiving.

We communicate nonverbally in many ways: through posture, gesture, use of the face and eyes, voice, physical attractiveness and clothing, touch, distance and territoriality, environment, and time.

It is difficult to interpret nonverbal cues with certainty. Mindfully focusing on other people's nonverbal behavior, as well as your own, can help. Perception checking can help verify hunches about your interpretations.

## Key Terms

**affect blend** The combination of two or more expressions, each showing a different emotion. *p. 182*

**affect displays** Facial expressions, body movements, and vocal traits that reveal emotional states. *p. 171*

**chronemics** The study of how humans use and structure time. *p. 189*

**disfluency** A nonlinguistic verbalization—for example, *um, er, ah. p. 183*

**emblems** Deliberate nonverbal behaviors with precise meanings, known to virtually all members of a cultural group. *p. 176*

**haptics** The study of touch. *p. 185*

**illustrators** Nonverbal behaviors that accompany and support verbal messages. *p. 176*

**intimate distance** One of Hall's four distance zones, ranging from skin contact to 18 inches. *p. 187*

**kinesics** The study of body movement, gesture, and posture. *p. 180*

**manipulators** Movements in which one part of the body grooms, massages, rubs, holds, fidgets, pinches, picks, or otherwise manipulates another part. *p. 181*

**monochronic** The use of time that emphasizes punctuality, schedules, and completing one task at a time. *p. 189*

**nonverbal communication** Messages expressed by other than linguistic means. *p. 169*

**paralanguage** Nonlinguistic means of vocal expression: rate, pitch, tone, and so on. *p. 182*

**personal distance** One of Hall's four distance zones, ranging from 18 inches to 4 feet. *p. 187*

**polychronic** The use of time that emphasizes flexible schedules in which multiple tasks are pursued at the same time. *p. 189*

**proxemics** The study of how people and animals use space. *p. 187*

**public distance** One of Hall's four distance zones, extending outward from 12 feet. *p. 187*

**social distance** One of Hall's four distance zones, ranging from 4 to 12 feet. *p. 187*

**territory** Fixed space that an individual assumes some right to occupy. *p. 188*

## Check Your Understanding

1. Explain how the characteristics of nonverbal communication outlined on pages 169–173 operate in a specific situation in your life.

2. Give examples of times when nonverbal behaviors served each of the following functions: repeating, substituting for, complementing, accenting, regulating, and contradicting verbal messages.

3. Identify situations when culture and gender influenced the nature of nonverbal communication.

4. Describe when and how you might appropriately use perception checking to share your interpretation of another person's nonverbal behavior.

## Activities

1. **Observing and Reporting Nonverbal Behavior** This exercise will give you a clear idea of the many nonverbal behaviors that are available to you whenever you encounter another person. It will also help prevent you from jumping to conclusions about the meaning of those behaviors without checking out your interpretations. You can try the exercise either in or outside of class, and the period of time over which you do it is flexible, from a single class period to several days. In any case, begin by choosing a partner, and then follow these directions:

   1. For the first period of time (however long you decide to make it), observe the way your partner behaves. Notice how he or she moves; his or her mannerisms, postures, way of speaking; how he or she dresses; and so on. To remember your observations, jot them down. If you're doing this exercise out of class

over an extended period of time, there's no need to let your observations interfere with whatever you'd normally be doing: Your only job here is to compile a list of your partner's behaviors. In this step, you should be careful not to interpret your partner's actions; just record what you see.

2. At the end of the time period, share what you've seen with your partner. He or she will do the same with you.

3. For the next period of time, your job is not only to observe your partner's behavior but also to interpret it. This time, in your conference, you should tell your partner what you thought his or her actions revealed. For example, if your partner dressed carelessly, did you think this meant that he or she overslept, that he or she is losing interest in his or her appearance, or that he or she was trying to be more comfortable? If you noticed him or her yawning frequently, did you think this meant that he or she was bored, tired from a late night, or sleepy after a big meal? Don't feel bad if your guesses weren't all correct. Remember that nonverbal clues tend to be ambiguous. You may be surprised how checking out the nonverbal clues you observe can help build a relationship with another person.

2. **Culture and Nonverbal Communication**

1. Identify at least three significant differences between nonverbal practices in two cultures or cocultures (e.g., ethnic, age, or socioeconomic groups) within your own society.

2. Describe the potential difficulties that could arise out of the differing nonverbal practices when members from the cultural groups interact. Are there any ways of avoiding these difficulties?

3. Now describe the advantages that might come from differing cultural nonverbal practices. How might people from diverse backgrounds profit by encountering one another's customs and norms?

3. **Kinesics in Action** You can appreciate the many ways kinesic cues operate by identifying examples from your own experience when body movement served each of the following nonverbal functions:

1. Repeating
2. Substituting
3. Complementing
4. Accenting
5. Regulating
6. Contradicting

7. **The Eyes Have It** Prove for yourself the role eye contact plays in social influence by trying a simple experiment.

1. Choose a situation in which you can make simple requests from a series of strangers. You might, for example, ask to cut in line to use a photocopying machine.

2. Make such a request to at least 20 people. Use the same words for each request but alternate your nonverbal behavior. Half the time, make direct eye contact, and the other half of the time avoid looking directly at the other person when you make your request.

3. Record your results, and see if your eye behavior played any role in generating compliance to your request.

4. If eye contact does make a difference, describe how you could apply your findings to real-life situations.

5. **Building Vocal Fluency** You can become more adept at both conveying and interpreting vocal messages by following these directions.

1. Join with a partner and designate one person A and the other B.

2. Partner A should choose a passage of 25 to 50 words from a newspaper or magazine, using his or her voice to convey one of the following attitudes:

   a. Egotism
   b. Friendliness
   c. Insecurity
   d. Irritation
   e. Confidence

3. Partner B should try to detect the emotion being conveyed.

4. Switch roles and repeat the process. Continue alternating roles until each of you has both conveyed and tried to interpret at least four emotions.

5. After completing the preceding steps, discuss the following questions:

   a. What vocal cues did you use to make your guesses?
   b. Were some emotions easier to guess than others?
   c. Given the accuracy of your guesses, how would you assess your ability to interpret vocal cues?
   d. How can you use your increased sensitivity to vocal cues to improve your everyday communication competence?

6. **The Rules of Touch** Like most types of nonverbal behavior, touching is governed by cultural and social rules.

Imagine you are writing a guidebook for visitors from another culture. Describe the rules that govern touching in the following relationships. In each case, describe how the gender of the participants affects the rules.

- An adult and a 5-year-old

- An adult and a 12-year-old

- Two good friends

- Boss and employee

7. **Distance Violations** You can test the importance of distance for yourself by violating the cultural rules for use of the proxemic zones outlined on pages 187–188.

   1. Join with a partner. Choose which one of you will be the experimenter and which will be the observer.

   2. In three situations, the experimenter should deliberately use the "wrong" amount of space for the context. Make the violations as subtle as possible. You might, for instance, gradually move into another person's intimate zone when personal distance would

be more appropriate. (Be careful not to make the violations too offensive!)

   3. The observer should record the verbal and nonverbal reactions of others when the distance zones are violated. After each experiment, inform the people involved about your motives and ask whether they were consciously aware of the reason for any discomfort they experienced.

## For Further Exploration

**For more resources about the nature of communication, see the *Understanding Human Communication* website at www.oup.com/us/adler.** There you will find a variety of free resources: "Media Room" clips from popular films and television shows to further illustrate important concepts, a list of books and articles, links to descriptions of feature films and television shows at the *Now Playing* website, study aids, and a self-test to check your understanding of the material in this chapter.

## SELF-ASSESSMENT

ANSWERS to "How Worldly Are Your Nonverbal Communication Skills?" from p. 181.

1. Thumb and forefinger form a circle, while the other three fingers are spread out.

2. Two men hold hands in public.

3. Pinkie and pointer finger point straight up, while thumb holds the two middle fingers down.

4. Palm is held flat out toward another person.

5. Hand is in fist with thumb poking out between the forefinger and middle finger.

*The gestures above match up to the meanings listed to the right.*

| | |
|---|---|
| **2** | We're a couple. (United States) |
| **1** | This is worthless. (France) |
| **3** | Hook 'em horns. (United States, made popular by University of Texas Longhorns fans) |
| **1** | Please give me money. (Japan) |
| **2** | We respect each other. (Arab countries) |
| **1** | OK. (United States) |
| **5** | I've got your nose! (often said playfully to children in the United States) |
| **4** | I'd like to smear excrement over your face. (Greece) |
| **3** | A sign of the devil. (Italy) |
| **1** | You're an a\*\*hole. (Latin America) |
| **4** | Please stop, or tell it to the hand. (United States) |

**CHAPTER 7**

# Understanding Interpersonal Communication

## Chapter Outline

## LEARNING OBJECTIVES

1 Identify the factors that shape interpersonal attraction.

2 Describe Knapp's model of relational development.

3 Explain how dialectical tensions shape communication in interpersonal relationships.

4 Describe characteristics that distinguish interpersonal relationships from impersonal ones.

5 Identify content and relational dimensions of messages, and describe how to discuss them via metacommunication.

6 Describe the dimensions and influences of intimacy in relationships.

7 Analyze the reasons for self-disclosure and apply the characteristics of effective and appropriate self-disclosure.

8 Recognize the functions served by lies, equivocation, and hints.

She is the quintessential girl next door, with dimples and an endearingly shy smile. He's an intense adventure seeker who has been a Hollywood heartthrob since she was in kindergarten. As a schoolgirl, she daydreamed about marrying him one day. In her mid-20s, the fantasy became reality. The two met and fell in love, and within 2 months, it was official: Katie Holmes and Tom Cruise were engaged to marry.

People who know Cruise were astonished at his transformation. On her television program, Oprah Winfrey marveled, "You are such an intensely, I mean, intensely, intensely, intensely private person. And then, now you are just out everywhere kissin' and a huggin'." Grinning broadly, Cruise replied by proclaiming, "I'm in love!" He leapt to his feet and raised his arms in a victory pose. Then, he sank to one knee and pumped his elbow toward his waist like a running back in the end zone. Finally he jumped on Winfrey's couch in a giddy jig.[1]

Elsewhere, the 26-year-old Holmes was less physically demonstrative, but she weighed in with abundant enthusiasm: "I've found the man of my dreams," she raved. "He's the most incredible man. He's so generous and kind, and he helps so many people, and, um, he makes me laugh like I've never laughed, and he's a great friend."[2]

The following year, the couple had a daughter and got married. Five and a half years later, Holmes announced that she was filing for divorce.

What happened?

***Tom Cruise and Katie Holmes's relationship reminds us that interpersonal relationships aren't easy. As you read this chapter, think about these questions as you consider your own relationships:***

- Recall times when communication felt most *personal* and most *impersonal*. What was the difference?

- Were there occasions when what *wasn't* being said was more important than the topic under discussion?

- Recall times when you tried to talk about your relationship. What happened?

- Did the nature of communication in your relationship change over time? How?

- Were there times when you didn't disclose all your thoughts and feelings? Why not?

This chapter will help you understand the role of communication during both the good and the challenging phases of close relationships. It begins by exploring the reasons we form relationships. It goes on to explore two ways of analyzing how communication operates throughout the lifetime of relationships. Next, it explores what kinds of communication make some relationships much more personal than others. It also looks at some ways—both subtle and obvious—that we show others how we regard them and what kind of relationship we are seeking with them. Finally, we will look at the role of self-disclosure in interpersonal communication.

# Why We Form Relationships

Sometimes we don't have a choice about our relationships: Children can't select their parents, and most workers aren't able to choose their bosses or colleagues. In many other cases, though, we seek out some people and actively avoid others. Social scientists have collected an impressive body of research on interpersonal attraction. The following are some of the factors they have identified that influence our choice of relational partners.

## Appearance

Most people claim that we should judge others on the basis of character, not appearance. The reality, however, is quite the opposite—at least in the early stages of a relationship. People are more likely to show romantic interest in people they consider physically attractive, both in person[3] and online.[4] This may be why unattractive people (based on reviewer rankings) are more likely than others to enhance the photos they post on online dating sites, although they usually report truthfully about other details of their lives.[5] At some level, we realize that appearance matters. However, we may overestimate its long-term effects.

Even if your appearance isn't beautiful by societal standards, consider these encouraging facts. Beauty can be a disadvantage. Sometimes, people have such high expectations of attractive people that they are disappointed when they don't measure up in other ways. For example, university students rated an unpleasant speaking voice more harshly when the speaker was attractive than when he or she wasn't.[6] Furthermore, physical factors become less important as a relationship progresses[7] and as our relational goals change. It's a phenomenon researchers call "mating versus dating": We tend to look for different qualities in life partners than we do in dating partners. Although the women in one study preferred to date muscular men, they considered men with average body shapes to be more appealing candidates for marriage.[8] As one social scientist put it, "attractive features may open doors, but apparently, it takes more than physical beauty to keep them open."[9]

## Similarity

A large body of research confirms that, in most cases, we like people who are similar to us.[10] For example, the more similar a married couple's personalities are, the more likely they are to report being happy and satisfied in their marriage.[11] Physical similarities predict attraction, to an extent. When given a choice of where to sit, we tend to gravitate toward people whose features are similar to own—those who also wear glasses or have the same color hair we do.[12] Researchers speculate that similarities are comfortable, and they may reduce our fear that the other person will reject us. However, there is limited evidence that physical similarity leads to long-term relationship success. In fact, in some studies, although people feel comfortable with strangers who look like them, they find those people less sexually attractive than others. The researchers quip that trustworthy does not equate to lust-worthy.[13]

Based on the (misguided) premise that look-alike couples are particularly compatible, a new online dating site, Find Your Facemate, promises to help you find your look-alike soul mate. The site touts the success of couples such as Maggie Gyllenhaal and Peter Sarsgaard. Actually, research shows that physical resemblance isn't a good predictor of relational longevity. Do your friends and romantic partners mostly look like you or different from you?

Attraction is greatest when we are similar to others in a high percentage of important areas. For example, two people who support each other's career goals, enjoy the same friends, and have similar beliefs about human rights can endure trivial disagreements about the merits of sushi or hip-hop music. But determining exactly which similarities are most important is a tricky matter. The online dating service eHarmony matches couples based on "29 dimensions of compatibility," and other online dating sites make similar promises. However, the long-term success of people matched by computer algorithms is no greater than that of couples who meet on their own.[14] Researchers who analyzed the data concluded that match-making software focuses on easy-to-measure factors such as hobbies, but it leaves out the most important factors of all—how we interact with each other once we start a relationship and how we handle stress as a couple. In short, it's great to have a lot in common, but long-term satisfaction hinges on the way we communicate once we're together.

One more caveat is in order. Evidence shows that we befriend people whose interests and attitudes *seem* similar to our own. This is at least partly an illusion, however. We tend to overestimate how similar we are to our friends and underestimate how similar we are to people we don't know well.[15] This can be a stumbling block for people who are obviously different from those around them in terms of skin color, native language, or national origin. They often feel socially isolated because people shy away from them, assuming they have little in common. In reality, there is strong evidence that, when we are willing to communicate in a friendly and open way with a range of people, our differences are not usually as great as we thought.[16]

## Complementarity

The folk wisdom that "opposites attract" seems to contradict the similarity principle just described. In truth, both are valid. Differences strengthen a relationship when they are *complementary*—when each partner's characteristics satisfy the other's needs. Individuals, for instance, are often likely to be attracted to each other when one partner is dominant and the other passive.[17] Relationships also work well when the partners agree that one will exercise control in certain areas ("You make the final decisions about money") and the other will exercise control in different areas ("I'll decide how we ought to decorate the place"). Strains occur when control issues are disputed.

When successful and unsuccessful couples are compared over a 20-year period, it becomes clear that partners in successful marriages are similar enough to satisfy each other physically and mentally but different enough to meet each other's needs and keep the relationship interesting. Successful couples find ways to keep a balance between their similarities and differences, adjusting to the changes that occur over the years.

Let's return to the example of Katie Holmes and Tom Cruise. Like many people who are attracted to each other, they initially assumed they had a great deal in common. During an interview in the early days of their relationship, Holmes remarked, "From the moment I met him it just felt like I'd known him forever."[18] However, some people who knew the couple well worried that the combination of her mild temperament and his headstrong intensity was not ideal. For example, during the famous "couch jumping" episode of *Oprah*, Cruise invited Holmes (who was backstage) to come out. Although he told Winfrey, "She's gonna run. . . . This is going to freak her out," he led the audience in chanting Katie's name. When she still did not emerge, the cameras followed Cruise backstage, where he chased and caught Holmes and then, holding her by the arms, propelled her on stage and into the spotlight. Perhaps it was meant as a playful bit of fun, but the sight of one adult coercing another into doing something she apparently did not want to do made some people uneasy. As this example illustrates, it can be tricky to predict the perfect balance between similarities and differences. We'll have more to say about balancing similarities and differences later in this chapter.

## Reciprocal Attraction

We are attracted to people who like us— usually.[19] The power of reciprocal attraction is especially strong in the early stages of a relationship. Conversely, we will probably not care for people who clearly dislike or seem indifferent toward us.

It's no mystery why reciprocal liking builds attractiveness. People who approve of us bolster our feelings of self-esteem. This approval is rewarding in its own right, and it can also confirm the part of our self-concept that says, "I'm a likable person."

Of course, we aren't drawn toward everyone who seems to like us. If we don't find the other person's attributes attractive, their interest can be a turn-off. Attraction has to be mutual to spark and maintain a relationship.

Awed by the beauty of their neighbor Penny, the nerdy protagonists in the TV sitcom *The Big Bang Theory* fall over themselves to impress her. Have you ever found yourself at a loss communicating with someone you considered to have superior talents or beauty?

## Competence

We like to be around talented people, probably because we hope their skills and abilities will rub off on us. On the other hand, we are uncomfortable around those who are *too* competent—probably because we look bad by comparison. Given these contrasting attitudes, it's no surprise that people are generally attracted to those who are talented but who have visible flaws that show that they are human, just like us.[20]

There are some qualifications to this principle. People with especially high or low self-esteem find "perfect" people more attractive than those who are competent but flawed, and some studies suggest that women tend to be more impressed by uniformly superior people of both sexes, whereas men tend to be more impressed by desirable but "human" others. On the whole, though, the principle stands: The best way to gain the liking of others is to be good at what you do but to admit your mistakes and flaws.

> cultural idiom

**on the other hand:**
from the other point of view

## Disclosure

Revealing important information about yourself through self-disclosure can help build liking.[21] Sometimes the basis of this liking comes from learning about how we are similar, either in experiences ("I broke off an engagement myself") or in attitudes ("I feel nervous with strangers, too"). Self-disclosure also builds liking because it is a sign of regard. When people share private information with you, it suggests that they respect and trust you—a kind of liking that we've already seen increases attractiveness. Disclosure plays an even more important role as relationships develop beyond their earliest stages.

Not all disclosure leads to liking. The information you reveal ought to be appropriate for the setting and stage of the relationship. You'll read more about self-disclosure later in this chapter.

## Proximity

In many cases, proximity leads to liking.[22] For instance, we're more likely to develop friendships with close neighbors than with distant ones, and chances are good that we'll choose a mate with whom we cross paths often. Facts like these are understandable when we consider that proximity allows us to get more information about other people and benefit from a relationship with them. Also, people in close proximity may be more similar to us than those not close. For example, if we live in the same neighborhood, odds are we share the same socioeconomic status. The Internet provides a new means for creating closeness, as users are able to experience "virtual proximity" in cyberspace.[23]

Familiarity, on the other hand, can also breed contempt. Spousal and child abuse are distressingly common. Most aggravated assaults occur within the family or among close neighbors. You are likely to develop strong feelings regarding others you encounter frequently, whether these feelings are positive or negative.

## Rewards

Some social scientists argue that all relationships—both impersonal and personal—are based on a semi-economic model called *social exchange theory*.[24] This model suggests that we often seek out people who can give us rewards that are greater than or equal to the costs we encounter in dealing with them. Rewards may be tangible (a nice place to live, a high-paying job) or intangible (prestige, emotional support, companionship). Costs are undesirable outcomes: unpleasant work, emotional pain, and so on. A simple formula captures the social exchange theory of why we form and maintain relationships:

$$\text{Rewards} - \text{Costs} = \text{Outcome}$$

According to social exchange theorists, we use this formula (usually unconsciously) to decide whether dealing with another person is a "good deal" or "not worth the effort," based on whether the outcome is positive or negative.

At its most blatant level, an exchange approach seems cold and calculating, but in some types of relationships it seems quite appropriate. A healthy business relationship is based on how well the parties help one another, and some friendships are based on an informal kind of barter: "I don't mind listening to the ups and downs of your love life because you rescue me when the house needs repairs." Even close relationships have an element of exchange. Friends and lovers often tolerate each other's quirks because the comfort and enjoyment they get make the less-than-pleasant times worth accepting. In more serious cases, social exchange explains why some people stay in abusive relationships. Sadly, these people often report that they would rather be in a bad relationship than have no relationship at all.

# Characteristics of Interpersonal Communication

What is interpersonal communication? How does it differ from other types of interaction? When and how are interpersonal messages communicated? Read on and see.

Will Smith and Jada Pinkett-Smith are two famous and attractive actors who seem to have forged a long-lasting (albeit unconventional) relationship. What factors are most important in your long-term relationships?

## What Makes Communication Interpersonal?

The most obvious way to define *interpersonal communication* is by looking at the number of people involved. In this sense we could consider all dyadic interaction as **contextually interpersonal communication**.

Although looking at communication by context is useful, this approach raises some problems. Consider, for example, a routine transaction between a sales clerk and customer, or the rushed exchange when you ask a stranger on the street for directions. Communication of this sort hardly seems interpersonal—or personal in any sense of the word. In fact, after transactions like this we commonly remark, "I might as well have been talking to a machine."

The impersonal nature of some two-person exchanges has led some scholars to say that *quality*, not quantity, is what distinguishes interpersonal communication. **Qualitatively interpersonal communication** occurs when people treat one another as unique individuals, regardless of the context in which the interaction occurs or the number of people involved.[25] When quality of interaction is the criterion, the opposite of interpersonal communication is *impersonal* interaction, not group, public, or mass communication.

The majority of our communication, even in dyadic contexts, is relatively impersonal. We chat pleasantly with shopkeepers or fellow passengers on the bus or plane; we discuss the weather or current events with most classmates and neighbors; we deal with coworkers in a polite way. Considering the number of people we communicate with, qualitatively interpersonal interaction is rather scarce. This scarcity isn't necessarily unfortunate: Most of us don't have the time or energy to create personal relationships with everyone we encounter—or even to act in a personal way all the time with the people we know and love best. In fact, the scarcity of qualitatively interpersonal communication contributes to its value. Like precious jewels and one-of-a-kind artwork, qualitatively interpersonal relationships are special because of their scarcity. You can get a sense of how interpersonal your relationships are by trying Activity 1 at the end of the chapter.

## Interpersonal Communication in Online Relationships

There's no question that mediated relationships pass the test of being contextually interpersonal. You can stay in touch via text messaging, IM, tweets, e-mail, and social networking websites more efficiently than in person. But what about the *quality* of mediated interaction? Is online communication a poor substitute for face-to-face contact, or is it a rich medium for developing close personal relationships?

Some observers have argued that mediated communication reduces the frequency and quality of face-to-face interaction.[26] As one critic put it, "[electronic] devices seem to wall us off from one another in some ways while both intensifying and yet perhaps also trivializing interpersonal contact in other ways."[27] Some evidence does suggest that mediated relationships can squeeze out face-to-face contacts. One survey revealed that people who relied heavily on the Internet to meet their communication needs grew to rely less and less on their face-to-face networks. More significantly, they tended to feel lonelier and more depressed as their online communication increased.[28] Some critics argue that communicators who strive to acquire a large number of "friends" on social networking websites like Facebook and Twitter are engaging in superficial, impersonal relationships. As one critic put it,

> the idea . . . is to attain as many of these not-really-friends as possible. . . . Like cheap wine, "friends" provide a high that can only be sustained by acquiring more and more of them. Quantity trumps quality.[29]

Despite criticism like this, a growing body of research confirms the claim that mediated communication can *enhance*, not diminish, the quantity and quality of interpersonal communication. For example, adolescents who use online communication typically have more cohesive friendships than other teens.[30] And adults (women especially) report that they use e-mail to stay in touch with relatives and that social media sites allow them to maintain friendships with people who live both nearby and far away.[31]

Even more significant than the amount of communication that occurs online is its quality: 55 percent of Internet users said that e-mail had improved communication with family, and 66 percent said that their contact with friends had increased because of e-mail. Among women, the rate of satisfaction was even higher: 60 percent reported better contact with family and 71 percent with friends. Families that use mediated communication—particularly cell phones—stay in touch more regularly.[32]

One quality of online communication is its potential to convey social support. Researchers note that online communication often boosts the well-being of people who are shy[33] and those who live in rural areas.[34] It is also valuable in reducing stress among young adults. University students who use Facebook typically experience less stress than their peers, especially when they consider their online friends to be supportive, interpersonally attractive, and trustworthy.[35]

Another quality of computer-mediated communication is its asynchronous nature. That is, it allows people to think about their messages before sending them. This can be an advantage. In a study of multimedia use by romantic partners,[36] one woman said she feels more genuine and in control when she has time to think about a message before she sends it. As she put it, "you can catch your mistakes or things that might offend the other person" rather than "blurting out" things you don't really mean. But another person interviewed in the same study felt that electronic communication is less genuine than face-to-face conversations because nonverbal cues are lacking and people can be more calculating in their responses. "Arguing over text messages is cheating because you don't have to immediately respond," he said, asserting that technology can be a "safeguard" that hides people's true feelings.

For some people, mediated channels make it easier to build close relationships. Sociolinguist Deborah Tannen describes a situation in which e-mail enhanced a relationship that wouldn't have developed to the same degree in person:

> E-mail deepened my friendship with Ralph. Though his office was next to mine, we rarely had extended conversations because he is shy. Face to face he mumbled so I could barely tell he was speaking. But when we both got on e-mail, I started receiving long, self-revealing messages; we poured our hearts out to each other. A friend discovered that e-mail opened up that kind of communication with her father. He would never talk much on the phone (as her mother would), but they have become close since they both got on line.[37]

> cultural idiom

**poured our hearts out:**
revealed our innermost thoughts and feelings

This story illustrates how online communication can provide rich opportunities for establishing depth and maintaining relationships. An Internet connection makes it possible to send and receive messages at any time of the day or night from people around the world. When face-to-face contact is impossible and telephone conversations difficult due to cost or time differences, computer-mediated messages are cheap, quick, and easy.

Researchers have found differences between mediated relationships that started online and those in which people rely on both mediated and face-to-face channels. Exclusively online relationships can develop rapidly because of the nature of the communication. Whereas face-to-face relationships often rely on shared activities and spending time together, online relationships rely entirely on communication. The focus on self-expression, combined with the somewhat anonymous nature of online interactions, tends to result in greater self-disclosure than that which takes place in budding face-to-face relationships.[38] On the other hand, without personal contact, communicators tend to idealize one another, creating the potential for disappointment once they actually meet in person. In one study, 68 percent of respondents reported that their online relationship terminated due to their first face-to-face interaction going poorly.[39]

## Content and Relational Messages

Virtually every verbal statement contains two kinds of messages. **Content messages**, which focus on the subject being discussed, are the most obvious. The content of such statements as "It's your turn to do the dishes" or "I'm busy Saturday night" is obvious.

Content messages aren't the only kind that are exchanged when two people interact. In addition, virtually all communication—both verbal and nonverbal—contains **relational messages**, which make statements about how the parties feel toward one another.[40] These relational messages express communicators' feelings and attitudes involving one or more dimensions, which are described here.

**Affinity**   One dimension of relational communication is **affinity**: the degree to which people like or appreciate one another. When Tom Cruise was asked what first attracted him to Katie Holmes, he didn't hesitate to answer: "She cares about other people. She's incredibly creative. She wants to live life. She's interested in people. She's very smart. She's funny."[41] Like him, we often associate our loved ones with a long list of admirable qualities.

**Respect**   **Respect** is the degree to which we admire others and hold them in esteem. Respect and affinity might seem identical, but they are actually different dimensions of a relationship.[42] For example, you might like a 3-year-old child tremendously without respecting her. Likewise, you could respect a boss or teacher's talents without liking him or her. Respect is a tremendously important and often overlooked ingredient in satisfying relationships. It is a better predictor of relational satisfaction than liking, or even loving.[43]

**Immediacy**   Communication scholars use the term **immediacy** to describe the degree of interest and attraction we feel toward and communicate to others. Immediacy is different than affinity. You can like someone (high affinity) but not demonstrate that feeling (low immediacy). Likewise, it's easy to imagine high affinity/high immediacy and low affinity/low immediacy, as well as low affinity and high immediacy.

**Control**   In every conversation and every relationship there is some distribution of **control**: the amount of influence communicators seek. Control can be distributed evenly among relational partners, or one person can have more and the other(s) less. An uneven distribution of control won't cause problems as long as everyone involved accepts that arrangement. Struggles arise, though, when people disagree on how control should be distributed in their relationship.

Speculation surrounding Tom Cruise and Katie Holmes's relationship has often focused on issues of control. T-shirts with the words "Free Katie" and "Run Katie Run" surfaced early on, in response to media reports that Cruise foisted his Scientology beliefs on Holmes, insisted (apparently against her wishes) that people call her Kate rather Katie, dictated how she traveled and the nature of publicity photos for her movies, and so on. The couple has not commented publicly on the power balance between them, so we should be careful not to give credence to

 **ON YOUR FEET**

*Reading Between the Lines*
Describe an incident in which someone heard the words you were saying but missed or misunderstood your underlying relational message. How did the person respond? What happened as a result? How might you have made your true meaning clearer?

Think of a close personal relationship. In what ways do you have power in the relationship? In what ways does your partner have power? Is the distribution of power and control in the relationship roughly equal? If not, who has more? What are the consequences of this power distribution?

rumors that may or may not be true. Instead, we can use the opportunity to consider the power dynamics in our own relationships.

You can get a feeling for how relational messages operate in everyday life by recalling the statements at the beginning of this section. Imagine two ways of saying, "It's your turn to do the dishes": one that is demanding and another that is matter of fact. Notice how the different nonverbal messages make statements about how the sender views control in this part of the relationship. The demanding tone says, in effect, "I have a right to tell you what to do around the house," whereas the matter-of-fact one suggests, "I'm just reminding you of something you might have overlooked." Likewise, you can easily visualize two ways to deliver the statement, "I'm busy Saturday night"—one with little affection and the other with much liking.

Notice that in each of these examples the relational dimension of the message was never discussed. In fact, most of the time we aren't conscious of the relational messages that bombard us every day. Sometimes we are unaware of relational messages because they match our belief about the amount of respect, immediacy, control, and affinity that is appropriate. For example, you probably won't be offended if your boss tells you to do a certain job, because you agree that supervisors have the right to direct employees. In other cases, however, conflicts arise over relational messages even though content is not disputed. If your boss delivers the order in a condescending, sarcastic, or abusive tone of voice, you probably will be offended. Your complaint wouldn't be with the order itself but rather would be with the way it was delivered. "I may work for this company," you might think, "but I'm not a slave or an idiot. I deserve to be treated like a human being."

How are relational messages communicated? As the boss-employee example suggests, they are usually expressed nonverbally. To test this fact for yourself, imagine how you could act while saying, "Can you help me for a minute?" in a way that communicates each of the following attitudes:

| | | |
|---|---|---|
| superiority | aloofness | friendliness |
| helplessness | sexual desire | irritation |

Although nonverbal behaviors are a good source of relational messages, remember that they are ambiguous. The sharp tone you take as a personal insult might be due to fatigue, and the interruption you take as an attempt to ignore your ideas might be a sign of pressure that has nothing to do with you. Before you jump to conclusions about relational clues, it's a good idea to practice the skill of perception checking that you learned in Chapter 2: "When you use that tone of voice to tell me it's my turn to do the dishes, I get the idea you're mad at me. Is that right?" If your interpretation was indeed correct, you can talk about the problem. On the other hand, if you were overreacting, the perception check can prevent a needless fight.

## Metacommunication

As the preceding example of perception checking shows, not all relational messages are nonverbal. Social scientists use the term **metacommunication** to describe messages that refer to other messages.[44] In other words, metacommunication is communication about communication. Whenever we discuss a relationship with others, we are metacommunicating: "It sounds like you're angry at me" or "I appreciate how honest you've been." As the cartoon on page 207 shows, even text messages can contain subtexts, otherwise known as metacommunicative dimensions. An e-mail or instant message that calls you an "idiot" might be a joking token of affection, or something quite the opposite. Given the fact that nonverbal cues are limited in computer-mediated communication, it's often important to supplement them with metacommunication (such as "just kidding").

Metacommunication is an important method of solving conflicts in a constructive manner. It allows us to look below the surface of a message, to the underlying meanings where the problem often lies. For example, consider a couple bickering because one partner wants to watch television, whereas the other wants to talk. Imagine how much better the chances of a positive outcome would be if they used metacommunication to examine the relational problems that were behind their quarrel: "Look, it's not the TV watching itself that bothers me. It's that I imagine you watch so much because you're mad at me or bored. Are you feeling bad about us?"

Metacommunication isn't just a tool for handling problems. It is also a way to reinforce the good aspects of a relationship: "I really appreciate it when you compliment me about my work in front of the boss." Comments like this serve two functions: First, they let others know that you value their behavior. Second, they boost the odds that the other people will continue the behavior in the future.

Despite the benefits of metacommunication, bringing relational issues out in the open does have its risks. Discussing problems can be interpreted in two ways. On the one hand, the other person might see it in a positive light—"our relationship is working because we can still talk things out." On the other hand, your desire to focus on the relationship might look like a bad omen—"our relationship isn't working if we have to keep talking it over." Furthermore, metacommunication does involve a certain degree of analysis ("It seems like you're angry at me"), and some people resent being analyzed. These cautions don't mean verbal metacommunication is a bad idea. They do suggest, though, that it's a tool that needs to be used carefully.

"She's texting me, but I think she's also subtexting me."

Source: © Cartoonbank.com

# Communication over the Relational Life Span

Qualitatively interpersonal relationships aren't stable. Instead, they are constantly changing. Communication scholars have described the way relationships develop and shift in two ways. We will examine each of them now.

## A Developmental Perspective

One of the best-known explanations of how communication operates in relationships was created by Mark Knapp, whose **developmental model** broke down the rise and fall of relationships into 10 stages, contained in the two broad phases of "coming together" and "coming apart."[45] Other researchers have suggested that any model of relational communication ought to contain a third part of the relational

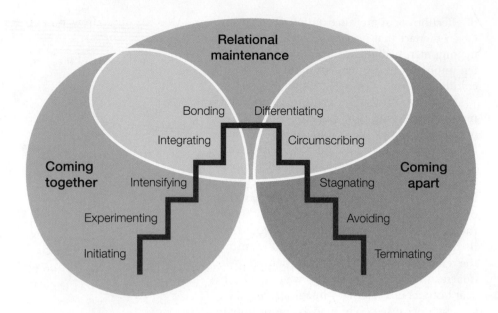

**FIGURE 7-1   Knapp's Stages of Relational Development**

process—a stage in which communication is aimed at keeping stable relationships operating smoothly and satisfactorily.[46] Figure 7-1 shows how Knapp's 10 stages fit into this three-part view of relational communication.

The following stages are especially descriptive of intimate, romantic relationships and close friendships. The pattern for other intimate relationships, such as families, would follow different paths.

**Initiating**   The stage of initiation involves the initial making of contact with another person. Knapp restricts this stage to conversation openers, both in initial contacts and in contacts with acquaintances: "Nice to meet you," "How's it going?" and so on.

Whatever your preference for opening remarks, this stage is important because you are formulating your first impressions and presenting yourself as interested in the other person.

Initiating relationships can be particularly hard for people who are shy. Making contact via the Internet can be helpful for people who have a hard time conversing in person. Researchers in one study found that shy people are more likely than others to prefer online dating.[47] The researchers found that many shy users employed the online service specifically to help overcome their inhibitions about initiating relationships in face-to-face settings.

**Experimenting**   In the stage of experimenting, conversation develops as people get acquainted by making "small talk." We ask: "Where are you from?" or "What do you do?" or "Do you know Josephine Mandoza? She lives in San Francisco, too."

Though small talk might seem meaningless, Knapp points out that it serves four purposes:

① It is a useful process for uncovering integrating topics and openings for more penetrating conversation.

② It can be an audition for a future friendship or a way of increasing the scope of a current relationship.

③ It provides a safe procedure for indicating who we are and how someone can come to know us better (reduction of uncertainty).

> cultural idiom

**small talk:**
unimportant or trivial conversation

④ It allows us to maintain a sense of community with our fellow human beings.

The relationship during this stage is generally pleasant and uncritical, and the commitments are minimal.

**Intensifying**    At the next stage, the kind of truly interpersonal relationship defined earlier in this chapter begins to develop. Several changes in communication patterns occur during intensifying. The expression of feelings toward the other becomes more common. Dating couples use a wide range of communication strategies to describe their feelings of attraction.[48] About a quarter of the time they express their feelings directly, using metacommunication to discuss the state of the relationship. More often they use less direct methods of communication: spending an increasing amount of time together, asking for support from each other, doing favors for the partner, giving tokens of affection, hinting and flirting, expressing feelings nonverbally, getting to know the partner's friends and family, and trying to look more physically attractive. Touching is more common during this stage than in either earlier or later ones.[49] Other changes mark the intensifying stage. Forms of address become more familiar. The parties begin to see themselves as "we" instead of as separate individuals. It is during the intensifying stage that individuals begin to directly express feelings of commitment to each other: "I'm so glad we met." "You're the best thing that's happened to me in a long time." It's often a time of intense emotion and optimism. Soon after Katie Holmes and Cruise were engaged, she proclaimed in an interview, "Tom and I will always be in our honeymoon phase."[50]

**Integrating**    As the relationship strengthens, the parties begin to take on an identity as a social unit. Invitations begin to come addressed to the couple. Social circles merge. The partners begin to take on each other's commitments: "Sure, we'll spend Thanksgiving with your family." Common property may begin to be designated—our apartment, our car, our song.[51] Partners develop their own rituals for everything from expressing intimacy to handling daily routines.[52] They even begin to speak alike, using common words and sentence patterns.[53] In this sense, the integration stage is a time when we give up some characteristics of our old selves and become different people.

As we become more integrated with others, our sense of obligation to them grows.[54] We feel obliged to provide a variety of resources such as class notes and money, whether or not the other person asks for them. When intimates do make requests of each other, they are relatively straightforward. Gone are the elaborate explanations, inducements, and apologies. In short, partners in an integrated relationship expect more from each other than they do in less intimate associations.

**Bonding**    During the bonding stage, the parties make symbolic public gestures to show the world that their relationship exists. The most common form of bonding in romantic relationships is a wedding ceremony or civil union. Bonding generates social support for the relationship. Both custom and law impose certain obligations on partners who have officially bonded.

Bonding marks a turning point in a relationship. Up to now the relationship may have developed at a steady pace: Experimenting gradually moved into intensifying and then into integrating. Now, however, there is a spurt of commitment. The public display and declaration of exclusivity make this a critical period in the relationship.

Relationships don't have to be romantic to have a bonding stage. Business contracts form a bond, as does being initiated into a fraternity or sorority. Acts like these "officialize" a relationship and involve a measure of public commitment.

Entertainment writers created the name TomKat to refer to Katie Holmes and Tom Cruise as a couple. The nickname drew attention to their relationship rather than their unique identities. In what ways have you established an integrated identity with people in your life? In what ways does an integrated identity enhance your relationships? Does it ever go too far?

Some people argue that Knapp's model of relational development and decline does not characterize nonromantic relationships well. Think of a nonromantic relationship of your own (e.g., parent/child, coworkers, friends). Construct a model describing communication stages in that relationship. Are the stages mostly similar to Knapp's or not? How does your model differ?

**Differentiating** Now that the two people have formed this commonality, they need to reestablish individual identities. This is the point at which the "hold me tight" orientation that has existed shifts, and "put me down" messages begin to occur. Partners use a variety of strategies to gain privacy from each other.[55] Sometimes they confront the other party directly, explaining that they don't want to continue a discussion. At other times they are less direct, offering nonverbal cues, changing the topic, or leaving the room.

Differentiation is likely to occur when a relationship begins to experience the first, inevitable stress. This desire for autonomy needn't be a negative experience, however. People need to be individuals as well as parts of a relationship, and differentiation is a necessary step toward autonomy. As you'll read later in this chapter, the key to successful differentiation is maintaining a commitment to the relationship while creating the space for being an individual as well.

**Circumscribing** In the circumscribing stage, communication between members decreases in quantity and quality. Restrictions and restraints characterize this stage, and dynamic communication becomes static. Rather than discuss a disagreement (which requires some degree of energy on both parts), members opt for withdrawal: either mental (silence or daydreaming and fantasizing) or physical (spending less time together). Circumscribing doesn't involve total avoidance, which comes later. Rather, it entails a certain shrinking of interest and commitment.

**Stagnating** If circumscribing continues, the relationship begins to stagnate. Members behave toward each other in old, familiar ways without much feeling. No growth occurs. The relationship is a shadow of its former self. We see stagnation in many workers who have lost enthusiasm for their job yet continue to go through the motions for years. The same sad event occurs for some couples who unenthusiastically have the same conversations, see the same people, and follow the same routines without any sense of joy or novelty.

**Avoiding** When stagnation becomes too unpleasant, parties in a relationship begin to create distance between each other. Sometimes this is done under the guise of excuses ("I've been sick lately and can't see you"), and sometimes it is done directly ("Please don't call me; I don't want to see you now"). In either case, by this point the handwriting about the relationship's future is clearly on the wall.

> cultural idiom
> **handwriting . . . is clearly on the wall:**
> an indication or foretelling of an unfortunate message

> cultural idiom
> **bitter jabs:**
> unkind comments

**Terminating** Characteristics of this final stage include summary dialogues about where the relationship has gone and the desire to dissociate. The relationship may end with a cordial dinner, a note left on the kitchen table, a phone call, or a legal document stating the dissolution. Depending on each person's feelings, this stage can be quite short, or it may be drawn out over time, with bitter jabs exchanged between the two people.

The deterioration of a relationship from bonding to circumscribing, stagnating, and avoiding isn't inevitable. One key difference between couples who get together again after a breakup and those who go their separate ways is how well they communicate about their dissatisfaction and negotiate for a mutually appealing fresh start. Unsuccessful couples deal with their problems by avoidance, indirectness, and less involvement with each other. By contrast, couples who "repair" their relationship communicate much more directly. They air their concerns and spend time and effort negotiating solutions to their problems.

Relationships don't always move toward termination in a straight line. Rather, they take a back-and-forth pattern, in which the trend is toward dissolution.[56]

One of the difficult aspects of a breakup often involves sharing the news with people around you. When Katie Holmes announced that she was filing for divorce, there was considerable publicity about it. Cruise's publicist issued a statement saying that "Tom is deeply saddened," but both Cruise and Holmes avoided badmouthing each other publicly. Instead, they stressed that, although they were no longer together, they had a shared interest in their daughter's well-being.

Although the communication surrounding relational termination can sometimes be cruel and painful, it doesn't have to be totally negative. Understanding each other's investment in the relationship and need for personal growth may dilute the hard feelings. In fact, many relationships aren't so much terminated as redefined. A divorced couple, for example, may find new, less intimate ways to relate to each other.

On the TV show *The Mindy Project*, Mindy (Mindy Kaling) and Danny (Chris Messina) are coworkers with a friendly, possibly flirtatious relationship. If they are headed toward a romantic relationship, in which stage of Knapp's developmental model would you say they are? How well does Knapp's model apply to nonromantic couples, such as coworkers or friends?

## A Dialectical Perspective

Developmental models like the one described in the preceding pages suggest that communication differs in important ways at various points in the life of a relationship. According to these stage-related models, the kinds of interactions that happen during initiating, experimenting, or intensifying are different from the interaction that occurs during differentiating, circumscribing, or avoiding.

### Understanding Communication Technology

## To End This Romance, Just Press "Send": Instant Messaging Altering the Way We Love

It was the middle of a workday 2 weeks ago, and Larry was deep into a meeting when a text message began scrolling across his cell phone screen. He glanced at it and thought: "You can't be serious."

It was no joke. His girlfriend was breaking up with him . . . again. And she was doing it by e-mail . . . again.

For the sixth time in 8 months, she had ended their relationship electronically rather than face-to-face. He had sensed trouble—he had been opening his e-mail with trepidation for weeks—so the previous day he had suggested that they meet in person to talk things over. But she nixed that, instead choosing to send the latest in what Larry had begun to consider part of a virtual genre: "the goodbye e-mail."

Understandably, he'd like to say his own goodbye to that genre. "E-mail is horrible," says Larry, 36, a U.S. Air Force sergeant from New Hampshire who asked that his last name not be used. "You just get to the point where you hate it. You can't have dialogue. You don't have that person in front of you. You just have that black-and-white text. It's a very cold way of communicating."

Cold, maybe. Popular, for sure. The use of e-mail and instant messaging to end intimate relationships is gaining popularity because instantaneous communication makes it easy—some say too easy—to just call the whole thing off. Want to avoid one of those squirmy, awkward breakup scenes? Want to control the dialogue while removing facial expressions, vocal inflections, and body language from the equation? A solution is as near as your keyboard or cell phone.

Sometimes there is a legitimate reason for wanting to avoid personal contact. Tara, a 32-year-old woman who lives near Boston, says her ex-husband was intimidating and emotionally abusive during their marriage. So when she wanted to end the marriage several years ago, she felt more comfortable doing so by sending a text message.

Tara says that since then she has ended several other relationships by e-mail. "I'm a softie, and I hate hurting people's feelings," she says. Recently she laid the groundwork for breaking her engagement with a series of e-mails to her fiancé. After ending the engagement last week, she reached a moment of truth, she says, and has decided that from now on, if she wants to call it quits, "The e-mail option is out."

This sort of back-and-forth might reflect what Lee Rainey, director of the Pew Internet & American Life Project, sees as a blurring of the boundaries in modern romance between the real and virtual realms. ●

Despite its value, a stage-related model isn't the only way to explain interaction in relationships. Some scholars suggest that communicators grapple with the same kinds of challenges whether a relationship is brand new or has lasted decades. They argue that communicators seek important but inherently incompatible goals throughout virtually all of their relationships. This **dialectical model** suggests that struggling to achieve these goals creates **dialectical tensions**: conflicts that arise when two opposing or incompatible forces exist simultaneously. In recent years, communication scholars have identified the dialectical tensions that make successful communication challenging.[57] They suggest that the struggle to manage these dialectical tensions creates the most powerful dynamics in relational communication. In the following pages we will discuss three powerful dialectical tensions.

**Connection Versus Autonomy**  No one is an island. Recognizing this fact, we seek out involvement with others. But, at the same time, we are unwilling to sacrifice our entire identity to even the most satisfying relationship. The conflicting desires for connection and independence are embodied in the *connection-autonomy dialectic*. Research on relational breakups demonstrates the consequences for relational partners who can't find a way to manage these very different personal needs.[58] Some of the most common reasons for relational breakups involve failure of partners to satisfy each other's needs for connection: "We barely spent any time together"; "He wasn't committed to the relationship"; "We had different needs." But other relational complaints involve excessive demands for connection: "I was feeling trapped"; "I needed freedom."

The levels of connection and autonomy that we seek can change over time. In his book *Intimate Behavior*, Desmond Morris suggests that each of us repeatedly goes through three stages: "Hold me tight," "Put me down," and "Leave me alone."[59] This cycle becomes apparent in the first years of life when children move from the "Hold me tight" stage that characterizes infancy into a new "Put me down" stage of exploring the world by crawling, walking, touching, and tasting. This move for independence isn't all in one direction: The same 3-year-old who insists, "I can do it myself" in August may cling to parents on the first day of preschool in September. As children grow into adolescents, the "Leave me alone" orientation becomes apparent. Teenagers who used to happily spend time with their parents now may groan at the thought of a family vacation or even the notion of sitting down at the dinner table each evening. More time is spent with friends or alone. Although this time can be painful for parents, most developmental experts recognize it as a necessary stage in moving from childhood to adulthood.

As the need for independence from family grows, adolescents take care of their "Hold me tight" needs by associating with their peers. Friendships during the teenage years are vital, and the level of closeness with contemporaries can be a barometer of happiness. This is the time when physical intimacy becomes an option, and sexual exploration may provide a new way of achieving closeness.

In adult relationships, the same cycle of intimacy and distance repeats itself. In marriages, for example, the "Hold me tight" bonds of the first year are often followed by a desire for independence. This need for autonomy can manifest itself in a number of ways, such as the desire to make friends or engage in activities that don't include the spouse, or the need to make a career move that might disrupt the relationship. As the discussion of relational stages later in this chapter will explain, this movement from closeness to autonomy may lead to the breakup of relationships, but it can also be part of a cycle that redefines the relationship in a new form that can recapture or even surpass the intimacy that existed in the past.

*Source:* Reprinted by special permission of King Features Syndicate.

**Predictability Versus Novelty**   Stability is important in relationships, but too much of it can lead to feelings of staleness. The *predictability-novelty dialectic* reflects this tension. Humorist Dave Barry exaggerates only slightly when he talks about the boredom that can come when husbands and wives know each other too well:

> After a decade or so of marriage, you know *everything* about your spouse, every habit and opinion and twitch and tic and minor skin growth. You could write a seventeen-pound book solely about the way your spouse *eats*. This kind of intimate knowledge can be very handy in certain situations—such as when you're on a TV quiz show where the object is to identify your spouse from the sound of his or her chewing—but it tends to lower the passion level of a relationship.[60]

Although too much familiarity can lead to the risk of boredom and stagnation, nobody wants a completely unpredictable relational partner. Too many surprises can threaten the foundations on which the relationship is based ("You're not the person I married!").

The challenge for communicators is to juggle the desire for predictability with the need for novelty that keeps the relationship fresh and interesting. People differ in their need and desire for stability and surprises, so there is no optimal mixture of the two. As you will read shortly, there are a number of strategies people can use to manage these contradictory drives.

**Openness Versus Privacy**   As Chapter 1 explained, disclosure is one characteristic of interpersonal relationships. Yet, along with the need for intimacy, we have an equally important need to maintain some space between ourselves and others. These sometimes conflicting drives create the *openness-privacy dialectic*.

Even the strongest interpersonal relationships require some distance. On a short-term basis, the desire for closeness waxes and wanes. Lovers may go through periods of much sharing and times of relative withdrawal. Likewise, they experience periods of passion and then periods of little physical contact. Friends have times of high disclosure during which they share almost every feeling and idea and then disengage for days, months, or even longer. Figure 7-2 illustrates some patterns of variation in openness uncovered in a study of college students' communication patterns.[61] The students reported the degree of openness in one of their important relationships—a friendship, romantic relationship, or marriage—over a range of 30 conversations. The graphs show a definite pattern of fluctuation between disclosure and privacy in every stage of the relationships.

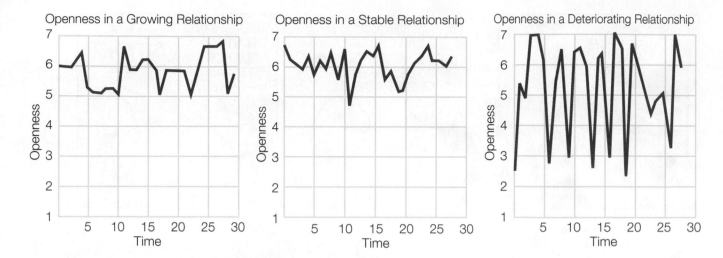

**FIGURE 7-2 Cyclical Phases of Openness and Withdrawal in Relationships**

**Strategies for Managing Dialectical Tensions** Managing the dialectical tensions outlined in these pages presents communication challenges. There are a number of strategies by which these challenges can be managed.[62] One of the least functional is *denial* that tensions exist. People in denial insist that "everything is fine," that the inevitable tugs of dialectical tensions really aren't a problem. For example, coworkers who claim that they're *always* happy to be members of the team and *never* see conflicts between their personal goals and the organization's are probably operating in a state of denial.

*Disorientation* is another response to dialectical tensions. In this response, communicators feel so overwhelmed and helpless that they are unable to confront their problems. In the face of dialectical tensions they might fight, freeze, or even leave the relationship. A couple who discover soon after the honeymoon that living a "happily ever after" conflict-free life is impossible might become so terrified that they would come to view their marriage as a mistake.

In the strategy of *selection*, communicators respond to one end of the dialectical spectrum and ignore the other. For example, a couple caught between the conflicting desires for stability and novelty might find their struggle to change too difficult to manage and choose to stick with predictable, if unexciting, patterns of relating to each other.

Communicators choose the strategy of *alternation* to alternate between one end of the dialectical spectrum at some times and the other end at other times. Friends, for example, might manage the autonomy-connection dialectic by alternating between times when they spend a large amount of time together and other times when they live independent lives.

A fifth strategy is *segmentation*, a tactic in which partners compartmentalize different areas of their relationship. For example, a couple might manage the openness-closedness dialectic by sharing almost all their feelings about mutual friends with each other but keeping certain parts of their past romantic histories private.

*Moderation* is a sixth strategy. This strategy is characterized by compromises, in which communicators choose to back off from expressing either end of the dialectical spectrum. Adult children, for example, might manage the revelation-concealment dialectic with their inquisitive parents by answering some (though not all) unwelcome parental questions.

Communicators can also respond to dialectical challenges by *reframing* them in terms that redefine the situation so that the apparent contradiction disappears. Consider a couple who wince when their friends characterize them as a "perfect couple." On one hand, they want to escape from the "perfect couple" label that feels confining, but on the other hand, they enjoy the admiration that comes with this identity. By pointing out to their friends that "ideal couples" aren't always blissfully happy, they can both be themselves and keep the admiration of their friends.

A final strategy for handling dialectical tensions is *reaffirmation*—acknowledging that dialectical tensions will never disappear and accepting or even embracing the challenges they present. The metaphorical view of relational life as a kind of roller coaster reflects this orientation, and communicators who use reaffirmation view dialectical tensions as part of the ride.

Even though a relationship may move back to a stage it has experienced before, it will never be the same. For example, most healthy, long-term relationships will go through several phases of experimenting, when the partners try out new ways of behaving with each other. Though each phase is characterized by the same general features, the specifics will feel different each time. As you learned in Chapter 1, communication is irreversible. Partners can never go back to "the way things were." Sometimes this fact may lead to regrets: It's impossible to take back a cruel comment or forget a crisis. On the other hand, the irreversibility of communication can make relationships exciting, because it lessens the chance for boredom.

In the TV drama *Grey's Anatomy*, Meredith (Ellen Pompeo) and Christina (Sandra Oh) are best friends who regularly rely on each other. Despite their closeness, each understands when the other needs time apart for herself. How do you balance the need for togetherness and independence in your close relationships?

# Intimacy in Interpersonal Relationships

Even the closest relationships involve a mixture of personal and interpersonal communication. We alternate between a "we" and a "me" orientation, sometimes focusing on connecting with others and at other times focusing on our own needs and interests. In the next few pages we will examine how our communication is affected by these apparently conflicting drives for intimacy and distance.

## Dimensions of Intimacy

The dictionary defines **intimacy** as arising from "close union, contact, association, or acquaintance." This definition suggests that the key element of intimacy is closeness, one element that "ordinary people" have reported as characterizing their intimate relationships.[63] However, it doesn't explain what *kinds* of closeness can create a state of intimacy. In truth, intimacy can have several qualities. The first is *physical*. Even before birth, the developing fetus experiences a kind of physical closeness with its mother that will never happen again, "floating in a warm fluid, curling inside a total embrace, swaying to the undulations of the moving body and hearing the beat of the pulsing heart."[64] As they grow up, fortunate children are continually nourished by physical intimacy: being rocked, fed, hugged, and held. As we grow older, the opportunities for physical intimacy are less regular, but still possible and important. Some, but by no means all, physical intimacy is sexual. In one survey, only one-quarter of the respondents (who were college students) stated that intimacy necessarily contained a romantic or sexual dimension.[65] Other

In the film *Friends with Benefits*, Dylan (Justin Timberlake) and Jamie (Mila Kunis) try to remain friends while becoming physically intimate without emotional entanglements. (Spoiler alert: It gets complicated.) Which dimensions of intimacy are most important to you? Do these dimensions relate to one another?

forms of physical intimacy include affectionate hugs, kisses, and even struggles. Companions who have endured physical challenges together—in athletics or emergencies, for example—form a bond that can last a lifetime.

In other cases, intimacy comes from *intellectual* sharing. Not every exchange of ideas counts as intimacy, of course. Talking about next week's midterm with your professor or classmates isn't likely to forge strong relational bonds. But when you engage another person in an exchange of important ideas, a kind of closeness develops that can be powerful and exciting.

A third quality of intimacy is *emotion*: exchanging important feelings. This chapter will offer several guidelines for disclosing your thoughts and feelings to others. If you follow those guidelines, you will probably recognize a qualitative change in your relationships.

If we define *intimacy* as being close to another person, then *shared activities* can provide another way to achieve this state. Shared activities can include everything from working side by side at a job to meeting regularly for exercise workouts. Although shared activities are no guarantee of intimacy, people who spend time together can develop unique ways of relating that transform the relationship from an impersonal one that could be done with anybody to one with interpersonal qualities. For example, both friendships and romantic relationships are often characterized by several forms of play. Partners invent private codes, fool around by acting like other people, tease each other, and play games—everything from having punning contests to arm wrestling.[66]

Some intimate relationships exhibit all four qualities: physical intimacy, intellectual exchanges, emotional disclosure, and shared activities. Other intimate relationships exhibit only one or two. Some relationships, of course, aren't intimate in any way. Acquaintances, roommates, and coworkers may never become intimate. In some cases even family members develop smooth but relatively impersonal relationships.

Not even the closest relationships always operate at the highest level of intimacy. At some times you might share all of your thoughts or feelings with a friend, family member, or lover, and at other times you might withdraw. You might freely share your feelings about one topic and stay more aloof in another one. The same principle holds for physical intimacy, which waxes and wanes in most relationships. The dialectical view of relational maintenance described later in this chapter explains how intimacy can wax and wane, even in the closest relationships.

## Male and Female Intimacy Styles

Until recently most social scientists believed that women are better at developing and maintaining intimate relationships than men. This belief grew from the assumption that the disclosure of personal information is the most important ingredient of intimacy. Most research *does* show that women (taken as a group, of course) are more willing than men to share their thoughts and feelings.[67] In terms of the amount and depth of information exchanged, female-female relationships are at the top of the disclosure list. Male-female relationships come in second, whereas relationships between men have less disclosure than any other type. At every age, women disclose more than men, and the information they disclose is more personal and more likely to involve feelings.

Through the mid-1980s many social scientists interpreted the relative lack of male self-disclosure as a sign that men are unwilling or even unable to develop close relationships. Some argued that the female trait of disclosing personal information and feelings makes them more "emotionally mature" and "interpersonally competent" than men. Personal growth programs and self-help books urged men to achieve closeness by learning to open up and share their feelings. Indeed, even today, magazines aimed at teen girls commonly depict boys as "shallow, highly sexual, emotionally inexpressive, and insecure."[68]

However, scholarship conducted in roughly the last two decades has begun to show that male-female differences aren't as great as they seem,[69] and emotional expression isn't the *only* way to develop close relationships. Unlike women, who value personal talk, men grow close to one another by doing things together. In one study, more than 75 percent of the men surveyed said that their most meaningful experiences with friends came from activities other than talking.[70] They reported that through shared activities they "grew on one another," developed feelings of interdependence, showed appreciation for one another, and demonstrated mutual liking. Likewise, men regarded practical help from other men as a measure of caring. Research like this shows that, for many men, closeness grows from activities that don't depend heavily on disclosure: A friend is a person who does things *for* you and *with* you. See the "Understanding Diversity" box below for more on male-female friendship patterns.

The difference between male and female measures of intimacy helps explain some of the stresses and misunderstandings that can arise between the sexes. For example, a woman who looks for emotional disclosure as a measure of affection may overlook an "inexpressive" man's efforts to show he cares by doing favors or spending time together. Fixing a leaky faucet or taking a hike may look like ways to avoid getting close, but to the man who proposes them, they may be measures of affection and bids for intimacy. Likewise, differing ideas about the timing and meaning of sex can lead to misunderstandings. Whereas many women think of sex as a way to express intimacy that has already developed, men are more likely to see it as a way to *create* that intimacy.[75] In this sense, the man who encourages sex early in a relationship or after a fight may not just be a testosterone-crazed lecher: He may view the shared activity as a way to build closeness. By contrast, the woman who views personal talk as the pathway to intimacy may resist the idea of physical closeness before the emotional side of the relationship has been discussed.

> cultural idiom
>
> **to open up:**
> talk about subjects that otherwise might be withheld

## Understanding Diversity

### Can Men and Women Be Just Friends?

It's an age-old question. And the answer depends on whom you ask. Women typically say yes. But men give a decidedly iffy answer. In a study of 88 pairs of college-age opposite-sex friends, most women said the friendship is purely platonic, with no romantic interest on either side.[71] The men were more likely to say that they secretly harbor romantic fantasies about their gal pals and they suspect (often wrongly, it seems) that the feeling is mutual.

Researchers speculate that men and women get their wires crossed partly because they communicate differently. Because women usually expect friends to be emotionally supportive and understanding, they engage in self-disclosure and empathy behaviors.[72] From the male perspective, this may feel like the trappings of romance rather than friendship. Men's same-sex friendships typically involve more independence, more friendly competition, and fewer intimate disclosures than women's do.[73] Those behaviors may not strike women as romantic.

So far, it seems there's still a gender gap where friendship is involved. But scientists encourage people to take heart. In the history of human development, male-female friendships are a recent development.[74] It may take a little practice. ●

## Personal Preferences for Intimacy

Some intimacy styles have less to do with gender than with personal preferences. Relationship counselor Gary Chapman[76] observes that people typically orient to one of five love languages: words of affirmation, quality time, acts of service, gifts, and physical touch. These languages reflect relationship maintenance behaviors well documented by communication scholars.[77] A brief description of each style is provided here. After reading about them, take the love language quiz on p. 219 to see which ones best describe you.

*Affirming words* include compliments, thanks, and statements that express love and commitment. Adult siblings frequently express affection this way,[78] as do parents[79] and romantic partners.[80] Even when you know someone loves and values you, it's often nice to hear it in words. For example, a study of couples who have been together for many years shows that the happiest of them continue to flirt with each other.[81]

*Quality time* might involve completing a task together, talking, or some other activity both partners enjoy. Grandparents and grandchildren indicate that sharing activities is one of the key factors in how close they feel to each other, and they feel a loss if their ability to do things together diminishes.[82] Research suggests that the quality of time we spend together is more important than the quantity.[83] The good news is that, even when people cannot be together physically, talking about quality time can be an important means of expressing love. Partners separated by military deployments often say they feel closer to each other just talking about everyday activities and future plans.[84]

*Acts of service* include running errands, playing caregiver to a friend who is sick, and other favors. Committed couples report that sharing daily tasks is the most frequent way they show their love and commitment.[85] Evidence shows that, although couples need not contribute in exactly the same ways, an overall sense that they are putting forth equal effort is essential to their long-term happiness.[86]

It may be no coincidence that we buy *gifts* for loved ones on Valentine's Day or other occasions. Evidence suggests that, for some people, receiving a gift—even an inexpensive or free one such as a flower from the garden—adds to a sense of being loved and valued.[87]

Finally, *physical touch* may involve a hug, a kiss, a pat on the back, or even having sex. For some people, touch is such a powerful indicator of intimacy that even an incidental touch can spur interest. In one study, a woman asked men in a bar for assistance in adding a key to her key ring.[88] She lightly touched some of the men but did not touch others. Afterward, researchers found that the men who had been touched were more romantically interested in the woman than the other men were. Touch is potent even in long-term relationships. Researchers in one study asked couples to increase the number of times they kissed each other. Six weeks later, the couples' stress levels and relational satisfaction, and even their cholesterol levels, had significantly improved.[89]

It's important to note that people attach different values to each of these love languages. You may feel that words are cheap, and that time spent together is the true measure of how much someone cares. But that doesn't mean everyone in your life feels the same way. Chapman proposes that the golden rule can lead us astray in this regard. If we value acts of service or gifts, we may go out of our way to provide them. But if our relational partner values touch or some other language, he or she may still feel unloved. "We cannot rely on our native tongue if our spouse [or other relational partner] does not understand it," Chapman says. "If we want him/her to feel the love we are trying to communicate, we must express it in his or her primary love language."[90]

## Your Love Languages

Answer the questions below to learn more about the love languages you prefer. Then ask people you know to fill out the quiz to learn more about their preferences.

1. You've had a stressful day working on a class project. The best thing your roommate can do for you is:
   a. Set aside distractions and spend some time with you
   b. Do your chores so you can put your feet up
   c. Give you a big hug
   d. Surprise you with a treat from your favorite bakery
   e. Tell you the team is lucky to have someone as talented as you

2. Your 5-year-old nephew is the apple of your eye. What are you most likely to do?
   a. Establish a ritual of going somewhere special together whenever you can
   b. Try to be available when he needs a helping hand or an arts and crafts partner
   c. Invite him to sit beside you while you read his favorite storybooks aloud
   d. Send him a little surprise
   e. Regularly tell him how proud you are of his talents and accomplishments

3. With which of the following do you most agree?
   a. The most lovable thing someone can do is give you his or her undivided attention
   b. A true friend is always willing to do nice things for you, even when you don't ask
   c. A loving touch says more than words can express
   d. Your dearest possessions are things that loved ones have given you
   e. People don't say "thank you" and "I love you" nearly enough

4. Your anniversary is coming up. Which of the following appeals to you most?
   a. An afternoon together, just the two of you
   b. A romantic, home-cooked dinner (you don't have to lift a finger)
   c. A relaxing massage by candlelight
   d. A mini photo-album of good times you have shared
   e. Finding little notes throughout the day that describe different things he or she loves about you

### INTERPRETING YOUR RESPONSES

For insight about your primary love languages, see which of the following best describes your answers.

#### Quality Time

If you answered "a" to one or more questions, you probably feel loved when people set aside life's distractions to spend time with you. Keep in mind that everyone defines quality time a bit differently. It may mean a thoughtful phone call during a busy day, a picnic in the park, or a few minutes every evening to share news about the day. Consider what "quality time" means to you and to the special people in your life.

#### Acts of Service

Answering "b" means you feel loved when people do thoughtful things for you such as washing your car, helping you with a repair job, bringing you breakfast in bed, or bathing the children so you can put your feet up. Even small gestures say "I love you" to people whose love language involves acts of service.

#### Physical Touch

Options labeled "c" are associated with the comfort and pleasure we get from physical affection. If your sweetheart texts to say, "Wish we were snuggled up together!" he or she is speaking the love language of touch. Physical touch includes sex but also friendly gestures such as a hug or a pat on the back.

#### Gifts

If you chose "d," chances are you treasure thoughtful gifts from loved ones. If you get a tear in your eye over things like a necktie, a finger puppet, a crayon drawing bestowed by a child, or a homemade ornament, gifts are probably an important love language to you.

#### Words of Affirmation

Options labeled "e" refer to words that make us feel loved and valued. These may be conveyed in a note from home, a homemade card or poem, a romantic letter, a song, or an unexpected text that simply says, "I love you." To people who speak this love language, hearing that they are loved (and why) is the sweetest message imaginable. ●

Our love language preferences may say something about the family or culture in which we grew up. In Muslim cultures, for instance, touch may be reserved for very intimate relationships only.[91] Following is more information about the impact of culture on intimate communication.

### Cultural Influences on Intimacy

The notion of how much intimacy is desirable and how to express it varies from one culture to another.[92] In most Asian cultures, emotions involving relationships are typically expressed less directly than in Western cultures. For example, in China, people adapt their speech to be more or less formal depending on the relative status and degree of intimacy between two people. These adaptations may be obvious to them, but not to people who are less familiar with the culture. It's easy to imagine how an American learning to speak Chinese could unwittingly take liberties that offend others.[93]

Culture also plays a role in shaping how much intimacy we display in different types of relationships. For instance, public displays of affection are taboo in Japan. Even holding hands is likely to raise eyebrows. But so-called love hotels, where couples may rent a room for a few hours, are prevalent. Affection is okay, just not in public spaces.[94]

In some collectivist cultures such as Taiwan and Japan, there is an especially great difference in the way members communicate with members of their "in-groups" (such as family and close friends) and with those they view as outsiders.[95] They generally do not reach out to strangers, often waiting until they are properly introduced before entering into conversations with them. Once introduced, they address outsiders with a degree of formality. They go to extremes to hide unfavorable information about in-group members from outsiders, on the principle that one doesn't wash dirty laundry in public. By contrast, members of more individualistic cultures like the United States and Australia make less of a distinction between personal relationships and casual ones. They act more familiar with strangers and disclose more personal information, making them excellent "cocktail party conversationalists."

> cultural idiom

**wash dirty laundry in public:**
disclose personal and private problems and concerns beyond one's family or group

# Self-Disclosure in Interpersonal Relationships

"We don't have any secrets," some people proudly claim. Opening up certainly is important. Earlier in this chapter you learned that one ingredient in qualitatively interpersonal relationships is disclosure. You've also read that we find others more attractive when they share certain private information with us. Given the obvious importance of self-disclosure, we need to take a closer look at the subject. Just what is it? When is it desirable? How can it best be done?

The best place to begin is with a definition. **Self-disclosure** is the process of deliberately revealing information about oneself that is significant and that would not normally be known by others. Let's take a closer look at some parts of this definition. Self-disclosure must be *deliberate*. If you accidentally mentioned to a friend that you were thinking about quitting a job or proposing marriage, that information would not fit into the category we are examining here. Self-disclosure must also be *significant*. Revealing relatively trivial information—the fact that you like fudge, for example—does not qualify as self-disclosure. The third requirement is that the information being revealed would *not be known by others*. There's nothing noteworthy about telling others that you are depressed or elated if they already know how you're feeling.

> cultural idiom

**opening up:**
talking about subjects that might otherwise be kept private

As Table 7-1 shows, people self-disclose for a variety of reasons. Some involve developing and maintaining relationships, but other reasons often drive revealing personal information. The reasons for disclosing vary from one situation to another, depending on several factors. The first important factor in whether we disclose seems to be how well we know the other person.[96] When the target of disclosure is a friend, the most frequent reason people give for volunteering personal information is relationship maintenance and enhancement. The second important reason is self-clarification—to sort out confusion, to understand ourselves better.

With strangers, reciprocity becomes the most common reason for disclosing. We offer information about ourselves to strangers to learn more about them, so we can decide whether and how to continue the relationship. The second most common reason is impression formation. We often reveal information about ourselves to strangers to make ourselves look good. This information, of course, is usually positive—at least in the early stages of a friendship.

*"There's something you need to know about me, Donna. I don't like people knowing things about me."*

## Models of Self-Disclosure

Over several decades, social scientists have created various models to represent and understand how self-disclosure operates in relationships. In the next few pages we will look at two of the best-known models.

Table 7-1  **Reasons for Self-Disclosure**

| Self-disclosure has the potential to improve and expand interpersonal relationships, but it serves other functions as well. As you read each of the following reasons why people reveal themselves, see which apply to you. | |
|---|---|
| **REASON** | **EXAMPLE/EXPLANATION** |
| Catharsis | "I need to get this off my chest . . ." |
| Self-clarification | "I'm really confused about something I did last night. If I tell you, maybe I can figure out why I did it . . ." |
| Self-validation | "I think I did the right thing. Let me tell you why I did it . . ." |
| Reciprocity | "I really like you . . ." (Hoping for a similar disclosure by the other person.) |
| Impression management | Salesperson to customer: "My boss would kill me for giving you this discount . . ." (Hoping disclosure will build trust.) |
| Relationship maintenance and enhancement | "I'm worried about the way things are going between us. Let's talk." Or, "I sure am glad we're together!" |
| Control | Employee to boss: "I got a job offer yesterday from our biggest competitor." (Hoping to get a raise.) |

*Source:* Adapted from Derlega, V. J., & Grezlak, J. (1979). Appropriateness of self-disclosure. In G. J. Chelune (Ed.), *Self-disclosure* (pp. 151–176). San Francisco, CA: Jossey-Bass.

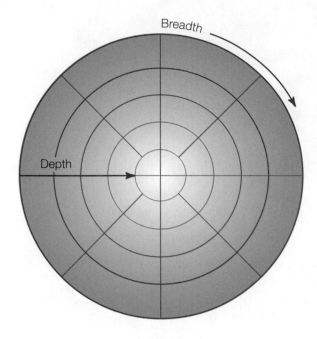

FIGURE 7-3  Social Penetration Model

**Breadth and Depth: Social Penetration**   Social psychologists Irwin Altman and Dalmas Taylor describe two ways in which communication can be more or less disclosing.[97] Their **social penetration model** is pictured in Figure 7-3. The first dimension of self-disclosure in this model involves the **breadth** of information volunteered—the range of subjects being discussed. For example, the breadth of disclosure in your relationship with a fellow worker will expand as you begin revealing information about your life away from the job, as well as on-the-job details. The second dimension of disclosure is the **depth** of the information being volunteered, the shift from relatively nonrevealing messages to more personal ones.

Depending on the breadth and depth of information shared, a relationship can be defined as casual or intimate. In a casual relationship, the breadth may be great, but not the depth. A more intimate relationship is likely to have high depth in at least one area. The most intimate relationships are those in which disclosure is great in both breadth and depth. Altman and Taylor see the development of a relationship as a progression from the periphery of their model to its center, a process that typically occurs over time. Each of your personal relationships probably has a different combination of breadth of subjects and depth of disclosure. Figure 7-4 pictures a student's self-disclosure in one relationship.

What makes the disclosure in some messages deeper than others? One way to measure depth is by how far it goes in two of the dimensions that define self-disclosure. Some revelations are certainly more *significant* than others. Consider the difference between saying, "I love my family" and "I love you." Other statements qualify as deep disclosure because they are *private*. Sharing a secret you've told to only a few close friends is certainly an act of self-disclosure, but it's even more revealing to divulge information that you've never told anyone.

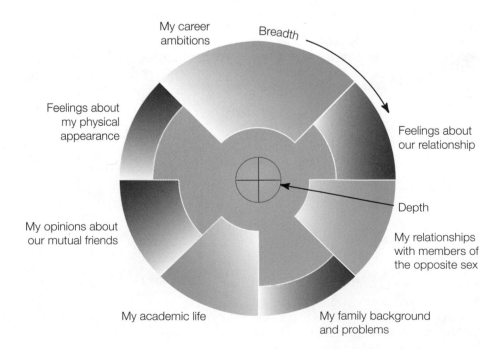

FIGURE 7-4  Sample Model of Social Penetration

**FIGURE 7-5** The Johari Window: Everything About You

**FIGURE 7-6** The Johari Window: Known to Self; Not Known to Self

**FIGURE 7-7** The Johari Window: Known to Others; Not Known to Others

**Self-Disclosure, Self-Awareness, and Relational Quality**   Another model that helps represent how self-disclosure operates is the **Johari Window**.[98] (The window takes its name from the first names of its creators, Joseph Luft and Harry Ingham.) Imagine a frame inside which is everything there is to know about you: your likes and dislikes, your goals, your secrets, your needs—everything. (See Figure 7-5.)

Of course, you aren't aware of everything about yourself. Like most people, you're probably discovering new things about yourself all the time. To represent this, we can divide the frame containing everything about you into two parts: the part you know about and the part you don't know about, as in Figure 7-6.

We can also divide this frame containing everything about you in another way. In this division the first part contains the things about you that others know, and the second part contains the things about you that you keep to yourself. Figure 7-7 represents this view.

When we impose these two divided frames one atop the other, we have a Johari Window. By looking at Figure 7-8 you can see the *everything about you* window divided into four parts.

Part 1 represents the information of which both you and the other person are aware. This part is your *open area*. Part 2 represents the *blind area*: information of which you are unaware but that the other person knows. You learn about information in the blind area primarily through feedback. Part 3 represents your *hidden area*: information that you know but aren't willing to reveal to others. Items in this hidden area become public primarily through self-disclosure, which is the focus of this chapter. Part 4 represents information that is *unknown* to both you and others. At first, the unknown area seems impossible to verify. After all, if neither you nor others know what it contains, how can you be sure it exists? We can deduce its existence because we are constantly discovering new things about ourselves. It is not unusual to discover, for example, that you have an unrecognized talent, strength, or weakness. Items move from the unknown area into the open area either directly when you disclose your insight or through one of the other areas first.

|  | Known to self | Not known to self |
|---|---|---|
| Known to others | 1 OPEN | 2 BLIND |
| Not known to others | 3 HIDDEN | 4 UNKNOWN |

**FIGURE 7-8** The Johari Window: Open; Blind; Hidden; Unknown

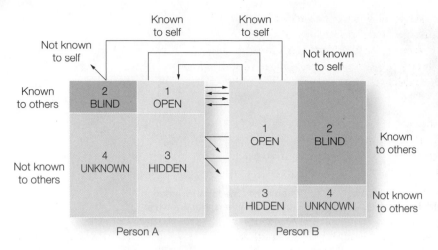

**FIGURE 7-9 The Johari Window: Self-Disclosure Levels in Two-Way Communication**

Interpersonal relationships of any depth are virtually impossible if the individuals involved have little open area. Going a step further, you can see that a relationship is limited by the individual who is less open, that is, who possesses the smaller open area. Figure 7-9 illustrates this situation with Johari Windows. A's window is set up in reverse so that A's and B's open areas are adjacent. Notice that the amount of communication (represented by the arrows connecting the two open areas) is dictated by the size of the smaller open area of A. The arrows originating from B's open area and being turned aside by A's hidden and blind areas represent unsuccessful attempts to communicate.

You have probably found yourself in situations that resemble Figure 7-9. Perhaps you have felt the frustration of not being able to get to know someone who was too reserved. Perhaps you have blocked another person's attempts to build a relationship with you in the same way. Whether you picture yourself more like Person A or Person B, the fact is that self-disclosure on both sides is necessary for the development of any interpersonal relationship. This chapter will describe just how much self-disclosure is optimal and of what type.

The Johari Window has many applications. When students in business communication classes partnered with the department store chain Target to craft a strategic communication plan, the Johari Window helped explain the teamwork process.[99] The students found that, as they got to know one another and try out new skills, aspects of themselves that were "blind" or "unknown" before diminished, and their "open" selves grew. Project leaders reported that the openness between them inspired teamwork and personal growth.

## Characteristics of Effective Self-Disclosure

Self-disclosure can certainly be valuable, but using it effectively requires an understanding of how it operates. Here are some findings from researchers that will help you decide when and how disclosure works best.

**Self-Disclosure Is Influenced by Culture**   The level of self-disclosure that is appropriate in one culture may seem completely inappropriate in another one. Disclosure is especially high in mainstream North American society, in which individualism encourages self-expression and attention to personal concerns. In contrast, in more collectivistic cultures, people may reveal little about themselves, in even in close relationships, and focus, instead, on issues affecting the group.[100]

Cultural differences like this mean that what counts as disclosing communication varies from one culture to another. If you were raised in the United States, you might view people from certain other cultures as undisclosing or even standoffish. But the amount of personal information that the nonnatives reveal might actually be quite personal and revealing according to the standards of their culture. The converse is also true: To members of some other cultures, North Americans probably appear like exhibitionists who spew personal information to anyone within earshot.

When communicating with people from different cultures, it's important to consider their standards for appropriate disclosure. Don't mistakenly judge them according to your own standards. Likewise, be sensitive about honoring their

> cultural idiom
**standoffish:**
unfriendly

> cultural idiom
**earshot:**
the distance at which one can hear
something or someone

standards when talking about yourself. In this sense, choosing the proper level of self-disclosure isn't too different from choosing the appropriate way of dressing or eating when encountering members of a different culture: What seems familiar and correct at home may not be suitable with strangers. As you read on, realize that the characteristics and guidelines that suit mainstream North American culture may not apply in other contexts.

**Self-Disclosure Usually Occurs in Dyads**    Although it is possible for people to disclose a great deal about themselves in groups, such communication usually occurs in one-to-one settings. Because revealing significant information about yourself involves a certain amount of risk, limiting the disclosure to one person at a time minimizes the chance that your disclosure will lead to unhappy consequences. One exception to this is the relatively new phenomenon of disclosing personal concerns online. There is evidence that bloggers who share their inner thoughts often gain social support and enlarge their social networks.[101] As you will see when reading the remainder of these tips for effective self-disclosure, however, it can be a risky prospect to self-disclose to such a large and unpredictable audience.

**Effective Self-Disclosure Is Usually Symmetrical**    Note in Figure 7-9 that the amount of successful, two-way communication (represented by the arrows connecting the two open areas) is dictated by the size of the smaller open area of A. The arrows that are originating from B's open area and being turned aside by A's hidden and blind areas represent unsuccessful attempts to communicate. In situations such as this, it's easy to imagine how B would soon limit the amount of disclosure to match that of A. On the other hand, if A were willing to match the degree of disclosure given by B, the relationship would move to a new level of intimacy. In either case, we can expect that, most often, the degree of disclosure between partners will soon stabilize at a symmetrical level.

**Effective Self-Disclosure Occurs Incrementally**    Although instances occur in which partners start their relationship by telling everything about themselves to each other, such cases are rare. In most cases, the amount of disclosure increases over time. We begin relationships by revealing relatively little about ourselves; then if our first bits of self-disclosure are well received and bring on similar responses from the other person, we're willing to reveal more. This principle is important to remember. It would usually be a mistake to assume that the way to build a strong relationship would be to reveal the most private details about yourself when first making contact with another person. Unless the circumstances are unique, such baring of your soul would be likely to scare potential partners away rather than bring them closer.

**Self-Disclosure Is Relatively Scarce**    Most conversations—even among friends—focus on everyday mundane topics and disclose little or no personal information.[102] Even partners in intimate relationships rarely talk about personal information.[103] Whether or not we open up to others is based on several criteria, some of which are listed in Table 7-2.

What is the optimal amount of self-disclosure? You might suspect that the correct answer is "the more, the better," at least in personal relationships. Research has shown that the matter isn't this simple, however. For example, imagine you have met an interesting person on an online dating site. The pressure is on to exchange enough information with each other to determine if you would like to take the relationship to the next stage. However, without the nonverbal cues that suggest how your disclosures are being received, you may be unsure how the other person is reacting to your disclosures, and you may worry that your online acquaintance will share your private information with others. Researchers

Table 7-2    Some Criteria Used to Reveal Family Secrets

**INTIMATE EXCHANGE**
Does the other person have a similar problem?
Would knowing the secret help the other person feel better?
Would knowing the secret help the other person manage his or her problem?

**EXPOSURE**
Will the other person find out this information, even if I don't tell him or her?
Is the other person asking me directly to reveal this information?

**URGENCY**
Is it very important that the other person know this information?
Will revealing this information make matters better?

**ACCEPTANCE**
Will the other person still accept me if I reveal this information?

**CONVERSATIONAL APPROPRIATENESS**
Will my disclosure fit into the conversation?
Has the topic of my disclosure come up in this conversation?

**RELATIONAL SECURITY**
Do I trust the other person with this information?
Do I feel close enough to this person to reveal the secret?

**IMPORTANT REASON**
Is there a pressing reason to reveal this information?

**PERMISSION**
Have other people involved in the secret given their permission for me to reveal it?
Would I feel okay telling the people involved that I have revealed the secret?

**MEMBERSHIP**
Is the person to whom I'm revealing the secret going to join this group (i.e., family)?

*Source:* Adapted from Vangelisti, A. L., Caughlin, J. P., & Timmerman, L. Criteria for revealing family secrets. *Communication Monographs, 68,* 1–27.

who studied people in this circumstance found that they were most comfortable disclosing private information if they proceeded slowly and developed trust in the other person and if the other person disclosed information about himself or herself.[104] One good measure of happiness is how well the level of disclosure matches the expectations of communicators: If we get what we believe is a reasonable amount of candor from others, we are happy. If they tell us too little—or even too much—we become less satisfied.

## Guidelines for Appropriate Self-Disclosure

One fear we've had while writing this chapter is that a few overenthusiastic readers may throw down their books and begin to share every personal detail of their lives with whomever they can find. As you can imagine, this kind of behavior isn't an example of effective interpersonal communication.

No single style of self-disclosure is appropriate for every situation. Let's take a look at some guidelines that can help you recognize how to express yourself in a way that's rewarding for you and the others involved.[105]

**Is the Other Person Important to You?**    There are several ways in which someone might be important. Perhaps you have an ongoing relationship deep enough so that sharing significant parts of yourself justifies keeping your present level of togetherness intact. Or perhaps the person to whom you're considering disclosing is someone with whom you've previously related on a less personal level. But now you see a chance to grow closer, and disclosure may be the path toward developing that personal relationship.

**Is the Risk of Disclosing Reasonable?**    Take a realistic look at the potential risks of self-disclosure. Even if the probable benefits are great, opening yourself up to almost certain rejection may be asking for trouble. For instance, it might be foolhardy to share your important feelings with someone you know is likely to betray your confidences or ridicule them. On the other hand, knowing that your partner is trustworthy and supportive makes the prospect of speaking out more reasonable.

Revealing personal thoughts and feelings can be especially risky on the job.[106] The politics of the workplace sometimes requires communicators to keep feelings to themselves in order to accomplish both personal and organizational goals. You might, for example, find the opinions of a boss or customer personally offensive but decide to bite your tongue rather than risk your job or lose goodwill for the company.

**Are the Amount and Type of Disclosure Appropriate?**    A third point to realize is that there are degrees of self-disclosure. Telling others about yourself isn't an all-or-nothing decision you must make. It's possible to share some facts, opinions, or feelings with one person while reserving riskier ones for others. In the same vein, before sharing very important information with someone who does matter to you, you might consider testing reactions by disclosing less personal data.

**Is the Disclosure Relevant to the Situation at Hand?**    The kind of disclosure that is often a characteristic of highly personal relationships usually isn't appropriate in less personal settings. For instance, a study of classroom communication revealed that sharing all feelings—both positive and negative—and being completely honest resulted in less cohesiveness than having a "relatively" honest climate in which pleasant but superficial relationships were the norm.[107]

Even in personal relationships—with close friends, family members, and so on—constant disclosure isn't a useful goal. The level of sharing in successful relationships rises and falls in cycles. You may go through a period of great disclosure and then spend another period of relative nondisclosure. Even during a phase of high disclosure, sharing *everything* about yourself isn't necessarily constructive. Usually the subject of appropriate self-disclosure involves the relationship rather than personal information.

**Is the Disclosure Reciprocated?**    There's nothing quite as disconcerting as talking your heart out to someone only to discover that the other person has yet to say anything to you that is half as revealing as what you've been saying. Unequal self-disclosure creates an unbalanced relationship, one doomed to fall apart.

There are few times when one-way disclosure is acceptable. Most of them involve formal, therapeutic relationships in which a client approaches a trained professional with the goal of resolving a problem. For instance, you wouldn't necessarily expect to hear about a physician's personal ailments during a visit to a medical office. Nonetheless, it's interesting to note that one frequently noted characteristic of effective psychotherapists, counselors, and teachers is a willingness to share their feelings about a relationship with their clients.

**Will the Effect Be Constructive?**    Self-disclosure can be a vicious tool if it's not used carefully. Psychologist George Bach suggests that every person has a psychological "belt line." Below that belt line are areas about which the person is extremely sensitive. Bach says that jabbing at a "below-the-belt" area is a surefire

> cultural idiom
> **opening yourself up:**
> letting yourself become vulnerable

> cultural idiom
> **to bite your tongue:**
> to remain silent

> cultural idiom
> **in the same vein:**
> related to this idea

> cultural idiom
> **talking your heart out:**
> revealing your innermost thoughts and feelings

way to disable another person, although usually at great cost to the relationship. It's important to consider the effects of your candor before opening up to others. Comments such as "I've always thought you were pretty unintelligent" or "Last year I made love to your best friend" *may* sometimes resolve old business and thus be constructive, but they also can be devastating—to the listener, to the relationship, and to your self-esteem.

**Is the Self-Disclosure Clear and Understandable?**   When you express yourself to others, it's important that you share yourself in a way that's intelligible. This means describing the *sources* of your message clearly. For instance, it's far better to describe another's behavior by saying, "When you don't answer my phone calls or drop by to visit anymore . . ." than to complain vaguely, "When you avoid me . . ."

It's also vital to express your *thoughts* and *feelings* explicitly. "I feel worried because I'm afraid you don't care about me" is more understandable than "I don't like the way things have been going."

# Lies, Equivocation, and Hinting

At first glance, our moral heritage leads us to abhor anything less than the truth. Ethicists point out that the very existence of a society seems based on a foundation of truthfulness.[108] Although isolated cultures do exist in which deceit is a norm, they are dysfunctional and on the verge of breakdown.

Although honesty is desirable in principle, it often has risky, potentially unpleasant consequences. This explains why communicators—even those with the best intentions—aren't always completely honest when they find themselves in situations when honesty would be uncomfortable.[109] Three common alternatives to self-disclosure are lies, equivocation, and hinting. We will take a closer look at each one.

## Lies

To most people, lying appears to be a breach of ethics. Although lying to gain unfair advantage over an unknowing victim seems clearly wrong, another kind of untruth isn't so easy to dismiss as completely unethical. White lies, more appropriately called **altruistic lies**, are defined (at least by the people who tell them) as being harmless, or even helpful, to the person to whom they are told.[110] As Table 7-3 shows, at least some of the lies we tell are indeed intended to be helpful, or at least relatively benign.

Whether or not they are innocent, altruistic lies are certainly common. Robert Feldman, a leading researcher in the field of deception, says that people lie more than they think. "People lie while they are getting acquainted an average of three times in a 10-minute period," he says.[111] "Participants in my studies actually are not aware that they are lying that much until they watch videos of their interactions." In a classic study, 130 subjects were asked to keep track of the truthfulness of their everyday conversational statements.[112] Only 38.5 percent of these statements—slightly more than a third—proved to be totally honest. In another experiment, subjects kept a log of all the lies they told over a 1-week period. Both men and women reported being untruthful in approximately one-fifth of their conversations that lasted more than 10 minutes.[113]

Lying varies by relationship. Dating couples lie to each other in about one-third of their interactions, and college students tell at least one lie to their mothers in fully half of their conversations. Overall, when people recorded their conversations over a 2-day period and later counted their own deceptions, their tallies confirmed the average lie rate: 3 fibs for every 10 minutes of conversation.[114]

What are the consequences of discovering that you've been lied to? In an interpersonal relationship, the discovery can be traumatic. As we grow closer to others,

Table 7-3   **Some Reasons for Lying**

| REASON | EXAMPLE |
|---|---|
| Acquire resources | "Oh, please let me add this class. If I don't get in, I'll never graduate on time!" |
| Protect resources | "I'd like to lend you the money, but I'm short myself." |
| Initiate and continue interaction | "Excuse me, I'm lost. Do you live around here?" |
| Avoid conflict | "It's not a big deal. We can do it your way. Really." |
| Avoid interaction or take leave | "That sounds like fun, but I'm busy Saturday night." "Oh, look what time it is! I've got to run!" |
| Present a competent image | "Sure, I understand. No problem." |
| Increase social desirability | "Yeah, I've done a fair amount of skiing." |

*Source:* Adapted from categories originally presented in Camden, C., Motley, M. T., & Wilson, A. White lies in interpersonal communication: A taxonomy and preliminary investigation of social motivations. *Western Journal of Speech Communication, 48,* 315.

our expectations about their honesty grow stronger. After all, discovering that you've been deceived requires you to redefine not only the lie you just uncovered but also many of the messages you previously took for granted. Was last week's compliment really sincere? Was your joke really funny, or was the other person's laughter a put-on? Does the other person care about you as much as he or she claimed?

Research has shown that deception does, in fact, threaten relationships.[115] Not all lies are equally devastating, however. Feelings like dismay and betrayal are greatest when the relationship is most intense, when the importance of the subject is high, and when there was previous suspicion that the other person wasn't being completely honest. Of these three factors, the importance of the information lied about proved to be the key factor in provoking a relational crisis. We may be able to cope with "misdemeanor" lying, but "felonies" are a grave threat. In fact, the discovery of major deception can lead to the end of the relationship. More than two-thirds of the subjects in one study reported that their relationship had ended since they discovered a lie. Furthermore, they attributed the breakup directly to the lie. If preserving a relationship is important, honesty—at least about important matters—really does appear to be the best policy.

## Equivocation

Lying isn't the only alternative to self-disclosure (see Figure 7-10). When faced with the choice between lying and telling an unpleasant truth, communicators can—and often do—equivocate. As Chapter 4 explained, **equivocal language** has two or more equally plausible meanings. Sometimes people send equivocal messages without meaning to, resulting in confusion. "I'll meet you at the apartment" could refer to more than one place. But other times we are deliberately vague. For instance, when a friend asks what you think of an awful outfit, you could say, "It's really unusual—one of a kind!" Likewise, if you are too angry to accept a friend's apology but don't want to appear petty, you might say, "Don't mention it."

The value of equivocation becomes clear when you consider the alternatives. Consider the dilemma of what to say when you've been given an unwanted present—an ugly painting, for example—and the giver asks what you think of it. How can you respond? On the one hand, you need to choose between telling the truth and lying. On the other hand, you have a choice of whether to make your response clear or vague. Figure 7-10 displays these choices. After considering the alternatives, it's clear that the first choice—an equivocal, true response—is far preferable to the other choices in several respects. First, it spares the receiver from

> cultural idiom
> **a put-on:**
> a false show of emotion

Equivocal

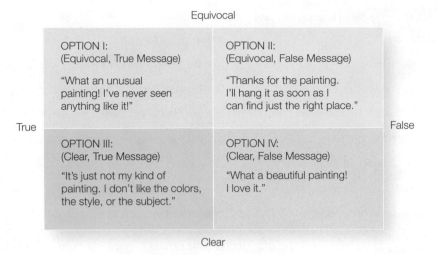

| OPTION I: | OPTION II: |
|---|---|
| (Equivocal, True Message) | (Equivocal, False Message) |
| "What an unusual painting! I've never seen anything like it!" | "Thanks for the painting. I'll hang it as soon as I can find just the right place." |

True | | False

| OPTION III: | OPTION IV: |
|---|---|
| (Clear, True Message) | (Clear, False Message) |
| "It's just not my kind of painting. I don't like the colors, the style, or the subject." | "What a beautiful painting! I love it." |

Clear

**FIGURE 7-10 Dimensions of Truthfulness and Equivocation**

> cultural idiom

**saving face:**
protecting one's dignity

**less taxing on:**
less demanding of

After receiving anonymous text messages threatening to expose their deepest secrets, characters on TV's *Pretty Little Liars* have to lie to protect themselves from humiliation and harm. Is it ever acceptable misrepresent yourself? What are the benefits and costs?

embarrassment. For example, rather than flatly saying "no" to an unappealing invitation, it may be kinder to say, "I have other plans"—even if those plans are to stay home and watch television.

Besides saving face for the recipient, honest equivocation can be less stressful for the sender than either telling the truth bluntly or lying. Because equivocation is often easier to take than the cold, hard truth, it spares the teller from feeling guilty. It's less taxing on the conscience to say, "I've never tasted anything like this" than to say, "This meal tastes terrible," even though the latter comment is more precise. Few people *want* to lie, and equivocation provides an alternative to deceit.[116]

A study by communication researcher Sandra Metts and her colleagues shows how equivocation can save face in difficult situations.[117] Several hundred college students were asked how they would turn down unwanted sexual overtures from a person whose feelings were important to them: either a close friend, a prospective date, or a dating partner. The majority of students chose a diplomatic reaction ("I just don't think I'm ready for this right now") as being more face saving and comfortable than a direct statement such as "I just don't feel sexually attracted to you." The diplomatic reaction seemed sufficiently clear to get the message across but not so blunt as to embarrass or even humiliate the other person. (Interestingly, men said they would be able to handle a direct rejection more comfortably than women. The researchers suggest that one reason for the difference is that men stereotypically initiate sexual offers and thus are more likely to expect rejection.)

Besides preventing embarrassment, equivocal language can also save the speaker from being caught lying. If a potential employer asks about your grades during a job interview, you would be safe saying, "I had a B average last semester," even though your overall grade average is closer to C. The statement isn't a complete answer, but it is honest as far as it goes. As one team of researchers put it, "equivocation is neither a false message nor a clear truth, but rather an alternative used precisely when both of these are to be avoided."[118]

Given these advantages, it's not surprising that most people will usually choose to equivocate rather than tell a lie. In a series of

## @Work

### Social Capital: Personal Relationships and Career Advancement

The old saying "It isn't what you know, it's *who* you know" is at least partly true. **Social capital** refers to the potential benefits that come from belonging to one or more social networks. An impressive body of research confirms that robust personal networks can pay off in your career.[123]

People with high social capital are more likely to find good jobs more quickly and be promoted early. They receive more positive performance evaluations from their bosses and earn larger bonuses. Social capital doesn't just benefit individuals. Group members who have rich and diverse personal networks enhance the performance of their teams, helping them generate more creative solutions and reach their goals more rapidly.

Social capital doesn't come only from close personal connections. Along with what sociologists call *strong ties*, we're linked to other networks by *weak ties*—relationships that are infrequent, but which have surprising value when it comes to seeking resources. Reaching out to a distant relative, former classmate, old neighbor, former coworker, or boss at the right time can get the information you need to succeed. Likewise, reaching out to casual contacts can prove beneficial—your seatmate on a recent flight, someone at the gym, or the person you met at a recent party.[124]

Along with contacts that you make and maintain through face-to-face and phone contact, online social networks can be a powerful tool for building and using social capital.[125] Business-oriented resources like LinkedIn can be helpful, as can "friends" on more general sites like Facebook. Within large organizations, company "intranets" can provide a way for employees to keep in touch.[126]

Whatever their nature, social networks can go beyond their obvious value as sources of friendship, providing you with the resources that can make a critical difference in your career success. ●

---

experiments, subjects chose between telling a face-saving lie, telling the truth, and equivocating. Only 6 percent chose the lie, and between 3 and 4 percent chose the hurtful truth. By contrast, more than 90 percent chose the equivocal response.[119] People *say* they prefer truth telling to equivocating, but given the choice, they prefer to finesse the truth.

## Hinting

Hints are more direct than equivocal statements. Whereas an equivocal message isn't necessarily aimed at changing others' behavior, a hint seeks to get the desired response from others. Some hints are designed to save the *receiver* from embarrassment:[120]

| DIRECT STATEMENT | FACE-SAVING HINT |
|---|---|
| I'm bored. I want to get out of this conversation. | You must be busy. I'd better let you go. |
| You aren't qualified for that job. | I've heard they only hire insiders for jobs like that. |

Other hints are strategies for saving the *sender* from embarrassment:

| DIRECT STATEMENT | FACE-SAVING HINT |
|---|---|
| Your smoking bothers me. | I'm pretty sure that smoking isn't permitted here. |
| I'd like to invite you out for lunch, but I don't want to risk a "no" answer to my invitation. | Gee, it's almost lunchtime. Have you ever eaten at that new Italian restaurant around the corner? |

The success of a hint depends on the other person's ability to pick up the unexpressed message. Your subtle remarks might go right over the head of an

> cultural idiom

**to pick up:**
to understand

**go right over the head of:**
fail to be understood by

insensitive receiver—or one who chooses not to respond to them. If this does happen, you still have the choice to be more direct. If the costs of a straightforward message seem too high, you can withdraw without risk.

It's easy to see why people choose hints, equivocations, and white lies instead of complete self-disclosure. These strategies provide a way to manage difficult situations that is easier than the alternatives for both the speaker and the receiver of the message. In this sense, successful liars, equivocators, and hinters can be said to possess a certain kind of communicative competence. On the other hand, there are certainly times when honesty is the right approach, even if it's painful. At times like these, evaders could be viewed as lacking the competence or the integrity to handle a situation most effectively.

Are hints, benign lies, and equivocations ethical alternatives to self-disclosure? Some of the examples in these pages suggest the answer is a qualified "yes." Many social scientists and philosophers agree. Some argue that the morality of a speaker's *motives* for lying ought to be judged, not the deceptive act itself.[121] Others ask whether the *effects* of a lie will be worth the deception. Ethicist Sissela Bok offers some circumstances in which deception may be justified: doing good, avoiding harm, and protecting a larger truth.[122] Perhaps the right questions to ask, then, are whether an indirect message is truly in the interests of the receiver, and whether this sort of evasion is the only effective way to behave. Bok suggests another way to check the justifiability of a lie: Imagine how others would respond if they knew what you were really thinking or feeling. Would they accept your reasons for not disclosing?

---

**Ethical Challenge**

## The Ethics of Lying and Equivocating

Research shows that virtually everyone hints, lies, and equivocates for a variety of reasons. Explore the ethical legitimacy of your lies and equivocations by following these directions:

1. For a 2-day period, keep track of the following:

    **a.** Your hints, lies, and equivocations.

    **b.** Your reason for taking one of these approaches in each situation.

    **c.** The positive and negative consequences (for you and the other person) of avoiding self-disclosure.

2. Based on your analysis of the information collected in Step 1, identify the ethical legitimacy of each type of nondisclosing communication. Are any sorts of deception justifiable? Which sorts are not? How would you feel if you discovered the other person had not been straightforward with you under similar circumstances?

---

## Summary

An interpersonal relationship is one in which two or more people meet one another's social needs to a greater or lesser degree. We form these relationships for a variety of reasons. Some of these reasons are rather straightforward (e.g., proximity, appearance, rewards), whereas others involve what can informally be called "chemistry" (e.g., similarity, mutual self-disclosure, reciprocal attraction).

Communication can be considered interpersonal according to either the context or the quality of interaction. Qualitatively interpersonal communication can occur both face-to-face and in mediated relationships. Communication in relationships consists of both content and relational messages. Explicit relational messages are termed *metacommunication*.

Some communication theorists suggest that intimate relationships pass through a series of stages, each of which is characterized by a unique mode of communication. These stages fall into three broad phases: coming together, relational maintenance, and coming apart. Although the movement within and between these stages does follow recognizable patterns, the amount and direction of movement are not predetermined. Some relationships move steadily toward termination, whereas others shift backward and forward as the partners redefine their desires for intimacy and distance.

Other theorists take a dialectical view, arguing that the same series of opposing desires operate throughout the entire span of relationships. These dialectical drives include autonomy versus connection, predictability versus novelty, and openness versus privacy. Because these opposing forces are inevitable, the challenge is to develop strategies for dealing with them that provide relational satisfaction.

Intimacy is a powerful need for most people. Intimacy can be created and expressed in a variety of ways: physically, emotionally, intellectually, and through shared activities. The notion of levels of intimacy has varied according to historical period, culture, and gender. Along with the desire for closeness, a need for distance is equally important. These opposing drives lead to conflicting communication behavior at different stages in people's lives and their relationships. The challenge is to communicate in a way that strikes a balance between intimacy and distance. Toward this end, recognizing the "love languages" that are most meaningful to you and significant others is an important step.

Self-disclosure is the process of deliberately revealing significant information about oneself that would not normally be known. The breadth and depth of self-disclosure can be described by the social penetration model. The Johari Window model reveals an individual's open, blind, hidden, and unknown areas. Complete self-disclosure is not common, nor is it always desirable. The chapter listed several guidelines to help determine when it is and is not appropriate. The chapter concluded by describing three widely used alternatives to self-disclosure: lies, equivocation, and hints. It discussed the conditions under which these alternatives can be appropriate.

## Key Terms

**affinity** The degree to which people like or appreciate one another. As with all relational messages, affinity is usually expressed nonverbally. *p. 205*

**altruistic lies** Deception intended to be unmalicious, or even helpful, to the person to whom it is told. *p. 228*

**breadth (of self-disclosure)** The range of topics about which an individual discloses. See also *Depth*. *p. 222*

**content message** A message that communicates information about the subject being discussed. See also *Relational message*. *p. 205*

**contextually interpersonal communication** Any communication that occurs between two individuals. See also *Qualitatively interpersonal communication*. *p. 203*

**control** The social need to influence others. *p. 205*

**depth (of self-disclosure)** The level of personal information a person reveals on a particular topic. See also *Breadth*. *p. 222*

**developmental models (of relational maintenance)** These models propose that the nature of communication is different in various stages of interpersonal relationships. *p. 207*

**dialectical model (of relational maintenance)** A model claiming that, throughout their lifetime, people in virtually all interpersonal relationships must deal with equally important, simultaneous, and opposing forces such as connection and autonomy, predictability and novelty, and openness versus privacy. *p. 212*

**dialectical tensions** Inherent conflicts that arise when two opposing or incompatible forces exist simultaneously. *p. 212*

**equivocal language** Language with more than one likely interpretation. *p. 229*

**immediacy** The degree of interest and attraction we feel toward and communicate to others. As with all relational messages, immediacy is usually expressed nonverbally. *p. 205*

**intimacy** A state of closeness between two (or sometimes more) people. Intimacy can be manifested in several ways: physically, intellectually, emotionally, and via shared activities. *p. 215*

**Johari Window** A model that describes the relationship between self-disclosure and self-awareness. *p. 223*

**metacommunication** Messages (usually relational) that refer to other messages; communication about communication. *p. 206*

**qualitatively interpersonal communication** Interaction in which people treat one another as unique individuals, regardless of the context in which the interaction occurs or the number of people involved. This concept contrasts with impersonal communication. See also *Contextually interpersonal communication*. *p. 203*

**relational message** A message that expresses the social relationship between two or more individuals. *p. 205*

**respect** The degree to which we hold others in esteem. *p. 205*

**self-disclosure** The process of deliberately revealing information about oneself that is significant and that would not normally be known by others. *p. 220*

**social capital** The potential benefits that come from belonging to one or more social networks. *p. 231*

**social penetration model** A model describing how intimacy can be achieved via the breadth and depth of self-disclosure. *p. 222*

## Check Your Understanding

1. Describe the factors that cause you to be attracted to someone with whom you are in a voluntary, ongoing relationship.

2. Identify the developmental stages you have experienced in an ongoing, voluntary relationship and the dialectical tensions that you have encountered in each stage.

3. Describe the extent and kinds of both interpersonal and impersonal communication in a familiar relationship. How satisfied are you with your findings? How might you change the mixture of communication types?

4. Identify the content and relational dimensions in a recent, significant communication encounter. Were the relational dimensions discussed or unspoken?

5. Which types of intimacy discussed on pages 218–219 characterize one of your close relationships? How satisfied are you with the types and levels of intimacy you have identified?

6. Describe the degree of self-disclosure in one of your close relationships. What functions do your disclosures serve? How satisfied are you with the nature of disclosures in this relationship?

7. Using the guidelines on pages 226–228, construct an effective, appropriate self-disclosing message you could deliver. Describe the reasons why you might or might not choose to deliver this message.

8. Which types of nondisclosing messages described on pages 228–231 do you characteristically use? Explain why you choose these types of nondisclosure, and evaluate whether your decisions to not fully disclose are ethical.

## Activities

1. **Interpersonal Communication: Context and Quality**

   1. Examine your interpersonal relationships in a contextual sense by making two lists. The first should contain all the two-person relationships in which you have participated during the past week. The second should contain all your relationships that have occurred in small group and public contexts. Are there any important differences that distinguish dyadic interaction from communication with a larger number of people?

   2. Now make a second set of two lists. The first one should describe all of your relationships that are interpersonal in a qualitative sense, and the second should describe all the two-person relationships that are more impersonal. Are you satisfied with the

number of qualitatively interpersonal relationships you have identified?

   3. Compare the lists you developed in Steps 1 and 2. See what useful information each one contains. What do your conclusions tell you about the difference between contextual and qualitative definitions of interpersonal communication?

2. **Identifying Relational Messages** To complete this exercise, you will need the help of a partner with whom you communicate on an ongoing basis.

   1. Pick three recent exchanges between you and your partner. Although any exchanges will do, the most interesting ones will be those in which you sensed that something significant (positive or negative) was going on that wasn't expressed overtly.

   2. For each exchange, identify both the content and relational messages that you were expressing. Identify relational messages in terms of dimensions such as affinity, respect, immediacy, and/or control.

   3. Explain the concept of relational messages to your partner, and ask him or her to identify the relational messages received from you during the same exchanges. How closely does your partner's perception match your analysis of the relational messages?

   4. Now identify the relational messages you interpreted your partner as sending during the three exchanges.

   5. Ask your partner to describe the relational messages he or she believed were sent to you on these occasions. How closely did your interpretation match your partner's explanation?

Based on your analysis of these three exchanges, answer the following questions:

   1. What significant kinds of relational messages are exchanged in your relationship?

   2. How accurate are you in decoding your partner's relational messages? How accurate is your partner in decoding your relational messages?

   3. What lessons have you learned from this exercise that can improve the quality of your relationship?

3. **Your I.Q. (Intimacy Quotient)** Answer the following questions as you think about your relationship with a person important in your life.

   1. What is the level of physical intimacy in your relationship?

   2. What intellectual intimacy do you share?

   3. How emotionally intimate are you? Is your emotional intimacy deeper in some ways than in others?

   4. Has your intimacy level changed over time? If so, in what ways?

After answering these questions, ask yourself how satisfied you are with the amount of intimacy in this relationship. Identify any changes you would like to occur, and describe the steps you could take to make them happen.

4. **Striking a Balance Between Intimacy and Distance** Choose an important interpersonal relationship with someone you encounter on a frequent, regular basis. You might choose a friend, family member, or romantic partner.

For at least a week, chart how your communication with this relational partner reflects your desire for either intimacy or distance. Use a 7-point scale, in which behavior seeking high intimacy receives a 7, whereas behavior seeking to avoid physical, intellectual, and/or emotional contact receives a 1. Use ratings from 2 through 6 to reflect intermediate stages. Record at least one rating per day, making more detailed entries if your desire for intimacy or distance changes during that period.

After charting your communication, reflect on what the results tell you about your personal desire for intimacy and distance. Consider the following questions:

1. Which state—intimacy or distance—seemed most desirable for you?

2. To the degree that you seek intimacy, which variety or varieties are most important to you: intellectual, emotional, and/or physical?

3. Was the pattern you charted during this week typical of your communication in this relationship over a longer period of time?

4. Do you seek the same mixture of intimacy and distance in other relationships?

5. Most important, are you satisfied with the results you discovered in this exercise? If not, how would you like to change your communication behavior?

5. **Juggling Dialectical Tensions** Identify one situation in which you are trying to manage dialectical tensions in your life. (Describe which of the dialectical forces described in this chapter are in operation.) Then answer these questions:

1. Which of the strategies for managing dialectical tensions listed on pages 214–215 do you use?

2. How effective is the strategy (or strategies) that you have chosen?

3. Would an alternative strategy be more effective for managing the tensions in this situation?

4. How might things go differently if you choose the alternative strategy?

6. **Love Languages** In an important relationship,

1. Identify the "love languages" that mean the most to you, and those that have the greatest value for your relational partner. (You may need to ask him or her.)

2. Describe how closely the ways you express your feelings for the other person match with his or her preferred modes.

3. Analyze how you might modify your communication to more closely match the preferred styles of appreciation and commitment.

7. **Reasons for Disclosing** Recall recent personal examples of times when you have disclosed personal information for each of the reasons listed in Table 7-1. Explain your answer by describing:

● The person who was the target of your self-disclosure

● The information you disclosed

● Your reason(s) for disclosing

Based on your findings, decide which of the reasons for self-disclosure are most characteristic of your communication. Note: In order to protect privacy, this exercise can be conducted in class by having each member submit anonymous entries.

8. **Effective Self-Disclosure** Choose a self-disclosing message that is important enough for you to consider sharing. Use the guidelines on pages 226–228 to craft the message in a way that maximizes the chances of having it received successfully. Share your message strategy with classmates, and get their opinion of whether it needs refinement.

## For Further Exploration

**For more resources about communication in interpersonal relationships, see the *Understanding Human Communication* website at www.oup.com/us/adler.** There you will find a variety of resources: "Media Room" clips from popular films and television shows to further illustrate important concepts, a list of books and articles, links to descriptions of feature films and television shows at the *Now Playing* website, study aids, and a self-test to check your understanding of the material in this chapter.

## CHAPTER 8

# Improving Interpersonal Relationships

## Chapter Outline

**LEARNING OBJECTIVES**

1 Describe the role of communication climate in interpersonal relationships and the types of messages that contribute to confirming and disconfirming climates.

2 Explain the unavoidable but potentially problematic role of conflict in interpersonal relationships.

3 Identify characteristics of nonassertive, directly aggressive, passive-aggressive, indirect, and assertive communications.

4 Describe the origins of and challenges presented by gender differences in conflict style.

5 Explain cultural differences in how direct and emotionally expressive people are during conflict.

6 Explain the differences among win–lose, lose–lose, compromising, and win–win approaches to conflict resolution.

# Words can hurt.

They can also heal. Just ask Kevin Curwick, a high school student in Minnesota. Concerned that some of his classmates were posting unkind comments about others on Twitter, he decided to do the opposite. Curwick, the captain of the Osseo High School football team, began a Twitter feed on which he anonymously posted kind comments about people, including

> "Shoutout to three cross country girls who stopped their race to help a girl from another team who had an asthma attack"

and

> "Ask any of _____'s friends, and they'll tell you about how caring and helping he is. He gives 100% in everything."

The gig was soon up. People realized Curwick was behind the kind messages. (No one was surprised.) But that was only the beginning. Students at other schools started similar Twitter accounts of their own. Soon the "nice it forward" movement spread nationwide and caught the eye of more than a few celebrities. Selena Gomez tweeted:

> If you haven't yet, you should DEFINITELY check out @OsseoNiceThings on twitter! . . . This tweet made my day, and I think that's the point of the account. It's really an eye-opener, and it helps you see the good in everyone. Go Kevin!

A host of other people (both famous and not) have posted messages on Osseo NiceThings as well. Curwick has been interviewed by Ryan Seacrest, among many others, and received scholarship offers from universities around the country who admire his spirit. Curwick shrugs off the attention, saying the spotlight shouldn't be on him, but on all the great people around us every day.

*Kevin Curwick's tale illustrates the constructive power of positive messages. But the novelty of his approach stands in contrast to the common and destructive tendency to criticize others online, often anonymously. What kinds of messages do you most commonly express?*

- Have you ever made or passed along a hurtful photo or comment about someone else using social media?

- What proportion of your face-to-face remarks about others is positive and/or constructive? What percentage is destructive or critical?

- The Golden Rule says we should behave toward others as we wish they would act toward us. How would your interpersonal communication change if you followed the Golden Rule more faithfully?

No matter how satisfying your relationships, there are almost certainly ways they could be better. At times even the best of friends, the closest of families, and the most productive coworkers become dissatisfied. Sometimes the people involved are unhappy with one another. At other times, one person's problem is unrelated to the relationship. In either case, there's a desire to communicate in a way that makes matters better.

The ideas in this chapter can help you improve the important relationships in your life. We'll begin by talking about the factors that make communication "climates" either positive or negative. Next we'll focus on methods for understanding and resolving interpersonal conflicts.

# Communication Climates in Interpersonal Relationships

Personal relationships are a lot like the weather. Some are fair and warm, whereas others are stormy and cold; some are polluted, and others healthy. Some relationships have stable climates, whereas others change dramatically—calm one moment and turbulent the next. You can't measure the interpersonal climate by looking at a thermometer or glancing at the sky, but it's there nonetheless. Every relationship has a feeling, a pervasive mood that colors the interactions of the participants. The term **communication climate** refers to the emotional tone of a relationship. A climate doesn't involve specific activities as much as the way people feel about one another as they carry out those activities. Consider two communication classes, for example. Both meet for the same length of time and follow the same syllabus. It's easy to imagine how one of these classes might be a friendly, comfortable place to learn, whereas the other might be cold and tense—even hostile. The same principle holds for families, coworkers, and other relationships: Communication climates are a function more of the way people feel about one another than of the tasks they perform.

Evidence suggests that healthy relationships make us feel better and even live longer than we might otherwise.[1] This is largely because loneliness and social isolation are linked to poor sleep, low motivation, and negativity.[2] By contrast, people with strong social support networks are likely to be active and well informed, to have help when they need it, and to feel confident that people will stand by them even when the going is tough.[3] The evidence is clear: The quality of our relationships establishes the quality of our lives.

> What adjectives would you use to describe the communication climate in one of your most important relationships. Sunny? Gloomy? Calm? Turbulent? What messages help create the climate you have described?

## Confirming and Disconfirming Messages

What makes some climates positive and others negative? A short but accurate answer is that the *communication climate is determined by the degree to which people see themselves as valued*. When we believe others view us as important, we are likely to feel good about our relationship. By contrast, the relational climate suffers when we think others don't appreciate or care about us.

Messages that show you are valued have been called **confirming responses**.[4] Kevin Curwick's positive tweets are a great example. Whether we post confirming responses publicly or offer them in person, they say "you exist," "you matter," "you're important." Actually, it's an oversimplification to talk about one type of confirming message. In truth, confirming communication occurs on three increasingly positive levels:[5]

- **Recognition:** The most fundamental act of confirmation is to recognize the other person. Recognition seems easy and obvious, and yet there are many times when we do not respond to others on this basic level. Failure to write or visit a friend is a common example. So is failure to return a phone message. Avoiding eye contact and not approaching someone you know on campus, at a party, or on the street can send a negative message. Of course, this lack of recognition may simply be an oversight. You might not notice your friend, or the pressures of work and school might prevent you from staying in touch. Nonetheless, if the other person *perceives* you as avoiding contact, the message has the effect of being disconfirming.

- **Acknowledgment:** Acknowledging the ideas and feelings of others is a stronger form of confirmation. Listening is probably the most common form of acknowledgment. Of course, counterfeit listening—ambushing, stage hogging, pseudolistening, and so on—has the opposite effect of acknowledgment. More active acknowledgment includes asking questions, paraphrasing, and reflecting. Not surprisingly, leaders who are supportive of others and their ideas are more successful than leaders who are more concerned with promoting their own image and ideas.[6] As you read in Chapter 5, reflecting the speaker's thoughts and feelings can be a powerful way to offer support when others have problems.

- **Endorsement:** Whereas acknowledgment means you are interested in another's ideas, endorsement means that you agree with them. It's easy to see why endorsement is the strongest type of confirming message, because it communicates the highest form of valuing. The most obvious form of endorsement is agreeing. We tend to be attracted to people who agree with us.[7] Fortunately, it isn't necessary to agree completely with another person in order to endorse her or his message. You can probably find something in the message that you endorse. "I can see why you were so angry," you might reply to a friend, even if you don't approve of his or her outburst. Of course, outright praise is a strong form of endorsement and one you can use surprisingly often after you look for opportunities to compliment others.

It's hard to overstate the importance of confirming messages. People who are generous with confirming statements are considered to be more appealing candidates for marriage than their less appreciative peers.[8] This preference is well founded. One of the most accurate ways to predict whether a marriage will last is to consider how negative a couple's communication is while they are dating.[9] This applies to both spoken words such as "thank you" and "I love you" and to nonverbal cues such as smiles and signs of affection.[10]

Positive, confirming messages are just as important in other relationships. For example, family members are most satisfied when they regularly encourage each other, joke around, and share news about their day.[11] And in the classroom, motivation and learning increase when teachers demonstrate a genuine interest and concern for students.[12]

Of course, some negative communication is to be expected. The important thing is to balance it with positive communication. People in satisfying relationships tend to maintain at least a 5:1 ratio of positive to negative statements.[13]

In contrast to confirming communication, messages that deny the value of others have been labeled **disconfirming responses**. These show a lack of regard for the other person by either disputing or ignoring some important part of that person's message.[14] *Disagreement* can certainly be disconfirming, especially if it goes beyond disputing the other person's ideas and attacks the speaker personally. However, disagreement is not the most damaging kind of disconfirmation. It may be tough to hear someone say, "I don't think that's a good idea," but a personal attack like "You're crazy" is even tougher to hear. Far worse than disagreements are responses that *ignore* others' ideas—or even their existence.

Table 8-1 lists a number of deliberate tactics that have been used to create distance in an undesired relationship. It's easy to see how each of them is inherently disconfirming.

As you read in Chapter 7, every message has a relational dimension along with its content. This means that, whether or not we are aware of the fact, we send and

Table 8-1    **Distancing Tactics**

| TACTIC | DESCRIPTION |
| --- | --- |
| Avoidance | Evading the other person. |
| Deception | Lying to or misleading the other person. |
| Degrading | Treating the other person with disrespect. |
| Detachment | Acting emotionally uninterested in the other person. |
| Discounting | Disregarding or minimizing the importance of what the other person says. |
| Humoring | Not taking the other person seriously. |
| Impersonality | Treating the other person like a stranger; interacting with her or him as a role rather than a unique individual. |
| Inattention | Not paying attention to the other person. |
| Nonimmediacy | Displaying verbal or nonverbal clues that minimize interest, closeness, or availability. |
| Reserve | Being unusually quiet and uncommunicative. |
| Restraint | Curtailing normal social behaviors. |
| Restriction of topics | Limiting conversation to less personal topics. |
| Shortening of interaction | Ending conversations as quickly as possible. |

*Source:* Adapted from Hess, J. A. (2002). Distance regulation in personal relationships: The development of a conceptual model and a test of representational validity. *Journal of Social and Personal Relationships, 19,* 663–683.

receive confirming and disconfirming messages virtually whenever we communicate. Serious conversations about our relationships may not be common, but we convey our attitudes about one another even when we talk about everyday matters. In other words, it isn't *what* we communicate about that shapes a relational climate so much as *how* we speak and act toward one another.

It's important to note that disconfirming messages, like virtually every other kind of communication, are a matter of perception. People usually doubt the sincerity of confirming messages that lack reinforcing nonverbal cues like friendly gestures and an earnest tone of voice.[15] And even when they are sincere, messages involving dramatic gestures and inflection may be perceived as domineering rather than supportive, especially when they are delivered by high-status individuals.[16] For example, when a parent or teacher says, "You are incredibly smart" with an intense look on her face, it may be received as veiled criticism ("So *why* are you acting this way?") rather than a compliment. We learn from these examples that the same message may be interpreted as confirming or disconfirming based on the nonverbal cues that accompany it.

Even doing nothing can be interpreted as disconfirming. Your failure to return a phone call or respond to the letter of an out-of-town friend might simply be the result of a busy schedule, but if the other person views the lack of contact as a sign that you don't value the relationship, the effect can be powerful.

In some cases it might be important or necessary to deliver a message that appears disconfirming, as when your best friend has a serious drinking problem. In that case, confirming messages may mask the problem. When challenging statements are necessary, they can come from a confirming place if they're grounded in concern for the other person ("I'm worried about you . . .") rather than in judgment

**Understanding Communication Technology**

## Can You Hear Me Now?

Thanks to technology, people have never been more connected—or more alienated.

I have traveled 36 hours to a conference on robotic technology in central Japan. The grand ballroom is Wi-Fi enabled, and the speaker is using the Web for his presentation. Laptops are open, fingers are flying. But the audience is not listening. Most seem to be doing their e-mail, downloading files, surfing the Web, or looking for a cartoon to illustrate an upcoming presentation. Every once in a while audience members give the speaker some attention, lowering their laptop screens in a kind of digital curtsy.

In the hallway outside the plenary session, attendees are on their phones or using laptops and PDAs to check their e-mail. Clusters of people chat with one another, making dinner plans, "networking" in that old sense of the term—the sense that implies sharing a meal. But at this conference it is clear that what people mostly want from public space is to be alone with their personal networks. It is good to come together physically, but it is more important to stay tethered to the people who define one's virtual identity, the identity that counts.

We live in techno-enthusiastic times, and we are most likely to celebrate our gadgets. Certainly the advertising that sells us our devices has us working from beautiful, remote locations that signal our status. We are connected, tethered, so important that our physical presence is no longer required. There is much talk of new efficiencies; we can work from anywhere and all the time. But tethered life is complex; it is helpful to measure our thrilling new networks against what they may be doing to us as people.  ●

Sherry Turkle

or evaluating ("You're ruining your life.") In one study, people were more successful at losing weight when their romantic partners gently challenged them than if they said nothing, but only if the challenges seemed to be motivated by love and if confirming messages outweighed the challenging ones.[17]

### How Communication Climates Develop

As soon as two people start to communicate, a relational climate begins to develop. If the messages are confirming, the climate is likely to be a positive one. If they disconfirm one another, the climate is likely to be hostile, cold, or defensive.

Verbal messages certainly contribute to the tone of a relationship, but many climate-shaping messages are nonverbal. The very act of approaching others is confirming, whereas avoiding them can be disconfirming. Smiles or frowns, the presence or absence of eye contact, tone of voice, the use of personal space—all these and other cues send messages about how the parties feel toward one another.

After a climate is formed, it can take on a life of its own and grow in a self-perpetuating **spiral**: a reciprocating communication pattern in which each person's message reinforces the other's.[18] In positive spirals, one partner's confirming message leads to a similar response from the other person. This positive reaction leads the first person to be even more

Early reports and a leaked video from the *American Idol* set suggested that feelings between judges Mariah Carey (left) and Nicki Minaj (right) were strained and sometimes openly hostile. How do you imagine this climate affected their working relationship? What messages shape the communication climate where you work and live?

reinforcing. Negative spirals are just as powerful, although they leave the partners feeling worse about themselves and each other. Research shows how spirals operate in relationships to reinforce the principle that "what goes around comes around." For example, when one partner refuses to talk about a sensitive issue, the other partner is likely to become frustrated and distant as well,[19] and when one person criticizes another, a tit-for-tat pattern of destructive criticism often emerges.[20] Conversely, when one partner shows empathy, the other is more likely to show empathy in return, and conflicts are more likely to be resolved to both people's satisfaction.[21]

> cultural idiom
> **what goes around comes around:** expect to be treated the way you treat others

**Escalatory conflict spirals** are the most visible way that disconfirming messages reinforce one another.[22] One attack leads to another until a skirmish escalates into a full-fledged battle. Although they are less obvious, **avoidance spirals** can also be destructive.[23] Rather than fighting, the parties slowly lessen their dependence on one another, withdraw, and become less invested in the relationship.

Spirals rarely go on indefinitely. Most relationships pass through cycles of progression and regression. If the spiral is negative, partners may find the exchange growing so unpleasant that they switch from negative to positive messages without discussing the matter. In other cases they may engage in metacommunication. "Hold on," one might say. "This is getting us nowhere." In some cases, however, partners pass the "point of no return," leading to the breakup of a relationship. Even positive spirals have their limit: Even the best relationships go through periods of conflict and withdrawal, although a combination of time and communication skills can eventually bring the partners back into greater harmony.

> cultural idiom
> **hold on:** wait

## Creating Positive Communication Climates

It's easy to see how disconfirming messages can pollute a communication climate. But what are some alternative ways of communicating that encourage positive relationships? The work of Jack Gibb gives a picture of what kinds of messages lead to both positive and negative spirals.[24]

After observing groups for several years, Gibb was able to isolate six types of defense-arousing communication and six contrasting behaviors that seemed to reduce the level of threat and defensiveness. The **Gibb categories** are listed in Table 8-2. Using the supportive types of communication and avoiding the defensive ones will increase the odds of creating and maintaining positive communication climates in your relationships.

**Evaluation Versus Description** The first type of defense-provoking behavior Gibb noted is **evaluative communication**. Most people become irritated at judgmental statements, which are likely to be interpreted as indicating a lack of regard.

**Table 8-2**    The Gibb Categories of Defensive and Supportive Behaviors

| DEFENSIVE BEHAVIORS | SUPPORTIVE BEHAVIORS |
| --- | --- |
| 1. Evaluation | 1. Description |
| 2. Control | 2. Problem orientation |
| 3. Strategy | 3. Spontaneity |
| 4. Neutrality | 4. Empathy |
| 5. Superiority | 5. Equality |
| 6. Certainty | 6. Provisionalism |

Evaluative language has often been described as **"you" language** because most such statements contain an accusatory use of that word. For example:

- You don't know what you're talking about.
- You're not doing your best.
- You smoke too much.

Unlike evaluative "you" language, **descriptive communication** focuses on the speaker's thoughts and feelings instead of judging the listener. One form of descriptive communication is **"I" language**.[25] Instead of putting the emphasis on judging another's behavior, the descriptive speaker explains the personal effect of the other's action. For instance, instead of saying, "You talk too much," a descriptive communicator would say, "When you don't give me a chance to say what's on my mind, I get frustrated." Notice that statements such as this include an account of the other person's behavior plus an explanation of its effect on the speaker and a description of the speaker's feelings.

**Control Versus Problem Orientation**    A second defense-provoking message involves some attempt to control the other person. A **controlling** message occurs when a sender seems to be imposing a solution on the receiver with little regard for the receiver's needs or interests. The control can range from relatively small matters (where to eat dinner or what television show to watch) to large ones (whether to remain in a relationship or how to spend a large sum of money).

The people most likely to use controlling behaviors are those with a fearful-avoidant adjustment style, meaning that they generally hold a low opinion of themselves and others.[26] In contrast, people with a secure attachment style (those who have positive feelings about themselves and others) are less likely to try to control other people. One implication is that people who engage in destructive behaviors are often motivated by how they feel on the inside rather than what their relational partners do or don't do.

By contrast, in **problem orientation**, communicators focus on finding a solution that satisfies both their needs and those of the others involved. The goal here isn't to "win" at the expense of your partner but rather to work out some arrangement in which everybody feels like a winner. The last section of this chapter has a great deal to say about "win–win" problem solving as a way to find problem-oriented solutions.

**Strategy Versus Spontaneity**    The third communication behavior that Gibb identified as creating a poor communication climate is **strategy**. A more accurate term to describe this type of behavior is *manipulation*. One of the surest ways to

*Source:* © Reprinted by special permission of the North America Syndicate.

make people defensive is to get caught trying to manipulate them. Nobody likes to be a guinea pig or a sucker, and even well-meant manipulation can cause bad feelings. Evidence suggests that manipulative attempts don't pay off for the perpetrator either. The relationships of manipulative people are typically less passionate and less fulfilling than other people's, and they score lower than average in terms of overall life satisfaction.[27]

**Spontaneity** is the label Gibb used as a contrast to strategy. A better term might be *honesty*. Despite the misleading label, spontaneous communication needn't be blurted out as soon as an idea comes to you. You might want to plan the wording of your message carefully so that you can express yourself clearly. The important thing is to be honest. A straightforward message may not always get what you want, but in the long run it's likely to pay dividends in a positive relational climate.

**Neutrality Versus Empathy**    Gibb used the term **neutrality** to describe a fourth behavior that arouses defensiveness. Probably a more descriptive term would be *indifference*. A neutral attitude is disconfirming because it communicates a lack of concern for the welfare of another and implies that the other person isn't very important to you.

The damaging effects of neutrality become apparent when you consider the hostility that most people have for the large, impersonal organizations with which they have to deal: "They think of me as a number instead of a person"; "I felt as if I were being handled by computers and not human beings." These two common statements reflect reactions to being handled in an indifferent way.

**Empathy** is an approach that confirms the other person. Having empathy means accepting another's feelings, putting yourself in another's place. This doesn't mean you need to agree with that person. Gibb noted the importance of nonverbal messages in communicating empathy. He found that facial and bodily expressions of concern are often more important to the receiver than the words used.

**Superiority Versus Equality**    **Superiority** is a fifth type of communication that creates a defensive climate. When it seems that people believe they are better than we are, a defensive response is likely.

We often meet people who possess knowledge or talents greater than ours. But your own experiences will tell you that it isn't necessary for these people to project an attitude of superiority. Gibb found ample evidence that many who have superior skills and talents are capable of conveying an attitude of **equality**. Such people communicate that, although they may have greater talent in certain areas, they see others as having just as much worth as human beings.

**Certainty Versus Provisionalism**    **Certainty** is a style of communication that is considered dogmatic and unyielding. Messages that suggest the speaker's mind is already made up are likely to generate defensiveness.

In contrast to dogmatic communication is **provisionalism**, in which people may have strong opinions but are willing to acknowledge that they don't have a corner on the truth and will change their stand if another position seems more reasonable.

There is no guarantee that using Gibb's supportive, confirming approach to communication will build a positive climate. But the chances for a constructive relationship will be greatest when communication consists of the kind of supportive approach described here. Besides boosting the odds of getting a positive response from others, supportive communication can leave you feeling better in a variety of ways: more in control of your relationships, more comfortable, and more positive toward others.

> cultural idiom
**to be a guinea pig or a sucker:**
to be taken advantage of

> cultural idiom
**in the long run:**
over an extended period of time

> cultural idiom
**mind is already made up:**
will not waiver from one's opinion

> cultural idiom
**boosting the odds of:**
increasing the chances of success of

# Understanding Interpersonal Conflict

Even the most supportive communication climate won't guarantee complete harmony. Regardless of what we may wish for or dream about, a conflict-free world just doesn't exist. Even the best communicators, the luckiest people, are bound to wind up in situations in which their needs don't match the needs of others. Money, time, power, sex, humor, and aesthetic taste, as well as a thousand other issues, arise and keep us from living in a state of perpetual agreement.

For many people the inevitability of conflict is a depressing fact. They think that the existence of ongoing conflict means that there's little chance for happy relationships with others. Effective communicators know differently, however. They realize that although it's impossible to *eliminate* conflict, there are ways to *manage* it effectively. And those effective communicators know the subject of this chapter—that managing conflict skillfully can open the door to healthier, stronger, and more satisfying relationships.

## The Nature of Conflict

Whatever form it may take, every interpersonal **conflict** involves an *expressed struggle between at least two interdependent parties who perceive incompatible goals, scarce resources, and interference from the other parties in achieving their goals.*[28] A closer look at the various parts of this definition helps to develop a clearer idea of how conflicts operate.

**Expressed Struggle**   A conflict doesn't exist unless both parties know that some disagreement exists. You may be upset for months because a neighbor's loud stereo keeps you from getting to sleep at night, but no conflict exists between the two of you until the neighbor learns about your problem. Of course, the expressed struggle doesn't have to be verbal. You can show your displeasure with somebody without saying a word. Giving a dirty look, using the silent treatment, and avoiding the other person are all ways of expressing yourself. But one way or another, both parties must know that a problem exists before they're in conflict.

**Perceived Incompatible Goals**   Conflicts often look as if one party's gain will be another's loss. For instance, consider the neighbor whose music keeps you awake at night. Does somebody have to lose? A neighbor who turns down the noise loses the enjoyment of hearing the music at full volume, but if the neighbor keeps the volume up, then you're still awake and unhappy.

But the goals in this situation really aren't completely incompatible—solutions do exist that allow both parties to get what they want. For instance, you could achieve peace and quiet by closing your windows and getting the neighbor to do the same. You might use a pair of earplugs. Or perhaps the neighbor could get a set of headphones and listen to the music at full volume without bothering anyone. If any of these solutions proves workable, then the conflict disappears.

Unfortunately, people often fail to see mutually satisfying answers to their problems.

> cultural idiom

**to wind up in:**
to end up being in

> cultural idiom

**open the door to:**
remove barriers to

> cultural idiom

**dirty look:**
facial expression indicating displeasure

In the sci-fi thriller *The Hunger Games*, young people are forced to fight one another to the death. Despite intense pressure, Katniss Everdeen (Jennifer Lawrence) finds ways to survive and win by collaborating with other contestants. In your experience, when is aggressive behavior promoted in today's society? What are the effects of this aggression?

And as long as they *perceive* their goals to be mutually exclusive, they create a self-fulfilling prophecy in which the conflict is very real.

**Perceived Scarce Resources**   In a conflict, people believe there isn't enough of some resource to go around. The most obvious example of a scarce resource is money—a cause of many conflicts. If a person asks for a raise in pay and the boss would rather keep the money or use it to expand the business, then the two parties are in conflict.

Time is another scarce commodity. As authors, we are constantly in the middle of struggles about how to use the limited time we have to spend. Should we work on this book? Visit with our partners? Spend time with our kids? Enjoy the luxury of being alone? With only 24 hours in a day, we're bound to end up in conflicts with our families, editors, students, and friends—all of whom want more of our time than we have available to give.

**Interdependence**   However antagonistic they might feel toward each other, the parties in a conflict are usually dependent on each other. The welfare and satisfaction of one depend on the actions of another. If this weren't true, then even in the face of scarce resources and incompatible goals, there would be no need for conflict. Interdependence exists between conflicting nations, social groups, organizations, friends, and lovers. In each case, if the two parties didn't need each other to solve the problem, both would go their separate ways. In fact, many conflicts go unresolved because the parties fail to understand their interdependence. One of the first steps toward resolving a conflict is to take the attitude that "we're in this together."

## Styles of Expressing Conflict

Communication scholars have identified a wide range of ways communicators handle conflicts.[29] Table 8-3 describes five ways people can act when their needs are not met. Each one has very different characteristics.

**Nonassertion**   The inability or unwillingness to express thoughts or feelings in a conflict is known as **nonassertion**. Sometimes nonassertion comes from a lack of confidence. At other times, people lack the awareness or skill to use a more direct means of expression.

Sometimes people know how to communicate in a straightforward way but choose to behave nonassertively. For example, women are less likely to clearly refuse an unwanted request for physical intimacy from a dating partner they would like to see in the future than from one they don't want to see again.[30]

One survey examined the conflict level of husbands and wives in normal "nondistressed" marriages. Over a 5-day period, spouses reported that their partner engaged in an average of 13 behaviors that were "displeasurable" to them but that they had only *1* confrontation during the same period.

Nonassertion can take a variety of forms. One is *avoidance*—either physical (steering clear of a friend after having an argument) or conversational (changing the topic, joking, or denying that a problem exists). People who avoid conflicts usually believe it's easier to put up with the status quo than to face the problem head-on and try to solve it. *Accommodation* is another type of nonassertive response. Accommodators deal with conflict by giving in, putting the other's needs ahead of their own.

Despite the obvious drawbacks of nonassertion, there are situations when accommodating or avoiding is a sensible approach. Avoidance may be the best course if a conflict is minor and short lived. For example, you might let a friend's annoying grumpiness pass without saying anything, knowing that he is having

> cultural idiom

**steering clear of:**
avoiding

**to face the problem head-on:**
to confront the problem directly

Table 8-3   **Individual Styles of Conflict**

| | NONASSERTIVE | DIRECTLY AGGRESSIVE | PASSIVE-AGGRESSIVE | INDIRECT | ASSERTIVE |
|---|---|---|---|---|---|
| **APPROACH TO OTHERS** | I'm not okay, you're okay. | I'm okay, you're not okay. | I'm okay, you're not okay. | I'm okay, you're not okay. (But I'll let you think you are.) | I'm okay, you're okay. |
| **DECISION MAKING** | Lets others choose. | Chooses for others. They know it. | Chooses for others. They don't know it. | Chooses for others. They don't know it. | Chooses for self. |
| **SELF-SUFFICIENCY** | Low. | High or low. | Looks high but usually low. | High or low. | Usually high. |
| **BEHAVIOR IN PROBLEM SITUATIONS** | Flees, gives in. | Outright attack. | Concealed attack. | Strategic, oblique behavior. | Direct confrontation. |
| **RESPONSE OF OTHERS** | Disrespect, guilt, anger, frustration. | Hurt, defensiveness, humiliation. | Confusion, frustration, feelings of manipulation. | Unknowing compliance or resistance. | Mutual respect. |
| **SUCCESS PATTERN** | Succeeds by luck or charity of others. | Beats out others. | Wins by manipulation. | Gains unwitting compliance of others. | Attempts "win–win" solutions. |

*Source:* Adapted with permission from Phelps, S., & Austin, N. (1975). *The assertive woman.* San Luis Obispo, CA: Impact, p. 11, © 1970, 1987, 1997, and 2000; and Gerald Piaget, American Orthopsychiatric Association, 1975. Further reproduction prohibited.

one of his rare bad days. Likewise, you might not complain to a neighbor whose loud music only rarely disturbs you. You may also reasonably choose to say nothing if the conflict occurs in an unimportant relationship, as with an acquaintance whose language you find offensive but whom you don't see often. Finally, you might choose to keep quiet if the risk of speaking up is too great: getting fired from a job you can't afford to lose, being humiliated in public, or even risking physical harm.

Assertiveness is most important when the issue and relationship matter a great deal. In one study, couples volunteered to be videotaped while they talked about sources of conflict in their marriages.[31] Researchers compared the couple's communication techniques to their marital satisfaction scores. They found that, when the issue was a relatively minor one, the happiest couples used indirect behaviors such as hinting. However, when the issue was of great concern, relationship satisfaction increased among the couples who addressed the issue assertively rather than indirectly. This was true even when the couples used communication techniques that are typically considered negative, such as blaming each other, making demands, or rejecting their partners' explanations. The researchers concluded that strong words should be used sparingly, but that overreacting is sometimes preferable to downplaying a serious concern.

**Direct Aggression**   Whereas nonasserters avoid conflicts, communicators who use direct aggression embrace them. A **directly aggressive message** confronts the other person in a way that attacks his or her position—and even the dignity of the receiver. Many directly aggressive responses are easy to spot: "You don't know what you're talking about." "That was a stupid thing to do." "What's the matter with you?" Other forms of direct aggression come more from nonverbal messages than from words. It's easy to imagine a hostile way of expressing statements like "What is it now?" or "I need some peace and quiet."

Verbal aggressiveness may get you what you want in the short run. Yelling "Shut up" might stop the other person from talking, and saying "Get it yourself" may save you from some exertion, but the relational damage of this approach probably isn't worth the cost. Direct aggression can be hurtful, and the consequences for the relationship can be long lasting.[32]

**Passive Aggression**    **Passive aggression** is far more subtle than its directly aggressive cousin. It occurs when a communicator expresses hostility in an obscure way. Psychologist George Bach terms this behavior "crazymaking"[36] and identifies several varieties. For example, *pseudoaccommodators* pretend to agree with you ("I'll be on time from now on") but don't comply with your request for change. *Guiltmakers* try to gain control by making you feel responsible for their choices: "I really should be studying, but I'll give you a ride." *Jokers* use humor as a weapon and then hide behind the complaint ("Where's your sense of humor?") when you object. *Trivial tyrannizers* do small things to drive you crazy instead of confronting you with their complaints: "forgetting" to take phone messages, playing the music

> cultural idiom

**in the short run:**
over a brief period of time

---

### @Work

## Dealing with Sexual Harassment

Sexual harassment takes many forms. It may arise between members of the same sex or between men and women. It can be a blatant sexual overture, or any verbal or nonverbal behavior that creates a "hostile work environment." The harasser can be a supervisor, peer, subordinate, or even someone outside the organization.

Thanks to enlightened company policies and government legislation, targets of sexual harassment have legal remedies. Although formal complaints are an assertive and powerful way to protect a target's rights, they can be time consuming, and those lodging the complaints sometimes experience depression, ridicule, isolation, and reprisal.[33]

As Chapter 1 explained, competent communication involves picking the most effective approach. Here are several options to consider if you or someone you care about experience harassment:[34]

1. *Consider dismissing the incident.* This nonassertive approach is only appropriate if you truly believe that the remark or behavior is trivial. Dismissing incidents that you believe are important can result in self-blame and diminished self-esteem. Even worse, it can lead to repetition of the offensive behavior.

2. *Tell the harasser to stop.* Assertively tell the harasser early that the behavior is unwelcome, and insist that it stop immediately. Your statement should be firm, but it doesn't have to be angry. Remember that many words or deeds that make you uncomfortable may not be deliberately hostile remarks.

3. *Write a personal letter to the harasser.* A written statement may help the harasser to understand what behavior you find offensive. Just as important, it can show that you take the problem seriously. Detail specifics about what happened, what behavior you want stopped, and how you felt. You may want to include a copy of your organization's sexual harassment policy. Keep a record of when you delivered your message.

4. *Ask a trusted third party to intervene.* This indirect approach can sometimes boost the odds of persuading the harasser to stop. The person you choose should be someone who you are convinced understands your discomfort and supports your opinion. Also, be sure this intermediary is someone the harasser respects and trusts.

5. *Use company channels.* Report the situation to your supervisor, personnel office, or a committee that has been set up to consider harassment complaints.

6. *File a legal complaint.* If all else fails or the incident is egregious, you may file a complaint with the federal Equal Employment Opportunity Commission or with your state agency. You have the right to obtain the services of an attorney regarding your legal options.[35] ●

**ON YOUR FEET**

Describe conflicts you've experienced that reflected each of these styles: indirect, passive-aggressive, directly aggressive, and assertive. Based on your observations, which styles were most successful in accomplishing the communicators' goals? Which styles were best for the relationship?

> cultural idiom

**test the waters:**
try

**softening the blow of:**
easing the effect of

> cultural idiom

**punch:**
force or effectiveness

too loud, and so on. *Withholders* punish their partners by keeping back something valuable, such as courtesy, affection, or humor.

**Indirect Communication**   The clearest communication is not necessarily the best approach. **Indirect communication** conveys a message in a roundabout manner, in order to save face for the recipient.[37] Although indirect communication lacks the clarity of an aggressive or assertive message, it involves more initiative than nonassertion. It also has none of the hostility of passive-aggressive crazymaking. The goal is to get what you want without arousing the hostility of the other person. Consider the case of the neighbor's loud music. One indirect approach would be to strike up a friendly conversation with the neighbor and ask if anything you are doing is too noisy for him, hoping he will get the hint.

Because it saves face for the other party, indirect communication is often kinder than blunt honesty. If your guests are staying too long, it's probably kinder to yawn and hint about your big day tomorrow than to bluntly ask them to leave. Likewise, if you're not interested in going out with someone who has asked you for a date, it may be more compassionate to claim that you're busy than to say, "I'm not interested in seeing you."

At other times we communicate indirectly in order to protect ourselves. You might, for example, test the waters by hinting instead of directly asking the boss for a raise, or by letting your partner know indirectly that you could use some affection, instead of asking outright. At times like these, an oblique approach may get the message across while softening the blow of a negative response.

The advantages of protecting oneself and saving face for others help explain why indirect communication is the most common way people make requests,[38] especially if we don't know the person well or if we feel intimidated about asking.[39] The risk of an indirect message, of course, is that the other party will misunderstand you or fail to get the message at all. There are also times when the importance of an idea is so great that hinting lacks the necessary punch. When clarity and directness are your goals, an assertive approach is in order.

**Assertion**   **Assertive** people handle conflicts by expressing their needs, thoughts, and feelings clearly and directly but without judging others or dictating to them. They have the attitude that most of the time it is possible to resolve problems to everyone's satisfaction. Possessing this attitude and the skills to bring it about doesn't guarantee that assertive communicators will always get what they want, but it does give them the best chance of doing so. An additional benefit of such an approach is that whether or not it satisfies a particular need, it maintains the self-respect of both the assertors and those with whom they interact. As a result, people who manage their conflicts assertively may experience feelings of discomfort while they are working through the problem. They usually feel better about themselves and one another afterward—quite a change from the outcomes of nonassertiveness or aggression.

---

Ethical Challenge

## Choosing an Ethical Conflict Style

At first glance, assertiveness seems like the most ethical communication style to use when you are faced with a conflict. The matter might not be so clear, however. Find out for yourself by following these steps.

1. Decide for yourself whether it is ever justifiable to use each of the other conflict styles: nonassertion, direct aggression, passive aggression, and indirect communication. Support your position on each style with examples from your own experience.

2. Explain your answer to classmates who disagree and listen to their arguments.

3. After hearing positions that differ from yours, work with your classmates to develop a code of ethics for expressing conflict messages.

## Characteristics of an Assertive Message

Knowing *about* assertive messages isn't the same as being able to express them. The next few pages describe a method for communicating assertively. It works for a variety of messages: your hopes, problems, complaints, and expressions of appreciation. Besides giving you a way to express yourself directly, this format also makes it easier for others to understand you. A complete assertive message has five parts:

**1. Behavioral Description**   As you learned in Chapter 4, a behavioral description is an objective picture of the behavior in question, without any judging or editorializing. Put in terms of Gibb's categories, it uses descriptive rather than evaluative language. Notice the difference between a behavioral description and an evaluative judgment:

- *Behavioral description*: "You asked me to tell you what I really thought about your idea, and then when I gave it to you, you told me I was too critical."

- *Evaluative judgment*: "Don't be so touchy! It's hypocritical to ask for my opinion and then get mad when I give it to you."

Judgmental words like "touchy" and "hypocritical" invite a defensive reaction. The target of your accusation can reply, "I'm not touchy or hypocritical!" It's harder to argue with the facts stated in an objective, behavioral description. Furthermore, the neutral language reduces the chances of a defensive reaction.

**2. Your Interpretation of the Other Person's Behavior**   This part is where you can use the perception-checking skill outlined in Chapter 2 (pages 61–62). Remember that a complete perception check includes two possible interpretations of the behavior: "Maybe you think I don't care because it took me 2 days to call you back. Is that it, or is there something else?"

Whether you offer just one interpretation or two, as described in Chapter 4, the key is to label your hunches as such instead of suggesting that you are positive about what the other person's behavior means.

**3. A Description of Your Feelings**   Expressing your feelings adds a new dimension to a message. For example, consider the difference between these two responses:

- "When you kiss me and nibble on my ear while we're watching television *[behavior]*, I think you probably want to make love *[interpretation]*, and *I feel excited.*"

- "When you kiss me and nibble on my ear while we're watching television *[behavior]*, I think you probably want to make love *[interpretation]*, and *I feel disgusted.*"

Likewise, adding feelings to the situation we have been examining makes the assertive message clearer:

- "When you said I was too critical after you asked me for my honest opinion *[behavior]*, it seemed to me that you really didn't want to hear a critical remark *[interpretation]*, and *I felt stupid for being honest [feeling].*"

**4. A Description of the Consequences**   A consequence statement explains what happens as a result of the behavior you have described, your interpretation, and the ensuing feeling. There are three kinds of consequences: What happens to you, the speaker ("When you tease me, I avoid you"), what happens to the target of the message ("When you drink too much, you start to drive dangerously"), or what happens to others ("When you play the radio so loud, it wakes up the baby").

**5. A Statement of Your Intentions**   Intention statements are the final element in the assertive format. They can communicate three kinds of messages:

> cultural idiom
>
> **touchy:**
> quickly offended with little provocation

- *Where you stand on an issue*: "I want you to know how much this bothers me." Or "I want you to know how much I appreciate your support."

- *Requests of others*: "I'd like to know whether you are angry." Or "I hope you'll come again."

- *Descriptions of how you plan to act in the future*: "Don't expect me ever to lend you anything again."

In our ongoing example, adding an intention statement would complete the assertive message:

- "When you said I was too critical after you asked me for my honest opinion *[behavior]*, it seemed to me that you really didn't want to hear a critical remark *[interpretation]*. That made me feel stupid for being honest *[feeling]*. Now I'm not sure whether I should tell you what I'm really thinking the next time you ask *[consequence]*. *I'd like to get it clear right now: Do you really want me to tell you what I think or not [intention]?*"

Before you try to deliver messages using the assertive format outlined here, there are a few points to remember. First, it isn't necessary or even wise always to put the elements in the order described here. As you can see from reviewing the examples on the preceding pages, it's sometimes best to begin by stating your feelings. In other cases, you can start by sharing your intentions or interpretations or by describing consequences.

You also ought to word your message in a way that suits your style of speaking. Instead of saying "I interpret your behavior to mean," you might choose to say, "I think . . ." or, "It seems to me . . ." or perhaps, "I get the idea. . . ." In the same way, you can express your intentions by saying, "I hope you'll understand (or do) . . ." or perhaps, "I wish you would. . . ." It's important that you get your message across, but you should do it in a way that sounds and feels genuine to you.

Realize that there are some cases in which you can combine two elements in a single phrase. For instance, the statement " . . . and ever since then I've been wanting to talk to you" expresses both a consequence and an intention. In the same way, saying, " . . . and after you said that, I felt confused" expresses a consequence and a feeling. Whether you combine elements or state them separately, the important point is to be sure that each one is present in your statement.

Finally, you need to realize that it isn't always possible to deliver messages such as the ones here all at one time, wrapped up in neat paragraphs. It will often be necessary to repeat or restate one part many times before your receiver truly understands what you're saying. As you've already read, there are many types of psychological and physical noise that make it difficult for us to understand one another. Just remember: You haven't communicated successfully until the receiver of your message understands everything you've said. In communication, as in many other activities, patience and persistence are essential.

## Gender and Conflict Style

The "Men Are from Mars, Women Are from Venus" theory of conflict has strong intuitive appeal. A body of research seems to support the notion that men and women typically do approach conflict differently.

Some differences are evident early on. By the time boys are 6, they tend to gravitate toward large groups in which there is a clear understanding of who outranks whom.[40] In this context, competition is often considered a way to earn respect and status. It's also common for boys to engage in physical tussles with each other, both as a form of play and as a means of settling disputes. Girls, on the other hand, tend to gravitate to one-on-one relationships. The emphasis is less on who

> cultural idiom

**on the other hand:**
from the other point of view

outranks whom and more on who is closest to whom. Even in a group, girls typically know who has best friend status. As a result, girls typically engage in more prosocial behaviors (offering compliments, showing empathy, providing emotional support) than boys do and more often shy away from direct confrontations.

Especially because children tend to have mostly same-sex friends, it's easy to imagine the misunderstandings that occur when they form other-sex relationships in their teen years and beyond. Girls may feel that boys are insensitive, boisterous, and emotionally distant, whereas boys may feel that girls are quick to get their feelings hurt but are reluctant to say outright what is bothering them. On the bright side, males typically appreciate the emotional support of their female friends. And women say they enjoy the freedom to be more frank and assertive with their male friends than they usually are with their female friends.[41]

**Origins of Gender Differences**    Biology explains some of the difference between the way men and women deal with conflict. During disagreements, men tend to experience greater physiological arousal than women, which comes in the form of increased heart rate and blood pressure. This may be why boys exhibit more aggressive behaviors than girls do, even when they are very young. About 1 in 20 male toddlers is frequently aggressive, compared with 1 in 100 female toddlers.[42]

Evolution may play a role as well. Because women are able to bear only a limited number of children, procreation has favored men who can successfully compete for their attention and demonstrate their superiority to other males. Moreover, in their traditional role as hunters and providers, men were challenged to be bold, physical, risk takers.[43] It may be that men have evolved to be more physical and competitive than women because—at least in years gone by—that was an advantage. By contrast, women have traditionally nurtured children. In that role, there is an advantage to creating safe environments, working in teams, and understanding the nuances of nonverbal communication because babies and children are often not verbally proficient.[44] This may explain why women are particularly sensitive to subtle cues and are more aligned to harmony and cooperation than to competition.

Although biology and evolution have some influence, as we grow up we learn to handle our emotions and to mimic our role models. This means that culture plays an important role as well.[45] We all know that there are powerful rewards for "acting like a lady" or "being a real man" and serious consequences for defying those expectations. In Western cultures, females are typically expected to be accommodating and males to be competitive. But these expectations can lead to frustrating double binds, as we will discuss next.

**Conflict Dilemmas**    Women face a double standard: They may be judged more harshly than men if they are assertive, but they may be overlooked if they aren't. Typically, women are more likely than men to use indirect strategies instead of confronting conflict head-on. They are also more likely to compromise and to give in to maintain relational harmony. This style works well in some situations, but not in others. In one study, men and women scored equally well on a set of mathematical challenges, but the men were twice as likely as the women to enter a tournament in which they could compete for cash prizes or raises based on their

In the film *Zero Dark Thirty*, Jessica Chastain plays Maya, the real-life intelligence expert who helped locate Osama bin Laden. As a woman in a male-dominated hierarchy, Maya is often overlooked and belittled. She gradually earns acceptance by being tireless, strong willed, and assertive—qualities typically associated with masculinity. Have you ever felt that the conflict style associated with your gender is either an asset or a limitation?

# How Assertive Are You?

Circle your answer to each question using the grid below. Note that the answers do not appear in alphabetical order.

1. You feel you deserve the new corner office that has just become available. What would you do?

   a. Hint around that you have outgrown your cubicle.

   b. Tell your coworkers, "You deserve it more than I do," but secretly ask the boss if you can have it.

   c. Meet with your supervisor and lay out the reasons you think you deserve the office.

   d. Threaten to quit if you aren't assigned to the office.

   e. Stay quiet and hope the boss realizes that you deserve the office.

2. Your best friend just called to cancel your weekend trip together at the last minute. This isn't the first time your friend has done this, and you are very disappointed. What do you do?

   a. Announce that the friendship is over. That's no way to treat someone you care about.

   b. Reassure your friend that it's okay and there are no hard feelings.

   c. Resolve to cancel the next trip yourself to teach your friend a lesson.

   d. Declare, "But I've already packed," hoping your friend will take the hint and decide to go after all.

   e. Say, "I feel disappointed, because I enjoy my time with you and because we have made nonrefundable deposits. Can we work this out?"

3. During a classroom discussion, a fellow student makes a comment that you find offensive. What do you do?

   a. Tell the instructor after class that the comment made you uncomfortable.

   b. Ignore it.

   c. Announce that the statement is the stupidest thing you have ever heard.

   d. Say nothing, but tell other people how much you dislike that person.

   e. Join the discussion, mention that you see the issue differently, and invite your classmate to explain why he or she feels that way.

4. You are on a first date when the other person suggests seeing a movie you are sure you will hate. What do you do?

   a. Lie and say you've already seen it.

   b. Say, "Sure!" How bad can it be?

   c. Say, "Okaaay" and raise your eyebrows in a way that suggests your date must be either stupid or kidding.

   d. Suggest that you engage in another activity instead.

   e. Proclaim that you'd rather stay home and watch old reruns than see that movie.

## EVALUATING YOUR RESPONSES

|        | Question 1 | Question 2 | Question 3 | Question 4 |
|--------|------------|------------|------------|------------|
| ROW 1  | e          | b          | b          | b          |
| ROW 2  | a          | d          | a          | b          |
| ROW 3  | b          | c          | d          | c          |
| ROW 4  | c          | e          | e          | d          |
| ROW 5  | d          | a          | c          | e          |

**Nonassertive**

If the majority of your answers appear on row 1, you rank low on the assertiveness scale. The people around you may be unable to guess when you have a preference or hurt feelings. It may seem that "going with the flow" is the way to go, but research suggests that relationships flounder when people don't share their likes and dislikes with one another. Try voicing your feelings more clearly. People may like you more for it.

**Indirect**

If the majority of your answers appear on row 2, you tend to know what you want, but you rely on subtlety to convey your preferences. This can be a strength, because you aren't likely to offend people. However, don't be surprised if people sometimes fail to notice when you are upset. Research suggests that indirect communication works well for small concerns, but not for big ones. When the issue is important to you, step up to say so.

**Passively Aggressive**

If the majority of your answers appear on row 3, you tend to be passive-aggressive. Rather than taking the bull by the horns, you are more likely to seek revenge, complain to people

around you, or use snide humor to make your point. These techniques can make the people around you feel belittled and frustrated. Plus, you are more likely to alienate people than to get your way in the long run. Try to break this habit by saying what you feel in a clear, calm way.

**Assertive**

If the majority of your answers appear on row 4, you have hit the bulls-eye in terms of healthy assertiveness. You tend to say what you feel without infringing on other people's right to do the same. Your combination of respectfulness

and self-confidence is likely to serve you well in relationships.

**Aggressive**

If the majority of your answers appear on row 5, you tend to overshoot assertive and land in the aggressive category instead. Although you may mean well, your comments are likely to offend and intimidate others. Try tuning it back a little by stating your opinions (gently) and encouraging others to do the same. If you refrain from name-calling and accusations, people are likely to take what you say more seriously. ●

performance.[46] As a result of their reluctance to compete, women may be overlooked for raises, promotions, and other forms of recognition, even though they are highly qualified.

Cultural norms present a dilemma for men as well. Men are typically rewarded for being competitive and assertive. But those behaviors can seem overly aggressive in close relationships. For example, when conflict arises with coworkers, friends, and loved ones, a competitive stance can make the situation worse.[47] That, coupled with men's high level of physical arousal in conflict conditions, can make interpersonal conflict particularly frustrating for them. They are more likely than women to withdraw if they become uncomfortable or fail to get their way.[48] Women may interpret this as indifference, but men often say they detach to avoid overreacting, physically and verbally, in the heat of the moment.

**Differences Online** Gender differences that appear in face-to-face communication also persist online. When researchers compared messages posted by male and female teenagers, they found that the boys typically used assertive language, such as boasts and sexual invitations, whereas the girls used mostly cooperative language, such as compliments and questions.[49] The teens' adherence to traditional gender roles was also evident nonverbally. The girls tended to post photos of themselves in seductive, receptive poses, and the boys in more rugged, dominant poses. These personae are likely to influence how they behave when conflict arises.

**Commonalities** General differences aside, it bears emphasizing that social expectations change over time and stereotypes do not always apply. The qualities men and women have in common far outnumber their differences. Put another way, although men and women differ on *average*, most of us live somewhere in the middle, where masculine and feminine styles frequently overlap.[50] For example, men and women are roughly the same in terms of how much closeness they desire in relationships and the value they place on sharing ideas and feelings.[51]

One danger is that we may stereotype others and even ourselves, based on differences that are fairly small or don't actually exist. People who assume that men are aggressive and women are accommodating may notice behavior that fits these stereotypes ("See how much he bosses her around? A typical man!"). On the other hand, behavior that doesn't fit these preconceived ideas (accommodating men, pushy women) goes unnoticed.

What, then, can we conclude about the influence of gender on conflict? Research has demonstrated that there are, indeed, some small but measurable differences in the two sexes. But, although men and women may have characteristically different conflict styles, the individual style of each communicator is more important than a person's sex in shaping the way he or she handles conflict.

## Conflict in Online Communication

Online communication has changed the nature of interpersonal conflict. Disagreements handled via texting, chatting, e-mail, and blogging can unfold differently than those that play out in person. Some of the characteristics of mediated communication described in Chapter 1 are especially important during conflicts.

**Delay**   The asynchronous nature of most mediated channels means that communicators aren't obliged to respond immediately to one another.

The inherent delays in mediated conflicts present both benefits and risks. On the upside, the chance to cool down and think carefully before replying can prevent aggressive blowups.[52] This is true on a personal and a global level. Researcher Donald Ellis commends inclusive chat rooms and discussion boards, calling them a "new public sphere" and a "deliberative democracy" in which people can share ideas and take their time considering a wide range of viewpoints.[53] On the other hand, participation requires active involvement. People can just as easily ignore online posts and fail to respond to e-mails, texts, and IMs. When they do reply, there's the temptation to craft insults and jabs that can make matters worse.

**Disinhibition**   The absence of face-to-face contact can make it easy to respond aggressively, without considering the consequences until it's too late. This is especially likely when people don't know one another well and when tensions are high. Researchers describe what they call a "flame war" (based on the term for inflammatory or blunt remarks online) that erupted in an online cancer support group.[54] It happened when the mother of a cancer patient posted her opinion that hospital beds needed by cancer patients were being taken up by "anorexic girls." Others weighed in to say she should be more compassionate and less judgmental. Eventually, the episode erupted into an online feud comprising nearly 100 posts by 30 of the 42 people in the support group. Capitalized words such as PISSED OFF, ATTACKING, and VULTURES screamed the participants' frustration. The researchers speculate that online communication can facilitate close ties, but people may post comments they wouldn't say to one another in person. Although it's easier to overlook the impact of a hostile approach at a virtual distance, remember that communication is irreversible: It's no more possible to retract a message that's been delivered than it is to "unsqueeze" a tube of toothpaste.

Rihanna and Chris Brown shared many details of their tumultuous relationship via Twitter, Instagram, and other channels. Their posts created a permanent record, despite their efforts to delete some after the fact. What digital record have you created? Do you ever wish you had hesitated before sending digital messages?

**Permanence**   Because e-mails and text messages come in written form, there's a permanent "transcript" that doesn't exist when communicators deal with conflict face-to-face. This record can help clarify misperceptions and faulty memories. On the other hand, the permanent documents that chronicle a conflict can stir up emotions that make it hard to forgive and forget.

If online communication seems to be making a conflict worse, you may want to consider shifting to a face-to-face approach. Although mediated conflict may feel easier at the time, it may create more lasting damage to the relationship.

## Cultural Influences on Conflict

The ways in which people communicate during conflicts vary widely from one culture to another. The kind of rational, calm, yet assertive approach that is the ideal for European American disagreements is not the norm in some other cultures.[55] For example, in traditional African American culture, conflict is characterized by a greater tolerance for expressions of intense emotions.[56] And ethnicity isn't the only factor that shapes a communicator's preferred conflict style: The degree of assimilation also plays an important role. For example, Latinos with strong cultural identities tend to seek accommodation and compromise more than those with weaker cultural ties.[57]

In individualistic cultures like that of the United States, the goals, rights, and needs of each person are considered important, and most people would agree that it is an individual's right to stand up for himself or herself. People in such cultures typically value direct communication in which you say outright what is bothering you.[58] By contrast, collectivist cultures (more common in Latin America and Asia) consider the concerns of the group to be more important than those of any individual. Preserving and honoring the face of the other person are prime goals, and communicators go to great lengths to avoid any communication that might risk embarrassing a conversational partner. In these cultures, the kind of assertive behavior that might seem perfectly appropriate to an American or Canadian would seem rude and insensitive.

As you might imagine, low-context cultures like that of the United States place a premium on being direct and literal. By contrast, high-context cultures like that of Japan value self-restraint and avoid confrontation. Communicators in these cultures derive meaning from a variety of unspoken rules, such as context, social conventions, and hints. For this reason, what seems like "beating around the bush" to an American would be polite to an Asian. In Japan, for example, even a simple request like "close the door" would be too straightforward.[59] A more indirect statement like "it is somewhat cold today" would be more appropriate. Or a Japanese person may glance at the door or tell a story about someone who got sick in a drafty room.[60] To take a more important example, Japanese are reluctant to simply say "no" to a request. A more likely answer would be, "Let me think about it for a while," which anyone familiar with Japanese culture would recognize as a refusal. When indirect communication is a cultural norm, it is unreasonable to expect more straightforward approaches to succeed.

From the examples so far, you might expect the United States to top the charts in terms of directness when it comes to conflict management. However, a mediating factor is at play—emotional expressiveness. In

> cultural idiom

**preserving and honoring the face:**
protecting and respecting the other's dignity

**beating around the bush:**
approaching something in an indirect way

The Kardashian sisters are well known from media accounts of their explosive arguments and just-as-quick acts of forgiveness. They attribute their passionate nature to their Armenian heritage. How much does culture account for the way you and others you know manage conflict? Can culture ever be an excuse for handling conflict badly?

## Understanding Diversity

### They Seem to Be Arguing

"The Italian language brings out the passion in me," declares Ewa Niemiec, who is fluent in Italian, English, and Polish.[64] Like many people who are multilingual, she feels that each language evokes a different feeling. Speaking English makes her feel polite, but Italian makes her "mouthy and loud." That's not necessarily bad, she says, unless people mistake the passion for conflict or aggression.

Once, when Niemiec interviewed for a job in Italian, she found herself "bickering" with her would-be boss. She's not unusual in finding that experience enjoyable. Members of many cultures consider verbal disputes to be a form of intimacy and even a game.

Misunderstandings may arise, however, when people from emotionally reserved cultures observe or interact with people from emotionally expressive ones. Americans visiting Greece, for example, often think they are witnessing an argument when they are overhearing a friendly conversation.[65] A comparative study of American and Italian nursery school children showed that one of the Italian children's favorite pastimes was a kind of heated debating that Italians call *discussione*, which Americans would regard as arguing.

Niemiec encourages people to overcome the idea that emotional language is confrontational. "If you're planning to travel or live in Italy," she says, "be prepared for a land of strong feelings, loud voices, and even bigger hand gestures." ●

---

this regard, the United States has a great deal in common with Asian cultures, namely, a preference for calm communication rather than heated displays of emotion.[61] From this perspective, it may seem rude, frightening, or incompetent to show intense emotion during conflict. Indeed, people who become passionate are warned about the danger of saying things they don't mean.

By contrast, in cultures that value emotional expressiveness, people who do *not* show passion are regarded as hiding their true feelings. African Americans, Arabs, Greeks, Italians, Cubans, and Russians are typically considered highly expressive.[62] To them, behaving calmly in a conflict episode may be a sign that a person is unconcerned, insincere, or untrustworthy.

With differences like these, it's easy to imagine how two friends, lovers, or fellow workers from different cultural backgrounds might have trouble finding a conflict style that is comfortable for them both. Sometimes we don't even understand our own reactions to conflict. Many Americans find that, although they usually consider themselves to be direct and individualistic, they are fairly accommodating when it comes to conflict management.[63] This may surprise them as much as it surprises other people.

## Managing Interpersonal Conflicts

It's helpful to understand how conflicts operate, but in itself that awareness isn't enough to help you manage them in your own life. The following pages describe several ways to communicate in the face of disagreement. As you read about them, consider which ones you use now, and whether others might serve you better.

### Methods for Conflict Resolution

Regardless of the relational style, gender, or culture of the participants, every conflict is a struggle to have one's goals met. Sometimes that struggle succeeds, and at other times it fails. In the remainder of this chapter we'll look at various approaches to resolving conflicts and see which ones are most promising.

**Win–Lose** Win–lose conflicts are ones in which one party achieves his or her goal at the expense of the other. People resort to this method of resolving disputes when they perceive a situation as being an "either–or" one: Either I get what I want, or you get your way. The most clear-cut examples of win–lose situations are certain games, such as baseball or poker, in which the rules require a winner and a loser. Some interpersonal issues seem to fit into this win–lose framework: two coworkers seeking a promotion to the same job, for instance, or a couple who disagree on how to spend their limited money.

Power is the distinguishing characteristic in win–lose problem solving, because it is necessary to defeat an opponent to get what you want. The most obvious kind of power is physical. Some parents threaten their children with warnings such as "Stop misbehaving, or I'll send you to your room." Adults who use physical power to deal with one another usually aren't so blunt, but the legal system is the implied threat: "Follow the rules, or we'll lock you up."

*"It's not enough that we succeed. Cats must also fail."*

*Source:* Cartoonbank 115108.

Real or implied force isn't the only kind of power used in conflicts. People who rely on authority of many types engage in win–lose methods without ever threatening physical coercion. In most jobs, supervisors have the potential to use authority in the assignment of working hours, job promotions, and desirable or undesirable tasks, and, of course, in the power to fire an unsatisfactory employee. Teachers can use the power of grades to coerce students to act in desired ways.

Even the usually admired democratic principle of majority rule is a win–lose method of resolving conflicts. However fair it may be, this system results in one group getting its way and another group being unsatisfied.

There are some circumstances when win–lose problem solving may be necessary, such as when there are truly scarce resources and where only one party can achieve satisfaction. For instance, if two suitors want to marry the same person, only one can succeed. And, to return to an earlier example, it's often true that only one applicant can be hired for a job. But don't be too willing to assume that your conflicts are necessarily win–lose: As you'll soon read, many situations that seem to require a loser can be resolved to everyone's satisfaction.

There is a second kind of situation in which win–lose is the best method. Even when cooperation is possible, if the other person insists on trying to defeat you, then the most logical response might be to defend yourself by fighting back. "It takes two to tango," the old cliché goes, and it also often takes two to cooperate.

A final and much less frequent justification for trying to defeat another person occurs when the other person is clearly behaving in a wrong manner and when defeating that person is the only way to stop the wrongful behavior. Few people would deny the importance of restraining a person who is deliberately harming others even if the aggressor's freedom is sacrificed in the process. Forcing wrong-doers to behave themselves is dangerous because of the wide difference in opinion between people about who is wrong and who is right. Given this difference, it would seem justifiable only in the most extreme circumstances to coerce others into behaving as we think they should.

**Lose–Lose** In **lose–lose problem solving**, neither side is satisfied with the outcome. Although the name of this approach is so discouraging that it's hard to imagine how anyone could willingly use it, in truth lose–lose is a fairly common way to handle conflicts. In many instances the parties will both strive to be winners, but as a result of the struggle, both end up losers. On the international scene many wars illustrate this sad point. A nation that gains military victory at the cost of thousands of lives, large amounts of resources, and a damaged national

> cultural idiom

**it takes two to tango:**
it takes two people to shape a relationship

Choose a conflict style different from yours and identify the assumptions on which it is based. Next, suggest how people with different styles can adapt their assumptions and behaviors to communicate in a more satisfying manner.

> cultural idiom

**haggling over:**
arguing about

consciousness hasn't truly won much. On an interpersonal level the same principle holds true. Most of us have seen battles of pride in which both parties strike out and both suffer.

**Compromise**   Unlike lose–lose outcomes, a **compromise** gives both parties at least some of what they wanted, though both sacrifice part of their goals. People usually settle for compromises when they see partial satisfaction as the best they can hope for. Although a compromise may be better than losing everything, this approach hardly seems to deserve the positive image it has with some people. In his valuable book on conflict resolution, management consultant Albert Filley makes an interesting observation about our attitudes toward this approach.[66] Why is it, he asks, that if someone says, "I will compromise my values," we view the action unfavorably, yet we talk admiringly about parties in a conflict who compromise to reach a solution? Although compromises may be the best obtainable result in some conflicts, it's important to realize that both people in a dispute can often work together to find much better solutions. In such cases *compromise* is a negative word.

Most of us are surrounded by the results of bad compromises. Consider a common example: the conflict between one person's desire to smoke cigarettes and another's need to breathe clean air. The win–lose outcomes of this conflict are obvious: Either the smoker abstains, or the nonsmoker gets polluted lungs—neither very satisfying. But a compromise in which the smoker gets to enjoy only a rare cigarette or must retreat outdoors and in which the nonsmoker still must inhale some fumes or feel like an ogre is hardly better. Both sides have lost a considerable amount of both comfort and goodwill. Of course, the costs involved in other compromises are even greater. For example, if a divorced couple compromises on child care by haggling over custody and then finally grudgingly agrees to split the time with their children, it's hard to say that anybody has won.

**Win–Win**   In **win–win problem solving**, the goal is to find a solution that satisfies the needs of everyone involved. Not only do the parties avoid trying to win at the other's expense, they also believe that by working together it is possible to find a solution that allows both to reach their goals.

Finding a win–win situation usually involves looking below the surface at what both parties are trying to achieve. Suppose you want a quiet evening at home tonight and your partner wants to go to a party. On the surface, only one of you can win. However, by listening carefully to each other, you realize you can both get your way. You don't feel like getting dressed up and talking to a room full of people. Your partner isn't crazy about that part of it either but would like to connect with two old friends who are going to be at the party. Once you understand the underlying goals, a solution presents itself: Invite those two friends over for a casual dinner at your place before they head off to the party. In this way, neither you nor your partner compromises on what you want to achieve. Indeed, the evening may be more enjoyable than either of you expected.

Although a win–win approach sounds ideal, it is not always possible, or even appropriate. Table 8-4 suggests some factors to consider when deciding which approach to take when facing a conflict. There will certainly be times when compromising is the most sensible approach. You will even encounter instances when pushing for your own solution is reasonable. Even more surprisingly, you will probably discover that there are times when it makes sense to willingly accept the loser's role.

## Steps in Win–Win Problem Solving

Although win–win problem solving is often the most desirable approach to managing conflicts, it is also one of the hardest to achieve. In spite of the challenge, it is definitely possible to become better at resolving conflicts. The following pages

Table 8-4    **Choosing the Most Appropriate Method of Conflict Resolution**

1. Consider deferring to the other person:
   - When you discover you are wrong
   - When the issue is more important to the other person than it is to you
   - To let others learn by making their own mistakes
   - When the long-term cost of winning may not be worth the short-term gains

2. Consider compromising:
   - When there is not enough time to seek a win–win outcome
   - When the issue is not important enough to negotiate at length
   - When the other person is not willing to seek a win–win outcome

3. Consider competing:
   - When the issue is important and the other person will take advantage of your noncompetitive approach

4. Consider cooperating:
   - When the issue is too important for a compromise
   - When a long-term relationship between you and the other person is important
   - When the other person is willing to cooperate

outline a method to increase your chances of being able to handle your conflicts in a win–win manner, so that both you and others have your needs met. As you learn to use this approach, you should find that more and more of your conflicts end up with win–win solutions. And even when total satisfaction isn't possible, this approach can preserve a positive relational climate.[67]

As it is presented here, win–win problem solving is a highly structured activity. After you have practiced the approach a number of times, this style of managing conflict will become almost second nature to you. You'll then be able to approach your conflicts without the need to follow the step-by-step approach. But for the time being, try to be patient, and trust the value of the following pattern. As you read on, imagine yourself applying it to a problem that's bothering you now.

**> cultural idiom**
**second nature:**
easy and natural

**Identify Your Problem and Unmet Needs**    Before you speak out, it's important to realize that the problem that is causing conflict is yours. Whether you want to return an unsatisfactory piece of merchandise, complain to noisy neighbors because your sleep is being disturbed, or request a change in working conditions from your employer, the problem is yours. Why? Because in each case *you* are the person who is dissatisfied. You are the one who has paid for the defective article; the merchant who sold it to you has the use of your good money. You are the one who is losing sleep as a result of your neighbors' activities; they are content to go on as before. You, not your boss, are the one who is unhappy with your working conditions.

Realizing that the problem is yours will make a big difference when the time comes to approach your partner. Instead of feeling and acting in an evaluative way, you'll be more likely to share your problem in a descriptive way, which will not only be more accurate but also will reduce the chance of a defensive reaction.

After you realize that the problem is yours, the next step is to identify the unmet needs that leave you feeling dissatisfied. Sometimes a relational need underlies the content of the issue at hand. Consider these cases:

- A friend hasn't returned some money you lent long ago. Your apparent need in this situation might be to get the cash back. But a little thought will probably show that this isn't the only, or even the main, thing you want. Even

> cultural idiom

**rolling in:**
possessing large amounts of

if you were rolling in money, you'd probably want the loan repaid because of your most important need: *to avoid feeling victimized by your friend's taking advantage of you.*

- Someone you care about who lives in a distant city has failed to respond to several letters. Your apparent need may be to get answers to the questions you've written about, but it's likely that there's another, more fundamental need: *the reassurance that you're still important enough to deserve a response.*

As you'll soon see, the ability to identify your real needs plays a key role in solving interpersonal problems. For now, the point to remember is that before you voice your problem to your partner, you ought to be clear about which of your needs aren't being met.

> cultural idiom

**frame of mind:**
mood, mental state

**to jump:**
to attack

**Make a Date**  Unconstructive fights often start because the initiator confronts a partner who isn't ready. There are many times when a person isn't in the right frame of mind to face a conflict: perhaps owing to fatigue, being in too much of a hurry to take the necessary time, being upset over another problem, or not feeling well. At times like these, it's unfair to "jump" a person without notice and expect to get full attention for your problem. If you do persist, you'll probably have an ugly fight on your hands.

After you have a clear idea of the problem, approach your partner with a request to try to solve it. For example: "Something's been bothering me. Can we talk about it?" If the answer is "yes," then you're ready to go further. If it isn't the right time to confront your partner, find a time that's agreeable to both of you.

**Describe Your Problem and Needs**  Your partner can't possibly meet your needs without knowing why you're upset and what you want. Therefore, it's up to you to describe your problem as specifically as possible. When you do so, it's important to use terms that aren't overly vague or abstract. Recall our discussion of behavioral descriptions in Chapter 4 when clarifying your problem and needs.

**Partner Checks Back**  After you've shared your problem and described what you need, it's important to make sure that your partner has understood what you've said. As you can remember from the discussion of listening in Chapter 5, there's a good chance—especially in a stressful conflict situation—of your words being misinterpreted.

**Solicit Your Partner's Needs**  After you've made your position clear, it's time to find out what your partner needs in order to feel satisfied about this issue. There are two reasons why it's important to discover your partner's needs. First, it's fair. After all, the other person has just as much right as you to feel satisfied, and if you expect help in meeting your needs, then it's reasonable that you behave in the same way. Second, just as an unhappy partner will make it hard for you to become satisfied, a happy one will be more likely to cooperate in letting you reach your goals. Thus, it is in your own self-interest to discover and meet your partner's needs.

You can learn about your partner's needs simply by asking about them: "Now I've told you what I want and why. Tell me what you need to feel okay about this." After your partner begins to talk, your job is to use the listening skills discussed earlier in this book to make sure you understand.

Think of a conflict in your life. What are the needs you want to have met? What might your partner's needs be? How would the relational climate be different if you strived to meet both of your needs?

**Check Your Understanding of Your Partner's Needs**  Paraphrase or ask questions about your partner's needs until you're certain you understand them. The surest way to accomplish this is to use the paraphrasing skills you learned in Chapter 5.

**Negotiate a Solution**  Now that you and your partner understand each other's needs, the goal becomes finding a way to meet them. This is done by trying to develop as many potential solutions as possible and then evaluating them to decide which one best meets the needs of both. The following steps can help communicators develop a mutually satisfying solution.

(1) **Identify and Define the Conflict.** We've discussed this process in the preceding pages. It consists of discovering each person's problem and needs, setting the stage for meeting all of them.

(2) **Generate a Number of Possible Solutions.** In this step the partners work together to think of as many means as possible to reach their stated ends. The key word here is *quantity*: It's important to generate as many ideas as you can think of without worrying about which ones are good or bad. Write down every thought that comes up, no matter how unworkable; sometimes a far-fetched idea will lead to a more workable one.

(3) **Evaluate the Alternative Solutions.** This is the time to talk about which solutions will work and which ones won't. It's important for all concerned to be honest about their willingness to accept an idea. If a solution is going to work, everyone involved has to support it.

(4) **Decide on the Best Solution.** Now that you've looked at all the alternatives, pick the one that looks best to everyone. It's important to be sure everybody understands the solution and is willing to try it out. Remember: Your decision doesn't have to be final, but it should look potentially successful.

**Follow Up on the Solution**   You can't be sure the solution will work until you try it out. After you've tested it for a while, it's a good idea to set aside some time to talk over how things are going. You may find that you need to make some changes or even rethink the whole problem. The idea is to keep on top of the problem, to keep using creativity to solve it.

> cultural idiom
**to keep on top of:**
to be in control of

Win–win solutions aren't always possible. There will be times when even the best-intentioned people simply won't be able to find a way of meeting all their needs. In cases like this, the process of negotiation has to include some compromising. But even then the preceding steps haven't been wasted. The genuine desire to learn what the other person wants and to try to satisfy those desires will build a climate of goodwill that can help you find the best solution to the present problem and also improve your relationship in the future.

## Summary

This chapter explored several factors that help make interpersonal relationships satisfying or unsatisfying. We began by defining *communication climate* as the emotional tone of a relationship as it is expressed in the messages being sent and received. We examined factors that contribute to positive and negative climates, learning that the underlying factor is the degree to which a person feels valued by others. We examined types of confirming and disconfirming messages and then looked in detail at Gibb's categories of defensiveness-arousing and supportive behaviors.

The second half of the chapter dealt with interpersonal conflict. We saw that conflict is a fact of life in every

relationship and that the way conflicts are handled plays a major role in the quality of a relationship. There are five ways people can behave when faced with a conflict: They can use nonassertive, directly aggressive, passive-aggressive, indirect, and assertive behaviors. Each of these approaches can be appropriate at times, but the chapter focused on assertive communication skills because of their value and novelty for most communicators. We saw that conflict styles are affected by both gender and culture.

There are four outcomes to conflicts: win–lose, lose–lose, compromise, and win–win. Win–win outcomes are often possible, if the parties possess the proper attitudes and skills. The final section of the chapter outlined the steps in win–win problem solving.

## Key Terms

**assertive communication** A style of communicating that directly expresses the sender's needs, thoughts, or feelings, delivered in a way that does not attack the receiver's dignity. *p. 250*

**avoidance spiral** A communication spiral in which the parties slowly reduce their dependence on one another, withdraw, and become less invested in the relationship. *p. 243*

**certainty** Messages that dogmatically imply that the speaker's position is correct and that the other person's ideas are not worth considering. These messages are likely to generate a defensive response. *p. 245*

**communication climate** The emotional tone of a relationship as it is expressed in the messages that the partners send and receive. *p. 239*

**compromise** An approach to conflict resolution in which both parties attain at least part of what they seek through self-sacrifice. *p. 260*

**confirming responses** A message that expresses respect and values the other person. *p. 239*

**conflict** An expressed struggle between at least two interdependent parties who perceive incompatible goals, scarce rewards, and interference from the other party in achieving their goals. *p. 246*

**controlling communication** Messages in which the sender tries to impose some sort of outcome on the receiver, usually resulting in a defensive reaction. *p. 244*

**descriptive communication** In terms of communication climate, a statement in which the speaker describes his or her position. See also *Evaluative communication*. *p. 244*

**direct aggression** An expression of the sender's thoughts or feelings or both that attacks the position and dignity of the receiver. *p. 248*

**disconfirming response** A message that expresses a lack of caring or respect for another person. *p. 240*

**empathy** The ability to project oneself into another person's point of view, so as to experience the other's thoughts and feelings. *p. 245*

**equality** When communicators show that they believe others have just as much worth as human beings as they do. *p. 245*

**escalatory spiral** A reciprocal pattern of communication in which messages, either confirming or disconfirming, between two or more communicators reinforce one another. *p. 243*

**evaluative communication** Messages in which the sender judges the receiver in some way, usually resulting in a defensive response. See also *"You" language*. *p. 243*

**Gibb categories** Six sets of contrasting styles of verbal and nonverbal behavior developed by Jack Gibb. Each set describes a communication style that is likely to arouse defensiveness and a contrasting style that is likely to prevent or reduce it. *p. 243*

**"I" language** Language that describes the speaker's position without evaluating others. Synonymous with *Description*. *p. 244*

**indirect communication** Hinting at a message instead of expressing thoughts and feelings directly. See also *Assertive communication; Passive aggression*. *p. 250*

**lose–lose problem solving** An approach to conflict resolution in which neither party achieves its goals. *p. 259*

**neutrality** A defense-arousing behavior in which the sender expresses indifference toward a receiver. *p. 245*

**nonassertion** The inability or unwillingness to express one's thoughts or feelings. *p. 247*

**passive aggression** An indirect expression of aggression, delivered in a way that allows the sender to maintain a facade of kindness. *p. 249*

**problem orientation** A supportive style of communication in which the communicators focus on working together to solve their problems instead of trying to impose their own solutions on one another. *p. 244*

**provisionalism** A supportive style of communication in which the sender expresses a willingness to consider the other person's position. *p. 245*

**spiral** A reciprocal communication pattern in which each person's message reinforces the other's. *p. 242*

**spontaneity** A supportive communication behavior in which the sender expresses a message without any attempt to manipulate the receiver. *p. 245*

**strategy** A defense-arousing style of communication in which the sender tries to manipulate or trick a receiver; also, the general term for any type of plan, as in the plan for a persuasive speech. *p. 244*

**superiority** A type of communication that suggests one person is better than the other. *p. 245*

**win–lose problem solving** An approach to conflict resolution in which one party reaches his or her goal at the expense of the other. *p. 259*

**win–win problem solving** An approach to conflict resolution in which the parties work together to satisfy all their goals. *p. 260*

**"you" language** Language that judges another person, increasing the likelihood of a defensive reaction. See also *Evaluative communication.* p. 244

## Check Your Understanding

1. Identify disconfirming messages and replace them with confirming ones, using the Gibb categories of supportive communication.

2. Describe the degree to which you use nonassertive, directly aggressive, passive-aggressive, indirect, and assertive messages, and then choose more satisfying responses as necessary.

3. Compose and deliver an assertive message, using the behavior-interpretation-feeling-consequence-intention format.

4. Consider how gender-related differences may influence you and people you know, when conflict arises. Describe an example from your experience of a conflict double bind.

5. Describe the misunderstandings that are likely to occur (a) when a person from a low-context and a high-context culture experience conflict and (b) when people from emotionally expressive and emotionally reserved cultures manage conflict together.

6. Apply the win–win approach to an interpersonal conflict.

## Activities

1. **Your Confirming and Disconfirming Messages** You can gain an understanding of how confirming and disconfirming messages create communication spirals by trying the following exercise.

    1. Think of an interpersonal relationship. Describe several confirming or disconfirming messages that have helped create and maintain the relational climate. Be sure to identify both verbal and nonverbal messages.

    2. Show how the messages you have identified have created either escalatory or de-escalatory conflict spirals. Describe how these spirals reach limits and what events cause them to stabilize or reverse.

2. **Constructing Supportive Messages** This exercise will give you practice in sending confirming messages that exhibit Gibb's categories of supportive behavior. You will find that you can communicate in a constructive way—even in conflict situations.

    1. Begin by recalling at least two situations in which you found yourself in an escalatory conflict spiral.

    2. Using the Gibb categories, identify your defense-arousing messages, both verbal and nonverbal.

    3. Now reconstruct the situations, writing a script in which you replace the defense-arousing behaviors with the supportive alternatives outlined by Gibb.

    4. If it seems appropriate, you may choose to approach the other people in each of the situations you have described here and attempt to replay the exchange. Otherwise, describe how you could use the supportive approach you developed in Step 3 in future exchanges.

3. **Constructing Assertive Messages** Develop your skill at expressing assertive messages by composing responses for each of the following situations:

    1. A neighbor's barking dog is keeping you awake at night.

    2. A friend hasn't repaid the $20 she borrowed 2 weeks ago.

    3. Your boss made what sounded like a sarcastic remark about the way you put school before work.

    4. An out-of-town friend phones at the last minute to cancel the weekend you planned to spend together.

    Now develop two assertive messages you could send to a real person in your life. Discuss how you could express these messages in a way that is appropriate for the situation and that fits your personal style.

4. **Problem Solving in Your Life**

    1. Recall as many conflicts as possible that you have had in one relationship. Identify which approach best characterizes each one: win–lose, lose–lose, compromise, or win–win.

    2. For each conflict, describe the consequences (for both you and the other person) of this approach.

    3. Based on your analysis, decide for yourself how successful you and your partner are at managing conflicts. Describe any differences in approach that would result in more satisfying outcomes. Discuss what steps you and your partner could take to make these changes.

## For Further Exploration

For more resources about improving interpersonal relationships, see the *Understanding Human Communication* website at www.oup.com/us/adler. There you will find a variety of resources: "Media Room" clips from popular films and television shows to further illustrate important concepts, a list of books and articles, links to descriptions of feature films and television shows at the *Now Playing* website, study aids, and a self-test to check your understanding of the material in this chapter.

CHAPTER 9

# Communicating in Groups and Teams

**9**

## Chapter Outline

## LEARNING OBJECTIVES

**1** Identify the characteristics that distinguish groups and teams from other collections of people.

**2** Distinguish between group and individual goals.

**3** Explain how groups are affected by rules, norms, roles, and patterns of interaction.

**4** Compare and contrast different leadership approaches.

**5** Knowledgeably discuss the roles that followers play and the sources of their power.

# Cows and kings

Cows and kings are an unlikely combination. But, together, they helped shape one of the most influential leaders of modern times.

This story began in the rolling hills of South Africa, where Nelson Mandela spent his boyhood days tending cattle. As a young cowhand, Mandela learned that the best way to lead wasn't to stand in front of the herd and proclaim, "Follow me!"[1] It was more effective to walk behind and offer encouragement. Mandela explains:

> When you want to get the cattle to move in a certain direction, you stand at the back . . . and then you get a few of the cleverer cattle to go to the front and move in the direction. . . . The rest of the cattle follow the few more-energetic cattle in the front, but you are really guiding them from the back.[2]

From this experience Mandela learned the value of putting followers first and "leading from behind."[3] He also grew to appreciate that each member of the herd is valuable, and that it's important not to lose even one of them.

Mandela learned other lessons about leadership by watching his guardian, a tribal ruler named Jongintaba. People would travel many miles on foot or horseback to meet with this wise elder. Once assembled, the group would sit in a circle and engage in heated debates that often lasted for hours.[4] Mandela observed that Jongintaba sat quietly during those meetings, listening until everyone's voice had been heard and all angles considered. Only then did he offer comment, in a calm, measured voice. Almost always, Mandela says, Jongintaba was able to identify a wise course of action that respected the best interests of everyone involved.[5] From this, Mandela learned the value of including diverse viewpoints, listening well, and thinking carefully and calmly as a leader.

No one could have predicted the degree to which Mandela's early leadership lessons would be put to the test. By the time he was a young man, South Africa was being torn apart by racist policies and poverty.[6] The country's white rulers established a government based on apartheid (from the Dutch word for "separate"). Over several decades, they confiscated black South Africans' property, restricted their voting rights, banned interracial marriages, designated coveted jobs as "white only," and relegated black residents to so-called homelands—impoverished slums with little medical care, poor sanitation, limited job opportunities, and few schools. By 1978, white South Africans claimed almost 90 percent of the land and the vast majority of the country's wealth, although they comprised less than 20 percent of the population.

Mandela took a steadfast approach to combating apartheid, working toward a peaceful solution to the injustice. He developed a reputation for listening carefully to people on all sides of the issue and speaking with well-considered wisdom and serenity, even when everyone else was agitated or panicked.[7] Although Mandela was imprisoned by the South African government for 27 years, he persevered. Today, he is considered one of the greatest civil rights leaders in history. In large part because of his influence, democracy has been restored in South Africa.[8]

Mandela recognized the necessity of collective action. This chapter will apply lessons he inspired about leadership and followership to groups in everyday affairs.

***Nelson Mandela recognized the importance of supporting followers by "leading from behind." Your own experience probably confirms that this principle is important even in everyday life.***

- Have you worked with a leader who appreciates and supports the contributions of team members? What kinds of communication conveyed the message that followers are important?

- How has confirmation of your value as a team member shaped your contributions to the group?

# The Nature of Groups and Teams

You are probably involved in groups and teams more than you realize. Some are informal, like friends and family, for example. Others are part of work and school: Project groups, work teams, and learning groups are common types. You may belong to some groups for fun (a band or athletic team) and others for profit (an investment group). Others center on personal growth (Bible study, exercise) or social advocacy (ACLU, Habitat for Humanity). You can probably think of more examples that illustrate how groups are a central part of life.

That doesn't mean that every group experience is a good one. Group work can be immensely gratifying, but it can also be only vaguely rewarding or even downright miserable. In some cases, it is easy to see why a group succeeds or fails, but in others, the reasons aren't immediately clear.[9] In many cases, the differences between success and failure, between satisfaction and frustration, involve communication. To see how, read on.

## What Is a Group?

Imagine that you're taking a test on group communication. Which of the following would you identify as groups?

> cultural idiom
> **gawking at:**
> staring at

- A crowd of onlookers gawking at a burning building
- Several passengers at an airline ticket counter discussing their hopes to find space on a crowded flight
- An army battalion

Because all these situations seem to involve groups, your experience as a canny test taker probably tells you that a commonsense answer will get you in trouble here, and you're right. When social scientists talk about *groups*, they use the word in a special way that excludes each of the preceding examples.

What are we talking about when we use the word *group*? For our purposes a **group** consists of a *small collection of people who interact with one another, usually face-to-face, over time in order to reach goals.* A closer examination of this definition will show why none of the collections of people described in the preceding quiz qualifies as a group.

**Interaction**   Without interaction, a collection of people isn't a group. Consider, for example, the onlookers at a fire. Though they all occupy the same area at a given time, they have virtually nothing to do with one another. Of course, if they should begin interacting—working together to give first aid to or rescue victims, for example—the situation would change. This requirement of interaction highlights the difference between true groups and collections of individuals who merely co-act, simultaneously engaging in a similar activity without communicating with one another. Students who passively listen to a lecture don't technically constitute a group until they begin to exchange messages verbally and nonverbally with one another and their instructor. (This explains why some students feel isolated even though they spend so much time on a crowded campus. Despite being surrounded by others, they really don't belong to any groups.)

**Interdependence**   In groups, members don't just interact: Group members are *interdependent.*[10] By contrast, when members don't need one another, they are a collection of individuals and not a group. Author John Krakauer captures this distinction in his account of climbers seeking to reach the peak of Mount Everest:

> [An] odd feeling of isolation hung in the air. We were a team in name only, I'd sadly come to realize. Although in a few hours we would leave camp as a group,

we would ascend as individuals, linked to one another by neither rope nor any deep sense of loyalty. Each client was in it for himself or herself, pretty much. And I was no different: I sincerely hoped Doug got to the top, for instance, yet I would do everything in my power to keep pushing on if he turned around.[11]

In a true group, the behavior of one person affects all the others in what can be called a "ripple effect."[12] Consider your own experience in family and work groups: When one member behaves poorly, his or her actions shape the way the entire group functions. The ripple effect can be positive as well as negative: Beneficial actions by some members help everyone.

**Time**    A collection of people who interact for a short while doesn't qualify as a group. As you'll soon read, groups who work together for any length of time begin to take on characteristics that aren't present in temporary aggregations. There are some occasions when a collection of individuals pulls together to tackle a goal quite quickly. A stirring example of this phenomenon occurred on September 11, 2001, when a group of passengers on United Airlines flight 93 banded together in a matter of minutes to thwart the efforts of hijackers who were attempting to crash the plane into the White House. Despite examples of ad hoc groups like this, most groups work together long enough to develop a sense of identity and history that shapes their ongoing effectiveness.

**THE FAR SIDE®    BY GARY LARSON**

**"And so you just threw everything together? ... Matthews, a posse is something you have to *organize*."**

**Size**    Our definition of *groups* included the word *small*. Most experts in the field set the lower limit of group size at three members.[13] This decision isn't arbitrary, because there are some significant differences between two- and three-person communication. For example, the only ways two people can resolve a conflict are to change each other's minds, give in, or compromise. In a larger group, however, there's a possibility of members forming alliances either to put increased pressure on dissenting members or to outvote them.

There is less agreement about the maximum number of people in a group.[14] Though no expert would call a 500-member army battalion a group in our sense of the word (it would be labeled an organization), most experts are reluctant to set an arbitrary upper limit. Probably the best description of smallness is the ability for each member to be able to know and react to every other member. It's sufficient to say that our focus in these pages will be on collections of people ranging in size from 3 to around 20.

Research suggests that the optimal size for a group is the smallest number of people capable of performing the task at hand effectively.[15] Generally speaking, as a group becomes larger, it is harder to schedule meetings, the members have less access to important information, and they have fewer chances to participate—three ingredients in a recipe for dissatisfaction.

## What Makes a Group a Team?

Teams share the same qualities as groups, but they take group work to a higher level. You probably know a team when you see it: Members are proud of their identity. They trust and value one another and cooperate. They seek, and often achieve, excellence. Teamwork doesn't come from *what* the group is doing, but *how* they do it.

Communication researchers Carl Larson and Frank LaFasto have spent their career interviewing members of more than 6,000 teams that were clearly winners.[16] The groups came from a wide range of enterprises, including a successful mountaineering expedition, a top cardiac surgery team, the developers of groundbreaking computer technology, and championship athletic teams. Although the goals of these high-achieving teams were varied, they shared several important characteristics.

The crew of the star ship *Enterprise* exhibits all the characteristics of a true team, despite individual differences. Have you ever belonged to a group that achieves this level of excellence?

- *Clear and inspiring shared goals.* Members of a winning team know why their group exists, and they believe that purpose is important and worthwhile. Ineffective groups have either lost sight of their purpose or do not believe that the goal is truly important.

- *A results-driven structure.* Members of winning teams focus on getting the job done in the most effective manner. They do whatever is necessary to accomplish the task. Less effective groups either are not organized at all or are structured in an inefficient manner, and their members don't care enough about the results to do what is necessary to get the job done.

- *Competent team members.* Members of winning teams have the skill necessary to accomplish their goals. Less effective groups lack people possessing one or more key skills.

- *Unified commitment.* People in successful teams put the group's goals above their personal interests. Although this commitment might seem like a sacrifice to others, for members of winning teams the personal rewards are worth the effort.

- *Collaborative climate.* Another word for collaboration is teamwork. People in successful groups trust and support one another.

- *Standards of excellence.* In winning teams, doing outstanding work is an important norm. Each member is expected to do his or her personal best. In less successful groups, getting by with the minimum amount of effort is the standard.

- *External support and recognition.* Successful teams need an appreciative audience that recognizes their effort and provides the resources necessary to get the job done. The audience may be a boss, or it may be the public the group is created to serve.

- *Principled leadership.* Winning teams usually have leaders who can create a vision of the group's purpose and challenge members to get the job done. Finally, they have the ability to unleash the talent of group members.

Despite these virtues, not all groups need to function as teams. If the goal is fairly simple, routine, or quickly accomplished, a group may accomplish it quite

**ON YOUR FEET**

*Experiencing a Real Team*
Describe a high-functioning team you have known. Which of the characteristics on page 271 did it exhibit? If you've never had the good fortune to experience a high-functioning team, describe the factors that led a less-stellar group to underperform.

adequately. For example, you may be effective working alone to solve a math problem or write a press release. But when the job requires a great deal of thought, collaboration, and creativity, nothing beats teamwork. This is because we literally have greater brain power when we work together and because most people feel more confident tackling complex issues when they share the challenge as a team.[17]

## Virtual and Face-to-Face Groups

The explosion of communication technologies has led to the growth of **virtual groups**—teams who interact with one another through mediated channels, without meeting face-to-face. With Web-enabled technology, members of a virtual group can swap ideas as easily as if they were in the same room.[18] Virtual groups can link members who are geographically disbursed—in different buildings, across town, and even around the globe. But even groups that are physically nearby can benefit by transacting some of their business online.

Virtual communication has clear advantages. Most obviously, getting together is fast and easy. A virtual team can meet whenever necessary, even if the members are widely separated. This ease of interaction isn't just useful in the business world. For most groups of students working on class projects, finding a convenient time to meet can be a major headache. Virtual groups don't face the same challenges.

A second advantage of virtual teams is the leveling of the status differences that can get in the way of effective group functioning. When people connect via computer networks, rank is much less prominent than when groups meet face-to-face.[19] This "leveling" effect also reduces gender differences, equalizing the contributions of men and women far more than occurs in face-to-face groups.[20]

Along with the benefits, virtual teams face communication challenges. Most of these involve building strong relationships. If part of the team is in one location and others are far away, the more distant members may feel left out and disconnected.[21] It can take a while for virtual groups to work out relating to one another, although initial problems are usually resolved within a short time.[22] Another danger is that people will feel less committed to the group or less accountable for their actions if they don't know their teammates well. Students who are part of group work in online classes sometimes find that team members are more likely than usual to shirk their responsibilities and avoid communication attempts.[23]

Experts offer the following communication tips to make the most of virtual interactions:[24]

- *Encourage socializing.* Building relationships is especially important when members don't have the chance to socialize in person. Make time for members to get acquainted and enjoy one another's company.

- *Strive for face time.* The richness of nonverbal cues and face-to-face communication is valuable in building a cohesive team. If possible, create opportunities for members to meet in one place, especially when the group is first formed.

- *Allow and encourage side channels.* As in face-to-face groups, members need a chance to work one to one. Phone calls, e-mails, and texting can be an efficient way to speed up the group's work.

- *Make expectations clear.* Are deadlines firm or negotiable? How much detail should a job contain? What does excellent work look like? Setting clear expectations will help members know what is acceptable and what isn't.

- *Provide training as necessary.* Not everybody joins a group with the same level of technological savvy. Make it easy for members to master the communication tools they need to make the team function effectively.

# Goals of Groups and Their Members

Whether or not members acknowledge the fact, two forces drive group communication. The first type involves **group goals**, the outcomes you seek to accomplish together. The second involves **individual goals**, the personal motives of each member.

## Group Goals

Most groups exist to achieve a collective *task*: win a contest, create a product, provide a service, and so on. Along with task goals like these, *social* goals can be equally important reasons for a group's existence: to meet other people and have fun together. Task and social goals aren't mutually exclusive: A working group will probably be more productive when members enjoy one another's company.

## Individual Goals

Some individual goals are related to the group's official reason for existing. For example, your primary motive for joining a class study group would probably be to master the course material, and you'd volunteer to help in a local health clinic to make a difference in your community. Other personal goals might be just about you: Your main reason for joining an exercise class or investment group might be to make new friends and have an enjoyable time with them.

Individual goals aren't necessarily harmful. In fact, they can help the larger group. A student seeking a top grade on a team project will probably help the team excel, and an employee aiming for a production bonus is likely to boost the performance of her work team.

Problems arise when individual motives conflict with the group's goal. You've probably experienced this situation. It is especially difficult when the individual goal is a **hidden agenda**. Consider an egocentric group member whose primary goal—which he would never admit— seems to be to hog the discussion. Or visualize an athlete whose goal of achieving personal glory might damage the team's overall effectiveness, or the effect of a member who engages in *social loafing*—lazy behavior that some members use to avoid doing their share of the work.

On the long-running reality series *Survivor*, the individual goals of contestants conflict with the challenges their tribe must solve to win the competition. What conflicts have you experienced between your personal goals and those of the groups to which you belong?

> Have you ever been part of a project in which one or more members seemed to care more about their personal goals than the group's main purpose? What were their personal goals? How did pursuit of them affect the team's functioning?

Ethical Challenge

## Rules for Hidden Agendas

Some hidden agendas are obviously harmful. Perhaps others are not. Give examples to illustrate the difference between harmful and benign hidden agendas. Next, develop a set of ethical guidelines that describes when you believe it is and is not ethical to participate in groups without stating any hidden agendas.

# Characteristics of Groups and Teams

Whatever their goals, all groups have certain characteristics in common. Understanding these characteristics is a first step to behaving more effectively in your own groups.

## Rules and Norms

Whether or not members know it, groups and teams have guidelines that govern members' behavior. You can appreciate this fact by comparing the ways you act in class or at work with the way you behave with your friends. The differences show that guidelines about how to communicate do exist.

**Rules** are official guidelines that govern what the group is supposed to do and how the members should behave. They are usually stated outright. In a classroom, rules include how absences will be treated, the firmness of deadlines, and so on.

Alongside the official rules is an equally powerful set of unspoken standards called **norms**. **Social norms** govern how we interact with one another (e.g., what kinds of humor are/aren't appropriate, how much socializing is acceptable on the job). **Procedural norms** guide operations and decision making (e.g., "We always start on time" or "When there's a disagreement, we try to reach consensus before forcing a vote"). **Task norms** govern how members get the job done (e.g., "Does the job have to be done perfectly, or is an adequate, if imperfect, solution good enough?").

Table 9-1 lists some typical rules and norms that operate in familiar groups. It is important to realize that our norms don't always match ideals. Consider punctuality, for example. A cultural norm in our society is that meetings should begin at the scheduled time, yet the norm in some groups is to delay talking about real business until 10 or so minutes into the meeting. On a more serious level, one cultural norm is that other people should be treated politely and with respect, but in some groups, members' failure to listen, sarcasm, and even outright hostility make the principle of civility a sham.

**Table 9-1**    Typical Rules and Norms in Two Types of Groups

| FAMILY | **RULES (EXPLICIT)** |
|---|---|
| | • If you don't do the chores, you don't get your allowance. |
| | • If you're going to be more than a half hour late, phone home so the others don't worry about you. |
| | • If the gas gauge reads "empty," fill up the tank before bringing the car home. |
| | • Don't make plans for Sunday nights. That's time for the family to spend together. |
| | • Daniel gets to watch *Sesame Street* from 5 to 6 P.M. |
| | **NORMS (UNSTATED)** |
| | • When Dad is in a bad mood, don't bring up problems. |
| | • Don't talk about Sheila's divorce. |
| | • It's okay to tease Lupe about being short, but don't make comments about Shana's complexion. |
| | • As long as the kids don't get in trouble, the parents won't ask detailed questions about what they do with their friends. |
| | • At family gatherings, try to change the subject when Uncle Max brings up politics. |
| ON-THE-JOB MEETINGS | **RULES (EXPLICIT)** |
| | • Regular meetings are held every Monday morning at 9 A.M. |
| | • The job of keeping minutes rotates from person to person. |
| | • Meetings last no more than an hour. |
| | • Don't leave the meetings to take phone calls except in emergencies. |
| | **NORMS (UNSTATED)** |
| | • Use first names. |
| | • It's okay to question the boss's ideas, but if she doesn't concede after the first remark, don't continue to object. |
| | • Tell jokes at the beginning of the meeting, but avoid sexual or ethnic topics. |
| | • It's okay to talk about "gut feelings," but back them up with hard facts. |
| | • Don't act upset when your ideas aren't accepted, even if you're unhappy. |

It is important to understand a group's norms. On the one hand, following them helps us fit in. On the other hand, we can sometimes help the group operate more effectively by recognizing norms that cause problems. For instance, in some groups a norm is to do things the way they have always been done. Pointing this out to members might be a way to change the unwritten rules and thereby improve the group's work.

## Patterns of Interaction

In interpersonal and public speaking settings, two-way information exchange is relatively uncomplicated. But in a group, the possibilities of complications increase exponentially. If there are five members in a group, there are 10 possible combinations for two-person conversations and 75 combinations involving more than two people. Besides the sheer quantity of information exchanged, the more complex structure of groups affects the flow of information in other ways, too.

A look at Figure 9-1 (which features a type of diagram usually called a **sociogram**) will suggest the number and complexity of interactions that can occur in a group. Arrows connecting members indicate remarks shared between them. Two-headed arrows represent two-way conversations, whereas one-headed arrows represent remarks that did not arouse a response. Arrows directed to the center of the circle indicate remarks made to the group as a whole. A network analysis of this sort can reveal both the amount of participation by each member and the recipients of every member's remarks.

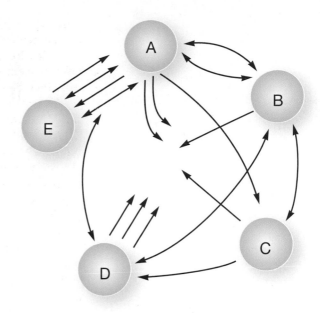

FIGURE 9-1 **Patterns of Interaction in a Five-Person Group**

In the group pictured in Figure 9-1, person E appears to be connected to the group only through a relationship with person A; E never addressed any other members, nor did they address E. Also notice that person A is the most active and best-connected member. A addressed remarks to the group as a whole and to every other member and was the object of remarks from three individuals as well.

Sociograms don't tell the whole story, because they do not indicate the quality of the messages being exchanged. Nonetheless, they are a useful tool in diagnosing group communication.

Physical arrangement influences communication in groups. It's obviously easier to interact with someone you can see well. Lack of visibility isn't a serious problem in dyadic settings, but it can be troublesome in groups. For example, group members seated in a circle are more likely to talk with persons across from them than with those on either side.[25] Different things happen when members are seated in rectangular arrangements. People seated at the ends of a rectangular table are usually considered to have the most influence on decisions,[26] and the farther apart people are at the table, the less friendly, talkative, and acquainted they typically are with one another.[27]

Figure 9-2 shows an **all-channel network** in which group members share the same information with everyone on the team. E-mails are a handy way to accomplish this. As you probably know from experience, it's nice to be in the loop, but too much sharing can lead to information overload.

Another option is a **chain network** (see Figure 9-2), in which information moves sequentially from one member to another. Chains are an efficient way to deliver simple verbal messages or to circulate written information when members can't manage to attend a meeting at one time, but they are not very reliable

Create a sociogram to describe communication in a group you know well. Does it mostly reflect an all-channel, chain, or network configuration? What are the implications of who communications with whom most often?

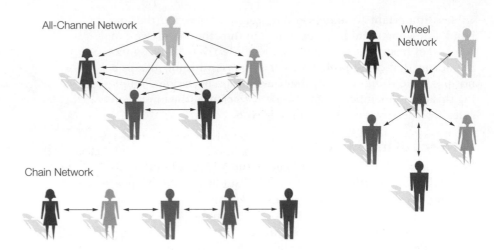

**FIGURE 9-2 Small Group Communication Networks**

for lengthy or complex verbal messages, because the content of the message can change as it passes from one person to another.

Another communication pattern is the **wheel network**, in which one person acts as a clearinghouse, receiving and relaying messages to all other members. Like chains, wheel networks are sometimes a practical choice, especially if one member is available to communicate with others all or most of the time. This person can become the informational hub who keeps track of messages and people. Groups sometimes use wheel networks when relationships are strained between two or more members. In cases like this, the central member can serve as a mediator or facilitator who manages messages as they flow among others. The success of a wheel network depends heavily on the skill of the **gatekeeper**, the person through whom information flows. If he or she is a skilled communicator, these mediated messages may help the group function effectively. But if the gatekeeper consciously or unconsciously distorts messages to suit personal goals or plays members off against one another, the group is likely to suffer.

Our communication patterns are shaped partly by the roles we play. You can probably think of people who always have the latest news, people who can be counted on to offer advice and sympathy, people who stay mostly to themselves, and so on. Next, we will look at the roles typically enacted by group and team members.

Communication norms among the four members of the "wolf pack" in *The Hangover* and its sequels would be considered outrageous by most people. What norms govern the groups to which you belong?

## Roles

**Roles** define patterns of behavior expected of members. Just like norms, some roles are officially recognized. These **formal roles** are assigned by an organization or group partly to establish order. Formal roles usually come with a label, such as *assistant coach, treasurer,* or *customer service representative*. By contrast, **informal roles** (sometimes called "functional roles") are rarely acknowledged by the group in words.[28]

Table 9-2 lists some of the most common informal roles in task-oriented groups. As the list shows, informal roles describe the functions members can fill rather than their formal

Table 9-2    **Functional Roles of Group Members**

| TASK ROLES | TYPICAL BEHAVIORS | EXAMPLES |
|---|---|---|
| 1. Initiator/contributor | Contributes ideas and suggestions; proposes solutions and decisions; proposes new ideas or states old ones in a novel fashion. | "How about taking a different approach to this chore? Suppose we . . ." |
| 2. Information seeker | Asks for clarification of comments in terms of their factual adequacy; asks for information or facts relevant to the problem; suggests information is needed before making decisions. | "Do you think the others will go for this?" "How much would the plan cost us?" "Does anybody know if those dates are available?" |
| 3. Information giver | Offers facts or generalizations that may relate to the group's task. | "I bet Chris would know the answer to that." "*Newsweek* ran an article on that a couple of months ago. It said . . ." |
| 4. Opinion seeker | Asks for clarification of opinions made by other members of the group and asks how people in the group feel. | "Does anyone else have an idea about this?" "That's an interesting idea, Ruth. How long would it take to get started?" |
| 5. Opinion giver | States beliefs or opinions having to do with suggestions made; indicates what the group's attitude should be. | "I think we ought to go with the second plan. It fits the conditions we face in the Concord plant best. . . ." |
| 6. Elaborator/clarifier | Elaborates ideas and other contributions; offers rationales for suggestions; tries to deduce how an idea or suggestion would work if adopted by the group. | "If we followed Lee's suggestion, each of us would need to make three calls." "Let's see . . . at 35 cents per brochure, the total cost would be $525." |
| 7. Coordinator | Clarifies the relationships among information, opinions, and ideas or suggests an integration of the information, opinions, and ideas of subgroups. | "John, you seem most concerned with potential problems. Mary sounds confident that they can all be solved. Why don't you list the problems one at a time, John, and Mary can respond to each one." |
| 8. Diagnostician | Indicates what the problems are. | "But you're missing the main thing, I think. The problem is that we can't afford . . ." |
| 9. Orienter/summarizer | Summarizes what has taken place; points out departures from agreed-on goals; tries to bring the group back to the central issues; raises questions about the direction in which the group is heading. | "Let's take stock of where we are. Helen and John take the position that we should act now. Bill says, 'Wait.' Rusty isn't sure. Can we set that aside for a moment and come back to it after we . . ." |
| 10. Energizer | Prods the group to action. | "Come on, guys. We've been wasting time. Let's get down to business." |
| 11. Procedure developer | Handles routine tasks such as seating arrangements, obtaining equipment, and handing out pertinent papers. | "I'll volunteer to see that the forms are printed and distributed." "I'd be happy to check on which of those dates are free." |
| 12. Secretary | Keeps notes on the group's progress. | "Just for the record, I'll put these decisions in the memo and get copies to everyone in the group." |
| 13. Evaluator/critic | Constructively analyzes group's accomplishments according to some set of standards; checks to see that consensus has been reached. | "Look, we said we only had two weeks, and this proposal will take at least three. Does that mean that it's out of the running, or do we need to change our original guidelines?" |

*(continued)*

Table 9-2 Functional Roles of Group Members *(continued)*

| SOCIAL/MAINTENANCE ROLES | TYPICAL BEHAVIORS | EXAMPLES |
|---|---|---|
| **1.** Supporter/encourager | Praises, agrees with, and accepts the contributions of others; offers warmth, solidarity, and recognition. | "I really like that idea, John." "Priscilla's suggestion sounds good to me. Could we discuss it further?" |
| **2.** Harmonizer | Reconciles disagreements; mediates differences; reduces tensions by giving group members a chance to explore their differences. | "I don't think you two are as far apart as you think. Henry, are you saying _____? Benson, you seem to be saying _____. Is that what you mean?" |
| **3.** Tension reliever | Jokes or in some other way reduces the formality of the situation; relaxes the group members. | "Let's take a break . . . maybe have a drink." "You're a tough cookie, Bob. I'm glad you're on our side!" |
| **4.** Conciliator | Offers new options when his or her own ideas are involved in a conflict; is willing to admit errors so as to maintain group cohesion. | "Looks like our solution is halfway between you and me, John. Can we look at the middle ground?" |
| **5.** Gatekeeper | Keeps communication channels open; encourages and facilitates interaction from those members who are usually silent. | "Susan, you haven't said anything about this yet. I know you've been studying the problem. What do you think about _____?" |
| **6.** Feeling expresser | Makes explicit the feelings, moods, and relationships in the group; shares his or her own feelings with others. | "I'm really glad we cleared things up today." "I'm just about worn out. Could we call it a day and start fresh tomorrow?" |
| **7.** Follower | Goes along with the movement of the group passively, accepting the ideas of others, sometimes serving as an audience. | "I agree. Yes, I see what you mean. If that's what the group wants to do, I'll go along." |

positions. Many unofficial roles may be filled by more than one member, and some of them may be filled by different people at different times. The important fact is that, at crucial times, the necessary informal roles must be filled by someone.

Notice that the informal roles listed in Table 9-2 fall into two categories: task and maintenance. **Task roles** help the group accomplish its goals, and **social roles** (also called "maintenance roles") help the relationships among the members run smoothly. Not all roles are constructive. Table 9-3 lists several **dysfunctional roles** that prevent a group from working effectively. As you might expect, research suggests that groups are most effective when people fulfill positive social roles and no one fulfills the dysfunctional ones.[29]

What is the optimal balance between task and social functions? According to Robert Bales, one of the earliest and most influential researchers in the area, the ideal ratio is 2:1, with task-related behavior dominating.[30] This ratio allows the group to get its work done while at the same time taking care of the personal needs and concerns of the members.

Groups can suffer from at least three role-related problems. The first occurs when one or more important informal roles (either task or social) go unfilled. For instance, there may be no information giver to provide vital knowledge or no harmonizer to smooth things over when members disagree.

There are other cases in which the problem isn't an absence of candidates to fill certain roles, but rather an overabundance of them. This

Research suggests that people bid for informal roles by trying them out, and that the roles are likely to stick if they suit the person's personality.[31] What unofficial role do you usually play? Does it suit your personality? What would happen in the group if you stopped fulfilling that role?

## Table 9-3    Dysfunctional Roles of Group Members

| DYSFUNCTIONAL ROLES | TYPICAL BEHAVIORS | EXAMPLES |
|---|---|---|
| **1.** Blocker | Interferes with progress by rejecting ideas or taking a negative stand on any and all issues; refuses to cooperate. | "Wait a minute! That's not right! That idea is absurd." "You can talk all day, but my mind is made up." |
| **2.** Aggressor | Struggles for status by deflating the status of others; boasts, criticizes. | "Wow, that's really swell! You turkeys have botched things again." "Your constant bickering is responsible for this mess. Let me tell you how you ought to do it." |
| **3.** Deserter | Withdraws in some way; remains indifferent, aloof, sometimes formal; daydreams; wanders from the subject, engages in irrelevant side conversations. | "I suppose that's right. . . . I really don't care." |
| **4.** Dominator | Interrupts and embarks on long monologues; is authoritative; tries to monopolize the group's time. | "Bill, you're just off base. What we should do is this. First . . ." |
| **5.** Recognition seeker | Attempts to gain attention in an exaggerated manner; usually boasts about past accomplishments; relates irrelevant personal experiences, usually in an attempt to gain sympathy. | "That reminds me of a guy I used to know . . ." "Let me tell you how I handled old Marris . . ." |
| **6.** Joker | Displays a lack of involvement in the group through inappropriate humor, horseplay, or cynicism. | "Why try to convince these guys? Let's just get the mob to snuff them out." "Hey, Carla, wanna be my roommate at the sales conference?" |
| **7.** Cynic | Discounts chances for the group's success. | "Sure, we could try that idea, but it probably won't solve the problem. Nothing we've tried so far has worked." |

*Source:* "Functional Roles of Group Members" and "Dysfunctional Roles of Group Members," adapted from Wilson, G., & Hanna, M. *Groups in context: Leadership and participation in decision-making groups,* pp. 144–146. © 1986. Reprinted by permission of McGraw-Hill Companies, Inc.

situation can lead to unstated competition between members that gets in the way of group effectiveness. You have probably seen groups in which two people both want to be the tension-relieving comedian. Sometimes, members become more concerned with occupying their pet position than with getting the group's job done.

Even when there is no competition over roles, a group's effectiveness can be threatened when one or more members suffer from "role fixation," acting out a specific role whether or not the situation requires it.[32] As you learned in Chapter 1, a key ingredient of communication competence is flexibility—the ability to choose the right behavior for a given situation. Members who always take the same role (even a constructive one) lack competence, and they hinder the group. As in other areas of life, too much of a good thing can be a problem. You can overcome the potential role-related problems by following these guidelines:

> cultural idiom

**occupying their pet position:**
playing their favorite role

- *Look for unfilled roles.* When a group seems to be experiencing problems, use the list in Table 9-2 as a kind of checklist to diagnose what roles might be unfilled.

- *Make sure unfilled roles are filled.* After you have identified unfilled roles, you may be able to help the group by filling them yourself. If key facts are missing, take the role of information seeker and try to dig them out. If nobody is keeping track of the group's work, offer to play secretary and take notes. Even if you are not suited by skill or temperament to a job, you can often encourage others to fill it.

- *Avoid role fixation.* Don't fall into familiar roles if they aren't needed. You may be a world-class coordinator or critic, but these talents will only annoy others if you use them when they aren't needed. In most cases your natural inclination to be a supporter might be just the ticket to help a group succeed, but if you find yourself in a group in which the members don't need or want this sort of support, your encouragement might become a nuisance.

- *Avoid dysfunctional roles.* Some of these roles can be personally gratifying, especially when you are frustrated with a group, but they do nothing to help the group succeed, and they can damage your reputation as a team player. Nobody needs a blocker, a joker, or any other of the dysfunctional roles listed in Table 9-3. Resist the temptation to indulge yourself by taking on any of them.

Two of the main roles people play are leader and follower. As you will see in the following section, both of them are integral to a team's success.

> cultural idiom

**just the ticket:**
the right thing

# Leadership and Communication

You don't have to be a social scientist to recognize the importance of good leadership. And the role that effective communication plays in leading well (and leading poorly) is obvious. But what communication skills make a leader effective? To discover answers to this question, read on.

## Approaches to Leadership

The question of effective leadership has occupied philosophers, rulers, and, more recently, social scientists, for centuries. The lessons learned by those who came before us can help you become more effective today.

**Trait Analysis**  More than 2,000 years ago, Aristotle proclaimed, "From the hour of their birth some are marked out for subjugation, and others for command."[33] This is a radical expression of **trait theories of leadership**, sometimes labeled as the "great man" (or "great woman") approach. Social scientists began their studies of leader effectiveness by conducting literally hundreds of studies that compared leaders to nonleaders. The results of all this research were mixed. Yet, as Table 9-4 shows, a number of distinguishing characteristics did emerge in several categories.

The majority of these categories involved social skills. For example, leaders talk more often and more fluently and are regarded as more popular, cooperative, and socially skillful.[34] Leaders also possess goal-related skills that help groups perform their tasks. They are somewhat more intelligent, possess more task-relevant information, and are more dependable than other members. Just as important, leaders want the role and act in ways that will help them achieve it. Finally, physical appearance seems to play a role in leadership. As a rule, leaders tend to be slightly taller, heavier, and physically more attractive than other members. They also seem to possess greater athletic ability and stamina.

Despite these general findings, trait theories have limited practical value. Later research has shown that many other factors are important in determining leader success and that not everyone who possesses these traits becomes a leader. Organizational researchers Warren Bennis and Burt Nanus interviewed 90 American leaders, including the founder of McDonald's, a professional football coach, and

Table 9-4    Some Traits Associated with Leaders

| FACTOR NO. | FACTORS APPEARING IN THREE OR MORE STUDIES | FREQUENCY |
|---|---|---|
| 1 | Social and interpersonal skills | 16 |
| 2 | Technical skills | 18 |
| 3 | Administrative skills | 12 |
| 4 | Leadership effectiveness and achievement | 15 |
| 5 | Social nearness, friendliness | 18 |
| 6 | Intellectual skills | 11 |
| 7 | Maintaining cohesive work group | 9 |
| 8 | Maintaining coordination and teamwork | 7 |
| 9 | Task motivation and application | 17 |
| 10 | General impression | 12 |
| 11 | Group task supportiveness | 17 |
| 12 | Maintaining standards of performance | 5 |
| 13 | Willingness to assume responsibility | 10 |
| 14 | Emotional balance and control | 15 |
| 15 | Informal group control | 4 |
| 16 | Nurturant behavior | 4 |
| 17 | Ethical conduct, personal integrity | 10 |
| 18 | Communication, verbality | 6 |
| 19 | Ascendance, dominance, decisiveness | 11 |
| 20 | Physical energy | 6 |
| 21 | Experience and activity | 4 |
| 22 | Mature, cultured manner | 3 |
| 23 | Courage, daring | 4 |
| 24 | Aloof, distant manner | 3 |
| 25 | Creative, independent manner | 5 |
| 26 | Conforming | 5 |

*Source:* Reprinted with permission of The Free Press, a division of Macmillan, Inc., from Bass, B. M. *Stodgill's handbook of leadership* (Rev. ed.). Copyright © 1974, 1981 by The Free Press.

the publisher of *Ebony.* Their analysis led to the conclusion that the principle that "leaders must be charismatic" is a myth.

Some are, most aren't. Among the ninety there were a few—but damned few—who probably correspond to our fantasies of some "divine inspiration," that "grace under stress" we associated with J.F.K. or the beguiling capacity to spellbind for which we remember Churchill. Our leaders were all "too human"; they were short and tall, articulate and inarticulate, dressed for success and dressed for failure, and there was virtually nothing in terms of physical appearance, personality, or style that set them apart from their followers. Our guess is that it operates in the other direction; that is, charisma is the result of effective leadership, not the other way around, and that those who are good at it are granted a certain amount of respect and even awe by their followers, which increases the bond of attraction between them.[35]

**Leadership Style**   As researchers began to realize that traits aren't the key to effective leadership, they began to look in other areas. Some scholars theorized that good leadership is a matter of communication style—the way leaders deal with members. Three basic approaches were identified. The first approach was an **authoritarian leadership style** that relied on legitimate, coercive, and reward power to influence others. The second approach was a **democratic leadership style**, which invited other members to share in decision making. The third approach was the **laissez-faire leadership style**, in which the leader gave up the power to dictate, transforming the group into a leaderless collection of equals. Early research suggested that the democratic style produced the highest-quality results,[36] but later research showed that matters weren't so simple.[37] For instance, groups with autocratic leaders proved more productive under stressful conditions, but democratically led groups did better when the situation was not stressful.[38]

Research showed that there is some merit to the styles approach. One extensive study of more than 12,000 managers showed that a democratic approach to leadership correlated highly with success. Effective managers usually sought the advice and opinions of their subordinates, whereas average or unsuccessful ones were more authoritarian and less concerned with the welfare or ideas of the people who reported to them.[39] Despite this fact, a democratic approach isn't always the best one. For example, an autocratic approach gets the job done much more quickly, which can be essential in situations where time is of the essence.

Some researchers have focused on leadership style from a different perspective. Robert R. Blake and Jane S. Mouton developed an approach based on the relationship between the designated leader's concern with the task and with the relationships among members.[40] Their **Leadership Grid** consists of a two-dimensional model pictured in Figure 9-3. The horizontal axis measures the leader's concern for production. This involves a focus on accomplishing the organizational task, with efficiency being the main concern. The vertical axis measures the leader's concern for people's feelings and ideas. Blake and Mouton suggest that the most effective leader is the one who adopts a 9,9 style, showing high concern for both task and relationships.

**Situational Approaches**   Most contemporary scholars are convinced that the best style of leadership varies from one set of circumstances to another.[41] In an effort to pin down which approach works best in a given situation, psychologist Fred Fiedler attempted to find out when a task-oriented approach was most effective and when a more relationship-oriented approach was most effective.[42] From his research, Fiedler developed a situational theory of leadership. Although the complete theory is too complex to describe here, the general conclusion of **situational leadership** is that a leader's style should change with the circumstances. A task-oriented approach works best when conditions are either highly favorable (good leader-member relations, strong leader power, and clear task structure) or highly unfavorable (poor leader-member relations, weak leader power, and an

> cultural idiom

**pin down:**
identify specifically

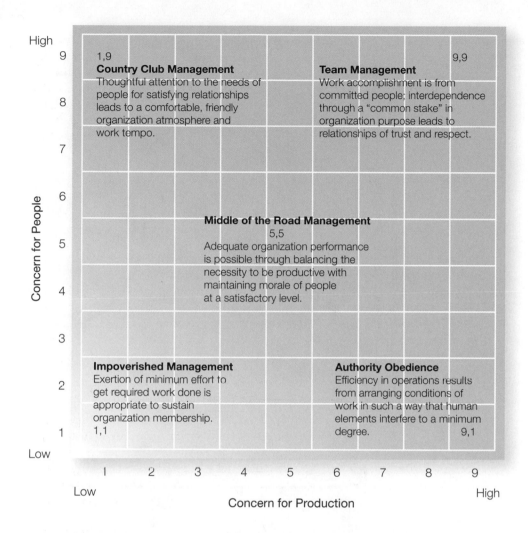

**FIGURE 9-3  The Leadership Grid®**

*Source:* The Leadership Grid® Figure from Blake, R. R., & McCanse, A. A. *Leadership dilemmas–grid solutions.*
Houston, TX: Gulf, p. 29. Copyright © 1991 by Scientific Methods, Inc. Reproduced by permission of the owners.

ambiguous task), whereas a more relationship-oriented approach is appropriate in moderately favorable or moderately unfavorable conditions.

More recently, some social scientists have suggested that a leader's focus on task or relational issues should vary according to the readiness of the group being led (see Figure 9-4).[43] Readiness involves the members' level of motivation, their willingness to take responsibility, and the amount of knowledge and experience they have in a given situation. For example, a new, inexperienced group would need more task-related direction, whereas a more experienced group might require more social support and less instruction about how to do the job. A well-seasoned group could probably handle the job well without much supervision at all. This approach suggests that, because an employee's readiness changes from one job to another, the best way to lead should vary as well.

## Leader–Member Relationships

No matter what their approach, leaders must communicate with group members. Researcher Karl Kuhnert[44] characterizes leaders as fitting into one of three approaches.

**FIGURE 9.4 Hersey and Blanchard's Leadership Model**

*Source:* Situational leadership behavior. In *Management of organizational behavior* (8th ed.). © 2001. Adapted/reprinted with permission of Center for Leadership Studies, Escondido, CA 92025. All Rights Reserved.

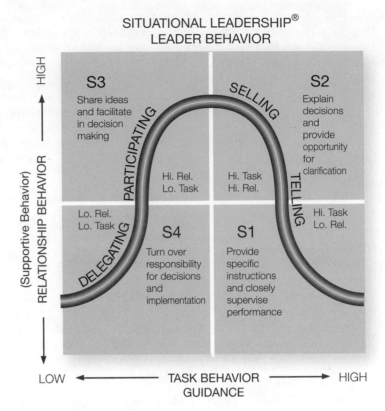

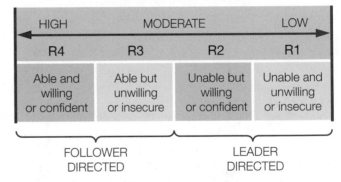

**Transactional Operators**    These leaders are motivated primarily by personal glory. They tend to take credit for successes and blame others for failures. As you might imagine, this doesn't lead to trusting relationships with team members. Because transactional operators are afraid of losing face and because they don't usually trust others, they tend to do as much as possible themselves. They delegate only if they run out of time or if they encounter tasks that are thankless or unpleasant. If you have ever worked with a transactional operator, you know the results: Team members comply if they feel they have no other choice, but they usually feel resentful and unappreciated. The team may have short-term success, but rarely does it last. People either work begrudgingly or leave at the first opportunity.

In the book *Good to Great*, James Collins[45] and his colleagues analyzed the 15 top-performing companies in the United States. They concluded that the best leaders aren't charismatic icons, but are often remarkably humble and content to let others take the spotlight. Collins concluded that charisma can actually be bad for business. For one thing, companies with charismatic leaders tend to base their images on the key figure. When a charismatic leader moves on or is involved in a scandal, the company's entire image is damaged. Second, people tend to be dazzled by charismatic leaders so much that they withhold unpleasant truths from them. And, third, charismatic leaders often focus on themselves rather than on the team or the mission. Collins advises: "The moment a leader allows himself [or herself] to become the primary reality people worry about rather than reality being the primary reality, you have a recipe for mediocrity, or worse."[46]

**Team Players**   Team players are the opposite of transactional operators. Their primary goal is to keep members happy and maintain harmony. A common word used to describe team players is *nice*. They smile a lot, listen, and offer lots of praise and encouragement.

The dark side of this approach is that team players may tell you what you want to hear in the moment (but not follow through later). They tend to let misbehavior slide because they abhor confrontations, and they have a hard time making decisions. People led by team players usually like the leaders personally, but they feel frustrated that the team is only moderately successful. In short, the leader is likable but not trustworthy, and major issues and problems go unaddressed. As a result, these leaders can inspire moderate goal fulfillment, but not long-term success.

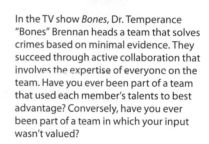

In the TV show *Bones*, Dr. Temperance "Bones" Brennan heads a team that solves crimes based on minimal evidence. They succeed through active collaboration that involves the expertise of everyone on the team. Have you ever been part of a team that used each member's talents to best advantage? Conversely, have you ever been part of a team in which your input wasn't valued?

**Transformational Leaders**   These leaders share the best qualities of team players. They respect the power of teamwork and positive morale. But transformational leaders avoid the pitfalls of striving for harmony at all costs. That's because their primary motivation isn't self, and it isn't harmony. It's something larger than either of those: *the mission of the group or organization.* Transformational leaders consider it their role to recruit great people and support them in accomplishing mutual goals they all feel passionate about. They listen to team members, support them, and honor their contributions. They also expect 100 percent effort.

Because they trust and empower team members, transformational leaders typically give people closest to the action the authority to make decisions. A reporter once asked Herb Kelleher, the founder of Southwest Airlines, if he was afraid of losing control. "I never had control and I never wanted it," he replied. "If you create an environment where the people truly participate, you don't need control."[47] Kelleher's philosophy has been demonstrably effective: Southwest is consistently among the world's most profitable airlines, and landing a mechanic's job there is more competitive than getting into Harvard.

Transformational leaders are willing to make tough calls when it's a leader's job to do so. They typically listen to people first, weigh all the factors, and, when they announce a decision, explain *why* they made it. Even when people don't agree with transformational leaders' decisions, they remain deeply loyal to them. The motto of transactional leaders could be, "It's about the team and the job, not me."

## Becoming a Leader

Even in groups that begin with no official leader, members can take on that role. **Emergent leaders** gain influence without being appointed by higher-ups. Juries elect forepersons, and committees elect chairpersons. Teams choose a captain.

# Your Leadership Approach

Check the item in each grouping below that *best* characterizes your beliefs as a leader.

**1.** I believe a leader's most important job is to:

___ a. Make sure people stay focused on the task at hand.

___ b. Help team members build strong relationships.

___ c. Make sure the workplace is an enjoyable environment.

**2.** When it comes to team members, I believe:

___ a. People have a natural inclination to work hard and do good work.

___ b. People work best when there are clear expectations and oversight.

___ c. People are most productive when they are happy and enjoying themselves.

**3.** When a problem arises, I am mostly likely to:

___ a. Solve it myself or smooth things over.

___ b. Ask team members' input on how to solve it.

___ c. Implement a new policy or procedure to avoid the same problem in the future.

**4.** If team members had to describe me in a few words, I would like them to be:

___ a. Competent and in control.

___ b. Pleasant and friendly.

___ c. Attentive and trustworthy.

**5.** When I see team members talking and laughing in the hallway, I am most likely to:

___ a. Feel frustrated that they are goofing off.

___ b. Share my latest joke with them.

___ c. Feel encouraged that they get along so well.

**EVALUATING YOUR RESPONSES**

Circle your answers on the grid below. Note that they do not appear in alphabetical order.

| Grouping 1 | Grouping 2 | Grouping 3 | Grouping 4 | Grouping 5 |
|:---:|:---:|:---:|:---:|:---:|
| b | a | b | c | c |
| a | b | c | a | a |
| c | c | a | b | b |

**Relationship Orientation**

If the majority of your answers appear in the yellow row, you are a relationship-oriented leader (upper half in the Blake and Mouton Leadership Grid; see Figure 9-3). You are likely to show team members a great deal of respect and attention, which often brings out the best in people. Most people consider this to be the ideal leadership style as long as your focus on relationships does not mean that you neglect task concerns.

**Task Orientation**

If your answers appear mostly in the green row, you are a task-oriented leader (lower half of the Leadership Grid). You tend to emphasize productivity and may be frustrated by inefficiency. The danger is that you will overlook relationships in your zeal to get the job done, which can be counterproductive in the long run.

**Country Club Orientation**

If most of your answers are in the blue row, you most closely resemble a country club leader (upper left in the Leadership Grid). Your focus on strong relationships and a pleasant work environment is likely to be appreciated by team members. However, you have a tendency to take that too far. A more moderate focus, in which you emphasize both relationships and tasks, may ultimately be more rewarding for everyone involved.

**Mixed Orientation**

If your answers are mostly spread all over the grid, you don't show a clear priority for either relationship or task goals. Perhaps you focus on both of them equally (as either a team or middle-of-the-road leader), or you may neglect both of them (an impoverished leader). It's important to consider that both relationships and tasks are highly important. If you pour your energy into both, pat yourself on the back. If you neglect one or both, reconsider your leadership approach. ●

## @Work

### "I'll Do It Myself"—Or Should I?

It's a rookie mistake some leaders never outgrow—the tendency to tackle a job instead of delegating. The reasons for doing it yourself seem appealing:

1. It's faster to do it myself.

2. Someone else might mess it up.

3. I don't want to ask others to do an unpleasant chore.

4. Other people are busy.

5. No one else knows how to do this.

6. It would take too long to train someone.

7. I like doing this task.

8. I wouldn't ask the team to do something I'm not willing to do myself.

9. If I'm not completing specific tasks, I might seem unnecessary.

The reasons to delegate aren't as numerous, but they are powerful:

1. As a leader, your most important job is to build high-performance, high-capacity teams,[48] and that doesn't happen when you do everything yourself.

2. Trying to do everything yourself slows down the process.

3. Leaders involved in tasks aren't available to lead.

4. Most team members, when asked, say they would gladly perform tasks on the boss's to-do list, if only he or she would listen to them more.

5. Leaders who try to do everything become tired, discouraged, and burned out.

The next time you're tempted to tackle the whole job yourself, ask whether delegating may be better for the team, yourself, and the task at hand. ●

---

Negotiating groups elect spokespeople. The subject of leadership emergence has been studied extensively.[49]

Emergent leaders don't always have official titles. A group of unhappy employees might urge one person to approach the boss and ask for a change. A team of students working on a class project might agree that one person is best suited to take the lead in organizing and presenting their work. Whether or not the role comes with a title, emergent leaders can gain influence in a variety of ways.[50]

Communication researchers have learned that emergent leaders gain influence, especially in newly formed groups, through a process of elimination in which potential candidates are gradually rejected for one reason or another until only one remains.[51]

This process occurs in two phases. In the first, members who are clearly unsuitable are rejected. Along with obvious incompetence, lack of involvement and dogmatism are causes for early disqualification. Once clearly unsuitable members have been eliminated, roughly half of the group's members may still be candidates for leadership. During this phase, the following kinds of behavior boost the odds of emerging as the formal or informal leader:

- *Frequent participation.* Talking won't guarantee that you will be recognized as a leader, but failing to speak up will almost certainly knock you out of the running.

- *Demonstrated competence.* Make sure your comments identify you as someone who can help the team succeed. Demonstrate the kinds of power described later in this chapter.

- *Assertion, not aggression.* It's fine to be assertive, but don't try to overpower other members. Even if you are right, your dogmatism is likely to alienate others.
- *Support of other members.* The endorsement of other members (some researchers have called them "lieutenants") increases your credibility and influence.
- *Provide a solution in a time of crisis.* How can the team get the necessary resources? Resolve a disagreement? Meet a deadline? Members who find answers to problems like these are likely to rise to a position of authority.

# Followership and Communication

"What are you, a leader or a follower?" we're asked, and we know which position is generally considered the better one. One reason is a fundamental misunderstanding about what it means to be a follower.

Despite the common belief that leaders are the most important group members, good followers are indispensable. Completing the self-assessment on the next page will help you appreciate why and will also help you gain a sense of the role you can play as a follower.

The self-assessment makes it clear that good followers aren't sheep who blindly follow the herd. According to management consultant Robert Kelley, effective followers "think for themselves, are very active, and have very positive energy."[52] He points out that many leaders have a special term for followers such as these. They call them "my right-hand person" or my "go-to person."

Successful executives agree. In a study of more than 300 senior-level leaders, 94 percent said that followers help shape leaders, not just the other way around.[53] In their view, effective followers and leaders share many of the same qualities, including honesty, competence, intelligence, and character. The executives also appreciated followers who were loyal, dependable, and cooperative. But they didn't define those qualities in terms of blind obedience. Indeed, almost all of the executives disagreed with the statement that good followers "simply do what they are told." Overall, the lesson seems to be that followership involves a sophisticated array of skills, a good measure of self-confidence, and a strong commitment to teamwork.

As an illustration of this, many people consider that Nelson Mandela's ability to empower followers is his most important quality as a leader. This was demonstrated most dramatically when the white South African government condemned Mandela to life in prison for inciting resistance to apartheid policies. The civil rights movement might have withered without Mandela, but it didn't. (As a more ordinary test of leadership, consider how well a workplace functions when the boss is away on vacation.) Even in Mandela's absence, people continued to be inspired by his wisdom and vision.

Sometimes called "the other Steve" in relation to his famous partner, Steve Wozniak was content to work mostly behind the scenes at Apple and let the more extroverted Steve Jobs take the limelight. How can you be a quiet yet important contributor to groups?

## Types of Followers

All followers don't communicate or contribute equally. Barbara Kellerman, a theorist who writes about both leaders and followers, describes how followers fall into five categories.[55] Which one best describes you?

## How Good a Follower Are You?

Check all of the following that apply to you in your role as a follower.

____ I think for myself.

____ I go above and beyond job requirements.

____ I am supportive of others.

____ I am goal oriented.

____ I focus on the end goal and help others stay focused as well.

____ I take the initiative to make improvements.

____ I realize that my ideas and experiences are essential to the success of the group.

____ I take the initiative to manage my time.

____ I frequently reflect on the job I am doing and how I can improve.

____ I keep learning.

____ I am a champion for new ideas.

If the majority of these statements describe you, pat yourself on the back. These are the qualities of an outstanding follower, according to Robert Kelley, author of *The Power of Followership*.[54]

**Isolates**   Isolates are indifferent to the overall goals of the organization and communicate very little with people outside their immediate environment.

**Bystanders**   Bystanders are aware of what's going on around them, but they tend to hang back and watch rather than play an active role. You may find yourself in a bystander role occasionally, especially when you are in a new situation. Because bystanders are usually not as emotionally involved as others, they can sometimes provide an objective, fresh perspective if you encourage them to share their thoughts.

**Participants**   Participants attempt to have an impact. Some participants support leaders' efforts, whereas others work in opposition. (Opposition isn't necessarily a bad quality in followers. Good followers *should* object when leaders are unethical or ineffective.)

**Activists**   Activists are more energetically and passionately engaged than participants. They, too, may act either in accordance with, or in opposition to, leaders' efforts. Their commitment is a plus in many ways. At the same time, activists sometimes have difficulty compromising and getting along with others.

**Diehards**   Diehards will, sometimes literally, sacrifice themselves for the cause. "Being a Diehard is all consuming. It is who you are. It determines what you do," Kellerman says.[56] Soldiers are a classic example, as are people who protest against oppressive rulers or fight for civil rights. Diehards may also work tirelessly in nonprofits or other organizations if they believe the services they provide are essential. Their commitment is unrivaled, but sometimes it's difficult to contain their enthusiasm, even when it runs counter to other peoples' goals.

## The Power of Followers

How influential and important are followers? The answer is "More than you might have imagined." To understand why, it's important to recognize that members are powerful.

Simply put, **power** is the ability to influence others. A few examples show that influence isn't just the domain of leaders:[57]

- In a tense meeting, apartment dwellers are arguing about overcrowded parking and late-night noise. One tenant cracks a joke and lightens up the tense atmosphere.
- A project team at work is trying to come up with a new way to attract customers. The youngest member, fresh from a college advertising class, suggests a winning idea.
- Workers are upset after the boss passes over a popular colleague and hires a newcomer for a management position. Despite their anger, they accept the decision after the colleague persuades them that she is not interested in a career move anyhow.

These examples suggest that power comes in a variety of forms. (See Table 9-5 for a summary.) The most obvious is **legitimate power** (sometimes called "position power")—influence that arises from the title one holds. Jobs like "supervisor," "professor," and "coach" all come with position power. Social scientists use the term **nominal leader** to label the person who is officially designated as being in charge of a group.

**Expert Power**   Expert power comes from what team members know or can do. If you're lost in the woods, it makes sense to follow the advice of a group member who has wilderness experience. If your computer crashes at a critical time, you turn to the team member with IT expertise. In groups it isn't sufficient to be an expert: The other members have to view you as one. This means it is important to make your qualifications known if you want others to give your opinions weight.

> cultural idiom
> **IT:**
> information technology

**Connection Power**   As its name implies, **connection power** comes from a member's ability to develop relationships that help the group reach its goal. For instance, a fundraising group seeking donations from local businesses might profit from the knowledge that one member has about which merchants are hospitable to the group's cause, and a team seeking guest speakers at a seminar might rely on a well-connected member to line up candidates.

**Reward Power**   Reward power exists when others are influenced by the granting or promise of desirable consequences. Rewards come in a variety of forms. Rewards don't come only from the official leader of a group. The goodwill of other members can sometimes be even more valuable. In a class group, for example, having your fellow students think highly of you might be a more powerful reward than the grade you could receive from the instructor. In fact, subordinates sometimes can reward nominal leaders just as much as the other way around. A boss might work hard to accommodate employees in order to keep them happy, for example.

**Coercive Power**   Coercive power comes from the threat or actual imposition of unpleasant consequences. Nominal leaders certainly can coerce members via compensation, assignments, and even termination from the group. But members also possess coercive power. Working with an unhappy, unmotivated teammate

Table 9-5    **Methods for Acquiring Power in Small Groups**

**Power isn't the only goal to seek in a group. Sometimes being a follower is a comfortable and legitimate role to play. But when you do seek power, the following methods outline specific ways to shape the way others behave and the decisions they make.**

**LEGITIMATE AUTHORITY**

1. Become an authority figure. If possible, get yourself appointed or elected to a position of leadership. Do so by following steps 2–5.
2. Speak up without dominating others. Power comes from visibility, but don't antagonize others by shutting them out.
3. Demonstrate competence on the subject. Enhance legitimate authority by demonstrating information and expertise power.
4. Follow group norms. Show that you respect the group's customs.
5. Gain the support of other members. Don't try to carve out authority on your own. Gain the visible support of other influential members.

**INFORMATION POWER**

1. Provide useful but scarce or restricted information. Show others that you possess information that isn't available elsewhere.
2. Be certain the information is accurate. One piece of mistaken information can waste the group's time, lead to bad decisions, and destroy your credibility. Check your facts before speaking up.

**EXPERT POWER**

1. Make sure members are aware of your qualifications. Let others know that you have expertise in the area being discussed.
2. Don't act superior. You will squander your authority if you imply your expertise makes you superior to others. Use your knowledge for the good of the group, not ego building.

**REWARD AND COERCIVE POWER**

1. Try to use rewards as a first resort and punishment as a last resort. People respond better to pleasant consequences than unpleasant ones, so take a positive approach first.
2. Make rewards and punishments clear in advance. Let people know your expectations and their consequences. Don't surprise them.
3. Be generous with praise. Let others know that you recognize their desirable behavior.

**REFERENT POWER**

1. Enhance your attractiveness to group members. Do whatever you can to gain the liking and respect of other members without compromising your principles.
2. Learn effective presentation skills. Present your ideas clearly and effectively in order to boost your credibility.

*Source:* Adapted from Rothwell, J. D. (1998). *In mixed company: Small group communication* (3rd ed.). Fort Worth, TX: Harcourt Brace, pp. 252–272. Reprinted with permission of Wadsworth, an imprint of the Wadsworth Group, a division of Thomson Learning. Fax 800-730-2215.

can be punishing. For this reason, it's important to keep members feeling satisfied . . . as long as you don't compromise the team's goals.

**Referent Power**    Referent power comes from the respect, liking, and trust others have for a member. If you have high referent power, you may be able to persuade others to follow your lead because they believe in you or because they are willing to do you a favor. Members acquire referent power by behaving in ways others in the group admire and by being genuinely likable. The kinds of confirming communication behaviors described in Chapter 8 can go a long way toward boosting referent power. Listening to others' ideas, honoring their contributions, and taking a win–win approach to meeting their needs lead to liking and respect.

After our look at various ways members can influence one another, three important characteristics of power in groups become clearer.[58]

- **Power is group centered.** Power isn't something an individual possesses. Instead, it is conferred by the group. You may be an expert on the subject being considered, but if the other members don't think you are qualified to talk, you won't have expert power. You might try to reward other people by praising their contributions, but if they don't value your compliments, then all the praise in the world won't influence them.

- **Power is distributed among group members.** Power rarely belongs to just one person. Even when a group has an official leader, other members usually have the power to affect what happens. This influence can be positive, coming from information, expertise, or social reinforcement. It can also be negative, coming from punishing behaviors such as criticizing or withholding the contributions that the group needs to succeed. You can appreciate how power is distributed among members by considering the effect just one member can have by not showing up for meetings or failing to carry out his or her part of the job.

- **Power isn't an either-or concept.** It's incorrect to assume that power is something that members either possess or lack. Rather, it is a matter of degree. Instead of talking about someone as "powerful" or "powerless," it's more accurate to talk about how much influence he or she exerts.

It's fitting that we end the chapter where we began, with the inspirational example of Nelson Mandela. Like all good followers, Mandela didn't simply do whatever leaders told him to do. He stood his ground when he believed their policies were unjust. Like all good leaders, he understood that true power lies in uniting and empowering people.

Mandela ultimately served nearly 30 years as a political prisoner. Then, in a remarkable turnaround in 1990, white South African president Frederik de Klerk released him from prison, and the two worked together to help the nation heal from more than 50 years of bloodshed, cruelty, and injustice. They were jointly awarded the Nobel Peace Prize in 1993. The following year, Mandela was elected as the first black president of South Africa. He has since won hundreds of leadership awards and has been lauded as one of the greatest leaders in history. As one biographer puts it, "Mandela brought together bitter enemies and unified a nation."[59]

## Summary

Groups and teams play an important role in many areas of our lives: families, education, employment, and friendships, to name a few. Groups possess several characteristics that distinguish them from other communication contexts. They involve interaction and interdependence over time among a small number of participants with the purpose of achieving one or more goals. Some groups achieve the status of teams. They embody a high level of shared goals and identity, commitment to a common cause, and high ideals. These qualities may be challenging to achieve, especially when group members are separated geographically, but even virtual teams can excel if they focus on developing strong relationships with one another.

Groups have their own goals, as do individual members. Member goals fall into two categories: task related and social. Sometimes individual and group goals are compatible, and sometimes they conflict.

Groups can be put into several classifications: learning, growth, problem solving, and social. All these types of groups share certain characteristics: the existence of group norms, individual roles for members, and patterns of interaction that are shaped by the group's structure.

No one leadership approach works well in all circumstances. Instead, leaders who understand the relative strengths of various styles are most likely to succeed. For the most part, leaders who focus on the overall mission, relationships, and task fulfillment accomplish more than those who are motivated by the desire to achieve personal glory or maintain harmony at all costs. There are many ways to become a leader. Evidence suggests that leaders often emerge through a process of elimination, which suggests that, whether or not we know it, we begin "auditioning" for leadership roles as soon as we join a group.

People often overlook the powerful roles that followers play in shaping innovations, challenging leaders, and pursuing important goals. Some followers tend to hang back, either because they are indifferent or because they prefer to watch and learn. Others take an active role—sometimes to the extent of putting their lives on the line for a cause. Followers embody many forms of power—either because they are respected as experts, because they are good relationship builders, because they are able to reward or coerce others, or because people like and admire them.

## Key Terms

**all-channel network** A communication network pattern in which group members are always together and share all information with one another. *p. 275*

**authoritarian leadership style** A leadership style in which the designated leader uses legitimate, coercive, and reward power to dictate the group's actions. *p. 282*

**chain network** A communication network in which information passes sequentially from one member to another. *p. 275*

**coercive power** The power to influence others by the threat or imposition of unpleasant consequences. *p. 290*

**connection power** The influence granted by virtue of a member's ability to develop relationships that help the group reach its goal. *p. 290*

**democratic leadership style** A style in which the nominal leader invites the group's participation in decision making. *p. 282*

**dysfunctional roles** Individual roles played by group members that inhibit the group's effective operation. *p. 278*

**emergent leader** A member who assumes leadership roles without being appointed by higher-ups. *p. 286*

**expert power** The ability to influence others by virtue of one's perceived expertise on the subject in question. *p. 290*

**formal role** A role assigned to a person by group members or an organization, usually to establish order. *p. 276*

**gatekeepers** Producers of mass messages who determine what messages will be delivered to consumers, how those messages will be constructed, and when they will be delivered. *p. 276*

**group** A small collection of people whose members interact with one another, usually face-to-face, over time in order to reach goals. *p. 269*

**group goals** Goals that a group collectively seeks to accomplish. See also *Individual goals*. *p. 273*

**hidden agendas** Individual goals that group members are unwilling to reveal. *p. 273*

**individual goals** Individual motives for joining a group. *p. 273*

**informal roles** Roles usually not explicitly recognized by a group that describe functions of group members, rather than their positions. These are sometimes called "functional roles." See also *Formal role*. *p. 276*

**laissez-faire leadership style** A style in which the designated leader gives up his or her formal role, transforming the group into a loose collection of individuals. *p. 282*

**Leadership Grid** A two-dimensional model that identifies leadership styles as a combination of concern for people and for the task at hand. *p. 282*

**legitimate power** The ability to influence a group owing to one's position in a group. See also *Nominal leader*. *p. 290*

**nominal leader** The person who is identified by title as the leader of a group. *p. 290*

**norms** Shared values, beliefs, behaviors, and procedures that govern a group's operation. *p. 274*

**power** The ability to influence others' thoughts and/or actions. *p. 290*

**procedural norms** Norms that describe rules for the group's operation. *p. 274*

**referent power** The ability to influence others by virtue of the degree to which one is liked or respected. *p. 291*

**reward power** The ability to influence others by the granting or promising of desirable consequences. *p. 290*

**roles** The patterns of behavior expected of group members. *p. 276*

**rule** An explicit, officially stated guideline that governs group functions and member behavior. *p. 274*

**situational leadership** A theory that argues that the most effective leadership style varies according to leader-member relations, the nominal leader's power, and the task structure. *p. 282*

**social norms** Group norms that govern the way members relate to one another. See also *Task norms. p. 274*

**social roles** Emotional roles concerned with maintaining smooth personal relationships among group members. Also termed "maintenance functions." *p. 278*

**sociogram** A graphic representation of the interaction patterns in a group. *p. 275*

**task norms** Group norms that govern the way members handle the job at hand. See also *Social norms. p. 274*

**task roles** Roles group members take on in order to help solve a problem. See also *Social roles. p. 278*

**trait theories of leadership** The belief that it is possible to identify leaders by personal traits, such as intelligence, appearance, or sociability. *p. 280*

**virtual groups** People who interact with one another via mediated channels, without meeting face-to-face. *p. 272*

**wheel network** A communication network in which a gatekeeper regulates the flow of information from all other members. *p. 276*

## Check Your Understanding

1. Make a list of groups to which you have belonged. Identify which of them functioned mostly like groups and which functioned mostly like teams. Did any of them embody the team qualities listed on page 271? If so, how did you achieve that? If not, what might have helped you be more effective?

2. Considering one of the groups or teams you just listed, draw three columns on a sheet of paper. In the first column, list your individual goals as a member of the team. In the second column, list the individual goals of another person on the team (based on that person's behavior). In the third column, list the group goals. How do the three columns compare? Were any of the individual goals you listed at odds with the team goals? If so, how?

3. Thinking about the same group or a different one, make a list of the written rules (if any) that governed how members should behave. Now list the unspoken norms (see page 274) about who talked to whom, what behavior was encouraged, how the work got done, what roles people played, and so on. Were the rules and norms consistent with each other? Which rules and norms helped the group succeed? Were there any that hampered the group's performance?

4. Try to think of leaders (people you know or famous figures) who embody each of the following leadership styles: autocratic, democratic, laissez-faire, transactional operator, team player, and transformational. In your opinion, which of these leaders has been most effective? Why do you think that is?

5. Why do you think people often overlook the important roles that followers play? Try to think of a follower who embodies each of the roles identified by Barbara Kellerman (pages 288–289). Which type of follower are you in different situations? What types of power (pages 290–291) do you most often embody as a follower?

## Activities

1. **Your Membership in Groups** To find out what roles groups play in your life, complete the following steps:

   1. Use the criteria of size, interaction, interdependence, time, and goals to identify the small groups to which you belong.

   2. Describe the importance of each group to you, and evaluate how satisfying the communication is in each one.

2. **Group and Individual Goals** Think about two groups to which you belong.

   1. What are your task-related goals in each?

   2. What are your social goals?

   3. Are your personal goals compatible or incompatible with those of other members?

   4. Are they compatible or incompatible with the group goals?

   5. What effect does the compatibility or incompatibility of goals have on the effectiveness of the group?

3. **Norms and Rules in Action** Describe the desirable norms and explicit rules you would like to see established in the following new groups, and describe the steps you could take to see that they are established.

   1. A group of classmates formed to develop and present a class research project

   2. A group of neighbors that is meeting for the first time to persuade the city to install a stop sign at a dangerous intersection

   3. A group of 8-year-olds you will be coaching in a team sport

4. A group of fellow employees who will be sharing new office space

4. **Choosing the Most Effective Leadership Style** Based on the self-assessment quiz on page 283, which leadership style (or styles) best characterizes you? Do you think your style changes based on the situation? If so, how? What are the advantages of the style you embody? What are some potential disadvantages?

5. **Followership and Power**

   1. Based on the self-assessment quiz on page 289 and your own experiences, what are your strengths as a follower? In what ways might you improve?

   2. Think of examples from groups you have belonged to or observed in which members had and used each type of power:

      Legitimate

      Coercive

      Reward

      Expert

      Connection

      Referent

   3. Describe the types of power you have possessed in groups. Evaluate whether your use of that power has helped or hindered the group's effectiveness.

 # For Further Exploration

**For more resources about the nature of small groups, see the *Understanding Human Communication* website at www.oup.com/us/adler.** There you will find a variety of resources: "Media Room" clips from popular films and television shows to further illustrate important concepts, a list of books and articles, links to descriptions of feature films and television shows at the *Now Playing* website, study aids, and a self-test to check your understanding of the material in this chapter.

## CHAPTER 10

# Solving Problems in Groups and Teams

## 10

## Chapter Outline

### LEARNING OBJECTIVES

1 Weigh the pros and cons of using a group to solve a problem.

2 Identify ways that teams can build strong foundations in terms of cohesiveness and team development.

3 Use a variety of the problem-solving formats (e.g., breakout groups, focus groups, symposia, reflective thinking, and dialogue) and decision-making methods to arrive at innovative solutions.

4 Identify common obstacles to effective functioning of a specific group and suggest more effective ways of communicating.

Susie Wee is excited. She's in a conference room, working with people who feel as close as the coffee cup across the table, although they are thousands of miles away. Wee calls it *cloud collaboration*—the ability to interact effortlessly and effectively with people in faraway places.

Breaking down barriers is one of Wee's specialties. She led the team that created the highly realistic cloud-collaboration technology. And think of her the next time you watch a video on your phone. She helped pioneer that technology, too.[1] Wee holds more than 40 technology patents, and her work has been published in more than 50 international journals.[2] She is regularly honored as one of the youngest, most innovative technology leaders in the United States.

Wee is the first to acknowledge that she hasn't achieved so many things on her own. "Teamwork is very important to me," she says.[3] "Innovation is all about using teamwork and creativity to solve hard problems."[4]

Wee talks about problems the way some people talk about chocolate cake. She savors them and can hardly wait for more. After all, she says, problems represent opportunities to change the world for the better. For example, there's the problem of interacting with colleagues in a different location. And there's the challenge of getting a hockey puck past defenders and into the net.

To explain, in addition to revolutionizing technology, Wee is an avid hockey player. She and her teammates on the San Jose Lady Sharks made it to the national championship a few years back. The experience strengthened her conviction that business and sports have a lot in common. One her favorite lessons on and off the ice is that "*any player of any ability* can create the spark needed to energize the team and turn the game around."[5] In other words, she says, teams need talent, but they also need commitment and energy.

To Wee, solving a tough challenge on the job can be as rewarding as playing on a sports team or getting together with friends. "[In] team sports, you're helping each other, coaching each other, trying to motivate each other, and trying to win games together," she says. "I've carried that forward to my management style."[6]

*Susie Wee's attitudes and accomplishments remind us that problems can be exciting opportunities. Think of groups to which you have belonged— perhaps your family, a group of friends, a project committee, or a sports team.*

- What problems and challenges have you addressed in each of those groups?

- How successful have your groups been?

- How enjoyable has the problem-solving process been?

- In your experience, what has made the difference between more and less successful groups?

## Problem Solving in Groups: When and Why

Perhaps because most people aren't aware of the problem-solving techniques available to them, groups sometimes get a bad name. You have probably heard the snide remark that "a camel is a horse designed by a committee." This unflattering reputation is at least partly justified. Most of us would wind up with a handsome sum if we had a dollar for every hour wasted in problem-solving groups.

On the other hand, teamwork has brought us computers, cars, space travel, the Internet, and many other innovations. As these examples illustrate, *solving problems*, as we define it here, doesn't refer only to situations in which something is wrong. Perhaps *meeting challenges* and *performing tasks* are better terms. After you recognize this, you can see that problem solving occupies a major part of life. Employers rank teamwork skills among the 10 most desired traits of people they hire.[7] Employees give teamwork high priority as well. They typically say that effective teamwork makes them feel more powerful and empowered than before, more appreciated, more successful, closer to their colleagues, and more confident that team members will support and encourage them in the future.[8]

In the blockbuster movie *The Avengers*, superheroes come together when global security is threatened. Each member has special skills necessary to help solve the problem, and they work together to succeed. What factors can help you decide when a problem needs to be solved by a group rather than alone?

Away from work, groups also meet to solve problems: Volunteer groups plan fundraisers; athletic teams work to improve their collective performance; neighbors meet to improve the quality of life where they live; educators and parents work together to improve schools—the list is almost endless.

All in all, groups do have their shortcomings, which we will discuss in a few pages. But extensive research has shown that, when these shortcomings can be avoided, groups are clearly the most effective way to handle many tasks.

## Advantages of Group Problem Solving

Years of research show that, in most cases, groups can produce more solutions to a problem than individuals working alone, and the solutions will be of higher quality. Groups have proved superior at a wide range of tasks—everything from assembling jigsaw puzzles to solving complex reasoning problems. There are several reasons why groups are effective.[9]

**Resources**    For many tasks, groups possess a greater collection of resources than do most individuals. Sometimes the resources are physical. For example, three or four people can put up a tent or dig a ditch better than a lone person. Pooled resources can also lead to qualitatively better solutions. Think, for instance, about times when you have studied with other students for a test and you discussed and learned material you might have overlooked if not for the group. Groups not only have more resources than individuals, but also, through interaction among the members, they are better able to mobilize them.

**Accuracy**    Another benefit of group work is the increased likelihood of catching errors. At one time or another, we all make stupid mistakes, like the man who built a boat in his basement and then wasn't able to get it out the door. Working in a group increases the chance that foolish errors like this won't slip by. Sometimes, of course, mistakes aren't so obvious, which makes groups even more valuable as an error-checking mechanism. Another side to the error-detecting story is the risk that group members will support one another in a bad idea. We'll discuss this problem later in this chapter when we focus on conformity.

**Commitment** Besides coming up with superior solutions, groups also generate a higher commitment to carrying them out. Members are most likely to accept solutions they have helped create, and they will work harder to carry out those solutions. This fact has led to the principle of participative decision making, in which people contribute to the decisions that will affect them. This is an especially important principle for those in authority, such as supervisors, teachers, and parents. As professors, we have seen the difference between the sullen compliance of students who have been forced to accept a policy with which they disagree and the much more willing cooperation of students when they help develop such a policy.

**Diversity** Working with others allows us to consider approaches and solutions we might not think of otherwise. Although we tend to think in terms of "lone geniuses" who make discoveries and solve the world's problems, most breakthroughs are actually the result of collective creativity—people working together to create options no one would have thought of alone.[10] One reason Susie Wee has been so effective is that she assembles highly diverse teams. Her former boss at Hewlett Packard puts it this way:

> Susie has that just innate ability to bring the right mix of people together to take a unique look at the problem. . . . For her, it's not about the leader. It's about: How do you bring the team together and bubble up the expertise and let everyone have a voice in the conversation?[11]

Although diversity is a benefit of teamwork, it requires special effort, especially when members come from different cultural backgrounds. For example, in teams that consist of both Asian and American members, Americans do most of the talking and are more likely than their Asian teammates to interject thoughts and ideas while other people are speaking.[12] And women may be dismayed to find

---

**Understanding Diversity**

## Maximizing the Effectiveness of Multicultural Teams

Italian clothier Carlo Rivetti made a bold step a few years ago. He realized that, although the clientele of his sportswear firm was multicultural, his staff wasn't. So he abandoned the one-designer model and recruited designers from a host of different countries. These days, the team is united by a common passion and shared vision, but they are diverse in terms of their tastes, languages, and customs. Coordinating the efforts of such a diverse team isn't simple, Rivetti says, but it is far more rewarding, creative, and client oriented.[14]

Travel and technology allow us to create more diverse teams than ever before. Evidence supports Rivetti's observation: Multicultural teams typically *are* more creative than homogenous teams or individuals.[15] But, as he says, they also present unique challenges. Communication researchers[16] offer the following tips to maximize the benefits and minimize the pitfalls of multicultural teams:

- Allow more time than usual for group development and discussions.

- Agree on clear guidelines for discussions, participation, and decision making.

- Use a variety of communication formats. Based on cultural preferences, people may be more or less comfortable speaking to the entire group, putting their thoughts in writing, speaking one on one, and so on.

- If possible, achieve an even distribution of people from various cultures. Research shows that being a "minority member" is especially challenging and not conducive to open communication.[17]

- Educate team members about the cultures represented. We are less likely to make unwarranted assumptions (that a person is lazy, disinterested, overbearing, or so on) if we understand the cultural patterns at play.

- Open your mind to new possibilities. Assumptions and too-quick solutions short-circuit the advantage of diverse perspectives.

The results of multicultural teams are usually worth the effort. As one analyst puts it, "diversity makes us smarter."[18]

that members of some cultures tend to dismiss their comments.[13] To make the most of multiculturalism and avoid some of the common pitfalls, see the "Understanding Diversity" box on the previous page.

## When to Use Groups for Problem Solving

Despite their advantages, groups aren't always the best way to solve a problem. Many jobs can be tackled more quickly, easily, and even more efficiently by one or more people working independently. Answering the following questions will help you decide when to solve a problem using a group and when to tackle it alone.[19]

**Is the Job Beyond the Capacity of One Person?**   Some jobs are simply too big for one person to manage. They may call for more information than a single person possesses or can gather. For example, a group of friends planning a large New Year's party will probably have a better event if they pool their ideas than if one person tries to think of everything. Some jobs also require more time and energy than one person can spare. Putting on the New Year's party could involve a variety of tasks: inviting the guests, hiring a band, finding a place large enough to hold the party, buying food and drinks, and so on. It's both unrealistic and unfair to expect one or two people to do all this work.

**Are Individuals' Tasks Interdependent?**   Remember that a group is more than a collection of individuals working side by side. The best tasks for groups are ones in which the individuals can help one another in some way. Think of a group of disgruntled renters considering how to protest unfair landlords. In order to get anywhere, they realize that they have to assign areas of responsibility to each member: researching the law, getting new members, publicizing their complaints, and so on. It's easy to see that these jobs are all interdependent: Getting new members, for example, will require publicity; and publicizing complaints will involve showing how the renters' legal rights are being violated.

Even when everyone is working on the same job, there can be interdependence if different members fulfill the various functional roles described in Chapter 9. Some people might be better at task-related roles like information giving, diagnosing, and summarizing. Others might contribute by filling social roles such as harmonizing, supporting, or relieving tension. People working independently simply don't have the breadth of resources to fill all these functions.

**Is There More Than One Decision or Solution?**   Groups are best suited to tackling problems that have no single, cut-and-dried answer: What's the best way to boost membership in a campus organization? How can funds be raised for a charity? What topic should the group choose for a class project? Gaining the perspectives of every member boosts the odds of finding high-quality answers to questions like these.

By contrast, a problem with only one solution won't take full advantage of a group's talents. For example, phoning merchants to get price quotes and looking up a series of books in the library don't require much creative thinking. Jobs like these can be handled by one or two people working alone. Of course, it may take a group meeting to decide how to divide the work to get the job done most efficiently.

**Is There Potential for Disagreement?**   Tackling a problem as a group is essential if you need the support of everyone involved. Consider a group of friends planning a vacation. Letting one or two people choose the destination, schedule, and budget would be asking for trouble, because their decisions would almost certainly disappoint at least some of the people who weren't consulted. It would be far smarter to involve everyone in the

> cultural idiom
> **cut-and-dried:**
> the usual thing
>
> **boosts the odds of:**
> increases the chances of success of

Think of an accomplishment that couldn't have been achieved by a single person acting alone. Then reflect on the problems you face, and decide which ones could best be tackled by a group.

most important decisions, even if doing so took more time. After the key decisions were settled, it might be fine to delegate relatively minor issues to one or two people.

## Setting the Stage for Problem Solving

Just as a poor blueprint or shaky foundation can weaken a house, all the problem-solving tips in the world won't mean much if you don't have a strong team. The following pages offer guidelines for building relationships and understanding the process teams go through as they work on a task.

### Basic Skills

Groups are most effective when members feel good about one another.[20] Susie Wee, whom we introduced at the beginning of the chapter, says she has learned that a little play makes for better work. In her experience, the best teams "like each other, have fun together, and celebrate each others' accomplishments."[21]

Probably the most important ingredient in good personal relationships is mutual respect, and the best way to demonstrate respect for the other person is to listen carefully. A more natural tendency, of course, is to assume that you understand the other members' positions and to interrupt or ignore them. Even if you are right, however, this tendency can create a residue of ill feelings. On the other hand, careful listening can at least improve the communication climate, and you may even learn something from your group mates.

### Building Cohesiveness

**Cohesiveness** can be defined as the degree to which members feel connected with and committed to their group. You might think of cohesiveness as the glue that bonds individuals together, giving them a collective sense of identity.

Highly cohesive groups communicate differently than less cohesive ones. Members spend more time interacting, and there are more expressions of positive feelings for one another. They report more satisfaction with the group and its work. In addition, people are more loyal to highly cohesive teams than to other ones. Cohesion keeps people coming back, even when the going is tough.

With characteristics like these, it's no surprise that highly cohesive groups have the potential to be productive. In fact, group cohesion is one of the strongest predictors of innovation, along with effective communication and encouragement.[22]

Despite its advantages, cohesiveness is no guarantee of success: If the group is united in supporting unproductive norms, members will feel close but won't get the job done. For example, consider a group of employees who have a boss they think is incompetent and unfair. They might grow quite cohesive in their opposition to the perceived tyranny, spending hours after (or during) work swapping complaints. They might even organize protests, work slowdowns, grievances to their union, or mass resignations. All these responses would boost cohesiveness, but they would not necessarily make the company more successful or help the employees.

Research has disclosed a curvilinear relationship between cohesiveness and productivity: Up to a certain point, productivity

In the *Harry Potter* films, Harry, Ron, and Hermione overcome a host of problems by sticking together and maintaining positive relationships. What factors help boost group cohesiveness? Why is cohesiveness so important?

increases as group members become a unified team. Beyond this point, however, the mutual attraction members feel for one another begins to interfere with the group's efficient functioning. Members may enjoy one another's company, but this enjoyment can keep them from focusing on the job at hand.

The goal, then, is to boost cohesiveness in a way that also helps get the job done. There are eight factors that can bring about these goals.

1. **Shared or compatible goals.** People draw closer when they share a similar aim or when their goals can be mutually satisfied. For example, members of a conservation group might have little in common until a part of the countryside they all value is threatened by development. Some members might value the land because of its beauty; others because it provides a place to hunt or fish; and still others because the nearby scenery increases the value of their property, but as long as their goals are compatible, this collection of individuals will find that a bond exists that draws them together.

2. **Progress toward goals.** While a group is making progress, members feel highly cohesive; when progress stops, cohesiveness decreases. All other things being equal, players on an athletic team feel closest when the team is winning. During extended losing streaks, it is likely that players will feel less positive about the team and less willing to identify themselves as members of the group.

3. **Shared norms and values.** Although successful groups will tolerate and even thrive on some differences in members' attitudes and behavior, wide variation in the group's definition of what actions or beliefs are proper will reduce cohesiveness. If enough members hold different ideas of what behavior is acceptable, the group is likely to break up. Disagreements over values or norms can fall into many areas, such as humor, finance, degree of candor, and proportion of time allotted to work and play.

4. **Lack of perceived threat between members.** Cohesive group members see no threat to their status, dignity, and material or emotional well-being. When such interpersonal threats do occur, they can be very destructive. Often competition arises within groups, and as a result members feel threatened. Sometimes there is a struggle over who will be the nominal leader. At other times, members view others as wanting to take over a functional role (problem solver, information giver, and so on), through either competition or criticism. Sometimes the threat is real, and sometimes it's only imagined, but in either case the group must neutralize it or face the consequences of reduced cohesiveness.

5. **Interdependence of members.** Groups become cohesive when their needs can be satisfied only with the help of other members. When a job can be done just as well by one person alone, the need for membership decreases. This factor explains the reason for food cooperatives, neighborhood yard sales, and community political campaigns. All these activities enable the participants to reach their goal more successfully than if they acted alone.

6. **Threat from outside the group.** When members perceive a threat to the group's existence or image (groups have self-concepts, just as individuals do), they grow closer together. Almost everyone knows of a family whose members seem to fight constantly among themselves until an outsider criticizes one of them. At this point, the internal bickering stops, and for the moment the group unites against its common enemy. The same principle often works on a larger scale when nations bind up their internal differences in the face of external aggression.

> cultural idiom

**bickering:**
quarreling

⑦ **Mutual attraction and friendship.** This factor is somewhat circular, because friendship and mutual attraction often are a result of the points just listed, yet groups often do become close simply because the members like one another. Social groups are a good example of a type of group that stays together because its members enjoy one another's company.

⑧ **Shared group experiences.** When members have been through some unusual or trying experience, they draw together. This explains why soldiers who have been in combat together often feel close and stay in touch for years after; it also accounts for the ordeal of fraternity pledging and other initiations. Many societies have rituals that all members share, thus increasing the group's cohesiveness.

To analyze how effective your problem-solving team is, take the self-assessment quiz on page 305.

## Developmental Stages in Problem-Solving Groups

When it comes to solving problems in groups, research shows that the shortest distance to a solution isn't always a straight line. Communication scholar Aubrey Fisher analyzed tape recordings of problem-solving groups and discovered that many successful groups seem to follow a four-stage process when arriving at a decision.[23] As you read about his findings, visualize how they have applied to problem-solving groups in your experience.

> cultural idiom

**sizing up:**
assessing

In the **orientation stage**, members approach the problem and one another tentatively. Rather than state their own position clearly and unambiguously, they test out possible ideas cautiously and rather politely. This cautiousness doesn't mean that members agree with one another; rather, they are sizing up the situation before asserting themselves. There is little outward disagreement at this stage, but it can be viewed as a calm before the storm.

After members understand the problem and become acquainted, a successful group enters the **conflict stage**. Members take strong positions and defend them against those who oppose their viewpoints. Coalitions are likely to form, and the discussion may become polarized. The conflict needn't be personal: It can focus

## Table 10-1 Some Communication Factors Associated with Group Productivity

| |
|---|
| The group contains the smallest number of members necessary to accomplish its goals. |
| Members care about and agree with the group's goals. |
| Members are clear about and accept their roles, which match the abilities of each member. |
| Group norms encourage high performance, quality, success, and innovation. |
| The group members have sufficient time together to develop a mature working unit and accomplish its goals. |
| The group is highly cohesive and cooperative. |
| The group spends time defining and discussing problems it must solve and decisions it must make. |
| Periods of conflict are frequent but brief, and the group has effective strategies for dealing with conflict. |
| The group has an open communication structure in which all members may participate. |
| The group gets, gives, and uses feedback about its effectiveness. |

*Source:* Adapted from research summarized in Wheelan, S. A., Murphy, D., Tsumaura, E., & Kline, S. F. (1998). Member perceptions of internal group dynamics and productivity. *Small Group Research, 29,* 371–393.

## How Effective Is Your Team?

Think of a team you belong to (or were part of in the past) with the goal of solving a problem or making the most of an opportunity. Select the number on each row that best describes your response.

| | Disagree | | | | Agree |
|---|---|---|---|---|---|
| 1. Team members know and like one another. | 1 | 2 | 3 | 4 | 5 |
| 2. We tend to shy away from issues about which we don't agree. | 1 | 2 | 3 | 4 | 5 |
| 3. We enjoy tackling challenging situations together. | 1 | 2 | 3 | 4 | 5 |
| 4. We enjoy one another's company so much that we often lose focus on what we are trying to achieve. | 1 | 2 | 3 | 4 | 5 |
| 5. We trust one another to be responsible and respectful. | 1 | 2 | 3 | 4 | 5 |
| 6. Members spend more energy competing with one another than cooperating with one another. | 1 | 2 | 3 | 4 | 5 |
| 7. We encourage everyone on the team to have input. | 1 | 2 | 3 | 4 | 5 |
| 8. We tend to spend more time complaining about issues than solving them. | 1 | 2 | 3 | 4 | 5 |
| 9. We approach challenges in a systematic and creative manner. | 1 | 2 | 3 | 4 | 5 |
| 10. Members aren't highly committed to the group or its purpose. | 1 | 2 | 3 | 4 | 5 |

### ANALYZING YOUR RESULTS

Add up the scores you indicated on the odd-numbered questions. Then reverse the scores on the even-numbered questions (5 = 1, 4 = 2, 3 = 3, 2 = 4, 1 = 5). Add both totals together and see how you did below.

### 40–50 points

Congratulations! You have created a team that is cohesive and goal oriented. Although there are likely to be ups and downs, if you maintain your focus on great results and effective teamwork, you are likely to be highly successful together.

### 30–39 points

You have potential, but this team isn't ready for the big leagues yet. The problem may be that you haven't taken the time to build strong relationships or that not everyone is inspired by the challenge before you. Teams who have high trust and high motivation are typically eager to focus on the issue, and they welcome diverse ideas. You'll find many tips in this chapter for strengthening your team's problem-solving potential.

### Less than 30 points

Either your team is very new or you are stuck in an unproductive groove. Over time, the less you accomplish, the less excited and confident members become, which means that commitment and cohesion suffer. Consider how you might turn things around. Perhaps you can host a dialogue session about the group process itself. When you better understand what is holding members back, you may be able to take positive steps to build a more cohesive and productive team. For more about the factors that enhance productivity, see Table 10-1. ●

> cultural idiom

**the give-and-take:**
sharing

on the issues at hand while preserving the members' respect for one another. Even when the climate does grow contentious, conflict seems to be a necessary stage in group development. The give-and-take of discussion tests the quality of ideas, and weaker ones may suffer a well-deserved death here.[24]

After a period of conflict, effective groups move to an **emergence stage**. One idea might emerge as the best one, or the group might combine the best parts of several plans into a new solution. As they approach consensus, members back off from their dogmatic positions. Statements become more tentative again: "I guess that's a pretty good idea," "I can see why you think that way."

Finally, an effective group reaches the **reinforcement stage**. At this point not only do members accept the group's decision, they also endorse it. Even if members disagree with the outcome, they do not voice their concerns. There is an unspoken drive toward consensus and harmony.

Ongoing groups can expect to move through this four-stage process with each new issue, such that their interaction takes on a cyclic pattern (see Figure 10-1). In fact, a group who deals with several issues at once might find itself in a different stage for each problem. In one series of studies, nearly 50 percent of the problem-solving groups examined followed this pattern.[25] The same research showed that a smaller percentage of groups (about 30 percent) didn't follow a cyclical pattern. Instead, they skipped the preliminary phases and focused on the solution.

What is the significance of the findings? They tell us that, like children growing toward adulthood, many groups can expect to pass through phases. Knowing that these phases are natural and predictable can be reassuring. It can help curb your impatience when the group is feeling its way through an orientation stage. It can also help you feel less threatened when the inevitable and necessary conflicts take place. Understanding the nature of emergence and reinforcement can help you know when it is time to stop arguing and seek consensus.

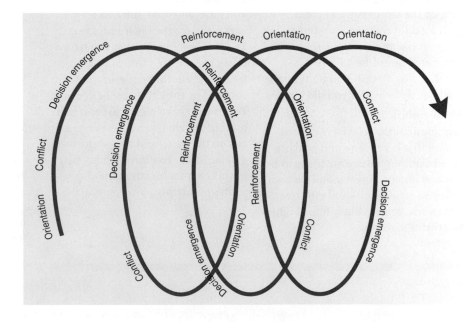

**FIGURE 10-1 Cyclical Stages in an Ongoing Problem-Solving Group**

*Source:* Brilhart, J. K., Galanes, G. J., & Adams, K. (2001). *Effective group discussion* (10th ed.). New York: McGraw-Hill, p. 289.

# Group Problem-Solving Strategies and Formats

Groups meet to solve problems in a variety of settings and for a wide range of reasons. The formats they use are also varied. Some groups meet before an audience to address a problem. The onlookers may be involved in, and affected by, the topic under discussion, like the citizens who attend a typical city council meeting or voters who attend a candidates' debate. In other cases, the audience members are simply interested spectators, as occurs in televised discussions such as *Meet the Press* and *Face the Nation*.

## Problem-Solving Formats

This list of problem-solving formats and approaches is not exhaustive, but it provides a sense of how a group's structure can shape its ability to come up with high-quality solutions.

**Breakout Group**    When the number of members is too large for effective discussion, **breakout groups** can be used to maximize effective participation. In this approach, subgroups (usually consisting of five to seven members) simultaneously address an issue and then report back to the group at large. The best ideas of each breakout group are then assembled to form a high-quality decision.

**Problem Census**    **Problem census** works especially well when some members are more vocal than others, because it equalizes participation. Members use a separate card to list each of their ideas. The leader collects all cards and reads them to the group one by one, posting each on a board visible to everyone. Because the name of the person who contributed each item isn't listed, issues are separated from personalities. As similar items are read, the leader posts and arranges them in clusters. After all items are read and posted, the leader and members consolidate similar items into a number of ideas that the group needs to address.

**Focus Group**    **Focus groups** are used as a market research tool to enable sponsoring organizations to learn how potential users or the public at large regards a new product or idea. Unlike some of the other groups discussed here, focus groups don't include decision makers or other members who claim any expertise on a subject. Instead, their comments are used by decision makers to figure out how people in the wider world might react to ideas.

**Parliamentary Procedure**    Problem-solving meetings can follow a variety of formats. A session that uses **parliamentary procedure** observes specific rules about how topics may be discussed and decisions made. The standard reference book for parliamentary procedure is the revised edition of *Robert's Rules of Order*. Although the parliamentary rules may seem stilted and cumbersome, when well used, they do keep a discussion on track and protect the rights of the minority against domination by the majority.

**Panel Discussion**    Another common problem-solving format is the **panel discussion**, in which the participants talk over the topic informally, much as they would in an ordinary conversation. A leader (called a "moderator," in public discussions) may help the discussion along by encouraging the comments of some members, cutting off overly talkative ones, and seeking consensus when the time comes for making a decision.

Contestants on *Celebrity Apprentice* have to make use of different problem-solving formats to help them succeed. Which formats do you think lead to the best possible solutions? How can groups decide which format is best to use in each situation?

**Symposium** In a **symposium** the participants divide the topic in a manner that allows each member to deliver in-depth information without interruption. Although this format lends itself to good explanations of each person's decision, the one-person-at-a-time nature of a symposium won't lead to a group decision. The contributions of the members must be followed by the give-and-take of an open discussion.

**Forum** A **forum** allows nonmembers to add their opinions to the group's deliberations before the group makes a decision. This approach is commonly used by public agencies to encourage the participation of citizens in the decisions that affect them.

**Dialogue** Sometimes the best way to tackle a problem is to stop trying to find a solution and listen. **Dialogue** is a process in which people let go of the notion that their ideas are superior to others' and instead try to understand the issue from many perspectives.[26] For example, if the problem is that some children in your community are not being immunized, you might invite a collection of diverse people together to talk about the issue. Perhaps you had assumed that parents were being irresponsible, but you learn by listening that some of them don't have transportation, can't afford the cost, or don't understand medical information very well. You will probably proceed very differently once you realize the complexities of the issue for some people.

In a genuine dialogue, members acknowledge that everything they "know" and believe is an assumption based on their own, unavoidably limited experiences. People engage in curious and open-minded discussion about that assumption.

---

@Work

## The Power of Constructive Dialogue

In a dialogue session, about 20 members of a large corporation explored ways to boost the effectiveness of their work team. One participant shared his belief that "people who come to work late are lazy and rude." Even members who thought the complaint was harsh listened respectfully as the speaker explained his ideas about what team members owe one another and the organization.

Another group member acknowledged that she had been arriving late recently and described a series of issues involving child care and transportation. She shared her frustration over the apparently impossible conflict between work obligations and family challenges, and her regret over letting down her colleagues. There was silence as the group pondered the dilemma she described.

Another member spoke out: "I don't have kids. You chose to have them. So your situation is not my problem." The emotional shockwaves in the room were evident on people's faces. The facilitator asked everyone to sit quietly for a few moments before responding.

One man in the group presented a different perspective: "Imagine we are a football team and we have just gotten new uniforms. We look great. We feel great. But the kicker says his feet hurt—his shoes are too small. Would we say, 'That's not our problem'?"

The session adjourned, as dialogues do, without any decisions being made, but leaving members with a good deal to think about. In the days that followed, many people approached the team member with child care problems to express their sympathy for her dilemma. Several said they had the opposite problem: They could come early, but they needed to leave a few minutes before the workday ended. They were able to make a time trade to suit the needs of everyone involved, without compromising the team's mission or inconveniencing the rest of the group.

In a follow-up dialogue, members of the team commented on how easily the situation was resolved once everyone understood one another. "Under different circumstances, we might have created a new policy we didn't need, which wouldn't have helped," said one team member. "Now we say, 'the kicker's feet hurt' any time we are tempted to jump to conclusions without listening first." ●

People may ask questions and suspend their own assumptions, but participants guard against either-or thinking. The goal is to understand one another better, not to reach a decision or debate an issue.

Through dialogue, observes theorist David Isaacs, problems are often not so much *solved* as *dissolved*.[27] The issue may cease to be a problem, or it may be so transformed that the solution is obvious or occurs without a formal decision. (For an example of an actual dialogue, see the @Work box on the previous page.)

## Solving Problems in Virtual Groups

Whether it's a group of students working on a class project from across town, a sales team sharing ideas and leads from the road, or a military group devising plans from across the globe, technology makes it possible to collaborate from virtually anywhere, either in real time or asynchronously.

Chapter 9 described some benefits of online collaboration. Members who might have kept quiet in face-to-face sessions may be more comfortable "speaking out" online. Also, online meetings often generate a permanent record of the proceedings, which can be convenient.

But where problem solving is concerned, virtual interaction presents some unique challenges as well as benefits. For one thing, if members can't see one another clearly, it may be difficult to convey and to understand one another's emotions and attitudes. For another, it may take virtual teams longer to reach decisions than those who meet face-to-face.[28] And whereas high-tech videoconferencing may make it feel that people are in the same room, other forms of interaction (such as typing messages) can be laborious. Because typing takes more time and effort than speaking, messages conveyed via computer can lack the detail of spoken ones. In some cases, members may not even bother to type out a message online that they would have shared in person. Finally, the string of separate messages that is generated in a computerized medium can be hard to track, sort out, and synthesize in a meaningful way.

---

### Understanding Communication Technology

## Developing Trust Long Distance

Trust is a feeling. We may not be able to say clearly why one person strikes us as trustworthy and another triggers our defenses. But if we could observe trust building in slow motion, we'd find that it's based on a collection of signals, some of them very subtle.

Nonverbal cues are usually the first evidence we consider. Does this person smile, make eye contact, show evidence of being friendly and interested in what we have to say, exhibit appropriate use of space and touch? Over time, we take into account patterns of behavior that suggest the person's underlying character and commitment. Is this person dependable, consistent in his or her actions, committed to the team, honest, and so on?[34]

Some of these factors are difficult to judge at a distance. But emerging research suggests that, with a little effort, trust can flourish among virtual team members. Experts' tips include the following:[35]

- Use video technology as often as possible to provide members with visual and nonverbal cues about one another.

- Pay particular attention to your nonverbal communication while you are on camera. Although it is tempting to leaf through papers on your desk, it may send the signal that you are disinterested.

- Show enthusiasm for the group's mission and tasks.

- Encourage members to share information about themselves. As you learned in Chapter 7, self-disclosure is an important way to demonstrate trust in others and to allow them to get to know you.

Trust typically rises in virtual teams who practice these simple principles, and as result, their performance improves as well.[36] ●

Research comparing the quality of decisions made by face-to-face and online groups is mixed. Evidence suggests that virtual teams can be as effective as others, but only if the members have cultivated trusting relationships with one another.[29] The growing body of research suggests that certain types of mediated communication work better than others. For example, asynchronous groups seem to make better decisions than those functioning in a "chat" mode.[30] Groups who have special decision-support software perform better than ones operating without this advantage.[31] Having a moderator also improves the effectiveness of online groups.[32] (For more on trust building in virtual teams, see the "Understanding Communication Technology" box on the previous page.)

Perhaps the most valuable lesson is that online meetings should not entirely replace face-to-face ones, but they can be a *supplement* to in-person sessions. Combining the two forms of interaction can help groups operate both efficiently and effectively.[33]

# Approaches and Stages in Problem Solving

> cultural idiom
> **live up to:**
> fulfill expectations

Groups may have the potential to solve problems effectively, but they don't always live up to this potential. What makes some groups succeed and others fail? Researchers have spent decades asking this question. To discover their findings, read on.

## A Structured Problem-Solving Approach

Although we often pride ourselves on facing problems, rationally intense emotions often hamper our problem-solving ability. This is especially true when frustration or anger leads us to lash out at others[37] or when we don't think things through clearly because we are overly optimistic that we know the right response.[38] Most theorists agree that problem-solving teams benefit from a healthy combination of rationality and creativity. Here, we discuss problem-solving models that incorporate both.

As early as 1910, John Dewey introduced his famous "reflective thinking" method as a systematic approach to solving problems.[39] Since then, other experts have suggested modifications of Dewey's approach. Some emphasize answering key questions, whereas others seek "ideal solutions" that meet the needs of all members. Research comparing various methods has clearly shown that, although no single approach is best for all situations, a structured procedure produces better results than "no pattern" discussions.[40]

The following problem-solving model contains the elements common to most structured approaches developed in the last century:

1. Identify the problem.
   a. Determine the group's goals.
   b. Determine individual members' goals.
2. Analyze the problem.
   a. Word the problem as a broad, open question.
   b. Identify criteria for success.
   c. Gather relevant information.
   d. Identify supporting and restraining forces.
3. Develop creative solutions through brainstorming or the nominal group technique.
   a. Avoid criticism at this stage.
   b. Encourage "freewheeling" ideas.

> cultural idiom
> **freewheeling:**
> unrestricted thinking

    **c.** Develop a large number of ideas.

    **d.** Combine two or more individual ideas.

④ Evaluate the solutions by asking the following:

    **a.** Which solution will best produce the desired changes?

    **b.** Which solution is most achievable?

    **c.** Which solution contains the fewest serious disadvantages?

⑤ Implement the plan.

    **a.** Identify specific tasks.

    **b.** Determine necessary resources.

    **c.** Define individual responsibilities.

    **d.** Provide for emergencies.

⑥ Follow up on the solution.

    **a.** Meet to evaluate progress.

    **b.** Revise the approach as necessary.

Competitors on *Project Runway* are presented with challenges such as creating high-fashion clothing out of newspaper or unusual fabric. Although the problem is defined for them, the solution relies on their creativity and, in some challenges, on how well they work with their teammates. When you are faced with a daunting challenge, how do you start? What process do you follow?

**Identify the Problem**   Sometimes a group's problem is easy to identify. The crew of a sinking ship, for example, doesn't need to conduct a discussion to understand that its goal is to avoid drowning or being eaten by a large fish.

There are many times, however, when the problems facing a group aren't so clear. As an example, think of an athletic team stuck deep in last place well into the season. At first the problem seems obvious: an inability to win any games. But a closer look at the situation might show that there are unmet goals and thus other problems. For instance, individual members may have goals that aren't tied directly to winning: making friends or receiving acknowledgment as good athletes, not to mention the simple goal of having fun playing in the recreational sense of the word. You can probably see that if the coach or team members took a simplistic view of the situation, looking only at the team's win–loss record, player errors, training methods, and so on, some important problems would probably go overlooked. In this situation, the team's performance could probably be best improved by working on the basic problems of the frustration of the players about having their personal needs unmet. What's the moral here? That the way to start understanding a group's problem is to identify the concerns of each member.

What about groups who don't have problems? Several friends planning a surprise birthday party and a family deciding where to go for its vacation don't seem to be in the dire straits of a losing athletic team: They simply want to have fun. In cases like these, it may be helpful to substitute the word *challenge* for the more gloomy word *problem*. However we express it, the same principle applies to all task-oriented groups: The best place to start work is to identify what each member seeks as a result of belonging to the group.

**Analyze the Problem**   After you have identified the general nature of the problem facing the group, you are ready to look at the problem in more detail. There are several steps you can follow to accomplish this important job.

**Word the Problem as a Broad, Open Question**   If you have ever seen a formal debate, you know that the issue under discussion is worded as a proposition:

> cultural idiom
> **dire straits:**
> an extremely difficult situation

"The United States should reduce its foreign aid expenditures," for example. Many problem-solving groups define their task in much the same way. "We ought to spend our vacation in the mountains," suggests one family member. The problem with phrasing problems as propositions (positions) is that such wording invites people to take sides. Though this approach is fine for formal debates (which are contests rather like football or card games), premature side taking creates unnecessary conflict in most problem-solving groups.

A far better approach is to state the problem as an open question that encourages exploratory thinking. Asking, "Should we vacation in the mountains or at the beach?" still forces members to choose sides. A far better approach involves asking a question to help define the general goals (interests) that came out during the problem-identification stage: "What do we want our vacation to accomplish?" (perhaps relaxation, adventure, or low cost).

Notice that this question is truly exploratory. It encourages the family members to work cooperatively, not forcing them to make a choice and then defend it. This absence of an either-or situation boosts the odds that members will listen openly to one another rather than listening selectively in defense of their own positions. There is even a chance that the cooperative, exploratory climate that comes from wording the question most broadly will help the family arrive at a consensus about where to vacation, eliminating the need to discuss the matter any further.

**Identify Criteria for Success**   Phrasing the challenge as an open-ended question will help the group identify the criteria for a successful solution. Imagine that a neighborhood task force asks the question, "How can we create a safer environment?" Developing an answer calls for clarifying what would count as the desired outcome. Fewer incidents reported to police? Less graffiti? More people on the street at night? Knowing what members want puts a group on the road to achieving its goal.

**Gather Relevant Information**   Groups often need to know important facts before they can make decisions or even understand the problem. We remember one group of students who were determined to do well on a class presentation. One of their goals, then, was "to get an A grade." They knew that, to do so, they would have to present a topic that interested both the instructor and the students in the audience. Their first job, then, was to do a bit of background research to find out what subjects would be well received. They interviewed the instructor, asking what topics had been successes and failures in previous semesters. They tested some possible subjects on a few classmates and noted their reactions. From this research they were able to modify their original question, "How can we choose and develop a topic that will earn us an A grade?" into a more specific one, "How can we choose and develop a topic that contains humor, action, and lots of information (to demonstrate our research skills to the instructor) and that contains practical information that will improve the audience's social life, academic standing, or financial condition?"

**Identify Supporting and Restraining Forces**   After members understand what they are seeking, the next step is to see what forces stand between the group and its goals. One useful tool for this approach is the **force field analysis**: a list of the forces that help and hinder the group.[41] By returning to our earlier example of the troubled sports team, we can see how the force field operates. Suppose the team defined its problem-question as "How can we (1) have more fun and (2) grow closer as friends?"

One restraining force in Area 1 (having more fun) was clearly the team's losing record. But, more interestingly, discussion revealed that another damper on enjoyment came from the coach's obsession with winning and his infectiously gloomy

> cultural idiom

**damper on:**
something that reduces or restricts

behavior when the team failed. The main restraining force in Area 2 (growing closer as friends) proved to be the lack of socializing among team members in nongame situations. The helping forces in Area 1 included the sense of humor possessed by several members and the confession by most players that winning wasn't nearly as important to them as everyone had suspected. The helping force in Area 2 was the desire of all team members to become better friends. In addition, the fact that members shared many interests was an important plus.

It's important to realize that most problems have many impelling and restraining forces, all of which need to be identified during this stage. This may call for another round of research. After the force field is laid out, the group is ready to move on to the next step: namely, deciding how to strengthen the impelling forces and weaken the restraining ones.

**Develop Creative Solutions**    After the group has set up a list of criteria for success, the next job is to develop a number of ways to reach its goal. Considering more than one solution is important, because the first solution may not be the best one. During this development stage, creativity is essential. The biggest danger is the tendency of members to defend their own idea and criticize others'. This kind of behavior leads to two problems. First, evaluative criticism almost guarantees a defensive reaction from members whose ideas have been attacked. Second, evaluative criticism stifles creativity. People who have just heard an idea rebuked, however politely, will find it hard even to think of more alternatives, let alone share them openly and risk possible criticism. The following strategies can keep groups creative and can maintain a positive climate.

**Brainstorm**    Probably the best-known strategy for encouraging creativity and avoiding the dangers just described is **brainstorming**.[42] There are four important rules connected with this strategy:

1. *Criticism is forbidden.* As we have already said, nothing will stop the flow of ideas more quickly than negative evaluation.

2. *"Freewheeling" is encouraged.* Sometimes even the most outlandish ideas prove workable, and even an impractical suggestion might trigger a workable idea.

3. *Quantity is sought.* The more ideas generated, the better the chance of coming up with a good one.

4. *Combination and improvement are desirable.* Members are encouraged to "piggyback" by modifying ideas already suggested and to combine previous suggestions.

Although brainstorming is a popular creativity booster, it isn't a guaranteed strategy for developing novel and high-quality ideas. In some experiments, individuals working alone were able to come up with a greater number of high-quality ideas than were small groups.[43] Nevertheless, brainstorming can help a group tap its creative potential.

**Use the Nominal Group Technique**    Because people in groups often can't resist the tendency to criticize one another's ideas, the **nominal group technique** was developed to let members brainstorm ideas without being attacked. As the following steps show, the pattern involves alternating cycles of individual work followed by discussion.

1. Each member works alone to develop a list of possible solutions.

2. In round-robin fashion, each member in turn offers one item from his or her list. The item is listed on a chart visible to everyone. Other members

**ON YOUR FEET**

*The Force Is with You—and Against You*
Describe a tough challenge faced by a team to which you've belonged. Construct a force field diagram that lists all the factors that acted in your favor and the factors that made it more difficult to succeed. Explain what your group did (or could have done) to maximize the beneficial forces and minimize the blocking ones.

> cultural idiom
**piggyback:**
add onto

> cultural idiom
**in round-robin fashion:**
go around in a circle, one after another

may ask questions to clarify an idea, but no evaluation is allowed during this step.

③ Each member privately ranks his or her choice of the ideas in order, from most preferable (5 points) to least preferable (1 point). The rankings are collected, and the top ideas are retained as the most promising solutions.

④ A free discussion of the top ideas is held. At this point critical thinking (though not personal criticism) is encouraged. The group continues to discuss until a decision is reached, either by majority vote or by consensus.

**Evaluate Possible Solutions**   After it has listed possible solutions, the group can evaluate the usefulness of each. One good way of identifying the most workable solutions is to ask three questions.

① *Will this proposal produce the desired changes?* One way to find out is to see whether it successfully overcomes the restraining forces in your force field analysis.

② *Can the proposal be implemented by the group?* Can the members strengthen supporting forces and weaken restraining ones? Can they influence others to do so? If not, the plan isn't a good one.

③ *Does the proposal contain any serious disadvantages?* Sometimes the cost of achieving a goal is too great. For example, one way to raise money for a group is to rob a bank. Although this plan might be workable, it causes more problems than it solves.

**Implement the Plan**   Everyone who makes New Year's resolutions knows the difference between making a decision and carrying it out. There are several important steps in developing and implementing a plan of action.

① *Identify specific tasks to be accomplished.* What needs to be done? Even a relatively simple job usually involves several steps. Now is the time to anticipate all the tasks facing the group. Remember everything now, and you will avoid a last-minute rush later.

② *Determine necessary resources.* Identify the equipment, material, and other resources the group will need in order to get the job done.

③ *Define individual responsibilities.* Who will do what? Do all the members know their jobs? The safest plan here is to put everyone's duties in writing, including the due date. This might sound compulsive, but experience shows that it increases the chance of having jobs done on time.

④ *Provide for emergencies.* Murphy's Law states, "Whatever can go wrong, will." Anyone experienced in group work knows the truth of this law. People forget their obligations, get sick, or quit. Machinery breaks down. (One corollary of Murphy's Law is "The Internet connection will be down whenever it's most needed.") Whenever possible, you ought to develop contingency plans to cover foreseeable problems. Probably the single best suggestion we can give here is to plan on having all work done well ahead of the deadline, knowing that, even with last-minute problems, your time cushion will allow you to finish on time.

> cultural idiom
**time cushion:**
extra time allowance

**Follow Up on the Solution**   Even the best plans usually require some modifications after they're put into practice. You can improve the group's effectiveness and minimize disappointment by following two steps.

① *Meet periodically to evaluate progress.* Follow-up meetings should be part of virtually every good plan. The best time to schedule these meetings is as you put the group's plan to work. At that time, a good leader or member will suggest: "Let's get together in a week (or a few days or a month, depending on the nature of the task). We can see how things are going and take care of any problems."

② *Revise the group's approach as necessary.* These follow-up meetings will often go beyond simply congratulating everyone for coming up with a good solution. Problems are bound to arise, and these periodic meetings, in which the key players are present, are the place to solve them.

Although these steps provide a useful outline for solving problems, they are most valuable as a general set of guidelines and not as a precise formula that every group should follow. As Table 10-2 suggests, certain parts of the model may need emphasis depending on the nature of the specific problem; the general approach will give virtually any group a useful way to consider and solve a problem.

Despite its advantages, the rational, systematic problem-solving approach isn't perfect. The old computer saying, "Garbage in, garbage out" applies here: If the group doesn't possess creative talent, a rational and systematic approach to solving problems won't do much good. Despite this, the rational approach does increase the odds that a group can solve problems successfully. Following the guidelines even imperfectly will help members analyze the problem, come up with solutions, and carry them out better than they could without a plan.

## Decision-Making Methods

There are several approaches a group can use to make decisions. We'll look at each of them now, examining their advantages and disadvantages.

**Consensus**   Consensus occurs when all members of a group support a decision. The advantages of consensus are obvious: Full participation can increase the quality of the decision as well as the commitment of the members to support it. Consensus is especially important in decisions on critical or complex matters; in such cases, methods using less input can diminish the quality of or enthusiasm for a decision. Despite its advantages, consensus also has its disadvantages. It takes a great deal of time, which makes it unsuitable for emergencies. In addition, it is often very frustrating: Emotions can run high on important matters, and patience in the face of such pressures is difficult. Because of the need to deal with these emotional pressures, consensus calls for more communication skill than do other

Table 10-2   **Adapting Problem-Solving Methods to Special Circumstances**

| CIRCUMSTANCES | METHOD |
| --- | --- |
| Members have strong feelings about the problem. | Consider allowing a period of emotional ventilation before systematic problem solving. |
| Task difficulty is high. | Follow the structure of the problem-solving method carefully. |
| There are many possible solutions. | Emphasize brainstorming. |
| A high level of member acceptance is required. | Carefully define the needs of all members, and seek solutions that satisfy all needs. |
| A high level of technical quality is required. | Emphasize evaluation of ideas; consider inviting outside experts. |

*Source:* Adapted from Brilhart, J., & Galanes, G. Adapting problem-solving methods. *Effective group discussion* (10th ed.), p. 291. Copyright © 2001. Reprinted by permission of McGraw-Hill Companies, Inc.

decision-making approaches. As with many things in life, consensus has high rewards, which come at a proportionately high cost.

**Majority Control**   A naive belief of many people (perhaps coming from overzealous high school civics teachers) is that the democratic method of majority rule is always superior. This method does have its advantages in matters in which the support of all members isn't necessary, but in more important matters it is risky. Remember that even if a 51 percent majority of the members favors a plan, 49 percent might still oppose it—hardly sweeping support for any decision that needs the support of all members in order to work.

Besides producing unhappy members, decisions made under majority rule are often inferior to decisions hashed out by a group until the members reach consensus.[44] Under majority rule, members who recognize that they are outvoted often participate less, and the deliberations usually end after a majority opinion has formed, even though minority viewpoints might be worthwhile.

**Expert Opinion**   Sometimes one group member will be defined as an expert and, as such, will be given the power to make decisions. This method can work well when that person's judgment is truly superior. For example, if a group of friends is backpacking in the wilderness, and one becomes injured, it would probably be foolish to argue with the advice of a doctor in the group. In most cases, however, matters aren't so simple. Who is the expert? There is often disagreement on this question. Sometimes a member thinks he or she is the best qualified to make a decision, but others disagree. In a case like this, the group probably won't support that person's advice, even if it is sound.

**Minority Control**   Sometimes a few members of a group decide matters. This approach works well with noncritical questions that would waste the whole group's time. In the form of a committee, a minority of members also can study an issue in greater detail than can the entire group. When an issue is so important that it needs the support of everyone, it's best at least to have the committee report its findings for the approval of all members.

**Authority Rule**   Authority rule is the approach most often used by autocratic leaders. Though it sounds dictatorial, there are times when such an approach has its advantages. This method is quick: There are cases when there simply isn't time for a group to decide what to do. The approach is also perfectly acceptable with routine matters that don't require discussion in order to gain approval. When overused, however, this approach causes problems. Much of the time, group decisions are of higher quality and gain more support from members than those made by an individual. Thus, failure to consult with members can lead to a decrease of effectiveness, even when the leader's decision is a reasonable one.

Which of these decision-making approaches is best? The answer can vary from one culture to another. People in more countries than ever before prefer a democratic style to an authoritarian style, in which leaders make decisions on their own.[45] This is probably because global communication has made human rights a high-priority issue. However, cultural differences still exist. For example, compared to Great Britain and the United States, people in Taiwan[46], Greece, and Cypress[47] are more accepting of leaders who make decisions on their own. As you may recall from Chapter 3, people in high-power-distance cultures such as these are

Characters in the *Toy Story* series of animated films must work together to solve problems. What skills in this chapter do they use? How can you and your teammates use these skills to address challenges you face?

more likely than others to revere authority figures and to accept their decisions without question.

Culture notwithstanding, the most effective approach in a given situation depends on the circumstances:

- **The type of decision:** Some decisions can best be made by an expert, whereas others will benefit from involving the entire group.
- **The importance of the decision:** If the decision is relatively unimportant, it's probably not worth involving all members of the group. By contrast, critical decisions probably require the participation, and ideally the buy-in, of all members.
- **Time available:** If time is short, it may not be possible to assemble the entire group for deliberations.[48]

When choosing a decision-making approach, weigh the pros and cons of each before you decide which one has the best chance of success in the situation your group is facing.

> What decision-making method (consensus, majority control, expert decision, minority control, or authority rule) are you most comfortable with? When might other methods be more productive?

## Overcoming Dangers in Group Discussion

Even groups with the best of intentions often find themselves unable to reach satisfying decisions. At other times, they make decisions that later prove to be wrong. Though there's no foolproof method of guaranteeing high-quality group work, there are several dangers to avoid.

### Information Underload and Overload

**Information underload** occurs when a group lacks information necessary to operate effectively. Sometimes the underload results from overlooking parts of a problem. We know of one group who scheduled a fundraising auction without considering what other events might attract potential donors. They later found that their event was scheduled opposite an important football game, resulting in a loss of sorely needed funds. In other cases, groups suffer from underload because they simply don't conduct enough research. For example, a group of partners starting a new business has to be aware of all the startup costs to avoid going bankrupt in the first months of operation. Overlooking one or two important items can make the difference between success and failure.

Sometimes groups can suffer from too much information. **Information overload** occurs when the rate or complexity of material is too great to manage. Having an abundance of information might seem like a blessing, but anyone who has tried to do conscientious library research has become aware of the paralysis that can result from being overwhelmed by an avalanche of books, magazine and newspaper articles, reviews, films, and research studies. When too much information exists, it is hard to sort out the essential from the unessential information.

Group expert J. Dan Rothwell offers several tips for coping with information overload.[49] First, specialize whenever possible. Try to parcel out areas of responsibility instead of expecting each member to explore every angle of the topic. Second, be selective: Take a quick look at each piece of information to see whether it has real value for your task. If it doesn't, move on to examine more promising material. Third, limit your search. Information specialists have discovered that there is often a curvilinear relationship between the amount of information a group possesses and the quality of its decision. After a certain point, gathering more material can slow you down without contributing to the quality of your group's decisions.

*Source:* © Original Artist. Reproduction rights obtainable from www.CartoonStock.com.

## Unequal Participation

The value of involving group members in making decisions, especially decisions that affect them, is great.[50] When people participate, their loyalty to the group increases. (Your own experience will probably show that most group dropouts were quiet and withdrawn.) Broad-based participation has a second advantage: It increases the amount of resources focused on the problem. As a result, the quality of the group's decisions goes up. Finally, participation increases members' loyalty to the decisions that they played a part in making.

The key to effective participation is balance. Domination by a few vocal or high-status members can reduce a group's ability to solve a problem effectively. One benefit of group decision making online is that participants tend to be blind to status differences that might sway them in person.[51] The moral to this story? Don't assume that quantity of speech or the status of the speaker automatically defines the quality of an idea. Instead, seek out and seriously consider the ideas of all members.

Not all participation is helpful, of course. It's better to remain quiet than to act out the dysfunctional roles described in Chapter 9—cynic, aggressor, dominator, and so on. Likewise, the comments of a member who is uninformed can waste time. Finally, downright ignorant or mistaken input can distract a group.

You can encourage the useful contributions of quiet members in a variety of ways. First, keep the group small. In groups with three or four members, participation is roughly equal, but after the size increases to between five and eight, there is a dramatic gap between the contributions of members.[52] Even in a large group, you can increase the contributions of quiet members by soliciting their opinions. This approach may seem obvious, but in their enthusiasm to speak out, more verbal communicators can overlook the people who don't speak up. When normally reticent members do offer information, reinforce their contributions. It isn't necessary to go overboard by gushing about a quiet person's brilliant remark, but a word of

> cultural idiom

**to go overboard:**
to do so much as to be excessive

**gushing about:**
being overly enthusiastic about

thanks and an acknowledgment of the value of an idea increase the odds that the contributor will speak up again in the future. Another strategy is to assign specific tasks to normally quiet members. The need to report on these tasks guarantees that they will speak up. A final strategy is to use the nominal group technique described earlier in this chapter, to guarantee that the ideas of all members are heard.

Different strategies can help when the problem is one or more members talking too much, especially when their remarks aren't helpful. If the talkative member is at all sensitive, withholding reinforcement can deliver a diplomatic hint that it may be time to listen more and speak less. A lack of response to an idea or suggestion can work as a hint to cut back on speaking. Don't confuse lack of reinforcement with punishment, however: Attacking a member for dominating the group is likely to trigger a defensive reaction and cause more harm than good. If the talkative member doesn't respond to subtle hints, politely expressing a desire to hear from other members can be effective. The next stage in this series of escalating strategies for dealing with dominating members is to question the relevance of remarks that are apparently off the wall: "I'm confused about what last Saturday's party has to do with the job we have to do today. Am I missing something?"

> cultural idiom
**off the wall:**
unconventional, ridiculous

## Ethical Challenge

## Dealing with Overly Talkative and Quiet Group Members

Balancing participation in group discussions can involve stifling some members and urging others to speak up when they would prefer to be silent. Explore the ethical justification for these actions by answering the following questions.

1. Are there any circumstances in which it is legitimate to place quiet group members in the position of speaking up when they would rather remain quiet? When does it become unreasonable to urge quiet members to participate?

2. Does discouraging talkative members ever violate the principles of free speech and tolerance for others' opinions? Describe when it is and is not appropriate to limit a member's contributions.

After developing your ethical guidelines, consider how willing you would feel if they were applied to you.

## Pressure to Conform

There's a strong tendency for group members to go along with the crowd, which often results in bad decisions. A classic study by Solomon Asch illustrated this point. College students were shown three lines of different lengths and asked to identify which of them matched a fourth line. Although the correct answer was obvious, the experiment was a setup: Asch had instructed all but one member of the experimental groups to vote for the wrong line. As a result, fully one-third of the uninformed subjects ignored their own good judgment and voted with the majority. If simple tasks like this one generate such conformity, it is easy to see that following the (sometimes mistaken) crowd is even more likely in the much more complex and ambiguous tasks that most groups face.

Even when there's no overt pressure to follow the majority, more subtle influences motivate members, especially in highly cohesive groups, to keep quiet rather than voice any thoughts that deviate from what appears to be the consensus. "Why rock the boat if I'm the only dissenter?" members think. "And if everybody else feels the same way, they're probably right."

> cultural idiom
**rock the boat:**
disturb a stable condition

With no dissent, the group begins to take on a feeling of invulnerability: an unquestioning belief that its ideas are correct and even morally right. As its position solidifies, outsiders who disagree can be viewed as the enemy, disloyal to what is obviously the only legitimate viewpoint. Social scientists use the term **groupthink** to describe a group's collective striving for unanimity that discourages realistic appraisals of alternatives to its chosen decision.[53] Groupthink has led to a number of disasters, including the United States' botched Bay of Pigs invasion of Cuba in the 1960s, the *Challenger* Space Shuttle disaster in 1986, and the corporate culture that led to the downfall of energy giant Enron in 2001. A more recent example is the Pennsylvania State University sex abuse scandal. Over 14 years, numerous people who knew about the abuse didn't report it because they feared they would lose their jobs or damage the institution's reputation if they went public.[54]

Several group practices can discourage this troublesome force.[55] A first step is to recognize the problem of groupthink as it begins to manifest itself. If agreement comes quickly and easily, the group may be avoiding the tough but necessary search for alternatives. Beyond vigilance, a second step to discourage groupthink is to minimize status differences. If the group has a nominal leader, he or she must be careful not to use the various types of power that come with the position to intimidate members. A third step involves developing a group norm that legitimizes disagreement. After members recognize that questioning one another's positions doesn't signal personal animosity or disloyalty, a constructive exchange of ideas can lead to top-quality solutions. Sometimes it can be helpful to designate a person or subgroup as a "devil's advocate" who reminds the others about the dangers of groupthink and challenges the trend toward consensus.

We opened this chapter with Susie Wee's enthusiasm for problem solving. In her view, developing high-tech software has a lot in common with playing on a sports team. In either case, challenge can be fun, especially when people work hard together to accomplish something that matters to them. We close with one more reflection, in which Wee encourages work teams to adopt the perspective of professional athletes. No matter how good they are, she says, champions never stop improving: "They still work hard to improve and build their skills. They continue to refine and perfect."[56] In the end, that's what teamwork and problem solving are all about.

> cultural idiom

**devil's advocate:**
one who argues against a widely held view in order to clarify issues

## Summary

Despite the bad reputation of groups in some quarters, research shows that they are often the most effective setting for problem solving. They command greater resources, both quantitatively and qualitatively, than do either individuals or collections of people working in isolation; their work can result in greater accuracy; and the participative nature of the solutions they produce generates greater commitment from members.

Groups aren't always the best forum for solving problems. They should be used when the problem is beyond the capacity of one person to solve, when tasks are interdependent, when there is more than one desired solution or decision, and when the agreement of all members is essential.

Groups who pay attention only to the task dimension of their interaction risk strains in the relationships among members. Many of these interpersonal problems can be avoided by using the skills described in Chapter 8 as well as by following the guidelines in this chapter for building group cohesiveness and encouraging participation.

Most groups can expect to move through several stages as they solve a problem. The first of these stages is orientation, during which the members get an initial sense of one another's positions. The conflict stage is characterized by partisanship and open debate over the merits of contending ideas. In the emergence stage, the group begins to move toward choosing a single solution. In the reinforcement stage, members endorse the group's decision.

Groups use a wide variety of discussion formats when solving problems. Some use parliamentary procedure to govern decision-making procedures. Others use moderated panel discussions, symposia, or forums. The best format depends on the nature of the problem and the characteristics of the group.

Because face-to-face meetings can be time consuming and difficult to arrange, computer-mediated communication can be a good alternative for some group tasks. Some group work can be handled via computer or teleconferencing, in which members communicate in real time over digital networks. Other tasks can be handled via asynchronous discussions, in which members exchange messages at their convenience. Mediated meetings provide a record of discussion, and they can make it easier for normally quiet members to participate, but they can take more time, and they lack the nonverbal richness of face-to-face conversation. Given the pros and cons of mediated meetings, smart communicators should give thoughtful consideration about when to use this approach.

Groups stand the best chance of developing effective solutions to problems if they begin their work by identifying the problem and recognizing the hidden needs of individual members. Their next step is to analyze the problem, including identification of forces both favoring and blocking progress. Only at this point should the group begin to develop possible solutions, taking care not to stifle creativity by evaluating any of them prematurely. During the implementation phase of the solution, the group should monitor the situation carefully and make any necessary changes in its plan.

Smart members will avoid some common dangers that threaten a group's effectiveness. They will make sure to get the information they need, without succumbing to overload. They will make sure that participation is equal by encouraging the contributions of quiet members and by keeping more talkative people on track. They will guard against groupthink by minimizing pressure on members to conform for the sake of harmony or approval.

## Key Terms

**brainstorming** A method for creatively generating ideas in groups by minimizing criticism and encouraging a large quantity of ideas without regard to their workability or ownership by individual members. *p. 313*

**breakout groups** A strategy used when the number of members is too large for effective discussion. Subgroups simultaneously address an issue and then report back to the group at large. *p. 307*

**cohesiveness** The totality of forces that causes members to feel themselves part of a group and makes them want to remain in that group. *p. 302*

**conflict stage** A stage in problem-solving groups when members openly defend their positions and question those of others. *p. 304*

**consensus** Agreement among group members about a decision. *p. 315*

**dialogue** A process in which people let go of the notion that their ideas are more correct or superior to others' and instead seek to understand an issue from many different perspectives. *p. 308*

**emergence stage** A stage in problem solving when the group moves from conflict toward a single solution. *p. 306*

**focus group** A procedure used in market research by sponsoring organizations to survey potential users or the public at large regarding a new product or idea. *p. 307*

**force field analysis** A method of problem analysis that identifies the forces contributing to resolution of the problem and the forces that inhibit its resolution. *p. 312*

**forum** A discussion format in which audience members are invited to add their comments to those of the official discussants. *p. 308*

**groupthink** A group's collective striving for unanimity that discourages realistic appraisals of alternatives to its chosen decision. *p. 319*

**information overload** The decline in efficiency that occurs when the rate of complexity of material is too great to manage. *p. 317*

**information underload** The decline in efficiency that occurs when there is a shortage of the information that is necessary to operate effectively. *p. 317*

**nominal group technique** A method for including the ideas of all group members in a problem-solving session. *p. 313*

**orientation stage** A stage in problem-solving groups when members become familiar with one another's position and tentatively volunteer their own. *p. 304*

**panel discussion** A discussion format in which participants consider a topic more or less conversationally, without formal procedural rules. Panel discussions may be facilitated by a moderator. *p. 307*

**parliamentary procedure** A problem-solving method in which specific rules govern the way issues may be discussed and decisions made. *p. 307*

**problem census** A technique used to equalize participation in groups when the goal is to identify important issues or problems. Members first put ideas on cards, which are then compiled by a leader to generate a comprehensive statement of the issue or problem. *p. 307*

**reinforcement stage** A stage in problem-solving groups when members endorse the decision they have made. *p. 306*

**symposium** A discussion format in which participants divide the topic in a manner that allows each member to deliver in-depth information without interruption. *p. 308*

## Check Your Understanding

1. Think of a challenge you've faced while belonging to a group (at work, with roommates or family, on a team, etc.). Considering the questions on page 301, evaluate whether it's better to tackle the problem collectively or to let members deal with it individually.

2. Assess the level of cohesiveness on a 1 (low) to 10 (high) scale in a group to which you currently belong or have belonged in the past. Using the factors on pages 303–304, describe the reasons for the cohesiveness level you identified, and develop recommendations for moving the group's cohesiveness toward the optimal level.

3. Imagine you and five other students have just been asked to engage in a team project to benefit a nonprofit organization of the team's choice. What problem-solving formats (review the options on pages 310–315) and decision-making methods (see pages 315–317) would you be most likely to use while deciding which organization to choose and what your project might involve? If we expanded the project to include the entire class (let's say 30 people), would your choice of formats change? Why or why not? How might your communication strategies differ if members meet virtually rather than in person?

4. Teamwork carries some inherent risks. Explain what strategies you would adopt in one of the groups you've identified above to make sure members get the right amount of information, that everyone participates equally, and that the team avoids groupthink.

## Activities

1. **When to Use Group Problem Solving** Explain which of the following tasks would best be managed by a group:

   1. Collecting and editing a list of films illustrating communication principles.

   2. Deciding what the group will eat for lunch at a one-day meeting.

   3. Choosing the topic for a class project.

   4. Finding which of six companies had the lowest auto insurance rates.

   5. Designing a survey to measure community attitudes toward a subsidy for local artists.

2. **The Pros and Cons of Cohesiveness** Based on the information on pages 303–304 and your own experiences, give examples of groups who meet each of the following descriptions:

   1. A level of cohesiveness so low that it interferes with productivity

   2. An optimal level of cohesiveness

   3. A level of cohesiveness so high that it interferes with productivity

   4. For your answers to 1 and 3, offer advice on how the level of cohesiveness could be adjusted to improve productivity.

   5. Are there ever situations in which maximizing cohesiveness is more important than maximizing productivity? Explain your answer, supporting it with examples.

3. **Stages in Group Development** Identify a problem-solving group, either from your personal experience or from a book or film. Analyze the group's approach to problem solving. Does it follow the cyclical model pictured in Figure 10-1? Does it follow a more linear approach? Or does the group follow no recognizable pattern at all?

4. **Increasing Group Creativity** You can improve your skill at increasing creativity in group discussions by trying the approaches described in *Understanding Human Communication*. Your group should begin by choosing one of the following problems:

   1. How can out-of-pocket student expenses (e.g., books, transportation) be decreased?

   2. How can the textbook you are using in this (or any other) class be improved?

   3. How could your class group (legally) earn the greatest amount of money between now and the end of the term?

   4. What strategies can be used effectively when you are confronted with employer discrimination or harassment? (Assume you want to keep the job.)

   5. Imagine that your group has been hired to develop a way of improving the course registration system at your institution. What three recommendations will be most effective?

   6. Choose either brainstorming or the nominal group technique to develop possible solutions to your chosen problem. Explain why you chose the method. Under what conditions would the other method be more appropriate?

5. **Choosing the Best Decision-Making Approach** Describe which of the decision-making approaches listed on pages 315–317 would be most appropriate in each of the following situations. Explain why your recommended approach is the best one for this situation.

   1. Four apartment mates must decide how to handle household chores.

2. A group of hikers and their experienced guide become lost in a snowstorm and debate whether to try to find their way to safety or to pitch camp and wait for the weather to clear.

3. After trying unsuccessfully to reach consensus, the partners in a new business venture cannot agree on the best name for their enterprise.

4. A 25-member ski club is looking for the cheapest airfare and lodging for its winter trip.

5. A passenger falls overboard during an afternoon sail on your friend's 20-foot sailboat. The wind is carrying the boat away from the passenger.

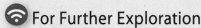 For Further Exploration

**For more resources about group problem solving, see the *Understanding Human Communication* website at www .oup.com/us/adler.** There you will find a variety of resources: "Media Room" clips from popular films and television shows to further illustrate important concepts, a list of books and articles, links to descriptions of feature films and television shows at the *Now Playing* website, study aids, and a self-test to check your understanding of the material in this chapter.

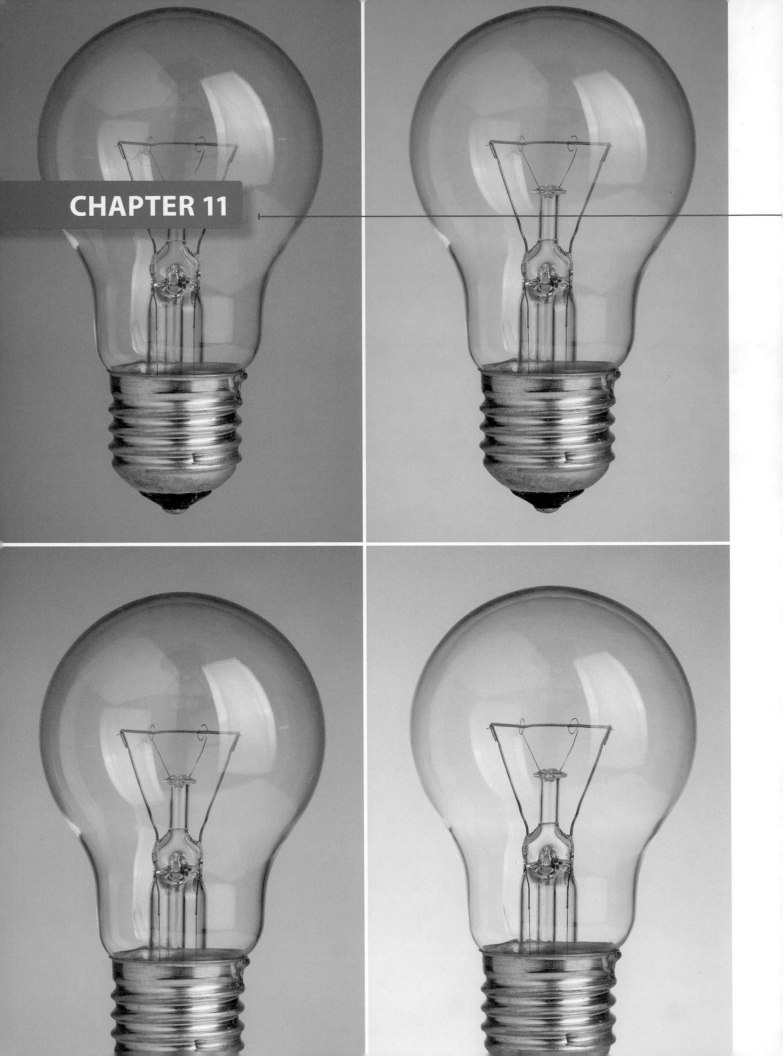

## CHAPTER 11

# Preparing and Presenting Your Speech

**11**

## Chapter Outline

### LEARNING OBJECTIVES

1 Choose an effective speaking topic.

2 Formulate a purpose statement and thesis statement that will help you develop that topic.

3 Analyze both the audience and occasion in any speaking situation.

4 Gather information on your chosen topic from a variety of sources.

5 Overcome debilitative stage fright.

6 Choose the most effective type of delivery for a particular speech.

Diane Sawyer famously dubbed Adora Svitak a "tiny literary giant." Svitak published her first book at age 7, and within 5 years was a well-known public speaker. Her TED talk, "What Adults Can Learn from Kids," which she presented at age 12, has been viewed more than 2 million times. The demand for her public appearances is so great that Svitak's parents created a TV studio in their basement, from which she speaks daily to audiences (mostly students and teachers) around the world. Companies such as Microsoft pay her $10,000 per speaking engagement.

Svitak's speaking skills arise from several factors. One is that she loves demonstrating her message—that children have more to offer than adults usually give them credit for. Another is that she does her homework. Svitak doesn't just propose the opinion that children can make a difference. She offers well-researched examples. A third strength is that Svitak handles words with great care, choosing and arranging them in ways that are artistic and powerful.

It's clear that Svitak knows her stuff when it comes to public speaking. Her success is no accident but rather the result of enthusiasm, hard work, practice, and a desire to connect with her audiences. Perhaps the reason she feels comfortable with large audiences is that she believes in mutual respect. She admires adults but does not feel intimidated by them. In fact, in the nicest tones possible, she tells adults to listen more. "It shouldn't just be a teacher at the head of the classroom telling students 'do this, do that,'" she maintains. "The students should teach their teachers. Learning between grown-ups and kids should be reciprocal."

Watch Svitak's talk by typing her name into the search window at www.ted.com. Then consider how well she displays the principles of public speaking in this chapter and the ones that follow. If you're like most people, you'll agree that we have a lot to learn from Adora Svitak.

*Adora Svitak chose to speak about the role of children in an adult society because she feels strongly about that topic. Imagine a topic that you feel so strongly about that you would talk about it in public without it being a speech assignment. Now think about these three questions:*

- What is your objective in speaking about this topic?

- What is your main idea?

- What information do you need to gather to support that idea?

You don't have to be a child prodigy like Adora Svitak to face the prospect of giving a public speech. In fact, even if you never took a course in which speech giving was required, you would almost certainly face the challenge of giving a speech at some point. It might be a job-related presentation, or something more personal, such as a wedding toast or a eulogy. You might find yourself speaking in favor of a civic-improvement project in your hometown or trying to persuade members of your club to deal more effectively with global problems like war, religious strife, or environmental threats.

Despite the potential benefits of effective speeches, many people view the prospect of standing before an audience with the same enthusiasm they have for a trip to the dentist or the tax auditor. In fact, giving a speech seems to be one of the most anxiety-producing things we can do: When asked to list their common fears, research subjects mention public speaking more often than they do insects, heights, accidents, and even death.[1]

There's no guarantee that the following chapters will make you love the idea of giving speeches, but we can promise that the information these chapters contain will give you the tools to design and deliver remarks that will be clear, interesting, and effective. And it's very likely that, as your skill grows, your confidence will too. This chapter will deal with your first steps in that process, through careful speech planning.

# Getting Started

Your first tasks are generally choosing a topic, determining your purpose, and finding information.

## Choosing Your Topic

The first question many student speakers face is, "What should I talk about?" When you need to choose a topic, you should try to pick one that is right for you, your audience, and the situation. You should try to choose a topic that interests you and that your audience will care about. Decide on your topic as early as possible. Those who wait until the last possible moment usually find that they don't have enough time to research, outline, and practice their speech.

## Defining Your Purpose

No one gives a speech—or expresses *any* kind of message—without having a reason to do so. Your first step in focusing your speech is to formulate a clear and precise statement of that purpose.

## Writing a Purpose Statement

Your **purpose statement** should be expressed in the form of a complete sentence that describes your **specific purpose**—exactly what you want your speech to accomplish. It should stem from your **general purpose**, which might be to inform, persuade, or entertain. Beyond that, though, there are three criteria for an effective purpose statement:

① **A purpose statement should be result oriented.** Having a *result orientation* means that your purpose is focused on the outcome you want to accomplish with your audience members. For example, if you were giving an informative talk on the high cost of college, this would be an inadequate purpose statement:

> *My purpose is to tell my audience about high college costs.*

As that statement is worded, your purpose is "to tell" an audience something, which suggests that the speech could be successful even if no one listened! A result-oriented purpose statement should refer to the response you want from your audience: It should tell what the audience members will know or be able to do after listening to your speech.

② **A purpose statement should be specific.** To be effective, a purpose statement should be worded specifically, with enough details so that you would be able to measure or test your audience, after your speech, to see if you had achieved your purpose. In the example given earlier, simply "knowing about high college costs" is too vague; you need something more specific, such as:

*After listening to my speech, my audience will be able to reduce college costs.*

This is an improvement, but it can be made still better by applying a third criterion:

③ **A purpose statement should be realistic.** It's fine to be ambitious, but you need to design a purpose that has a reasonable chance of success. You can appreciate the importance of having a realistic goal by looking at some unrealistic ones, such as "My purpose is to convince my audience to make federal budget deficits illegal." Unless your audience happens to be a joint session of Congress, it won't have the power to change U.S. fiscal policy. But any audience can write its congressional representatives or sign a petition. In your speech on college costs, it would be impossible for your audience members to change the entire structure of college financing. So a better purpose statement for this speech might sound something like this:

*After listening to my speech, my audience will be able to list four simple steps to lower their college expenses.*

Consider the following sets of purpose statements:

| LESS EFFECTIVE | MORE EFFECTIVE |
| --- | --- |
| To talk about professional wrestling (not receiver oriented) | After listening to my speech, my audience will understand that kids who imitate professional wrestlers can be seriously hurt. |
| To tell my audience about gun control (not specific) | After my speech, the audience will be able to list five ways to keep guns out of the hands of criminals. |

You probably won't include your purpose statement word-for-word in your actual speech. Rather than being aimed at your listeners, a specific purpose statement usually is a tool to keep you focused on your goal as you plan your speech.

## Stating Your Thesis

> Describe someone you consider an effective public speaker. This could be someone you know personally, such as a teacher, or someone you know only through the media, such as a celebrity or other public figure. What is it about this person that makes him or her effective?

After you have defined the purpose, you are ready to start planning what is arguably the most important sentence in your entire speech. The **thesis statement** tells your listeners the central idea of your speech. It is the one idea that you want your audience to remember after it has forgotten everything else you had to say. The thesis statement for a speech about winning in small claims court might be worded like this:

*Arguing a case on your own in small claims court is a simple, five-step process that can give you the same results you would achieve with a lawyer.*

Unlike your purpose statement, your thesis statement is almost always delivered directly to your audience. The thesis statement is usually formulated later in the speech-making process, after you have done some research on your topic. The progression from topic to purpose to thesis is, therefore, another focusing process, as you can see in the following example:

*Topic:* Organ donation

*Specific Purpose:* After listening to my speech, audience members will recognize the importance of organ donation and will sign an organ donor's card for themselves.

*Thesis:* Because not enough of us choose to become organ donors, thousands of us needlessly die every year. You can help prevent this needless dying.

# Analyzing the Speaking Situation

There are two components to analyze in any speaking situation: the audience and the occasion. To be successful, every choice you make in putting together your speech—your purpose, topic, and all the material you use to develop your speech—must be appropriate to both of these components.

## The Listener: Audience Analysis

**Audience analysis** involves identifying and adapting your remarks to the most pertinent characteristics of your listeners.

**Audience Purpose**  Just as you have a purpose for speaking, audience members have a reason for gathering. Sometimes virtually all the members of your audience will have the same, obvious goal. Expectant parents at a natural childbirth class are all seeking a healthy delivery, and people attending an investment seminar are looking for ways to increase their net worth.

In the film *Flight*, pilot Whip Whitaker (Denzel Washington) tries to salvage his career after managing a successful crash landing by convincing authorities that he can overcome his addictions. How might he define the purpose and thesis of his speech?

There are other times, however, when audience purpose can't be so easily defined. In some instances, different listeners will have different goals, some of which might not be apparent to the speaker. Consider a church congregation, for example. Whereas most members might listen to a sermon with the hope of applying religious principles to their lives, a few might be interested in being entertained or in merely appearing pious. In the same way, the listeners in your speech class probably have a variety of motives for attending. Becoming aware of as many of these motives as possible will help you predict what will interest them. Observing audience demographics helps you make that prediction.

**Demographics**  **Demographics** are characteristics of your audience that can be categorized, such as cultural differences, age, gender, group membership, number of people, and so on. Demographic characteristics might affect your speech planning in a number of ways.[2] For example:

- **Cultural diversity.** Do audience members differ in terms of race, religion, or national origin? The guideline here might be, *Do not exclude or offend any portion of your audience on the basis of cultural differences.* If there is a dominant cultural group represented, you might decide to speak to it, but remember that the point is to analyze, not stereotype, your audience. If you talk down to any segment of your listeners, you have probably stereotyped them.

  > cultural idiom
  > **talk down to:**
  > speak to in a condescending way

- **Gender.** Although masculine and feminine stereotypes are declining, it is still important to think about how gender can affect the way you choose and approach a topic. Every speech teacher has a horror story about a student getting up in front of a class composed primarily, but not entirely, of men and speaking on a subject such as "Picking Up Babes."

  > cultural idiom
  > **picking up babes:**
  > offensive term for making the acquaintance of women or girls with sexual purposes in mind

- **Age.** Our interests vary and change with our age. These differences may run relatively deep; our approach to literature, films, finance, health, and long-term success may change dramatically over just a few years, perhaps from graphic novels to serious literature, from punk to classical music, or from hip-hop to epic poetry.

- **Group membership.** Groups generally form around shared interests among the members. By examining the groups to which they belong, you can surmise audience members' political leanings (Campus Reform Party, College Democrats, Young Republicans), religious beliefs (Catholic Youth

Organization, Hillel, or Muslim Students' Association), or occupation (Bartenders Union or National Communication Association). Group membership is often an important consideration in college classes. Consider the difference between a "typical" college day class and one that meets in the evening. At many colleges the evening students are generally older and tend to belong to civic groups, church clubs, and the local chamber of commerce. Daytime students are more likely to belong to sororities and fraternities, sports clubs, and social action groups.

> cultural idiom
**stuffy:**
impersonal, not relating to the audience

- **Number of people.** Topic appropriateness varies with the size of an audience. With a small audience you can be less formal and more intimate; you can, for example, talk more about your feelings and personal experiences. If you gave a speech before 5 people as impersonally as if they were a standing-room-only crowd in a lecture hall, they would probably find you stuffy. On the other hand, if you talked to 300 people about your unhappy childhood, you'd probably make them uncomfortable.

You have to decide which demographics of your audience are important for a particular speech. For example, when Sneha Polisetti, a student at James Madison University in Virginia, gave a speech on the loss of Native American culture, she knew she had to broaden the appeal of her topic beyond the small demographic referred to in her speech. She adapted to her broader audience this way:

> When the Native American cultures that are tied closely to America's story are lost, we all lose a part of our identity and history, whether we're Native Americans or not.[3]

These five demographic characteristics are important examples, but the list goes on. Other demographic characteristics that might be important in a college classroom include the following:

- Educational level
- Economic status
- Hometown
- Year in school
- Major subject
- Ethnic background

A final factor to consider in audience analysis concerns members' attitudes, beliefs, and values.

---

**Ethical Challenge**

## Adapting to Speaking Situations

How much adaptation is ethical? How far would you go to be effective with an audience? Try the following exercise with your classmates.

1. Prepare, in advance, three index cards: one with a possible topic for a speech, one with a possible audience, and one with a possible occasion.

2. Form groups of four members each. Mark the back of each card with "A" for "audience," "T" for "topic," or "O" for "occasion," and turn the cards face down.

3. Take one card from each of the other members.

4. Turn the cards over. For each set, decide which characteristics of the audience, topic, and occasion would most likely affect the way the speech was developed.

5. Discuss the adaptation that would be necessary in each situation and the role ethics would play in determining how far you would go.

**Attitudes, Beliefs, and Values**    Audience members' feelings about you, your subject, and your intentions for them are central issues in audience analysis. One way to approach these issues is through a consideration of attitudes, beliefs, and values.[4] Attitudes, beliefs, and values reside in human consciousness like layers of an onion (see Figure 11-1). **Attitudes** lie closest to the surface. They reflect a predisposition to view you or your topic in a favorable or unfavorable way. **Beliefs** lie a little deeper and deal with the truth of something. **Values** are deeply rooted feelings about a concept's inherent worth or worthiness. You can begin to appreciate the usefulness of these concepts by considering an example. Suppose you were a dentist trying to persuade a group of patients to floss their teeth more often. Consider how audience analysis would help you design the most promising approach:

> *Attitudes.* How do your listeners feel about the importance of dental hygiene? If they recognize its importance, you can proceed confidently, knowing they'll probably want to hear what you have to say. On the other hand, if they are vaguely disgusted by even thinking about the topic, you will need to begin by making them want to listen.
>
> *Beliefs.* Does your audience accept the relationship between regular flossing and dental health? Or do you need to inform them about the consequences of neglecting this daily ritual?
>
> *Values.* Which underlying values matter most to your listeners: Health? Attractiveness? Career success? The approach you'll use will depend on the answer to these questions.

*"I'll tell you what this election is about. It's about homework, and pitiful allowances, and having to clean your room. It's also about candy, and ice cream, and staying up late."*

Experts in audience analysis, such as professional speechwriters, often try to concentrate on values. As one team of researchers pointed out, "values have the advantage of being comparatively small in number, and owing to their abstract nature, are more likely to be shared by large numbers of people."[5] Stable American values include the ideas of good citizenship, a strong work ethic, tolerance of differing political views, individualism, and justice for all. Michael Kelley, a student at Kansas State University, appealed to his audience's values when he wanted to make the point that unemployment discrimination was unfair:

> Jobless discrimination occurs when a company or business refuses to employ an individual unless they are already employed elsewhere. This should alarm us for several reasons. The Bureau of Labor Statistics, as of April 6, 2012, points out that there are 5.3 million Americans who have been unemployed for seven months or more because of the recession. It's not fair to discriminate against them. . . . We need to make jobless discrimination just as illegal as refusing to hire someone because of their sex, race or religion.[6]

Kelley pointed out that discriminating against unemployed people was basically unfair; his analysis had suggested that the value of fairness would be important to his audience. You can often make an inference about audience members' attitudes by recognizing the beliefs and values they are likely to hold. In this example, Kelley knew that his audience, made up mostly of idealistic college students and professors, would dislike the idea of unfair discrimination.

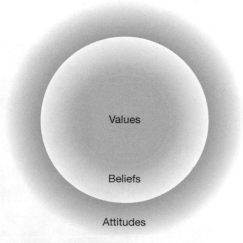

Values

Beliefs

Attitudes

**FIGURE 11-1  Structure of Values, Beliefs, and Attitudes**

ON YOUR FEET

*Attitudes, Beliefs, and Values*
Find a persuasive appeal in an advertisement, newspaper editorial, or another source. Identify an attitude or value that the source of the message is appealing to. Explain why, in your opinion, this appeal is or is not effective.

The analysis of hidden psychological states can be extremely helpful in audience analysis. For example, a religious group might hold the value of "obeying God's word." For some fundamentalists this might lead to the belief, based on their religious training, that women are not meant to perform the same functions in society as men. This, in turn, might lead to the attitude that women ought not to pursue careers as firefighters, police officers, or construction workers.

You can also make a judgment about one attitude your audience members hold based on your knowledge of other attitudes they hold. If your audience is made up of undergraduates who have a positive attitude toward liberation movements, it is a good bet they also have a positive attitude toward civil rights and ecology. If they have a negative attitude toward collegiate sports, they may also have a negative attitude toward fraternities and sororities. This should suggest not only some appropriate topics for each audience but also ways that those topics could be developed.

## The Occasion

The second phase in analyzing a speaking situation focuses on the occasion. The occasion of a speech is determined by the circumstances surrounding it. Three of these circumstances are time, place, and audience expectations.

**Time**  Your speech occupies an interval of time that is surrounded by other events. For example, other speeches might be presented before or after yours, or comments might be made that set a certain tone or mood. External events such as elections, the start of a new semester, or even the weather can color the occasion in one way or another. The date on which you give your speech might have some historical significance. If that historical significance relates in some way to your topic, you can use it to help build audience interest.

The time available for your speech is also an essential consideration. You should choose a topic that is broad enough to say something worthwhile but brief enough to fit your limits. "Wealth," for example, might be an inherently interesting topic to some college students, but it would be difficult to cover such a broad topic in a 10-minute speech and still say anything significant. However, a topic like "How to Make Extra Money in Your Spare Time" could conceivably be covered in 10 minutes in enough depth to make it worthwhile. All speeches have limits, whether or not they are explicitly stated. If you are invited to say a few words, and you present a few volumes, you might not be invited back.

**Place**  Your speech also occupies a physical space. The beauty or squalor of your surroundings and the noise or stuffiness of the room should all be taken into consideration. These physical surroundings can be referred to in your speech if appropriate. If you were talking about world poverty, for example, you could compare your surroundings to those that might be found in a poorer country.

**Audience Expectations**  Finally, your speech is surrounded by audience expectations. A speech presented in a college class, or a TED talk like Adora Svitak's (which we mentioned at the beginning of this chapter), is usually expected to reflect a high level of thought and intelligence. This doesn't necessarily mean that it has to be boring or humorless; wit and humor are, after all, indicative of intelligence. But it does mean that you have to put a little more effort into your presentation than if you were discussing the same subject with friends over coffee.

Former Alaska governor Sarah Palin delights in skewering political figures and viewpoints that conflict with her conservative beliefs and values. This motivates her supporters and antagonizes those who disagree with her. How successful is Palin at reaching her target audience? How can you craft your remarks to appeal to the attitudes, beliefs, and values of your most important listeners?

In the movie *Bridesmaids*, Annie (Kristen Wiig) and Helen (Rose Byrne) try to outdo each other with dueling speeches (and breaking into song) instead of offering traditional engagement party toasts. Have you ever experienced a speech that didn't fit the occasion?

When you are considering the occasion of your speech, it pays to remember that every occasion is unique. Although there are obvious differences among the occasions of a college class, a church sermon, and a bachelor party "roast," there are also many subtle differences that will apply only to the circumstances of each unique event.

> cultural idiom

**bachelor party:**
a men-only gathering of the groom and his friends just prior to his wedding

**roast:**
an entertaining program in which the guest of honor is teased in an affectionate manner

# Gathering Information

This discussion about planning a speech purpose and analyzing the speech situation makes it apparent that it takes time, interest, and knowledge to develop a topic well. Setting aside a block of time to reflect on your own ideas is essential. However, you will also need to gather information from outside sources.

By this time you are probably familiar with both web searches and library research as forms of gathering information. Sometimes, however, speakers overlook interviewing, personal observation, and survey research as equally effective methods of gathering information. Let's review all these methods here and perhaps provide a new perspective on one or more of them.

### Online Research

The ease of using search engines like Google has made them the popular favorite for speech research. But students are sometimes so grateful to have found a website dealing with their topic that they forget to evaluate it. Like any other written sources you would use, websites should be accurate and rational. Beyond that, there are three specific criteria that you can use to evaluate the quality of a website. They are listed in the checklist on page 335.

In the case of some special search engines, like Google Scholar, the criteria of credibility, objectivity, and currency will be practically guaranteed. However, these guidelines are especially important when accessing information from Wikipedia, the popular online encyclopedia. Because anyone can edit a Wikipedia article at any time, many professors forbid the use of it as a primary resource. Others allow

@Work

## Sample Analysis of a Speaking Situation

**Audience:** Employees in the Production Department of my company

**Situation:** Training session on sexual harassment

Management has realized that our company is at risk of being slapped with a harassment lawsuit. The most likely offenders are several "good old boys" who have worked in the Production Department a long time. They are really nice guys, and I know they view their jokes and comments as good-natured fun and not harassment. On the other hand, several female employees have complained about being offended by these men.

One of my duties as an intern in the Human Resources Department of my company is to share the latest information on sexual harassment with employees. My bosses know that this topic has been covered in my classes, and they decided I should pass it along.

**Purpose:** After I am finished speaking, I want audience members to view sexual harassment as a legitimate concern and to be careful to avoid communicating in a way that might be perceived as harassing.

**Analysis:** This is a tricky situation for me: First of all, these guys will be a captive audience, forced to listen to a subject that they find annoying. Also, I am younger than anyone in my audience, and I'm a woman. In fact, I've been the target of some of the behavior I'm being asked to discourage! There's a strong risk that the men who are the target of my remarks won't take me seriously, so I have to change their attitude about the subject and me.

I know that scolding and threatening these men would be a big mistake. Even if they didn't object out loud, they would probably regard me as some sort of chip-on-the-shoulder feminist and consider the advice I offered as "politically correct" and out of touch with the way the real world operates.

To avoid this sort of negative reaction, I need to separate myself from the law that they dislike, taking the position of sharing with them "here's what I've learned about how it works." I might even give them a few examples of harassment suits that I think were frivolous, so we can agree that some people are much too sensitive. That common ground will help put us on the same side. Then I can emphasize that they don't have to agree with the law to follow it. I'll tell stories of people like them who suffered as targets of harassment suits, pointing out that even an unfair accusation of harassment could make all of our lives miserable. My basic argument will be that potentially harassing behavior "isn't worth it."

I also hope to use my age and gender as advantages. A couple of the men have told me that they have daughters my age. I could ask the group to imagine how they would feel if their daughters were the targets of suggestive comments and sexual jokes. I'll tell them that I know how angry and protective my dad would feel, and I'll tell them that I know that, as good fathers, they'd feel the same way. I could also ask them to think about how they would feel if their wives, sisters, or mothers were the targets of jokes that made those women feel uncomfortable.

I don't think any speech will totally reverse attitudes that were built over these men's lifetimes, but I do think that getting on their side will be much more effective than labeling them as insensitive sexist pigs and threatening them with lawsuits. ●

Wikipedia to be used for general information and inspiration. Most will allow its use when articles have references to external sources (whether online or not) and the student reads the references and checks whether they really do support what the article says.

However you use the Web, remember that it is a good addition to, but *not* a substitute for, library research. Library experts help you make sense of and determine the validity of the information you find. And a library can be a great environment for concentration, a place of quiet with minimum distractions that is rare in our media age.

Consider the following three criteria when choosing a website for online research:

☐ **Credibility.** Anyone can establish a website, so it is important to evaluate where your information is coming from. Who wrote the page? Anonymous sources should not be used. If the sources *are* listed, are their credentials listed? What institution publishes the document? Remember that a handsome site design doesn't guarantee high-quality information, but misspellings and grammatical mistakes are good signs of low quality.

☐ **Objectivity.** What opinions (if any) are expressed by the author? The domain names .edu, .gov, .org, or .net are generally preferable to .com, because if the page is a mask for advertising, the information might be biased.

☐ **Currency.** When was the page produced? When was it updated? How up-to-date are the links? If any of the links are dead, the information might not be current.

## Library Research

Libraries, like people, tend to be unique. Although many of your library's resources will be available online through your school's website, it can be extremely rewarding to get to know your library in person, to see what kind of special collections and services it offers, and just to find out where everything is. There are, however, a few resources that are common to most libraries, including the library catalog, reference works, periodicals, nonprint materials, and databases.

**The Library Catalog**    The library catalog is an ancient and noble information-storing device. Once housed in long rows of oak drawers, catalogs are now computerized, but they remain your key to all the books and other materials in the library. Each work is filed according to subject, author, and title, so you can look for general topics as well as for specific books and authors.

**Reference Works**    Reference works will also be listed in the library catalog. There are encyclopedias galore, even specialized ones such as *The Historical Dictionary of American Slang* and *The Encyclopedia of American History*, and you can collect a lot of facts in a short time in the reference room. Reference works are good for uncovering basic information, definitions, descriptions, and sources for further investigation.

**Periodicals**    Magazines, journals, and newspapers are good resources for finding recently published material on interesting topics. Specialized indexes such as *Psychological Abstracts* can be used to find articles in specific fields, and newspaper indexes such as *The New York Times Index* can be used to find online newspaper articles. Periodicals are a good source of high-interest, up-to-date information on your topic.

**Nonprint Materials**    Most libraries are also treasuries of nonprint and audio-visual materials. Films, records, tapes, and videotapes can be used not only as research tools but also as aids during your presentation.

**Databases**    Libraries have access to databases that are not available to home users without hefty subscription fees. **Databases** are computerized collections of highly credible information from a wide variety of sources. One popular collection of databases is Lexis-Nexis, which contains millions of articles from news services, magazines, scholarly journals, conference papers, books, law journals, and other sources. Other popular databases include ProQuest, Factiva, and Academic Search Premier, and there are dozens of specialized databases, such as Communication and Mass Media Complete. Database searches are slightly different from web searches; they generally don't respond well to long strings of terms or searches worded as questions. With databases it is best to use one or two key terms with a connector such as AND, OR, or NOT.[7] Once you learn this technique and a few other rules (perhaps with a librarian's help), you will be able to locate dozens of articles on your topic in just a few minutes.

## Interviewing

An information-gathering interview allows you to view your topic from an expert's perspective, to take advantage of that expert's experience, research, and thought. You can also use an interview to stimulate your own thinking. Often the interview will save you hours of Internet or library research and allow you to present ideas that you could not have uncovered any other way. And because an interview is an interaction with an expert, many ideas that otherwise might be unclear can become more understandable through questions and answers. Interviews can be conducted face-to-face, by telephone, or by e-mail. If you do use an interview for research, you might want to read the section on that type of interview in the appendix.

## Survey Research

One advantage of **survey research**—the distribution of questionnaires for people to respond to—is that it can give you up-to-date answers concerning "the way things are" for a specific audience. For example, if you handed out questionnaires a week or so before presenting a speech on the possible dangers of body piercing, you could present information like this in your speech:

> According to a survey I conducted last week, 90 percent of the students in this class believe that body piercing is basically safe. Only 10 percent are familiar with the scarring and injury that can result from this practice. Two of you, in fact, have experienced serious infections from body piercing: one from a pierced tongue and one from a simple pierced ear.

That statement would be of immediate interest to your audience members because *they* were the ones who were surveyed. Another advantage of conducting your own survey is that it is one of the best ways to find out about your audience: It is, in fact, *the* best way to collect the demographic data mentioned earlier. The one disadvantage of conducting your own survey is that, if it is used as evidence, it might not have as much credibility as published evidence found in the library. But the advantages seem to outweigh the disadvantages of survey research in public speaking.

No matter how you gather your information, remember that it is the *quality* rather than the quantity of the research that is most important. The key is to determine carefully what type of research will answer the questions you need to have answered. Sometimes only one type of research will be necessary; at other times every type mentioned here will have to be used. Generally, you will collect far more information than you'll use in your speech, but the winnowing process will ensure that the research you do use is of high quality.

Along with improving the quality of what you say, effective research will also minimize the anxiety of actually giving a speech. Let's take a close look at that form of anxiety.

# Managing Communication Apprehension

The terror that strikes the hearts of so many beginning speakers is commonly known as *stage fright* or *speech anxiety* and is called *communication apprehension* by communication scholars.[8] Whatever term you choose, the important point to realize is that fear about speaking can be managed in a way that works for you rather than against you.

## Facilitative and Debilitative Communication Apprehension

Although communication apprehension is a very real problem for many speakers, it is definitely a problem that can be overcome. Interestingly enough, the first step in feeling less apprehensive about speaking is to realize that a certain amount of nervousness is not only natural but also facilitative. That is, **facilitative communication apprehension** is a factor that can help improve your performance. Just as totally relaxed actors or musicians aren't likely to perform at the top of their potential, speakers think more rapidly and express themselves more energetically when their level of tension is moderate.

It is only when the level of anxiety is intense that it becomes **debilitative**, inhibiting effective self-expression. Intense fear causes trouble in two ways. First, the strong emotion keeps you from thinking clearly.[9] This has been shown to be a problem even in the preparation process: Students who are highly anxious about giving a speech will find the preliminary steps, including research and organization, to be more difficult.[10] Second, intense fear leads to an urge to do something, anything, to make the problem go away. This urge to escape often causes a speaker to speed up delivery, which results in a rapid, almost machine-gun style. As you can imagine, this boost in speaking rate leads to even more mistakes, which only add to the speaker's anxiety. Thus, a relatively small amount of nervousness can begin to feed on itself until it grows into a serious problem.

## Sources of Debilitative Communication Apprehension

Before we describe how to manage debilitative communication apprehension, let's consider why people are afflicted with the problem in the first place.[11]

**Previous Negative Experience**   People often feel apprehensive about speech giving because of unpleasant past experiences. Most of us are uncomfortable doing *anything* in public, especially if it is a form of performance in which our talents and abilities are being evaluated. An unpleasant experience in one type of performance can cause you to expect that a future similar situation will also be unpleasant.[12] These expectations can be realized through the self-fulfilling prophecies discussed in Chapter 3. A traumatic failure at an earlier speech and low self-esteem from critical parents during childhood are common examples of experiences that can cause later communication apprehension.

You might object to the idea that past experiences cause communication apprehension. After all, not everyone who has bungled a speech or had critical parents is debilitated in the future. To understand why some people are affected more strongly than others by past experiences, we need to consider another cause of communication apprehension.

**Irrational Thinking**   Cognitive psychologists argue that it is not events that cause people to feel nervous but rather the beliefs they have about those events. Certain irrational beliefs leave people feeling unnecessarily apprehensive. Psychologist

Actress Kim Basinger had such severe communication apprehension as a child that her parents had her tested for autism. The HBO film *Panic: A Film about Coping* features commentary from Basinger about her struggles with anxiety. How might Basinger have benefited from the advice in these pages? How can you use this advice to feel less anxious?

Albert Ellis lists several such beliefs, or examples of **irrational thinking**, which we will call "fallacies" because of their illogical nature.[13]

- **Catastrophic failure.** People who succumb to the **fallacy of catastrophic failure** operate on the assumption that if something bad can happen, it probably will. Their thoughts before a speech resemble these:

  "As soon as I stand up to speak, I'll forget everything I wanted to say."

  "Everyone will think my ideas are stupid."

  "Somebody will probably laugh at me."

  Although it is naive to imagine that all your speeches will be totally successful, it is equally naive to assume they will all fail miserably. One way to escape the fallacy of catastrophic failure is to take a more realistic look at the situation. Would your audience members really hoot you off the stage? Will they really think your ideas are stupid? Even if you did forget your remarks for a moment, would the results be a genuine disaster? It helps to remember that nervousness is more apparent to the speaker than to the audience.[14] Beginning public speakers, when congratulated for their poise during a speech, are apt to say, "Are you kidding? I was dying up there."

- **Perfection.** Speakers who succumb to the **fallacy of perfection** expect themselves to behave flawlessly. Whereas such a standard of perfection might serve as a target and a source of inspiration (like the desire to make a hole in one while golfing), it is totally unrealistic to expect that you will write and deliver a perfect speech, especially as a beginner. It helps to remember that audiences don't expect you to be perfect.

- **Approval.** The mistaken belief called the **fallacy of approval** is based on the idea that it is vital—not just desirable—to gain the approval of everyone in the audience. It is rare that even the best speakers please everyone, especially on topics that are at all controversial. To paraphrase Abraham Lincoln, you can't please all the people all the time, and it is irrational to expect you will.

- **Overgeneralization.** The **fallacy of overgeneralization** might also be labeled the fallacy of exaggeration, because it occurs when a person blows one poor experience out of proportion. Consider these examples:

  "I'm so stupid! I mispronounced that word."

  "I completely blew it—I forgot one of my supporting points."

  "My hands were shaking. The audience must have thought I was crazy."

  A second type of exaggeration occurs when a speaker treats occasional lapses as if they were the rule rather than the exception. This sort of mistake usually involves extreme labels, such as "always" or "never."

  "I always forget what I want to say."

  "I can never come up with a good topic."

  "I can't do anything right."

## Overcoming Debilitative Communication Apprehension

There are five strategies that can help you manage debilitative communication apprehension:

> cultural idiom

**hoot:**
express rude and disparaging remarks

> cultural idiom

**a hole in one:**
hitting the golf ball in the hole with one swing of the club, a perfect shot

> cultural idiom

**blows ... out of proportion:**
exaggerates

## Speech Anxiety

1. What is your overall level of anxiety about speech making?

   **a.** Nonexistent

   **b.** Moderate

   **c.** Severe

2. Are you in control of your speech anxiety, or is your speech anxiety in control of you?

   **a.** I'm in control

   **b.** Half and half

   **c.** Anxiety is in control

What level of the following do you experience while speaking?

3. Sweating/sweaty palms

   **a.** Nonexistent

   **b.** Moderate

   **c.** Severe

4. Rapid breathing

   **a.** Nonexistent

   **b.** Moderate

   **c.** Severe

5. Restless energy

   **a.** Nonexistent

   **b.** Moderate

   **c.** Severe

6. Forgetting what you wanted to say

   **a.** Nonexistent

   **b.** Moderate

   **c.** Severe

Give yourself one point for every "a," two points for every "b," and three points for every "c." If your score is:

6 to 9 You have nerves of steel. You're probably a natural public speaker.

10 to 13 You are the typical public speaker. Read the strategies discussed in the next section to learn how to improve your skills.

14 to 18 You tend to have significant apprehension about public speaking. You need to consider each strategy below carefully. Although you will benefit from the tips provided, you should keep in mind that some of the greatest speakers of all time have considered themselves highly anxious. ●

---

- **Use nervousness to your advantage.** Paralyzing fear is obviously a problem, but a little nervousness can actually help you deliver a successful speech. Being completely calm can take away the passion that is one element of a good speech. Use the strategies below to control your anxiety, but don't try to completely eliminate it.

- **Understand the difference between rational and irrational fears.** Some fears about speaking are rational. For example, you ought to be worried if you haven't properly prepared for your speech. But fears based on the fallacies you just read about aren't constructive. It's not realistic to expect that you'll deliver a perfect speech, and it's not rational to indulge in catastrophic fantasies about what might go wrong.

- **Maintain a receiver orientation.** Paying too much attention to your own feelings—even when you're feeling good about yourself—will take energy away from communicating with your listeners. Concentrate on your audience members rather than on yourself. Focus your energy on keeping them interested, and on making sure they understand you.

- **Keep a positive attitude.** Build and maintain a positive attitude toward your audience, your speech, and yourself as a speaker. Some communication consultants suggest that public speakers should concentrate on three statements immediately before speaking. The three statements are as follows:

  I'm glad I have the chance to talk about this topic.

  I know what I'm talking about.

  I care about my audience.

  Repeating these statements (until you believe them) can help you maintain a positive attitude.

  Another technique for building a positive attitude is known as **visualization**.[15] This technique has been used successfully with athletes. It requires you to use your imagination to visualize the successful completion of your speech. Visualization can help make the self-fulfilling prophecy discussed in Chapter 3 work in your favor.

- **Be prepared!** Preparation is the most important key to controlling communication apprehension. You can feel confident if you know from practice that your remarks are well organized and supported and your delivery is smooth. Researchers have determined that the highest level of communication apprehension occurs just before speaking, the second highest level at the time the assignment is announced and explained, and the lowest level during the time you spend preparing your speech.[16] You should take advantage of this relatively low-stress time to work through the problems that would tend to make you nervous during the actual speech. For example, if your anxiety is based on a fear of forgetting what you are going to say, make sure that your note cards are complete and effective, and that you have practiced your speech thoroughly (we'll go into speech practice in more detail in a moment). If, on the other hand, your great fear is "sounding stupid," then getting started early with lots of research and advance thinking is the key to relieving your communication apprehension.

One of the first things you'll want to consider is the type of delivery you will use.

## Choosing a Type of Delivery

There are four basic types of delivery: extemporaneous, impromptu, manuscript, and memorized. Each type creates a different impression and is appropriate under different conditions. Any speech may incorporate more than one of these types of delivery. For purposes of discussion, however, it is best to consider them separately.

### Extemporaneous

An **extemporaneous speech** is planned in advance but presented in a direct, spontaneous manner. Extemporaneous speeches are conversational in tone, which means that they give the audience members the impression that you are talking to them, directly and honestly. Extemporaneous speaking is the most common type of delivery in both the classroom and the "outside" world.

### Impromptu

An **impromptu speech** is given off the top of one's head, without preparation. This type of speech is spontaneous by definition, but it is a delivery style that is necessary

> cultural idiom

**off the top of one's head:**
with little time to plan or think about

for informal talks, group discussions, and comments on others' speeches. It is also a highly effective training aid that teaches you to think on your feet and to organize your thoughts quickly.

## Manuscript

**Manuscript speeches** are read word for word from a prepared text. They are necessary when you are speaking for the record, as when speaking at legal proceedings or when presenting scientific findings. The greatest disadvantage of a manuscript speech is the lack of spontaneity that may result.

## Memorized

**Memorized speeches**—those learned by heart—are the most difficult and often the least effective. They often seem excessively formal. However, like manuscript speeches, they may be necessary on special occasions. They are used in oratory contests, and they are used as training devices for memory.

There is one guideline that is true for each type of speech: Practice.

> **cultural idiom**
> **for the record:**
> word-for-word documentation

> What type of delivery do you prefer? Why?

## Practicing the Speech

A smooth and natural delivery is the result of extensive practice. Get to know your material until you feel comfortable with your presentation. One way to do that is to go through some or all steps listed in the checklist on page 342.

Adora Svitak, whose profile appeared at the beginning of this chapter, practiced her speech while writing it:

> As far as preparation for the speech, I wrote a rough draft and actually practiced the speech even as I was making changes. I found that reading it aloud helped me find any structural/organizational errors or places where I could make my wording more effective. As someone who tends to write on the convoluted side, reading it aloud throughout the writing process was key to preparation.[19]

In each of these steps, critique your speech according to the guidelines that follow.

## Guidelines for Delivery

Let's examine some nonverbal aspects of presenting a speech. As you read in Chapter 6, nonverbal behavior can change, or even contradict, the meaning of the words a speaker utters. If audience members want to interpret how you feel about something, they are likely to trust your nonverbal communication more than the words you speak. If you tell them, "It's great to be here today," but you stand before them slouched over with your hands in your pockets and an expression on your face like you're about to be shot, they are likely to discount what you say. This might cause your audience members to react negatively to your speech, and their negative reaction might make you even more nervous. This cycle of speaker and audience reinforcing each other's feelings can work for you, though, if you approach a subject with genuine enthusiasm. Enthusiasm is shown through both the visual and auditory aspects of your delivery.

### Visual Aspects of Delivery

Visual aspects of delivery include appearance, movement, posture, facial expression, and eye contact.

In the timeless comedy *Bridget Jones's Diary*, Bridget (Renée Zellweger) delivers a hilariously awkward speech that manages to offend several audience members in only a few paragraphs. (To watch it, type "Bridget Jones speech" into your search engine.) How might Bridget have done a better (if less amusing) job? How can you avoid the kinds of mistakes Bridget makes?

## CHECKLIST > **Practicing Your Presentation**

☐ First, present the speech to yourself. "Talk through" the entire speech, including your examples and forms of support. Don't skip through parts of your speech as you practice by using placeholders such as "This is where I present my statistics" or "This is where I explain about photosynthesis." Make sure you know how you plan to present your statistics and explanations.

☐ Tape-record the speech, and listen to it. Because we hear our own voices partially through our cranial bone structure, we are sometimes surprised at what we sound like to others. Videotaping has been proven to be an especially effective tool for rehearsals, giving you an idea of what you look like, as well as what you sound like.[17]

☐ Present the speech in front of a small group of friends or relatives.[18]

☐ Present the speech to at least one listener in the room in which you will present the final speech (or, if that room is not available, a similar room).

> cultural idiom

**flashy:**
showy, gaudy

**Appearance**    Appearance is not a presentation variable as much as a preparation variable. Some communication consultants suggest new clothes, new glasses, and new hairstyles for their clients. In case you consider any of these, be forewarned that you should be attractive to your audience but not flashy. Research suggests that audiences like speakers who are similar to them, but they prefer the similarity to be shown conservatively.[20] Speakers, it seems, are perceived to be more credible when they look businesslike. Part of looking businesslike, of course, is looking like you took care in the preparation of your wardrobe and appearance.

**Movement**    The way you walk to the front of your audience will express your confidence and enthusiasm. And after you begin speaking, nervous energy can cause your body to shake and twitch, and that can be distressing both to you and to your audience. One way to control involuntary movement is to move voluntarily when you feel the need to move. Don't feel that you have to stand in one spot or that all your gestures need to be carefully planned. Simply get involved in your message, and let your involvement create the motivation for your movement. That way, when you move, you will emphasize what you are saying in the same way you would emphasize it if you were talking to a group of friends.

Describe a speaker you have observed whose delivery is memorable—in either a good or a bad way. What visual and vocal elements of the speech do you recall that stood out, and how did they help or hinder the speaker from succeeding? How can you make your delivery more effective?

Movement can also help you maintain contact with all members of your audience. Those closest to you will feel the greatest contact. This creates what is known as the "action zone" in the typical classroom, within the area of the front and center of the room. Movement enables you to extend this action zone, to include in it people who would otherwise remain uninvolved. Without overdoing it, you should feel free to move toward, away from, or from side to side in front of your audience.

Remember: Move with the understanding that it will add to the meaning of the words you use. It is difficult to bang your fist on a podium or take a step without conveying emphasis. Make the emphasis natural by allowing your message to create your motivation to move.

**Posture**    Generally speaking, good posture means standing with your spine relatively straight, your shoulders relatively squared off, and your feet angled out to keep your body from falling over sideways. In other words, rather than standing at military attention, you should be comfortably erect.

Good posture can help you control nervousness by allowing your breathing apparatus to work properly; when your brain receives enough oxygen, it's easier for you to think clearly. Good posture also increases your audience contact because the audience members will feel that you are interested enough in them to stand formally, yet relaxed enough to be at ease with them.

**Facial Expression**   The expression on your face can be more meaningful to an audience than the words you say. Try it yourself with a mirror. Say, "You're a terrific audience," for example, with a smirk, with a warm smile, with a deadpan expression, and then with a scowl. It just doesn't mean the same thing. But don't try to fake it. Like your movement, your facial expressions will reflect your genuine involvement with your message.

**Eye Contact**   Eye contact is perhaps the most important nonverbal facet of delivery. Eye contact not only increases your direct contact with your audience but also can be used to help you control your nervousness. Direct eye contact is a form of reality testing. The most frightening aspect of speaking is the unknown. How will the audience react? What will it think? Direct eye contact allows you to test your perception of your audience as you speak. Usually, especially in a college class, you will find that your audience is more "with" you than you think. By deliberately establishing contact with any apparently bored audience members, you might find that they are interested, they just aren't showing that interest because they don't think anyone is looking.

To maintain eye contact, you could try to meet the eyes of each member of your audience squarely at least once during any given presentation. After you have made definite eye contact, move on to another audience member. You can learn to do this quickly, so you can visually latch on to every member of a good-sized class in a relatively short time.

The characteristics of appearance, movement, posture, facial expression, and eye contact are visual, nonverbal facets of delivery. Now consider the auditory nonverbal messages that you might send during a presentation.

## Auditory Aspects of Delivery

As you read in Chapter 6, your paralanguage—the way you use your voice—says a good deal about you, especially about your sincerity and enthusiasm. In addition, using your voice well can help you control your nervousness. It's another cycle: Controlling your vocal characteristics will decrease your nervousness, which will enable you to control your voice even more. But this cycle can also work in the opposite direction. If your voice is out of control, your nerves will probably be in the same state. Controlling your voice is mostly a matter of recognizing and using appropriate volume, rate, pitch, and articulation.

**Volume**   The loudness of your voice is determined by the amount of air you push past the vocal folds in your throat. The key to controlling volume, then, is controlling the amount of air you use. The key to determining the right volume is audience contact. Your delivery should be loud enough so that your audience members can hear everything you say but not so loud that they feel you are talking to someone in the next room. Too much volume is seldom the problem for beginning speakers. Usually they either are not loud enough or have a tendency to fade off at the end of a thought. Sometimes, when they lose faith in an idea in midsentence, they compromise by mumbling the end of the sentence so that it isn't quite coherent.

**Rate**   There is a range of personal differences in speaking speed, or **rate**. Daniel Webster, for example, is said to have spoken at around 90 words per minute, whereas one actor who is known for his fast-talking commercials speaks at about 250. Normal speaking speed, however, is between 120 and 150 words per minute.

If you talk much more slowly than that, you may tend to lull your audience to sleep. Faster speaking rates are stereotypically associated with speaker competence,[21] but if you speak too rapidly, you will tend to be unintelligible. Once again, your involvement in your message is the key to achieving an effective rate.

**Pitch**  The highness or lowness of your voice—**pitch**—is controlled by the frequency at which your vocal folds vibrate as you push air through them. Because taut vocal folds vibrate at a greater frequency, pitch is influenced by muscular tension. This explains why nervous speakers have a tendency occasionally to "squeak," whereas relaxed speakers seem to be more in control. Pitch will tend to follow rate and volume. As you speed up or become louder, your pitch will have a tendency to rise. If your range in pitch is too narrow, your voice will have a singsong quality. If it is too wide, you may sound overly dramatic. You should control your pitch so that your listeners believe you are talking with them rather than performing in front of them. Once again, your involvement in your message should take care of this naturally for you.

When considering volume, rate, and pitch, keep emphasis in mind. Remember that a change in volume, pitch, or rate will result in emphasis. If you pause or speed up, your rate will suggest emphasis. Words you whisper or scream will be emphasized by their volume.

**Articulation**  The final auditory nonverbal behavior, articulation, is perhaps the most important. For our purposes here, **articulation** means pronouncing all the parts of all the necessary words and nothing else.

It is not our purpose to condemn regional or ethnic dialects within this discussion. It is true that a considerable amount of research suggests that regional dialects can cause negative impressions,[22] but our purpose here is to suggest careful, not standardized, articulation. Incorrect articulation is usually nothing more than careless articulation. It is caused by (1) leaving off parts of words (deletion), (2) replacing parts of words (substitution), (3) adding parts to words (addition), or (4) overlapping two or more words (slurring).

**Deletion**  The most common mistake in articulation is **deletion**, or leaving off part of a word. As you are thinking the complete word, it is often difficult to recognize that you are saying only part of it. The most common deletions occur at the ends of words, especially -*ing* words. *Going, doing,* and *stopping* become *goin', doin',* and *stoppin'*. Parts of words can be left off in the middle, too, as in *terr'iss* for *terrorist, Innernet* for *Internet,* and *asst* for *asked*.

**Substitution**  **Substitution** takes place when you replace part of a word with an incorrect sound. The ending -*th* is often replaced at the end of a word with a single *t,* as when *with* becomes *wit*. The *th*- sound is also a problem at the beginning of words, as *this, that,* and *those* have a tendency to become *dis, dat,* and *dose*. (This tendency is especially prevalent in many parts of the northeastern United States.)

**Addition**  The articulation problem of **addition** is caused by adding extra parts to words, such as *incentative* instead of *incentive, athalete* instead of *athlete,* and *orientated* instead of *oriented*. Sometimes this type of addition is caused by incorrect word choice, as when *irregardless* is used for *regardless*.

Another type of addition is the use of "tag questions," such as *you know?* or *you see?* or *right?* at the end of sentences. To have every other sentence punctuated with one of these barely audible superfluous phrases can be annoying.

Probably the worst type of addition, or at least the most common, is the use of *uh* and *anda* between words. *Anda* is often stuck between two words when *and* isn't even needed. If you find yourself doing that, you might want just to pause or swallow instead.[23]

## Understanding Diversity

## A Compendium of American Dialects

The following is a short glossary of examples of regionalized pronunciation (with apologies to all residents who find them exaggerated).

**Appalachian Hill Country**

**Bile** To bring water to 212 degrees

**Cowcumber** A vittle you make pickles out of

**Hern** Not his'n

**Tard** Exhausted

**Bawlamerese (Spoken around Baltimore)**

**Arn** What you do with an arnin board

**Blow** The opposite of above

**Pleece** Two or more po-leece

**Torst** Tourist

**Boston**

**Back** The outer covering of a tree trunk

**Had licka** Hard liquor

**Moa** The opposite of less

**Pahk** To leave your car somewhere, as in, "Pahk the cah in Haavaad Yahd"

**NooYorkese**

**Huh** The opposite of him

**Mel pew?** May I help you?

**Reg you la caw fee** Coffee with milk and sugar

**Pock** A place with trees and muggers

**Philadelphia**

**Fluffya** The name of the city

**Mayan** The opposite of yours

**Pork** A wooded recreational area

**Tail** What you use to dry off with after a shower

**Southern**

**Abode** A plank of wood

**Bidness** Such as, "Mistah Cottah's paynut bidness"

**Shurf** A local law enforcement officer

**Watt** The color of the Watt House in Wushinton

**Texas**

**Ah stay** Iced tea

**Bayer** A beverage made from hops

**Pars** A town in Texas. Also, the capital of France

**Awful Tar** The famous tall structure in Pars, France

Other interesting regionalisms can be found at the Slanguistics website, www.slanguage.com. ●

**Slurring** Slurring is caused by trying to say two or more words at once—or at least overlapping the end of one word with the beginning of the next. Word pairs ending with *of* are the worst offenders in this category. *Sort of* becomes *sorta, kind of* becomes *kinda*, and *because of* becomes *becausa*. Word combinations ending with *to* are often slurred, as when *want to* becomes *wanna*. Sometimes even more than two words are blended together, as when *that is the way* becomes *thatsaway*. Careful articulation means using your lips, teeth, tongue, and jaw to bite off your words, cleanly and separately, one at a time.

# Sample Speech

Adora Svitak was born in 1997. She was 12 years old when she gave the following speech at the TED conference in Long Beach, California, in 2010.

As a very young person planning to address an audience of older intellectuals, authors, and other notables who had paid $7,500 each to hear a 4-day series of speeches, Svitak had to do some serious analysis of her audience and occasion. In the end, she decided that no matter how distinguished her audience members were, they would still hold the universal human desire for a better future. She would refer to this in her speech:

> The goal is not to turn kids into your kind of adult, but rather better adults than you have been, which may be a little challenging considering your credentials.

Svitak also found another way to analyze the occasion of her speech:

> I also analyzed previous TED speakers. Indeed, you can get to know a lot about the ethos of a conference (and by extension, its audience) by considering past speeches.[24]

Svitak defined her speech purpose as follows:

> After listening to this speech, my audience members will be encouraged to listen and learn from kids, and to trust them and expect more from them.

She worded her thesis statement this way:

> Learning between grown-ups and kids should be reciprocal.

Svitak gathered information carefully and chose well-researched examples such as these:

> Now, what have kids done? Well, Anne Frank touched millions with her powerful account of the Holocaust, Ruby Bridges helped end segregation in the United States, and most recently, Charlie Simpson helped to raise 120,000 pounds for Haiti on his little bike.

She found visual aids to illustrate each of those examples, which she prepared in the form of Prezi slides (a dynamic form of PowerPoint that is available at www .prezi.com).

She chose a combination of memorized and manuscript-style speaking:

> I chose to speak holding a manuscript mainly because the short preparation time before I went to the conference, as well as the number of changes I'd made the night before, made me want to have it on hand for the sake of confidence. I found the confidence I gained from holding the manuscript made me feel freer to improvise. However, in the future, I'd definitely prefer to memorize what I plan to say.

In terms of speech anxiety, Svitak felt she had an advantage over better-known speakers:

> Like probably anyone about to address an audience, I definitely felt some nervousness; luckily, it was tempered by the kindness of everyone at TED and the energy I felt as I ran onstage. You just have to realistically understand that you're giving a speech, not saving the world, but also just accept the nerves calmly instead of trying to fight them. However, it also helped that I was at this point pretty much a complete unknown to the audience, unburdened by too many prior expectations (versus a speaker like, say, James Cameron, who everyone probably knew a bit about).

Finally, Svitak said of her TED experience:

> I learned that the quality of an audience and the energy in the room can be amazing sources for the quality and energy in your speech. After speaking at a wide range of conferences, I realized that oftentimes if the crowd is a sleepy group around breakfast time, you have to work way harder to make people enthusiastic. Drawing energy from the crowd is great, but you also have to be prepared to create it.

**SAMPLE SPEECH** | What Adults Can Learn from Kids    **Adora Svitak**

**1**   Now, I want to start with a question: When was the last time you were called childish? For kids like me, being called childish can be a frequent occurrence. Every time we make irrational demands, exhibit irresponsible behavior, or display any other signs of being normal American citizens, we are called childish. Which really bothers me. After all, take a look at these events: imperialism and colonization, world wars, George W. Bush. Ask yourself, who's responsible? Adults.

The sharp focus of Svitak's introduction was made possible by her consideration of her purpose and the formation of her thesis statement. She shows Prezi slides illustrating each of her examples.

**2**   Now, what have kids done? Well, Anne Frank touched millions with her powerful account of the Holocaust, Ruby Bridges helped to end segregation in the United States, and, most recently, Charlie Simpson helped to raise 120,000 pounds for Haiti on his little bike.

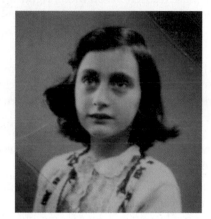

She had researched her examples carefully, uncovering many more than we see here, but choosing just the ones that best fit her purpose. Again, she illustrates them with slides.

**3**   So, as you can see evidenced by such examples, age has absolutely nothing to do with it. The traits the word *childish* addresses are seen so often in adults that we should abolish this age-discriminatory word when it comes to criticizing behavior associated with irresponsibility and irrational thinking.

This was an applause line, and Svitak thanked her audience politely for it.

**4**   Then again, who's to say that certain types of irrational thinking aren't exactly what the world needs? Maybe you've had grand plans before but stopped yourself, thinking, "That's impossible," or, "That costs too much," or, "That won't benefit me." For better or worse, we kids aren't hampered as much when it comes to thinking about reasons why not to do things.

Again, she chooses specific examples to make her point.

**5**   Kids can be full of inspiring aspirations and hopeful thinking. Like my wish that no one went hungry or that everything were a free kind of utopia. How many of you still dream like that and believe in the possibilities? Sometimes a knowledge of history and the past failures of utopian ideals can be a burden because you know that if everything were free, then the food stocks would become depleted and scarce and lead to chaos. On the other hand, we kids still dream about perfection. And that's a good thing because in order to make anything a reality, you have to dream about it first.

She backs up her ideas about the advantages of children's ideas by recognizing the history of utopian ideals.

**6**   In many ways, our audacity to imagine helps push the boundaries of possibility. For instance, the Museum of Glass in Tacoma, Washington, my home state—yoo-hoo Washington!—has a program called Kids Design Glass, and kids draw their own ideas for glass art. Now, the resident artist said they got some of their best ideas through the program because kids don't think about the limitations of how hard it can be to blow glass into certain shapes; they just think of good ideas. Now, when you think of glass, you might think of colorful Chihuly designs or maybe Italian vases, but kids challenge glass artists to go beyond that into the realm of broken-hearted snakes and bacon boys, who you can see has meat vision.

Both "yoo-hoo Washington!" and "meat vision" are designed as laugh lines, and they are successful. Again, slides are used to illustrate.

**7** Now, our inherent wisdom doesn't have to be insider's knowledge. Kids already do a lot of learning from adults, and we have a lot to share. I think that adults should start learning from kids. Now, I do most of my speaking in front of an education crowd, teachers and students, and I like this analogy: It shouldn't just be a teacher at the head of the classroom telling students, "Do this, do that." The students should teach their teachers. Learning between grown-ups and kids should be reciprocal. The reality, unfortunately, is a little different, and it has a lot to do with trust, or a lack of it.

**8** Now, if you don't trust someone, you place restrictions on them, right? If I doubt my older sister's ability to pay back the 10 percent interest I established on her last loan, I'm going to withhold her ability to get more money from me until she pays it back. True story, by the way.

This well-chosen example from personal experience elicits a healthy laugh from her audience.

**9** Now, adults seem to have a prevalently restrictive attitude towards kids from every "don't do that, don't do this" in the school handbook to restrictions on school Internet use. As history points out, regimes become oppressive when they're fearful about keeping control. And although adults may not be quite at the level of totalitarian regimes, kids have no, or very little, say in making the rules, when really the attitude should be reciprocal, meaning that the adult population should learn and take into account the wishes of the younger population.

A well-chosen historical truth that the audience can relate to.

**10** Now, what's even worse than restriction is that adults often underestimate kids' abilities. We love challenges, but when expectations are low, trust me, we will sink to them. My own parents had anything but low expectations for me and my sister. Okay, so they didn't tell us to become doctors or lawyers or anything like that, but my dad did read to us about Aristotle and pioneer germ fighters when lots of other kids were hearing "The Wheels on the Bus Go Round and Round." Well, we heard that one too, but "Pioneer Germ Fighters" totally rules.

Another Prezi slide. Another laugh line.

**11** I loved to write from the age of 4, and when I was 6 my mom bought me my own laptop equipped with Microsoft Word. Thank you Bill Gates and thank you Ma. I wrote over 300 short stories on that little laptop, and I wanted to get published. Instead of just scoffing at this heresy that a kid wanted to get published or saying wait until you're older, my parents were really supportive. Many publishers were not quite so encouraging, one large children's publisher ironically saying that they didn't work with children—children's publisher not working with children? I don't know, you're kind of alienating a large client there. Now, one publisher, Action Publishing, was willing to take that leap and trust me and to listen to what I had to say. They published my first book, *Flying Fingers*—you see it here—and from there on, it's gone to speaking at hundreds of schools, keynoting to thousands of educators and finally, today, speaking to you.

Again, a slide to show what her book looks like.

**12** I appreciate your attention today, because to show that you truly care, you listen. But there's a problem with this rosy picture of kids being so much better than adults. Kids grow up and become adults just like you. (Laughter) Or just like you? Really? The goal is not to turn kids into your kind of adult, but rather better adults than you have been, which may be a little challenging considering your credentials. (Laughter) But the way progress happens is because new generations and new eras grow and develop and become better than the previous ones. It's the reason we're not in the Dark Ages anymore. No matter your position or place in life, it is imperative to create opportunities for children so that we can grow up to blow you away. (Laughter)

*Her audience analysis is manifested in her reference to the audience members' credentials.*

13 Adults and fellow TEDsters, you need to listen and learn from kids and trust us and expect more from us. You must lend an ear today, because we are the leaders of tomorrow, which means we're going to be taking care of you when you're old and senile. No, just kidding. No, really, we are going to be the next generation, the ones who will bring this world forward. And in case you don't think that this really has meaning for you, remember that cloning is possible, and that involves going through childhood again, in which case you'll want to be heard just like my generation. Now, the world needs opportunities for new leaders and new ideas. Kids need opportunities to lead and succeed. Are you ready to make the match? Because the world's problems shouldn't be the human family's heirloom. Thank you.[25]

*Shows slide: "You must lend an ear today, because we are the leaders of tomorrow."*

## Summary

This chapter dealt with your first tasks in preparing a speech: choosing and developing a topic. Some guidelines for choosing a topic include these: Look for a topic early and stick with it, choose a topic you find interesting, and choose a topic you already know something about.

One of your tasks is to understand your purpose so that you can stick to it as you prepare your speech. General purposes include entertaining, informing, and persuading. Specific purposes are expressed in the form of purpose statements, which must be result oriented, specific, and realistic.

Your next task is to formulate a thesis statement, which tells what the central idea of your speech is. Another early task is to analyze the speaking situation, including the audience and the occasion. When analyzing your audience, you should consider the audience purpose, demographics, attitudes, beliefs, and values. When analyzing the occasion, you should consider the time (and date) your speech will take place, the time available, the location, and audience expectations.

Although much of your speech will be based on personal reflection about your own ideas and experiences, it is usually necessary to gather some information from outside sources. Techniques for doing so include interviewing and surveys, as well as Internet and library research.

Carefully considering each of these preliminary tasks will enable you to avoid debilitative (as opposed to facilitative) communication apprehension. Sources of debilitative communication apprehension include irrational thinking, which might include a belief in one or more of the following fallacies: the fallacy of catastrophic failure (something is going to ruin this presentation), the fallacy of perfection (a good speaker never does anything wrong), the fallacy of absolute approval (everyone has to like you), and the fallacy of overgeneralization (you always mess up speeches). There are several methods of overcoming communication apprehension. The first is to remember that nervousness is natural, and to use it to your advantage. The others include being rational, receiver oriented, positive, and prepared.

There are four types of delivery: extemporaneous, impromptu, manuscript, and memorized. In each type, the speaker must be concerned with both visual and auditory aspects of the presentation. Visual aspects include appearance, movement, posture, facial expression, and eye contact. Auditory aspects include volume, rate, pitch, and articulation. The four most common articulation problems are deletion, substitution, addition, and slurring of word sounds.

Throughout all these preliminary tasks, you will be organizing information and choosing supporting material. These processes will be discussed in the next chapter.

## Key Terms

**addition** The articulation error that involves adding extra parts to words. *p. 344*

**articulation** The process of pronouncing all the necessary parts of a word. *p. 344*

**attitude** The predisposition to respond to an idea, person, or thing favorably or unfavorably. *p. 331*

**audience analysis** A consideration of characteristics, including the type, goals, demographics, beliefs, attitudes, and values of listeners. *p. 329*

**belief** An underlying conviction about the truth of an idea, often based on cultural training. *p. 331*

**database** A computerized collection of information that can be searched in a variety of ways to locate information that the user is seeking. *p. 335*

**debilitative communication apprehension** An intense level of anxiety about speaking before an audience, resulting in poor performance. *p. 337*

**deletion** An articulation error that involves leaving off parts of words. *p. 344*

**demographics** Audience characteristics that can be analyzed statistically, such as age, gender, education, and group membership. *p. 329*

**extemporaneous speech** A speech that is planned in advance but presented in a direct, conversational manner. *p. 340*

**facilitative communication apprehension** A moderate level of anxiety about speaking before an audience that helps improve the speaker's performance. *p. 337*

**fallacy of approval** The irrational belief that it is vital to win the approval of virtually every person a communicator deals with. *p. 338*

**fallacy of catastrophic failure** The irrational belief that the worst possible outcome will probably occur. *p. 338*

**fallacy of overgeneralization** Irrational beliefs in which (1) conclusions (usually negative) are based on limited evidence or (2) communicators exaggerate their shortcomings. *p. 338*

**fallacy of perfection** The irrational belief that a worthwhile communicator should be able to handle every situation with complete confidence and skill. *p. 338*

**general purpose** One of three basic ways a speaker seeks to affect an audience: to entertain, inform, or persuade. *p. 327*

**impromptu speech** A speech given "off the top of one's head," without preparation. *p. 340*

**irrational thinking** Beliefs that have no basis in reality or logic; one source of debilitative communication apprehension. *p. 338*

**manuscript speech** A speech that is read word for word from a prepared text. *p. 341*

**memorized speech** A speech learned and delivered by rote without a written text. *p. 341*

**pitch** The highness or lowness of one's voice. *p. 344*

**purpose statement** A complete sentence that describes precisely what a speaker wants to accomplish. *p. 327*

**rate** The speed at which a speaker utters words. *p. 343*

**slurring** The articulation error that involves overlapping the end of one word with the beginning of the next. *p. 345*

**specific purpose** The precise effect that the speaker wants to have on an audience. It is expressed in the form of a purpose statement. *p. 327*

**substitution** The articulation error that involves replacing part of a word with an incorrect sound. *p. 344*

**survey research** Information gathering in which the responses of a sample of a population are collected to disclose information about the larger group. *p. 336*

**thesis statement** A complete sentence describing the central idea of a speech. *p. 328*

**value** A deeply rooted belief about a concept's inherent worth. *p. 331*

**visualization** A technique for behavior rehearsal (e.g., for a speech) that involves imagining the successful completion of the task. *p. 340*

## Check Your Understanding

When it is time for you to prepare a speech assignment for your class, answer the following questions:

1. Why do you believe your topic has the potential to be effective for your specific audience?

2. Did your purpose statement and thesis statement follow the guidelines on pp. 327–328?

3. What characteristics of your audience and occasion made a difference in how you presented your speech?

4. What was the most effective piece of research that you found for your speech?

5. Would you consider yourself highly, moderately, or not particularly anxious about public speaking? What is the source of any anxiety you feel?

6. Why did you choose the type of delivery that you did?

## Activities

1. **Formulating Purpose Statements** Write a specific purpose statement for each of the following speeches:

1. An after-dinner speech at an awards banquet in which you will honor a team who has a winning, but not championship, record. (You pick the team. For example: "After listening to my speech, my audience members will appreciate the individual sacrifices made by the members of the chess team.")

2. A classroom speech in which you explain how to do something. (Again, you choose the topic: "After listening to my speech, my audience members will know at least three ways to maximize their comfort and convenience on an economy class flight.")

3. A campaign speech in which you support the candidate of your choice. (For example: "After listening to my speech, my audience members will consider voting for Alexandra Rodman in order to clean up student government.")

Answer the following questions about each of the purpose statements you make up: Is it result oriented? Is it precise? Is it attainable?

2. **Formulating Thesis Statements** Turn each of the following purpose statements into a statement that expresses a possible thesis. For example, if you had a purpose statement such as this:

> After listening to my speech, my audience will recognize the primary advantages and disadvantages of home teeth bleaching.

you might turn it into a thesis statement such as this:

> Home bleaching your teeth can significantly improve your appearance, but watch out for injury to the gums and damaged teeth.

1. At the end of my speech, the audience members will be willing to sign my petition supporting the local needle exchange program for drug addicts.

2. After listening to my speech, the audience members will be able to list five disadvantages of tattoos.

3. During my speech on the trials and tribulations of writing a research paper, the audience members will show their interest by paying attention and their amusement by occasionally laughing.

3. **Gathering Information** Break up into groups of eight or fewer. Select a topic of your own choosing or one of the following:

1. Who came up with the idea of latitude and longitude lines, and how do they work?

2. College athletes are exploited by the schools they play for.

3. Our jury system does not work.

4. U.S. schools are not safe.

5. What are the steps in the design and construction of the Macy's Thanksgiving Day parade balloons?

6. What do modern-day witches believe?

7. What does it mean to be innumerate, and how many people suffer from this problem?

Assign each member of your group a different research source:

1. Internet search engine

2. Library catalog

3. Reference works

4. Periodicals

5. Databases

6. Talk to a librarian.

7. Talk to a professor.

8. Conduct a survey of your other class members.

During the next class period, report back to the class on which research sources were most productive.

4. **Communication Apprehension: A Personal Analysis** To analyze your own reaction to communication apprehension, think back to your last public speech, and rate yourself on how rational, receiver oriented, positive, and prepared you were. How did these attributes affect your anxiety level?

5. **Types of Delivery** Identify at least one speech you have seen presented using the four types of delivery: extemporaneous, impromptu, manuscript, or memorized. For this speech, decide whether the type of delivery was effective for the topic, speaker, and situation. Explain why or why not. If the speech was not effective, suggest a more appropriate type.

6. **Articulation Exercises** Tongue twisters can be used to practice careful articulation out loud. Try these two classics:

1. She sells seashells down by the seashore.

2. Peter Piper picked a peck of pickled peppers.

Now make up some of your own and try them out. Make twisters for both consonant sounds ("Frank's friendly face flushed furiously") and vowel sounds ("Oliver oiled the old annoying oddity").

## For Further Exploration

For more resources about preliminary considerations in planning a speech, see the *Understanding Human Communication* website at www.oup.com/us/adler. There you will find a variety of resources: a list of books and articles, links to descriptions of feature films and television shows at the Now Playing website, study aids, and a self-test to check your understanding of the material in this chapter.

CHAPTER 12

For every one textbook
you use one paycheck

Passing a class depends
alot on having the
class textbook

# Organization and Support

## 12

## Chapter Outline

### LEARNING OBJECTIVES

1. Construct an effective speech outline using the organizing principles described in this chapter.

2. Develop an effective introduction, conclusion, and transitions.

3. Choose supporting material for a speech to make your points clear, interesting, memorable, and convincing.

Competing on a speech team has a lot in common with TV news reporting. Just ask Curt Casper, who has done both.

These days Casper is a sports and news reporter at KPTM-TV in Omaha, Nebraska. But he first honed his public speaking skills on the Hastings College forensics team. (Forensics is the process of considering evidence to reach a sound conclusion, whether it's making a speech or solving a crime.)

When Casper applied for the job at KPTM, the news director said he had never seen a résumé that included the words "speech/forensics." He asked Casper, "How would your experience in public speaking help you in this career?" Curt gave him examples, such as impromptu speaking competitions, in which he was given 2 minutes to prepare a 5-minute speech inspired by one quotation, and extemporaneous speaking competitions, in which he had 30 minutes to prepare a 7-minute answer to a question about national or world events using credible sources to back up his information. Casper explained the similarities between those competitions and news reporting. He got the job.

After Casper proved himself to be an effective newscaster, his news director praised the value of a background in public speaking, especially for a career in reporting.

"I use my speech skills every day," says Casper, who feels that public speaking has taught him to be a quick and effective researcher, to choose words carefully, and to speak within time limits. His two biggest lessons—as both a public speaker and a news reporter—have been to find strong supporting material and to organize it in a way that makes sense to an audience. As you'll see in the sample speech at the end of this chapter, Casper began making good use of these skills when he was still in college.

***Public speaking skills helped Curt Casper attain his "dream job." See if you can answer the following questions about your own career aspirations.***

- What is your dream job?

- What communication skills could help you attain that job?

- How would public speaking relate to such a career choice?

As Curt Casper learned as both a public speaker and a newscaster, *knowing* what you are talking about and *communicating* that knowledge aren't the same thing. It's frustrating to realize you aren't expressing your thoughts clearly, and it's equally unpleasant to be unable to follow what a speaker is saying because the material is too jumbled. In the following pages, you will learn methods of organizing and supporting your thoughts effectively.

## Structuring Your Speech

As discussed in Chapter 2, people tend to arrange their perceptions in some meaningful way in order to make sense of the world. Being clear to your audience, however, isn't the only benefit of good organization: Structuring a message effectively will help you refine your own ideas and construct more persuasive messages.

A good speech is like a good building: Both grow from a careful plan. Chapter 11 showed you how to begin this planning by formulating a purpose, analyzing your audience, and conducting research. You apply that information to the structure of the speech through outlining. Like any other plan, a speech outline is the framework on which your message is built. It contains your main ideas and shows how they relate to one another and to your thesis. Virtually every speech outline ought to follow the basic structure outlined in Figure 12-1.

This **basic speech structure** demonstrates the old aphorism for speakers: "Tell what you're going to say, say it, and then tell what you said." Although this structure sounds redundant, the research on listening cited in Chapter 5 demonstrates that receivers forget much of what they hear. The clear, repetitive nature of the basic speech structure reduces the potential for memory loss, because audiences have a tendency to listen more carefully during the beginning and ending of a speech.[1] Your outline will reflect this basic speech structure.

Outlines come in all shapes and sizes, but the three types that are most important to us here are working outlines, formal outlines, and speaking notes.

### Your Working Outline

A **working outline** is a construction tool used to map out your speech. The working outline will probably follow the basic speech structure, but only in rough form. It is for your eyes only, and you'll probably create several drafts as you refine your ideas. As your ideas solidify, your outline will change accordingly, becoming more polished as you go along.

### Your Formal Outline

A **formal outline** such as the one shown on page 356 uses a consistent format and set of symbols to identify the structure of ideas.

A formal outline serves several purposes. In simplified form, it can be displayed as a visual aid or distributed as a handout. It can also serve as a record of a speech that was delivered; many organizations send outlines to members who miss meetings at which presentations were given. Finally, in speech classes, instructors often use speech outlines to analyze student speeches. When one is used for that purpose, it is usually a full-sentence outline and includes the purpose, thesis, and topic or title. Most instructors also require a bibliography of sources at the end of the outline. The bibliography should include full research citations, the correct form for which can be found in any style guide, such as *The Craft of Research*, by Wayne Booth et al.[2] There are at least six standard bibliographic styles. Whichever style you use, you should be consistent in form and remember the two primary functions of a bibliographic citation: to demonstrate the credibility of your source and to enable the readers—in this case, your professor or your fellow students—to find the source if they want to check its accuracy or explore your topic in more detail.

Another person should be able to understand the basic ideas included in your speech by reading the formal outline. In fact, that's one test of the effectiveness of your outline. See if the outline on page 356 passes this test for you.

### Your Speaking Notes

Like your working outline, your speaking notes are for your use only, so the format is up to you. Many teachers suggest that speaking notes should be in the form of a brief keyword outline, with just enough information listed to jog your memory but not enough to get lost in.

Many teachers also suggest that you fit your notes on one side of one 3-by-5-inch note card. Other teachers recommend that you also have your introduction and conclusion on note cards, and still others recommend that your longer quotations be written out on note cards. Curt Casper's notes for his speech on suicide survivors (see the sample outline, page 356) might look like the ones in Figure 12-2.

**Introduction**
   I. Attention-getter
   II. Preview

**Body**
   I.
   II.
   III. ⎬ Three to five
   IV.   main points
   V.

**Conclusion**
   I. Review
   II. Final remarks

**FIGURE 12-1  Basic Speech Structure**

Do you usually make outlines for term papers, essay responses on exams, and class presentations? If not, how could you benefit from outlining more often?

# Speech Outline

The following outline is for the sample speech at the end of this chapter, which Curt Casper presented at a national event in college. A bibliography for this speech can be found on page 373.

## Suicide Survivor Support

### INTRODUCTION

I. Attention-getter: My father's suicide had a powerful impact on my family.

II. Thesis statement: We can change the stigma of suicide if we stop survivors from suffering alone.

III. Preview main points.

### BODY

I. We need to recognize the reasons suicide survivors (family and friends of those who commit suicide) do not receive the help they deserve.

  A. The deficiencies in survivor support can be found on a societal level.

    1. Society's refusal to use the word *suicide* sets up a social stigma.

    2. Religious doctrine increases this social stigma.

    3. Even media guidelines increase the stigma.

  B. The deficiencies in survivor support can be found on an economic level.

    1. Survivors are left with funeral, counseling, and living expenses.

    2. Survivors might not be eligible for life insurance payouts.

    3. Survivors might not use the money they do receive wisely.

II. We need to examine the impact of that lack of help.

  A. A suicide can cause more grief than most normal deaths.

  B. A suicide can cause post-traumatic stress disorder.

III. We need to examine some possible solutions.

  A. Survivor support solutions can and should be facilitated on a societal level.

    1. One part of the solution would be to require insurance companies to give back the premiums that were paid before the suicide.

    2. Another part of the solution would be to use the word *suicide* when talking to survivors.

  B. Survivor support solutions can and should be facilitated on an individual level.

    1. If you have a friend who is a survivor, just be there for him or her.

    2. If you are a survivor yourself, share your story with others in similar situations.

      a. Make survivors realize that they are not at fault for what happened.

      b. Become part of a LOSS team.

      c. Make sure you also get the help you need.

## Conclusion

I. Review main points.

II. I have seen firsthand how a suicide can destroy a family.

III. I know my dad would have wanted us to move on and know that everything is okay.

# Principles of Outlining

Over the years, a series of rules or principles for the construction of outlines has evolved. These rules are based on the use of the standard symbols and format discussed next.

## Standard Symbols

A speech outline generally uses the following symbols:

I. Main point (roman numeral)

  A. Subpoint (capital letter)

    1. Sub-subpoint (standard number)

      a. Sub-subsubpoint (lowercase letter)

In the examples in this chapter, the major divisions of the speech—introduction, body, and conclusion—are not given in symbols. They are listed by name, and the roman numerals for their main points begin anew in each division. An alternative form is to list these major divisions with roman numerals, main points with capital letters, and so on.

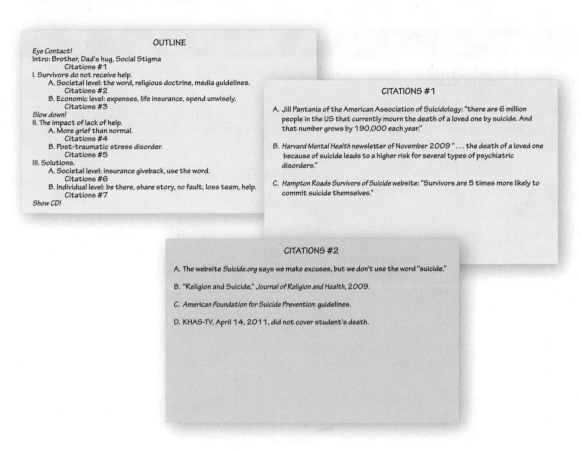

**OUTLINE**

*Eye Contact!*
Intro: Brother, Dad's hug, Social Stigma
　　　Citations #1
I. Survivors do not receive help.
　　A. Societal level: the word, religious doctrine, media guidelines.
　　　　Citations #2
　　B. Economic level: expenses, life insurance, spend unwisely.
　　　　Citations #3
*Slow down!*
II. The impact of lack of help.
　　A. More grief than normal.
　　　　Citations #4
　　B. Post-traumatic stress disorder.
　　　　Citations #5
III. Solutions.
　　A. Societal level: insurance giveback, use the word.
　　　　Citations #6
　　B. Individual level: be there, share story, no fault, loss team, help.
　　　　Citations #7
*Show CD!*

**CITATIONS #1**

A. Jill Pantania of the American Association of Suicidology: "there are 6 million people in the US that currently mourn the death of a loved one by suicide. And that number grows by 190,000 each year."

B. *Harvard Mental Health* newsletter of November 2009 "... the death of a loved one because of suicide leads to a higher risk for several types of psychiatric disorders."

C. *Hampton Roads Survivors of Suicide* website: "Survivors are 5 times more likely to commit suicide themselves."

**CITATIONS #2**

A. The website *Suicide.org* says we make excuses, but we don't use the word "suicide."

B. "Religion and Suicide," *Journal of Religion and Health*, 2009.

C. *American Foundation for Suicide Prevention*: guidelines.

D. KHAS-TV, April 14, 2011, did not cover student's death.

**FIGURE 12 2** **Speaking Notes** These speaking notes are based on the outline on page 356. The entire set would be eight cards, including one for the outline and seven for citations.

## Standard Format

In the sample outlines in this chapter, notice that each symbol is indented a number of spaces from the symbol above it. Besides keeping the outline neat, the indentation of different-order ideas is actually the key to the technique of outlining; it enables you to coordinate and order ideas in the form in which they are most comprehensible to the human mind. If the standard format is used in your working outline, it will help you create a well-organized speech. If it is used in speaking notes, it will help you remember everything you want to say.

Proper outline form is based on a few rules and guidelines, the first of which is the rule of division.

## The Rule of Division

In formal outlines, main points and subpoints always represent a division of a whole. Because it is impossible to divide something into fewer than two parts, you always have at least two main points for every topic. Then, if your main points are divided, you will always have at least two subpoints, and so on. Thus, the rule for formal outlines is as follows: Never a "1" without a "II," never an "A" without a "B," and so on.

Three to five is considered to be the ideal number of main points. It is also considered best to divide those main points into three to five subpoints, when necessary and possible. Notice how Curt Casper divided the body of his topic as shown in the sample outline on page 356.

**SELF-ASSESSMENT**

## Main Points and Subpoints

To get an idea of your ability to distinguish main points from subpoints, set the "timer" function on your mobile phone and see how long it takes you to fit the following concepts for a speech entitled "The College Application Process" into outline form:

| CONCEPTS | RECOMMENDED OUTLINE FORM |
|---|---|
| Participation in extracurricular activities | I. |
| Visit and evaluate college websites | A. |
| Prepare application materials | B. |
| Career ambitions | II. |
| Choose desired college | A. |
| Letters of recommendation | B. |
| Write personal statement | C. |
| Visit and evaluate college campuses | III. |
| Choose interesting topic | A. |
| Test scores | B. |
| Include important personal details | 1. |
| Volunteer work | 2. |
| Transcripts | 3. |

You can score yourself as follows:

30 seconds or less: Congratulations, organization comes naturally to you.

31 to 60 seconds: You have typical skills in this area.

61 to 90 seconds: Give yourself extra time while building your speech outline. ●

## The Rule of Parallel Wording

Your main points should be worded in a similar, or "parallel," manner. For example, if you are developing a speech against capital punishment, your main points might look like this:

I. Capital punishment is not effective: It is not a deterrent to crime.
II. Capital punishment is not constitutional: It does not comply with the Eighth Amendment.
III. Capital punishment is not civilized: It does not allow for a reverence for life.

Whenever possible, subpoints should also be worded in a parallel manner. For your points to be worded in a parallel manner, they should each contain one, and only one, idea. (After all, they can't really be parallel if one is longer or contains more ideas than the others.) This will enable you to completely develop one idea before moving on to another one in your speech. If you were discussing cures for indigestion, your topic might be divided incorrectly if your main points looked like this:

I. "Preventive cures" help you before eating.
II. "Participation cures" help you during and after eating.

You might actually have three ideas there and thus three main points:

I.  Prevention cures (before eating)
II.  Participation cures (during eating)
III.  Postparticipation cures (after eating)

# Organizing Your Outline into a Logical Pattern

An outline should reflect a logical order for your points. You might arrange them from newest to oldest, largest to smallest, best to worst, or in a number of other ways that follow. The organizing pattern you choose ought to be the one that best develops your thesis.

## Time Patterns

Arrangement according to **time patterns**, or chronology, is one of the most common patterns of organization. The period of time could be anything from centuries to seconds. In a speech on airline food, a time pattern might look like this:

I.  Early airline food: a gourmet treat
II.  The middle period: institutional food at 30,000 feet
III.  Today's airline food: the passenger starves

Arranging points according to the steps that make up a process is another form of time patterning. The topic "Recording a Hit Song" might use this type of patterning:

I.  Record the demo CD.
II.  Tape a YouTube video.
III.  Get a recording company to listen and view.

Time patterns are also the basis of **climax patterns**, which are used to create suspense. For example, if you wanted to create suspense in a speech about military intervention, you could chronologically trace the steps that eventually led us into Afghanistan or Iraq in such a way that you build up your audience's curiosity. If you told of these steps through the eyes of a soldier who entered military service right before one of those wars, you would be building suspense as your audience wonders what will become of that soldier.

The climax pattern can also be reversed. When it is, it is called *anticlimactic* organization. If you started your military intervention speech by telling the audience that you were going to explain why a specific soldier was killed in a specific war, and then you went on to explain the things that caused that soldier to become involved in that war, you would be using anticlimactic organization. This pattern is helpful when you have an essentially uninterested audience, and you need to build interest early in your speech to get the audience to listen to the rest of it.

## Space Patterns

**Space patterns** are organized according to area. The area could be stated in terms of continents or centimeters or anything in between. If you were discussing the Great Lakes, for example, you could arrange them from west to east:

I.  Superior
II.  Michigan
III.  Huron
IV.  Erie
V.  Ontario

**ON YOUR FEET**

*Outlining*
Present a 1-minute talk on the principles of outlining. Use only a formal outline for your presentation.

One of the greatest speakers of the 20th century, Dr. Martin Luther King Jr., knew well how to construct a speech and how to conclude with passion. What best practices can you use to boost the impact when organizing your speeches?

## Topic Patterns

A topical arrangement or **topic pattern** is based on types or categories. These categories could be either well known or original; both have their advantages. For example, a division of college students according to well-known categories might look like this:

I. Freshmen
II. Sophomores
III. Juniors
IV. Seniors

Well-known categories are advantageous because audiences quickly understand them. But familiarity also has its disadvantages. One disadvantage is the "Oh, this again" syndrome. If the members of an audience feel they have nothing new to learn about the components of your topic, they might not listen to you. To avoid this, you could invent original categories that freshen up your topic by suggesting an original analysis. For example, original categories for "college students" might look like this:

I. Grinds: Students who go to every class and read every assignment before it is due.
II. Renaissance students: Students who find a satisfying balance of scholarly and social pursuits.
III. Burnouts: Students who have a difficult time finding the classroom, let alone doing the work.

Sometimes topics are arranged in the order that will be easiest for your audience to remember. To return to our Great Lakes example, the names of the lakes could be arranged so their first letters spell the word "HOMES." Words used in this way are known as *mnemonics*. Carol Koehler, a professor of communication and medicine, uses the mnemonic "CARE" to describe the characteristics of a caring doctor:

C stands for *concentrate*. Physicians should pay attention with their eyes and ears . . .

A stands for *acknowledge*. Show them that you are listening . . .

R stands for *response*. Clarify issues by asking questions, providing periodic recaps . . .

E stands for *exercise emotional control*. When your "hot buttons" are pushed . . .[3]

## Problem-Solution Patterns

The **problem-solution pattern**, as you might guess from its no-nonsense name, describes what's wrong and proposes a way to make things better. It is usually (but not always) divisible into two distinct parts, as in this example:

I. The Problem: Addiction (which could then be broken down into addiction to cigarettes, alcohol, prescribed drugs, and street drugs)
II. The Solution: A national addiction institute (which would study the root causes of addiction in the same way that the National Cancer Institute studies the root causes of cancer)

We will discuss this pattern in more detail in Chapter 14.

## Nontraditional Patterns of Organization

In addition to the traditional patterns usually taught in public speaking classes, researchers are looking at other organizational patterns commonly used by women and ethnic speakers. For example, Cheryl Jorgenson-Earp is exploring a number of alternative patterns that women have used historically. She argues that many speakers are uncomfortable with the standard organization patterns because of cultural backgrounds or personal inclinations. As alternatives, she proposes several less direct and more "organic" patterns that provide a clear structure for a speech but have a less linear form.

One of these is the wave pattern. In this pattern the speaker uses repetitions and variations of themes and ideas. The major points of the speech come at the crest of the wave. The speaker follows these with a variety of examples leading up to another crest, where she repeats the theme or makes another major point.

Perhaps the most famous speech that illustrates this pattern is the Reverend Martin Luther King Jr.'s "I Have a Dream." King used this memorable line as the crest of a wave that he followed with examples of what he saw in his dream; then he repeated the line. He ended with a "peak" conclusion that emerged from the final wave in the speech—repetition and variation on the phrase "Let freedom ring."

An excerpt from Sojourner Truth's "Ain't I a Woman?" speech also illustrates this pattern:

That man over there says that women need to be helped into carriages, and lifted over ditches, and to have the best place everywhere. Nobody ever helps me into carriages, or over mud-puddles, or gives me any best place!

And ain't I a woman?

Look at me! Look at my arm! I have ploughed and planted, and gathered into barns, and no man could head me!

And ain't I a woman?

I could work as much and eat as much as a man—when I could get it—and bear the lash as well!

And ain't I a woman?

I have borne thirteen children and seen them most all sold off to slavery, and when I cried out with my mother's grief, none but Jesus heard me!

And ain't I a woman? ●

Jaffe, C. (2007). *Public speaking: Concepts and skills for a diverse society* (5th ed.). Boston: Wadsworth, © 2007. Reprinted with permission of Wadsworth, an imprint of the Wadsworth Group, a division of Thomson Learning.

Why is diversity important in the messages you send and receive? Why is message organization such an important factor?

## Cause-Effect Patterns

**Cause-effect patterns** are similar to problem-solution patterns in that they are basically two-part patterns: First you discuss something that happened, and then you discuss its effects.

A variation of this pattern reverses the order and presents the effects first and then the causes. Persuasive speeches often have effect-cause or cause-effect as the first two main points. Elizabeth Hallum, a student at Arizona State University, organized the first two points of a speech on "workplace revenge"[4] like this:

I. The effects of the problem
   A. Lost productivity
   B. Costs of sabotage
II. The causes of the problem
   A. Employees feeling alienated
   B. Employers' light treatment of incidents of revenge

Think of an idea that you could present to your class. Which pattern of organization would be most effective for that presentation?

The third main point in this type of persuasive speech is often "solutions," and the fourth main point is often "the desired audience behavior." Hallum's final points were as follows:

III. Solutions: Support the National Employee Rights Institute.
IV. Desired Audience Response: Log on to www.disgruntled.com.

Cause-effect and problem-solution patterns are often combined in various arrangements. In the sample speech at the end of this chapter, Curt Casper uses a problem-effect-solution pattern. One extension of the problem-solution organizational pattern is Monroe's Motivated Sequence.

### Monroe's Motivated Sequence

The Motivated Sequence was proposed by a scholar named Alan Monroe in the 1930s.[5] In this persuasive pattern, the problem is broken down into an attention step and a need step, and the solution is broken down into a satisfaction step, a visualization step, and an action step. In a speech on "random acts of kindness,"[6] the Motivated Sequence might break down like this:

I. The attention step draws attention to your subject. ("Just the other day Ron saved George's life with a small, random, seemingly unimportant act of kindness.")
II. The need step establishes the problem. ("Millions of Americans suffer from depression, a life-threatening disease.")
III. The satisfaction step proposes a solution. ("One random act of kindness can lift a person from depression.")
IV. The visualization step describes the results of the solution. ("Imagine yourself having that kind of effect on another person.")
V. The action step is a direct appeal for the audience to do something. ("Try a random act of kindness today!")

Chapter 14 has more to say about the organization of persuasive speeches.

 **ON YOUR FEET**

*Motivated Sequence*
Outline a persuasive topic in just five sentences, one for each step of the Motivated Sequence.

## Using Transitions

**Transitions** keep your message moving forward. They perform the following functions:

They tell how the introduction relates to the body of the speech.

They tell how one main point relates to the next main point.

They tell how your subpoints relate to the points they are part of.

They tell how your supporting points relate to the points they support.

Transitions, to be effective, should refer to the previous point and to the upcoming point, showing how they relate to each other and to the thesis. They usually sound something like this:

"Like [previous point], another important consideration in [topic] is [upcoming point]."

"But _____ isn't the only thing we have to worry about. _____ is even more potentially dangerous."

"Yes, the problem is obvious. But what are the solutions? Well, one possible solution is . . ."

Sometimes a transition includes an internal review (a restatement of preceding points), an internal preview (a look ahead to upcoming points), or both:

"So far we've discussed _____ , _____ , and _____ . Our next points are _____ , _____ , and _____ ."

You can find several examples of transitions in the sample speech at the end of this chapter.

# Beginning and Ending the Speech

The **introduction** and **conclusion** of a speech are vitally important, although they usually will occupy less than 20 percent of your speaking time. Listeners form their impression of a speaker early, and they remember what they hear last; it is, therefore, vital to make those few moments at the beginning and end of your speech work to your advantage.

## The Introduction

There are four functions of a speech introduction. It serves to capture the audience's attention, preview the main points, set the mood and tone of the speech, and demonstrate the importance of the topic.

**Capturing Attention**    There are several ways to capture an audience's attention. The checklist on this page shows how some of these ways might be used in a speech entitled "Communication Between Plants and Humans."

**Previewing Main Points**    After you capture the attention of the audience, an effective introduction will almost always state the speaker's thesis and give the

 ON YOUR FEET

*Grabbing Attention*
Introduce any idea to your class in no more than 30 seconds. Then ask for a show of hands: Who would like to hear more?

---

**CHECKLIST >** **Capturing Audience Attention**

☐ **Refer to the audience.** The technique of referring to the audience is especially effective if it is complimentary: "Julio's speech last week about how animals communicate was so interesting that I decided to explore a related topic: Whether people can communicate with plants!"

☐ **Refer to the occasion.** A reference to the occasion could allude to the event of your speech: "Our assignment is to focus on an aspect of *human* communication. Given this guideline, it seems appropriate to talk about whether humans can communicate with plants."

☐ **Refer to the relationship between the audience and the subject.** "It's fair to say that all of us here believe it's important to care for our environment. What you'll learn today will make you care about that environment in a whole new way."

☐ **Refer to something familiar to the audience.** "Most of us have talked to our pets. Today, you'll learn that there are other conversational partners around the house."

☐ **Cite a startling fact or opinion.** "See that lilac bush outside the window? At this very moment it might be reacting to the joys and anxieties that you are

experiencing in this classroom." *Or,* "There is now actual scientific evidence that plants appreciate human company, kind words, and classical music."

☐ **Ask a question.** "Have you ever wondered why some people seem able to grow beautiful, healthy plants effortlessly, whereas others couldn't make a weed grow in the best soil? Perhaps it's because they have better relationships with those plants."

☐ **Tell an anecdote.** "The other night, while taking a walk in the country, I happened on a small garden that was rich with vegetation. But it wasn't the lushness of the plants that caught my eye. There, in the middle of the garden, was a man who was talking quite animatedly to a giant sunflower."

☐ **Use a quotation.** "Max Thornton, the naturalist, recently said, 'Psychobiology has proven that plants can communicate. Now humans need to learn how to listen to them.'"

☐ **Tell an (appropriate) joke.** "We once worried about people who talked to plants, but that's no longer the case. Now we only worry if the plants talk back."

listeners an idea of the upcoming main points. Katherine Graham, the former publisher of the *Washington Post*, addressed a group of businessmen and their wives in this way:

> I am delighted to be here. It is a privilege to address you. And I am especially glad the rules have been bent for tonight, allowing so many of you to bring along your husbands. I think it's nice for them to get out once in a while and see how the other half lives. Gentlemen, we welcome you.
>
> Actually, I have other reasons for appreciating this chance to talk with you tonight. It gives me an opportunity to address some current questions about the press and its responsibilities—whom we are responsible to, what we are responsible for, and generally how responsible our performance has been.[7]

Thus, Graham previewed her main points:

① To explain whom the press is responsible to

② To explain what the press is responsible for

③ To explain how responsible the press has been

Sometimes your preview of main points will be even more straightforward:

> "I have three points to discuss: They are _____ , _____ , and _____ ."

Sometimes you will not want to refer directly to your main points in your introduction. Your reasons for not doing so might be based on a plan calling for suspense, humorous effect, or stalling for time to win over a hostile audience. In that case, you might preview only your thesis:

> "I am going to say a few words about _____ ."
>
> "Did you ever wonder about _____ ?"
>
> "_____ is one of the most important issues facing us today."

**Setting the Mood and Tone of Your Speech**  Notice, in the example just given, how Katherine Graham began her speech by joking with her audience. She was a powerful woman speaking before an all-male organization; the only women in the audience were the members' wives. That is why Ms. Graham felt it necessary to put her audience members at ease by joking with them about women's traditional role in society. By beginning in this manner, she assured the men that she would not berate them for the sexist bylaws of their organization. She also showed them that she was going to approach her topic with wit and intelligence. Thus, she set the mood and tone for her entire speech. Imagine how different that mood and tone would have been if she had begun this way:

> Before I start today, I would just like to say that I would never have accepted your invitation to speak here had I known that your organization does not accept women as members. Just where do you Cro-Magnons get off, excluding more than half the human race from your little club?

**Demonstrating the Importance of Your Topic to Your Audience**  Your audience members will listen to you more carefully if your speech relates to them as individuals. Based on your audience analysis, you should state directly *why* your topic is of importance to your audience members. This importance should be related as closely as possible to their specific needs at that specific time. For example, Stephanie Hamilton, a student at North Dakota State University, presented a speech

 ON YOUR FEET

*Setting the Tone*

Present a brief introduction for a speech, but alter the tone you set by preparing three different versions.

about loopholes in the justice system when crimes of violence occur on cruise ships. After telling the story of a rape aboard ship, she established the importance of her topic this way:

> Each year, millions of people take to the seas on cruises. Many of us have taken cruises of our own or plan to take one someday, and practically everyone knows at least someone who has taken a cruise. Even if we will never take a cruise, we are a part of society and a possible target for crime. If someone were found guilty of a crime, would we want them free? That is exactly what is happening without laws of recourse in place for our protection. We don't need to let our family, friends, neighbors or ourselves be taken advantage of and never given justice.[8]

**Establishing Credibility**  One final consideration for your introduction is to establish your credibility to speak on your topic. One way to do this is to be *well prepared*. Another is to *appear confident* as soon as you face your audience. A third technique is to *tell your audience about your personal experience* with the topic, in order to establish why it is important to you. Curt Casper, in the sample speech found at the end of this chapter, used all three of these techniques. His first sentence says it all: "It is the four-year anniversary since my dad decided to drive in front of a train, dying by suicide."

In the *Anchorman* comedies, newscaster Ron Burgundy (Will Ferrell) reads the same opening and closing statements every night. Even if you haven't seen the films, it's easy to imagine the effect of his approach. How can you make your delivery most authentic?

## The Conclusion

The conclusion, like the introduction, is an especially important part of your speech. The conclusion has three essential functions: to restate the thesis, to review your main points, and to provide a memorable final remark.

You can review your thesis either by repeating it or by paraphrasing it. Or you might devise a striking summary statement for your conclusion to help your audience remember your thesis. Grant Anderson, a student at Minnesota State University, gave a speech against the policy of rejecting blood donations from homosexuals. He ended his conclusion with this statement: "The gay community still has a whole host of issues to contend with, but together all of us can all take a step forward by recognizing this unjust and discriminatory measure. So stand up and raise whatever arm they poke you in to draw blood and say 'Blood is Blood' no matter who you are."[9] Grant's statement was concise but memorable.

Your main points can also be reviewed artistically. For example, first look back at that example introduction by Katherine Graham, and then read her conclusion to that speech:

> So instead of seeking flat and absolute answers to the kinds of problems I have discussed tonight, what we should be trying to foster is respect for one another's conception of where duty lies, and understanding of the real worlds in which we try to do our best. And we should be hoping for the energy and sense to keep on arguing and questioning, because there is no better sign that our society is healthy and strong.

Let's take a closer look at how and why this conclusion was effective. Graham posed three questions in her introduction. She dealt with those questions in her speech and reminded her audience, in her conclusion, that she had answered the questions.

| PREVIEW (FROM INTRODUCTION OF SPEECH) | REVIEW (FROM CONCLUSION) |
|---|---|
| 1. To whom is the press responsible? | 1. To its own conception of where its duty lies |
| 2. What is the press responsible for? | 2. For doing its best in the "real world" |
| 3. How responsible has the press been? | 3. It has done its best |

## CHECKLIST > Effective Conclusions

You can make your final remarks most effective by avoiding the following mistakes:

☐ **Do not end abruptly.** Make sure that your conclusion accomplishes everything it is supposed to accomplish. Develop it fully. You might want to use signposts such as "Finally . . . ," "In conclusion . . . ," or "To sum up what I've been talking about here . . ." to let your audience know that you have reached the conclusion of the speech.

☐ **Don't ramble, either.** Prepare a definite conclusion, and never, never end by mumbling something like "Well, I guess that's about all I wanted to say . . ."

☐ **Don't introduce new points.** The worst kind of rambling is "Oh, yes, and something I forgot to mention is . . ."

☐ **Don't apologize.** Don't say, "I'm sorry I didn't have more time to research this subject," or use any of those sad songs. They will only highlight the possible weaknesses of your speech, and there's a good chance those weaknesses were far more apparent to you than to your audience. It's best to end strong. You can use any of the attention-getters suggested for the introduction to make the conclusion memorable. In fact, one kind of effective closing is to refer to the attention-getter you used in your introduction and remind your audience how it applies to the points you made in your speech.

> cultural idiom

**sad songs:**
statements meant to elicit sympathy

# Supporting Material

It is important to organize ideas clearly and logically. But clarity and logic by themselves won't guarantee that you'll interest, enlighten, or persuade others; these results call for the use of supporting materials. These materials—the facts and information that back up and prove your ideas and opinions—are the flesh that fills out the skeleton of your speech.

## Functions of Supporting Material

There are four functions of supporting material.

**To Clarify**   As explained in Chapter 4, people of different backgrounds tend to attach different meanings to words. Supporting material can help you overcome this potential source of confusion by helping you clarify key terms and ideas. For example, when Jacoby Cochran, a student at Bradley University in Illinois, spoke on the dangers of "special administrative measures," or SAMs, he needed to clarify what he meant by his key term. He used supporting material in this way:

> AlterNet of June 13, 2011, explains that SAMs are measures including limited communication, solitary confinement, the withholding of evidence and enhanced interrogation, enacted against individuals convicted or suspected of mob or terrorist ties. In the most extreme circumstances, such as keeping a known mob boss from running an organization from inside prison, SAMs have

@Work

## Organizing Business Presentations

When top business executives plan an important speech, they often call in a communication consultant to help organize their remarks. Even though they are experts, executives are so close to the topic of their message that they may have difficulty arranging their ideas so others will understand or be motivated by them.

Consultants stress how important organization and message structure are in giving presentations. Seminar leader and corporate trainer T. Stephen Eggleston sums up the basic approach: "Any presentation . . . regardless of complexity . . . should consist of the same four basic parts: an opening, body, summary and closing."[10]

Ethel Cook, a Massachusetts consultant, is very specific about how much time should be spent on each section of a speech. "In timing your presentation," she says, "an ideal breakdown would be:

Opening—10 to 20 percent
Body—65 to 75 percent
Closing—10 to 20 percent."[11]

Within the body of a presentation, business coach Vadim Kotelnikov gives his clients a step-by-step procedure to organize their ideas. "List all the points you plan to cover," he advises. "Group them in sections and put your list of sections in the order that best achieves your objectives. Begin with the most important topics."[12]

Toastmasters International, an organization that runs training programs for business professionals, suggests alternative organizational patterns:

To organize your ideas into an effective proposal, use an approach developed in the field of journalism—the "inverted pyramid." In the "inverted pyramid" format, the most important information is given in the first few paragraphs. As you present the pitch, the information becomes less and less crucial. This way, your presentation can be cut short, yet remain effective.[13]

While each consultant may offer specific tips, all agree that clear organization is essential when a business speaker wants his or her ideas to be understood and appreciated. ●

---

Imagine a business presentation you might have to make in your future career. Why would organization be important in such a presentation?

---

See the appendix of this book for more on work-related communication.

---

proven beneficial, but their recent expansions have elevated them from a rarely used, extreme holding measure to a legal basis for torture, detentions without charge or trial, and the shredding of constitutional rights.[14]

**To Prove** A second function of support is to be used as evidence, to prove the truth of what you are saying. If you were giving a speech on what is known as the immigration crisis, you might want to point out that concerns about immigration are nothing new. The following could be used to prove that point:

A prominent American once said about immigrants, "Few of their children in the country learn English. . . . The signs in our streets have inscriptions in both languages. . . . Unless the stream of their importation could be turned they will soon so outnumber us that all the advantages we have will not be able to preserve our language, and even our government will become precarious." This sentiment did not emerge from the rancorous debate over the immigration bill defeated not long ago in the Senate. It was not the lament of some . . . candidate intent on wooing bedrock conservative votes. Guess again. Voicing this grievance was Benjamin Franklin. And the language so vexing to him was the German spoken by new arrivals to Pennsylvania in the 1750s, a wave of immigrants whom Franklin viewed as the "most stupid of their nation."[15]

**To Make Interesting**   A third function of support is to make an idea interesting or to catch your audience's attention. For example, when Nathan Dunn, a student at Oklahoma City College, spoke about how special education students are sometimes treated, he started with this concrete example:

> For most high school seniors, their biggest problems revolve around getting into college, getting a job, or finding a date to the prom. Unfortunately, Andre McCollins of Canton, Massachusetts, is not most high school seniors. In October 2002, Andre was an 18-year-old student at the Judge Rotenberg Educational Center, a residential school for students with developmental disabilities less than 20 miles from where we are right now. One morning, Andre did not respond to a staff member asking him to take off his coat. In response, staff members tied him to a board face down, for 7 hours, with no breaks for food, water, or bathroom use. More horrifying, though, was that staff members electrically shocked Andre 31 times while he was tied down. The school's classroom cameras captured the whole day on a video the school fought to keep secret for years.[16]

**To Make Memorable**   A final function of supporting materials, related to the preceding one, is to make a point memorable. We have already mentioned the importance of "memorable" statements in a speech conclusion; use of supporting material in the introduction and body of the speech provides another way to help your audience retain important information. When Chris Griesinger of Eastern Michigan University spoke about the importance of pain management, he wanted his audience to remember the severity of the problem, so he used the following as supporting material:

> Every year the National Committee on Treatment of Intractable Pain receives letters from people sharing their stories of loved ones who died in pain. One letter reads, "I lost my mother to cancer. Her pain was so horrid that she lost her mind and ate her bottom lip completely off from clenching her top teeth so tightly. My 13-year-old sister and I watched this for 6 weeks."[17]

## Types of Supporting Material

As you may have noted, each function of support could be fulfilled by several different types of material. Let's take a look at these different types of supporting material.

**Definitions**   It's a good idea to give your audience members definitions of your key terms, especially if those terms are unfamiliar to them or are being used in an unusual way. A good definition is simple and concise. When Elizabeth Hobbs, a student at Truman State University in Missouri, gave a speech on U.S. torture policy, she needed to define a key term, *extraordinary rendition*:

> "Extraordinary rendition" is the phrase used by the CIA to describe the U.S. practice of secretly sending terrorist suspects to countries where torture is routine.[18]

**Examples**   An **example** is a specific case that is used to demonstrate a general idea. Examples can be either factual or hypothetical, personal or borrowed. In Elizabeth Hobbs's speech on U.S. torture policy, she used the following example:

> He was kidnapped while making a business trip to Macedonia. To be transported to a secret prison in Afghanistan, he was beaten, his underwear was forcibly removed and he was put into a diaper, and chained spread eagle inside the plane. In Afghanistan he was beaten, interrogated and put into solitary confinement. To get out, he started a hunger strike, but after 37 days without food, a feeding

tube was forced through his nose and into his stomach. Nearly 5 months later he was released, with no explanation of his imprisonment.

Does this sound like Chile under the Pinochet regime? Prisoner abuse in Uzbekistan? A Russian gulag? It wasn't. This is a story of a victim of America's War on Terror.[19]

**Hypothetical examples** can often be more powerful than factual examples, because hypothetical examples ask audience members to imagine something, thus causing them to become active participants in the thought. Stephanie Wideman of the University of West Florida used a hypothetical example to start off her speech on oil prices:

The year is 2020. One day you are asked not to come into work, not because of a holiday, but instead because there is not enough energy available to power your office. You see, it is not that the power is out, but that they are out of power.[20]

**Statistics**   **Statistics** are numbers that are arranged or organized to show that a fact or principle is true for a large percentage of cases. Statistics are actually collections of examples, which is why they are often more effective as proof than are isolated examples. Here's the way a newspaper columnist used statistics to prove a point about gun violence:

I had coffee the other day with Marian Wright Edelman, president of the Children's Defense Fund, and she mentioned that since the murders of Robert Kennedy and the Rev. Martin Luther King Jr. in 1968, well over a million Americans have been killed by firearms in the United States. That's more than the combined U.S. combat deaths in all the wars in all of American history. "We're losing eight children and teenagers a day to gun violence," she said. "As far as young people are concerned, we lose the equivalent of the massacre at Virginia Tech about every 4 days."[21]

Because statistics can be powerful proof, you have certain rules to follow when using them. You should make sure that they make sense and that they come from a credible source. You should also cite the source of the statistic when you use it. A final rule is based on effectiveness rather than ethics. You should reduce the statistic to a concrete image if possible. For example, $1 billion in $100 bills would be about the same height as a 60-story building. Using concrete images such as this will make your statistics more than "just numbers" when you use them. For example, one observer expressed the idea of Bill Gates's wealth this way:

Examine Bill Gates' wealth compared to yours: Consider the average American of reasonable but modest wealth. Perhaps he has a net worth of $100,000. Mr. Gates' worth is 400,000 times larger. Which means that if something costs $100,000 to him, to Bill it's as though it costs 25 cents. So for example, you might think a new Lamborghini Diablo would cost $250,000, but in Bill Gates dollars that's 63 cents.[22]

**Analogies/Comparison-Contrast**   We use **analogies**, or comparisons, all the time, often in the form of figures of speech, such as similes and metaphors. A simile is a direct comparison that usually uses *like* or *as*, whereas a metaphor is an implied comparison that does not use *like* or *as*. So if you said that the rush of refugees from a war-torn country was "like a tidal wave," you would be using a simile. If you used the expression "a tidal wave of refugees," you would be using a metaphor.

> Recall a recent occasion in which you tried to change the mind of one or more people. What were your arguments? Which forms of support did you use to back them up?

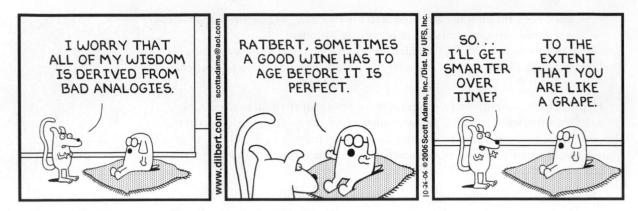

*Source:* DILBERT: Scott Adams, Inc./Dist. by United Feature Syndicate, Inc.

Analogies are extended metaphors. They can be used to compare or contrast an unknown concept with a known one. For example, here's how one writer made her point against separate Academy Awards for men and women:

> Many hours into the 82nd Academy Awards ceremony this Sunday, the Oscar for best actor will go to Morgan Freeman, Jeff Bridges, George Clooney, Colin Firth, or Jeremy Renner. Suppose, however, that the Academy of Motion Picture Arts and Sciences presented separate honors for best white actor and best non-white actor, and that Mr. Freeman was prohibited from competing against the likes of Mr. Clooney and Mr. Bridges. Surely, the Academy would be derided as intolerant and out of touch; public outcry would swiftly ensure that Oscar nominations never again fell along racial lines.
>
> Why, then, is it considered acceptable to segregate nominations by sex, offering different Oscars for best actor and best actress?[23]

**Anecdotes**    An **anecdote** is a brief story with a point, often (but not always) based on personal experience. (The word *anecdote* comes from the Greek, meaning "unpublished item.") Ronald Reagan was famous for his use of anecdotes. In his farewell address, when he wanted to make the point that America stood as a symbol of freedom to people in other lands, he used the following anecdote:

> It was back in the early eighties, at the height of the boat people, and a sailor was hard at work on the carrier *Midway*, which was patrolling the South China sea. The sailor, like most American servicemen, was young, smart and fiercely observant. The crew spied on the horizon a leaky little boat—and crammed inside were refugees from Indochina hoping to get to America. The *Midway* sent a small launch to bring them to the ship, and safety. As the refugees made their way through the choppy seas, one spied the sailor on deck, and stood up and called out to him. He yelled, "Hello American Sailor—Hello Freedom Man."
>
> A small moment with a big meaning, a moment the sailor, who wrote it in a letter, couldn't get out of his mind. And when I saw it, neither could I.[24]

**Quotations/Testimonies**    Using a familiar, artistically stated saying will enable you to take advantage of someone else's memorable wording. For example, if you were giving a speech on personal integrity, you might quote Mark Twain, who said, "Always do right. This will gratify some people, and astonish the rest." A quotation like that fits Alexander Pope's definition of "true wit": "What was often thought, but ne'er so well expressed."

You can also use quotations as **testimony**, to prove a point by using the support of someone who is more authoritative or experienced on the subject than you are. When Rajiv Khanna, a student at Newman University in Kansas, wanted to prove that the distortion of history was a serious problem, he used testimony this way:

> Eugene Genovese, Professor Emeritus of History at Emory University, states in the July 11 issue of the *Chronicle of Higher Education*, "The distortion of history remains a serious problem to the academic community and the country at large." He continues, "As individuals who are history-making animals, we remain rooted in the past, and we are shaped by our society's version of its history."[25]

Sometimes testimony can be paraphrased. For example, when one business executive was talking on the subject of diversity, he used a conversation he had with Jesse Jackson Sr., an African American leader, as testimony:

In the film *Lincoln*, Daniel Day-Lewis captures the 16th U.S. president's use of folksy anecdotes to clarify ideas for his listeners. How can you use stories effectively to get your points across?

> At one point in our conversation, Jesse talked about the stages of advancement toward a society where diversity is fully valued. He said the first stage was emancipation—the end of slavery. The second stage was the right to vote and the third stage was the political power to actively participate in government—to be part of city hall, the Governor's office and Capitol Hill. Jesse was clearly focused, though, on the fourth stage—which he described as the ability to participate fully in the prosperity that this nation enjoys. In other words, economic power.[26]

**Ethical Challenge**

## The Ethics of Support

Have you ever "stretched" supporting material to help it conform to a point you were trying to make? (An example might be citing an "expert" for an idea of your own when discussing a social issue with a friend.) How far can you stretch the facts without violating ethical standards?

## Styles of Support: Narration and Citation

Most of the forms of support discussed in the preceding section could be presented in either of two ways: through narration or through citation. **Narration** involves telling a story with your information. You put it in the form of a small drama, with a beginning, middle, and end. For example, Evan McCarley of the University of Mississippi narrated the following example in his speech on the importance of drug courts:

> Oakland contractor Josef Corbin has a lot to be proud of. Last year his firm, Corbin Building Inc., posted revenue of over 3 million dollars after funding dozens of urban restoration projects. His company was ranked as one of the 800 fastest-growing companies in the country, all due to what his friends call his motivation for success. Unfortunately, until 1996 Corbin used this motivation to rob and steal on the streets of San Francisco to support a heroin and cocaine habit. But when he was charged with possession in 1996, Josef was given the option to participate in a state drug court, a program targeted at those recently charged with drug use, possession, or distribution. The drug court offers

offenders free drug treatment, therapy, employment, education, and weekly meetings with a judge, parole officer and other accused drug offenders.[27]

**Citation**, unlike narration, is a simple statement of the facts. Citation is shorter and more precise than narration, in the sense that the source is carefully stated. Citation will always include such phrases as, "According to the July 25, 2010, edition of *Time* magazine," or, "As Mr. Smith made clear in an interview last April 24." Evan McCarley cited statistics later in his speech on drug courts:

> Fortunately, Corbin's story, as reported in the May 30th *San Francisco Chronicle*, is not unique, since there are currently over 300 drug courts operating in 21 states, turning first-time and repeat offenders into successful citizens with a 70% success rate.[29]

Some forms of support, such as anecdotes, are inherently more likely to be expressed as narration. Statistics, on the other hand, are nearly always cited rather than narrated. However, when you are using examples, quotation/testimony, definitions, and analogies, you often have a choice.

## Sample Speech

The following sample speech was presented by Curt Casper, whose story began this chapter. When Curt was a senior at Hastings College in 2011, he presented this speech at the Interstate Oratorical Association Annual Contest, hosted by James Madison University. He won second place in the tournament, but the speech was important to him for more than that.

Curt chose his topic because of his intimate experience with it:

> My dad committed suicide when I was a senior in high school. I strongly believed my voice and speech mattered through showing others what my family went

---

### Understanding Communication Technology

## Plagiarism in a Digital Age

Some experts believe that the Web is redefining how students understand the concept of authorship and originality. After all, the Internet is the home of file sharing that allows us to download music, movies, and TV programs without payment. Google and Wikipedia are our main portals to random free information, also. It all seems to belong to us, residing on our computer as it does. Information wants to be free.

According to one expert on the topic, "Now we have a whole generation of students who've grown up with information that just seems to be hanging out there in cyberspace and doesn't seem to have an author. It's possible to believe this information is just out there for anyone to take."[28] Other experts beg to differ. They say students are fully aware of what plagiarism is, online or off, and they know it's cheating. It's just that it's so easy to copy and paste online material, and students like to save time wherever they can.

Public speaking instructors are on the front lines of those fighting plagiarism, because it's so important for successful student speakers to speak from the heart, in their own words and with their own voice. Plus, citing research enhances credibility. Plagiarism in public speaking isn't just cheating, it's ineffective.

The general rule for the digital age is as follows: Thou shalt not cut and paste into a final draft—not for a paper, and not for a speech. Cutting and pasting is fine for research, but everything that's cut and pasted should be placed in a separate "research" file, complete with a full citation for the website you found it in. Then switch to your "draft" file to put everything in your own words, and go back to the research file to find the attribution information when you need to cite facts and ideas that you got from those sources. ●

Have you ever had a problem with online plagiarism? What was the outcome?

through when my dad did this. I wanted people in my shoes to have the opportunity to get help, the opportunity to know there is hope, and that it will get better.[30]

Curt used a simple problem-effect-solution organizational structure, as seen in his outline, presented on page 356.

Curt collected his supporting material from a wide range of sources, as seen in the following bibliography:

## Bibliography

American Association of Suicidology. (2009). *Survivors of suicide fact sheet.* Washington, D.C.: American Association of Suicidology.

American Foundation for Suicide Prevention. (2011). *For the media.* Retrieved March 15, 2011, from American Foundation for Suicide Prevention: http://www.afsp.org/media

American Foundation for Suicide Prevention. (2011). *Out of the darkness community walks.* (EABnet.) Retrieved March 15, 2011, from SOS-walk.org: http://www.sos-walk.org/sos/index.htm

Belau, D. (2011, March 16). LOSS team. (C. Casper, E-mail)

Caruso, K. (2011). *Suicide survivors: Coping with rumors and gossip.* Retrieved March 15, 2011, from suicide.org: http://www.suicide.org/suicide-survivors-coping-with-rumors-and-gossip.html

Cerel, J., Jordan, J. R., & Duberstein, P. R. (2008). The impact of suicide on the family. *Crisis Intervention and Suicide Prevention, 29*(1), 38–44.

Evans, D. (2011, February 28). Accidental death becomes suicide when insurers dodge payouts. *Bloomberg Markets Magazine.* http://www.bloomberg.com/news/2011-03-01/accidental-death-becomes-suicide-when-insurers-dodge-paying-life-benefits.html

Gearing, R. E., & Lizardi, D. (2009, October). Religion and suicide. *Journal of Religion and Health, 48*(3), 332–341.

Hudenko, D., & Crenshaw, D. (2010, October 5). *The relationship between PTSD and suicide.* Retrieved March 15, 2011, from National Center for PTSD: http://www.ptsd.va.gov/professional/pages/ptsd-suicide.asp

Harvard Mental Health. (2009, November). Supporting survivors of suicide loss. *Harvard Mental Health Letter, 4*, 5.

Hopkins, K. (2010, July 15). Suicides, attempts spike again in western Alaska villages. *Anchorage Daily News*, 1.

Insurance.com. (2007, May 17). *Will mental illness affect your life insurance cost?* Retrieved March 15, 2011, from insurance.com: http://www.insurance.com/life-insurance/health-and-life-insurance/will-mental-illness-affect-your-life-insurance-cost.aspx

Johnson, C. (2011, March 15). Compensability clauses. (C. Casper, Interviewer)

KHAS-TV. (2011, April 17). Suicide coverage. (C. Casper, Interviewer)

National Endowment for Financial Education. (2011). *Surviving a suicide loss: A financial guide.* New York: American Foundation for Suicide Prevention.

Patania, J. (2011, March 16). Program assistant for American Association Suicidology. (C. Casper, Interviewer)

University of Nebraska Public Policy Center. (2010). *2010 Nebraska State Suicide Prevention Summit.* Hastings: University of Nebraska-Lincoln.

As you read Curt's speech below, notice how he carefully chooses various types of supporting material to back up what he has to say.

**SAMPLE SPEECH** Survivor Support                                    **Curt Casper**

1   It is the 4-year anniversary since my dad decided to drive in front of a train, dying by suicide. My family has never been the same. My little brother, Blake, who was 10 at the time, has now been in more than a dozen different homes and has been diagnosed with post-traumatic stress syndrome three times. While there was initial help from friends and relatives, the support system quickly went away, and there was nowhere my family could turn to for help.

*Curt begins with a startling statement about his personal experience. This sets the tone for the speech.*

2   Three days before my dad killed himself, I received a hug asking for help. I refused to see the pain that my dad was suffering and kept it to myself. Six months later, I wanted to drive in front of a train, because I blamed myself.

*He expands on his personal experience with another powerful statement.*

3   My brother and I are not alone. Jill Pantania of the American Association of Suicidology recently told me, "There are 6 million people in the U.S. that currently mourn the death of a loved one by suicide. And that number grows by 190,000 each year."

*He backs up his personal experience with statistics from an interview.*

4   Our society is suffering from a mental health stigma. We cannot change this stigma until we stop suicide survivors from suffering alone. Suicide survivors include friends, families, and loved ones who are left behind to deal with a suicide. The *Harvard Mental Health* newsletter of November 2009 notes that the death of a loved one because of suicide leads to a higher risk for several types of psychiatric disorders. According to the Hampton Roads Survivors of Suicide website, "survivors are five times more likely to commit suicide themselves." In other words, suicide isn't the end of a problem for anyone—it's often the starting point for more crises. We all have to become the support that survivors so desperately need.

*Here Curt states his thesis, defines a key term ("suicide survivors"), and provides statistics.*

5   Today, I'd like to tell you how we can all facilitate survivor support. First, though, we need to recognize the reasons suicide survivors do not receive the help they deserve. Second, we need to examine the impact of that lack of help. And then finally, we can consider some possible solutions to give survivors the hope they deserve.

*A transition in the form of a preview of main points.*

6   The deficiencies in survivor support can be found on both a societal and economic level.

*Another transition, in the form of a preview of two subpoints.*

7   First, it can take a while to get over a suicide because our society refuses to use the word *suicide*. The website suicide.org says we as a society make up excuses for the suicide, like "it was his time to go"; yet we don't use the word *suicide*.

*He backs up his first subpoint with information from a website . . .*

8   This negative connotation regarding suicide is furthered by religious doctrine, because some religions believe that suicide is a one-way ticket to hell. This is confirmed in the essay "Religion and Suicide," published in the *Journal of Religion and Health* in 2009.

*. . . and a printed essay . . .*

9   There are even guidelines in place restricting the use of the word in the media, according to the American Foundation for Suicide Prevention. For instance, KHAS-TV said in a personal correspondence on April 14, 2011, that they did not cover a student's death in December because it was suicide, yet in March they covered a student's death because she died from a skiing accident and not from suicide. These guidelines are in place to prevent other suicides. However, these same guidelines implicitly affirm the messages of guilt and stigma for the family and other survivors.

*. . . and an example that he found in an e-mail interview.*

10  Second, as the National Endowment for Financial Education states, "someone getting over a suicide will face financial turmoil." Life insurance companies do not provide benefits if a suicide occurs within 24 months of signing with the company. This is known as the "suicide clause." In some cases, this makes it difficult to pay for the funeral arrangements and other financial obligations. For example, one mother in Nebraska lost her husband to suicide 10 months after

*He introduces his second subpoint with a citation and then backs it up with an example.*

signing with the insurance company. She could not even afford to send her son, who witnessed his father shooting himself, to counseling. In other cases the money *is* received, but it is received in one large sum, and survivors feel guilty about receiving it. They might not want to touch the money, or they might just waste it, rather than saving it for a time of need.

**11** With an understanding of the causes that undermine survivor support, we can consider the impact of this lack of support, including profound grief and post-traumatic stress disorder on the part of the survivor.

A clearly stated transition from his first to his second main point.

**12** First, a suicide causes more grief than most normal deaths, as there are unanswered questions. Survivors wonder, "why" and "what could I have done," which can lead to depression and further suicides, as noted by the *Journal of Crisis Intervention and Suicide Prevention* in 2008. For example, a small community in Alaska, Yukon-Kuskwim Delta, saw nine people between the ages of 17 and 22 commit suicide within only a few weeks of each other. According to the *Anchorage Daily News* of July 15, 2010, there was a chain reaction as each person was affected by the previous death. Alaska is not alone; my campus experienced the suicide cycle back in December.

Several examples, from research and personal experience.

**13** Second, because denial and shock are often the first emotions felt by survivors, it can take years for bereavement, creating a condition known as post-traumatic stress disorder, or PTSD. On average, it takes 4.5 years after a suicide before a survivor *seeks* help. I learned that from Dr. Dan Belau, a mental health advocate, in personal correspondence during March 2011. According to Dr. Belau, PTSD leads to nightmares and flashbacks, ultimately making it difficult for a survivor to effectively function in society. We have all seen the effects of post-traumatic stress on soldiers fighting overseas, but often people don't realize that we are at war *here* with suicide.

His next subpoint.

**14** The National Center for PTSD website, which I accessed in October 2010, says there is a "direct link between survivors of suicide and PTSD." Even small events, like seeing someone else's dad come to watch your sports event or come to a birthday party can result in a paralysis of emotions for survivors—even many years after the suicide.

Although Curt words this example as a generality, his audience knows he is referring to personal experience here, which provides a sort of transition to his next, personal statement.

**15** I was eventually able to get help, and I no longer blame myself. I have not contemplated suicide since I got the help I needed. However, many survivors simply do not get help. Survivor support solutions can and should be facilitated on two levels: through survivor supporters and through survivors themselves.

A transition in the form of a preview of final subpoints.

**16** First, our lawmakers could be survivor supporters by easing the red tape on insurance policies. Insurance agent Caleb Johnson, in a personal interview on March 15, 2011, says, "A simple solution would be to set a standard that insurance companies give back the premiums that were paid before the suicide." If someone is willing to spend money on insurance, they should know their loved ones would be taken care of if a suicide occurs. If you wanted to become a survivor supporter, you could encourage insurance reform by sending a brief e-mail about this issue to your local lawmakers.

First subpoint is developed with a quotation.

**17** On a more personal level, if you have a friend who is a survivor, just be there for them by giving them a list of resources. I've prepared a CD with this type of resources, such as inexpensive but effective counselors, along with a list of websites that can help supporters and survivors. I'd be glad to give you a copy of this CD after my speech.

Direct statement of next subpoint.

**18** As a survivor supporter, you need to use the word *suicide* when talking to survivors. This will ease their grief, because it will help make suicide visible. While attending an Active Minds Conference, I was able to see a display of 1,100 backpacks that represents the number of collegiate suicides annually. The display,

A subpoint developed with a descriptive anecdote.

entitled *Send Silence Packing*, travels across the nation to show the effects suicide has on all. There are stories of survivors who have dealt with a suicide in
each backpack. In addition, the cool part is, you can get the backpacks in your
communities—that information will also be available at the end of my speech.

**19** Second, I urge survivors to share their stories to help others in similar situations.
I use my story, because I know I cannot change what happened to my dad, but by
sharing my story I can help other families.

**20** The first step is for survivors to realize that they are not at fault for what happened.
Yes, the grief is going to be difficult to handle, but it can get easier. We as a community of survivors need to be there for each other. I am currently a member of
a LOSS team, which is a group of individuals who are survivors and want to help
other survivors. When there is a suicide in the area, the team is dispatched to the
family. Dr. Dan Belau, the mental health advocate I mentioned earlier, told me,
"The time it takes for a survivor to seek help changes from 4.5 years to 39 days"
when resources like the LOSS team are provided.

LOSS stands for Local Outreach to Suicide Survivors. Curt felt the acronym was intuitive and did not require an explanation. Do you agree?

**21** Finally, survivors, remember it's never too late to request the help you deserve. If
it takes 4.5 years to get the courage and seek unsolicited help, how long might it
take before we come to terms with the event? Survivor support cannot be rushed;
there is no statute of limitations on grief.

**22** I realize this is a tough topic to talk about. That's why I have created this CD with
a list of resources that can help you and survivors. Please take one of these. In fact,
take a few of them so you can give them to others, because while a survivor will
never know the reasons why a suicide occurs, having a better understanding of
how to deal with the loss will help ease the grieving mind.

Curt picks up the CD here so audience members can see it.

**23** I have seen firsthand how a suicide can destroy a family. In light of the 4-year anniversary of my father's death, I hope that my brother, Blake, and the rest of my
family will be able to pick up the pieces and begin to rebuild our family. And,
while the road to recovery will still be tough and has been tough, I know my dad
would have wanted us to move on and know that everything is okay.[31]

Powerful personal experience is used as supporting material in this conclusion.

## Summary

This chapter dealt with speech organization and supporting material. Speech organization is a process that begins
with the formulation of a thesis statement to express the
central idea of a speech. The thesis is established in the
introduction, developed in the body, and reviewed in
the conclusion of a structured speech. The introduction
will also gain the audience's attention, preview the main
points, set the mood and tone of the speech, and demonstrate the importance of the topic to the audience. The
conclusion will review your thesis and/or main points and
supply the audience with a memory aid.

Organizing the body of the speech will begin with a list
of points you might want to make. These points are then
organized according to the principles of outlining. They are
divided, coordinated, and placed in a logical order. Transitions from point to point help make this order apparent
to your audience. Organization follows a pattern, such as
time, space, topic, problem-solution, cause-effect, Motivated Sequence, or climax arrangements.

Supporting materials are the facts and information you
use to back up what you say. Supporting material has four
purposes: to clarify, to make interesting, to make memorable, and to prove.

Types of support include *definitions* of key terms; *examples*, which can be real or hypothetical; *statistics*, which
show that a fact or principle is true for a large percentage of

cases; *analogies*, which compare or contrast an unknown or unfamiliar concept with a known or familiar one; *anecdotes*, which add a lively, personal touch; and *quotations and testimony*, which are used for memorable wording as well as ideas from a well-known or authoritative source. Any piece of support might combine two or more of these types. Support may be narrated (told in story form) or cited (stated briefly).

## Key Terms

**analogy** An extended comparison that can be used as supporting material in a speech. *p. 369*

**anecdote** A brief, personal story used to illustrate or support a point in a speech. *p. 370*

**basic speech structure** The division of a speech into introduction, body, and conclusion. *p. 355*

**cause-effect pattern** An organizing plan for a speech that demonstrates how one or more events result in another event or events. *p. 361*

**citation** A brief statement of supporting material in a speech. *p. 372*

**climax pattern** An organizing plan for a speech that builds ideas to the point of maximum interest or tension. *p. 359*

**conclusion (of a speech)** The final structural unit of a speech, in which the main points are reviewed and final remarks are made to motivate the audience to act or help listeners remember key ideas. *p. 363*

**example** A specific case that is used to demonstrate a general idea. *p. 368*

**formal outline** A consistent format and set of symbols used to identify the structure of ideas. *p. 355*

**hypothetical example** An example that asks an audience to imagine an object or event. *p. 369*

**introduction (of a speech)** The first structural unit of a speech, in which the speaker captures the audience's attention and previews the main points to be covered. *p. 363*

**narration** The presentation of speech supporting material as a story with a beginning, middle, and end. *p. 371*

**problem-solution pattern** An organizing pattern for a speech that describes an unsatisfactory state of affairs and then proposes a plan to remedy the problem. *p. 360*

**space pattern** An organizing plan in a speech that arranges points according to their physical location. *p. 359*

**statistic** Numbers arranged or organized to show how a fact or principle is true for a large percentage of cases. *p. 369*

**testimony** Supporting material that proves or illustrates a point by citing an authoritative source. *p. 370*

**time pattern** An organizing plan for a speech based on chronology. *p. 359*

**topic pattern** An organizing plan for a speech that arranges points according to logical types or categories. *p. 360*

**transition** A phrase that connects ideas in a speech by showing how one relates to the other. *p. 362*

**working outline** A constantly changing organizational aid used in planning a speech. *p. 355*

## Check Your Understanding

1. Which of the organizing principles for outlining from pages 356–359 do you need to work on in your own outlining? Which ones come naturally to you?

2. What are the primary characteristics of introductions, conclusions, and transitions? Why is each important?

3. Which one of the goals of supporting material, as outlined on pages 366–368, do you consider most important? Why?

## Activities

1. **Dividing Ideas** For practice in the principle of division, divide each of the following into three to five subcategories:

   1. Clothing
   2. Academic studies
   3. Crime
   4. Health care
   5. Fun
   6. Charities

2. **Organizational Effectiveness** Take any written statement at least three paragraphs long that you consider effective. This statement might be an editorial in your local newspaper, a short magazine article, or even a section of one of your textbooks. Outline this statement according to the rules discussed here. Was the statement well organized? Did its organization contribute to its effectiveness?

3. **The Functions of Support** For practice in recognizing the functions of support, identify three instances of support in each of the speeches at the end of Chapters 13 and 14. Explain the function of each instance of support. (Keep in mind that any instance of support *could* perform more than one function.)

## For Further Exploration

For more resources about organization and support, see the *Understanding Human Communication* website at www .oup.com/us/adler. There you will find a variety of resources: "Media Room" clips from popular films and television shows to further illustrate important concepts, a list of books and articles, links to descriptions of feature films and television shows at the *Now Playing* website, study aids, and a self-test to check your understanding of the material in this chapter.

**CHAPTER 13**

# Informative Speaking

**13**

## Chapter Outline

### LEARNING OBJECTIVES

1. Create information hunger by stressing the relevance of your material to your listeners' needs.

2. Use the strategies outlined in this chapter to organize unfamiliar information in an understandable manner.

3. Emphasize important points in your speech.

4. Generate audience involvement.

5. Use visual aids effectively.

**ShaoLan Hsueh is a radical.** Or rather, her approach to teaching Chinese is.

As the daughter of a calligrapher in Taiwan, Hsueh spent 15 years mastering the symbols that represent Chinese words. Because there are more than 20,000 of these symbols in all, many people consider Chinese the most difficult language in the world.

"It must seem as impenetrable as the Great Wall of China," Hsueh acknowledges. "Over the years I often wondered if I could find a way to break down this wall."[1] She may have done just that.

Hsueh has designed an easy-to-learn system she calls Chineasy. It's based on eight simple characters for words such as *person, tree, sun,* and *moon.* Once people understand them, the meaning of 30 or 40 additional symbols becomes apparent, and so on. Soon, Hsueh says, people can quickly learn enough to read Chinese road signs, menus, and newspapers.

The idea is catching on. Chineasy has achieved worldwide attention, and Hsueh is in demand as a public speaker. You will find her TED talk, which has been viewed more than 700,000 times, at the end of this chapter.

*ShaoLan Hsueh's TED talk demonstrates that even complicated topics can be explained clearly.*

- What speakers have you encountered who have the ability to present difficult concepts in a clear and interesting way? What lessons can you learn from them?

- What complicated topics would you like to explain in a clearer and more interesting way? How can you do so by applying the information in this chapter?

> cultural idiom

**rain down on:**
fall like rain, overwhelm

Have you noticed that there's a lot of information going around these days? Some people call it the age of information; others call it the age of information glut, data smog, and clutter. There are, in fact, a hundred names for it, but they all deal with the same idea: There is just too much information. And the amount of information is increasing exponentially. One information expert estimates that every 2 days now we create as much information as we did from the dawn of civilization up until 2003.[2]

Social scientists tell us that the information glut leads to **information overload**, which is a form of psychological stress that occurs when people become confused and have trouble sorting through all the information that is available to them.[3] Some experts use another term, **information anxiety**, for the same phenomenon. To check on how information overload affects you personally, do the self-assessment on p. 381.

As ShaoLan Hsueh discovered when planning her speech on the Chineasy method, the informative speaker's responsibility is not just to provide new information. Informative speaking, when it's done effectively, seeks to relieve information overload by turning information into **knowledge** for an audience. Information is the raw materials, the sometimes-contradictory facts and competing claims that rain down on public consciousness. Knowledge is what you get when you are able to make sense of and use those raw materials. Effective public speakers filter, organize, and illustrate information in order to reach small audiences with messages tailored for them, in an environment in which they can see if the audience is "getting it." If they aren't, the speaker can adjust the message and work with the audience until they do.

Informative speaking goes on all around you: in your professors' lectures or in a mechanic's explanation of how to keep your car from breaking down. You engage in this type of speaking frequently whether you realize it or not. Sometimes it is formal, as when you give a report in class. At other times, it is more casual, as when you tell a friend how to prepare your favorite dish. The main objective of this chapter is to give you the skills you need to enhance all of your informative speaking.

## SELF-ASSESSMENT

### Are You Overloaded with Information?

Problems in informative speaking are often the result of information overload—on the part of both the speaker and the audience. For each statement to the right, select "often," "sometimes," or "seldom" to assess your level of information overload.

**1.** I forget information I need to know.

    Often        Sometimes        Seldom

**2.** I have difficulty concentrating on important tasks.

    Often        Sometimes        Seldom

**3.** When I go online, I feel anxious about the work that I don't have time to do.

    Often        Sometimes        Seldom

**4.** I have e-mail messages sitting in my inbox that are more than 2 weeks old.

    Often        Sometimes        Seldom

**5.** I constantly check my online services because I am afraid that if I don't, I will never catch up.

    Often        Sometimes        Seldom

**6.** I find myself easily distracted by things that allow me to avoid work I need to do.

    Often        Sometimes        Seldom

**7.** I feel fatigued by the amount of information I encounter.

    Often        Sometimes        Seldom

**8.** I delay making decisions because of too many choices.

    Often        Sometimes        Seldom

**9.** I make wrong decisions because of too many choices.

    Often        Sometimes        Seldom

**10.** I spend too much time seeking information that is *nice to know* rather than information that I *need to know*.

    Often        Sometimes        Seldom

Scoring: Give yourself 3 points for each "often," 2 points for each "sometimes," and 1 point for each "seldom." If your score is:

10–15: Information overload is not a big problem for you. However, it's probably still a significant problem for at least some members of your audience, so try to follow the guidelines for informative speaking outlined in this chapter.

16–24: You have a normal level of information overload. The guidelines in this chapter will help you be a more effective speaker.

25–30: You have a high level of information overload. Along with observing the guidelines in this chapter, you might also want to search online for guidelines to help you overcome this problem. ●

# Types of Informative Speaking

There are several types of informative speaking. The primary types have to do with the content and purpose of the speech.

## By Content

Informative speeches are generally categorized according to their content, including the following types:

**Speeches About Objects**   This type of informative speech is about anything that is tangible (that is, capable of being seen or touched). Speeches about objects might include an appreciation of the Grand Canyon (or any other natural wonder) or a demonstration of the newest smartphone (or any other product).

**Speeches About Processes**   A process is any series of actions that leads to a specific result. If you spoke on the process of aging, the process of learning to juggle, or the process of breaking into a social networking business, you would be giving this type of speech.

**Speeches About Events**   You would be giving this type of informative speech if your topic dealt with anything notable that happened, was happening, or might happen: an upcoming protest against hydraulic fracturing ("fracking"), for example, or the prospects of your favorite baseball team winning the national championship.

**Speeches About Concepts**   Concepts include intangible ideas, such as beliefs, theories, ideas, and principles. If you gave an informative speech about postmodernism, vegetarianism, or any other "ism," you would be giving this type of speech. Other topics would include everything from New Age religions to theories about extraterrestrial life to rules for making millions of dollars.

## By Purpose

We also distinguish among types of informative speeches depending on the speaker's purpose. We ask, "Does the speaker seek to describe, explain, or instruct?"

**Descriptions**   A speech of **description** is the most straightforward type of informative speech. You might introduce a new product like a wearable computer to a group of customers, or you might describe what a career in nursing would be like. Whatever its topic, a descriptive speech uses details to create a "word picture" of the essential factors that make that thing what it is.

**Explanations**   Explanations clarify ideas and concepts that are already known but not understood by an audience. For example, your audience members might already know that a U.S. national debt exists, but they might be baffled by the reasons why it has become so large. Explanations often deal with the question of *why* or *how*. Why do we have to wait until the age of 21 to drink legally? How did China evolve from an impoverished economy to a world power in a single generation? Why did tuition need to be increased this semester?

**Instructions**   Instructions teach something to the audience in a logical, step-by-step manner. They are the basis of training programs and orientations. They often deal with the question of *how to*. This type of speech sometimes features a demonstration or a visual aid. Thus, if you were giving instructions on "how to promote your career via social networking sites," you might demonstrate by showing the

---

### ON YOUR FEET

*Content and Purpose*

Choose a topic for an informative speech. Briefly explain to your classmates why you have chosen this topic and what you hope to accomplish by presenting it. Listen carefully to their reactions and see if you need to adjust your idea.

social media profile of successful people. For instructions on "how to perform CPR," you could use a volunteer or a dummy.

These types of informative speeches aren't mutually exclusive. As you'll see in the sample speech at the end of this chapter, there is considerable overlap, as when you give a speech about objects that has the purpose of explaining them. Still, even this imperfect categorization demonstrates how wide a range of informative topics is available. One final distinction we need to make, however, is the difference between an informative and a persuasive speech topic.

Sushi chef Toshio Suzuki presents a training session on preparing raw fish at Oceana in New York. Even when an audience is interested in a topic, it takes skill for a speaker to present material in a way that is understandable.

# Informative Versus Persuasive Topics

There are many similarities between an informative and a persuasive speech. In an informative speech, for example, you are constantly trying to "persuade" your audience to listen, understand, and remember. In a persuasive speech, you "inform" your audience about your arguments, your evidence, and so on. However, two basic characteristics differentiate an informative topic from a persuasive topic.

## An Informative Topic Tends to Be Noncontroversial

In an informative speech, you generally do not present information that your audience is likely to disagree with. Again, this is a matter of degree. For example, you might want to give a purely informative talk on the differences between hospital births and home-based midwife births by simply describing what the practitioners of each method believe and do. By contrast, a talk either boosting or criticizing one method over the other would clearly be persuasive.

The noncontroversial nature of informative speaking does not mean that your speech topic should be uninteresting to your audience; rather, it means that your approach to it should not engender conflict. You could speak about the animal rights movement, for example, by explaining the points of view of both sides in an interesting but objective manner.

## The Informative Speaker Does Not Intend to Change Audience Attitudes

The informative speaker does seek a response (such as attention and interest) from the listener and does try to make the topic important to the audience. But the speaker's primary intent is not to change attitudes or to make the audience members *feel* differently about the topic. For example, an informative speaker might explain how a microwave oven works but will not try to "sell" a specific brand of oven to the audience.

The speaker's intent is best expressed in a specific informative purpose statement, which brings us to the first of our techniques of informative speaking.

Find an interesting informative speech online. (For example, see www.ted.com.) How would you categorize this speech by content and purpose?

 ON YOUR FEET

*Informative vs. Persuasive Approaches*
Pick a speech topic that interests you. Describe two speeches on this topic, one informative and the other persuasive.

## How Culture Affects Information

Cultural background is always a part of informative speaking, although it's not always easy to spot. Sometimes this is because of ethnocentrism, the belief in the inherent superiority of one's own ethnic group or culture. According to communication scholars Larry Samovar and Richard Porter, ethnocentrism is exemplified by what is taught in schools.

Each culture, whether consciously or unconsciously, tends to glorify its historical, scientific, and artistic accomplishments while frequently minimizing the accomplishments of other cultures. In this way, schools in all cultures, whether or not they intend to, teach ethnocentrism. For instance, the next time you look at a world map, notice that the United States is prominently located in the center—unless, of course, you are looking at a Chinese or Russian map. Many students in the United States, if asked to identify the great books of the world, would likely produce a list of books mainly by Western, white, male authors. This attitude of subtle ethnocentrism, or the reinforcing of the values, beliefs, and prejudices of the culture, is not a uniquely American phenomenon. Studying only the Koran in Iranian schools or only the Old Testament in Israeli classrooms is also a quiet form of ethnocentrism. ●

How would culture affect the informative topic you have chosen?

From Samovar, L., & Porter, R. (2010) *Communication between cultures* (5th ed.). Boston: Wadsworth. ©2010. Reprinted with permission of Wadsworth, an imprint of the Wadsworth Group, a division of Cengage Learning.

# Techniques of Informative Speaking

The techniques of informative speaking are based on a number of principles of human communication in general, and public speaking specifically, that we have discussed in earlier chapters. The most important principles to apply to informative speaking include those that help an audience understand and care about your speech. Let's look at how these principles apply to specific techniques.

## Define a Specific Informative Purpose

As Chapter 11 explained, any good speech must be based on a purpose statement that is audience oriented, precise, and attainable. When you are preparing an informative speech, it is especially important to define in advance, for yourself, a clear informative purpose. An **informative purpose statement** will generally be worded to stress audience knowledge, ability, or both:

*"I know so much that I don't know where to begin."*

*Source:* © The New Yorker Collection 1987 James Stevenson from cartoonbank.com. All Rights Reserved.

> After listening to my speech, my audience will be able to recall the three most important questions to ask when shopping for a smartphone.

> After listening to my speech, my audience will be able to identify the four reasons that online memes go viral.

> After listening to my speech, my audience will be able to discuss the pros and cons of using drones in warfare.

Notice that in each of these purpose statements a specific verb such as *to recall*, *to identify*, or *to discuss* points out what the audience will be able to do after hearing the speech. Other key verbs for informative purpose statements include these:

| | | | | |
|---|---|---|---|---|
| Accomplish | Choose | Explain | Name | Recognize |
| Analyze | Contrast | Integrate | Operate | Review |
| Apply | Describe | List | Perform | Summarize |

## CHECKLIST > **Techniques of Informative Speaking**

- [ ] Define a specific informative purpose.
- [ ] Create information hunger by relating to audience needs.
- [ ] Make it easy for audience members to listen.
  - Limit the amount of information presented.
  - Use familiar information to introduce unfamiliar information.
  - Start with simple information before moving to more complex ideas.
- [ ] Use clear, simple language.
- [ ] Use clear organization and structure.
- [ ] Support and illustrate your points.
  - Provide interesting, relevant facts and examples, citing your sources.
  - Use visual aids that help make your points clear, interesting, and memorable.
- [ ] Emphasize important points.
  - Repeat key information in more than one way.
  - Use signposts: words or phrases that highlight what you are about to say.
- [ ] Generate audience involvement.
  - Personalize the speech.
  - Use audience participation.
  - Use volunteers.
  - Have a question-and-answer period at the end.

---

A clear purpose statement will lead to a clear thesis statement. As you remember from Chapter 11, a thesis statement presents the central idea of your speech. Sometimes your thesis statement for an informative speech will just preview the central idea:

> Today's smartphones have so many features that it is difficult for the uninformed consumer to make a choice.

> Understanding how memes go viral could make you very wealthy someday.

> Soldiers and civilians have different views on the morality of drones.

At other times, the thesis statement for an informative speech will delineate the main points of that speech:

> When shopping for a smartphone, the informed consumer seeks to balance price, dependability, and user friendliness.

> The four basic principles of aerodynamics—lift, thrust, drag, and gravity—can explain why memes go viral.

> Drones can save warrior lives but cost the lives of civilians.

Setting a clear informative purpose will help keep you focused as you prepare and present your speech.

## Create Information Hunger

An effective informative speech creates **information hunger**: a reason for your audience members to want to listen to and learn from your speech. To do so, you can use the analysis of communication functions discussed in Chapter 1 as a guide. You read there that communication of all types helps us meet our physical needs, identity needs, social needs, and practical needs. In informative speaking, you could tap into your audience members' physical needs by relating your topic to their survival or to the improvement of their living conditions. If you gave a speech on food (eating it, cooking it, or shopping for it), you would be dealing with that basic physical need. In the same way, you could appeal to identity needs by showing your audience members how to be respected—or simply by showing them that you respect them. You could relate to social needs by showing them how your topic could help them be well liked. Finally, you can relate your topic to practical audience needs by telling your audience members how to succeed in their courses, their job search, or their quest for the perfect outfit.

> Think about an effective informative presentation you've seen recently. How did it connect with your needs?

## Make It Easy to Listen

Keep in mind the complex nature of listening, discussed in Chapter 5, and make it easy for your audience members to hear, pay attention, understand, and remember. This means first that you should speak clearly and with enough volume to be heard by all your listeners. It also means that as you put your speech together you should take into consideration techniques that recognize the way human beings process information.

**Limit the Amount of Information You Present**   Remember that you probably won't have enough time to transmit all your research to your audience in one sitting. It's better to make careful choices about the three to five main ideas you want to get across and then develop those ideas fully. Remember, too much information leads to overload, anxiety, and a lack of attention on the part of your audience. You will notice in the sample speech at the end of this chapter that ShaoLan Hsueh bases her system of learning Chinese on just eight simple characters.

**Use Familiar Information to Increase Understanding of the Unfamiliar**   Move your audience members from familiar information (on the basis of your audience analysis) to your newer information. For example, if you are giving a speech about how the stock market works, you could compare the daily activity of a broker with that of a salesperson in a retail store, or you could compare the idea of capital growth (a new concept to some listeners) with interest earned in a savings account (a more familiar concept). In the sample speech at the end of this chapter, you'll notice that ShaoLan Hsueh connects Chinese characters with common images that her audience is familiar with.

---

Ethical Challenge

## The Ethics of Simplicity

Often, persuasive speakers use language that is purposely complicated or obscure in order to keep the audience uninformed about some idea or piece of information. Informative rather than persuasive intent can often help clear the air. Find any sales message (a print ad or television commercial, for example) or political message (a campaign speech, perhaps) and see if you can transform it into an informative speech. What are the differences?

---

**Use Simple Information to Build Up Understanding of Complex Information**   Just as you move your audience members from the familiar to the unfamiliar, you can move them from the simple to the complex. An average college audience, for example, can understand the complexities of genetic modification if you begin with the concept of inherited characteristics. Again, ShaoLan Hsueh's sample speech begins with simple images and moves on to more complex characters.

## Use Clear, Simple Language

Another technique for effective informative speaking is to use clear language, which means using precise, simple wording and avoiding jargon. As you plan your speech, consult online dictionaries such as Dictionary.com to make sure you are selecting precise vocabulary. Remember that picking the right word seldom means using a word that is unfamiliar to your audience; in fact, just the opposite is true. Important ideas do not have to sound complicated. Along with simple, precise vocabulary, you should also strive for direct, short sentence structure. For example, when Warren Buffet, one of the world's most successful investors, wanted to explain the impact of taxes on investing, he didn't use unusual vocabulary or complicated sentences. He explained it like this:

> Suppose that an investor you admire and trust comes to you with an investment idea. "This is a good one," he says enthusiastically. "I'm in it, and I think you should be, too." Would your reply possibly be this? "Well, it all depends on what my tax rate will be on the gain you're saying we're going to make. If the taxes are too high, I would rather leave the money in my savings account, earning a quarter of 1 percent." So let's forget about the rich and ultrarich going on strike and stuffing their ample funds under their mattresses if—gasp—capital gains rates and ordinary income rates are increased. The ultrarich, including me, will forever pursue investment opportunities.[4]

Sheryl Sandberg, chief operating officer and member of the board of Facebook, has earned a reputation for exploring socially important topics in a way that holds the attention of a mass audience.

Each idea within that explanation is stated directly, using simple, clear language.

## Use a Clear Organization and Structure

Because of the way humans process information (that is, in a limited number of chunks at any one time),[5] organization is extremely important in an informative speech. Rules for structure may be mere suggestions for other types of speeches, but for informative speeches they are ironclad.

Chapter 12 discusses some of these rules:

- Limit your speech to three to five main points.
- Divide, coordinate, and order those main points.
- Use a strong introduction that previews your ideas.
- Use a conclusion that reviews your ideas and makes them memorable.
- Use transitions, internal summaries, and internal previews.

> cultural idiom
> **ironclad:**
> mandatory

The repetition that is inherent in strong organization will help your audience members understand and remember those points. This will be especially true if you use a well-organized introduction, body, and conclusion.

**The Introduction**  The following principles of organization from Chapter 12 become especially important in the introduction of an informative speech:

1. Establish the importance of your topic to your audience.
2. Preview the thesis, the one central idea you want your audience to remember.
3. Preview your main points.

For example, Kevin Allocca, the trends manager at YouTube, began his TED talk "Why Videos Go Viral" with the following introduction:

> I professionally watch YouTube videos. It's true. So we're going to talk a little bit today about how videos go viral and then why that even matters. Web video has

made it so that any of us or any of the creative things that we do can become completely famous in a part of our world's culture. Any one of you could be famous on the Internet by next Saturday. But there are over 48 hours of video uploaded to YouTube every minute. And of that, only a tiny percentage ever goes viral and gets tons of views and becomes a cultural moment. So how does it happen? Three things: tastemakers, communities of participation, and unexpectedness.[6]

**The Body**   In the body of an informative speech, the following organizational principles take on special importance:

1. Limit your division of main points to three to five subpoints.
2. Use transitions, internal summaries, and internal previews.
3. Order your points in the way that they will be easiest to understand and remember.

Kevin Allocca followed these principles for organizing his speech on why some videos go viral and some do not. He developed his speech with the following three main points:

I. Tastemakers: Tastemakers like Jimmy Kimmel introduce us to new and interesting things and bring them to a larger audience.
II. Communities of participation: A community of people who share this big inside joke start talking about it and doing things with it.
III. Unexpectedness: In a world where more than 2 days of video get uploaded every minute, only those that are truly unique can go viral.

**The Conclusion**   Organizational principles are also important in the conclusion of an informative speech:

1. Review your main points.
2. Remind your audience members of the importance of your topic to them.
3. Provide your audience with a memory aid.

For example, this is how Kevin Allocca concluded his speech on viral videos:

> Tastemakers, creative participating communities, complete unexpectedness, these are characteristics of a new kind of media and a new kind of culture where anyone has access and the audience defines the popularity. One of the biggest stars in the world right now, Justin Bieber, got his start on YouTube. No one has to green-light your idea. And we all now feel some ownership in our own pop culture. And these are not characteristics of old media, and they're barely true of the media of today, but they will define the entertainment of the future.

## Use Supporting Material Effectively

Another technique for effective informative speaking has to do with the supporting material discussed in Chapter 12. All of the purposes of support (to clarify, to prove, to make interesting, to make memorable) are essential to informative speaking. Therefore, you should be careful to support your thesis in every way possible. Notice the way in which ShaoLan Hsueh uses solid supporting material in the sample speech at the end of this chapter. In particular, notice her use of visuals, which can grab your audience members' attention and keep them attuned to your topic throughout your speech.

You should also try to briefly explain where your supporting material came from. These **vocal citations** build the credibility of your explanations and increase audience trust in the accuracy of what you are saying. For example, when Kerry Konda of Northern State University in South Dakota gave a speech on post-traumatic stress disorder, he used the following vocal citation:

Some instructors point out that students naturally organize ideas in the order in which those ideas occurred to them, rather than for strategic effect. Do you agree?

The *Journal of the American Medical Association* published a report on a study conducted by Charles Hoge, Jennifer Auchterlonie, and Charles Milliken which found 1 in 5 soldiers returning from Iraq and Afghanistan suffered from post-traumatic stress disorder, a statistic that rivals the Vietnam experience.[7]

By telling concisely and simply where his information came from, Konda reassured his audience that his statistics were credible.

## Emphasize Important Points

One specific principle of informative speaking is to stress the important points in your speech through repetition and the use of signposts.

**Repetition**    Repetition is one of the age-old rules of learning. Human beings are more likely to comprehend information that is stated more than once. This is especially true in a speaking situation, because, unlike a written paper, your audience members cannot go back to reread something they have missed. If their minds have wandered the first time you say something, they just might pick it up the second time.

Of course, simply repeating something in the same words might bore the audience members who actually are paying attention, so effective speakers learn to say the same thing in more than one way. Kathy Levine, a student at Oregon State University, used this technique in her speech on contaminated dental water:

> The problem of dirty dental water is widespread. In a nationwide *20/20* investigation, the water used in approximately 90% of dental offices is dirtier than the water found in public toilets. This means that 9 out of 10 dental offices are using dirty water on their patients.[8]

Redundancy can be effective when you use it to emphasize important points.[9] It is ineffective only when (1) you are redundant with obvious, trivial, or boring points or (2) you run an important point into the ground. There is no sure rule for making certain you have not overemphasized a point. You just have to use your best judgment to make sure that you have stated the point enough that your audience members get it without repeating it so often that they want to give it back.

**Signposts**    Another way to emphasize important material is by using **signposts**: words or phrases that emphasize the importance of what you are about to say. You can state, simply enough, "What I'm about to say is important," or you can use some variation of that statement: "But listen to this . . . ," or "The most important thing to remember is . . . ," or "The three keys to this situation are . . . ," and so on.

## Generate Audience Involvement

The final technique for effective informative speaking is to get your audience involved in your speech. **Audience involvement** is the level of commitment and attention that listeners devote to a speech. Educational psychologists have long known that the best way to teach people something is to have them do it; social psychologists have added to this rule by proving, in many studies, that involvement in a message increases audience comprehension of, and agreement with, that message.

There are many ways to encourage audience involvement in your speech. One way is by following the rules for good delivery by maintaining enthusiasm, energy, eye contact, and so on. Other ways include personalizing your speech, using audience participation, using volunteers, and having a question-and-answer period.

**Personalize Your Speech**    One way to encourage audience involvement is to give audience members a human being to connect to. In other words, don't be afraid to be yourself and to inject a little of your own personality into the speech. If you happen to be good at storytelling, make a narration part of your speech. If humor is a personal strength, be funny. If you feel passion about your topic, show it. Certainly if you have any experience that relates to your topic, use it.

Kathryn Schulz, author of *Being Wrong* and a self-proclaimed "wrongologist," personalized her TED speech, "Being Wrong," this way:

> So it's 1995, I'm in college, and a friend and I go on a road trip from Providence, Rhode Island, to Portland, Oregon. And you know, we're young and unemployed, so we do the whole thing on back roads through state parks and national forests—basically the longest route we can possibly take. And somewhere in the middle of South Dakota, I turn to my friend and I ask her a question that's been bothering me for 2,000 miles. "What's up with the Chinese character I keep seeing by the side of the road?"
>
> My friend looks at me totally blankly. There's actually a gentleman in the front row who's doing a perfect imitation of her look. (Laughter) And I'm like, "You know, all the signs we keep seeing with the Chinese character on them." She just stares at me for a few moments, and then she cracks up, because she figures out what I'm talking about. And what I'm talking about is this:

> (Laughter) Right, the famous Chinese character for picnic area.[10]

Another way to personalize your speech is to link it to the experience of audience members . . . maybe even naming one or more.

**Use Audience Participation** Audience participation, having your listeners actually do something during your speech, is another way to increase their involvement in your message. For example, if you were giving a demonstration on isometric exercises (which don't require too much room for movement), you could have the entire audience stand up and do one or two sample exercises. If you were explaining how to fill out a federal income-tax form, you could give each class member a sample form to fill out as you explain it. Outlines and checklists can be used in a similar manner for just about any speech. Here's how one student organization used audience participation to demonstrate the various restrictions that were once placed on voting rights:

> Voting is something that a lot of us may take for granted. Today, the only requirements for voting are that you are a U.S. citizen aged 18 or older who has lived in the same place for at least 30 days and that you have registered. But it hasn't always been that way. Americans have had to struggle for the right to vote. I'd like to illustrate this by asking everyone to please stand.
>
> [Wait, prod class to stand.]
>
> I'm going to ask some questions. If you answer no to any question, please sit down.
>
> Have you resided at the same address for at least 1 year? If not, sit down. Residency requirements of more than 30 days weren't abolished until 1970.

Are you white? If not, sit down. The 15th Amendment gave non-whites the right to vote in 1870, but many states didn't enforce it until the late 1960s.

Are you male? If not, sit down. The 19th Amendment only gave women the right to vote in 1920.

Do you own a home? If not, sit down. Through the mid-1800s only property owners could vote.

Are you Protestant? If not, sit down. That's right. Religious requirements existed in the early days throughout the country.[11]

**Use Volunteers**    Some points or actions are more easily demonstrated with one or two volunteers. Selecting volunteers from the audience will increase the psychological involvement of all audience members, because they will tend to identify with the volunteers.

Kathryn Schulz, in her speech on being wrong, subtly enlisted volunteers when she wanted to impress an important point on her audience. She began by addressing a rhetorical question to her entire audience but then directed it to a few individuals in the front row:

> So let me ask you guys something—or actually, let me ask you guys something, because you're right here: How does it feel—emotionally—how does it feel to be wrong?

Schulz then listened to the responses and repeated them for the rest of the audience:

> Dreadful. Thumbs down. Embarrassing. . . . Thank you, these are great answers, but they're answers to a different question. You guys are answering the question: How does it feel to *realize* you're wrong? When we're wrong about something—not when we realize it, but before that—*it feels like being right.*

**Have a Question-and-Answer Period**    One way to increase audience involvement that is nearly always appropriate if time allows is to answer questions at the end of your speech. You should encourage your audience to ask questions. Solicit questions and be patient waiting for the first one. Often no one wants to ask the first question. When the questions do start coming, the following suggestions might increase your effectiveness in answering them:

1. Listen to the substance of the question. Don't zero in on irrelevant details; listen for the big picture, the basic, overall question that is being asked. If you are not really sure what the substance of a question is, ask the questioner to paraphrase it. Don't be afraid to let the questioners do their share of the work.

2. Paraphrase confusing or quietly asked questions. Use the active listening skills described in Chapter 5. You can paraphrase the question in just a few words: "If I understand your question, you are asking _____. Is that right?"

3. Avoid defensive reactions to questions. Even if the questioner seems to be calling you a liar or stupid or biased, try to listen to the substance of the question and not to the possible personality attack.

**Rubes®**    **By Leigh Rubin**

"In order to adequately demonstrate just how many ways there are to skin a cat, I'll need a volunteer from the audience."

*Source:* "Rubes" by Leigh Rubin. By permission of Leigh Rubin and Creators Syndicate.

> cultural idiom
> **zero in on:**
> focus directly on

ON YOUR FEET

*Using Audience Participation*
Present one point from the informative speech you are preparing. To demonstrate your point, find a way to use audience participation from your entire class or from a volunteer or two. After this demonstration, invite suggestions for improvement.

④ Answer the question briefly. Then check the questioner's comprehension of your answer by observing his or her nonverbal response or by asking, "Does that answer your question?"

# Using Visual Aids

**Visual aids** are graphic devices used in a speech to illustrate or support ideas. Although they can be used in any type of speech, they are especially important in informative speeches. For example, they can be extremely useful when you want to show how things look (photos of your trek to Nepal or the effects of malnutrition) or how things work (a demonstration of a new ski binding or a diagram of how seawater is made drinkable). Visual aids can also show how things relate to one another (a graph showing the relationships among gender, education, and income). In the sample speech at the end of this chapter, ShaoLan Hsueh demonstrates how effective visual aids can be.

## Types of Visual Aids

There is a wide variety of types of visual aids. The most common types include the following.

**Objects and Models**   Sometimes the most effective visual aid is the actual thing you are talking about. This is true when the thing you are talking about is portable enough to carry and simple enough to use during a demonstration before an audience: a piece of sports equipment such as a lacrosse racket or a small piece of weight-training equipment. **Models** are scaled representations of the object you are discussing and are used when that object is too large (the new campus arts complex) or too small (a DNA molecule) or simply don't exist anymore (a *Tyrannosaurus rex*).

**Diagrams**   A **diagram** is any kind of line drawing that shows the most important properties of an object. Diagrams do not try to show everything but just those parts of a thing that the audience most needs to be aware of and understand. Blueprints and architectural plans are common types of diagrams, as are maps and organizational charts. A diagram is most appropriate when you need to simplify a complex object or phenomenon and make it more understandable to the audience. Figure 13-1 shows a humorous depiction of one student's perception of what was covered on a final exam, in the form of a Venn diagram.

**Word and Number Charts**   **Word charts** and **number charts** are visual depictions of key facts or statistics. Your audience will understand and remember these facts and numbers better if you show them than if you just talk about them. Many speakers arrange the main points of their speech, often in outline form, as a word chart. Other speakers list their main statistics. In the sample speech at the end of this chapter, ShaoLan Hsueh uses a number chart in her sample speech to allow her audience to keep track visually of an important point: that 20,000 characters are needed for Chinese language scholarship, 1,000 characters are needed for basic literacy, and 200 are needed to read road signs and restaurant menus—but you can build up to all these numbers from eight basic characters (see Figure 13-2).

**Pie Charts**   **Pie charts** are shaped as circles with wedges cut into them. They are used to show divisions of any whole: where your tax dollars go, the percentage of the population involved in various occupations, and so

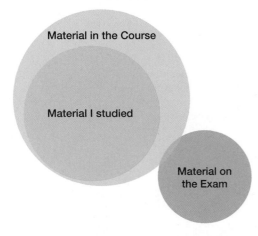

**FINAL EXAMS**

Material in the Course

Material I studied

Material on the Exam

FIGURE 13-1 **Venn Diagram: Student Perception of Final Exam**

on. Pie charts are often made up of percentages that add up to 100 percent. Usually, the wedges of the pie are organized from largest to smallest. The pie chart in Figure 13-3 represents one's person's perception of "people who find you on Facebook," and Figure 13-4 shows how the U.S. government adapted a pie chart for a new nutrition diagram. Coincidentally, Figure 13-4 is also a **pictogram**, which is a visual aid that conveys its meaning through images of an actual object.

**Bar and Column Charts**    **Bar charts**, such as the one shown in Figure 13-5, compare two or more values by stretching them out in the form of horizontal rectangles. **Column charts**, such as the one shown in Figure 13-6, perform the same function as bar charts but use vertical rectangles.

**Line Charts**    A **line chart** maps out the direction of a moving point; it is ideally suited for showing changes over time. The time element is usually placed on the horizontal axis so that the line visually represents the trend over time. Figure 13-7 is a line chart.

## Media for Presenting Visual Aids

Obviously, many types and variations of visual aids can be used in any speech. And a variety of materials can be used to present these aids.

20,000
1,000
200
8

FIGURE 13-2 Number Chart

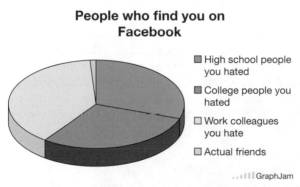

FIGURE 13-3 Pie Chart

FIGURE 13-4 Adaptation of a Pie Chart

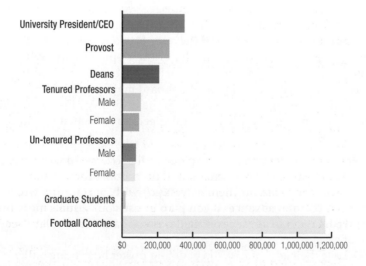

FIGURE 13-5 Bar Chart: College Salaries

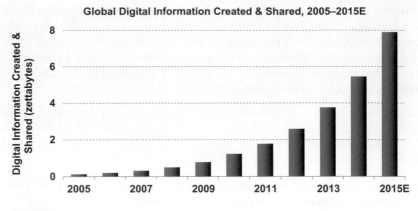

**FIGURE 13-6 Column Chart: Global Digital Information Created and Shared**
*Source:* IDC report "Extracting Value from Chaos" 6/11.

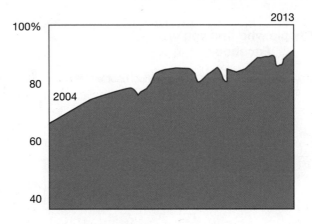

**FIGURE 13-7 Line Chart: Percentage of American Adults Who Own a Cell Phone, 2004–2013**

**Chalkboards, Whiteboards, and Polymer Marking Surfaces** The major advantage of these write-as-you-go media is their spontaneity. With them you can create your visual aid as you speak, including items generated from audience responses. Along with the odor of whiteboard markers and the squeaking of chalk, a major disadvantage of these media is the difficulty of preparing visual aids on them in advance, especially if several speeches are scheduled in the same room at the same hour.

**Flip Pads and Poster Board** Flip pads are like oversized writing tablets attached to a portable easel. Flip pads enable you to combine the spontaneity of the chalkboard (you can write on them as you go) with portability, which enables you to prepare them in advance. If you plan to use your visuals more than once, you can prepare them in advance on rigid poster board and display them on the same type of easel.

Despite their advantages, flip pads and poster boards are bulky, and preparing professional-looking exhibits on them requires a fair amount of artistic ability.

**Handouts**  The major advantage of handouts is that audience members can take away the information they contain after your speech. For this reason, handouts are excellent memory and reference aids. The major disadvantage is that they are distracting when handed out during a speech: First, there is the distraction of passing them out, and second, there is the distraction of having them in front of the audience members while you have gone on to something else. It's best, therefore, to pass them out at the end of the speech so audience members can use them as take-aways.

**Projectors**  When your audience is too large to view handheld images, projectors are an ideal tool. *Digital projectors* allow you to use screen images directly from a computer screen, making them the most direct way to use computer software presentations. Projectors allow you to use room-sized images, rather than displaying images on screens that are too small for audiences to see well, such as laptops.

In this photo director James Cameron uses digital projectors to enhance the ideas he presents at iEX 2013 (idea Exchange 2013), a conference to explore the intersection of creativity with technology for storytelling.

**Other Electronic Media**  A wide range of other electronic media are available as presentation aids. Audio aids such as CDs can supply information that could not be presented any other way (comparing musical styles, for example, or demonstrating the differences in the sounds of gas and diesel engines), but in most cases you should use them sparingly. Remember that your presentation already relies heavily on your audience's sense of hearing; it's better to use a visual aid, if possible, than to overwork the audio.

Of course, there are audiovisual aids, including DVDs. These should also be used sparingly, however, because they allow audience members to receive information passively, thus relieving them of the responsibility of becoming active participants in the presentation. The general rule when using these media is *Don't let them get in the way of the direct, person-to-person contact that is the primary advantage of public speaking.*

## Rules for Using Visual Aids

It's easy to see that each type of visual aid and each medium for its presentation have their own advantages and disadvantages. No matter which type you use, however, there are a few rules to follow.

**Simplicity**  Keep your visual aids simple. Your goal is to clarify, not confuse. Use only key words or phrases, not sentences. The "rule of seven" states that each exhibit you use should contain no more than seven lines of text, each with no more than seven words. Keep all printing horizontal. Omit all nonessential details.

**Size**  Visual aids should be large enough for your entire audience to see them at one time but portable enough for you to get them out of the way when they no longer pertain to the point you are making.

**Attractiveness**  Visual aids should be visually interesting and as neat as possible. If you don't have the necessary artistic or computer skills, try to get help from a friend or at the computer or audiovisual center on your campus.

# The Pros and Cons of Presentation Software

PowerPoint is by far the most popular form of work presentation today. In fact, as one expert points out, "Today there are great tracts of corporate America where to appear at a meeting without PowerPoint would be unwelcome and vaguely pretentious, like wearing no shoes."[12] Prezi, as an enhanced form of PowerPoint, is subject to many of the same advantages and criticisms.

**The Pros**  The advantages of PowerPoint are well known. Proponents say that PowerPoint slides can focus the attention of audience members on important information at the appropriate time. The slides also help listeners appreciate the relationship between different pieces of information. By doing so, they make the logical structure of an argument more transparent.

Some experts think the primary advantage of PowerPoint is that it forces otherwise befuddled speakers to organize their thoughts in advance. Most, however, insist that its primary benefit is in providing two channels of information rather than just one. This gives audiences a visual source of information that is a more efficient way to learn than just by listening. One psychology professor puts it this way: "We are visual creatures. Visual things stay put, whereas sounds fade. If you zone out for 30 seconds—and who doesn't?—it is nice to be able to glance up on the screen and see what you missed."[13]

**The Cons**  For all its popularity, PowerPoint has been receiving some bad press lately, being featured in articles with such downbeat titles as "PowerPoint Is Evil"[14] and "Does PowerPoint Make You Stupid?"[15] But the statement that truly put the anti-PowerPoint argument on the map was a 23-page pamphlet with a less dramatic title, *The Cognitive Style of PowerPoint*,[16] because it was authored by Edward R. Tufte, a well-respected author of several influential books on the effective design of visual aids.

According to Tufte, the use of low-content PowerPoint slides trivializes important information. It encourages oversimplification by asking the presenter to summarize key concepts in as few words as possible—the ever-present bullet points.

Tufte also insists that PowerPoint makes it easier for a speaker to hide lies and logical fallacies. When dazzling slides are used, the audience stays respectfully still, and a speaker can quickly move past gross generalizations, imprecise logic, superficial reasoning, and misleading conclusions.

Perhaps most seriously, opponents of PowerPoint say that it is an enemy of interaction, that it interferes with the spontaneous give-and-take that is so important in effective public speaking. One expert summarized this effect by saying, "Instead of human contact, we are given human display."[17]

**The Middle Ground?**  PowerPoint proponents say that it is just a tool, one that can be used effectively or ineffectively. They are the first to admit that a poorly done PowerPoint presentation can be boring and ineffective, such as the infamous "triple delivery," in which precisely the same text is seen on the screen, spoken aloud, and printed on the handout in front of you. One proponent insists, "Tufte is correct in that most talks are horrible and most PowerPoint slides are bad—but that's not PowerPoint's fault. Most writing is awful, too, but I don't go railing against pencils or chalk."[18]

PowerPoint proponents say that PowerPoint should not be allowed to overpower a presentation—it should be just one element of a speech, not the whole thing. They point out that even before the advent of the personal computer, some people argued that speeches with visual aids stressed format over content. PowerPoint just makes it extremely easy to stress impressive format over less-than-impressive content, but that's a tendency that the effective speaker recognizes and works against. Thus, proponents say, the arguments for and against PowerPoint are really the arguments for and against visual aids. These arguments are merely accentuated now that they apply to one of the most influential media technologies of our day. Opponents shake their heads sadly at this explanation and insist that every technology changes the humans that use it in some way, and sometimes those changes are subtle and dangerous. ●

After reviewing the pros and cons of PowerPoint, would you say that PowerPoint is a benefit or detriment to effective public speaking? Why?

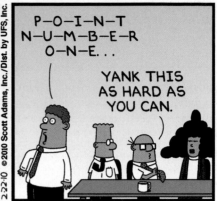

**Appropriateness**  Visuals must be appropriate to all the components of the speaking situation—you, your audience, and your topic—and they must emphasize the point you are trying to make. Don't make the mistake of using a visual aid that looks good but has only a weak link to the point you want to make—such as showing a map of a city transit system while talking about the condition of the individual cars.

**Reliability**  You must be in control of your visual aid at all times. Test all electronic media (projectors, computers, and so on) in advance, preferably in the room where you will speak. Just to be safe, have nonelectronic backups ready in case of disaster. Be conservative when you choose demonstrations: Wild animals, chemical reactions, and gimmicks meant to shock a crowd can often backfire.

When it comes time for you to use the visual aid, remember one more point: Talk to your audience, not to your visual aid. Some speakers become so wrapped up in their props that they turn their backs on their audience and sacrifice all their eye contact.

> cultural idiom
> **gimmicks:**
> clever means of drawing attention
>
> **wrapped up in:**
> giving all one's attention to something

### Using Presentation Software

Several specialized programs exist just to produce visual aids. Among the most popular of these programs are Microsoft PowerPoint, Apple's Keynote, and Prezi.

In its simplest form, presentation software lets you build an effective slide show out of your basic outline. You can choose color-coordinated backgrounds and consistent formatting that match the tone and purpose of your presentation. Most presentation software programs contain a clip art library that allows you to choose images to accompany your words. They also allow you to import images from outside sources and to build your own charts.

If you would like to learn more about using PowerPoint, Keynote, and Prezi, there are several Web-based tutorial programs, which you can find easily by typing the name of your preferred program into your favorite search engine.

# Sample Speech

The sample speech for this chapter was presented by ShaoLan Hsueh, whose profile began this chapter. The speech was presented at a TED conference in 2013.[19] Her purpose is to introduce a method of learning to read Chinese and to demonstrate that method's efficiency. Her purpose statement could be worded like this:

> After listening to my speech, my audience will be able to identify eight basic characters of the Chinese language.

Her thesis statement might be worded this way:

> Eight basic characters can be used to build a workable vocabulary for reading Chinese.

Throughout this speech Hsueh makes it easy for her audience members to hear, pay attention, understand, and remember. She does this by limiting the amount of information she presents, by using information and images to increase understanding of the unfamiliar, and by using simple information to build up an understanding of more complex information.

Her organization is based on a limited number of fundamental characters; she then demonstrates how these characters can be used to exponentially increase one's knowledge of Chinese. She does this efficiently by using a series of well-designed visuals and effective analogies throughout. You can find her complete set of slides on this book's companion website, www.oup.com/us/adler.

---

**SAMPLE SPEECH** | **Learn to Read Chinese . . . with Ease!**   **ShaoLan Hsueh**

**1** Growing up in Taiwan as the daughter of a calligrapher, one of my most treasured memories was my mother showing me the beauty, the shape, and the form of Chinese characters. Ever since then, I was fascinated by this incredible language.

Her introduction personalizes the speech, while establishing her credibility at the same time.

**2** But to an outsider, it seems to be as impenetrable as the Great Wall of China. Over the past few years, I've been wondering if I can break down this wall, so anyone who wants to understand and appreciate the beauty of this sophisticated language could do so. I started thinking about how a new, fast method of learning Chinese might be useful.

**3** Since the age of 5, I started to learn how to draw every single stroke for each character in the correct sequence. I learned new characters every day during the course of the next 15 years. Since we only have 5 minutes, it's better that we have a fast and simpler way.

**4** [Slide; see p. 393] A Chinese scholar would understand 20,000 characters. You only need 1,000 to understand the basic literacy. The top 200 will allow you to comprehend 40 percent of basic literature—enough to read road signs, restaurant menus, to understand the basic idea of the Web pages or the newspapers. Today I'm going to start with eight to show you how the method works. You are ready?

**5** [Slide] Open your mouth as wide as possible until it's square. You get a mouth.

[Slide] This is a person going for a walk. Person.

[Slide] If the shape of the fire is a person with two arms on both sides, as if she was yelling frantically, "Help! I'm on fire!"—this symbol actually is originally from the shape of the flame, but I like to think that way. Whichever works for you.

[Slide] This is a tree. Tree.

[Slide] This is a mountain.

[Slide] The sun.

[Slide] The moon.

[Slide] The symbol of the door looks like a pair of saloon doors in the Wild West.

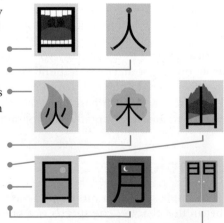

*Radicals* is used here in its most basic sense, meaning "fundamentals" or "roots." Considering the level of her audience, ShaoLan did not believe she had to define this term beyond her reference to "building blocks."

**6** I call these eight characters radicals. They are the building blocks for you to create lots more characters.

[Slide] A person.

[Slide] If someone walks behind, that is "to follow."

[Slide] As the old saying goes, two is company, three is a crowd.

[Slide] If a person stretched their arms wide, this person is saying, "It was this big."

7   [Slide] The person inside the mouth, the person is trapped. He's a prisoner, just like Jonah inside the whale.

person

follow
(two people)

crowd
(three people)

big
(person with arms wide)

prisoner
(person inside a mouth)

[Slide] One tree is a tree. Two trees together, we have the woods. Three trees together, we create the forest.

tree

woods
(two trees)

forest
(three trees)

[Slide] Put a plank underneath the tree, we have the foundation.

[Slide] Put a mouth on the top of the tree, that's "idiot." (Laughter) Easy to remember, since a talking tree is pretty idiotic.

foundation
(plank below a tree)

idiot
(mouth above a tree)

[Slide] Remember fire? Two fires together, I get really hot. Three fires together, that's a lot of flames.

[Slide] Set the fire underneath the two trees, it's burning.

8   . . . So we have gone through almost 30 characters. By using this method, the first 8 radicals will allow you to build 32. The next group of 8 characters will build an extra 32. So with very little effort, you will be able to learn a couple hundred characters, which is the same as a Chinese 8-year-old.

9   So after we know the characters, we start building phrases. [Slide] For example, the mountain and the fire together, we have fire mountain. It's a volcano.

fire

hot (two fires)

flame (three fires)

burning
(fire under two trees)

(fire)

(mountain)

火山
volcano

[Slide] A mouth which tells you where to get out is an exit. This is a slide to remind me that I should stop talking and get off of the stage. Thank you.

Her mission accomplished, she ends quickly. For a different audience, this might have seemed abrupt. For a TED audience, it was perfect.

## Summary

This chapter classified informative speaking based on content (speeches about objects, processes, events, and concepts) and purpose (descriptions, explanations, and instructions). Next, it discussed the differences between informative and persuasive speaking. It then suggested techniques for effective informative speaking. These techniques include using a specific informative purpose that stresses audience knowledge and/or ability, creating information hunger by tapping into audience needs, and making it easy to listen by limiting the amount of information you present, by using familiar information to increase understanding of the unfamiliar, and by using simple information to build up understanding of complex information. Other techniques include emphasizing important points through repetition and signposts; using clear organization and structure; using effective supporting materials, including visual aids; using clear language (language that uses precise, simple vocabulary and avoids jargon); and involving the audience through audience participation, the use of volunteers, and a question-and-answer period.

## Key Terms

**audience involvement** The level of commitment and attention that listeners devote to a speech. *p. 389*

**audience participation** Listener activity during a speech; a technique to increase audience involvement. *p. 390*

**bar chart** A visual aid that compares two or more values by showing them as elongated horizontal rectangles. *p. 393*

**column chart** A visual aid that compares two or more values by showing them as elongated vertical rectangles. *p. 393*

**description** A type of speech that uses details to create a "word picture" of the essential factors that make that thing what it is. *p. 382*

**diagram** A line drawing that shows the most important components of an object. *p. 392*

**explanations** Speeches or presentations that clarify ideas and concepts already known but not understood by an audience. *p. 382*

**information anxiety** The psychological stress that occurs when dealing with too much information. *p. 380*

**information hunger** Audience desire, created by a speaker, to learn information. *p. 385*

**information overload** The decline in efficiency that occurs when the rate of complexity of material is too great to manage. *p. 380*

**informative purpose statement** A complete statement of the objective of a speech, worded to stress audience knowledge and/or ability. *p. 384*

**instructions** Remarks that teach something to an audience in a logical, step-by-step manner. *p. 382*

**knowledge** The understanding acquired by making sense of the raw material of information. *p. 380*

**line chart** A visual aid consisting of a grid that maps out the direction of a trend by plotting a series of points. *p. 393*

**model (in speeches and presentations)** A replica of an object being discussed. It is usually used when it would be difficult or impossible to use the actual object. *p. 392*

**number chart** A visual aid that lists numbers in tabular form in order to clarify information. *p. 392*

**pictogram** A visual aid that conveys its meaning through an image of an actual object. *p. 393*

**pie chart** A visual aid that divides a circle into wedges, representing percentages of the whole. *p. 392*

**signpost** A phrase that emphasizes the importance of upcoming material in a speech. *p. 389*

**visual aids** Graphic devices used in a speech to illustrate or support ideas. *p. 392*

**vocal citation** A simple, concise, spoken statement of the source of your evidence. *p. 388*

**word chart** A visual aid that lists words or terms in tabular form in order to clarify information. *p. 392*

## Check Your Understanding

For each of the following questions, please refer to your informative speech topic.

1. What are the ways in which you can generate information hunger with this topic?

2. Give examples of the strategies that can be used to organize unfamiliar information.

3. Identify ways of emphasizing important points in your speech.

4. How could you generate audience involvement?

5. What visual aids would you use for your speech?

## Activities

1. **Informative Purpose Statements** For practice in defining informative speech purposes, reword the following statements so that they specifically point out what the audience will be able to do after hearing the speech.

    1. My talk today is about building a wood deck.

    2. My purpose is to tell you about vintage car restoration.

    3. I am going to talk about toilet training.

    4. I'd like to talk to you today about sexist language.

    5. There are six basic types of machines.

    6. The two sides of the brain have different functions.

    7. Do you realize that many of you are sleep deprived?

2. **Effective Repetition** Create a list of three statements, or use the three that follow. Restate each of these ideas in three different ways.

    1. The magazine *Modern Maturity* has a circulation of more than 20 million readers.

    2. Before buying a used car, you should have it checked out by an independent mechanic.

    3. One hundred thousand pounds of dandelions are imported into the United States annually for medical purposes.

3. **Using Clear Language** For practice in using clear language, select an article from any issue of a professional journal in your major field. Using the suggestions in this chapter, rewrite a paragraph from the article so that it will be clear and interesting to a layperson.

4. **Inventing Visual Aids** Take any sample speech. Analyze it for where visual aids might be effective. Describe the visual aids that you think will work best. Compare the visuals you devise with those of your classmates.

## For Further Exploration

For more resources about informative speaking, see the *Understanding Human Communication* website at www.oup.com/us/adler. There you will find a variety of resources: "Media Room" clips from popular films and television shows to further illustrate important concepts, a list of books and articles, links to descriptions of feature films and television shows at the *Now Playing* website, study aids, and a self-test to check your understanding of the material in this chapter.

**CHAPTER 14**

# Persuasive Speaking

**14**

## Chapter Outline

### LEARNING OBJECTIVES

1 Formulate an effective persuasive strategy to convince or actuate an audience.

2 Formulate your persuasive strategy based on ethical guidelines.

3 Bolster your credibility as a speaker by enhancing your competence, character, and charisma.

4 Build persuasive arguments through audience analysis, solid evidence, and careful reasoning.

5 Organize a persuasive speech for greatest audience effect.

**"I want my 2-year-old to be a rapper,"** proclaims Tunette Powell.[1]

The 27-year-old mother of two acknowledges that she might change her mind about that career choice down the road. But for now, she says, the idea that rapping gives the toddler a "freestyle" way to express himself is sweet indeed.

She should know. Although Powell is now a published author and a nationally recognized speaker, it took many years to find her own voice. She was born to a mother with limited education and a father who was addicted to crack cocaine and often in trouble with the law. Growing up, Powell felt silently trapped in a "room" she didn't create. Eventually, she says, she realized that the door wasn't locked.

These days Powell inspires audiences and readers to unlock the barriers that hold them back. "We can't change what room we were born into. . . . We can't change who our parents are. We can't change what city we were born into, what home we were born into," she tells an audience at the University of Nebraska–Omaha (UNO).[2] "But we can choose to leave that room. We can choose to open doors and open possibilities."

Powell's door opener was self-expression. But she didn't know that at first. In her first semester of college, she was an unmotivated student who often skipped class and made low grades. There seemed to be a locked door between her and the degree she hoped to earn. "I had to change," she says, "to adapt myself to fit into that lock."[3]

A transformative moment in Powell's life occurred when—in a moment of deep distress—she started to put her feelings on paper. The effort blossomed into a place on the university's forensics team and, eventually, a national title as a persuasive speaker.[4] She graduated with a degree in speech communication in 2012 and recently published her critically acclaimed first book, *The Other Woman*, about her life and her father's struggles.

Powell's style combines the power of a polished and passionate storyteller, a rap lyricist, and a been-there-and-survived adult who isn't afraid of life's darker moments and knows how to connect with audiences who have experienced a few of their own. She acknowledges that doors don't always open easily but encourages people to not be afraid of that. "It's just going to take a little bit more work," she says. "And every time the door gets tougher, the rewards are greater."[5]

Powell now travels the country talking about growing up with a father addicted to drugs. One of her speeches appears at the end of this chapter.

***Tunette Powell is a model of how persuasive speaking can change lives.***

- What persuasive messages have moved you?

- What audiences would you hope to reach through your own public speaking? How would you like to change the way they think and act?

How persuasion works and how to accomplish it successfully are complex topics. Our understanding of persuasion begins with classical wisdom and extends to the latest psychological research. We begin by looking at what we really mean by the term.

# Characteristics of Persuasion

**Persuasion** is the process of motivating someone, through communication, to change a particular belief, attitude, or behavior. Implicit in this definition are several characteristics of persuasion.

## Persuasion Is Not Coercive

Persuasion is not the same thing as coercion. If you put someone in a headlock and said, "Do this, or I'll choke you," you would be acting coercively. Besides being illegal, this approach would be ineffective. As soon as the authorities came and took you away, the person would stop following your demands.

The failure of coercion to achieve lasting results is also apparent in less dramatic circumstances. Children whose parents are coercive often rebel as soon as they can; students who perform from fear of an instructor's threats rarely appreciate the subject matter; and employees who work for abusive and demanding employers are often unproductive and eager to switch jobs as soon as possible. Persuasion, by contrast, makes a listener *want* to think or act differently.

## Persuasion Is Usually Incremental

Attitudes do not normally change instantly or dramatically. Persuasion is a process. When it is successful, it generally succeeds over time, in increments, and usually small increments at that. The realistic speaker, therefore, establishes goals and expectations that reflect this characteristic of persuasion.

Communication scientists explain this characteristic of persuasion through **social judgment theory**.[6] This theory tells us that when members of an audience hear a persuasive appeal, they compare it to opinions that they already hold. The preexisting opinion is called an **anchor**, but around this anchor there exist what are called **latitudes of acceptance**, **latitudes of rejection**, and **latitudes of non-commitment**. A diagram of any opinion, therefore, might look something like Figure 14-1.

People who care very strongly about a particular point of view will have a very narrow latitude of noncommitment. People who care less strongly will have a wider latitude of noncommitment. Research suggests that audience members simply will not respond to appeals that fall within their latitude of rejection. This means that persuasion in the real world takes place in a series of small movements. One persuasive speech may be but a single step in an overall persuasive

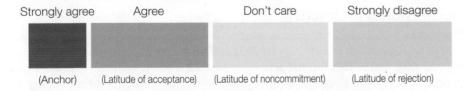

FIGURE 14-1 **Latitudes of Acceptance, Rejection, and Noncommitment**

campaign. The best example of this is the various communications that take place during the months of a political campaign. Candidates watch the opinion polls carefully, adjusting their appeals to the latitudes of acceptance and noncommitment of the uncommitted voters.

Public speakers who heed the principle of social judgment theory tend to seek realistic, if modest, goals in their speeches. For example, if you were hoping to change audience views on the pro-life/pro-choice question, social judgment theory suggests that the first step would be to consider a range of arguments such as this:

Abortion is a sin.

Abortion should be absolutely illegal.

Abortion should be allowed only in cases of rape and incest.

A woman should be required to have her husband's permission to have an abortion.

A girl under the age of 18 should be required to have a parent's permission before she has an abortion.

Abortion should be allowed during the first 3 months of pregnancy.

A girl under the age of 18 should not be required to have a parent's permission before she has an abortion.

A woman should not be required to have her husband's permission to have an abortion.

Abortion is a woman's personal decision.

Abortion should be discouraged but legal.

Abortion should be available anytime to anyone.

Abortion should be considered simply a form of birth control.

You could then arrange these positions on a continuum and estimate how listeners would react to each one. The statement that best represented the listeners' point of view would be their anchor. Other items that might also seem reasonable to them would make up their latitude of acceptance. Opinions that they would reject would make up their latitude of rejection. Those statements that are left would be the listeners' latitude of noncommitment.

Social judgment theory suggests that the best chance of changing audience attitudes would come by presenting an argument based on a position that fell somewhere within the listeners' latitude of noncommitment—even if this wasn't the position that you ultimately wanted them to accept. If you pushed too hard by arguing a position in your audience's latitude of rejection, your appeals would probably backfire, making your audience *more* opposed to you than before.

## Persuasion Is Interactive

The transactional model of communication described in Chapter 1 makes it clear that persuasion is not something you do *to* audience members but rather something you do *with* them. This mutual activity is best seen in an argument between two people, in which an openness to opposing arguments is essential to resolution. As one observer has pointed out,

Arguments are not won by shouting down opponents. They are won by changing opponents' minds—something that can happen only if we give opposing

> cultural idiom

**backfire:**
produce a result opposite of the one intended

arguments a respectful hearing and still persuade their advocates that there is something wrong with those arguments. In the course of this activity, we may well decide that there is something wrong with our own.[7]

Even in public communication, both speaker and audience are active. This might be manifested in the speaker taking an audience survey *before* a speech, a sensitivity to audience reactions *during* a speech, or an open-minded question-and-answer period *after* a speech.

## Persuasion Can Be Ethical

Even when they understand the difference between persuasion and coercion, some people are still uncomfortable with the idea of persuasive speaking. They see it as the work of high-pressure hucksters: salespeople with their feet stuck in the door, unscrupulous politicians taking advantage of beleaguered taxpayers, and so on. Indeed, many of the principles we are about to discuss have been used by unethical speakers for unethical purposes, but that is not what all—or even most—persuasion is about. Ethical persuasion plays a necessary and worthwhile role in everyone's life.

It is through ethical persuasion that we influence others' lives in worthwhile ways. The person who says, "I do not want to influence other people," is really saying, "I do not want to get involved with other people," and that is an abandonment of one's responsibilities as a human being. Look at the good you can accomplish through persuasion: You can convince a loved one to give up smoking or to not keep a firearm in the house; you can get members of your community to conserve energy or to join together to refurbish a park; you can persuade an employer to hire you for a job in which your own talents, interests, and abilities will be put to their best use.

Persuasion is considered ethical if it conforms to accepted standards. But what are the standards today? If your plan is selfish and not in the best interest of your audience members, but you are honest about your motives—is that ethical? If your plan is in the best interest of your audience members, yet you lie to them to get them to accept the plan—is that ethical? Philosophers and rhetoricians have argued for centuries over questions like these.

There are many ways to define **ethical persuasion**.[8] For our purpose, we will consider it as *communication in the best interest of the audience that does not depend on false or misleading information to change an audience's attitude or behavior.* The best way to appreciate the value of this simple definition is to consider the many strategies listed in Table 14-1 that do not fit it. For example, faking enthusiasm about a speech topic, plagiarizing material from another source and passing it off as your own, and making up statistics to support your case are clearly unethical.

Besides being wrong on moral grounds, unethical attempts at persuasion have a major practical disadvantage: If your deception is uncovered, your credibility will suffer. If, for example, prospective buyers uncover your attempt to withhold a structural flaw in the condominium you are trying to sell, they will probably suspect that the property has other hidden problems. Likewise, if your speech instructor suspects that you are lifting material from other sources without giving credit, your entire presentation will be suspect. One unethical act can cast doubt on future truthful statements. Thus, for pragmatic as well as moral reasons, honesty really is the best policy.

Tunette Powell's speech at the end of this chapter is an example of an honest, ethical speech.

> What does an ethical persuasive speaker need to do to ensure that he or she is sharing a well-founded message?

> cultural idiom
**lifting material:**
using another's words or ideas as one's own

Table 14-1    **Unethical Communication Behaviors**

1. Committing Plagiarism
   a. Claiming someone else's ideas as your own
   b. Quoting without citing the source

2. Relaying False Information
   a. Deliberate lying
   b. Ignorant misstatement
   c. Deliberate distortion and suppression of material
   d. Fallacious reasoning to misrepresent truth

3. Withholding Information; Suppression
   a. About self (speaker); not disclosing private motives or special interests
   b. About speech purpose
   c. About sources (not revealing sources; plagiarism)
   d. About evidence; omission of certain evidence (card stacking)
   e. About opposing arguments; presenting only one side

4. Appearing to Be What One Is Not; Insincerity
   a. In words, saying what one does not mean or believe
   b. In delivery (for example, feigning enthusiasm)

5. Using Emotional Appeals to Hinder Truth
   a. Using emotional appeals as a substitute or cover-up for lack of sound reasoning and valid evidence
   b. Failing to use balanced appeals

*Source:* Adapted from Andersen, M. K. (1979). *An analysis of the treatment of ethos in selected speech communication textbooks* (Unpublished dissertation). University of Michigan, Ann Arbor, pp. 244–247.

---

**Ethical Challenge**

Analyzing
Communication
Behaviors

Read Table 14-1 carefully. The behaviors listed there are presented in what some (but certainly not all) communication experts would describe as "most serious to least serious" ethical faults. Do you agree or disagree with the order of this list? Explain your answer, and whether or not you would change the order of any of these behaviors. Are there any other behaviors that you would add to this list?

---

# Categorizing Types of Persuasion

There are several ways to categorize the types of persuasive attempts you will make as a speaker. What kinds of subjects will you focus on? What results will you be seeking? How will you go about getting those results? In the following pages we will look at each of these questions.

## By Types of Proposition

Persuasive topics fall into one of three categories, depending on the type of thesis statement (referred to as a "proposition" in persuasion) that you are advancing. The three categories are propositions of fact, propositions of value, and propositions of policy.

**Propositions of Fact**    Some persuasive messages focus on **propositions of fact**: issues in which there are two or more sides about conflicting information, in which listeners are required to choose the truth for themselves. Some questions of fact are these:

> The National Security Agency was/was not justified in listening in to the phone calls of everyday citizens.

> Windmills are/are not a practical way for the private homeowner to create clean energy.

> Bottled water is/is not healthier for you than tap water.

These examples show that many questions of fact can't be settled with a simple "yes" or "no" or with an objective piece of information. Rather, they are open to debate, and answering them requires careful examination and interpretation of evidence, usually collected from a variety of sources. That's why it is possible to debate questions of fact, and that's why these propositions form the basis of persuasive speeches and not informative ones.

**Propositions of Value**    **Propositions of value** go beyond issues of truth or falsity and explore the worth of some idea, person, or object. Propositions of value include the following:

> Cheerleaders are/are not just as valuable as the athletes on the field.

> The United States is/is not justified in attacking countries that harbor terrorist organizations.

> The use of laboratory animals for scientific experiments is/is not cruel and immoral.

In order to deal with most propositions of value, you will have to explore certain propositions of fact. For example, you won't be able to debate whether the experimental use of animals in research is immoral—a proposition of value—until you have dealt with propositions of fact such as how many animals are used in experiments and whether experts believe they actually suffer.

**Propositions of Policy**    **Propositions of policy** go one step beyond questions of fact or value: They recommend a specific course of action (a "policy"). Some questions of policy are these:

> The World Bank should/should not create a program of microloans for citizens of impoverished nations.

> The Electoral College should/should not be abolished.

> Genetic engineering of plants and livestock is/is not an appropriate way to increase the food supply.

Looking at persuasion according to the type of proposition is a convenient way to generate topics for a persuasive speech, because each type of proposition suggests different topics. Selected topics could also be handled differently depending on how they are approached. For example, a campaign speech could be approached as a proposition of fact ("Candidate X has done more for this community than the opponent"), a proposition of value ("Candidate X is a better person than the opponent"), or a proposition of policy ("We should get out and vote for Candidate X"). Remember, however, that a fully developed persuasive speech is likely to contain all three types of propositions. If you were preparing a speech advocating that college athletes should be paid in cash for their talents (a proposition of policy), you might want to first prove that the practice is already widespread (a proposition of fact) and that it is unfair to athletes from other schools (a proposition of value).

## By Desired Outcome

We can also categorize persuasion according to two major outcomes: convincing and actuating.

**Convincing**   When you set about to **convince** an audience, you want to change the way its members think. When we say that convincing an audience changes the way its members think, we do not mean that you have to swing them from one belief or attitude to a completely different one. Sometimes audience members will already think the way you want them to, but they will not be firmly enough committed to that way of thinking. When that is the case, you reinforce, or strengthen, their opinions. For example, if your audience already believed that the federal budget should be balanced but did not consider the idea important, your job would be to reinforce members' current beliefs. Reinforcing is still a type of change, however, because you are causing an audience to adhere more strongly to a belief or attitude. In other cases, a speech to convince will begin to shift attitudes without bringing about a total change of thinking. For example, an effective speech to convince might get a group of skeptics to consider the possibility that bilingual education is/isn't a good idea.

**Actuating**   When you set about to **actuate** an audience, you want to move its members to a specific behavior. Whereas a speech to convince might move an audience to action, it won't be any specific action that you have recommended. In a speech to actuate, you do recommend that specific action.

There are two types of action you can ask for—adoption or discontinuance. The former asks an audience to engage in a new behavior; the latter asks an audience to stop behaving in an established way. If you gave a speech for a political candidate and then asked for contributions to that candidate's campaign, you would be asking your audience to adopt a new behavior. If you gave a speech against smoking and then asked your audience members to sign a pledge to quit, you would be asking them to discontinue an established behavior.

## By Directness of Approach

We can also categorize persuasion according to the directness of approach employed by the speaker.

**Direct Persuasion**   In **direct persuasion** the speaker will make his or her purpose clear, usually by stating it outright early in the speech. This is the best strategy to use with a friendly audience, especially when you are asking for a response that the audience is reasonably likely to give you. Direct persuasion is the kind we hear in most academic situations. Eugene Nemirovskiy, a student at Glendale Community College in California, used direct

Bill Clinton used a direct form of persuasion when he spoke in support of Barack Obama at the 2012 Democratic National Convention. Will you be direct or indirect in your next persuasive speech?

persuasion in his speech about America's mental health care system. Part of his introduction announced his intention to persuade in this way:

> The Virginia Tech shooter, Seung-Hui Cho, was released from a psychiatric hospital and ordered by the court to go to an outpatient treatment center. He never received care and no one enforced the court order. In Brooklyn, this past June, Esmin Green keeled over and died on the floor of a psychiatric emergency room while she waited for help. She waited for more than 24 hours. . . . In fixing health care we've forgotten mental health care. There's no parallel thing happening in other health care fields. People are not languishing or being neglected in cardiology wards across America. . . . In order to cure our mental health care systems we must first uncover what needs to be fixed, then, second, why the problems occur, and finally offer some viable solutions.[9]

**Indirect Persuasion**    **Indirect persuasion** disguises or deemphasizes the speaker's persuasive purpose in some way. The question, "Is a season ticket to the symphony worth the money?" (when you intend to prove that it is) is based on indirect persuasion, as is any strategy that does not express the speaker's purpose at the outset.

Indirect persuasion is sometimes easy to spot. A television commercial that shows us attractive young men and women romping in the surf on a beautiful day and then flashes the product name on the screen is pretty indisputably indirect persuasion. Political oratory also is sometimes indirect persuasion, and it is sometimes more difficult to identify as such. A political hopeful might be ostensibly speaking on some great social issue when the real persuasive message is "Please remember my name, and vote for me in the next election."

In public speaking, indirect persuasion is usually disguised as informative speaking, but this approach isn't necessarily unethical. In fact, it is probably the best approach to use when your audience is hostile to either you or your topic. It is also often necessary to use the indirect approach to get a hearing from listeners who would tune you out if you took a more direct approach. Under such circumstances, you might want to ease into your speech slowly.[10] You might take some time to make your audience feel good about you or the social action you are advocating. If you are speaking in favor of your candidacy for city council, but you are in favor of a tax increase and your audience is not, you might talk for a while about the benefits that a well-financed city council can provide to the community. You might even want to change your desired audience response. Rather than trying to get audience members to rush out to vote for you, you might want them simply to read a policy statement that you have written or become more informed on a particular issue. The one thing you cannot do in this instance is to begin by saying, "My appearance here today has nothing to do with my candidacy for city council." That would be a false statement. It is more than indirect; it is untrue and therefore unethical.

The test of the ethics of an indirect approach would be whether you would express your persuasive purpose directly if asked to do so. In other words, if someone in the audience stopped you and asked, "Don't you want us to vote for you for city council?" You would admit to it rather than deny your true purpose, if you were ethical.

> cultural idiom
> **tune you out:**
> stop listening to you

 ON YOUR FEET

*Direct or Indirect Persuasion?*
Find a current political speech online and give a brief summary of its persuasive appeal. Would you categorize the speech as direct or indirect persuasion? Why?

## Creating the Persuasive Message

Persuasive speaking has been defined as "reason-giving discourse." Its principal technique, therefore, involves proposing claims and then backing those claims up with reasons that are true. Preparing an effective persuasive speech isn't easy, but it can be made easier by observing a few simple rules. These include the following: Set a clear, persuasive purpose; structure the message carefully; use solid evidence; and avoid fallacies.

## Set a Clear, Persuasive Purpose

Remember that your objective in a persuasive speech is to move the audience to a specific, attainable attitude or behavior. In a speech to convince, the purpose statement will probably stress an attitude:

> After listening to my speech, my audience members will agree that steps should be taken to save whales from extinction.

In a speech to actuate, the purpose statement will stress behavior:

> After listening to my speech, my audience members will sign my petition.

As Chapter 11 explained, your purpose statement should always be specific, attainable, and worded from the audience's point of view. "The purpose of my speech is to save the whales" is not a purpose statement that has been carefully thought out. Your audience members wouldn't be able to jump into the ocean and save the whales, even if your speech motivated them into a frenzy. They might, however, be able to support a specific piece of legislation.

A clear, specific purpose statement will help you stay on track throughout all the stages of preparation of your persuasive speech. Because the main purpose of your speech is to have an effect on your audience, you have a continual test that you can use for every idea, every piece of evidence, and every organizational structure that you think of using. The question you ask is "Will this help me to get the audience members to think/feel/behave in the manner I have described in my purpose statement?" If the answer is "yes," you forge ahead.

## Structure the Message Carefully

A sample structure of the body of a persuasive speech is outlined in Figure 14-2. With this structure, if your objective is to convince, you concentrate on the first two components: establishing the problem and describing the solution. If your objective is to actuate, you add the third component, describing the desired audience reaction.

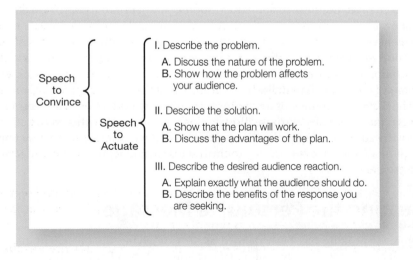

**FIGURE 14-2  Sample Structure for a Persuasive Speech**

There are, of course, other structures for persuasive speeches. This one can be used as a basic model, however, because it is easily applied to most persuasive topics.

**Describe the Problem**    In order to convince an audience that something needs to be changed, you have to show members that a problem exists. After all, if your listeners don't recognize the problem, they won't find your arguments for a solution very important. An effective description of the problem will answer two questions, either directly or indirectly.

**What Is the Nature of the Problem?**    Your audience members might not recognize that the topic you are discussing is a problem at all, so your first task is to convince them that there is something wrong with the present state of affairs. For example, if your thesis were "This town needs a shelter for homeless families," you would need to show that there are, indeed, homeless families and that the plight of these homeless families is serious.

Your approach to defining your problem will depend largely on your audience analysis, as discussed in Chapter 11. If your prespeech analysis shows that your audience may not feel sympathetic to your topic, you will need to explain why your topic is, indeed, a problem that your audience should recognize. In a speech about the plight of the homeless, you might need to establish that most homeless people are not lazy, able-bodied drifters who choose to panhandle and steal instead of work. You could cite respected authorities, give examples, and maybe even show photographs to demonstrate that some homeless people are hardworking but unlucky parents and innocent children who lack shelter owing to forces beyond their control.

**How Does the Problem Affect Your Audience?**    It's not enough to prove that a problem exists. Your next challenge is to show your listeners that the problem affects them in some way. This is relatively easy in some cases: the high cost of tuition, the lack of convenient parking near campus, the quality of food in the student center. In other cases, you will need to spell out the impact to your listeners more clearly. Hope Stallings, a student at Berry College in Georgia, presented a speech on deferred prosecution agreements for large corporations. She connected this topic to her audience in the following way:

> What do Morgan Stanley, Wachovia, Fannie Mae, Merrill Lynch, and AIG all have in common? You might say that they all contributed to the credit crisis in September, and according to the *Washington Post* of March 5, 2009, the ensuing $787 billion government bailout of big business. And you'd be right—partially. You see, these corporations have something else in common. In the past 5 years, each has been indicted on criminal charges like fraud. Never heard about the trials or verdict? That's because in spite of their fraudulent behavior, these corporations never went to court. They avoided the media spotlight, investor scrutiny, and public outrage by entering into deferred prosecution agreements. The *Record* of July 21, 2008, explains that deferred prosecution agreements allow corporations to avoid criminal convictions by paying a small fine out of court. In other words, these companies paid our government to ensure that we remain ignorant, and we have, right up to the collapse of our economy and our personal financial security.[11]

The problem section of a persuasive speech is often broken up into segments discussing the cause and the effect of the problem. (The sample speech at the end of this chapter is an example of this type of organization.)

**Describe the Solution**    Your next step in persuading your audience members is to convince them that there is an answer to the problem you have just introduced. To describe your solution, you should answer two questions:

> cultural idiom

**get back on their feet:**
return to a financially stable lifestyle

> cultural idiom

**paint a . . . picture:**
describe in detail

**Will the Solution Work?**   A skeptical audience might agree with the desirability of your solution but still not believe that it has a chance of succeeding. In the homeless speech discussed previously, you would need to prove that the establishment of a shelter can help unlucky families get back on their feet—especially if your audience analysis shows that some listeners might view such a shelter as a way of coddling people who are too lazy to work.

**What Advantages Will Result from Your Solution?**   You need to describe in specific terms how your solution will lead to the desired changes. This is the step in which you will paint a vivid picture of the benefits of your proposal. In the speech proposing a shelter for homeless families, the benefits you describe would probably include these:

1. Families will have a safe place to stay, free of the danger of living on the street.
2. Parents will have the resources that will help them find jobs: an address, telephone, clothes washers, and showers.
3. The police won't have to apply antivagrancy laws (such as prohibitions against sleeping in cars) to people who aren't the intended target of those laws.
4. The community (including your listeners) won't need to feel guilty about ignoring the plight of unfortunate citizens.

**Describe the Desired Audience Response**   When you want to go beyond simply a strategy to convince your audience members and use a strategy to actuate them to follow your solution, you need to describe exactly what you want them to do. This action step, like the previous ones, should answer two questions:

**What Can the Audience Do to Put Your Solution into Action?**   Make the behavior you are asking your audience members to adopt as clear and simple as possible for them. If you want them to vote in a referendum, tell them when and where to go to vote and how to go about registering, if necessary (some activists even provide transportation). If you're asking them to support a legislative change, don't expect them to write their congressional representative. *You* write the letter or draft a petition and ask them to sign it. If you're asking for a donation, pass the hat at the conclusion of your speech, or give audience members a stamped, addressed envelope and simple forms that they can return easily.

**What Are the Direct Rewards of This Response?**   Your solution might be important to society, but your audience members will be most likely to adopt it if you can show that they will get a personal payoff. Show that supporting legislation to reduce acid rain will produce a wide range of benefits, from reduced lung damage to healthier forests to longer life for their car's paint. Explain that saying "no" to a second drink before driving will not only save lives but also help your listeners avoid expensive court costs, keep their insurance rates low, and prevent personal humiliation. Show how helping to establish and staff a homeless shelter can lead to personal feelings of satisfaction and provide an impressive demonstration of community service on a job-seeking résumé.

On the reality TV series *Shark Tank*, budding entrepreneurs pitch their ideas to potential investors. What persuasive strategies distinguish successful contestants from unsuccessful ones? How can you adapt these strategies to your persuasive appeals?

**Adapt the Model Persuasive Structure**   Describing the problem and the solution makes up the basic structure for any persuasive speech. However, you don't have to analyze too many successful persuasive speeches to realize that the best of them do far more than the basic minimum. In one adaptation of the basic model, the speaker will combine the solution with the desired audience response. Another adaptation is known as the Motivated Sequence.

The **Motivated Sequence**, mentioned in Chapter 12 as a persuasive organization pattern (see Table 14.2), was proposed by a scholar named Alan Monroe in the 1930s and is still widely in use today.[12] In the Motivated Sequence, the problem is broken down into an attention step and a need step, and the solution is broken down into a satisfaction step, a visualization step, and an action step. In a speech on "organ donation," the Motivated Sequence might break down like this:

I. The attention step draws attention to your subject. ("Someday, someone you know may be on an organ donation list; it might even be you.")

II. The need step establishes the problem. ("There is a lack of life-saving organs.")

III. The satisfaction step proposes a solution. ("Organ donation benefits both the donor's family and the recipient.")

IV. The visualization step describes the results of the solution. ("Donating an organ could be one of the greatest gifts you could ever give.")

V. The action step is a direct appeal for the audience to do something. ("Sign an organ donor card today.")

## Use Solid Evidence

All the forms of support discussed in Chapter 12 can be used to back up your persuasive arguments.[13] Your objective here is not to find supporting material that just clarifies your ideas, but rather to find the perfect example, statistic, definition, analogy, anecdote, or testimony to establish the truth of your claim in the mind of this specific audience.

You choose **evidence** that strongly supports your claim, and you should feel free to use **emotional evidence**, which is supporting material that evokes audience feelings such as fear, anger, sympathy, pride, or reverence. Emotional evidence is an ethical fault only when it is used to obscure the truth (see Table 14-1, page 408). It is ethical, however, to use emotion to give impact to a truth.

Whatever type of evidence you use, you should cite your sources carefully. It is important that your audience know that your sources are credible, unbiased, and current. If you are quoting the source of an interview, give a full statement of the source's credentials:

> According to Sean Wilentz, Dayton–Stockton Professor of History, Director of American Studies at Princeton University, and the author of several books on this topic . . .

Table 14-2   **Monroe's Motivated Sequence—The Five Steps**

| STEP | FUNCTION | IDEAL AUDIENCE RESPONSE |
|------|----------|--------------------------|
| _____ 1. Attention | To get the audience to listen | "I want to hear what you have to say." |
| _____ 2. Need | To get the audience to feel a need or want | "I agree. I have that need/want." |
| _____ 3. Satisfaction | To tell the audience how to fill a need or want | "I see your solution will work." |
| _____ 4. Visualization | To get the audience to see the benefits of a solution | "This is a great idea." |
| _____ 5. Action | To get the audience to take action | "I want it." |

If the currency of the interview is important, you might add, "I spoke to Professor Wilentz just last week . . ." If you are quoting an article, give a quick statement of the author's credentials and the full date and title of the magazine:

> According to Professor Sean Wilentz of Princeton University, in an article in the April 21, 2006, *Rolling Stone Magazine* . . .

You do not need to give the title of the article (although you may, if it helps in any way) or the page number. If you are quoting from a book, include a quick statement of the author's credentials:

> According to Professor Sean Wilentz of Princeton University, in his book *The Rise of American Democracy* . . .

You don't need to include the copyright date unless it's important to authenticate the currency of the quotation, and you don't have to mention the publisher or city of publication unless it's relevant to your topic. Generally, if you're unsure about how to cite your sources in a speech, you should err in the direction of too much information rather than too little.

Carefully cited sources are part of a well-reasoned argument. This brings us to our next step in creating a persuasive message.

> **How can you tell if evidence will be effective?**

## Avoid Fallacies

A **fallacy** (from the Latin word meaning "false") is an error in logic. Although the original meaning of the term implied purposeful deception, most logical fallacies are not recognized as such by those who use them. Scholars have devoted lives and volumes to the description of various types of logical fallacies.[14] Here are some of the most common ones to keep in mind when building your persuasive argument:[15]

**Attack on the Person Instead of the Argument (*Ad Hominem*)**   In an *ad hominem* **fallacy** the speaker attacks the integrity of a person in order to weaken the argument. At its crudest level, an *ad hominem* argument is easy to detect. "How can you believe that fat slob?" is hardly persuasive. It takes critical thinking to catch more subtle *ad hominem* arguments, however. Consider this one: "All this talk about 'family values' is hypocritical. Take Senator _____, who made a speech about the 'sanctity of marriage' last year. Now it turns out he was having an affair with his secretary, and his wife is suing him for divorce." Although the senator certainly does seem to be a hypocrite, his behavior doesn't necessarily weaken the merits of family values.

**Reduction to the Absurd (*Reductio Ad Absurdum*)**   A *reductio ad absurdum* **fallacy** unfairly attacks an argument by extending it to such extreme lengths that it looks ridiculous. "If we allow developers to build homes in one section of this area, soon we will have no open spaces left. Fresh air and wildlife will be a thing of the past." "If we allow the administration to raise tuition this year, soon they will be raising it every year, and before we know it only the wealthiest students will be able to go to school here." This extension of reasoning doesn't make any sense: Developing one area doesn't necessarily mean that other areas have to be developed, and one tuition increase doesn't mean that others will occur. Any of these policies might be unwise or unfair, but the *ad absurdum* reasoning doesn't prove it.

**Either-Or**   An **either-or fallacy** sets up false alternatives, suggesting that if the inferior one must be rejected, then the other must be accepted. An angry citizen used either-or thinking to support a proposed city ordinance: "Either we outlaw alcohol in city parks, or there will be no way to get rid of drunks." This reasoning overlooks the possibility that there may be other ways to control public

**ON YOUR FEET**

*Logical Fallacies*

Choose one of the logical fallacies discussed here and give an example of how it might be used in an argument. Then show how it could be corrected with more effective reasoning.

drunkenness besides banning all alcoholic beverages. The old saying "America, love it or leave it" provides another example of either-or reasoning. For instance, when an Asian-born college professor pointed out examples of lingering discrimination in the United States, some suggested that if she didn't like her adopted country, she should return to her native home—ignoring that it is possible to admire a country and still envision ways to make it a better place.

**False Cause (*Post Hoc Ergo Propter Hoc*)**    A *post hoc* fallacy mistakenly assumes that one event causes another because they occur sequentially. An old (and not especially funny) joke illustrates the *post hoc* fallacy. Mac approaches Jack and asks, "Hey, why are you snapping your fingers?" Jack replies, "To keep the elephants away." Mac is incredulous: "What are you talking about? There aren't any elephants within a thousand miles of here." Jack smiles and keeps on snapping: "I know. Works pretty well, doesn't it?"

In real life, *post hoc* fallacies aren't always so easy to detect. For example, one critic of education pointed out that the increase in sexual promiscuity among adolescents began about the same time as prayer in public schools was prohibited by the courts. A causal link in this case may exist: Decreased emphasis on spirituality could contribute to promiscuity. But it would take evidence to establish a *definite* connection between the two phenomena.

**Appeal to Authority (*Argumentum Ad Verecundiam*)**    An *argumentum ad verecundiam* **fallacy** involves relying on the testimony of someone who is not an authority in the case being argued. Relying on experts is not a fallacy, of course. A movie star might be just the right person to offer advice on how to seem more glamorous, and a professional athlete could be the best person to comment on what it takes to succeed in organized sports. But an *ad verecundiam* fallacy occurs when the movie star promotes a political candidate or the athlete tells us why we should buy a certain kind of automobile. When considering endorsements and claims, it's smart to ask yourself whether the source is qualified to make them.

## Understanding Diversity

### Cultural Differences in Persuasion

Different individuals have a tendency to view persuasion differently, and often these differences are based on cultural background. Even the ability to recognize logical argument is, to a certain extent, culturally determined. Not all cultures use logic in the same way that the European-American culture does. The influence of the dominant culture is seen even in the way we talk about argumentation. When we talk about "defending" ideas and "attacking our opponent's position," we are using male-oriented militaristic/aggressive terms. Logic is also based on a trust in objective reality, on information that is verifiable through our senses. As one researcher points out, such a perspective can be culturally influenced:

> Western culture assumes a reality that is materialist and limited to comprehension via the five senses. African

culture assumes a reality that is both material and spiritual viewed as one and the same.[16]

The way logic is viewed differs between Eastern and Western Hemisphere cultures, also. As Larry A. Samovar and Richard E. Porter point out:

> Westerners discover truth by active searching and the application of Aristotelian modes of reasoning. On the contrary, many Easterners wait patiently, and if truth is to be known it will make itself apparent.[17]

It is because of cultural differences such as these that speech experts have always recommended a blending of logical and emotional evidence. ●

**Bandwagon Appeal (*Argumentum Ad Populum*)**  An *argumentum ad populum fallacy* is based on the often-dubious notion that, just because many people favor an idea, you should, too. Sometimes, of course, the mass appeal of an idea can be a sign of its merit. If most of your friends have enjoyed a film or a new book, there is probably a good chance that you will, too. But in other cases widespread acceptance of an idea is no guarantee of its validity. In the face of almost universal belief to the contrary, Galileo reasoned accurately that the earth is not the center of the universe, and he suffered for his convictions. The lesson here is simple to comprehend but often difficult to follow: When faced with an idea, don't just follow the crowd. Consider the facts carefully and make up your own mind.

> cultural idiom

**follow the crowd:**
do what the majority does

## Adapting to the Audience

It is important to know as much as possible about your audience for a persuasive speech. For one thing, you should appeal to the values of your audience whenever possible, even if they are not *your* strongest values. This advice does not mean you should pretend to believe in something. According to our definition of *ethical persuasion*, pretense is against the rules. It does mean, however, that you have to stress those values that are felt most forcefully by the members of your audience.[18]

In addition, you should analyze your audience carefully to predict the type of response you will get. Sometimes you have to pick out one part of your audience— a **target audience**, the subgroup you must persuade to reach your goal—and aim your speech mostly at those members. Some of your audience members might be so opposed to what you are advocating that you have no hope of reaching them. Still others might already agree with you, so they do not need to be persuaded. A middle portion of your audience members might be undecided or uncommitted, and they would be the most productive target for your appeals.

Of course, you need not ignore that portion of your audience that does not fit your target. For example, if you were giving a speech against smoking, your target might be the smokers in your class. Your main purpose would be to get them to quit, but at the same time, you could convince the nonsmokers not to start and to use their influence to help their smoking friends quit.

All of the methods of audience analysis described in Chapter 11—surveys, observation, interviews, and research—are valuable in collecting information about your audience for a persuasive speech.

### Establish Common Ground

It helps to stress as many similarities as possible between yourself and your audience members. This technique helps prove that you understand them: If not, why should they listen to you? Also, if you share a lot of common ground, it shows you agree on many things; therefore, it should be easy to settle one disagreement—the one related to the attitude or behavior you would like them to change.

Celebrities such as Angelina Jolie and George Clooney regularly speak out on issues they feel strongly about. Here, as a special envoy for refugees, Angelina Jolie speaks before the Security Council at the United Nations to urge the world's nations to prioritize the fight against war zone rape. What characteristics of her audience did she have to consider to make her speech effective?

The manager of public affairs for *Playboy* magazine gave a good demonstration of establishing common ground when he reminded a group of Southern Baptists that they shared some important values with him:

> I am sure we are all aware of the seeming incongruity of a representative of *Playboy* magazine speaking to an assemblage of representatives of the Southern Baptist convention. I was intrigued by the invitation when it came last fall, though I was not surprised. I am grateful for your genuine and warm hospitality, and I am flattered (although again not surprised) by the implication that I would have something to say that could have meaning to you people. Both *Playboy* and the Baptists have indeed been considering many of the same issues and ethical problems; and even if we have not arrived at the same conclusions, I am impressed and gratified by your openness and willingness to listen to our views.[19]

## Organize According to the Expected Response

It is much easier to get an audience to agree with you if the members have already agreed with you on a previous point. Therefore, you should arrange your points in a persuasive speech so you develop a "yes" response. In effect, you get your audience into the habit of agreeing with you. For example, if you were giving a speech on the donation of body organs, you might begin by asking the audience members if they would like to be able to get a kidney if they needed one. Then you might ask them if they would like to have a major role in curbing tragic and needless dying. The presumed response to both questions is "yes." It is only when you have built a pattern of "yes" responses that you would ask the audience to sign organ donor cards.

An example of a speaker who was careful to organize material according to expected audience response is the late Robert Kennedy. Kennedy, when speaking on civil rights before a group of South Africans who believed in racial discrimination, arranged his ideas so that he spoke first on values that he and his audience shared—values like independence and freedom.[20]

If audience members are already basically in agreement with you, you can organize your material to reinforce their attitudes quickly and then spend most of your time convincing them to take a specific course of action. If, on the other hand, they are hostile to your ideas, you have to spend more time getting the first "yes" out of them.

## Neutralize Potential Hostility

One of the trickier problems in audience adaptation occurs when you face an audience hostile to you or your ideas. Hostile audiences are those who have a significant number of members who feel adversely about you, your topic, or the speech situation. Members of a hostile audience could range from unfriendly to violent. Two guidelines for handling this type of audience are (1) show that you understand their point of view and (2) if possible, use appropriate humor. A good example of a speaker who observed these guidelines was First Lady and literacy activist Barbara Bush when she was invited to speak at the commencement exercises at Wellesley College in 1990. After the invitation was announced, 150 graduating seniors at the prestigious women's college signed a petition in protest. They wrote, in part:

> We are outraged by this choice and feel it is important to make ourselves heard immediately. Wellesley teaches us that we will be rewarded on the basis of our own work, not on that of a spouse. To honor Barbara Bush as a commencement speaker is to honor a woman who has gained recognition through the achievements of her husband.[21]

Bush decided to honor her speaking obligation, knowing that these 150 students and others who shared their view would be in the audience of 5,000 people. Bush diffused most of this hostility by presenting a speech that stressed that everyone should follow her personal dream and be tolerant of the dreams of others:

> For over 50 years, it was said that the winner of Wellesley's annual hoop race would be the first to get married. Now they say the winner will be the first to become a C.E.O. Both of these stereotypes show too little tolerance. . . . So I offer you today a new legend: the winner of the hoop race will be the first to realize her dream, not society's dream, her own personal dream.[22]

---

**Ethical Challenge**

Adapting to a Hostile Audience

How far would you go in adapting to a hostile audience? What forms would that adaptation take? Discuss this question with your classmates, using a specific speech situation as an example. You can make up the speech situation or choose one of the following:

1. Speaking before a group of advertising executives about your firm belief that there should be heavy governmental penalties for false or deceptive advertising

2. Speaking before a group of Catholic bishops about your belief in reproductive choice

3. Speaking before a group of animal rights advocates about advances in interspecies (animal to human) organ transplants

---

# Building Credibility as a Speaker

**Credibility** refers to the believability of a speaker. Credibility isn't an objective quality; rather, it is a perception in the minds of the audience. In a class such as the one you're taking now, students often wonder how they can build their credibility. After all, the members of the class tend to know one another well by the time the speech assignments roll around. This familiarity illustrates why it's important to earn a good reputation before you speak, through your class comments and the general attitude you've shown.

> cultural idiom
> **roll around:**
> occur, arrive

It is also possible for credibility to change during a speaking event. In fact, researchers speak in terms of initial credibility (what you have when you first get up to speak), derived credibility (what you acquire while speaking), and terminal credibility (what you have after you finish speaking). It is not uncommon for a student with low initial credibility to earn increased credibility while speaking and to finish with much higher terminal credibility.

Without credibility, you won't be able to convince your listeners that your ideas are worth accepting, even if your material is outstanding. On the other hand, if you can develop a high degree of credibility in the eyes of your listeners, they will be likely to open up to ideas they wouldn't otherwise accept. Members of an audience form judgments about the credibility of a speaker based on their perception of many characteristics, the most important of which might be called the "three Cs" of credibility: competence, character, and charisma.[23]

## Competence

*Competence* refers to the speaker's expertise on the topic. Sometimes this competence can come from personal experience that will lead your audience to regard you as an authority on the topic you are discussing. If everyone in the audience knows you've earned big profits in the stock market, they will probably take your investment advice seriously. If you say that you lost 25 pounds from a

## Persuasive Speech

Use the following self-assessment for a persuasive speech you have presented or plan to present.

**1.** Have you set a clear, persuasive purpose?

    I've done my best.       I've got work to do.       I've barely started.

**2.** Is your purpose in the best interest of the audience?

    I've done my best.       I've got work to do.       I've barely started.

**3.** Have you structured the message to achieve a "yes" response?

    I've done my best.       I've got work to do.       I've barely started.

**4.** Have you used solid evidence for each point?

    I've done my best.       I've got work to do.       I've barely started.

**5.** Have you used solid reasoning for each point?

    I've done my best.       I've got work to do.       I've barely started.

**6.** Have you adapted to your audience?

    I've done my best.       I've got work to do.       I've barely started.

**7.** Have you built your own credibility?

    I've done my best.       I've got work to do.       I've barely started.

**8.** Is your information true to the best of your knowledge?

    I've done my best.       I've got work to do.       I've barely started.

Scoring on this assessment is self-evident: For every area in which you've got work left to do, do it.

---

diet-and-exercise program, most audience members will be likely to respect your opinions on weight loss.

The other way to be seen as competent is to be well prepared for speaking. A speech that is well researched, organized, and presented will greatly increase the audience's perception of the speaker's competence. Your personal credibility will therefore be enhanced by the credibility of your evidence, including the sources you cite, the examples you choose, the way you present statistics, the quality of your visual aids, and the precision of your language.

## Character

Competence is the first component of being believed by an audience. The second is being trusted, which is a matter of character. *Character* involves the audience's perception of at least two ingredients: honesty and impartiality. You should try to find ways to talk about yourself (without boasting, of course) that demonstrate your integrity. You might describe how much time you spent researching the subject or demonstrate your open-mindedness by telling your audience that you changed your mind after your investigation. For example, if you were giving a speech arguing against a proposed tax cut in your community, you might begin this way:

> You might say I'm an expert on the municipal services of this town. As a lifelong resident, I owe a debt to its schools and recreation programs. I've been protected by its police and firefighters and served by its hospitals, roads, and sanitation crews.
>
> I'm also a taxpayer who's on a tight budget. When I first heard about the tax cut that's been proposed, I liked the idea. But then I did some in-depth

@Work

## Persuasion Skills in the World of Sales

The skills you develop while learning to prepare persuasive speeches are generalizable to a number of important skills in the world of work. The advice of business consultant George Rodriguez makes it clear that the process of developing a successful sales plan is very much like the planning involved in building a persuasive speech.

"A sales plan is basically your strategic and tactical plan for achieving your marketing objectives," Rodriguez explains. "It is a step-by-step and detailed process that will show how you will acquire new business; and how you will gain more business from your existing customer base."[24]

The process of audience analysis is as important in sales-plan development as it is in persuasive speaking. "The first step is to clearly identify your target markets," Rodriquez says. "Who are more likely to buy your product? The more defined your target market, the better. Your target market can be defined as high-income men ages 30–60 who love to buy the latest electronic gadgets; or mothers with babies 0–12 months old living in urban areas."

And don't forget the guideline that persuasion is interactive. "Prospects are more likely to purchase if you can talk to them about solving their problems," Rodriguez points out.

Rodriguez is far from alone in pointing out the importance of thinking in terms of problems and solutions. Business consultant Barbara Sanfilippo advises her clients to "prepare, prepare, and plan your calls. Today's customers and prospects have very little time to waste. They want solutions. A sales consultant who demonstrates a keen understanding of customers' needs and shows up prepared will earn the business."[25] Sanfilippo suggests reviewing the customer's website and interviewing key people in advance of the meeting.

Sanfilippo also points out the importance of building credibility: "How can you stand out from the pack of sales professionals and consultants all offering similar services?" she asks rhetorically. "Establish Credibility and Differentiate!"

But George Rodriguez probably has the last word in how valuable training in persuasive speaking is to the sales professional. Before you make that first sales call, he says, "You may want to take courses on how to improve your confidence and presentation skills." ●

---

investigation into the possible effects, not just to my tax bill but to the quality of life of our entire community. I looked into our municipal expenses and into the expenses of similar communities where tax cuts have been mandated by law.

### Charisma

*Charisma* is spoken about in the popular press as an almost indefinable, mystical quality. Even the dictionary defines it as "a special quality of leadership that captures the popular imagination and inspires unswerving allegiance and devotion." Luckily, communication scholars favor a more down-to-earth definition. For them, charisma is the audience's perception of two factors: the speaker's enthusiasm and likability. Whatever the definition, history and research have both shown us that audiences are more likely to be persuaded by a charismatic speaker than by a less charismatic one who delivers the same information.

Enthusiasm is sometimes called "dynamism" by communication scholars. Your enthusiasm will mostly be perceived from how you deliver your remarks, not from what you say. The nonverbal parts of your speech will show far better than your words that you believe in what you are saying. Is your voice animated and sincere? Do your gestures reflect your enthusiasm? Do your facial expression and eye contact show you care about your audience?

You can boost your likability by showing that you like and respect your audience. Insincere flattery will probably boomerang, but if you can find a way to give your listeners a genuine compliment, they'll be more receptive to your ideas.

> cultural idiom
> **down-to-earth:**
> practical

> cultural idiom
> **boomerang:**
> create a negative effect

Building your personal credibility through a recognition of the roles of competence, character, and charisma is an important component of your persuasive strategy. When combined with a careful consideration of audience adaptation, persuasive structure, and persuasive purpose, it will enable you to formulate the most effective strategy possible.

---

**CHECKLIST > Ethos, Pathos, and Logos**

The Greek philosopher Aristotle divided the means of persuasion into three types of appeal: **ethos**, **pathos**, and **logos**. Use the following checklist to make sure you are using all three means in your persuasive speeches.

☐ **Ethos (credibility), or ethical appeal:** Have you established your credibility as a speaker so that your audience believes you to be trustworthy?

☐ **Pathos (emotions):** Have you used emotional appeals effectively to make your case?

☐ **Logos (logic):** Have you made logical arguments to appeal to the audience's sense of reasoning? This was Aristotle's favorite, and the most important form of appeal we have discussed in this chapter.

---

# Sample Speech

The sample speech for this chapter was presented by Tunette Powell, who was profiled at the beginning of this chapter. When Powell gave this speech, she was a student and member of the forensics team at the University of Nebraska–Omaha. She was coached by Abbie Syrek and Vanessa Hatfield-Reeker. With this speech, Powell won first place at the Interstate Oratorical Association Annual Contest, hosted by Emerson College in 2012.

Powell's thesis statement could be worded this way:

The U.S. government should change the focus of its war on drugs.

Her purpose statement could be worded as follows:

After listening to my speech, my audience members will agree that the government should decriminalize drug addiction.

Powell carefully organized her argument in a problem-effects-solution format, arranging her points for maximum persuasive impact. Her persuasive organization can be seen in the following outline. (Parenthetical numbers refer to paragraphs in the speech.)

**INTRODUCTION**
  I. Attention-getter (1)
 II. Statement of thesis (2–4)
III. Preview of main points (5–6)

**BODY**
  I. We are the problem, for two reasons. (7–9)
     A. We demonize addiction as a moral rather than a public health issue. (8)
     B. We put addicts behind bars rather than giving them treatment. (9)
 II. This problem has a number of serious negative effects on the addict and society. (10–15)

A. When addicts go to prison, they go from being sick to being criminals. (12)

    1. They are released without treatment. (12)

    2. They are released without employment prospects. (13)

B. When addicts go to prison, society's tax dollars are wasted. (14–15)

III. Solutions can be found on personal, organizational, and governmental levels. (16–18)

A. Personal solutions involve both attitudes and actions. (17)

    1. Each of us must change our attitudes about addiction.

    2. Each of us should get involved to promote rehabilitation.

B. Organizational solutions include A New Path. (18)

C. Governmental solutions involve a needed change of policy. (19)

    1. Government policy should change to reflect the differences between possession and distribution. (19)

    2. Government policy should change to decriminalize the use of drugs. (20)

**CONCLUSION (21)**

  I. Review of main points

  II. Restatement of thesis

  III. Final remarks

As you read Powell's speech, notice how she expands on this outline as she develops her argument point by point. Notice also how she uses solid evidence throughout, including emotional evidence. Her research was culled from the following bibliography:

## Bibliography

Addiction a brain disorder, not just bad behavior. (2011, August 16). *USA Today.*

Amen, H. (2011, July 1). 10 years of drug decriminalization in Portugal has reduced addiction, crime. *Matador Magazine.*

Carmichael, M. (2010, June 28). The case for treating drug addicts in prison. *News Weekly.*

Herman, C., & Whalen, K. (Filmmakers). (2010). *Tulia Texas: The war on drugs* [Documentary]. United States: PBS.

Jackson, S. (2011, May 6). Beyond prisons. *Yes Magazine, 58.* 1–75.

A New Path. (2012, February 17). Retrieved from http://anewpathsite.org/

Office of National Drug Control Policy. (2011). Retrieved from http://www.drugsense.org/cms/wodclock

Public Safety Performance Project. (2011). *Pew Research Center.* Retrieved from http://www.pewcenteronthestates.org/topic_category.aspx?category=528

Reinberg, S. (2011, September 10). Study: More U.S. adults using illegal drugs. *USA Today.*

Schuessler, J. (2012, March 7). Drug policy as race policy: Best seller galvanizes the debate. *The New York Times,* p. 1C.

The science of drug abuse and addiction. (2011). *National Institute on Drug Abuse.* Retrieved from http://www.drugabuse.gov/

Southern Center for Human Rights. (2011, October 6). Retrieved from http://www.schr.org/safety/criminalization

Skolnick, A. (2011, February 9). Runaway prison costs trash state budgets. *The Fiscal Times*.

Szalavitz, M. (2011, September 27). Drugs, risk and the myth of the "evil" addict. *New York Times*. Retrieved from http://opinionator.blogs.nytimes.com/2011/09/27/drugs-risk-and-the-myth-of-the-evil-addict/?scp=2&sq=Maia%20Szalavitz&st=cse

Uniform crime report. (2011, October). *Federal Bureau of Investigation*. Retrieved from http://www.fbi.gov/about-us/cjis/ucr/ucr

Williams, K. (2011, October 3). Recovery month 2011: Getting rid of addiction stigma. *Huffington Post*. Retrieved from http://www.huffingtonpost.com/kimberly-williams/the-problem-is-not-the-pe_b_989742.html

**SAMPLE SPEECH** | It's Not the Addict, It's the Drug: Redefining America's War on Drugs > | **Tunette Powell**

**1** Bruce Callis grew up in one of the poorest projects in San Antonio, Texas. His mother was a housekeeper; his father, a full-time alcoholic. Bruce downed his first beer at age 13, smoked marijuana at 14, and at 21 he was addicted to crack cocaine. By the time he was 30 Bruce was convicted of possession of crack cocaine and sentenced to 15 years behind bars.

*Attention-getter: A high-impact introduction uses an example that personalizes the problem.*

**2** Forty years ago, Richard Nixon launched the "War on Drugs" to eliminate drug use and the illegal drug trade in our country. Sadly, Nixon and presidents after him waged the wrong war. This 40-year fight has become less about preventing drug distribution and more about the criminalization of addiction. According to the *New York Times* of March 7, 2012, the United States currently incarcerates 2.3 million people, of which 23 percent are nonviolent drug offenders.

*Direct statement of the thesis, demonstrating that this is direct persuasion. Statistics from trustworthy sources increase Powell's credibility on this topic.*

**3** Yes, drug distribution in our country is a serious concern, but according to the Law Office for the Southern Center for Human Rights, our misguided attitudes and policies toward drugs has created a culture that is intolerant of addiction. Although many people recognize addiction as a disease, we are still more likely to punish people for it than to help them with recovery.

*Here Powell expands on her thesis statement, explaining the basic problem she will address in the rest of her speech.*

**4** According to the Office of National Drug Control Policy, "The U.S. federal government spent over $15 billion dollars in 2010 on the War on Drugs, at a rate of about $500 per second." But the cost of criminalizing addiction isn't just paid in dollars, it is paid in lives. According to the summer 2011 issue of *YES* magazine, only one-fifth of addicts behind bars have adequate access to rehabilitation programs, making it almost impossible for them to recover and become functioning members of society, which hurts not only them but society as a whole.

*Powell could have also broken down this statistic to $41 million a day, $1.7 million an hour, or $28.5 thousand a minute. Which is more memorable?*

**5** Today, let's set aside what we've previously been told about drug use in America and focus on the person behind the addiction by discussing the problems, impacts, and solutions of criminalizing addiction. Attitude is the paint that can change the color of any room. And the walls of America are in dire need of a touch-up.

*Preview of main points.*

**6** According to the *USA Today* of September 10, 2011, over 20 million Americans struggling with addictions never receive help with recovery. Let's ask ourselves not *what* the problem is, but *who* the problem is.

*Powell continues to establish the problem with solid evidence from a reliable source.*

**7** *We* are the problem for two reasons. One, we demonize addiction as dirty and morally wrong, and, two, our policies reinforce this by putting addicts behind bars without rehabilitation.

*Statement of the first main point, preview of the first two subpoints.*

**8** First, we are guilty of branding addiction as morally wrong when it is really an issue of public health. Maia Szalavitz wrote in the *New York Times* on September 27, 2011, "Prejudice against people based on the substances they use is one of the few remaining acceptable biases." She explains that we are blinded by a cultural perception that addicts are expendable; that they "*deserve* to die because they have violated the law and aren't taking responsibility for the consequences of their actions." Just proving her point further, in response to the article one reader exclaimed, "Is it really in the social interest to save the lives of junkies who overdose?"

*She chooses powerful quotations from a reliable source to develop her first subpoint.*

**9** Unfortunately, this voice is only one in a chorus of intolerance toward addicts, which leads to our second problem: We incarcerate addicts instead of giving them treatment. As we discussed earlier, the United States currently incarcerates over 500,000 nonviolent drug users, all despite this: As *USA Today* explained on August 16, 2011, two decades of neuroscience have uncovered how addiction hijacks different parts of the brain and changes the cognitive and behavioral functions of drug users.

*Development of the second subpoint.*

**10** According to the National Institute on Drug Abuse in 2011, "addiction is a chronic disease similar to other chronic diseases such as type II diabetes, cancer, and cardiovascular disease." If cancer were treated the same as addiction, we would refuse treatment to inmates suffering from lung cancer simply because they had a history of smoking cigarettes. According to *News Weekly* on June 28, 2010, only one-fifth of prison inmates get any form of drug treatment, and nowhere does our public health policy stipulate that such treatment has to be "effective."

*A powerful analogy used as proof.*

**11** Bruce Callis was in and out of prison from his early 20s to his late 40s. Most prisons didn't offer him treatment, and the ones that did were ineffective. Criminalizing addictions results in two alarming impacts: on the addict and society.

*A return to her personal example and a preview of the next main point.*

**12** According to a 2011 Public Safety Performance Project conducted by the Pew Research Center, 4 out of 10 drug offenders returned to state prison within 3 years of their release. And with little treatment available, this shouldn't surprise us. A cycle is created the first time an addict goes to prison. They go from a sick person to a criminal. The addict is then released back into society. The sickness is ignored, and the cycle repeats itself all over again.

*The first subpoint of the second main point.*

**13** As previously cited, neuroscience journalist Maia Szalavitz points out, "Even when drug users are released, their criminal record makes it impossible for them to find meaningful employment." So not only are many addicts fighting disease without medical assistance, but many do so as unemployed, sometimes homeless, members of our society.

*Evidence from a reliable source.*

**14** This leads to startling social impacts. According to *Uniform Crime Reports*, published by the FBI in October of 2011, every 20 seconds someone in America is arrested for violating a drug law. However, many of these arrests are for drug possession with no intent to distribute. For example, according to that same report, approximately 900,000 people in 2009 were arrested for marijuana, of which 89 percent were charged with possession with no intent to distribute.

*Transition to the next point.*

**15** Our economy is in a state of emergency, yet our eagerness to criminalize drugs and put users behind bars is costing us billions of dollars a year. *The Fiscal Times* reported on February 9th, 2011, that in California alone it costs about $45,000 per year to incarcerate a drug user; the same price as one year at Harvard University with room and board. By contrast, rehabilitation would cost less than $5,000 per year. Our tax dollars continue to be wasted on room and board for inmates who will never benefit or recover as long as they're incarcerated.

*Another powerful analogy, with statistics.*

**16** Bruce Callis was released from prison for the final time when he was 47 years old. After 1 week his son found him slumped over at a bus station, high on crack and barely able to walk. Notice that nowhere in Callis's story have I mentioned drug

*Return to the personal example; a preview of the final main point.*

treatment, only incarceration. What can we do to help people like him? Let's look at personal, organizational, and governmental solutions.

17 Our personal solution comes first, because it is the foundation for all other solutions: We must change our attitudes about addiction. Dr. Ellen Friedman, a psychologist, told the *Huffington Post* on October 3, 2011, "The profile of the addict as an amoral thrill-seeker is . . . scientifically wrong." We don't shame people for cancer diagnoses; we cannot continue to demonize drug users.

*Again, an excellent coupling of an analogy with statistical evidence.*

18 Second, we have to get involved to promote rehabilitation and fight incarceration for nonviolent drug users. There are existing organizations that need our support, such as A New Path, an organization that is dedicated to reducing the stigma of addictive illness and advocates for therapeutic rather than punitive drug policies. Visit their website at anewpathsite.org. This organization publishes updates on national drug legislation; check it out to learn more about legislation in your area.

*Desired audience behavior.*

19 On a governmental level, the first step is for policy to reflect the differences between possession and distribution, which would greatly reduce the number of drug users behind bars. This would help law enforcement distinguish between the *crime* of distributing drugs and the *person* who is addicted to them.

20 Finally, perhaps our government can look to Portugal, which has set a noble example. Ten years ago, Portugal decriminalized the use of drugs, according to *Matador Magazine* in July 2011. People caught using illegal substances are sent before a panel of psychologists and social workers instead of a judge in a criminal court. *Matador Magazine* reported that since the 2001 law was enacted, the number of addicts has been cut in half. Portugal is a real-life example of what happens when a country treats drug addiction as a health issue and not a criminal one.

*Example/analogy used as evidence.*

21 Now is the time to separate the War on Drugs from the war on addiction. Today you've heard the problems, impacts, and solutions of criminalizing addictions. Bruce Callis is 50 years old now. And he is still struggling with his addiction. While you all are sitting out there listening to this, I'm living it. Bruce Callis is my father, and for my entire life, I have watched our misguided system destroy him. The irony here is that we live in a society where we are told to recycle. We recycle paper, aluminum, and old electronics. But why don't we ever consider recycling the most precious thing on earth—the human life.[26]

*A review of the main points and a restatement of the thesis.*

## Summary

Persuasion—the act of moving someone, through communication, toward a belief, attitude, or behavior—can be both worthwhile and ethical. Ethical persuasion requires that the speaker be sincere and honest and avoid such behaviors as plagiarism. It also requires that the persuasion be in the best interest of the audience.

Persuasion can be categorized according to the type of proposition (fact, value, or policy), outcome (convincing or actuating), or approach (direct or indirect). A persuasive strategy is put into effect through the use of several techniques.

These include setting a specific, clear persuasive purpose, structuring the message carefully, using solid evidence (including emotional evidence), using careful reasoning, adapting to the audience, and building credibility as a speaker.

A typical structure for a speech to convince requires you to explain what the problem is and then propose a solution. For a speech to actuate, you also have to ask for a desired audience response. The basic three-pronged structure can be adapted to more elaborate persuasive plans, but the basic components will remain a part of any persuasive strategy.

For each of these components, you need to analyze the arguments your audience will have against accepting what you say and then answer those arguments.

In adapting to your audience, you should establish common ground, organize your speech in such a way that you can expect a "yes" response along each step of your persuasive plan, and take special care with a hostile audience. In building credibility, you should keep in mind the audience's perception of your competence, character, and charisma.

## Key Terms

**actuate** To move members of an audience toward a specific behavior. *p. 410*

**ad hominem fallacy** A fallacious argument that attacks the integrity of a person to weaken his or her position. *p. 416*

**anchor** The position supported by audience members before a persuasion attempt. *p. 405*

**argumentum ad populum fallacy** Fallacious reasoning based on the dubious notion that because many people favor an idea, you should, too. *p. 418*

**argumentum ad verecundiam fallacy** Fallacious reasoning that tries to support a belief by relying on the testimony of someone who is not an authority on the issue being argued. *p. 417*

**convincing** A speech goal that aims at changing audience members' beliefs, values, or attitudes. *p. 410*

**credibility** The believability of a speaker or other source of information. *p. 420*

**direct persuasion** Persuasion that does not try to hide or disguise the speaker's persuasive purpose. *p. 410*

**either-or fallacy** Fallacious reasoning that sets up false alternatives, suggesting that if the inferior one must be rejected, then the other must be accepted. *p. 416*

**emotional evidence** Evidence that arouses emotional reactions in an audience. *p. 415*

**ethical persuasion** Persuasion in an audience's best interest that does not depend on false or misleading information to induce change in that audience. *p. 407*

**ethos** A speaker's credibility or ethical appeal. *p. 423*

**evidence** Material used to prove a point, such as testimony, statistics, and examples. *p. 415*

**fallacy** An error in logic. *p. 416*

**indirect persuasion** Persuasion that disguises or deemphasizes the speaker's persuasive goal. *p. 411*

**latitude of acceptance** In social judgment theory, statements that a receiver would not reject. *p. 405*

**latitude of noncommitment** In social judgment theory, statements that a receiver would not care strongly about one way or another. *p. 405*

**latitude of rejection** In social judgment theory, statements that a receiver could not possibly accept. *p. 405*

**logos** A speaker's use of logical arguments to appeal to an audience's sense of reasoning. *p. 423*

**Motivated Sequence** A five-step plan used in persuasive speaking; also known as Monroe's Motivated Sequence. *p. 415*

**pathos** A speaker's use of emotional appeals to persuade an audience. *p. 423*

**persuasion** The act of motivating a listener, through communication, to change a particular belief, attitude, value, or behavior. *p. 405*

**post hoc fallacy** Fallacious reasoning that mistakenly assumes that one event causes another because they occur sequentially. *p. 417*

**proposition of fact** A claim bearing on issue in which there are two or more sides of conflicting factual evidence. *p. 409*

**proposition of policy** A claim bearing on issue that involves adopting or rejecting a specific course of action. *p. 409*

**proposition of value** A claim bearing on issue involving the worth of some idea, person, or object. *p. 409*

**reductio ad absurdum fallacy** Fallacious reasoning that unfairly attacks an argument by extending it to such extreme lengths that it looks ridiculous. *p. 416*

**social judgment theory** An explanation of attitude change that posits that opinions will change only in small increments and only when the target opinions lie within the receiver's latitudes of acceptance and noncommitment. *p. 405*

**target audience** That part of an audience that must be influenced in order to achieve a persuasive goal. *p. 418*

## Check Your Understanding

Answer the following for a persuasive speech you have presented or plan to present:

1. What was your persuasive strategy for this speech?

2. Which guidelines did you use to make sure your speech was ethical?

3. How did you bolster your credibility as a speaker? Give specific examples.

4. Which guidelines did you use to check the effectiveness of your persuasive arguments?

5. How did you organize your speech for the desired effect on your audience?

## Activities

1. **Audience Latitudes of Acceptance** To better understand the concept of latitudes of acceptance, rejection, and noncommitment, formulate a list of perspectives on a topic of your choice. This list should contain 8 to 10 statements that represent a variety of attitudes, such as the list pertaining to the pro-life/pro-choice issue on page 406. Arrange this list from your own point of view, from most

acceptable to least acceptable. Then circle the single statement that best represents your own point of view. This will be your "anchor." Underline those items that also seem reasonable. These make up your latitude of acceptance on this issue. Then cross out the numbers in front of any items that express opinions that you cannot accept. These make up your latitude of rejection. Those statements that are left would be your latitude of noncommitment. Do you agree that someone seeking to persuade you on this issue would do best by advancing propositions that fall within this latitude of noncommitment?

2. **Personal Persuasion** When was the last time you changed your attitude about something after discussing it with someone? In your opinion, was this persuasion interactive? Not coercive? Incremental? Ethical? Explain your answer.

3. **Propositions of Fact, Value, and Policy** Which of the following are propositions of fact, propositions of value, and propositions of policy?

   1. "Three Strikes" laws that put felons away for life after their third conviction are/are not fair.

   2. Elder care should/should not be the responsibility of the government.

   3. The mercury in dental fillings is/is not healthy for the dental patient.

   4. Congressional pay raises should/should not be delayed until an election has intervened.

   5. Third-party candidates strengthen/weaken American democracy.

   6. National medical insurance should/should not be provided to all citizens of the United States.

   7. Elderly people who are wealthy do/do not receive too many Social Security benefits.

   8. Tobacco advertising should/should not be banned from all media.

   9. Domestic violence is/is not on the rise.

   10. Pit bulls are/are not dangerous animals.

4. **Structuring Persuasive Speeches** For practice in structuring persuasive speeches, choose one of the following topics, and provide a full-sentence outline that conforms to the outline in Figure 14-2, page 412.

   1. It should/should not be more difficult to purchase a handgun.

   2. Public relations messages that appear in news reports should/should not be labeled as advertising.

   3. Newspaper recycling is/is not important for the environment.

   4. Police should/should not be required to carry nonlethal weapons only.

   5. Parole should/should not be abolished.

6. The capital of the United States should/should not be moved to a more central location.

7. We should/should not ban capital punishment.

8. Bilingual education should/should not be offered in all schools in which students speak English as a second language.

5. **Find the Fallacy** Test your ability to detect shaky reasoning by identifying which fallacy is exhibited in each of the following statements.

   a. *Ad hominem*        d. *Post hoc*

   b. *Ad absurdum*       e. *Ad verecundiam*

   c. Either-or           f. *Ad populum*

   1. Some companies claim to be in favor of protecting the environment, but you can't trust them. Businesses exist to make a profit, and the cost of saving the earth is just another expense to be cut.

   2. Take it from me, imported cars are much better than domestics. I used to buy only American, but the cars made here are all junk.

   3. Rap music ought to be boycotted. After all, the number of assaults on police officers went up right after rap became popular.

   4. Carpooling to cut down on the parking problem is a stupid idea. Look around—nobody carpools!

   5. I know that staying in the sun can cause cancer, but if I start worrying about every environmental risk I'll have to stay inside a bomb shelter breathing filtered air, never drive a car or ride my bike, and I won't be able to eat anything.

   6. The biblical account of creation is just another fairy tale. You can't seriously consider the arguments of those Bible-thumping, know-nothing fundamentalists, can you?

6. **The Credibility of Persuaders** Identify someone who tries to persuade you via public speaking or mass communication. This person might be a politician, a teacher, a member of the clergy, a coach, a boss, or anyone else. Analyze this person's credibility in terms of the three dimensions discussed in the chapter. Which dimension is most important in terms of this person's effectiveness?

## For Further Exploration

For more resources about persuasive speaking, see the *Understanding Human Communication* website at www.oup.com/us/adler. There you will find a variety of resources: "Media Room" clips from popular films and television shows to further illustrate important concepts, a list of books and articles, links to descriptions of feature films and television shows at the *Now Playing* website, study aids, and a self-test to check your understanding of the material in this chapter.

# APPENDIX

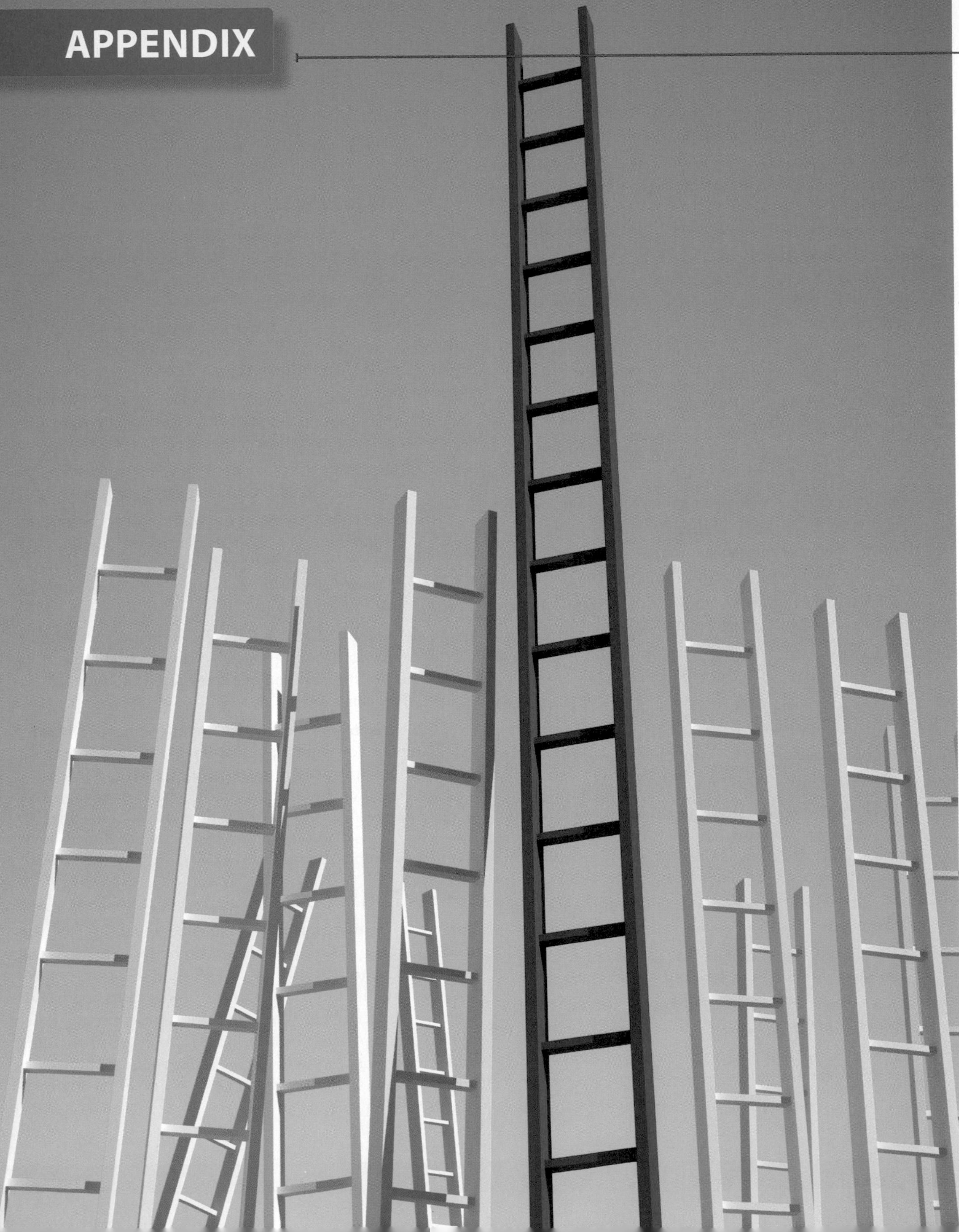

# Communicating for Career Success

## Chapter Outline

Take a look at job descriptions in any online posting or print publication. No matter what kind of work—entry-level jobs, highly technical professional positions, and management—you're likely to see "excellent communication skills" listed as a job requirement.

Communication skills are not just important on the job—they're necessary to get hired in the first place. Before you receive a job offer, you'll need to demonstrate to a potential employer that you will bring value to the organization that will be paying you.

This appendix outlines the strategies and skills that can help you identify, secure, and perform a job that fits your talents and interests. Applying the information in these pages won't guarantee career success. But it will certainly boost the odds.

# Employment Strategies

In a perfect world, the person with the best qualifications will get a job. In reality, the person who knows the most about getting hired often gets the desired position. Though job-getting skills are no substitute for qualifications after the actual work begins, they are necessary if you are going to be hired in the first place. The following guidelines will increase your chances of success.

## Cultivate Personal Networks

Everybody belongs to personal networks—interlocking relationships linked by communication. Yours probably include friends, family, school, and community. Beyond the everyday value of communicating with these people, career-related **networking** is the strategic process of deliberately meeting people and maintaining contacts that result in information, advice, and leads that enhance one's career. Rich networks provide the kind of social capital described in the "@Work" box on page 231 of Chapter 7.

Once you think about it, the potential value of networking is obvious. If you're looking for a job, personal contacts can tell you about positions that may not even be public yet. When many candidates seek the same job, people you know can put in a good word for you with potential employers and also give you tips on how to pursue the position you're seeking.

The number of jobs found through networking is staggering. It exceeds the number of those that come from Web searches, headhunters, or other formal means.[1] Some research suggests that less than 10 percent of job seekers find employment by using the Internet.[2] One study of more than 150,000 jobs found that more people were hired by referrals than by any other source.[3] Another survey conducted by global resources company DBM revealed that 75 percent of job seekers obtained their current positions through personal networking.[4] The reverse is also true: Most employers find good employees through their personal networks.[5]

**Networking Strategies**    Here are some tips that will enhance your networking skills.[6]

(1) **View everyone as a networking prospect.** Besides the people in your immediate everyday networks, you have access to a wealth of other contacts: former coworkers, neighbors and schoolmates, people you've met at social and community events, professional people whose services you have used . . . the list can be quite long and diverse.

(2) **Seek referrals.** Each contact in your immediate network has connections to people you don't already know and who might be able to help you. Social

scientists examined the "six degrees of separation" hypothesis by studying more than 45,000 messages exchanged in more than 150 countries. They discovered that the average number of links separating any two people in the world is indeed a half dozen.[7] You can take advantage of this principle by only seeking people removed from your personal network by just one degree: If you ask 10 people for referrals, and each of them knows 10 others who might be able to help, you have the potential of support from 100 information givers.

(3) **Show appreciation.** The best way to repay people who help you is by expressing gratitude for their help. Beyond a sincere thank-you, take the time to let your contacts know when their help has made a difference in your career advancement. Besides being the right thing to do, your expressions of thanks will distinguish you as the kind of person worth helping again in the future.

**Networking on the Web**    In addition to personal networking, there are plenty of websites where job seekers can make themselves known to prospective employers. It can't hurt to join at least a few professional networking sites and set up a basic profile. Many business professionals maintain a presence on these six sites, and sometimes more.

**LinkedIn** (www.linkedin.com) has about 200 million members across the globe, and its website represents more than 150 industries. There is no charge to become a basic member, but there are more advanced networking tools available for a membership fee. On LinkedIn, members create their own profile page, including information about work experience and education, and then create connections to people they know. Through a network of connections that already exist, users can ask for referrals, introductions, and business opportunities. LinkedIn is a way to get to know people who may be able to help you professionally, through people you already know.

**SunZu** (ecademy.com) does not report membership numbers, so it is impossible to say how many users it has, but it is a well-known site among professional networkers. Basic membership is free, and users have the option to upgrade to two more advanced networking levels for a fee. Through SunZu, users learn about networking events and can even arrange one-on-one meetings with other members. Members create a profile page and can then send messages to other members, depending on each person's membership level. Higher levels offer greater access to users. There is a space for blog postings, ratings of businesses, and personal testimonials.

**Xing** (xing.com) reports about 6 million members, mainly in Europe and China. Although this site does not have a blogging feature, it allows members to create a profile page, join groups, send messages to other members, and learn about offline events. A free basic membership on Xing will allow you to have an online presence if someone performs an online search of your name, but you will need to pay for more advanced features on the site.

**Ryze** (ryze.com) is a professional networking site with roughly 500,000 members. Similar to the sites already mentioned, a paid membership gets you more options but is not required to join and have a basic profile. Ryze boasts more than 1,000 groups you can join once you are a member. There are no blogs, but the ability to join the network groups is the highlight of this site.

**Plaxo** (plaxo.com) has 50 million members and counting. It offers users a free membership that allows them to show off what they are doing online by linking other websites and services to their profile. For example, your Plaxo profile can link to your Flickr account to show off your photos and even announce "new updates" anytime you post on another linked website. As with most other sites, a paid upgrade will allow you to explore more networking tools on the site but is not necessary.

**Facebook** (www.facebook.com) is the world's largest social networking site, but it shouldn't be a primary tool for career-related communication. As you'll read elsewhere in this appendix (pages A-20–A-21), you should be mindful of how information posted there will be regarded by people with whom you deal professionally.

## Conduct Informational Interviews

Sooner or later your networking and personal research are likely to point you toward people whose knowledge, experience, and contacts could shape your career. These may be people you already know but whom you suddenly view in a new way: a successful neighbor or relative, for example. In other cases, you may casually meet someone who you realize could be a great career asset, perhaps at a social event, or even as a seatmate on the train or plane. Finally, you may read or hear about a total stranger whose perspective could transform your career.

**Goals of Informational Interviews**    Regardless of the source, with a little initiative and planning you can approach these contacts and request an **informational interview**: a structured meeting in which you seek answers from a source whose knowledge can help enhance your success.

The best informational interview has three goals:

(1) To *conduct research* that helps you understand a job, organization, or field

(2) To *be remembered favorably* by the person you are interviewing (so he or she may mention you to others who can also advance your career)

(3) To *gain referrals* to other people who might also be willing to help you

**Contacting Informational Interviewees**    Unless you know a prospective interviewee well, the best approach is usually to make your first contact in writing. A phone call might be easier, but it runs at least two risks. First, you may miss the person and be forced to leave a voice mail message that can either be too short to explain yourself or too long to hold your recipient's attention. Even if the potential interviewee answers your call, you may have caught him or her at a bad time. With an e-mail, or even a snail mail letter, you can carefully edit your introduction until it's just right and assume that the recipient will read it whenever he or she is ready.

In your written message, you should do the following (see Figure A-1):

- Introduce yourself.
- Explain your reason for the interview (emphasizing that you're seeking information, not asking for a job).
- Identify the amount of time your questions are likely to take. (Don't ask for more than 1 hour. The shorter the amount of time you request, the better are your odds of being seen.)
- State a range of dates when you are available to meet. Be as flexible as possible.

**Questions to Ask in an Informational Interview**    More than any other factor, the questions you ask and the way you ask them will determine the success or failure of an interview. Truly good questions rarely come spontaneously, even to the best of interviewers.

The first thing to realize is that a career-related informational interview is ultimately about *you*, and not the person you're talking with. Fascinating as it might be, dwelling on the life story of the person you're interviewing isn't likely to help advance your career. Instead, probe your interviewee for information that will

TO:        Roland Sanchez

FROM:     Andrew Kao <akao@webmail.com>

SUBJECT:  Seeking your advice

DATE:      February 18, 2014

Dear Mr. Sanchez:

As an aspiring entrepreneur, I was interested to read the recent article in the *Washington Post* about your success in growing NX solutions from scratch to an internationally renowned consulting firm.

My purpose in writing is to seek your advice about career paths. I am in my final year as an international business major in the University of Maryland's Robert H. Smith School of Business. I expect to receive my bachelor of science degree in December with honors.

I'm fascinated with the idea of building a career similar to yours and want to approach that goal in the best way. Several options seem attractive, including graduate school, employment with a large firm, or employment with a small but promising firm where I may be able to have a bigger impact.

I would be most grateful for the chance to meet with you and gain the benefit of your advice. All of my classes are in the morning, so I am available in the afternoon on any day when you may be available for a short informational phone call or meeting.

I look forward to hearing from you via e-mail or phone, and I hope we can set up a time to talk soon. My contact information is below.

Thanks in advance for any help you can offer.

Sincerely,

Andrew Kao

akao@webmail.com

(555) 555-4800

FIGURE A-1 Letter Seeking an Informational Interview

help you succeed. You can appreciate the difference by comparing these types of questions:

| FOCUSED ON INFORMATIONAL INTERVIEWEE (LESS EFFECTIVE) | FOCUSED ON YOU (BETTER) |
|---|---|
| Did you go to graduate school? Where? Why? | Do you think it would be helpful for me to go to graduate school? Where? Why? (Or why not?) |
| What was your first job? | What kinds of jobs do you think would be good for me in the early stages of my career? |
| What do you think helped you become successful in your career? | What lessons have you learned in your career that you think could help me become as successful as you are? |

Don't fall into the trap of making this a journalistic interview. If you've told your interviewee up front that you're seeking career advice, it will be clear that you are the focus of this conversation.

Once you're clear about the topics you want to cover, you can design questions that will get the information you're seeking. There are a number of question types, each of which has its own uses.

(1) **Factual versus opinion questions:** As their name implies, **factual questions** are usually straightforward requests for information: "What are the three fastest-growing companies in this field?" or "What's the average entry-level salary in this field?" By contrast, **opinion questions** ask for the interviewer's evaluation: "What parts of the country do you think will offer the best chance for advancement in the next few years?" or "How important do you think it is to be bilingual?" When planning an interview, ask yourself whether you're more interested in facts or opinions and plan your questions accordingly.

(2) **Open versus closed questions:** **Closed questions** call for a specific, usually concise answer: "Do you think I should rent or lease?" or "Is the code for that software open source or proprietary?"

By contrast, **open questions** invite the interviewee to reply in whatever way he or she chooses: "What do you think about the risks of working for an Internet start-up company?" or "Why did you say that accounting is a must-take course?"

Developing good open questions takes time and thought. Questions that are poorly worded or ones that are too broad or too narrow to get the information you seek can be a waste of time. A good list of open-ended questions can help in several ways. First, you will almost certainly have enough lengthy responses to fill the allotted time, soothing a common fear of inexperienced interviewers. Your open questions, inviting comment as they do, will also make your subject feel more comfortable. Second, the way in which your subject chooses to answer your open questions will tell you more about him or her than you could probably learn by asking only more restrictive closed questions, which can be answered in a few words.

(3) **Direct versus indirect questions:** Most of the time the best way to get information is to ask a **direct question**. There are times, however, when a subject won't be willing to give a candid response. This sort of situation usually occurs when a straightforward reply would be embarrassing or risky. For

instance, you probably wouldn't want to ask questions like "What's your salary?" or "Do you ever have to compromise your ethical standards?"

At times like these it's wise to seek information by using **indirect questions**, which do not directly request the information you are seeking. Instead of the direct questions above, you could ask, "What kind of salary might I expect if I ever held a position like yours?" or "Are there any ethical dilemmas that come with this kind of job?"

④ **Primary versus secondary questions**: Sometimes you'll need to ask only an initial, primary question to get the fact or opinion you need in a given content area. But more often you will need to follow up your first question with others to give you all the information you need. These follow-ups are called secondary questions.

> *Primary question*: "In your opinion, who are the best people for me to ask about careers in the financial planning field?"

> *Secondary questions*: "How could I meet them?" "Do you think they'd be willing to help?" "How could each one help me?"

Sometimes an interviewer can follow up with secondary responses that aren't really questions. Simple **probes**—interjections, silences, and other brief remarks—can open up or direct an interviewee and uncover useful information.

**Interviewer:**  "What traits are you looking for in a new employee?"

**Respondent:**  "Flexibility is the most important thing for us."

**Interviewer:**  "Flexibility?"

**Respondent:**  "Yes. Things change so rapidly in our organization that we need people who can adapt to whatever happens next."

It can be smart to develop a list of secondary questions to each primary one. In many cases, however, the best follow-ups will occur to you during the interview, depending on how the respondent answers your first question. As you ask and probe, be sure each secondary question you ask helps achieve your goal. It's easy to wind up taking an interesting digression, only to discover that you didn't get the information you were after.

> cultural idiom
> **to wind up:**
> to bring to an end, to finish

⑤ **Neutral versus leading questions**: A **neutral question** gives the interviewee a chance to respond without any influence from the interviewer. By contrast, a **leading question** is one in which the interviewer—either directly or indirectly—signals the desired answer. Unless you're a litigator or salesperson, there are almost no cases when a leading question is useful.

A few examples illustrate the difference between these two types of questions:

| NEUTRAL QUESTION | LEADING QUESTION |
| --- | --- |
| What do you think about my idea? | I've worked very hard on this idea, and I'm proud of it. What do you think? |
| Do you think sexism is a problem in this industry? | What examples of sexism have you seen in this industry? |

⑥ **Hypothetical questions**: A **hypothetical question** seeks a response by proposing a "what-if" situation. "If your own son or daughter were considering the career I've asked you about, what would you say?"

Hypothetical questions can encourage interviewees to offer information they wouldn't volunteer if asked directly. For instance, your interviewee might not be comfortable criticizing specific organizations in your field, but you could get the information you're seeking by asking, "If you had to rank the top five or six nonprofits in this community, what would the list look like?"

**After the Informational Interview** Good manners call for sending a note of thanks to the interviewer who has taken time to give you advice and information. Such a note can also be strategically savvy: It serves as a tangible reminder of you, and it provides a written record of your name and contact information. It can be smart to keep your contact alive by sending follow-up messages letting your interviewee know how you have put his or her advice to good use. If the interviewee has referred you to other people, be sure to let him or her know the results of your conversations with those people.

## The Selection Interview

For many people the short time spent facing a potential employer is the most important interview of a lifetime. A **selection interview** may occur when you are being considered for employment, but it may also occur when you are being evaluated for promotion or reassignment. In an academic setting, selection interviews are often part of the process of being chosen for an award, a scholarship, or admission to a graduate program. Being chosen for the position you seek depends on making a good impression on the person or people who can hire you, and your interviewing skills can make the difference between receiving a job offer and being an also-ran.

> cultural idiom
> **an also-ran:**
> an unsuccessful applicant

### Preparing for the Interview

A good interview begins long before you sit down to face the other person. There are several steps you can take to boost your chances for success.

**Do Your Research** Displaying your knowledge of an organization in an interview is a terrific way to show potential employers that you are a motivated and savvy person. Along with what you've learned from informational interviews, diligent Web browsing can reveal a wealth of information about a prospective employer and the field in which you want to work. (See the "Online Research" section on page 333 in Chapter 11 for details on searching tools and strategies.)

Most business firms, government agencies, and nonprofit agencies have websites that will help you understand their mission. If you're lucky, those websites will also contain the names of people you'll want to know about and possibly refer to during an interview.

Beyond an organization's own website, you can almost certainly find what others have published about the places where you might want to work. In your search engine, type the name of the organization and/or key people who work there. You are likely to be pleased and surprised at what you learn. Use your research to prepare a few questions that may be good to ask at the end of the interview (see "Ask Good Questions of Your Own" on p. A-16).

**Create or Update Your Résumé and Cover Letter** No matter how extensive and supportive your network, you will need a polished résumé to provide a snapshot of your professional strengths and achievements. For guidelines on the various types of résumés, type "create résumé" into your favorite search engine. Figure A-2 illustrates a common format for this document.

A flawed résumé can do more harm than good, so be sure to proofread carefully. It's smart to have a staff member at your school's career center critique your

## CAMILLA DORANTES

camilla.dorantes@connectmail.net          Phone: (223) 242-3554

### SUMMARY OF QUALIFICATIONS

- Academic background in political and economic dimensions of environmental policy
- Experience working in commercial and nonprofit organizations related to sustainability
- Strong work ethic and ability to work independently as necessary

### EDUCATION

**Current: University of Southern California**

Graduating (Bachelor of Science degree) in May 2014

Major in Global Studies, Pacific Rim Studies Emphasis

**Fall 2013: Tokyo International Studies University (Fulbright Junior Scholar)**

Japanese language program, ethnographic study of contemporary Japanese culture

### RELATED EXPERIENCE

**December 2013–February 2014: Undergraduate Research Fellow, University of Southern California**

In Asia, analyzed the effectiveness of committees designed to create international environmental policy. Interviewed officials from municipal government, business, and nonprofit sectors in Japan, China, and Singapore.

**January 2013–present: Correspondent, Environmental Policy blog (http://greenpolicy.org)**

Published dispatches on insights gained from travels in Asia for the award-winning website.

**September 2012–October 2012: Assistant Coordinator, International Environmental Treaty**

Assisted in coordinating media and fundraising events to educate public and recruited volunteers for this campaign to promote and protect environmental rights around the world.

**March 2012–May 2012: International Green Research Intern, Southern California World Trade Center**

Conducted individualized, in-depth sales and marketing research for the Trade Center's members.

**January 2012–March 2012: Intern, Greenpeace San Diego**

Conducted research to identify immediate environmental threats across California; helped develop funding proposals for major donors.

### LANGUAGES

Fluency in Spanish

Competence in Japanese

**FIGURE A-2 Sample Résumé**

résumé. The final document should be clear, honest, succinct, and free of typos and other errors, and ideally it should fit on one page.

You may need to upload your résumé to an employer's website when applying for a position, and you may benefit from posting your résumé to online job banks (sometimes called job boards) such as SimplyHired, Indeed, CareerBuilder, Dice, Monster, Computer Jobs, and US.jobs.

When submitting your résumé for a specific position, include a cover letter that creates a positive first impression. This letter gives you a chance to make the case for why you would be a good hire. As one expert put it, a cover letter is "an introduction, a sales pitch, and a proposal for further action all in one."[8]

Cover letters should be sent to a specific individual. If you don't know the appropriate person, call the company and ask for the individual's name. Be certain that you get the spelling and title correct. Like the sample in Figure A-3, a good cover letter should include the following information:

- Within the first lines, a statement of what position you are applying for, how you know of the position, and any connection you have to the company. If you are responding to an advertisement, mention the job title, number, and publication. If you are writing at the suggestion of a mutual acquaintance or as a result of your research, say so.

- An introduction (or reintroduction) of yourself if the reader may not know (or remember) who you are.

- A brief description of your most impressive accomplishments that are relevant to the job at hand. Remember: Don't just say you can help the organization. Offer some specific evidence that backs up your claim.

- A demonstration of your knowledge of the company.

- A statement regarding the next step you hope to take—usually a request for an interview. If you must, mention any pertinent information about limits on your availability, but keep these to an absolute minimum.

- A final, cordial expression of appreciation to the reader for considering you.

When posting your résumé and cover letter online or e-mailing them, ensure that they display correctly by taking the following steps:

- Create your documents in a word processing program, but save the final versions as a PDF file.

- If you are e-mailing a résumé and cover letter, include them as attachments. Don't paste the résumé in the body of your e-mail, because the formatting may not transfer properly.

- Be aware that once you post or e-mail your résumé, there is no guarantee of where it may be sent or copied. If you are posting to a publicly viewable website, you may want to protect your privacy by including your e-mail address but not your home address or phone number.

**Prepare for Likely Questions** Regardless of the organization and job, most interviewers have similar concerns, which they explore with similar questions. Here are some of the most common ones, with commentary on how you can prepare to answer them.

① **Tell me something about yourself.** This broad, opening question gives you a chance to describe what qualities you possess that can help the employer (e.g., enthusiastic, motivated, entrepreneurial). Be sure to keep your answer focused on the job for which you're applying—this isn't a time to talk about your hobbies, family, or pet peeves.

EDWARD R. ROMERO
2312 Haynes Rd.
Warren, OH 44481
(330) 164-1411        erm@ohcom.com

January 9, 2014

Ms. Alicia Hastings
Director of Human Resources
St. Bonaventure Health System
Youngstown, OH 44501

Re: **Occupational Therapist Job Application** (2014-01-1667)

Dear Ms. Hastings:

Having just completed six years as an Emergency Medical Technician and Occupational Therapist with the U.S. Army, I was very interested to read about the recently posted job opportunity as an Occupational Therapist with the St. Bonaventure Health System.

As the attached résumé describes in detail, my background includes extensive experience working with both inpatients in acute care settings and outpatients in rehabilitation units. Letters of recommendation and military commendations detail my success at working with patients on both the physical and emotional challenges. My experiences in adverse conditions have taught me the importance of composure under stress and working in teams.

I am looking for the opportunity to utilize my expertise on my return to the civilian world. Youngstown is my home town, and I would welcome the chance to contribute to the community and hospital that helped make me who I am.

I will be returning to the Youngstown area in mid-January and would welcome the chance to meet with you in person. In the meantime, I'm happy to provide any information you may require via phone or e-mail.

Thank you in advice for considering my application.

Sincerely,

*Edward Romero.*

**FIGURE A-3** Sample Cover Letter

2. **What makes you think you're qualified to work for this company?** This question may sound like an attack, but it really is another way of asking, "How can you help us?" It gives you another chance to show how your skills and interests fit with the company's goals. Prepare for a question like this by making a table with three columns: one listing your main qualifications (e.g., demonstrated sales success), one listing specific examples of each qualification, and one explaining how these qualifications would benefit your prospective employer.

3. **What accomplishments have given you the most satisfaction?** The accomplishments you choose needn't be directly related to former employment, but they should demonstrate qualities that would help you be successful in the job for which you're interviewing. Your accomplishments might demonstrate creativity, perseverance in the face of obstacles, self-control, or dependability.

4. **Why do you want to work for us?** As the research cited in Table A-1 shows, employers are impressed by candidates who have done their homework about the organization. This question offers you the chance to demonstrate your knowledge of the employer's organization and to show how your talents fit with its goals.

5. **What college subjects did you like most and least?** Whatever your answer, show how your preferences about schoolwork relate to the job for which you are applying. Sometimes the connection between college courses and a job is obvious. At other times, though, you can show how apparently unrelated subjects do illustrate your readiness for a job. For example, you might say, "I really enjoyed cultural anthropology courses because they showed me the importance of understanding different cultures. I think that those courses would help me a lot in relating to your overseas customers and suppliers."

6. **Where do you see yourself in 5 years?** This familiar question is really asking, "How ambitious are you?" "How well do your plans fit with this company's goals?" "How realistic are you?" If you have studied the industry and the company, your answer will reflect an understanding of the workplace realities and a sense of personal planning that should impress an employer.

7. **What major problems have you faced, and how have you dealt with them?** The specific problems aren't as important as the way you responded to them. What (admirable) qualities did you demonstrate as you grappled with the problems you have chosen to describe? Perseverance? Calmness? Creativity? You may even choose to describe a problem you didn't handle well, to show what you learned from the experience that can help you in the future.

8. **What are your greatest strengths and weaknesses?** The "strength" question offers another chance to sell yourself. As you choose an answer, identify qualities that apply to employment. "I'm a pretty good athlete" isn't a persuasive answer, unless you can show how your athletic skill is job related. For instance, you might talk about being a team player, having competitive drive, or having the ability to work hard and not quit in the face of adversity.

   Whatever answer you give to the "weakness" question, try to show how your awareness of your flaws makes you a desirable person to hire. There are four ways to respond to this question:

   - *Discuss a weakness that can also be viewed as a strength.*

   "When I'm involved in a big project, I tend to work too hard, and I can wear myself out."

## Table A-1    Communication Behaviors of Successful and Unsuccessful Interviewees

|  | UNSUCCESSFUL INTERVIEWEES | SUCCESSFUL INTERVIEWEES |
|---|---|---|
| **STATEMENTS ABOUT THE POSITION** | Had only vague ideas of what they wanted to do; changed "ideal job" up to six times during the interview. | Were specific and consistent about the position they wanted; were able to tell why they wanted the position. |
| **USE OF COMPANY NAME** | Rarely used the company name. | Referred to the company by name four times as often as unsuccessful interviewees. |
| **KNOWLEDGE ABOUT COMPANY AND POSITION** | Made it clear that they were using the interview to learn about the company and what it offered. | Made it clear that they had researched the company; referred to specific brochures, journals, or people who had given them information. |
| **LEVEL OF INTEREST, ENTHUSIASM** | Responded neutrally to interviewer's statements: "Okay," "I see." Indicated reservations about company or location. | Expressed approval of information provided by the interviewer nonverbally and verbally: "That's great!" Explicitly indicated desire to work for this particular company. |
| **PICKING UP ON INTERVIEWER'S CLUES** | Gave vague or negative answers even when a positive answer was clearly desired ("How are your math skills?"). | Answered positively and confidently—and backed up the claim with a specific example of "problem solving" or "toughness." |
| **USE OF INDUSTRY TERMS AND TECHNICAL JARGON** | Used almost no industry terms. | Used industry terms: "point of purchase display," "NCR charge," "two-column approach," "direct mail." |
| **USE OF SPECIFICS IN ANSWERS** | Gave short answers—10 words or fewer, sometimes only one word; did not elaborate. Gave general responses: "Fairly well." | Supported claims with specific personal experiences, comparisons, statistics, statements of teachers and employers. |
| **QUESTIONS ASKED BY INTERVIEWEE** | Asked a small number of general questions. | Asked specific questions based on knowledge of the industry and the company. Personalized questions: "What would my duties be?" |
| **CONTROL OF TIME AND TOPICS** | Interviewee talked 37 percent of the interview time, initiated 36 percent of the comments. | Interviewee talked 55 percent of the total time, initiated subjects 56 percent of the time. |

*Source:* Based on research reported by Einhorn, L. J. (1981, July). An inner view of the job interview: An investigation of successful communicative behaviors. *Communication Education, 30,* 217–228.

- *Discuss a weakness that is not related to the job at hand, and end your answer with a strength that is related to the job.*

  (for a job in sales) "I'm not very interested in accounting. I'd much rather work with people, selling a product I believe in."

  (for a job in accounting) "I'm not great at sales and marketing. I'm at my best working with numbers and talking to people about them."

- *Discuss a weakness the interviewer already knows about from your résumé, application, or the interview.*

  "I don't have a lot of experience in multimedia design at this early stage of my career. But my experience in other kinds of computer programming and my internship in graphic arts have convinced me that I can learn quickly."

- *Discuss a weakness you have been working to remedy.*

"I know being bilingual is important for this job. That's why I've enrolled in a Spanish course."

⑨ **What are your salary requirements?** Your answer should be based on knowledge of the prevailing compensation rates in the industry and geography in question. Shooting too high can knock you out of consideration, whereas shooting too low can cost you dearly. Give your answer by naming a salary range and backing up your numbers: "Based on the research I've done about compensation in this area, I'd expect to start somewhere between $35,000 and $38,500." As you give your answer, watch the interviewer. If he or she seems to respond favorably, you're in good shape. If you notice signs of disapproval, follow up: ". . . depending, of course, on benefits and how quickly I could expect to be promoted. However, salary isn't the most important criterion for me in choosing a job, and I won't necessarily accept the highest offer I get. I'm interested in going somewhere where I can get good experience and use my talents to make a real contribution." It's important to know your "bottom line" for compensation in advance so you don't end up accepting an offer at a salary you can't afford to take.

> cultural idiom
**bottom line:**
minimum requirements

**Dress for Success**   First impressions can make or break an interview. Research shows that many interviewers form their opinions about applicants within the first 4 minutes of conversation.[9] Physical attractiveness is a major influence on how applicants are rated, so it makes sense to do everything possible to look your best. The basic rules apply, no matter what the job or company: Be well groomed and neatly dressed, and don't overdo it with too much makeup or flashy clothes.

The proper style of clothing can vary from one type of job or organization to another. A good rule of thumb is to come dressed as you would for the first day of work. When in doubt, it's best to dress formally and conservatively. It's unlikely that an employer will think less of you for being overdressed, but looking too casual can be taken as a sign that you don't take the job or the interview seriously.

> cultural idiom
**rule of thumb:**
practical plan of action

**Take Copies of Your Résumé and Samples of Past Work**   Arrive at the interview with materials that will help the employer learn more about why you are ready, willing, and able to do the job. Take extra copies of your résumé. If appropriate, take copies of your past work: reports you've helped prepare, performance reviews by former employers, drawings or designs you have created for work or school, letters of commendation, and so on. Besides demonstrating your qualifications, items like these demonstrate that you know how to sell yourself. Take along the names, addresses, and phone numbers of any references you haven't listed in your résumé. And be prepared to take notes: you'll need something to write on and a pen or pencil.

**Know When and Where to Go**   Don't risk sabotaging the interview before it begins by showing up late. Be sure you're clear about the time and location of the meeting. Research parking or public transportation to be sure you aren't held up by delays. There's virtually no good excuse for showing up late. Even if the interviewer is forgiving, a bad start is likely to shake your confidence and impair your performance.

**Reframe Your Anxiety as Enthusiasm**   Feeling anxious about an employment interview is understandable. After all, the stakes are high—especially if you really want the job.

Managing your feelings in interviews calls for the same approach described in the "Managing Communication Apprehension" section of Chapter 11 (see pages 337–340). Realize that a certain amount of anxiety is understandable. If you can reframe those feelings as *excitement* about the prospect of holding a great job, the feelings can even work to your advantage.

If feelings of anxiety get out of hand, consider whether you are indulging yourself with any of the fallacies of catastrophic failure or perfection. Following the guidelines on pages 337–338 can help shrink your concerns and give you ways of managing them.

## During and After the Interview

Once the time comes for your interview, keep the following tips in mind to make it a success.

**Follow the Interviewer's Lead**    Let the interviewer set the tone of the session. Along with topics and verbal style, pay attention to the kinds of nonverbal cues described in Chapter 6: the interviewer's posture, gestures, vocal qualities, and so on. If he or she is informal, you can loosen up and be yourself, but if he or she is formal and proper, you should act the same way. A great deal depends on the personal chemistry between interviewer and applicant, so try to match the interviewer's style without becoming phony. If the tone of the interview doesn't fit well with you, this may be a signal that you won't feel comfortable with this company. It may be smart to see whether the interviewer's approach represents the whole company, by either asking for a short tour or speaking with other employees on your own. This desire to learn about the company shows that you are a thinking person who takes the job seriously, so your curiosity isn't likely to offend the interviewer.

> cultural idiom
> **the personal chemistry:**
> how two people get along with or react to each other

**Keep Your Answers Succinct and Specific**    It's easy to rattle on in an interview, either out of enthusiasm, a desire to show off your knowledge, or nervousness, but in most cases long answers are not a good idea. The interviewer probably has lots of ground to cover, and long-winded answers won't help this task. A good rule of thumb is to keep your responses under 2 minutes. While keeping your comments succinct, be sure to provide specific examples to support your statements.

> cultural idiom
> **to rattle on:**
> to utter responses that are excessively wordy
>
> **ground to cover:**
> topics to discuss
>
> **long-winded:**
> speaking for a long time
>
> **go overboard:**
> do so much as to be excessive

**Keep on the Subject**    It is sometimes tempting to go overboard with your answers, sidetracking the discussion into areas that won't help the interviewer. Try to keep your focus on the topic at hand. If you worry that your responses have gone off topic, it may be a good idea to ask the interviewer whether your responses are helpful and then adjust them accordingly.

**Describe Relevant Challenges, Actions, and Results**    Most sophisticated employers realize that past performance can be the best predictor of future behavior. For that reason, there is an increasing trend toward **behavioral interviews**—sessions that explore specifics of the applicant's past performance as it relates to the job at hand. Typical behavioral questions include the following:

Describe a time you needed to work as part of a team.

Tell me about a time when you had to think on your feet to handle a challenging situation.

Describe a time when you were faced with an ethical dilemma, and discuss how you handled it.

When faced with behavioral questions, answer in a way that shows the prospective employer how your past performance demonstrates your ability to handle the job you are now seeking. One format for constructing such answers has three parts:

① Offer specific examples of a situation, and how you handled it.

② Show the result of your behavior.

③ Draw a connection between the incident you've described and the job you are seeking.

Here are some examples of good answers to behavioral questions:

**Q:** Give an example of a time when you were faced with an overwhelming amount of work.

**A:** Last year I was chairperson of the committee that organized a triathlon to raise money for a friend who had enormous medical bills after being in a car accident. When I took on the job, I had no idea how big it was: logistics, publicity, fund-raising, legal—it was huge. And some of the people who originally offered to help backed out halfway through the planning. At first I tried to do everything myself, but after a while I realized that this was not going to work. So I wound up recruiting more people, and my job turned out to be supporting and encouraging them rather than doing it all. If I'm lucky enough to get this job, that's the approach I'd take as a manager.

**Q:** Tell me about a time when you had to work with someone you didn't like, or someone who didn't like you.

**A:** A very talented teammate in my marketing class term project kept making somewhat sexist jokes, even after I told him they made me uncomfortable. Changing teams wasn't possible, and I figured complaining to the professor would jeopardize our success on the project. So I did my best to act professionally, even in the face of those jokes. We got the job done and received an outstanding evaluation, so I guess my discomfort was worth it. What I learned from this experience is that we don't always get to choose the people we work with, and that sometimes you have to put the job ahead of personal feelings.

**Ask Good Questions of Your Own**   Besides answering the employer's questions, the selection interview is also a chance for you to learn whether the job and organization are right for you. In this sense, the potential boss and the prospective employee are interviewing each other.

Near the end of the interview, you'll probably be asked if you have any questions. You might feel as if you already know all the important facts about the job, but asking questions based on your knowledge of the industry, the company, and the position can produce some useful information, as well as show the interviewer that you are realistically assessing the fit between yourself and the organization. The following list offers examples of good questions to ask:

- Why is this position open now? How often has it been filled in the past 5 years? What have been the primary reasons people have left it in the past?
- What is the biggest problem facing your staff now? How have past and current employees dealt with this problem?
- What are the primary results you would like to see me produce?
- How would you describe the management style I could expect from my supervisors?
- Where could a person go who is successful in this position? Within what time frame?

Important note: You should not ask about salary or benefits during a selection interview unless you have been offered the position.

**Follow Up with a Thank-You Note Shortly After the Interview**   Follow up your interview with a prompt, sincere, and personalized note of thanks to the interviewer. Do not underestimate the importance of this step: A thoughtful and well-written thank-you note can set you apart from other candidates, and not writing a thank-you note within a day of your interview can eliminate you from the running.

A good thank-you should do the following:

- Express your appreciation for the chance to get acquainted with the company.
- Reinforce why you see a good fit between you and the job, highlighting your demonstrated skills.
- Let the interviewer know that the conversation left you excited about the chance of becoming associated with it.

Most employment advisors agree that this is one situation in which a handwritten message can be appropriate, though many interviewers expect a thank-you within 24 hours. Whether your thank-you message is handwritten or e-mailed, reread it carefully several times, and have a skilled proofreader review it, as a mistake here can damage your prospects. One job seeker ruined her chances of employment by mentioning the "report" (instead of "rapport") that she felt with the interviewer.

The following checklist summarizes the keys to successful interviewing discussed above.

---

**CHECKLIST > Successful Interviewing**

**BEFORE THE INTERVIEW**

- ☐ Do your research.
- ☐ Create or update your résumé.
- ☐ Prepare for likely questions.
- ☐ Dress for success.
- ☐ Take copies of your résumé and samples of past work.
- ☐ Know when and where to go.
- ☐ Reframe your anxiety as enthusiasm.

**DURING AND AFTER THE INTERVIEW**

- ☐ Follow the interviewer's lead.
- ☐ Keep your answers succinct and specific.
- ☐ Keep on the subject.
- ☐ Describe relevant challenges, actions, and results.
- ☐ Ask good questions of your own.
- ☐ Follow up with a thank-you note shortly after the interview.

---

## Interviewing and the Law

Most laws governing what topics can and can't be covered in job interviews boil down to two simple principles: First, questions may not be aimed at discriminating on the basis of race, color, religion, gender, sexual orientation, disabilities, national origin, or age. Second, questions must be related to what the U.S. government's Equal Employment Opportunity Commission (EEOC) calls *bona fide occupational qualifications*. In other words, prospective employers may only ask about topics that are related to the job at hand. Another basic principle is that employers should ask the same job-related questions of all candidates. For example, if an interviewer asks whether one candidate has international experience, he or she should ask all others the same question.

These principles help distinguish between legal and illegal questions:

| ILLEGAL | LEGAL |
| --- | --- |
| Were you born in Latin America? | Fluency in Spanish is an important part of this job. Are you fluent in that language? |
| If you don't mind my asking, how did you get that limp? | Being on your feet for several hours per day is part of this job. Do you have any physical conditions that would make it hard to do that? |
| Do you have any children at home? | Are you able to work occasional nights and weekends? |
| Please tell me about any political clubs or organizations to which you belong. | Tell me about any job-related organizations you belong to that you think will enhance your ability to do this job. |

Despite the law, there is a good chance that interviewers will ask illegal questions. This will probably have more to do with being uninformed than with being malicious. Still, when faced with a question that's not legal, you will need to know how to respond tactfully. There are several options:

① *Answer without objecting.* Answer the question, even though you know it is probably unlawful: "No, I'm not married. But I'm engaged." Recognize, though, that this could open the door for other illegal questions—and perhaps even discrimination in hiring decisions.

② *Seek explanation.* Ask the interviewer firmly and respectfully to explain why this question is related to the job: "I'm having a hard time seeing how my marital status relates to my ability to do this job. Can you explain?"

③ *Redirect.* Shift the focus of the interview away from a question that isn't job related and toward the requirements of the position itself: "What you've said so far suggests that age is not as important for this position as knowledge of accounting. Can you tell me more about the kinds of accounting that are part of this job?"

④ *Refuse.* Explain politely but firmly that you will not provide the information requested: "I'd rather not talk about my religion. That's a very private and personal matter for me."

⑤ *Withdraw.* End the interview immediately and leave, stating your reasons firmly but professionally: "I'm very uncomfortable with these questions about my personal life, and I don't see a good fit between me and this organization. Thank you for your time."

There's no absolutely correct way to handle illegal questions. The option you choose will depend on several factors: the likely intent of the interviewer, the nature of the questions, and, of course, your desire for the job—and finally, your "gut level" of comfort with the whole situation.

## Communicating for Career Advancement

Careful, strategic communication (or its absence), whether in person or through mediated channels, can enhance (or damage) your career, from before you begin looking for a job until the day you retire. In the remaining pages, you'll read tips on how to manage the way others regard you, and how to handle yourself in ways that distinguish you as the kind of capable person who is an asset to any organization.

## Managing Your Online Identity

The "@Work" box in Chapter 2 (page 67) describes the importance of managing your identity on the job. That sort of identity management extends into cyberspace and deserves special consideration.

You almost certainly have an online identity. If someone plugged your name into a search engine like Google, at least a few hits would probably surface. The information that shows up about you in cyberspace is more than a curiosity or ego booster: It can either enhance or damage your career prospects.

By now you probably have been warned about the risks of posting potentially embarrassing information about yourself online, especially if you're looking for a job. According to the *New York Times*, 70 percent of U.S. recruiters report having rejected job candidates because of personal information online.[10]

Notwithstanding these cautionary tales, it's worth detailing the dimensions of your online identity that can either enhance or damage your chances of getting a job or getting promoted. According to the creators of ClaimID, a service designed to help users control their online identities, Web-based information that can shape your career success falls into one of four categories.[11] Each calls for different management strategies.

**Information by You, About Yourself**    This category includes social networking profiles, professional profiles, tweets, Facebook comments and photos, and personal websites you have created and intentionally posted where anybody can view them. (See the box on page A-20 for more information about constructing your own website.) It may also include a detailed résumé, or information you've entered into a job-search site such as Monster or LinkedIn.

Self-authored information gives you a chance to promote yourself in ways that go beyond the one- or two-page résumé you bring to a job interview. If you've contributed to a worthy project, participated in volunteer work, or won any awards, create a place online that features these accomplishments and interests.

When posting information about yourself online, be sure to consider how it will look to all viewers. You may be proud of your membership in the National Rifle Association or Planned Parenthood, but a prospective employer might not find your affiliations so admirable. Political philosophy, religious affiliations, and even your musical preferences may all be better kept private, or at least behind a secure firewall where only the people you know and trust will see them. You may not realize just how much of what you post on social media, for example, is viewable to anyone who does a Web search for your name: Google yourself and see what comes up.

**Information by Others, About You**    This category includes everything viewable online that anyone has ever said about you. Some websites are organized specifically to capture comments about individuals. Students can rate their professors (ratemyprofessors.com), friends can rate one another (ratemyeverything.net), and you can rate the attractiveness of strangers (hotornot.com). Commentary on these sites can be insensitive, unfair, and even blatantly false, but it can damage your reputation nonetheless. Even if your name isn't listed on a dedicated website, searchers may find random posts about you by typing your name into a simple search. One waitress was shocked to find that a customer's review of the restaurant where she worked mentioned her by name as having a bad attitude.

If you discover incorrect, unfair, and potentially damaging information about yourself online, and if you are unable to remove it yourself, you might consider seeking professional help to set the record straight. For example, reputationdefender .com will monitor your online identity and contact offending websites, asking them to remove unflattering information. Other services that help people take

## Constructing a Personal Website

Designing your own site can give you the personal, creative touches that a predesigned site can't offer. If getting a job is your goal, your personal website should be focused on maintaining a professional image. You can include hobbies and interests unrelated to your skills and industry, but they should not be the focus of your site. The best way to make sure people can find your site is to choose a domain name that captures your complete real name (e.g., yourname.com). If your name is not available, make sure at least your complete last name is included in your domain name (e.g., yournamedesign.com). The next step is to use one of the many free services to construct your website. Popular services include Weebly, Google Sites, and Wix.

An important part of your personal website is your photo. Most employers are not allowed to request a photo with your résumé submission; however, appearance does matter to them. Help employers find out that you look like an excellent future employee by posting your photo on the homepage of your site. Make sure you don't confuse a nice appearance with being attractive. Overt attempts at appearing attractive can come across as too sexual or tacky. Physical attractiveness is not as important as looking put-together. Choose an outfit that shows you can work with clients outside the workplace and will represent the company well. Save personal photos for your password-protected social networking sites, and include only one or two professional photos on your website that is open to the public.

Once you create your website, you may want to monitor its success. Google Trends (google.com/trends) is a free program that can monitor your personal and business websites. Google Trends can show you two important pieces of information: how often a set of keywords, either your name or your company's name, appears on the Web and also how frequently people search for it. Using a tool called "Hot Searches," you can see how often people search for your company over a span of time.

---

back control of their online identity include Naymz.com, Reputation.com, and ClaimID. Of course, a far less extensive and burdensome approach is to minimize the chances of reputation damage by being on your best public behavior.

Information about you can also come from belonging to groups that post membership information online for unrestricted viewing. You may not have intended for inquiring minds to know that you belong to Yahoo's Mysticism and Witchcraft Interest Group or Meetup.com's Obsessive Compulsive Support Group, but unless you're careful, that information can become public. One employee learned the hard way that group membership isn't necessarily private when she sent an e-mail to her boss from her Yahoo account. The boss was surprised to find, underneath his reply confirmation, the message, "Shelly has just posted a comment on the Pregnant Career Women's Message Board."

**Information by You, Not About You**    This category includes anything that you have created online that isn't self-referential. It can include text-based material, such as school projects and your reviews of music or films. It can also include nontextual information, such as your art or music portfolio. This sort of information can showcase your talents in ways that are likely to impress current or potential employers or clients.

You can steer potential readers to this sort of material by compiling it all in a single place online. You don't have to be a Web designer to pull this off: Resources like Blogger are free and easy to use.

Once your online showcase is set up, you can reference it in your résumé and other job-seeking materials. Beyond this, you can steer Web surfers to your blog by including your full name in the blog's URL and title. This approach ensures that searchers will find it when they type your name into their search engine.

Along with potentially career-enhancing material, there's a risk that you may have posted material that will reflect poorly on you. Almost any griping, complaining, gossiping, or bad-mouthing can come back to haunt you, even if it was justified.

**Information Not by You, Not About You**    This category involves material that turns up in a search when others' names are identical or similar to yours. Nobody is likely to confuse you with the John or Jane Doe who is currently doing research in Antarctica, but sometimes mistaken identity can be less obvious. One job seeker Googled herself out of curiosity, only to find that the first hit was the Facebook page of another person with the same name. She clicked the link and was taken to a personal profile loaded with immature comments.

If a search of your name generates potentially damaging hits of people who are unrelated to you, consider distinguishing yourself by including your middle name or middle initial on your résumé and all other information you post where online seekers might find it.

## Distinguishing Yourself on the Job

Once you're on the job, distinguishing yourself from the pack can be a challenge. It can be hard to figure out which behaviors cast you in a positive light, and which might give the impression you are a self-promoting "suck-up." Here are a few guidelines that will serve you well.

**Communicate in a Principled Manner**    Communicating with integrity isn't always easy. Management can favor business practices that put the company before the customers that it serves and can even reward employees who support ethical transgressions.[12] The culture in some organizations favors bad-mouthing, competing, and "working the system." One employee recalls how her colleagues joked about ways to be the least productive while getting paid the most.

Principled communication means following your own set of ethics rather than relying on the approval of others. You don't need to explicitly state that you don't like what's being said, or chastise coworkers for bad behavior. You can simply lead by example. A good policy is to avoid any type of communication that you will not feel good about later, and try not to say anything about anyone that you would not say in his or her presence.

World-renowned leadership consultant Stephen Covey emphasizes that principled communication is not as difficult as it seems:

> Correct principles are like compasses: They are always pointing the way. And if we know how to read them, we won't get lost, confused, or fooled by conflicting voices and values. Principles such as fairness, equity, justice, integrity, honesty, and trust are not invented by us: They are the laws of the universe that pertain to human relationships and organizations. They are part of the human condition, consciousness, and conscience.[13]

Taking the high road may seem to have short-term costs, but the long-term benefits justify this approach. Covey explains the long-term benefits of principled communication this way:

> People instinctively trust those whose personalities are founded upon correct principles. We have evidence of this in our long-term relationships. We learn that technique is relatively unimportant compared to trust, which is the result of our trustworthiness over time. When trust is high, we communicate easily, effortlessly, instantaneously. We can make mistakes, and others will still capture our meaning. But when trust is low, communication is exhausting, time-consuming, ineffective, and inordinately difficult.[14]

**Use Gossip Wisely**    Malicious gossip is another behavior that may provide short-term satisfaction but can damage your career. Besides reflecting character defects,[15] gossiping can mark you as untrustworthy.

In addition to making a bad impression, gossip can be hurtful. "Gossip is high stakes," says Sam Chapman, the CEO of Empower, the public relations agency that banned gossip. "It's emotionally lethal. It's leading to suicides." He urges executives to make it clear that they don't engage in gossip and says that their employees will follow the example.

Avoiding malicious talk doesn't mean all gossip is bad. In fact, researchers have found that certain types of workplace gossip can help people unite during struggles, form positive alliances, and engage in healthy competition. For example, when workers gossip about someone who got fired, they learn what happens to people who break the rules, and it may motivate employees to work harder or create greater loyalties to their company.[16]

One key to identifying benign or even helpful gossip lies in its intention. If your juicy information is helpful to others, it may be worth sharing. Are personnel changes coming? Have you heard something important about a new policy? But be careful not to break a promise to keep the information confidential.

Along with usefulness, a second criterion for "good" gossip is its tone. One executive proposed this test: Before you start talking, stop and ask yourself, "Is it kind?"[17] Stories and information spread through word of mouth don't always have to be negative or malicious. If someone at work received an award or completed a major project, go ahead and spread the word. People who speak kindly of others get noticed.

In sum, it's unrealistic to avoid talking about other people; just make sure, when you do, that you aren't casting a shadow on your own character by denigrating the target of your story.

**Exceed Others' Expectations**   Bare-minimum performance may not get you fired, but neither will it get you noticed. One method for standing out is to do more than what's required by your job description.[18]

Positively exceeding expectations may mean

- Finishing a job ahead of schedule
- Providing more information than was requested
- Doing a better job than others anticipated

The ways in which you can go above and beyond depend a lot on the type of organization in which you work. If you're not sure what you could be doing, consider volunteering to serve on a committee, offering to help orient a new employee, showing up to work on a weekend or after hours (if it's allowed), offering to deliver a presentation, or tackling a job that keeps getting delayed due to other work demands. The few minutes or hours jobs like this take will be well worth the reputation they earn you.

**Greet People**   Most career-minded people have been advised to learn names as a method of standing out. Although learning names is an important networking tool, a simple hello can also have a powerful impact.[19] Greet people even if you don't know their names.

If you can't remember someone's name, you can always say, "This is really embarrassing because I know who you are, but I've forgotten your name." Everyone forgets names, but few people risk their own embarrassment by asking. Making it a priority to reach out to others will in turn help them remember you.

**Sweat the Small Stuff**   You may have heard the phrase *don't sweat the small stuff*. In fact, making a good impression requires paying attention to every detail.

Situations in which details seem unimportant are exactly the situations you can use to stand out from the average employee. A common faux pas committed by new employees is thinking that mediated messages don't require the same etiquette as face-to-face interactions. Even if you are just shooting your boss a quick reply or confirmation, make sure you have a salutation, body, and closing, and always use proper grammar, spelling, and punctuation. Using "I" instead of "i" and "you" instead of "u" is imperative to any business correspondence, no matter how casual. In a world of text messaging, we are so accustomed to shortcutting our communication that we rarely realize the bad impression it makes at work. Take a moment to compose e-mails that sound articulate, professional, and respectful.

Besides making sure the work you do is impeccable, pay attention to the way you present yourself in career-related contexts. Casual use of slang and profanity risks offending others. It's smart to heed advice from the *Wall Street Journal*: "Tiny missteps may derail your career. You appear unpolished when you talk like an adolescent, or curse at colleagues."[20]

How you look can be just as important as what you say. No one wants to hire or promote someone they fear won't represent the company well. One executive recruiter warns, "Outdated clothes, frayed cuffs, messy hair, scuffed shoes or excess cleavage also signal poor judgment."[21]

Behaving professionally can distinguish you from the pack. A now-successful businesswoman recalls that her big break came when the boss chose her to accompany him to an important trade show. When she asked why he chose her instead of others with more experience, he replied that she was the only employee who he knew wouldn't embarrass the company.

**Ask Questions**   Don't fake understanding. When you aren't sure about an idea, assignment, or procedure, ask for clarification. To justify your request for clarification, consider prefacing questions with something like "I really want to understand what you're saying . . . " or "I want to make sure I get this right."

## Summary

Beyond professional qualifications, strategic planning and effective communication can enhance your career. Developing relationships, knowing what to do in an interview, and distinguishing yourself at work can provide an edge in a competitive, demanding workplace.

Developing relationships with people who can help you is integral to success. You can develop and maintain personal networks by viewing everyone as a networking prospect, seeking referrals, and showing appreciation whenever you receive help. Making a name for yourself online through professional websites is also important. Conducting informational interviews with those who have experience, expertise, and contacts can enhance your career prospects.

Selection interviews can be a critically important part of career advancement. Before an interview, conduct background research, create an impressive résumé, and prepare for questions that the interviewer is likely to ask. During the interview make sure to let the interviewer take the lead. Keep your answers succinct and on topic, and be prepared for the interviewer to ask you to demonstrate a skill or respond to a specific situation. Don't forget to plan questions to ask the interviewer at the end.

Managing your professional identity can create the desired impression. Online information about you speaks volumes to others. It is important to monitor and control information about yourself that others create, as well as what you create and post yourself.

Getting ahead isn't always about seeking a new place of employment. You can receive a promotion or reassignment by distinguishing yourself at your current workplace. Get noticed by communicating in a principled manner. Exceed the expectations of your superiors, get to know people at work, and pay attention to details. Asking questions instead of assuming can help you perform in a way that shows initiative. In sum, being qualified for a job or promotion isn't enough: Help others help you by standing out in a way that makes you a desirable employee in whom they want to invest.

## Key Terms

**behavioral interview** A session that explores the specifics of the applicant's past performance as it relates to the job at hand. *p. A-15*

**closed question** An interview question that can be answered in a few words. *p. A-6*

**direct question** An interview question that makes a straightforward request for information. *p. A-6*

**factual question** An interview question that investigates matters of fact. See also *Opinion question. p. A-6*

**hypothetical question** A question that seeks a response by proposing a "what-if" situation. *p. A-7*

**indirect question** An interview question that does not directly request the information being sought. See also *Direct question. p. A-7*

**informational interview** An interview intended to collect facts and opinions from the respondent. *p. A-4*

**leading question** A question in which the interviewer—either directly or indirectly—signals the desired answer. *p. A-7*

**networking** The strategic process of deliberately meeting people and maintaining contacts that results in information, advice, and leads that enhance one's career. *p. A-2*

**neutral question** A question that gives the interviewee a chance to respond without any influence from the interviewer. *p. A-7*

**open question** An interview question that requires the interviewee to respond in detail. See also *Closed question. p. A-6*

**opinion question** An interview question seeking the interviewee's opinion. See also *Factual question. p. A-6*

**probe** An interjection, silence, or brief remark designed to open up or direct an interviewee. *p. A-7*

**selection interview** An interview in which a candidate is evaluated for a new position—either initial employment, promotion, or reassignment. *p. A-8*

## For Further Exploration

**For more resources about communicating for career success, see the *Understanding Human Communication* website at www.oup.com/us/adler.** There you will find a variety of resources: "Media Room" clips from popular films and television shows to further illustrate important concepts, a list of books and articles, links to descriptions of feature films and television shows at the *Now Playing* website, study aids, and a self-test to check your understanding of the material in this chapter.

# Notes

## CHAPTER 1

1. See, for example, 100 most powerful people in healthcare. (2002, August 26). *Modern Healthcare, 32*, 7, and 100 most powerful people in healthcare. (2008, August 25), *Modern Healthcare, 38*, 56.
2. Studer, Q. (nd). *Speakers on healthcare*. Retrieved September 21, 2012, from http://www.speakersonhealthcare.com/speakers/ Quint_Studer.php.
3. Verderber, R., Elder, A., & Weiler, E. *A study of communication time usage among college students*. Unpublished study, University of Cincinnati, 1976.
4. Outzen, R. (2005 July 7). The story of a fire starter. *Independent News*. Retrieved September 11, 2012, from http://www.inweekly .net/article.asp?artID=1624.
5. Gergen, K. (1991). *The saturated self: Dilemmas of identity in contemporary life*. New York: Basic Books, p. 158.
6. Mottet, T. P., & Richmond V. P. (2001). Student nonverbal communication and its influence on teachers and teaching: A review of literature. In J. L. Chesebro & J. C. McCroskey (Eds.), *Communication for teachers* (pp. 47–61). Needham Heights, MA: Allyn & Bacon.
7. Weeks, J. (2001, February 25). Conversations with Jeff Weeks: Quint Studer. *WSRE television*
8. Shannon, C. E., & Weaver, W. (1949). *The mathematical theory of communication*. Urbana: University of Illinois Press.
9. See, for example, Dunne, M. & Ng, S. H. (1994). Simultaneous speech in small group conversation: All-together-now and one-at-a-time? *Journal of Language and Social Psychology, 13*, 45–71.
10. The issue of intentionality has been a matter of debate by communication theorists. For a sample of the arguments on both sides, see Greene, J. O. (Ed.). (1997). *Message production: Advances in communication theory*. New York: Erlbaum; Motley, M. T. (1990). On whether one can(not) communicate: An examination via traditional communication postulates. *Western Journal of Speech Communication, 54*, 1–20; Bavelas, J. B. (1990). Behaving and communicating: A reply to Motley. *Western Journal of Speech Communication, 54*, 593–602; and Stewart, J. (1991). A postmodern look at traditional communication postulates. *Western Journal of Speech Communication, 55*, 354–379.
11. For an in-depth look at this topic, see Cunningham, S. B. (2012). Intrapersonal communication: A review and critique. In S. Deetz (Ed.), *Communication yearbook* 15 (pp. 597–620). Newbury Park, CA: Sage.
12. Wheeler, L., & Nelek, J. (1977). Sex differences in social participation. *Journal of Personality and Social Psychology, 35*, 742–754.
13. John, J. (1953). The distribution of free-forming small group size. *American Sociological Review, 18*, 569–570.
14. Jenks, I. (2009). Living on the future edge. *Presentation handout, 21st Century Fluency Project*. Kelowna, BC, Canada: The Info Savvy Group.
15. United Nations Cyberschoolbus. (nd). Retrieved February 2, 2010, from http://www.un.org/Pubs/CyberSchoolBus/aboutus .html.
16. Aristotle. (1991). *On rhetoric: A theory of civic discourse* (George A. Kennedy, Trans.). New York: Oxford University Press.
17. See, for example, Peters, J. D., Durham, J., & Simonson, P. (1997). *Mass communication and American social thought: Key texts: 1919– 1968*. Lanham, MD: Rowman and Littlefield.
18. Heath, R. L., & Bryant, J. (2000). *Human communication theory and research*. Hillsdale, NJ: Lawrence Erlbaum.
19. Ibid.
20. O'Sullivan, P. B. (2009, May 25). *Masspersonal communication: Rethinking the mass-interpersonal divide*. Paper presented at the annual meeting of the International Communication Association, New York. Retrieved from http://www.allacademic.com/meta/ p14277_index.html.
21. Lenhart, A., Madden, M., & Smith, A. (2007, December). Teens and social media. *Pew Internet & American Life Project*. Retrieved January 16, 2010, from http://www.pewinternet.org/Reports/2007/Teens -and-Social-Media/I.Summary-of-Findings.aspx?r=1.
22. Johnson, S. (2009, June 5). How Twitter will change the way we live. *Time*. Retrieved from http://www.time.com/time/magazine/ article/0,9171,1902818,00.html.
23. Surinder, K. S., & Cooper, R. B. (2003). Exploring the core concepts of media richness theory: The impact of cue multiplicity and feedback immediacy on decision quality. *Journal of Management Information Systems, 20*, 263–299.
24. Severin, W. J., & Tankard, J. W. (1997). *Communication theories: Origins, methods, and uses in the mass media* (4th ed.). New York: Longman, pp. 197–214.
25. Ruggiero, T. E. (2000). Uses and gratifications theory in the 21st century. *Mass Communication & Society, 3*, 3–37. For a somewhat different categorization of uses and gratifications, see Joinson, A. N. (2008, April 5–10). "Looking at," "looking up" or "keeping up with" people? Motives and uses of Facebook. In *Proceedings of the 26th annual SIGCHI Conference on Human Factors in Computing Systems* (Florence, Italy) (pp. 1027–1036). New York: ACM.
26. Lengel, R. H., & Daft, R. L. (1988). The selection of communication media as an executive skill. *Academy of Management Executive, 2*, 225–232.

27. Miss Seattle insists she doesn't hate Seattle after Twitter rant. (2012, March 7). *ABC News*. Retrieved August 28, 2012, from http://abcnews.go.com/blogs/headlines/2012/03/miss-seattle-insists-she-doesnt-hate-seattle-after-twitter-rant.

28. Lenhart, A.. (2009, December). Teens and sexting. *Pew Internet & American Life Project* 4. Retrieved January 10, 2009, from http://www.pewinternet.org/Reports/2009/Teens-and-Sexting.aspx.

29. MTV-AP Digital Abuse Study. (2009). Executive summary. Retrieved from http://www.athinline.org/MTV-AP_Digital_Abuse_Study_Executive_Summary.pdf.

30. "Sexting" and suicide. (2009, December 16). *Psychology Today Online*. Retrieved from http://www.psychologytoday.com/blog/gender-and-schooling/200912/sexting-and-suicide.

31. Bauerlein, M.. (2009, September 4). Why Gen-Y Johnny can't read nonverbal cues. *Wall Street Journal*. Retrieved from http://online.wsj.com/article/SB10001424052970203863204574348493483201758.html.

32. Watts, S. A. (2007). Evaluative feedback: Perspectives on media effects. *Journal of Computer-Mediated Communication, 12*. Retrieved January 29, 2010, from http://jcmc.indiana.edu/vol12/issue2/watts.html. See also Turnage, A. K. (2007). E-mail behaviors and organizational conflict. *Journal of Computer-Mediated Communication, 13*(1), article 3. Retrieved January 16, 2009, from http://jcmc.indiana.edu/vol13/issue1/turnage.html.

33. LeBlanc, J. C. (2012, October 20). *Cyberbullying and suicide: A retrospective analysis of 21 cases*. Presented at the American Academy of Pediatrics National Conference, New Orleans. Retrieved December 6, 2012, from https://aap.confex.com/aap/2012/webprogram/Paper18782.html.

34. National Crime Prevention Council. (2007). Executive research summary "teens and cyberbullying." Retrieved January 19, 2010, from http://www.ncpc.org.

35. Caplan, S. E. (2005). A social skill account of problematic Internet use. *Journal of Communication, 55*, 721–736; Schiffrin, H., Edelman, A., Falkenstein, M., & Stewart C. (2010). Associations among computer-mediated communication, relationships, and well-being. *Cyberpsychology, Behavior, and Social Networking, 13*, 1–14; Morrison, C. M., & Gore, H. (2010). The relationship between excessive Internet use and depression: A questionnaire-based study of 1,319 young people and adults. *Psychopathology, 43*, 121–126.

36. Ibid., Caplan (2005).

37. Ko, C., Yen, J., Chen, C., Chen, S., & Yen, C. (2005). Proposed diagnostic criteria of Internet addiction for adolescents. *The Journal of Nervous and Mental Disease, 11*, 728–733.

38. Young, K. (1998). *Caught in the net: How to recognize the signs of Internet addiction and a winning strategy for recovery*. Malden, MA: Wiley.

39. See, for example, Teens Creating Content. (2007). *Pew Internet & American Life Project*. Retrieved February 2, 2010, from http://www.pewinternet.org/Reports/2007/Teens-and-Social-Media/3-Teens-creating-content/18-Videos-are-not-restricted-as-often-as-photos.aspx?r=1.

40. Strayer, D. L., Drews, F. A., Crouch, D. J., & Johnston, W. A. (2005). Why do cell phone conversations interfere with driving? In W. R. Walker & D. Herrmann (Eds.), *Cognitive technology: Transforming thought and society* (pp. 51–68). Jefferson, NC: McFarland.

41. U.S. Department of Transportation, National Highway Safety Administration. (2010, September). Traffic safety facts. Retrieved December 6, 2012, from http://www.distraction.gov/research/PDF-Files/Distracted-Driving-2009.pdf.

42. Strayer, D. L., & Drew, F. A. (2004, Winter). Profiles in driver distraction: Effects of cell phone conversations on younger and older drivers. *Human Factors, 46*, 640–649.

43. Nationwide Mutual Insurance Company. (2007). 2007 report. Retrieved January 10, 2010, from http://www.nationwide.com/newsroom/nationwide-fights-dwd.jsp.

44. Study conducted by Virginia Tech Transportation Institute. (2009). *Virginia Tech News*. Retrieved January 10, 2009, from http://www.vtnews.vt.edu/story.php?relyear=2009&itemno=571.

45. For a summary of the link between social support and health, see Duck, S. (1992). Staying healthy . . . with a little help from our friends? In *Human Relationships* (2nd ed.). Newbury Park, CA: Sage.

46. Cohen, S., Doyle, W. J., Skoner, D. P., Rabin, B. S., & Gwaltney, J. M. (1997). Social ties and susceptibility to the common cold. *Journal of the American Medical Association, 277*, 1940–1944.

47. Three articles in the *Journal of the American Medical Association, 267* (1992, January 22/29) focus on the link between psychosocial influences and coronary heart disease: Case, R. B., Moss, A. J., Case, N., McDermott, M., & Eberly, S. Living alone after myocardial infarction (pp. 515–519); Williams, R. B., Barefoot, J. C., Calif, R. M., Haney, T. L., Saunders, W. B., Pryon, D. B., . . . Mark, D. B. Prognostic importance of social and economic resources among medically treated patients with angiographically documented coronary artery disease (pp. 520–524); and Ruberman, R. Psychosocial influences on mortality of patients with coronary heart disease (pp. 559–560).

48. Stewart, J. (2004). *Bridges, not walls: A book about interpersonal communication* (9th ed.). New York: McGraw-Hill, p. 11.

49. Shattuck, R. (1980). *The forbidden experiment: The story of the wild boy of Aveyron*. New York: Farrar, Straus & Giroux, p. 37.

50. For a fascinating account of Genie's story, see Rymer, R. (1993). *Genie: An abused child's flight from silence*. New York: HarperCollins. Linguist Susan Curtiss (1977) provides a more specialized account of the case in her book *Genie: A psycholinguistic study of a modern-day "wild child."* San Diego, CA: Academic Press.

51. Rubin, R. B., Perse, E. M., & Barbato, C. A. (1988). Conceptualization and measurement of interpersonal communication motives. *Human Communication Research, 14*, 602–628.

52. Goldschmidt, W. (1990). *The human career: The self in the symbolic world*. Cambridge, MA: Basil Blackmun.

53. *Job Outlook 2004, National Association of Colleges and Employers*. Retrieved from http://www.jobweb.com/joboutlook/2004outlook.

54. Peterson, M. S. (1997). Personnel interviewers' perceptions of the importance and adequacy of applicants' communication skills. *Communication Education, 46*, 287–291.

55. Martin, M. W., & Anderson, C. M. (1995). Roommate similarity: Are roommates who are similar in their communication traits more satisfied? *Communication Research Reports, 12*, 46–52.

56. Kirchler, E. (1988). Marital happiness and interaction in everyday surroundings: A time-sample diary approach for couples. *Journal of Social and Personal Relationships, 5*, 375–382.

57. Rubin, R. B., & Graham, E. E. (1988). Communication correlates of college success: An exploratory investigation. *Communication Education, 37*, 14–27.

58. Duran, R. L., & Kelly, L. (1988). The influence of communicative competence on perceived task, social and physical attraction. *Communication Quarterly, 36*, 41–49.

59. For a thorough review of this topic, see Spitzberg, B. H., & Cupach, W. R. (1989). *Handbook of interpersonal competence research*. New York: Springer-Verlag.

60. See Wiemann, J. M., Takai, J., Ota, H., & Wiemann, M. (1997). A relational model of communication competence. In B. Kovacic (Ed.), *Emerging theories of human communication* (pp. 25–44). Albany: SUNY. These goals, and the strategies used to achieve them, needn't be conscious. See Fitzsimons, G. M., & Bargh, J. A. (2003). Thinking of you: Nonconscious pursuit of interpersonal goals

associated with relationship partners. *Journal of Personality and Social Psychology, 84,* 148–164.

61. For a review of the research citing the importance of flexibility, see Martin, M. M., & Anderson, C. M. (1998). The cognitive flexibility scale: Three validity studies. *Communication Reports, 11,* 1–9.

62. For a discussion of the trait versus state assessments of communication, see Infante, D. A., Rancer, A. S., & Womack, D. F. (1996). *Building communication theory* (3rd ed.). Prospect Heights, IL: Waveland Press, pp. 159–160. For a specific discussion of trait versus state definitions of communication competence, see Cupach, W. R., & Spitzberg, B. H. (1983). Trait versus state: A comparison of dispositional and situational measures of interpersonal communication competence. *Western Journal of Speech Communication, 47,* 364–379.

63. Burleson, B. R., & Samter, W. (1994). A social skills approach to relationship maintenance. In D. Canary & L. Stafford (Eds.), *Communication and relationship maintenance.* San Diego, CA: Academic Press, p. 12.

64. Guerrero, L. K., Andersen, P. A., Jorgensen, P. F., Spitzberg, B. H., & Eloy, S. V. (1995). Coping with the green-eyed monster: Conceptualizing and measuring communicative responses to romantic jealousy. *Western Journal of Communication, 59,* 270–304.

65. See O'Keefe, B. J. (1988). The logic of message design: Individual differences in reasoning about communication. *Communication Monographs, 55,* 80–103.

66. See, for example, Heisel, A. D., McCroskey, J. C., & Richmond, V. P. (1999). Testing theoretical relationships and nonrelationships of genetically-based predictors: Getting started with communibiology. *Communication Research Reports, 16,* 1–9; and McCroskey, J. C., & Beatty, K. J. (2000). The communibiological perspective: Implications for communication in instruction. *Communication Education, 49,* 1–6.

67. Kline, S. L., & Clinton, B. L. (1998). Developments in children's persuasive message practices. *Communication Education, 47,* 120–136.

68. de Turck, M. A., & Miller, G. R. (1990). Training observers to detect deception: Effects of self-monitoring and rehearsal. *Human Communication Research, 16,* 603–620.

69. Rubin, R. B., Graham, E. E., & Mignerey, J. T. (1990). A longitudinal study of college students' communication competence. *Communication Education, 39,* 1–14.

70. See, for example, Martin, R. (1992). Relational cognition complexity and relational communication in personal relationships. *Communication Monographs, 59,* 150–163; Stacks, D. W., & Murphy, M. A. (1993). Conversational sensitivity: Further validation and extension. *Communication Reports, 6,* 18–24; and Vangelisti, A. L., & Draughton, S. M. (1987). The nature and correlates of conversational sensitivity. *Human Communication Research, 14,* 167–202.

71. Research summarized in Hamachek, D. E. (1987). *Encounters with the self* (2nd ed.). Fort Worth, TX: Holt, Rinehart and Winston, p. 8. See also Daly, J. A., Vangelisti, A. L., & Daughton, S. M. (1995). The nature and correlates of conversational sensitivity. In Redmond, M. V. (Ed.), *Interpersonal communication: Readings in theory and research* (pp. 271–283). Fort Worth, TX: Harcourt Brace.

72. Kruger, J., & Dunning, D. (1999). Unskilled and unaware of it: How difficulties in recognizing one's own incompetence lead to inflated self-assessments. *Journal of Personality and Social Psychology, 77,* 1121–1134.

73. Adapted from the work of Hart, R. P. as reported by Knapp, M. L. (1984) in *Interpersonal communication and human relationships* (pp. 342–344). Boston: Allyn & Bacon. See also Hart, R. P., & Burks, D. M. (1972). Rhetorical sensitivity and social interaction. *Speech Monographs, 39,* 75–91; and Hart, R. P., Carlson, R. E., & Eadie, W. F. (1980). Attitudes toward communication and the assessment of rhetorical sensitivity. *Communication Monographs, 47,* 1–22.

74. Adapted from McCroskey, J. C., & Wheeless, L. R. (1976). *Introduction to human communication* (pp. 3–10). Boston: Allyn & Bacon.

75. Smith, J. L., Ickes, W., & Hodges, S. (Eds.). (2010). *Managing interpersonal sensitivity: Knowing when—and when not—to understand others.* Hauppauge, NY: Nova Science.

76. Pearce, W. B., & Pearce, K. A. (2000). Extending the theory of the coordinated management of meaning (CMM) through a community dialogue process. *Communication Theory, 10,* 405–423. See also Griffin, E. M. (2003). *A first look at communication theory* (5th ed.). New York: McGraw-Hill, pp. 66–81.

77. Meerloo, J. A. M. (1952). *Conversation and communication.* Madison, CT: International Universities Press, p. 91.

78. For a detailed rationale of the position argued in this section, see Stamp, G. H., & Knapp, M. L. (1990). The construct of intent in interpersonal communication. *Quarterly Journal of Speech, 76,* 282–299. See also Stewart, J. (1991). A postmodern look at traditional communication postulates. *Western Journal of Speech Communication, 55,* 354–379.

79. For a thorough discussion of communication difficulties, see Coupland, N., Giles, H., & Wiemann, J. M. (Eds.). (1991). *"Miscommunication" and problematic talk.* Newbury Park, CA: Sage, 1991.

80. Leonardi, P. M., Treem, J. W., & Jackson, M. H. (2010). The connectivity paradox: Using technology to both decrease and increase perceptions of distance in distributed work arrangements. *Journal of Applied Communication Research, 38,* 85–105.

81. McCroskey, J. C., & Wheeless, L. R. (1976). *Introduction to human communication.* Boston: Allyn & Bacon, p. 5.

## CHAPTER 2

1. The quotes in this profile are taken from two sources: Cain, S. (2011). Hi, I'm Susan Cain. Retrieved October 23, 2012, from http://www.thepowerofintroverts.com/about-the-author and S. Cain. (2012, March). The power of introverts. *TED [Technology Entertainment and Design]: Ideas Worth Spreading.* Retrieved from http://www.ted.com/talks/susan_cain_the_power_of_introverts .html.

2. Cain, S. (2012). *Quiet: The power of introverts in a world that can't stop talking.* New York: Crown.

3. Hamachek, D. (1992). *Encounters with the self* (3rd ed.). Fort Worth, TX: Holt, Rinehart and Winston, pp. 5–8. See also Campbell, J. D., & Lavallee, L. F. (1993). Who am I? The role of self-concept confusion in understanding the behavior of people with low self-esteem. In R. F. Baumeister (Ed.), *Self-esteem: The puzzle of low self-regard* (pp. 3–20). New York: Plenum Press.

4. Baumeister, R. F. (2005). *The cultural animal: Human nature, meaning, and social life.* New York: Oxford University Press; and Baumeister, R. F., Campbell, J. D., Krueger, J. I., & Vohs, K. D. Does high self-esteem cause better performance, interpersonal success, happiness, or healthier lifestyles? *Psychological Science in the Public Interest, 4,* 1–44.

5. Vohs, K. D., & Heatherton, T. F. (2004). Ego threats elicit different social comparison process among high and low self-esteem people: Implications for interpersonal perceptions. *Social Cognition, 22,* 168–191.

6. For more, see Kandler, C., Riemann, R., & Kämpfe, N. (2009). Genetic and environmental mediation between measures of personality and family environment in twins reared together. *Behavioral Genetics, 39,* 24–35, and Caspi, A., Harrington, H., Milne, B., Amell, J. W., Theodore, R. F., & Moffitt, T. E. (2003). Children's behavioral styles at age 3 are linked to their adult personality traits at age 26. *Journal of Personality, 71,* 495–514. doi: 10.1111/1467-6494.7104001.

7. Ashton, M. C., Lee, K., Perugini, M., Szarota, P., de Vries, R. E., Di Blas, L., . . . De Raad, B. (2004, February). A six-factor structure of personality-descriptive adjectives: Solutions from psycholexical studies in seven languages. *Journal of Personality and Social Psychology, 86*(2), 356–366.

8. See Gong, P., Zheng, A., Zhang, K, Lei, X., Li, F., Chen, D., . . . Zhang, F. (2010). Association analysis between 12 genetic variants of ten genes and personality traits in a young Chinese Han population. *Journal of Molecular Neuroscience, 42*, 120–126, and Heck, A., Lieb, R., Ellgas, A., Pfister, H., Lucae, S., Roeske, D., . . . Ising, M. (2009). Investigation of 17 candidate genes for personality traits confirms effects of the HTR2A gene on novelty seeking. *Genes, Brain and Behavior, 8*, 464–472. doi: 10.1111/j.1601-183X.2009.00494.x.

9. Cole, J. G., & McCroskey, J. C. (2000). Temperament and socio-communicative orientation. *Communication Research Reports, 17*, 105–114.

10. Heisel, A. D., McCroskey, J. C., & Richmond, V. P. (1999). Testing theoretical relationships and non-relationships of genetically-based predictors: Getting started with communibiology. *Communication Research Reports, 16*, 1–9.

11. Cole, J. G., & McCroskey, J. C. (2000). Temperament and socio-communicative orientation. *Communication Research Reports, 17*, 105–114.

12. Wigley, C. J. (1998). Verbal aggressiveness. In J. C. McCroskey, J. A. Daly, M. M. Martin, & M. J. Beatty (Eds.), *Personality and communication: Trait perspectives* (pp. 191–214). New York: Hampton.

13. McCroskey, J. C., Heisel, A. D., & Richmond, V. P. (2001). Eysenck's big three and communication traits: Three correlational studies. *Communication Monographs, 68*, 360–366.

14. McCroskey, J. C., & Richmond, V. (1980). *The quiet ones: Communication apprehension and shyness.* Dubuque, IA: Gorsuch Scarisbrick. See also Bouchard, T. J., Lykken, D. T., McGue, M., & Segal, N. L. (1990, October 12). Sources of human psychological differences—the Minnesota study of twins reared apart. *Science, 250*, 223–228.

15. Dweck, C. (2008). Can personality be changed? The role of beliefs in personality and change. *Current Directions in Psychological Science, 6*, 391–394.

16. Begney, S. (2008, December 1). When DNA is not destiny. *Newsweek, 152*, 14.

17. See also Keltikangas, J. (1990). The stability of self-concept during adolescence and early adulthood: A six-year follow-up study. *Journal of General Psychology, 117*, 361–369.

18. Kubric, K. N., & Chory, R. M. (2007). Exposure to television makeover programs and perceptions of self. *Communication Research Reports, 24*, 283–291.

19. López-Guimerà, G., Levine, M. P., Sánchez-Carracedo, D., & Fauquet J. (2010). Influence of mass media on body image and eating disordered attitudes and behaviors in females: A review of effects and processes. *Media Psychology, 13*, 387–416.

20. Servaes, J. (1989). Cultural identity and modes of communication. In J. A. Anderson (Ed.), *Communication yearbook* 12 (pp. 386–434). Newbury Park, CA: Sage, p. 396.

21. Bharti, A. (1985). The self in Hindu thought and action. In *Culture and self: Asian and Western perspectives* (pp. 185–230). New York: Tavistock.

22. Gudykunst, W. B., & Ting-Toomey, S. (1988). *Culture and interpersonal communication.* Newbury Park, CA: Sage.

23. Samovar, L. A., Porter, R. E., & McDaniel, E. R. (2007). *Communication between cultures* (7th ed.). Boston, MA: Cengage, p. 91.

24. Alberts, J. K., Kellar-Guenther, U., & Corman, S. R. (1996). That's not funny: Understanding recipients' responses to teasing. *Western Journal of Communication, 60*, 337–357.

25. Katzer, C., Fetchenhauer, D., & Belschak, F. (2009). Cyberbullying: Who are the victims? A comparison of victimization in Internet chatrooms and victimization in school. *Journal of Media Psychology: Theories, Methods, and Applications, 21*, 25–36.

26. MacIntyre, P. D., & Thivierge, K. A. (1995). The effects of speaker personality on anticipated reactions to public speaking. *Communication Research Reports, 12*, 125–133.

27. DiPaola, B. M., Roloff, M. E., & Peters, K. M. (2010). College students' expectations of conflict intensity: A self-fulfilling prophecy. *Communication Quarterly, 58*(1), 59–76.

28. Stinson, D. A., Cameron, J. J., Wood, J. V., Gaucher, D., & Holmes J. G. (2009). Deconstructing the "reign of error": Interpersonal warmth explains the self-fulfilling prophecy of anticipated acceptance. *Personality and Social Psychology, 35*, 1165–1178.

29. Dimberg, U., & Söderkvist, S. (2011). The voluntary facial action technique: A method to test the facial feedback hypothesis. *Journal of Nonverbal Behavior, 35*, 17–33.

30. Holmes, J. G. (2002). Interpersonal expectations as the building blocks of social cognition: An interdependence theory perspective. *Personal Relationships, 9*, 1–26.

31. Rosenthal R. & Jacobson, L. (1968). *Pygmalion in the classroom.* New York: Holt, Rinehart and Winston.

32. For a detailed discussion of how self-fulfilling prophecies operate in relationships, see Watzlawick, P. (2005). Self-fulfilling prophecies. In J. O'Brien & P. Kollock (Eds.), *The production of reality* (3rd ed., pp. 382–394). Thousand Oaks, CA: Pine Forge Press.

33. James, W. (1920). *The letters of William James* (H. James, Ed.). Boston, p. 462.

34. Fletcher, G. J. O., Fincham, F. D., Cramer, L., & Heron, N. (1987). The role of attributions in the development of dating relationships. *Journal of Personality and Social Psychology, 53*, 481–489.

35. Knobloch, L. K., Miller, L. E., Bond, B. J., & Mannone, S. E. (2007). Relational uncertainty and message processing in marriage. *Communication Monographs, 74*, 154–180.

36. Macrae, C. N., & Bodenhausen, G. V. (2001). Social cognition: Categorical person perception. *British Journal of Psychology, 92*, 239–256.

37. Matthys, W., & Cohen-Kettenis, P. (1994). Boys' and girls' perceptions of peers in middle childhood: Differences and similarities. *Journal of Genetic Psychology, 155*, 15–24.

38. Heisler, J., & Crabill, S. (2006). Who are "stinkybug" and "packerfan4"? Email pseudonyms and participants' perceptions of demography, productivity, and personality. *Journal of Computer-Mediated Communication, 12*, article 6. Retrieved from http://jcmc.indiana.edu/vol12/issue1/heisler.html.

39. Manusov, V., Winchatz, M. R., &. Manning, L. M. (1997). Acting out our minds: Incorporating behavior into models of stereotype-based expectancies for cross-cultural interactions. *Communication Monographs, 64*, 119–139.

40. Merolla, A. J. (2008). Communicating forgiveness in friendships and dating relationships. *Communication Studies, 59*, 114–131.

41. Clark, A. (2000). *A theory of sentience.* New York: Oxford University Press.

42. Miró, E., Cano, M. C., Espinoza-Fernández, L., & Beula-Casal, G. (2003). Time estimation during prolonged sleep deprivation and its relation to activation measures. *Human Factors, 45*, 148–159.

43. Alaimo, K., Olson, C. M., & Frongillo, E. A. (2001). Food insufficiency and American school-aged children's cognitive, academic, and psychosocial development. *Pediatrics, 108*, 44–53.

44. Koukkari, W. L., & Sothern, R. B. (2006). *Introducing biological rhythms: A primer on the temporal organization of life, with implications for health, society, reproduction and the natural environment.* New York: Springer.

45. Hasler, B. P., & Troxel, W. M. (2010). Couples' nighttime sleep efficiency and concordance: Evidence of bidirectional associations with daytime relationship functioning. *Psychosomatic Medicine, 72*, 794–801.

46. Goldstein, S. (2008). Current literature in ADHD. *Journal of Attention Disorders, 11*, 614–616.

47. Von Briesen, P. D. (2007). Pragmatic language skills of adolescents with ADHD. *DAI, 68*(5-B), 3430.

48. Babinski, D. E., Pelham W. E., Jr., Molina, B. S. G., Gnagy, E. M., Waschbusch, D. A., Yu, J., & Karch, K. M. (2011). Late adolescent and young adult outcomes of girls diagnosed with ADHD in childhood: An exploratory investigation. *Journal of Attention Disorders, 15*, 204–214.

49. National Institute of Mental Health. (2008, April 3). *Attention deficit hyperactivity disorder.* Retrieved from http://www.nimh.nih.gov/health/publications/attention-deficit-hyperactivity-disorder/index.shtml

50. Bem, S. L. (1974). The measurement of psychological androgyny. *Journal of Consulting and Clinical Psychology, 42*, 155–162.

51. Choi, Y. S., Gray, H. M., & Ambady, N. (2005). The glimpsed world: Unintended communication and unintended perception. In R. R. Hassin, J. S. Uleman, & J. A. Bargh (Eds.), *The new unconscious* (pp. 309–333). New York: Oxford University Press.

52. Versalle, A., & McDowell, E. E. (2004–2005). The attitudes of men and women concerning gender differences in grief. *Omega: Journal of Death and Dying, 50*, 53–67.

53. Ibid.

54. Hanzal, A., Segrin, C., & Dorros, S. M. (2008). The role of marital status and age on men's and women's reactions to touch from a relational partner. *Journal of Nonverbal Behavior, 32*, 21–35.

55. Dougherty, D. S. (2001). Sexual harassment as [dys]functional process: A feminist standpoint analysis. *Journal of Applied Communication Research, 29*, 372–402; Ohse, D.M., & Stockwell, M.S. (2008). Age comparisons in workplace sexual harassment perceptions. *Sex Roles, 59*, 240–253.

56. Singer, J. K., Miller, L. C., & Murphy, S. (1998). *Sexual harassment and memory: How repetition of behavior and personal experience relate to judgments of sexual harassment.* Paper presented at the annual conference of the International Communication Association, Jerusalem.

57. Solomon, D. H., & Williams, M. L. M. (1997). Perceptions of social-sexual communication at work: The effects of message, situation, and observer characteristics on judgments of sexual harassment. *Journal of Applied Communication Research, 25*, 197–216.

58. Zimbardo, P. G. (1971). *The psychological power and pathology of imprisonment.* Statement prepared for the U.S. House of Representatives Committee on the Judiciary, Subcommittee No. 3, Robert Kastemeyer, Chairman. Unpublished manuscript, Stanford University. See also Zimbardo, P. G. (1977). *Shyness: What it is, what to do about it.* Reading, MA: Addison-Wesley.

59. Swami, V., & Furnham, A. (2008). *The psychology of physical attraction.* New York: Routledge/Taylor & Francis.

60. Gonzaga, G. G., Haselton, M. G., Smurda J., Davies, M., & Poore, J. C. (2008). Love, desire, and the suppression of thoughts of romantic alternatives. *Evolution and Human Behavior, 29*, 119–126.

61. Shaw, C. L. M. (1997). Personal narrative: Revealing self and reflecting other. *Human Communication Research, 24*, 302–319.

62. Sias, P. M. (1996). Constructing perceptions of differential treatment: An analysis of coworkers' discourse. *Communication Monographs, 63*, 171–187.

63. Martz, J. M., Verette, J., Arriaga, X. B., Slovik, L. F., Cox, C. L., & Rusbult, C. E. (1998). Positive illusion in close relationships. *Personal Relationships, 5*, 159–181.

64. Pearson, J. C. (2000). Positive distortion: "The most beautiful woman in the world." In K. M. Galvin & P. J. Cooper (Eds.), *Making connections: Readings in relational communication* (2nd ed., pp. 184–190). Los Angeles, CA: Roxbury.

65. Summarized in Hamachek, D. E. (1982). *Encounters with others.* New York: Holt, Rinehart and Winston, pp. 23–30.

66. Willis, J., & Todorov, A. (2006). First impressions: Making up your mind after a 100-ms exposure to a face. *Psychological Science, 17*, 592–598.

67. Nelson, T. D. (2005). Ageism: Prejudice against our featured future self. *Journal of Social Issues, 61*, 207–221.

68. Zenmore, S. E., Fiske, S. T., & Kim H. J. (2000). Gender stereotypes and the dynamics of social interaction. In T. Eckes & H. M. Trautner (Eds.), *The developmental social psychology of gender* (pp. 207–241). Mahwah, NJ: Erlbaum.

69. Allen, M. (1998). Methodological considerations when examining a gendered world. In D. J. Canary & K. Dindia (Eds.), *Handbook of sex differences and similarities in communication* (pp. 427–444). Mahwah, NJ: Erlbaum.

70. Allen, B. (1995). "Diversity" and organizational communication. *Journal of Applied Communication Research, 23*, 143–155. See also Buttny, R. (1997). Reported speech in talking race on campus. *Human Communication Research, 23*, 477–506.

71. Burgess, M. R., Dill, K. E., Stermer, S., Burgess, S. R., & Brown, B. P. (2011). Playing with prejudice: The prevalence and consequences of racial stereotypes in video games. *Media Psychology, 14*(3), 289–311. doi:10.1080/15213269.2011.596467.

72. Block, C. J., Aumann, K., & Chelin, A. (2012). Assessing stereotypes of black and white managers: A diagnostic approach. *Journal of Applied Social Psychology.* Advance online publication retrieved online from http://onlinelibrary.wiley.com/doi/10.1111/j.1559-1816.2012.01014.x/abstract.

73. For a review of these perceptual biases, see Hamachek, D. (1992) *Encounters with the self* (3rd ed.). Fort Worth, TX: Harcourt Brace Jovanovich. See also Bradbury, T. N., & Fincham, F. D. (1990). Attributions in marriage: Review and critique. *Psychological Bulletin, 107*, 3–33. For information on the self-serving bias, see Shepperd, J., Malone, W., & Sweeny, K. (2008). Exploring causes of the self-serving bias. *Social and Personality Psychology Compass, 2/2*, 895–908.

74. Sypher, B., & Sypher, H. E. (1984, January). Seeing ourselves as others see us. *Communication Research, 11*, 97–115.

75. Reported by Myers, D. (1980, May). The inflated self. *Psychology Today, 14*, 16.

76. See, for example, Kanouse, D. E., & Hanson, L. R. (1972). Negativity in evaluations. In E. E. Jones, D. E. Kanouse, H. H. Kelley, R. E. Nisbett, S. Valins, & B. Weiner (Eds.), *Attribution: Perceiving the causes of behavior* (pp. 47–62). Morristown, NJ: General Learning Press.

77. Marek, C. I., Wanzer, M. B., & Knapp, J. L. (2004). An exploratory investigation of the relationship between roommates' first impressions and subsequent communication patterns. *Communication Research Reports, 21*, 210–220.

78. See, for example, Baron, P. (1974). Self-esteem, ingratiation, and evaluation of unknown others. *Journal of Personality and Social Psychology, 30*, 104–109; and Walster, E. (1965). The effect of self-esteem on romantic liking. *Journal of Experimental and Social Psychology, 1*, 184–197.

79. Henningsen, D., Henningsen, M., McWorthy, E., McWorthy, C., & McWorthy, L. (2011). Exploring the effects of sex and mode of presentation in perceptions of dating goals in video-dating. *Journal of Communication, 61*(4), 641–658. doi:10.1111/j.1460-2466.2011.01564.x.

80. See, for example, Walther, J. B., DeAndrea, D. C., & Tong, S. T. (2009, November). *Computer-mediated communication versus vocal*

*communication in the amelioration of stereotypes: A replication with three theoretical models.* Paper presented at the annual meeting of the National Communication Association, Chicago, IL.

81. Okdie, B. M., Guadgno, R. E., Bemien, F. J., Geers, A. L., & Mclarney-Vesotski, A. R. (2011). Getting to know you: Face-to-face versus online interactions. *Computers in Human Behavior, 27,* 153–159.

82. Pempek, T. A., Yermolayeva, Y. A., & Calvert, S. L. (2009). College students' social networking experiences on Facebook. *Journal of Applied Developmental Psychology, 30,* 227–238.

83. Gill, A. J., Oberlander, J. & Austin. E. (2005). Rating email personality at zero acquaintance. *Personality and Individual Differences, 40,* 497–507.

84. Walther, J. B., Loh, T., & Granka, L. (2005). Let me count the ways: The interchange of verbal and nonverbal cues in computer-mediated and face-to-face affinity. *Journal of Language and Social Psychology, 24,* 36–65.

85. Lea, M. & Spears, R. (1992). Paralanguage and social perception in computer-mediated communication. *Journal of Organizational Computing, 2,* 321–341.

86. Walther, J. B., & Tidwell, L. C. (1995). Nonverbal cues in computer-mediated communication, and the effect of chronemics on relational communication. *Journal of Organizational Computing, 5,* 355–378.

87. Stiff, J. B., Dillard, J. P., Somera, L., Kim, H., & Sleight, C. (1988). Empathy, communication, and prosocial behavior. *Communication Monographs, 55,* 198–213.

88. Goleman, D. (1995). *Emotional intelligence: Why it can matter more than I.Q.* New York: Bantam.

89. Lennon, R. & Eisenberg, N. (1987). Gender and age differences in empathy and sympathy. In N. Eisenberg & J. Strayer (Eds.), *Empathy and its development.* Cambridge: Cambridge University Press.

90. Walter, H. (2012). Social cognitive neuroscience of empathy: Concepts, circuits, and genes. *Emotion Review, 4,* 9–17.

91. Miklikowka, M., Duriez, M., & Soenens, B. (2011). Family roots of empathy-related characteristics: The role of perceived maternal and paternal needs support in adolescence. *Developmental Psychology, 47,* 1342–1352.

92. Peterson, T. R. & Horton, C. C. (1995). Rooted in the soil: How understanding the perspectives of landowners can enhance the management of environmental disputes. *Quarterly Journal of Speech, 81,* 139–166.

93. Shaw, C. M., & Edwards, R. (1997). Self-concepts and self-presentation of males and females: Similarities and differences. *Communication Reports, 10,* 56–62.

94. Goffman, E. (1971). *The presentation of self in everyday life.* Garden City, NY: Doubleday, and Goffman, E. (1971). *Relations in public.* New York: Basic Books.

95. Cupach, W. R., & Metts, S. (1994). *Facework.* Thousand Oaks, CA: Sage. See also Brown, P., & Levinson, S. C. (1987). *Politeness: Some universals in language usage.* Cambridge: Cambridge University Press.

96. Sharkey, W. F., Park, H. S., & Kim, R. K.. (2004). Intentional self embarrassment. *Communication Studies, 55,* 379–399.

97. Urciuoli, B. (2009). The political topography of Spanish and English: The view from a New York Puerto Rican neighborhood. *American Ethnologist, 10,* 295–310.

98. Stewart, J., & Logan, C. (1998). *Together: Communicating interpersonally* (5th ed.). New York: McGraw-Hill, p. 120.

99. Leary, M. R., & Kowalski, R. M. (1990). Impression management: A literature review and two-component model. *Psychological Bulletin, 107,* 34–47.

100. Brightman, V., Segal, A., Werther, P., & Steiner, J. (1975). Ethological study of facial expression in response to taste stimuli. *Journal of Dental Research, 54,* 141.

101. Chovil, N. (1991). Social determinants of facial displays. *Journal of Nonverbal Behavior, 15,* 141–154.

102. See note 99, Leary and Kowalski (1990).

103. Snyder, M. (1979). Self-monitoring processes. In L. Berkowitz (Ed.), *Advances in experimental social psychology* (pp. 85–128). New York: Academic Press, and M. Snyder. (1983, March). The many me's of the self-monitor. *Psychology Today, 34f.*

104. The following discussion is based on material in Hamachek, D. (1992). *Encounters with the self* (3rd ed.). Fort Worth, TX: Holt, Rinehart and Winston, pp. 24–26.

105. Fleming, P., & Sturdy, A. (2009). "Just be yourself!": Towards neo-normative control in organisations? *Employee Relations, 31,* 569–583.

106. Ragins, B. R. (2008). Disclosure disconnects: Antecedents and consequences of disclosing invisible stigmas across life domains. *Academy of Management Review, 33,* 194–215.

107. Ragins, B. R., Singh, R., & Cornwell, J. M. (2007). Making the invisible visible: Fear and disclosure of sexual orientation at work. *Journal of Applied Psychology, 92,* 1103–1118.

108. Pachankis, J. E. (2007). The psychological implications of concealing a stigma: A cognitive-affective-behavioral model. *Psychological Bulletin, 133,* 328–345.

109. Coleman, L. M., & DePaulo, B. M. (1991). Uncovering the human spirit: Moving beyond disability and "missed" communications. In N. Coupland, H. Giles, & J. M. Wiemann (Eds.), *"Miscommunication" and problematic talk* (pp. 61–84). Newbury Park, CA: Sage.

110. Siibak, A. (2009). Constructing the self through the photo selection: Visual impression management on social networking websites. *Cyberpsychology: Journal of Psychosocial Research on Cyberspace, 3,* article 1. Retrieved December 13, 2012, from http://www.cyberpsychology.eu/view.php?cisloclanku=2009061501&article=1.

111. Hancock, J. T., & Durham, P. J. (2001) Impression formation in computer-mediated communication revisited: An analysis of the breadth and intensity of impressions. *Communication Research, 28,* 325–347.

112. Suler, J. R. (2002). Identity management in cyberspace. *Journal of Applied Psychoanalytic Studies, 4,* 455–459.

113. Gibbs, J. L., Ellison, N. B., & Heino, R. D. (2006). Self-presentation in online personals: The role of anticipated future interaction, self-disclosure, and perceived success in Internet dating. *Communication Research, 33,* 1–26.

114. See, for example, Chandler, D. (nd). Personal home pages and the construction of identities on the Web. Retrieved May 8, 2006, from http://www.aber.ac.uk/~dgc/webident.html.

115. Symonds, S. (2011, November 2). Creating video game avatars [Web log post]. Retrieved December 17, 2012, from http://www.icheg.org/blog/chegheads/2011/11/creating-video-game-avatars.

116. Levine, K. (2007, July 31). Alter egos in a virtual world. *National Public Radio.* Retrieved December 17, 2012, from http://www.npr.org/templates/story/story.php?storyId=12263532.

117. Ibid., paragraphs 7 and 10.

118. Martey, R., & Consalvo, M. (2011). Performing the looking-glass self: Avatar appearance and group identity in Second Life. *Popular Communication, 9*(3), 165–180. doi:10.1080/15405702.2011.583830.

119. Nowak, K. L., Hamilton, M. A., & Hammond, C. C. (2009). The effect of image features on judgments of homophily, credibility, and intention to use as avatars in future interactions. *Media Psychology, 12*(1), 50–76. doi:10.1080/15213260802669433.

120. Toma, C., Hancock, J., & Ellison N. (2008). Separating fact from fiction: An examination of deceptive self-presentation in online dating profiles. *Personality and Social Psychology Bulletin, 34,* 1023–1036.

## CHAPTER 3

1. Wang, J. (2012, September 21). China sends more students aboard than any other country. *The Epoch Times.* Retrieved January 17, 2013, from http://www.theepochtimes.com/n2/china-news/china-sends-more-students-abroad-than-any-other-country-295022.html.
2. Kroeber, A. L., & Kluckholn, C. (1952). *Culture: A critical review of concepts and definitions.* Harvard University, Peabody Museum of American Archeology and Ethnology Papers 47.
3. Samovar, L. A., & Porter, R. E. (2007). *Communication between cultures* (6th ed.). Belmont, CA: Wadsworth, 2007, quote on p. 395.
4. Buzzanell, P. M. (1999). Tensions and burdens in employment interviewing processes: Perspectives of non-dominant group members. *Journal of Business Communication, 36,* 143–162.
5. Ferguson, G. M., & Cramer, P. (2007). Self-esteem among Jamaican children: Exploring the impact of skin color and rural/urban residence. *Journal of Applied Developmental Psychology, 28,* 345–359.
6. Golash-Boza, T., & Darity, W. (2008). Latino racial choices: The effects of skin colour and discrimination on Latinos' and Latinas' racial self-identifications. *Ethnic & Racial Studies, 31,* 899–934.
7. Brown, H. K., Ouellette-Kuntz, H., Lysaght, R., & Burge, P. (2011). Students' behavioural intentions towards peers with disability. *Journal of Applied Research in Intellectual Disabilities, 24,* 322–332. doi:10.1111/j.1468-3148.2010.00616.x.
8. Binder, J., Brown, R., Zagefka, H., Funke, F., Kessler, T., Mummendey, A., . . . Leyens. J.-F. (2009). Does contact reduce prejudice or does prejudice reduce contact? A longitudinal test of the contact hypothesis among majority and minority groups in three European countries. *Journal of Personality & Social Psychology, 96*(4), 843–856.
9. Bryan, C. (2009, August 8). Michelle Obama's dark skin inspired women of color all over the world. *Examiner.com.* Retrieved December 26, 2012, from http://www.examiner.com/article/michelle-obama-s-dark-skin-inspires-women-of-color-all-over-the-world.
10. Duggan, M. & Brenner, J. (2013). The demographics of social media users. *Pew Internet & American Life Project.* Retrieved from http://www.pewinternet.org/Reports/2013/Social-media-users.aspx.
11. Collier, M. J. (1996). Communication competence problematics in ethnic relationships. *Communication Monographs, 63,* 314–336. See also Kline, S., Horton, B. W., & Zhang, S. (2008). How we think, feel and express love: A cross-cultural comparison between American and East Asian culture. *International Journal of Intercultural Relations, 32,* 200–214.
12. Tajfel, H. & Turner, J. C. (1986). The social identity theory of inter-group behavior. In S. Worchel & L. W. Austin (Eds.), *Psychology of intergroup relations* (pp. 7–24). Chicago: Nelson-Hall.
13. Gudykunst, W. B., & Matsumoto, Y. (1996). Cross-cultural variability of communication in personal relationships. In W. B. Gudykunst, S. Ting-Toomey, & T. Nishida (Eds.), *Communication in personal relationships across cultures* (pp. 19–56). Newbury Park, CA: Sage, pp. 19–56.
14. Triandis, H. C. (1995). *Individualism and collectivism.* Boulder, CO: Westview.
15. Servaes, J. (1989). Cultural identity and modes of communication. In J. A. Anderson (Ed.), *Communication yearbook 12* (pp. 383–416). Newbury Park, CA: Sage.
16. Samovar, L. A., & Porter, R. E. (2004). *Communication between cultures* (5th ed.). Belmont, CA: Wadsworth.
17. Gudykunst, W. B. (1993a). *Communication in Japan and the United States.* Albany: State University of New York Press.
18. D. A. Cai & E. L. Fink. (2002). Conflict style differences between individualists and collectivists. *Communication Monographs, 69,* 67–87.
19. See Triandis, H. C., Bontempo, R., Villareal, M., Asai, M., & Lucca, N. (1988). Individualism and collectivism: Cross-cultural perspectives of self-ingroup relationships. *Journal of Personality and Social Psychology, 54,* 323–338.
20. See, for example, Moss, G., Kubacki, K., Hersh, M., & Gunn, R. (2007). Knowledge management in higher education: A comparison of individualistic and collectivist cultures. *European Journal of Education, 42,* 377–394.
21. Merkin., R. S. (2009). Cross-cultural communication patterns—Korean and American communication. *Journal of Intercultural Communication, 20,* 5.
22. Wu, S., & Keysar, B. (2007). Cultural effects on perspective taking. *Psychological Science, 18,* 600–606.
23. Ting-Toomey, S. (1988). A face-negotiation theory. In Y. Kim & W. Gudykunst (Eds.), *Theory in interpersonal communication.* Newbury Park, CA: Sage.
24. Hall, E. T. (1959). *Beyond culture.* New York: Doubleday.
25. Yuan-shan, C., Chun-yin Doris, C., & Miao-Hsia, C. (2011). American and Chinese complaints: Strategy use from a cross-cultural perspective. *Intercultural Pragmatics, 8,* 253–275.
26. Leets, L. (1993). Explaining perceptions of racist speech. *Communication Research, 28,* 676–706, and Leets, L. (1993). Disentangling perceptions of subtle racist speech: A cultural perspective. *Journal of Language and Social Psychology, 22,* 1–24.
27. Hofstede, G. (2001). *Culture's consequences: Comparing values, behaviors, institutions, and organizations across nations* (2nd ed.). Thousand Oaks, CA: Sage.
28. Ibid.
29. Cohen, A. (2007). One nation, many cultures: A cross-cultural study of the relationship between personal cultural values and commitment in the workplace to in-role performance and organizational citizenship behavior. *Cross-Cultural Research: The Journal of Comparative Social Science, 41,* 273–300.
30. Dailey, R. M., Giles, H., & Jansma, L. L. (2005). Language attitudes in an Anglo-Hispanic context: The role of the linguistic landscape. *Language & Communication, 25*(1), 27–38.
31. Basso, K. (2012). "To give up on words": Silence in Western Apache culture. In L. Monogahn, J. E. Goodman, & J. M. Robinson (Eds.), *A cultural approach to interpersonal communication: Essential readings* (2nd ed., pp. 73–83). Malden, MA: Blackwell, quote on p. 84.
32. Hofstede, G. (2001). *Culture's consequences: Comparing values, behaviors, institutions, and organizations across nations* (2nd ed.). Thousand Oaks, CA: Sage.
33. Ibid.
34. Ayoun, B., Palakurthi, R., & Moreo, P. (2010). Cultural influences on strategic behavior of hotel executives: Masculinity and femininity. *International Journal of Hospitality & Tourism Administration, 11,* 1–21.
35. What about Taiwan? (n.d.). *The Hofstede Centre.* Retrieved from http://geert-hofstede.com/taiwan.html.
36. The androgyny revolution. (2007, December 12). *The Yale Globalist.* Retrieved from http://tyglobalist.org/in-the-magazine/theme/the-androgyny-revolution.

37. Ten things everyone should know about race. (2003). *Race—The power of an illusion.* California Newsreel, Public Broadcasting System. Retrieved from http://www.pbs.org/race/000_About/002_04-background-01-x.htm.

38. Interview with Jonathan Marks. (2003). Background readings for *Race—The power of an illusion.* California Newsreel, Public Broadcasting System. Retrieved from http://www.pbs.org/race/000_About/002_04-background-01-08.htm.

39. Samovar, L. A., Porter, R. E., McDaniel, E. R. (2013). *Communication between cultures* (8th ed.). Boston, MA: Wadsworth.

40. Saulny, S. (2011, October 12). In strangers' glances at family, tensions linger. *The New York Times.* Retrieved December 27, 2012, from http://www.nytimes.com/2011/10/13/us/for-mixed-family-old-racial-tensions-remain-part-of-life.html?pagewanted=1&_r=0&ref=raceremixed.

41. Bonam, C. M., & Shih, M. (2009). Exploring multiracial individual's comfort with intimate interracial relationships. *Journal of Social Issues, 65,* 87–103.

42. For a summary of research on this subject, see Bradac, J. J. (1990). Language attitudes and impression formation. In H. Giles & W. P. Robinson (Eds.), *The handbook of language and social psychology* (pp. 387–413). Chichester, England: Wiley. See also Ng, S. H., & Bradac, J. J. (1993). *Power in language: Verbal communication and social influence.* Newbury Park, CA: Sage.

43. Bailey, R. W. (2003). Ideologies, attitudes, and perceptions. *American Speech, 88,* 115–143.

44. Frumkin, L. (2007). Influences of accent and ethnic background on perceptions of eyewitness testimony. *Psychology, Crime & Law, 13,* 317–331.

45. Gluszek, A., & Dovidio, J. F. (2010). Perceptions of bias, communication difficulties, and belonging in the United States. *Journal of Language & Social Psychology, 29,* 224–234.

46. Tannen, D. (2005). *Conversational style: Analyzing talk among friends* (Rev. ed.). New York: Oxford University Press.

47. Tannen, D. (2012, October 18). Would you please let me finish. . . . *New York Times,* p. A33.

48. Birdwhistell, R. L. (1970). *Kinesics and context.* Philadelphia: University of Philadelphia Press, pp. 30–31.

49. Andersen, P., Lustig, M., & Anderson, J. (1987). *Changes in latitude, changes in attitude: The relationship between climate, latitude, and interpersonal communication predispositions.* Paper presented at the annual convention of the Speech Communication Association, Boston. Andersen, P., Lustig, M., & Andersen, J. (1988). *Regional patterns of communication in the United States: Empirical tests.* Paper presented at the annual convention of the Speech Communication Association, New Orleans.

50. What is LGBTQ? (n.d.). Iknowmine.org., sponsored by Alaska Native Tribal Health Consortium, Community Health Services. Retrieved from http://www.iknowmine.org/for-youth/what-is-glbt.

51. Federal Bureau of Investigation. (2012, December 10). Hate crimes accounting: Annual report. Retrieved from http://www.fbi.gov/news/stories/2012/december/annual-hate-crimes-report-released/annual-hate-crimes-report-released.

52. All of the statements by Anderson Cooper in this paragraph are from Sullivan, A. (2012, July 2). Anderson Cooper: "The fact is, I'm gay." *The Dish.* Retrieved from http://dish.andrewsullivan.com/2012/07/02/anderson-cooper-the-fact-is-im-gay/.

53. Potter, J. E. (2002). Do ask, do tell. *Annals of Internal Medicine, 137*(5), 341–343, quote on p. 342.

54. Russell, G. M., & Bohan, J. S. (2005, December). The gay generational gap: Communicating across the LGBT generational divide. *Institute for Gay and Lesbian Strategic Studies, 8*(1), 1–8, quote on p. 3.

55. About the It Gets Better Project. (2013). Retrieved from http://www.itgetsbetter.org/pages/about-it-gets-better-project/.

56. Dan Savage: It gets better. (2013, January 14). *Take part.* Retrieved from http://www.takepart.com/video/dan-savage-it-gets-better.

57. Milevsky, A., Shifra Niman, D., Raab, A., & Gross, R. (2011). A phenomenological examination of dating attitudes in ultra-orthodox Jewish emerging adult women. *Mental Health, Religion & Culture, 14,* 311–322. doi:10.1080/13674670903585105.

58. U.S. religious landscape survey. Religious beliefs and practices: Diverse and politically relevant. (2008, June). *The Pew Charitable Trust forum on religion and public life.* Retrieved December 27, 2012, from http://religions.pewforum.org/pdf/report2-religious-landscape-study-full.pdf.

59. Bartkowski, J. P., Xiaohe, X., & Fondren, K. M. (2011). Faith, family, and teen dating: Examining the effects of personal and household religiosity on adolescent romantic relationships. *Review of Religious Research, 52,* 248–265.

60. Reiter, M. J., & Gee, C. B. (2008). Open communication and partner support in intercultural and interfaith romantic relationships: A relational maintenance approach. *Journal of Social & Personal Relationships, 25,* 539–559. doi:10.1177/0265407508090872.

61. Colaner, C. (2009). Exploring the communication of evangelical families: The association between evangelical gender role ideology and family communication patterns. *Communication Studies, 60,* 97–113. doi:10.1080/10510970902834833ß.

62. See note 58, U.S. religious landscape survey (2008, June).

63. Stone, K. G. (1995, February 19). Disability act everyone's responsibility in America. *Albuquerque Journal,* p. H3.

64. Solomon, A. (2012). *Far from the tree: Parents, children, and the search for identity.* New York: Scribner, pp. 68–69.

65. Braithwaite, D. O. & Labrecque, D. (1994). Responding to the Americans with Disabilities Act: Contributions of interpersonal communication research and training. *Journal of Applied Communication Research, 22,* 285–94. See also Braithwaite, D. O. (1991). "Just how much did that wheelchair cost?": Management of privacy boundaries by persons with disabilities. *Western Journal of Speech Communication, 55,* 254–275. See also Colvert, A. L., & Smith, J. (2000). What is reasonable? Workplace communication and people who are disabled. In D. O. Braithwaite and T. L. Thompson (Eds.), *Handbook of communication and people with disabilities: Research and application* (pp. 116–130). Mahwah, NJ: Erlbaum.

66. Fitch, V. (1985). The psychological tasks of old age. *Naropa Institute Journal of Psychology, 3,* 90–106.

67. Gergen, K. J., & Gergen, M. M. (2000). The new aging: Self construction and social values. In K. W. Schae & J. Hendricks (Eds.), *The societal impact of the aging process* (pp. 281–306). New York: Springer.

68. Bailey, T. A. (2010). Ageism and media discourse: Newspaper framing of middle age. *Florida Communication Journal, 38,* 43–56.

69. Frijters, P., & Beatoon, T. (2012). The mystery of the U-shaped relationship between happiness and age. *Journal of Economic Behavior & Organization, 82,* 525–542.

70. Giles, H., Ballard, D., & McCann, R. M. (2002). Perceptions of intergenerational communication across cultures: An Italian case. *Perceptual and Motor Skills, 95,* 583–591.

71. Ryan, E. B., & Butler, R. N. (1996). Communication, aging, and health: Toward understanding health provider relationships with older clients. *Health Communication, 8,* 191–197.

72. Harwood, J. (2007). *Understanding communication and aging: Developing knowledge and awareness.* Newbury Park, CA: Sage, p. 79.

73. Kroger, J., Martinussen, M., & Marcia, J. E. (2010). Identity status change during adolescence and young adulthood: A meta-analysis. *Journal of Adolescence, 33,* 683–698.

74. Galanaki, E. P. (2012). The imaginary audience and the personal fable: A test of Elkind's theory of adolescent egocentrism. *Psychology, 3*, 457–466.

75. Myers, K. K., & Sadaghiani, K. (2010). Millennials in the workplace: A communication perspective on Millennials' organizational relationships and performance. *Journal of Business and Psychology*, 225–238. doi: 10.1007/s10869-010-9173-7.

76. Lucas, K. (2011). The working class promise: A communicative account of mobility-based ambivalences. *Communication Monographs, 78*, 347–369.

77. Stuber, J. M. (2006). Talk of class. *Journal of Contemporary Ethnography, 35*, 285–318, quote on p. 306.

78. Kim, Y. K., & Sax, L. J. (2009). Student–faculty interaction in research universities: Differences by student gender, race, social class, and first-generation status. *Research in Higher Education, 50*, 437–459. doi: 10.1007/s11163-009-9127-x.

79. Kaufman, P. (2003). Learning to not labor: How working-class individuals construct middle-class identities. *Sociological Quarterly, 44*, 481–504.

80. Lubrano., A. (2004). *Limbo: Blue-collar roots, white-collar dreams.* Hoboken, NJ: John Wiley and Sons, and Lucas, K. (2011). The working class promise: A communicative account of mobility-based ambivalences. *Communication Monographs, 78*, 347–369. doi: 10.1080/03637751.2011.589461. For a case study on social class mobility, see Lucas, K. (2010). Moving up: The challenges of communicating a new social class identity. In D. O. Braithwaite & J. T. Wood (Eds.), *Casing interpersonal communication: Case studies in personal and social relationships* (pp. 17–24). Dubuque, IA: Kendall-Hunt.

81. Orbe, M. P., & Groscurth, C. R. (2004). A co-cultural theoretical analysis of communicating on campus and at home: Exploring the negotiation strategies of first generation college (FGC) students. *Qualitative Research Reports in Communication, 5*, 41–47.

82. Ibid, p. 45.

83. National Youth Violence Prevention Resource Center. (2007, December 20). Gangs fact sheet. Retrieved from http://www.safeyouth.org/scripts/facts/gangs.asp.

84. Andrlik, T. (2007, February 18). Legends of unbelievable Nordstrom service [Web log post]. Retrieved January 1, 2013, from http://toddand.com/2007/02/18/legends-of-unbelievable-nordstrom-service/.

85. Hartnell, C. A., Ou, A., & Kinicki, A. (2011). Organizational culture and organizational effectiveness: A meta-analytic investigation of the competing values framework's theoretical suppositions. *Journal of Applied Psychology, 96*(4), 677–694.

86. Arasaratnam, L. A. (2006). Further testing of a new model of intercultural communication competence. *Communication Research Reports, 23*, 93–99.

87. Pettigrew, T. F. & Tropp, L. R. (2000). Does intergroup contact reduce prejudice? Recent meta-analytic findings. In S. Oskamp (Ed.), *Reducing prejudice and discrimination: Social psychological perspectives* (pp. 93–114). Mahwah, NJ: Erlbaum.

88. Pettigrew, T. F., & Tropp, L. R. (2006, May). A meta-analytic test of intergroup contact theory. *Journal of Personality and Social Psychology, 90*, 751–783.

89. Kassing, J. W. (1997). Development of the intercultural willingness to communicate scale. *Communication Research Reports, 14*, 399–407.

90. Amichai-Hamburger, Y. & McKenna, K. Y. A. (2006). The contact hypothesis reconsidered: Interacting via the Internet. *Journal of Computer-Mediated Communication, 11*. Retrieved February 2, 2010, from http://jcmc.indiana.edu/vol11/issue3/amichai-hamburger.html.

91. Iyer, P. (1990). *The lady and the monk: Four seasons in Kyoto.* New York: Vintage, pp. 129–130.

92. Ibid., pp. 220–221.

93. Steves, R. (1996, May–September). Culture shock. *Europe through the Back Door Newsletter, 50*, 9.

94. Kim, M. S., Hunter, J. E., Miyahara, A., Horvath, A. M., Bresnahan, M., & Yoon, H. (1996). Individual- vs. culture-level dimensions of individualism and collectivism: Effects on preferred conversational styles. *Communication Monographs, 63*, 28–49.

95. Berger, C. R. (1979). Beyond initial interactions: Uncertainty, understanding, and the development of interpersonal relationships. In H. Giles & R. St. Clair (Eds.), *Language and social psychology* (pp. 122–144). Oxford: Blackwell.

96. Carrell, L. J. (1997). Diversity in the communication curriculum: Impact on student empathy. *Communication Education, 46*, 234–244.

97. Oberg, K. (1960). Cultural shock: Adjustment to new cultural environments. *Practical Anthropology, 7*, 177–182.

98. Ibid.

99. Bruhwiler, B. (2012, November 12). Culture shock! [Web log post]. Retrieved December 18, 2012, from http://www.joburgexpat.com/2012/11/culture-shock.html.

100. Chang, L. C.-N. (2011). My culture shock experience. *ETC: A Review of General Semantics, 68*(4), 403–405.

101. Kim, Y. Y. (2008). Intercultural personhood: Globalization and a way of being. *International Journal of Intercultural Relations, 32*, 359–368.

102. Kim, Y. Y. (2005). Adapting to a new culture: An integrative communication theory. In W. B. Gudykunst (Ed.), *Theorizing about intercultural communication* (pp. 375–400). Thousand Oaks, CA: Sage.

103. See note 101, Kim (2008).

## CHAPTER 4

1. Wang, W. S. Y. (1982). Language and derivative systems. In W. S. Y. Wang (Ed.), *Human communication: Language and its psychobiological basis.* San Francisco: Freeman, p. 36.

2. Sacks, O. (1989). *Seeing voices: A journey into the world of the deaf.* Berkeley: University of California Press, p. 17.

3. Adapted from O'Brien, J., & Kollock, P. (2001). *The production of reality* (3rd ed.). Thousand Oaks, CA: Pine Forge Press, p. 66.

4. Henneberger, M. (1999). Misunderstanding of word embarrasses Washington's new mayor. *New York Times.* Retrieved from http://www.nyt.com.

5. Ogden, C. K., & Richards, I. A. (1923). *The meaning of meaning.* New York: Harcourt Brace, p. 11.

6. Duck, S. (1994). Steady as she goes: Maintenance as a shared meaning system. In D. J. Caharg & L. Stafford (Eds.), *Communication and relational maintenance* (pp. 49–60). San Diego, CA: Academic Press.

7. Gaudin, S. (2011, March 25). OMG! Text shorthand makes the Oxford English Dictionary. *Computerworld.* Retrieved from http://www.computerworld.com/s/article/9215079/OMG_Text_shorthand_makes_the_dictionary.

8. Pearce, W. B., & Cronen, V. (1980). *Communication, action, and meaning.* New York: Praeger. See also Barge, J. K. (2004). Articulating CMM as a practical theory. *Human Systems: The Journal of Systemic Consultation and Management, 15*, 193–204, and Griffin, E. M. (2006). *A first look at communication theory* (6th ed.). New York: McGraw-Hill.

9. Genesis 2:19. This biblical reference was noted by. Mader, D. C. (1992, May). *The politically correct textbook: Trends in publishers' guidelines for the representation of marginalized groups.* Paper

presented at the annual convention of the Eastern Communication Association, Portland, ME.

10. Smith, G. W. (1998). The political impact of name sounds. *Communication Monographs, 65,* 154–172.

11. Fryer, R. G., & Levitt, S. D. (2004). The causes and consequences of distinctively black names. *Quarterly Journal of Economics, 119,* 767–805.

12. VanLear, C. A. (1991). Testing a cyclical model of communicative openness in relationship development. *Communication Monographs, 58,* 337–361.

13. Varadarajan, T. (1999, July 26). Big names, big battles. *New York Times.* Retrieved from http://aolsvc.aol.com/computercenter/internet/index.adp.

14. Cotton, J. L., O'Neill, B. S., & Griffin, A. (2008). The 'name game': Affective and hiring reactions to first names. *Journal of Managerial Psychology, 23,* 18–39.

15. Brunning, J. L., Polinko, N. K., Zerbst, J. I., & Buckingham, J. T. (2000). The effect on expected job success of the connotative meanings of names and nicknames. *Journal of Social Psychology, 140,* 197–201.

16. Coffey, B., & McLaughlin, P. A. (2009). Do masculine names help female lawyers become judges? Evidence from South Carolina. *American Law and Economics Review, 11,* 112–133.

17. Naftulin, D. H., Ware, J. E., Jr., & Donnelly, F. A. (1973, July). The Doctor Fox Lecture: A paradigm of educational seduction. *Journal of Medical Education, 48,* 630–635. See also Cory, C. T. (Ed.). (1980, May). Bafflegab pays. *Psychology Today, 13,* 12, and Marsh, H. W., & Ware, J. E., Jr. (1982). Effects of expressiveness, content coverage, and incentive on multidimensional student rating scales: New interpretations of the 'Dr. Fox' effect. *Journal of Educational Psychology, 74,* 126–134.

18. Armstrong, J. S. (1980). Unintelligible management research and academic prestige. *Interfaces, 10,* 80–86.

19. For a summary of research on this subject, see Bradac, J. J. (1990). Language attitudes and impression formation. In H. Giles & W. P. Robinson (Eds.). *The handbook of language and social psychology* (pp. 387–412). Chichester, England: Wiley.

20. Giles, H., & Poseland, P. F. (1975). *Speech style and social evaluation.* New York: Academic Press.

21. Miller, C., & Swift, K. (1991). *Words and women.* New York: Harper Collins, p. 27.

22. For a discussion of racist language, see Bosmajian, H. A. (1983). *The language of oppression.* Lanham, MD: University Press of America.

23. See note 9, Mader (1992, May, p. 5).

24. Kirkland, S. L., Greenberg, J., & Pysczynski, T. (1987). Further evidence of the deleterious effects of overheard derogatory ethnic labels: Derogation beyond the target. *Personality and Social Psychology Bulletin, 12,* 216–227.

25. For a review of the relationship between power and language, see Liska, J. (1992). Dominance-seeking language strategies: Please eat the floor, dogbreath, or I'll rip your lungs out, O.K.? In S. A. Deetz (Ed.), *Communication yearbook* 15 (pp. 427–456). Newbury Park, CA: Sage. See also Burrell, N. A., & Koper, R. J. (1994). The efficacy of powerful/powerless language on persuasiveness/credibility: A meta-analytic review. In R. W. Preiss & M. Allen (Eds.), *Prospects and precautions in the use of meta-analysis* (pp. 235–255). Dubuque, IA: Brown & Benchmark.

26. Hosman, L. A. (1989). The evaluative consequences of hedges, hesitations, and intensifiers: Powerful and powerless speech styles. *Human Communication Research, 15,* 383–406. Hosman, L. A. & Siltanen, S. A. (2006). Powerful and powerless language forms: Their consequences for impression formation, attributions of control of self and control of others, cognitive responses, and message memory. *Journal of Language and Social Psychology, 25,* 33–46.

27. Ng, S. H., & Bradac, J. J. (1993). *Power in language: Verbal communication and social influence.* Newbury Park, CA: Sage. See also Reid, S. A., & Ng, S. H. (1999). Language, power, and intergroup relations. *Journal of Social Issues, 55,* 119–139.

28. Parton, S., Siltanen, S. A., Hosman, L. A., & Langenderfer, J. (2002). Employment interview outcomes and speech style effects. *Journal of Language and Social Psychology, 21,* 144–161.

29. Reid, S. A., Keerie, N., Palomares, N. A. (2003). Language, gender salience, and social influence. *Journal of Language and Social Psychology, 22,* 210–233.

30. Guenzi, P., & Georges, L. (2010). Interpersonal trust in commercial relationships: Antecedents and consequences of customer trust in the salesperson. *European Journal of Marketing, 44,* 114–138.

31. Tannen, D. (1994). *Talking from 9 to 5.* New York: Morrow, p. 101.

32. Geddes, D. (1992). Sex roles in management: The impact of varying power of speech style on union members' perception of satisfaction and effectiveness. *Journal of Psychology, 126,* 589–607.

33. Samovar, L. A., & Porter, R. E. (1998). *Communication between cultures* (3rd ed.). Belmont, CA: Wadsworth ITP, pp. 58–59.

34. For a summary of scholarship supporting the notion of linguistic determinism, see Boroditsky, L. (2010, July 23). Lost in translation. *Wall Street Journal Online.* Retrieved August 11, 2010, from http://online.wsj.com/article/NA_WSJ_PUB :SB10001424052748703467304575383131592767868.html.

35. Whorf, B. (1956). The relation of habitual thought and behavior to language. In J. B. Carroll (Ed.), *Language, thought, and reality* (pp. 134–159). Cambridge, MA: MIT Press. See also Hoijer, H. (1994). The Sapir-Whorf hypothesis. In Larry A. Samovar & Richard E. Porter (Eds.), *Intercultural communication: A reader* (7th ed., pp. 194–200). Belmont, CA: Wadsworth.

36. Martin, L., & Pullum, G. (1991). *The great Eskimo vocabulary hoax.* Chicago: University of Chicago Press.

37. Giles, H., & Franklyn-Stokes, A. (1989). Communicator characteristics. In M. K. Asante & W. B. Gudykunst (Eds.), *Handbook of international and intercultural communication* (pp. 117–144). Newbury Park, CA: Sage.

38. For a critique, see Pinker, S. (1994). *The language instinct: How the mind creates language.* New York: Perennial. For support, see Lee, P. (1996). *The Whorf theory complex—A critical reconstruction.* Amsterdam: John Benjamins.

39. Giles, H., Coupland, J., & Coupland, N. (Eds.). (1991). *Contexts of accommodation: Developments in applied sociolinguistics.* Cambridge: Cambridge University Press.

40. See, for example, Bell, R. A., & Healey, J. G. (1992). Idiomatic communication and interpersonal solidarity in friends' relational cultures. *Human Communication Research, 18,* 307–335, and Bell, R. A., Buerkel-Rothfuss, N., & Gore, K. E. (1987). Did you bring the yarmulke for the Cabbage Patch Kid? The idiomatic communication of young lovers. *Human Communication Research, 14,* 47–67.

41. Cassell, J., & Tversky, D. (2005). The language of online intercultural community formation. *Journal of Computer-Mediated Communication, 10,* Article 2.

42. OMG: IM slang is invading everyday English. (2006, February 18). *NPR Weekend Edition.* Retrieved from http://www.npr.org/templates/story/story.php?storyId=5221618.

43. Maass, A., Salvi, D., Arcuri, L., & Semin, G. R. (1989). Language use in intergroup context. *Journal of Personality and Social Psychology, 57,* 981–993.

44. Weiner, M., & Mehrabian, A. (1968). *A language within language.* New York: Appleton-Century-Crofts.

45. Kubanyu, E. S., Richard, D. C., Bower, G. B., & Muraoka, M. Y. (1992). Impact of assertive and accusatory communication of distress and anger: A verbal component analysis. *Aggressive Behavior, 18,* 337–347.

46. Scott, T. L. (2000, November 27). Teens before their time. *Time,* p. 22.

47. Motley M. T., & Reeder, H. M. (1995). Unwanted escalation of sexual intimacy: Male and female perceptions of connotations and relational consequences of resistance messages. *Communication Monographs, 62,* 356–382.

48. Wallstein, T. (1986). Measuring the vague meanings of probability terms. *Journal of Experimental Psychology: General, 115,* 348–365.

49. Labov, T. (1992). Social and language boundaries among adolescents. *American Speech, 4,* 339–366.

50. UCLA slang. (DATE). Retrieved October 24, 2001, from http://www.cs.rpi.edu/~kennyz/doc/humor/slang.humor.

51. Kakutani, M. (2000, July 2). Computer slang scoffs at wetware. *Santa Barbara News-Press,* p. D1.

52. Myer, M., & Fleming, C. (1994, August 15). Silicon screenings. *Newsweek,* p. 63.

53. Twitter killing English, says actor. (2011, October 29). *Herald Sun.* Retrieved from http://www.heraldsun.com.au/entertainment/twitter-killing-english-says-actor/story-e6frf96x-1226179939640.

54. Henry, J. (2013, January 20). Art of essay-writing damaged by Twitter and Facebook, Cambridge don warns. *The Telegraph.* Retrieved from http://www.telegraph.co.uk/technology/social-media/9813109/Art-of-essay-writing-damaged-by-Twitter-and-Facebook-Cambridge-don-warns.html.

55. Evans, N., & Levinson, S. C. (2009). The myth of language universals: Language diversity and its importance for cognitive science. *Behavioral and Brain Sciences, 32,* 429–492.

56. Knapp, A. (2011, October 31). No, Twitter isn't ruining the English language. *Forbes.* Retrieved from http://www.forbes.com/sites/alexknapp/2011/10/31/no-twitter-isnt-ruining-the-english-language/.

57. OMG! The impact of social media on the English language [Web log post]. (2012, August 28). Retrieved from http://blogs.imediaconnection.com/blog/2012/08/28/omg-the-impact-of-social-media-on-the-english-language/.

58. Twitter all atwitter over newborn girl allegedly named Hashtag Jameson. (2012, November 28). *New York Daily News.* Retrieved from http://www.nydailynews.com/news/world/remains-unclear-hashtag-infant-actual-post-twitter-themed-spoof-article-1.1209420.

59. Mabillard, A. (2000). Words Shakespeare invented. *Shakespeare Online.* Retrieved from http://www.shakespeare-online.com/biography/wordsinvented.html.

60. Hayakawa, S. I. (1964). *Language in thought and action.* New York: Harcourt Brace.

61. Eisenberg, E. M. (1984). Ambiguity as strategy in organizational communication. *Communication Monographs, 51,* 227–242, and Eisenberg, E. M., & Witten, M. G. (1987). Reconsidering openness in organizational communication. *Academy of Management Review, 12,* 418–426.

62. Alberts, J. K. (1988). An analysis of couples' conversational complaints. *Communication Monographs, 55,* 184–197.

63. Streisand, B. (1992). Crystal Award speech delivered at the Crystal Awards, Women in Film luncheon.

64. Morrison, B. (2000). What you won't hear the pilot say. *USA Today,* p. A1.

65. Eisenberg, E. M. (Ed.). (2007). *Strategic ambiguities: Essays on communication, organization and identity.* Thousand Oaks, CA: Sage.

66. For detailed discussions of the relationship between gender and communication, see Canary, D. J., & Emmers-Sommer, T. M.

(1997). *Sex and gender differences in personal relationships.* New York: Guilford; Wood, J. (1994). *Gendered lives: Communication, gender, and culture.* Belmont, CA: Wadsworth; and Pearson, J. C. (1994). *Gender and communication* (2nd ed.). Madison, WI: Brown & Benchmark.

67. Sehulster, J. R. (2006). Things we talk about, how frequently, and to whom: Frequency of topics in everyday conversation as a function of gender, age, and marital status. *The American Journal of Psychology, 119,* 407–432.

68. Clark, R. A. (1998). A comparison of topics and objectives in a cross section of young men's and women's everyday conversations. In D. J. Canary & K. Dindia (Eds.), *Sex differences and similarities in communication: Critical essays and empirical investigations of sex and gender in interaction* (pp. 303–310). Mahwah, NJ: Erlbaum.

69. Wood, J. T. (2001). *Gendered lives: Communication, gender, and culture* (4th ed.). Belmont, CA: Wadsworth, p. 141.

70. Sherman, M. A., & Haas, A. (1984, June). Man to man, woman to woman. *Psychology Today, 17,* 72–73.

71. Haas, A., & Sherman, M. A. (1982). Conversational topic as a function of role and gender. *Psychological Reports, 51,* 453–454.

72. Mehl, M. R., Vazire, S., Ramírez-Esparza, N., Slatcher, R. B., & Pennebaker, J. W. (2007, July). Are women really more talkative than men? *Science, 317,* 82.

73. For a summary of research on the difference between male and female conversational behavior, see Giles, H., & Street, R. L., Jr. (1985). Communication characteristics and behavior. In M. L. Knapp & G. R. Miller (Eds.), *Handbook of interpersonal communication* (pp. 205–261). Beverly Hills, CA: Sage, and A. Kohn. (1988, February). Girl talk, guy talk. *Psychology Today, 22,* 65–66.

74. Fox, A. B., Bukatko, D., Hallahan, M., & Crawford, M. (2007). The medium makes a difference: Gender similarities and differences in instant messaging. *Journal of Language and Social Psychology, 26,* 389–397.

75. Carli, L. L. (1990). Gender, language, and influence. *Journal of Personality and Social Psychology, 59,* 941–951.

76. Canary, D. J., & Hause, K. S. (1993). Is there any reason to research sex differences in communication? *Communication Quarterly, 41,* 129–144.

77. Zahn, C. J. (1989). The bases for differing evaluations of male and female speech: Evidence from ratings of transcribed conversation. *Communication Monographs, 56,* 59–74. See also Grob, L. M., Meyers, R. A., & Schuh, R. (1997). Powerful? Powerless language use in group interactions: Sex differences or similarities? *Communication Quarterly, 45,* 282–303.

78. Wood, J. T., & Dindia, K. (1998). What's the difference? A dialogue about differences and similarities between women and men. In D. J. Canary & K. Dindia (Eds.), *Sex differences and similarities in communication: Critical essays and empirical investigations of sex and gender in interaction* (pp. 19–39). Mahwah, NJ: Erlbaum.

79. Rubin, D. L., Greene, K., & Schneider, D. (1994). Adopting gender-inclusive language reforms: Diachronic and synchronic variation. *Journal of Language and Social Psychology, 13,* 91–114.

80. Eisenegger, C, Haushofer, J., & Fehr, E. (2011). The role of testosterone in social interaction. *Trends in Cognitive Sciences, 15*(1), 263–271. See also Baker, S. (2007, January 1). The sex hormone secrets. *Psychology Today.* Retrieved from http://www.psychologytoday.com/articles/200612/the-sex-hormone-secrets.

81. Jones, A.C., & Josephs, R. A. (2006). Interspecies hormonal interactions between man and the domestic dog (Canis familiaris). *Hormones and Behavior, 50*(3), 393–400.

82. Pennebaker, J. W., Groom, C. J., Loew, D., & Dabbs, J. M. (2004). Testosterone as a social inhibitor: Two case studies of the effect of testosterone treatment on language. *Journal of Abnormal Psychology, 113*(1), 172.

83. Chen, C. P., Cheng, D. Z., Luo, Y.-J. (2011). Estrogen impacts on emotion: Psychological, neuroscience and endocrine studies. *Science China Life, 41*(11). Retrieved from http://www.eurekalert.org/pub_releases/2012-01/sicp-tio010912.php.

84. Dabbs, J.M., & Dabbs, M.G. (2000). *Heroes, rogues and lovers: On testosterone and behavior.* New York: McGraw-Hill.

85. How common is PMS? (2010). Premenstrual syndrome (PMS) fact sheet. U.S. Department of Health and Human Services. Retrieved from http://womenshealth.gov/publications/our-publications/fact-sheet/premenstrual-syndrome.cfm#ẹ.

86. Yong, E. (2009, April 7). Do testosterone and oestrogen affect our attitudes to fairness, trust, risk and altruism? *Discover.* Retrieved from https://blogs.discovermagazine.com/notrocketscience/2009/04/07/do-testosterone-and-oestrogen-affect-our-attitudes-to-fairness-trust-risk-and-altruism/.

87. See, for example, Geddes, D. (1992). Sex roles in management: The impact of varying power of speech style on union members' perception of satisfaction and effectiveness. *Journal of Psychology, 126*, 589–607.

## CHAPTER 5

1. Isay, D. (Ed.). (2007). *Listening is an act of love: A celebration of American life from the StoryCorps projects.* New York: Penguin Press, p. 15.

2. Franzblau, R.N. (1966). *New York Post.* Reprinted by 2Inspire Daily.com. Retrieved from http://www.2inspiredaily.com/Daily_Motivational_Quotes_Detail.asp?uid=3075&cat=Honesty.

3. See note 1, Isay (2007).

4. Ibid., p. 250.

5. The fact that changed everything: David Isay and StoryCorps. (n.d.). *GOOD Worldwide, LLC.* Retrieved from http://www.good.is/posts/the-fact-that-changed-everything-david-isay-and-storycorps.

6. StoryCorps: About us. (2013). Retrieved from http://storycorps.org/about/.

7. "One on 1: StoryCorps founder Dave Isay documents everyday lives." (2011, May 9). *NY1 News.* Retrieved from http://www.ny1.com/content/features/138771/one-on-1-storycorps-founder-dave-isay-documents-everyday-lives

8. StoryCorps National Day of Listening. (2012). Retrieved from http://nationaldayoflistening.org/.

9. Covey, S. (1989). *The seven habits of highly effective people.* New York: Simon & Schuster.

10. Brockner, J., & Ames, D. (2010). Not just holding forth: The effect of listening on leadership effectiveness (December 1, 2010). *Social Science Electronic Publishing.* Retrieved from http://papers.ssrn.com/sol3/papers.cfm?abstract_id=1916263.

11. Ames, D., Maissen, L. B., & Brockner, J. (2012). The role of listening in interpersonal influence. *Journal of Research in Personality, 46*, 345–349.

12. Kalargyrou, V., & Woods, R. H. (2011). Wanted: Training competencies for the twenty-first century. *International Journal of Contemporary Hospitality Management, 23*(3), 361–376.

13. Davis, J., Foley, A., Crigger, N., & Brannigan, M. C. (2008). Healthcare and listening: A relationship for caring. *International Journal of Listening, 22*(2), 168–175.

14. Helms, M. M., & Haynes, P. J. (1992). Are you really listening? The benefit of effective intra-organizational listening. *Journal of Managerial Psychology, 7*(6), 17–21. Retrieved from http://ezproxy.lib.uwf.edu/login?url=http://search.proquest.com/docview/215888773?accountid=14787.

15. See note 12, Kalargyrou & Woods (2011).

16. Brownell, J., & Wolvin, A. D. (2010). *What every student should know about listening.* Boston, MA: Allyn & Bacon; Wolvin, A. D.

(1984). Meeting the communication needs of the adult learner. *Communication Education, 33*, 267–271.

17. Prager, K. J., & Buhrmester, D. (1998). Intimacy and need fulfillment in couple relationships. *Journal of Social and Personal Relationships, 15*, 435–469. See also Birditt, K., & Antonucci, T. C. (2008). Life sustaining irritations? Relationship quality and mortality in the context of chronic illness. *Social Science & Medicine, 67*, 1291–1299.

18. Campbell, L., Simpson, J. A., Boldry, J. G., & Rubin, H. (2010, July). Trust, variability in relationship evaluations, and relationship processes. *Journal of Personality and Social Psychology, 99*, 14–31.

19. Hjalone, K. K., & Pecchioni, L. L. (2001). Relational listening: A grounded theoretical model. *Communication Reports, 14*, 59–71.

20. Jalongo, M. (2010). Listening in early childhood: An interdisciplinary review of the literature. *International Journal of Listening, 24*, 1–18.

21. Horowitz, S. (2012, Novembver 11). The science and art of listening. *New York Times,* p. SR10.

22. Powers, W. G., & Witt, P. L. (2008). Expanding the theoretical framework of communication fidelity. *Communication Quarterly, 56*, 247–267; Fitch-Hauser, M., Powers, W. G., O'Brien, K., & Hanson, S. (2007). Extending the conceptualization of listening fidelity. *International Journal of Listening, 21*, 81–91; Powers, W. G., & Bodie, G. D. (2003). Listening fidelity: Seeking congruence between cognitions of the listener and the sender. *International Journal of Listening, 17*, 19–31.

23. Nichols, R. G. (1948). Factors in listening comprehension. *Speech Monographs, 15*, 154–163.

24. Imhof, M. (2002). In the eye of the beholder: Children's perception of good and poor listening behavior. *International Journal of Listening, 16*, 40–57.

25. Lewis, M. H., & Reinsch, N. L., Jr. (1988). Listening in organizational environments. *Journal of Business Communication, 25*, 49–67.

26. Thomas, T. L., & Levine, T. R. (1994). Disentangling listening and verbal recall: Related but separate constructs? *Human Communication Research, 21*, 103–127.

27. See note 23, Nichols (1948).

28. Cowan, N., & AuBuchon, A. M. (2008). Short-term memory loss over time without retroactive stimulus interference. *Psychonomic Bulletin and Review, 15*, 230–235.

29. Brownell, J. (1990). Perceptions of effective listeners: A management study. *Journal of Business Communication, 27*, 401–415.

30. Rautalinko, E., Lisper, H., & Ekehammar, B. (2007). Reflective listening in counseling: Effects of training time and evaluator social skills. *American Journal of Psychotherapy, 61*, 191–209.

31. Reported by Nichols, R., & Stevens, L. (1957, September–October). Listening to people. *Harvard Business Review, 35*, 85–92.

32. Imhof, M. (2008). What have you listened to in school today? *International Journal of Listening, 22*, 1–12.

33. Lawson, K. (2012). The real power of parental reading aloud: Exploring the affective and attentional dimensions. *Australian Journal of Education, 56*, 257–272.

34. See note 32, Imhof (2008).

35. Winter, W., Ferreira, A., & Bowers, N. (1973). Decision-making in married and unrelated couples. *Family Process, 12*, 83–94.

36. Langer, E. (1990). *Mindfulness.* Reading, MA: Addison-Wesley.

37. Burgoon, J. K., Berger, C. R., & Waldron, V. R. (2000). Mindfulness and interpersonal communication. *Journal of Social Issues, 56*, 105–127. See note 36, Langer (1990, p. 90).

38. Nichols, R. G. (1987, September). Listening is a ten-part skill. *Nation's Business, 75*, 40.

39. Vangelisti, A. L., Knapp, M. L., & Daly, J. A. (1990). Conversational narcissism. *Communication Monographs, 57*, 251–274.

40. McComb, K. B., & Jablin, F. M. (1984). Verbal correlates of interviewer empathic listening and employment interview outcomes. *Communication Monographs, 51*, 353–371.

41. Hansen, J. (2007). *24/7: How cell phones and the Internet change the way we live, work, and play.* New York: Praeger. See also Turner, J. W., & Reinsch, N. L. (2007). The business communicator as presence allocator: Multicommunicating, equivocality, and status at work. *Journal of Business Communication, 44*, 36–58.

42. Sarampalis, A., Kalluri, S., Edwards, B., & Hafter, E. (2009). Objective measures of listening effort: Effects of background noise and noise reduction. *Journal of Speech, Language & Hearing Research, 52*, 1230–1240.

43. Info stupidity. (2005, April 30). *New Scientist, 186*, 6–7.

44. Lin, L. (2009, September 15). Breadth-biased versus focused cognitive control in media multitasking behaviors. *Proceedings of the National Academy of Sciences, 106*, 15521–15522. Retrieved from http://www.pnas.org/content/106/37/15521.full.pdf.

45. Ophir, E., Nass, C., & Wagner, A. (2009). Cognitive control in media multitaskers. *Proceedings of the National Academy of Sciences, 106*, 15583–15587.

46. Drullman, R., & Smoorenburg, G. F. (1997). Audio-visual perception of compressed speech by profoundly hearing-impaired subjects. *Audiology, 36*, 165–177.

47. Listen to this: Hearing problems can stress relationships. (2008). Retrieved from http://www.energizer.com/livehealthy/#listentothis. See also D. N. Shafer, (2007). Hearing loss hinders relationships. *ASHA Leader, 12*, 5–7.

48. Kline, N. (1999). *Time to think: Listening to ignite the human mind.* London: Ward Lock, p. 21.

49. Menz, F., & Al-Roubaie, A. (2008). Interruptions, status and gender in medical interviews: The harder you brake, the longer it takes. *Discourse & Society, 19*, 645–666.

50. Imhof, M. (2003). The social construction of the listener: Listening behaviors across situations, perceived listener status, and cultures. *Communication Research Reports, 20*, 357–366.

51. Zohoori, A. (2013). A cross-cultural comparison of the HURIER Listening Profile among Iranian and U.S. students. *International Journal of Listening, 27*, 50–60.

52. Imhof, M. (2003). The social construction of the listener: Listening behaviors across situations, perceived listener status, and cultures. *Communication Research Reports, 20*, 357–366.

53. Weger, H., Jr., Castle, G. R., & Emmett, M. C. (2010). Active listening in peer interviews: The influence of message paraphrasing on perceptions of listening skill. *International Journal of Listening, 24*, 34–49.

54. Remer, R., & De Mesquita, P. (1990). Teaching and learning the skills of interpersonal confrontation. In D. Cahn (Ed.), *Intimates in conflict: A communication perspective* (pp. 225–252). Norwood, NJ: Erlbaum, p. 242.

55. Villaume, W. A., & Bodie, G. D. (2007). Discovering the listener within us: The impact of trait-like personality variables and communicator styles on preferences for listening style. *International Journal of Listening, 21*, 102–123.

56. Gearhart, C. G., & Bodie, G. D. (2011). Active-empathic listening as a general social skill: Evidence from bivariate and canonical correlations. *Communication Reports, 24*, 86–98. doi: 10.1080/08934215.2011.610731.

57. Paraschos, S. (2013). Unconventional doctoring: A medical student's reflections on total suffering. *Journal of Palliative Medicine, 16*, 325.

58. Huerta-Wong, J. E., & Schoech, R. (2010). Experiential learning and learning environments: The case of active listening skills. *Journal of Social Work Education, 46*, 85–101.

59. Luedtke, K. (1987, January 7). What good is free speech if no one listens? *Los Angeles Times.* Retrieved from http://articles.latimes.com/1987-01-07/local/me-2347_1_free-speech.

60. Adapted from Infante, D. A. (1988). *Arguing constructively.* Prospect Heights, IL: Waveland, pp. 71–75.

61. Sprague, J., & Stuart, D. (1992). *The speaker's handbook* (3rd ed.). Fort Worth, TX: Harcourt Brace Jovanovich, p. 172.

62. Gearhart, C. C., Denham, J. P., & Bodie, G. D. (2013, November). *Listening is a goal-directed activity.* Paper presented at the annual meeting of the National Communiation Association, Washington, DC.

63. Bodie, G. D., Vickery, A. J., & Gearhart, C. C. (2013). The nature of supportive listening, I: Exploring the relation between supportive listeners and supportive people. *International Journal of Listening, 27*, 39–49.

64. Chia, H. L. (2009). Exploring facets of a social network to explicate the status of social support and its effects on stress. *Social Behavior & Personality: An International Journal, 37*(5), 701–710. See also Segrin, C., & Domschke, T. (2011). Social support, loneliness, recuperative processes, and their direct and indirect effects on health. *Health Communication, 26*, 221–232.

65. Giles, L. C., Glonek, G. F., Luszcz, M. A., & Andrews, G. R. (2005, July). Effect of social networks on 10-year survival in very old Australians: The Australian longitudinal study of aging. *Journal of Epidemiology & Community Health, 59*(7), 574–579.

66. Robinson, J. D., & Tian, Y. (2009). Cancer patients and the provision of informational social support. *Health Communication, 24*, 381–390.

67. See research cited in Burleson, B. (1994). Comforting messages: Their significance and effects. In J. A. Daly & J. M. Wiemann (Eds.), *Communicating strategically: Strategies in interpersonal communication* (pp. 3–28). Hillside, NJ: Erlbaum.

68. For a summary of research on online support groups, see Walther, J. B., & Boyd, S. (2002). Attraction to computer-mediated social support. In C. A. Lin & D. Atkin (Eds.), *Communication technology and society: Audience adoption and uses* (pp. 153–188). Cresskill, NJ: Hampton Press.

69. Tanis, M. (2007). Online support groups. In A. Joinson, K. McKenna, T. Postmes, & U. Reips (Eds.), *The Oxford handbook of Internet psychology* (pp. 137–152). Oxford: Oxford University Press.

70. Humorous example of social media monitoring: Sydney University [Web log post]. (2009, September 7). Retrieved from http://www.altimetergroup.com/2009/09/humorous-example-of-social-media-monitoring-sydney-university.html.

71. Caruso, R. (2011). A real example of effectie social media monitoring and engagement. *Bundle Post.* Retrieved from http://bundlepost.wordpress.com/2011/11/07/a-real-example-of-effective-social-media-monitoring-and-engagement/.

72. Petrocelli, T. (2012, December 20). One rule with social media and social networking: Don't be creepy [Web log post]. Retrieved from http://www.esg-global.com/blogs/one-rule-with-social-media-and-social-networking-dont-be-creepy/.

73. For a comprehensive discussion of gender similarities and differences in social support, see Burleson, B. R. (2002, Winter). Psychological mediators of sex differences in emotional support: A reflection on the mosaic. *Communication Reports, 15*, 71–79.

74. Weaver, J. B., & Kirtley, M. D. (1995). Listening styles and empathy. *Southern Communication Journal, 60*, 131–140.

75. Currona, C. E., Suhr, J. A., & MacFarlane, R. (1990). Interpersonal transactions and the psychological sense of support. In S. Duck & R. Silver (Eds.), *Personal relationships and social support* (pp. 30–45). London: Sage.

76. Goldsmith, D. J., & Fitch, K. (1997). The normative context of advice as social support. *Human Communication Research, 23*, 454–476.

77. Goldsmith, D. J., & Fitch, K. (1997). The normative context of advice as social support. *Human Communication Research, 23,* 454–476. See also Goldsmith, D. J., & MacGeorge, E. L. (2000). The impact of politeness and relationship on perceived quality of advice about a problem. *Human Communication Research, 26,* 234–263. See also Burleson, B. (2008). What counts as effective emotional support?" In M. T. Motley (Ed.), *Studies in Applied Interpersonal Communication* (pp. 207–227). Thousand Oaks, CA: Sage.

78. Goldsmith, D. (1994, November). *The sequential placement of advice.* Paper presented at the annual convention of the Speech Communication Association, New Orleans.

79. Burleson, B. R. (2008). What counts as effective emotional support? In M. T. Motley (Ed.), *Studies in applied interpersonal communication* (pp. 2-7-227). Thousand Oaks, CA: Sage.

80. Goldsmith, D. (2000). Soliciting advice: The role of sequential placement in mitigating face threat. *Communication Monographs, 67,* 1–19.

81. MacGeorge, E. L., Feng, B., & Thompson, E. R. (2008). "Good" and "bad" advice: How to advise more effectively. In M. T. Motley (Ed.), *Studies in applied interpersonal communication* (pp. 145–164). Thousand Oaks, CA: Sage.

82. Goldsmith, D. J., & MacGeorge, E. L. (2000). The impact of politeness and relationship on perceived quality of advice about a problem. *Human Communication Research, 26,* 234–263. See also Miczo, N., & Burgoon, J. K. (2008). Facework and nonverbal behavior in social support interactions within romantic dyads. In M. T. Motley (Ed.), *Studies in applied interpersonal communication* (pp. 244–266). Thousand Oaks, CA: Sage.

83. See, for example, Pearlin, L., & McCall, M. (1990). Occupational stress and marital support: A description of microprocesses. In J. Eckenrode & S. Gore (Eds.), *Stress between work and family* (pp. 39–60). New York: Plenum.

84. Hample, D. (2006). Anti-comforting messages. In K. M. Galvin & P. J. Cooper (Eds.), *Making connections: Readings in relational communication* (4th ed., pp. 222–227). Los Angeles, CA: Roxbury.

85. Davidowitz, M., & Myrim, R. D. (1984). Responding to the bereaved: An analysis of "helping" statements. *Death Education, 8,* 1–10. See also Servaty-Seib, H. L., & Burleson, B. R. (2008). Bereaved adolescents' evaluations of the helpfulness of support-intended statements. *Journal of Social and Personal Relationships, 24,* 207–223.

86. Helping adults, children cope with grief. (2001, September 13). *Washington Post.* Retrieved from http://www.washingtonpost.com/wp-dyn/articles/A23679-2001Sep13.html.

87. Adapted from Burleson, B. R. (1994). Comforting messages: Features, functions, and outcomes. In J. A. Daly & J. M. Wiemann (Eds.), *Strategic interpersonal communication* (pp. 135–161). Hillsdale, NJ: Erlbaum, p. 140.

88. Gottman, J. M. (1999). *The marriage clinic: A scientifically-based marital therapy.* New York: Norton, p. 10.

89. Lewis, T., & Manusov, V. (2009). Listening to another's distress in everyday relationships. *Communication Quarterly, 57,* 282–301.

90. Hosman, L. A. (1987). The evaluational consequences of topic reciprocity and self-disclosure reciprocity. *Communication Monographs, 54,* 420–435.

91. Clark, R. A., & Delia, J. G. (1997). Individuals' preferences for friends' approaches to providing support in distressing situations. *Communication Reports, 10,* 115–121.

92. Day, A. L., & Livingstone, H. A. (2003). Gender differences in perceptions of stressors and utilization of social support among university students. *Canadian Journal of Behavioural Science, 35,* 73–83.

93. See, for example, Silver, R., & Wortman, C. (1981). Coping with undesirable life events. In J. Garber & M. Seligman (Eds.), *Human helplessness: Theory and applications* (pp. 279–340). New York: Academic Press, and Young, C. R., Giles, D. E., & Plantz, M. C. (1982). Natural networks: Help-giving and help-seeking in two rural communities. *American Journal of Community Psychology, 10,* 457–469.

94. See note 91, Clark & Delia (1997).

95. Burleson, B. (2008). What counts as effective emotional support?" In M. T. Motley (Ed.), *Studies in Applied Interpersonal Communication* (pp. 207–227). Thousand Oaks, CA: Sage.

96. Young, R. W., & Cates, C. M. (2004). Emotional and directive listening in peer mentoring. *International Journal of Listening, 18,* 21–33.

97. Mankell, H. (2011, December 10). The art of listening. *New York Times.* Retrieved from http://www.nytimes.com/2011/12/11/opinion/sunday/in-africa-the-art-of-listening.html?_r=0.

## CHAPTER 6

1. Gossom, T., Jr. (2008). *Walk-on: My reluctant journey to integration at Auburn University.* Ann Arbor, MI: State Street Press, p. 13.

2. For a survey of the issues surrounding the definition of nonverbal communication, see Knapp, M., & Hall, J. A. (2010). *Nonverbal communication in human interaction* (6th ed.). Belmont, CA: Wadsworth, Chapter 1.

3. Keating, C. F. (2006). Why and how the silent self speaks volumes. In V. Manusov & M. L. Patterson (Eds.), *The SAGE handbook of nonverbal communication* (pp. 321–340). Thousand Oaks, CA: Sage.

4. Manusov, F. (1991, Summer). Perceiving nonverbal messages: Effects of immediacy and encoded intent on receiver judgments. *Western Journal of Speech Communication, 55,* 235–253.

5. For a discussion of intentionality, see note 2, Knapp & Hall (2010, pp. 9–12).

6. Palmer, M. T., & Simmons, K. B. (1995). Communicating intentions through nonverbal behaviors: Conscious and nonconscious encoding of liking. *Human Communication Research, 22,* 128–160.

7. Dennis, A. R., Kinney, S. T., & Hung, Y. T. (1999). Gender differences in the effects of media richness. *Small Group Research, 30,* 405–437.

8. See Smith, S. W. (1994). Perceptual processing of nonverbal relational messages. In D. E. Hewes (Ed.), *The cognitive bases of interpersonal communication* (pp. 87–110). Hillsdale, NJ: Erlbaum.

9. Burgeon, J., Buller, D., Hale, J., & de Turck, M. (1984, Spring). Relational messages associated with nonverbal behaviors. *Human Communication Research, 10,* 351–378.

10. Lim, G. Y., & Roloff, M. E. (1999). Attributing sexual consent. *Journal of Applied Communication Research, 27,* 1–23.

11. Safeway clerks object to "service with a smile." (1998, September 2). *San Francisco Chronicle.*

12. Druckmann, D., Rozelle, R. M., & Baxter, J. C. (1982). *Nonverbal communication: Survey, theory, and research.* Newbury Park, CA: Sage.

13. Motley, M. T., & Camden, C. T. (1988, Winter). Facial expression of emotion: A comparison of posed expressions versus spontaneous expressions in an interpersonal communication setting. *Western Journal of Speech Communication, 52,* 1–22.

14. See, for example, Rosenthal, R., Hall, J. A., Matteg, M. R. D., Rogers, P. L., & Archer, D. (1979). *Sensitivity to nonverbal communication: The PONS test.* Baltimore, MD: Johns Hopkins University Press.

15. Hall, J. A. (1979). Gender, gender roles, and nonverbal communication skills. In R. Rosenthal (Ed.), *Skill in nonverbal communication: Individual differences* (pp. 32–67). Cambridge, MA: Oelgeschlager, Gunn, and Hain, pp. 32–67.

16. Research supporting these claims is cited in Burgoon, J. K., & Hoobler, G. D. (2002). Nonverbal signals. In M. L. Knapp & J. A. Daly (Eds.)., *Handbook of interpersonal communication* (3rd ed., pp. 240–299). Thousand Oaks, CA: Sage.

17. Jones, S. E., & LeBaron, C. D. (2002). Research on the relationship between verbal and nonverbal communication: Emerging interactions. *Journal of Communication, 52*, 499–521.

18. Rourke, B. P. (1989). *Nonverbal learning disabilities: The syndrome and the model.* New York: Guilford Press.

19. Fudge, E. S. (n.d.). Nonverbal learning disorder syndrome? Retrieved from http://www.nldontheweb.org/fudge.htm.

20. Ekman, P., & Friesen, W. (1975). *Unmasking the face.* New York: Prentice Hall.

21. Birdwhistell, R. (1970). *Kinesics and context.* Philadelphia: University of Pennsylvania Press, Chapter 9.

22. Ekman, P., Friesen, W. V., & Baer, J. (1984, May). The international language of gestures. *Psychology Today, 18*, 64–69.

23. Hall, E. (1969). *The hidden dimension.* Garden City, NY: Anchor Books.

24. Ibid.

25. Rubin, D. L. (1986). "Nobody play by the rules he know": Ethnic interference in classroom questioning events. In Y. Y. Kim (Ed.), *International and intercultural communication yearbook* (pp. 158–177). Beverly Hills, CA: Sage.

26. Warnecke, A. M., Masters, R. D., & Kempter, G. (1992). The roots of nationalism: Nonverbal behavior and xenophobia. *Ethnology and Sociobiology, 13*, 267–282.

27. Weitz, S. (Ed.). (1974). *Nonverbal communication: Readings with commentary.* New York: Oxford University Press.

28. For a comparison of Japanese and Arab nonverbal communication norms, see Leathers, D. G. (1986). *Successful nonverbal communication.* New York: Macmillan, pp. 258–261.

29. Booth-Butterfield, M., & Jordan, F. (1988). *"Act like us": Communication adaptation among racially homogeneous and heterogeneous groups.* Paper presented at the Speech Communication Association meeting, New Orleans.

30. For a review, see Tabak, J. A., & Zayas, V. (2012). The roles of featural and configural face processing in snap judgments of sexual orientation. *PLoS ONE, 7*(5), e36671.

31. Woolery, L. M. (2007). Gaydar: A social-cognitive analysis. *Journal of Homosexuality, 53*(3), 9–17.

32. Rule, N.O. (2010). Sexual orientation perception involves gendered facial cues. *Personality and Social Psychology Bulletin, 36*(10), 1318–1331.

33. Hall, J. A. (2006). Women and men's nonverbal communication. In V. Manusov & M. L. Patterson (Eds.), *The Sage handbook of nonverbal communication* (pp. 201–218). Thousand Oaks, CA: Sage.

34. Canary, D. J., & Emmers-Sommer, T. M. (1997). *Sex and gender differences in personal relationships.* New York: Guilford Press.

35. Knöfler, T., & Imhof, M. (2007). Does sexual orientation have an impact on nonverbal behavior in interpersonal communication? *Journal of Nonverbal Behavior, 31*, 189–204.

36. Hall, J. A., Carter, J. D., & Horgan, T. G. (2001). Status roles and recall of nonverbal cues. *Journal of Nonverbal Behavior, 25*, 79–100.

37. Cross, E. S., & Franz, E. A. (2003, March 30–April 1). *Talking hands: Observation of bimanual gestures as a facilitative working memory mechanism.* Paper presented at the Cognitive Neuroscience Society 10th Annual Meeting, New York.

38. Derks, D., Bos, A. E. R., & von Grumbkow, J. (2001). Emoticons and social interaction on the Internet: The importance of social context. *Computers in Human Behavior, 23*, 842–849.

39. See note 23, Hall (1969).

40. Kleinke, C. R. (1977). Compliance to requests made by gazing and touching experimenters in field settings. *Journal of Experimental Social Psychology, 13*, 218–233.

41. Argyle, M. F., Alkema, F., & Gilmour, R. (1971). The communication of friendly and hostile attitudes: Verbal and nonverbal signals. *European Journal of Social Psychology, 1*, 385–402.

42. Buller, D. B., & Burgoon, J. K. (1994). Deception: Strategic and nonstrategic communication. In J. Daly & J. M. Wiemann (Eds.), *Interpersonal communication* (pp. 191–223). Hillsdale, NJ: Erlbaum.

43. Burgoon, J. K., Buller, D. B., Guerrero, L. K., & Feldman, C. M. (1994). Interpersonal deception: VI. Effects on preinteractional and international factors on deceiver and observer perceptions of deception success. *Communication Studies, 45*, 263–280, and Burgoon, J. K., Buller, D. B., & Guerrero, L. K. (1995). Interpersonal deception: IX. Effects of social skill and nonverbal communication on deception success and detection accuracy. *Journal of Language and Social Psychology, 14*, 289–311.

44. Riggio, R. G., & Freeman, H. S. (1983). Individual differences and cues to deception. *Journal of Personality and Social Psychology, 45*, 899–915.

45. Vrij, A. (2006). Nonverbal communication and deception. In V. Manusov & M. L. Patterson (Eds.), *The SAGE handbook of nonverbal communication* (pp. 341–359). Thousand Oaks, CA: Sage.

46. DePaulo, B. M., Lindsay, J. J., Malone, B. E., Muhlenbruck, L., Charlton, K., & Cooper, H. (2003). Cues to deception. *Psychological Bulletin, 129*, 74–118, and Vrig, A., Edward, K., Roberts, K. P., & Bull, R. (2000). Detecting deceit via analysis of verbal and nonverbal behavior. *Journal of Nonverbal Behavior, 24*, 239–263.

47. Dunbar, N. E., Ramirez, A., Jr., & Burgoon, J. K. (2003). The effects of participation on the ability to judge deceit. *Communication Reports, 16*, 23–33.

48. Vrig, A., Akehurst, L., Soukara, S., & Bull, R. (2004). Detecting deceit via analyses of verbal and nonverbal behavior in children and adults. *Human Communication Research, 30*, 8–41.

49. Millar, M. G., & Millar, K. U. (1998). The effects of suspicion on the recall of cues to make veracity judgments. *Communication Reports, 11*, 57–64.

50. McCornack, S. A., & Parks, M. R. (1990). What women know that men don't: Sex differences in determining the truth behind deceptive messages. *Journal of Social and Personal Relationships, 7*, 107–118.

51. McCornack, S. A., & Levine, T. R. (1990). When lovers become leery: The relationship between suspicion and accuracy in detecting deception. *Communication Monographs, 7*, 219–230.

52. deTurck, M. A. (1991). Training observers to detect spontaneous deception: Effects of gender. *Communication Reports, 4*, 81–89.

53. Burgoon, J. K., & Levine, T. R. (2010). Advances in deception detection. In S. W. Smith & S. R. Wilson (Eds.), *New directions in interpersonal communication research* (pp. 201–220). Thousand Oaks, CA: Sage.

54. Guerrero, L. K., & Floyd, K. (2006). *Nonverbal communication in close relationships.* Mahwah, NJ: Erlbaum.

55. Levine, T. (2009). To catch a liar. *Communication Currents, 4*, 1–2.

56. Maurer, R. E., & Tindall, J. H. (1983). Effect of postural congruence on client's perception of counselor empathy. *Journal of Counseling Psychology, 30*, 158–163.

57. Manusov, V. (1995). Reacting to changes in nonverbal behaviors: Relational satisfaction and adaptation patterns in romantic dyads. *Human Communication Research, 21*, 456–477.

58. Myers, M. B., Templer, D., & Brown, R. (1984). Coping ability of women who become victims of rape. *Journal of Consulting and Clinical Psychology, 52*, 73–78. See also Rubenstein, C. (1980, August). Body language that speaks to muggers. *Psychology Today,*

*20*, 20, and Meer, J. (1984, May). Profile of a victim. *Psychology Today, 24,* 76.

59. Hall, J. A., Coats, E. J., & Smith LeBeau, L. (2005). Nonverbal behavior and the vertical dimension of social relations: A meta-analysis. *Psychological Bulletin, 131,* 898–924.

60. Carney, D. R., Cuddy, A .J., & Yap, A. J. (2010). Power posing: Brief nonverbal displays affect neuroendocrine levels and risk tolerance. *Psychological Science, 21,* 1363–1368.

61. Iverson, J. M. (1999). How to get to the cafeteria: Gesture and speech in blind and sighted children's spatial descriptions. *Developmental Psychology, 35,* 1132–1142.

62. Ekman, P. (1985). *Telling lies: Clues to deceit in the marketplace, politics, and marriage.* New York: Norton, pp. 109–110.

63. Donaghy, W., & Dooley, B. F. (1994). Head movement, gender, and deceptive communication. *Communication Reports, 7,* 67–75.

64. Ekman, P., & Friesen, W. V. (1974). Nonverbal behavior and psychopathology. In R. J. Friedman & M. N. Katz (Eds.), *The psychology of depression: Contemporary theory and research* (pp. 202–232). Washington, DC: J. Winston.

65. Sutton, R., & Rafaeli, A. (1988). Untangling the relationship between displayed emotions and organizational sales: The case of convenience stores. *Academy of Management Journal, 31,* 461–487, p. 463.

66. Matsumoto, D. (2006). Culture and nonverbal behavior. In V. Manusov & M. L. Patterson (Eds.), *The SAGE handbook of nonverbal communication* (pp. 219–235). Thousand Oaks, CA: Sage.

67. Edman, P., Friesen, W. V., & Ellsworth, P. (1972). *Emotion in the human face: Guidelines for research and an integration of findings.* Elmsford, NY: Pergamon.

68. Kleinke, C. L. (1986). Gaze and eye contact: A research review. *Psychological Bulletin, 100,* 78–100.

69. Starkweather, J. A. (1961). Vocal communication of personality and human feeling. *Journal of Communication, II,* 69, 63–71; and Scherer, K. R., Koiwunaki, J., & Rosenthal, R. (1972). Minimal cues in the vocal communication of affect: Judging emotions from content-masked speech. *Journal of Psycholinguistic Speech, I,* 269–285. See also Cox, F. S., & Olney, C. (1985). *Vocalic communication of relational messages.* Paper delivered at the annual meeting of the Speech Communication Association, Denver.

70. Burns, K. L., & Beier, E. G. (1973). Significance of vocal and visual channels for the decoding of emotional meaning. *Journal of Communication, 23,* 118–130. See also Hegstrom, T. G. (1979). Message impact: What percentage is nonverbal? *Western Journal of Speech Communication, 43,* 134–143, and McMahan, E. M. (1976). Nonverbal communication as a function of attribution in impression formation. *Communication Monographs, 43,* 287–294.

71. Mehrabian, A., & Weiner, M. (1967). Decoding of inconsistent communications. *Journal of Personality and Social Psychology, 6,* 109–114.

72. Buller, D., & Aune, K. (1992). The effects of speech rate similarity on compliance: Application of communication accommodation theory. *Western Journal of Communication, 56,* 37–53. See also Buller, D., LePoire, B. A., Aune, K., & Eloy, S. V. (1992). Social perceptions as mediators of the effect of speech rate similarity on compliance. *Human Communication Research, 19,* 286–311, and Francis, J., & Wales, R. (1994). Speech a la mode: Prosodic cues, message interpretation, and impression formation. *Journal of Language and Social Psychology, 13,* 34–44.

73. Kimble, C. E., & Seidel, S. D. (1991). Vocal signs of confidence. *Journal of Nonverbal Behavior, 15,* 99–105.

74. Tusing, K. J., & Dillard, J. P. (2000). The sounds of dominance: Vocal precursors of perceived dominance during interpersonal influence. *Human Communication Research, 26,* 148–171.

75. Zuckerman, M., & Driver, R. E. (1989). What sounds beautiful is good: The vocal attractiveness stereotype. *Journal of Nonverbal Behavior, 13,* 67–82.

76. Hosoda, M., & Stone-Romero, E. (2010). The effects of foreign accents on employment-related decisions. *Journal of Managerial Psychology, 25,* 113–132.

77. For a summary, see Knapp, M. L., & Hall, J. A. (1992). *Nonverbal communication in human interaction* (3rd ed.). New York: Holt, Rinehart and Winston, pp. 93–132. See also Hensley, W. (1992). Why does the best looking person in the room always seem to be surrounded by admirers? *Psychological Reports, 70,* 457–469.

78. Bennett, J. (2010, July 19). The beauty advantage. *Newsweek.* Retrieved from http://www.newsweek.com/2010/07/19/the-beauty-advantage.html.

79. Guerrero, L. K., & Hecht, M. L. (2008). *The nonverbal communication reader: Classic and contemporary readings* (3rd ed.). Long Grove, IL: Waveland Press.

80. Persico, N., Postlewaite, A., & Silverman, D. (2004). The effect of adolescent experience of labor market outcomes: The case of height. *Journal of Political Economy, 112,* 1019–1053.

81. Yee, N., & Bailenson, J. N. (2008). A method for longitudinal behavioral data collection in Second Life. *Presence, 17,* 594–596.

82. Ritts, V., Patterson, M. L., & Tubbs, M. E. (1992). Expectations, impressions, and judgments of physically attractive students: A review. *Review of Educational Research, 62,* 413–426.

83. Abdala, K. F., Knapp, M. L., & Theune, K. E. (2002). Interaction appearance theory: Changing perceptions of physical attractiveness through social interaction. *Communication Theory, 12,* 8–40.

84. Bickman, L. (1974). The social power of a uniform. *Journal of Applied Social Psychology, 4,* 47–61.

85. Lawrence, S. G., & Watson, M. (1991). Getting others to help: The effectiveness of professional uniforms in charitable fund raising. *Journal of Applied Communication Research, 19,* 170–185.

86. Rehman, S. U., Nietert, P. J., Cope, D. W., & Kilpatrick, A. O. (2005). What to wear today? Effect of doctor's attire on the trust and confidence of patients. *The American Journal of Medicine, 118,* 1279–1286.

87. Bickman, L. (1974, April). Social roles and uniforms: Clothes make the person. *Psychology Today, 7,* 48–51.

88. Temple, L. E., & Loewen, K. R. (1993). Perceptions of power: First impressions of a woman wearing a jacket. *Perceptual and Motor Skills, 76,* 339–348.

89. Hoult, T. F. (1954). Experimental measurement of clothing as a factor in some social ratings of selected American men. *American Sociological Review, 19,* 326–327.

90. Hart, S., Field, T., Hernandez-Reif, M., & Lundy, B. (1998). Preschoolers' cognitive performance improves following massage. *Early Child Development and Care, 143,* 59–64. For more about the role of touch in relationships, see Keltner, D. (2009). *Born to be good: The science of a meaningful life.* New York: Norton, pp. 173–198.

91. Montagu, A. (1972). *Touching: The human significance of the skin.* New York: Harper & Row, p. 93.

92. Yarrow, L. J. (1963). Research in dimension of early maternal care. *Merrill-Palmer Quarterly, 9,* 101–122.

93. Hall, E. (1996). Touch, status, and gender at professional meetings. *Journal of Nonverbal Behavior, 20,* 23–44.

94. Gueguen, N., & Vion, M. (2009). The effect of a practitioner's touch on a patient's medication compliance. *Psychology, Health and Medicine, 14,* 689–694.

95. Segrin, C. (1993). The effects of nonverbal behavior on outcomes of compliance gaining attempts. *Communication Studies, 11,* 169–187.

96. Hornik, J. (1992). Effects of physical contact on customers' shopping time and behavior. *Marketing Letters, 3,* 49–55.

97. Smith, D. E., Gier, J. A., & Willis, F. N. (1982). Interpersonal touch and compliance with a marketing request. *Basic and Applied Social Psychology, 3,* 35–38.

98. Field, T., Lasko, D., Mundy, P., Henteleff, T., Kabat, S., Talpins, S., & Dowling, M. (1997). Brief report: Autistic children's attentiveness and responsivity improve after touch therapy. *Journal of Autism and Developmental Disorders, 27,* 333–338.

99. Kraus, M. W., Huang, C., & Keltner, D. (2010). Tactile communication, cooperation, and performance: An ethological study of the NBA. *Emotion. 10,* 745–749.

100. See, for example, Segrin, C. (1993). The effects of nonverbal behavior on outcomes of compliance gaining attempts. *Communication Studies, 11,* 169–187.

101. Kleinke, C. R. (1977). Compliance to requests made by gazing and touching experimenters in field settings. *Journal of Experimental Social Psychology, 13,* 218–223.

102. Willis, F. N., & Hamm, H. K. (1980). The use of interpersonal touch in securing compliance. *Journal of Nonverbal Behavior, 5,* 49–55.

103. Crusco, A. H., & Wetzel, C. G. (1984). The Midas touch: Effects of interpersonal touch on restaurant tipping. *Personality and Social Psychology Bulletin, 10,* 512–517.

104. Chan, Y. K. (1999). Density, crowding, and factors intervening in their relationship: Evidence from a hyper-dense metropolis. *Social-Indicators-Research, 48,* 103–124.

105. See note 23, Hall (1969, pp. 113–130).

106. Hackman, M., & Walker, K. (1990). Instructional communication in the televised classroom: The effects of system design and teacher immediacy. *Communication Education, 39,* 196–206. See also McCroskey, J. C., & Richmond, V. P. (1992). Increasing teacher influence through immediacy. In V. P. Richmond & J. C. McCroskey (Eds.), *Power in the classroom: Communication, control, and concern* (pp. 101–119). Hillsdale, NJ: Erlbaum.

107. Conlee, C., Olvera, J., & Vagim, N. (1993). The relationships among physician nonverbal immediacy and measures of patient satisfaction with physician care. *Communication Reports, 6,* 25–33.

108. Mehrabian, A. (1976). *Public places and personal spaces: The psychology of work, play, and living environments.* New York: Basic Books, p. 69.

109. Sadalla, E. (1987). Identity and symbolism in housing. *Environment and Behavior, 19,* 569–587.

110. Maslow, A. H., & Mintz, N. L. (1956). Effects of esthetic surroundings. *Journal of Psychology, 41,* 247–254.

111. Sommer, R. (1969). *Personal space: The behavioral basis of design.* Englewood Cliffs, NJ: Prentice-Hall, p. 78.

112. Ibid., p. 35.

113. Ballard, D. I., & Seibold, D. R. (2000). Time orientation and temporal variation across work groups: Implications for group and organizational communication. *Western Journal of Communication, 64,* 218–242.

114. Levine, R. (1997). *A geography of time: The temporal misadventures of a social psychologist.* New York: Basic Books.

115. See, for example, Hill, O. W., Block, R. A., & Buggie, S. E. (2000). Culture and beliefs about time: Comparisons among black Americans, black Africans, and white Americans. *Journal of Psychology, 134,* 443–457.

116. Levine, R., & Wolff, E. (1985, March). Social time: The heartbeat of culture. *Psychology Today, 19,* 28–35. See also Levine, R. (1987, April). Waiting is a power game. *Psychology Today, 21,* 24–33.

117. Burgoon, J. K., Buller, D. B., & Woodall, W. G. (1996). *Nonverbal communication.* New York: McGraw-Hill, p. 148.

118. Carlson, E. N. (2013). Overcoming barriers to self-knowledge: Mindfulness as a path to seeing yourself as you really are. *Perspectives on Psychological Science, 8,* 173–186.

## CHAPTER 7

1. Tom Cruise: Couch jumping for Katie Holmes [Television series episode]. (2005). In *The Oprah Winfrey Show.* New York: ABC. Retrieved October 30, 2012, from http://abcnews.go.com/Entertainment/video/tom-cruise-couch-jumping-for-katie-holmes-16680590.

2. Haskell, R. (2005, August). Holmes, sweet Holmes. *W Magazine.* Retrieved October 30, 2012, from http://www.wmagazine.com/celebrities/archive/katie_holmes

3. Lemay, E. P., Jr., Clark, M. S., & Greenberg, A. (2010). What is beautiful is good because what is beautiful is desired: Physical attractiveness stereotyping as projection of interpersonal goals. *Personality and Social Psychology Bulletin, 36,* 339–353.

4. Wang, S., Moon, S., Kwon, K., Evans, C. A., & Stefanone, M. A. (2010). Face off: Implications of visual cues on initiating friendship on Facebook. *Computers in Human Behavior, 26,* 226–234.

5. Toma, C. L., & Hancock, J. T. (2010). Looks and lies: The role of physical attractiveness in online dating self-presentation and deception. *Communication Research, 37,* 335–351.

6. Zuckerman, M., & Sinicropi, V. (2011). When physical and vocal attractiveness differ: Effects on favorability of interpersonal impressions. *Journal of Nonverbal Behavior, 35,* 75–86.

7. Albada, K. F. (2002). Interaction appearance theory: Changing perceptions of physical attractiveness through social interaction. *Communication Theory, 12,* 8–41.

8. Alley, T. R., & McCanless, E. R. (2002). *Body shape and muscularity preferences in short-term and long-term relationships.* Presented at the Biennial International Conference on Human Ethology, Vienna.

9. Hamachek, D. (1982). *Encounters with others: Interpersonal relationships and you.* New York: Holt, Rinehart and Winston.

10. See, for example, Byrne, D. (1997). An overview (and underview) of research and theory within the attraction paradigm. *Journal of Social and Personal Relationships, 14,* 417–431. For a discussion of some ways in which similarity does not enhance relational longevity, see Shiota, M. N., & Levenson, R. W. (2007). Birds of a feather don't always fly farthest: Similarity in big five personality predicts more negative marital satisfaction trajectories in long-term marriages. *Psychology and Aging, 22,* 667–675.

11. Luo, S., & Klohnen, E. (2005). Assortive mating and marital quality in newlyweds: A couple-centered approach. *Journal of Personality and Social Psychology, 88,* 304–326. See also Amodio, D. M., & Showers, C. J. (2005). Similarity breeds liking revisited: The moderating role of commitment. *Journal of Social and Personal Relationships, 22,* 817–836.

12. Mackinnon, S. P., Jordan, C., & Wilson, A. (2011). Birds of a feather sit together: Physical similarity predicts seating distance. *Personality and Social Psychology Bulletin, 37,* 879–892.

13. DeBruine, L. M. (2005). Trustworthy but not lust-worthy: Context-specific effects of facial resemblance. *Proceedings of the Royal Society of London B, 272,* 919–922.

14. Finkel, E. J., Eastwick, P. W., Karney, B. R., Reis, H. T., & Sprecher, S. (2012). Online dating: A critical analysis from the perspective of psychological science. *Psychological Science in the Public Interest, 13*(1), 3–66.

15. Duck, S. W. (2011). Similarity and perceived similarity of personal constructs as influences on friendship choice. *British Journal of Clinical Psychology, 12,* 1–6.

16. Sias, P. M., Drzewiecka, J. A., Meares, M., Bent, R., Konomi, Y., Ortega, M., & White, C. (2008). Intercultural friendship development. *Communication Reports, 21*, 1–13.

17. Heatherington, L., Escudero, V., & Friedlander, M. L. (2005). Couple interaction during problem discussions: Toward an integrative methodology. *Journal of Family Communication, 5*, 191–207.

18. Haskell, R. (2005, August). Holmes, sweet Holmes. *W Magazine*. Retrieved October 30, 2012, from http://www.wmagazine.com/celebrities/archive/katie_holmes.

19. Specher, S. (1998). Insiders' perspectives on reasons for attraction to a close other. *Social Psychology Quarterly, 61*, 287–300.

20. Aronson, E. (2008). *The social animal* (9th ed.). New York: Worth/Freeman. See Chapter 9: "Liking, Loving, and Interpersonal Sensitivity."

21. Dindia, K. (2002). Self-disclosure research: Knowledge through meta-analysis. In M. Allen & R. W. Preiss (Eds.), *Interpersonal communication research: Advances through meta-analysis* (pp. 169–185). Mahwah, NJ: Erlbaum.

22. Flora, C. (2004, January/February). Close quarters. *Psychology Today, 37*, 15–16.

23. Haythornthwaite, C., Kazmer, M. M., & Robbins, J. (2000). Community development among distance learners: Temporal and technological dimensions. *Journal of Computer-Mediated Communication, 6*, Issue 1, Article 2. Retrieved from http://jcmc.indiana.edu/vol6/issue1/haythornthwaite.html.

24. See, for example, Roloff, M. E. (1981). *Interpersonal communication: The social exchange approach.* Beverly Hills, CA: Sage.

25. For a discussion of the characteristics of impersonal and interpersonal communication, see Bochner, A. P. (1984). The functions of human communication in interpersonal bonding. In C. C. Arnold & J. W. Bowers (Eds.), *Handbook of rhetorical and communication theory* (pp. 544–621). Boston: Allyn and Bacon, p. 550; Trenholm, S., & Jensen, A. (1987). *Interpersonal communication.* Belmont, CA: Wadsworth, p. 37; and Stewart, J., Zediker, K. E., & Witteborn, S. (2007). *Together: Communicating interpersonally: A social construction approach.* New York: Oxford University Press.

26. O'Toole, K. (2000, February 16). Study takes early look at social consequences of Net use. *Stanford Online Report.* Retrieved July 18, 2013, from http://www.stanford.edu/dept/news/report/news/february16/internetsurvey-216.html.

27. Craig, R. T. (2007). Issue forum introduction: Mobile media and communication: What are the important questions? *Communication Monographs, 74*, 386.

28. Kraut, R., Patterson, M., Lundmark, V., Kiesler, S., Mukophadhyay, T., & Scherlis, W. (1998). Internet paradox: A social technology that reduces social involvement and psychological well-being? *American Psychologist, 53*, 1017–1031.

29. Daum, M. (2009, March 7). The age of friendaholism. *Los Angeles Times*, p. B 13. For an extensive critique of false intimacy in social networking sites, see Deresiewicz, W. (2009, December 6). Faux friendship. *The Chronicle of Higher Education.* Retrieved June 8, 2010, from http://chronicle.com/article/The-End-of-Solitude/3708/.

30. Lee, S. J. (2009). Online communication and adolescent social ties: Who benefits more from Internet use? *Journal of Computer-Mediated Communication, 14*, 509–531.

31. Houser, M. L., Fleuriet, C., & Estrada, D. (2012). The cyber factor: An analysis of relational maintenance through the use of computer-mediated communication. *Communication Research Reports, 29*, 34–43.

32. Wellman, B., Smith, A., Wells, A., & Kennedy, T. (2008). Networked families. In *Pew Internet and American Life Project.* Washington, DC: Pew Research center.

33. Hammick, J.K. & Lee, M.J. (2013, in press). Do shy people feel less communication apprehension online? The effects of virtual reality on the relationship between personality characteristics and communication outcomes. *Computers in Human Behavior.*

34. Park, N., Strover, S., & Straubhaar, J. (2011). *Benefits of Internet use for communication in a rural area: Relationships between online communication and perceived social support.* Presented at the annual meeting of the International Communication Association, Boston, MA.

35. Wright, K. B. (2012). Emotional support and perceived stress among college students using Facebook.com: An exploration of the relationship between source perceptions and emotional support. *Communication Research Reports, 29*, 175–184.

36. Hales, K. D. (2012). *Multimedia use for relational maintenance in romantic couples.* Presented at the annual meeting of the International Communication Association, Phoenix AZ.

37. Tannen, D. (1994, May 16). High tech gender gap. *Newsweek*, p. 52–53.

38. Reingold, H. (1993). *The virtual community.* New York: Addison-Wesley. See also Wallace, P. (1999). *The psychology of the Internet.* Cambridge, MA: Cambridge University Press.

39. Walther, J. B. (1996). Computer-mediated communication: Impersonal, interpersonal, and hyper-personal interaction. *Communication Research, 23*, 3–43.

40. See Dillard, J. P., Solomon, D. H., & Palmer, M. T. (1999). Structuring the concept of relational communication. *Communication Monographs, 66*, 46–55.

41. Tom Cruise in 2005: "I'm in Love" [Television series episode]. (2005). *The View.* New York: ABC. Retrieved October 30, 2012, from http://abcnews.go.com/Entertainment/video/tom-cruise-says-hes-in-love-with-katie-holmes-in-2005-interview-16680603.

42. Lim, T. S., & Bowers, J. W. (1991). Facework: Solidarity, approbation, and tact. *Human Communication Research, 17*, 415–450.

43. Frei, J. R., & Shaver, P. R. (2002). Respect in close relationships: Prototype, definition, self-report assessment, and initial correlates. *Personal Relationships, 9*, 121–139.

44. See Rossiter, C. M., Jr. (1974). Instruction in metacommunication. *Central States Speech Journal, 25*, 36–42, and Wilmot, W. W. (1980). Metacommunication: A reexamination and extension. In D. Nimmo (Ed.), *Communication yearbook* 4. New Brunswick, NJ: Transaction.

45. Knapp, M. L., & Vangelisti, A. L. (2009). *Interpersonal communication and human relationships* (6th ed.). Boston: Allyn and Bacon.

46. Canary, D. J., & Stafford, L. (Eds.). (1994). *Communication and relational maintenance.* San Diego, CA: Academic Press. See also Lee, J. (1998). Effective maintenance Communication in superior-subordinate relationships. *Western Journal of Communication, 62*, 181–208.

47. Whitty, M. T., & Buchanan, T. (2009). Looking for love in so many places: Characteristics of online daters and speed daters. *Interpersona: An International Journal of Personal Relationships, 3*(2), 63–86.

48. Tolhuizen, J. H. (1989). Communication strategies for intensifying dating relationships: Identification, use and structure. *Journal of Social and Personal Relationships, 6*, 413–434.

49. Guerrero, L. K., & Andersen, P. A. (1991). The waxing and waning of relational intimacy: Touch as a function of relational stage, gender and touch avoidance. *Journal of Social and Personal Relationships, 8*, 147–165.

50. See note 2, Haskell (2005, August).

51. Baxter, L. A. (1987). Symbols of relationship identity in relationship culture. *Journal of Social and Personal Relationships, 4*, 261–280.

52. Bruess, C. J., & Pearson, J. C. (1995, November). *Like sands through the hour glass: These are the rituals functioning in day-to-day married lives.* Paper delivered at the Speech Communication Association convention, San Antonio, TX.

53. Giles, H., & Poseland, P. F. (1975). *Speech style and social evaluation.* London: Academic Press.

54. Roloff, M., Janiszewski, C. A., McGrath, M. A., Burns, C. S., & Manrai, L. A. (1988). Acquiring resources from intimates: When obligation substitutes for persuasion. *Human Communication Research, 14,* 364–396.

55. Burgoon, J. K., Parrott, R., LePoire, B. A., Kelley, D. L., Walther, J. B., & Perry, D. (1989). Maintaining and restoring privacy through different types of relationships. *Journal of Social and Personal Relationships, 6,* 131–158.

56. Battaglia, D. M., Richard, F. D., Datteri, D. L., & Lord, C. G. (1998). Breaking up is (relatively) easy to do: A script for the dissolution of close relationships. *Journal of Social and Personal Relationships, 15,* 829–845.

57. See, for example, Baxter, L. A., & Montgomery, B. M. (1998). A guide to dialectical approaches to studying personal relationships. In B. M. Montgomery & L. A. Baxter (Eds.), *Dialectical approaches to studying personal relationships* (pp. 1–16). New York: Erlbaum, and Ebert, L. A., & Duck, S. W. (1997). Rethinking satisfaction in personal relationships from a dialectical perspective. In R. J. Sternberg & M. Hojjatr (Eds.), *Satisfaction in close relationships* (pp. 190–217). New York: Guilford.

58. Summarized by Baxter, L. A. (1994). A dialogic approach to relationship maintenance. In D. J. Canary & L. Stafford (Eds.), *Communication and relational maintenance* (pp. 233–254). San Diego, CA: Academic Press.

59. Morris, D. (1971). *Intimate behavior.* New York: Kodansha Globe, pp. 21–29.

60. Barry, D. (1990). *Dave Barry turns 40.* New York: Fawcett, p. 47.

61. VanLear, C. A. (1991). Testing a cyclical model of communicative openness in relationship development. *Communication Monographs, 58,* 337–361.

62. Adapted from Baxter, L. A., & Montgomery, B. M. (1998). A guide to dialectical approaches to studying personal relationships. In B. M. Montgomery & L. A. Baxter (Eds.), *Dialectical approaches to studying persnal relatinships* (pp. 1–16). New York: Erlbaum.

63. Register, L. M., & Henley, T. B. (1992). The phenomenology of intimacy. *Journal of Social and Personal Relationships, 9,* 467–481.

64. Morris, D. (1973). *Intimate behavior.* New York: Bantam, p. 7.

65. Floyd, K. (1996). Meanings for closeness and intimacy in friendship. *Journal of Social and Personal Relationships, 13,* 85–107.

66. Baxter, L. A. (1994). A dialogic approach to relationship maintenance. In D. Canar & L. Stafford (Eds.), *Communication and relational maintenance* (pp. 233–254). San Diego, CA: Academic Press.

67. Bond, B. J. (2009). He posted, she posted: Gender differences in self-disclosure on social network sites. *Rocky Mountain Communication Review, 6*(2), 29–37.

68. Firminger, K. B. (2006). Is he boyfriend material? *Men & Masculinities, 8*(3), 298–308, p. 298.

69. MacGeorge, E. L., Graves, A. R., Feng, B., Gillihan, S. J., & Burleson, B. R. (2004). The myth of gender cultures: Similarities outweigh differences in men's and women's provision of and responses to supportive communication. *Sex Roles, 50,* 143–175.

70. Wood, J. T., & Inman, C. C. (1993). In a different mode: Masculine styles of communicating closeness. *Journal of Applied Communication Research, 21,* 279–295. See also Swain, S. (1989). Covert intimacy in men's friendships: Closeness in men's friendships. In B. J. Risman & P. Schwartz (Eds.), *Gender in intimate relationships: A microstructural approach* (pp. 71–86). Belmont, CA: Wadsworth.

71. Bleske-Rechek, A., Somers, E., Micke, C., Erickson, L., Matteson, L., Stocco, C., . . . Ritchie, L. (2012). Burden or benefit? Attraction in cross-sex friendship. *Journal of Social and Personal Relationships, 29,* 569–596.

72. Hall, J. A. (2011). Sex differences in friendship expectations: A meta-analysis. *Journal of Social and Personal Relationships, 28,* 723–747.

73. Ibid.

74. Ward, A. F. (2012, October 23). Men and women can't be "just friends." *Scientific American.* Retrieved from http://www.scientificamerican.com/article.cfm?id=men-and-women-cant-be-just-friends.

75. Elliott, S., & Umberson, O. (2008). The performance of desire: Gender and sexual negotiation in long-term marriages. *Journal of Marriage & Family, 70,* 391–406.

76. Chapman, G. (2010). *The five love languages: The secret to love that lasts.* Chicago: Northfield.

77. Egbert, N., & Polk, D. (2006). Speaking the language of relational maintenance: A validity test of Chapman's (1992) *Five Love Languages. Communication Research Reports, 23*(1), 19–26.

78. Myers, S. A., Byrnes, K. A., Frisby, B. N., & Mansson, D. H. (2011). Adult siblings' use of affectionate communication as a strategic and routine relational maintenance behavior. *Communication Research Reports, 28,* 151–158.

79. Perry Carson, C. K., Carson, D. K., Thomas, K., & Jackman-Brown, J. (2007). Self-reported parenting behavior and child temperament in families of toddlers with and without speech-language delay. *Communication Disorders Quarterly, 28,* 155–165.

80. Horan, S. M., & Booth-Butterfield, M. (2010). Investing in affection: An investigation of affection exchange theory and relational qualities. *Communication Quarterly, 58,* 394–413.

81. Frisby, B. N., & Booth-Butterfield, M. (2012). The "how" and "why" of flirtatious communication between marital partners. *Communication Quarterly, 60,* 465–480.

82. Kam, J., & Nussbaum, J. (2008). *Exploring the dynamic nature of the grandparent-grandchild relationship.* Presented at the annual meeting of the National Communication Association, San Diego, CA.

83. Emmers-Sommer, T. M. (2004). The effect of communication quality and quantity indicatros on intimacy and relational satisfaction. *Journal of Social and Personal Relationships, 21,* 399–411.

84. Merolla, A. J. (2010). Relational maintenance during military deployment: Perspectives of wives of deployed US soldiers. *Journal of Applied Communication Research, 38*(1), 4–26.

85. Haas, S. M., & Stafford, L. (2005). Maintenance behaviors in same-sex and marital relationships: A matched sample comparison. *Journal of Family Communication, 5,* 43–60.

86. Ibid.

87. Soin, R. (2011). Romantic gift giving as chore or pleasure: The effects of attachment orientations on gift giving perceptions. *Journal of Business Research, 64,* 113–118.

88. Guéguen, N. (2010). The effect of a woman's incidental tactile contact on men's later behavior. *Social Behavior & Personality: An International Journal, 38,* 257–266.

89. Floyd, K., Boren, J. P., & Hannawa, A. F. (2009). Kissing in marital and cohabiting relationships: Effects of blood lipids, stress, and relationship satisfaction. *Western Journal of Communication, 73,* 113–133.

90. Chapman, G. (1995). *The five love languages: How to express heartfelt commitment to your mate.* Chicago: Northfield, p. 17.

91. Huang, W.-J. (2005). An Asian perspective on relationship and marriage education. *Family Process, 44,* 161–173.

92. For a useful survey of cultural differences in interpersonal communication, see Gudykunst, W. B., Ting-Toomey, S., & Nishida,

T. (Eds.). (1996). *Communication in personal relationships across cultures.* Thousand Oaks, CA: Sage.

93. Park, Y. S., & Kim, B. S. K. (2008). Asian and European American cultural values and communication style among Asian American and European American college students. *Cultural Diversity and Ethnic Minority Psychology, 14,* 47–56.

94. Lin, H. S. (2008, May). Private love in public sphere: Love hotels and the transformation of intimacy in contemporary Japan. *Asian Studies Review, 32,* 31–56.

95. Triandis, H. C. (1994). *Culture and social behavior.* New York: McGraw-Hill, p. 230. See also Doronto, P. M., Nishida, T., & Nakayama, S. I. (2005, September). Uncertainty, anxiety, and avoidance in communication with strangers. *International Journal of Intercultural Relations, 29,* 549–560.

96. Rosenfeld, L. B., & Kendrick, W. L. (1984, Fall). Choosing to be open: Subjective reasons for self-disclosing. *Western Journal of Speech Communication, 48,* 326–343.

97. Altman, I., & Taylor, D. A. (1973). *Social penetration: The development of interpersonal relationships.* New York: Holt, Rinehart and Winston.

98. Luft, J. (1969). *Of human interaction.* Palo Alto, CA: National Press.

99. Brzovic, K., & Matz, S. I. (2008). Students advise Fortune 500 company: Designing a problem-based learning community. *Business Communication Quarterly, 72,* 21–34.

100. Chen, Y., & Nakazawa, M. (2009). Influences of culture on self-disclosure as relationally situated in intercultural and interracial friendships from a social penetration perspective. *Journal of Intercultural Communication Research, 38*(2), 77–98.

101. Ko, H.-C., & Kuo, F.-Y. (2009, February 10). Can blogging enhance subjective well-being through self-disclosure? *CyberPsychology & Behavior, 12,* 75–79.

102. Duck, S., & Miell, D. E. (1991). Charting the development of personal relationships. In R. Gilmour & S. Duck (Eds.), *Studying interpersonal interaction* (pp. 323–336). Hillsdale, NJ: Erlbaum.

103. Duck, S. (1991). Some evident truths about conversations in everyday relationships: All communications are not created equal. *Human Communication Research, 18,* 228–267.

104. Gibbs, J. L., Ellison, N. B., & Lai, C. (2011). First comes love, then comes Google: An investigation of uncertainty reduction strategies and self-disclosure in online dating. *Communication Research, 38,* 70–100.

105. Summarized in Pearson, J. (1989). *Communication in the family.* New York: Harper & Row, pp. 252–257.

106. Eisenberg, E. M., & Witten, M. G. (1987). Reconsidering openness in organizational communication. *Academy of Management Review, 12,* 418–428.

107. Rosenfeld, L. B., & Gilbert, J. R. (1989). The measurement of cohesion and its relationship to dimensions of self-disclosure in classroom settings. *Small Group Behavior, 20,* 291–301.

108. Jaksa, J. A., & Pritchard, M. (1994). *Communication ethics: Methods of analysis* (2nd ed.). Belmont, CA: Wadsworth, pp. 65–66.

109. O'Hair, D., & Cody, M. J. (1993). Interpersonal deception: The dark side of interpersonal communication? In B. H. Spitzberg & W. R. Cupach (Eds.), *The dark side of interpersonal communication.* Hillsdale, NJ: Erlbaum.

110. Kaplar, M. E., & Gordon, A. K. (2004). The enigma of altruistic lying: Perspective differences in what motivates and justifies lie telling within romantic relationships. *Personal Relationships, 11,* 489–507.

111. Harrell, E. (2009, August 19). Why we lie so much. *Time.* Retrieved from http://www.time.com/time/health/article/0,8599,1917215,00.html.

112. Turner, R. E., Edgley, C., & Olmstead, G. (1975). Information control in conversation: Honesty is not always the best policy. *Kansas Journal of Sociology, 11,* 69–89.

113. Bell, K. L., & DePaulo, B. M. (1996). Liking and lying. *Basic and Applied Social Psychology, 18,* 243–266.

114. Feldman, R. S., Forrest, J. A., & Happ, B. R. (2002). Self-presentation and verbal deception: Do self-presenters lie more? *Basic and Applied Social Psychology, 24,* 163–170.

115. McCornack, S. A., & Levine, T. R. (1990). When lies are uncovered: Emotional and relational outcomes of discovered deception. *Communication Monographs, 57,* 119–138.

116. See Hamilton, M. A., & Mineo, P. J. (1998). A framework for understanding equivocation. *Journal of Language and Social Psychology, 17,* 3–35.

117. Metts, S., Cupach, W. R., & Imahori, T. T. (1992). Perceptions of sexual compliance-resisting messages in three types of cross-sex relationships. *Western Journal of Communication, 56,* 1–17.

118. Bavelas, J. B., Black, A., Chovil, N., & Mullett, J. (1990). *Equivocal communication.* Newbury Park, CA: Sage, p. 171.

119. Ibid.

120. Motley, M. T. (1992). Mindfulness in solving communicators' dilemmas. *Communication Monographs, 59,* 306–314.

121. See note 118, Bavelas et al. (1990).

122. Bok, S. (1978). *Lying: Moral choice in public and private life.* New York: Pantheon.

123. For a summary of the link between social capital and career success, see Krebs, V. (2008). Social capital: The key to success for the 21st century organization. *International Association for Human Resources Journal, 12,* 38–42. See also Seibert, S. E., Kraimer, M. L., & Liden, R. C. (2001). A social capital theory of career success. *Academy of Management Journal, 44,* 219–237.

124. Granovetter, M. S. (1973). The strength of weak ties. *American Journal of Sociology, 78,* 1360–1380.

125. Ellison, N. B., Steinfield, C., & Lampe, C. (2007). The benefits of Facebook "friends": Social capital and college students' use of online social network sites. *Journal of Computer-Mediated Communication, 12*(4), Article 1. Retrieved from http://jcmc.indiana.edu/vol12/issue4/ellison.html.

126. Steinfield, C., DiMicco, J. M., Ellison, N. B., & Lampe, C. (2009, June 25–27). Bowling online: Social networking and social capital within the organization. In *Proceedings of the Fourth International Conference on Communities and Technologies (University Park, PA, June 25–27, 2009)* (pp. 245–254). New York: Association for Computing Machinery.

## CHAPTER 8

1. Giles, L. C., Glonek, G. F., Luszcz, M. A., & Andrews, G. R. (2005, July). Effect of social networks on 10-year survival in very old Australians: The Australian longitudinal study of aging. *Journal of Epidemiology & Community Health, 59*(7), 574–579.

2. Segrin, C., & Passalacqua, S. A. (2010). Functions of loneliness, social support, health behaviors, and stress in association with poor health. *Health Communication, 25,* 312–322.

3. Segrin, C., & Domschke, T. (2011). Social support, loneliness, recuperative processes, and their direct and indirect effects on health. *Health Communication, 26,* 221–232.

4. Cissna, K. N. L., & Seiburg, E. (1995). Patterns of interactional confirmation and disconfirmation. In J. Stewart (Ed.), *Bridges not walls: A book about interpersonal communication* (6th ed., pp. 237–246). New York: McGraw-Hill.

5. Ibid.

6. De Vries, R. E., Bakker-Pieper, A., & Oostenveld, W. (2010). Leadership = communication? The relations of leaders'

communication styles with leadership styles, knowledge sharing and leadership outcomes. *Journal of Business & Psychology, 25,* 367–380.

7. Singh, R., & Simons, J. J. P. (2010). Attitudes and attraction: Optimism and weight as explanations for the similarity-dissimilarity asymmetry. *Social and Personality Psychology Compass, 12,* 1206–1219.

8. Imai, T., & Vangelisti, A. L. (2011). *The influence of plans to marry in dating couples on relationship quality, confirmation, and desire for evaluation.* Presented at the annual meeting of the International Communication Association, Boston, MA.

9. Markman, H. J., Rhoades, G. K., Stanley, S. M., & Ragan, E. P. (2010). The premarital communication roots of marital distress and divorce: The first five years of marriage. *Journal of Family Psychology, 24,* 289–298.

10. Spott, J., Pyle, C., & Punyanunt-Carter, N. (2010). Positive and negative nonverbal behaviors in relationships: A study of relationship satisfaction and longevity. *Human Communication, 13,* 29–41.

11. Burns, M. E., & Pearson, J. C. (2011). An exploration of family communication environment, everyday talk, and family satisfaction. *Communication Studies, 62*(2), 171–185.

12. Ellis, K. (2004). The impact of perceived teacher confirmation on receiver apprehension, motivation, and learning. *Communication Education, 53,* 1–20.

13. Gottman, J. M., Driver, J., & Tabares, A. (2002). Building the sound marital house: An empirically derived couple therapy. In A. S. Gurman & N. S. Jacobson (Eds.), *Clinical handbook of couple therapy* (3rd ed., pp. 373–400). New York: Guilford Press.

14. For a discussion of reactions to disconfirming responses, see Vangelisti, A. L., & Crumley, L. P. (1998). Reactions to messages that hurt: The influence of relational contexts. *Communication Monographs, 64,* 173–196. See also Cortina, L. M., Magley, V. J., Williams, J. H., & Langhout, R. D. (2001). Incivility in the workplace: Incidence and impact. *Journal of Occupational Health Psychology, 6,* 64–80.

15. Dailey, R. M. (2008). Assessing the contribution of nonverbal behaviors in displays of confirmation during parent-adolescent interactions: An actor-partner interdependence model. *Journal of Family Communication, 8,* 62–91.

16. Ibid.

17. Dailey, R. M., Romo, L., & Thompson, C. (2011). Confirmation in couples' communication about weight management: An analysis of how both partners contribute to individuals' health behaviors and conversational outcomes. *Human Communication Research, 37,* 553–582.

18. See Wilmot, W. W. (1987). *Dyadic communication.* New York: Random House, pp. 149–158, and Andersson, L. M., & Pearson, C. M. (1999). Tit for tat? The spiraling effect of incivility in the workplace. *Academy of Management Review, 24,* 452–471. See also Olson, L. N., & Braithwaite, D. O. (2004). "If you hit me again, I'll hit you back": Conflict management strategies of individuals experiencing aggression during conflicts. *Communication Studies, 55,* 271–286.

19. Harper, M. S., & Welsh, D. P. (2007). Keeping quiet: Self-silencing and its association with relational and individual functioning among adolescent romantic couples. *Journal of Social & Personal Relationships, 24,* 99–116.

20. Peterson, K. M., & Smith, D. A. (2010). To what does perceived criticism refer? Constructive, destructive, and general criticism. *Journal of Family Psychology, 24,* 97–100.

21. Bates, C. E., & Samp, J. A. (2011). Examining the effects of planning and empathic accuracy on communication in relational and nonrelational conflict interactions. *Communication Studies, 62,* 207–223.

22. Wilmot, W. W., & Hocker, J. L. (2007). *Interpersonal conflict* (7th ed.). New York: McGraw-Hill, pp. 21–22.

23. Ibid., pp. 23–24.

24. Gibb, J. (1961). Defensive communication. *Journal of Communication, 11,* 141–148. See also Eadie, W. F. (1982). Defensive communication revisited: A critical examination of Gibb's theory. *Southern Speech Communication Journal, 47,* 163–177.

25. For a review of research supporting the effectiveness of "I" language, see Proctor, R. F., II, & Wilcox, J. R. (1993). An exploratory analysis of responses to owned messages in interpersonal communication. *Et Cetera: A Review of General Semantics, 50,* 201–220. See also Proctor, R. F., II. (1989). Responsibility or egocentrism?: The paradox of owned messages. *Speech Association of Minnesota Journal, 16,* 59–60.

26. Goodboy, A. K., & Bolkan, S. (2011). Attachment and the use of negative relational maintenance behaviors in romantic relationships. *Communication Research Reports, 28,* 327–336.

27. Ali, F., & Chamorro-Premuzic, T. (2010). The dark side of love and life satisfaction: Associations with intimate relationships, psychopathy and Machiavellianism. *Personality and Individual Differences, 48,* 228–233.

28. Sillars, A. L. (2009). Interpersonal conflict. In C. Berger, M. Roloff, & D. R. Roskos-Ewoldsen (Eds.), *Handbook of communication science* (2nd ed., pp. 273–289). Thousand Oaks, CA: Sage.

29. See, for example, Baxter, L. A., Wilmot, W. W., Simmons, C. A., & Swartz, A. (1993). Ways of doing conflict: A folk taxonomy of conflict events in personal relationships. In P. J. Kalbfleisch (Ed.), *Interpersonal communication: Evolving interpersonal relationships* (pp. 89–107). Hillsdale, NJ: Erlbaum.

30. Lannutti, P. J., & Monahan, J. I. (2004). "Not now, maybe later": The influence of relationship type, request persistence, and alcohol consumption on women's refusal strategies. *Communication Studies, 55,* 362–377.

31. McNulty, J. K., & Russell, V. (2010). When "negative" behaviors are positive: A contextual analysis of the long-term effects of problem-solving behaviors on changes in relationship satisfaction. *Journal of Personality & Social Psychology, 98,* 587–604.

32. Meyer, J. R. (2004). Effect of verbal aggressiveness on the perceived importance of secondary goals in messages. *Communication Studies, 55,* 168–184.

33. New Mexico Commission on the Status of Women. (2002). *Dealing with sexual harassment.* Retrieved June 17, 2010, from http://www.womenscommission.state.nm.us/Publications/sexhbrochre.pdf.

34. Adapted from Adler, R. B., & Elmhorst, J. M. (2010). *Communicating at work: Principles and practices for business and the professions* (10th ed., pp. 118–119). New York: McGraw-Hill.

35. For information on filing a formal complaint, see http://www.eeoc.gov/laws/types/sexual_harassment.cfm.

36. Bach, G. R., & Goldberg, H. (1974). *Creative aggression.* Garden City, NY: Doubleday.

37. See Kellermann, K., & Shea, B. C. (1996). Threats, suggestions, hints, and promises: Gaining compliance efficiently and politely. *Communication Quarterly, 44,* 145–465.

38. Jordan, J., & Roloff, M. E. (1990). Acquiring assistance from others: The effect of indirect requests and relational intimacy on verbal compliance. *Human Communication Research, 16,* 519–555.

39. Curl, T. S., & Drew, P. (2008). Contingency and action: A comparison of two forms of requesting. *Research on Language & Social Interaction, 41,* 129–153.

40. Information in this paragraph is from Rose, A. J., & Rudolph, K. D. (2006). A review of sex differences in peer relationship

processes: Potential trade-offs for the emotional and behavioral development of girls and boys. *Psychological Bulletin, 132,* 98–131.

41. Holmstrom, A. J. (2009). Sex and gender similarities and differences in communication values in same-sex and cross-sex friendships. *Communication Quarterly, 57,* 224–238.

42. Baillargeon, R. H., Zoccolillo, M., Keenan, K., Côté, S., Pérusse, D., Wu, H.-X., . . . Tremblay, R. E. (2007). Gender differencds in physical aggression: A prospective population-based survey of children before and after 2 years of age. *Developmental Psychology, 43,* 13–26.

43. Daly, M., & Wilson, M. (1983). *Sex, evolution, and behavior* (2nd ed.). Belmont, CA: Wadsworth.

44. Joseph, R. (2000). The evolution of sex differences in language, sexuality, and visual-spatial skills. *Archives of Sexual Behavior, 29,* 35–66.

45. Root, A., & Rubin, K. H. (2010). Gender and parents' reactions to children's emotion during the preschool years. *New Directions for Child & Adolescent Development, 128,* 51–64.

46. Niederle, M., & Versterlund, L. (2007). Do women shy away from competition? Do men complete too much? *Quarterly Journal of Economics, 122,* 1067–1101.

47. The information in this paragraph is drawn from research summarized by Wood, J. T. (2005). *Gendered lives* (6th ed.). Belmont, CA: Wadsworth.

48. Ibid.

49. Kapidzic, S., & Herring, S. C. (2011). Gender, communication, and self-presentation in teen chatrooms revisisted: Have patterns changed? *Journal of Computer-Mediated Communication, 17,* 39–59.

50. Carothers, B. J., & Reis, H. T. (2013). Men and women are from Earth: Examining the latent structure of gender. *Journal of Personality and Social Psychology, 104,* 385–407.

51. Tan, R., Overall, N. C., & Taylor, J. K. (2012). Let's talk about us: Attachment, relationship-focused disclosure, and relationship quality. *Personal Relationships, 19,* 521–534.

52. University of Colorado Conflict Research Consortium. (n.d.). *Shuttle diplomacy/mediated communication.* Boulder, CO: International Online Training Program on Intractable Conflict. Retrieved June 16, 2010, from http://www.colorado.edu/conflict/peace/treatment/shuttle.htm.

53. Ellis, D. G. (2010). Online deliberative discourse and conflict resolution. *Landscapes of Violence, 1,* article 6. Retrieved from http://scholarworks.umass.edu/lov/vol1/iss1/6.

54. Aakhus, M., & Rumsey, E. (2010). Crafting supportive communication online: A communication design analysis of conflict in an online support group. *Journal of Applied Communication Research, 38,* 65–84.

55. For a more detailed discussion of culture, conflict, and context, see Gudykunst, W. B., & Ting-Toomey, S. (1988). *Culture and interpersonal communication.* Newbury Park, CA: Sage, pp. 153–160.

56. Hammer, M. R. (2009). Solving problems and resolving conflict using the Intercultural Style Model and Inventory. In M. A. Moodian (Ed.), *Contemporary leadership and intercultural competence* (pp. 219–232). Thousand Oaks, CA: Sage.

57. Ting-Toomey, S., Yee-Jung, K. K., Shapiro, R. B., Garcia, W., & Wright, T. (1994, November). *Ethnic identity salience and conflict styles in four ethnic groups: African Americans, Asian Americans, European Americans, and Latino Americans.* Paper presented at the annual conference of the Speech Communication Association, New Orleans.

58. Hammer, M. R. (2009). Solving problems and resolving conflict using the Intercultural Style Model and Inventory. In M. A. Moodian (Ed.), *Contemporary leadership and intercultural competence* (pp. 219–232). Thousand Oaks, CA: Sage.

59. Okabe, K. (1987). Indirect speech acts of the Japanese. In L. Kincaid (Ed.), *Communication theory: Eastern and Western perspectives* (pp. 127–136). San Diego, CA: Academic Press.

60. Kim-Jo, T., Benet-Martinez, V., & Ozer, D. J. (2010). Culture and interpersonal conflict resolution styles: Role of acculturation. *Journal of Cross-Cultural Psychology, 41,* 264–269.

61. Information in this paragraph is from Hammer (2009), see note 56.

62. Ibid.

63. Ibid.

64. Niemiec, E. (2010, September 27). Emotions and Italians. Retrieved from http://www.lifeinitaly.com/italian/emotions.

65. The following research is summarized in Tannen, D. (1990). *You just don't understand: Women and men in conversation.* New York: William and Morrow, p. 160.

66. Filley, A. C. (1975). *Interpersonal conflict resolution.* Glenview, IL: Scott Foresman, p. 23.

67. For a brief discussion of constructive problem solving, see Gallo, A. (2009, May 11). The right way to fight. *Harvard Business Review.* Retrieved June 16, 2010, from http://blogs.hbr.org/hmu/2010/05/the-right-way-to-fight.html.

## CHAPTER 9

1. Stengel, R. (2009). *Mandela's way: Lessons on life, love, and courage.* New York: Random House.

2. Stengel, R. (2008, July 9). Mandela: His 8 lessons of leadership. *Time.* Retrieved from http://www.time.com/time/magazine/article/0,9171,1821659-1,00.html.

3. Mandela in his own words. (2008, June 26). CNN. Retrieved from http://edition.cnn.com/2008/WORLD/africa/06/24/mandela.quotes/.

4. Sampson, A. (1999). *Mandela: The authorized biography.* New York: Knopf.

5. See note 2, Stengel (2008).

6. Information in this paragraph is from Marquard, L. (1969). *The people and policies of South Africa* (4th ed.). New York: Oxford University Press.

7. See note 4, Sampson (1999).

8. Limb, P. (2008). *Nelson Mandela: A biography.* Westport, CT: Greenwood Press.

9. For a more detailed discussion of the advantages and disadvantages of working in groups, see Beebe, S. A., & Masterson, J. T. (2003). *Communicating in small groups: Principles and practices* (9th ed.). Needham Heights, MA: Allyn & Bacon.

10. Marby, E. A. (1999). The systems metaphor in group communication. In L. R. Frey (Ed.), *Handbook of group communication theory and research* (pp. 71–91). Thousand Oaks, CA: Sage.

11. Krakauer, J. (1997). *Into thin air.* New York: Anchor, pp. 212–213.

12. Rothwell, J. D. (2004). *In mixed company: Small group communication* (5th ed.). Belmont, CA: Wadsworth, pp. 29–31.

13. Is your team too big? Too small? What's the right number? (2006, June 14). Knowledge@Wharton. Retrieved January 26, 2009, from Knowledge@Wharton, http://knowledge.wharton.upenn.edu/article.cfm?articleid=1501.

14. Lowry, P., Roberts, T. L., Romano, N. C., Jr., Cheney, P. D., & Hightower, R. T. (2006). The impact of group size and social presence on small-group communication. *Small Group Research, 37,* 631–661.

15. Hackman, J. (1987). The design of work teams. In J. Lorsch (Ed.), *Handbook of organizational behavior* (pp. 315–342). Englewood Cliffs, NJ: Prentice Hall.

16. LaFasto, F., & Carson, C. (2001). When teams work best: 6,000 team members and leaders tell what it takes to succeed. Thousand

Oaks, CA: Sage. Larson, C. E., & LaFasto, F. M. J. (1989). *Teamwork: What must go right, what can go wrong.* Thousand Oaks, CA: Sage.

17. Kirschner, F., Paas, F., & Kirschner, P. A. (2010). Superiority of collaborative learning with complex tasks: A research note on alternative affective explanation. *Computers in Human Behavior, 27,* 53–57.

18. See, for example, Powell, A., Piccoli, G., & Ives, B. (2004). Virtual teams: A review of current literature and directions for future research. *ACM SIGMIS Database, 35,* 6–16. See also Walther, J. B., & Bazarova, N. (2008). Validation and application of electronic propinquity theory to computer-mediated communication in groups. *Communication Research, 35,* 622–645.

19. Herndon, S. L. (1997, January). Theory and practice: Implications for the implementation of communication technology in organizations. *Journal of Business Communication, 34,* 121–129.

20. Anderson, D. M., & Haddad, C. J. (2005). Gender, voice and learning in online course environments. *Journal of Asynchronous Learning Networks, 9,* 3–14.

21. Schaefer, R. A. B., & Erskine, L. (2012). Virtual team meetings: Reflections on a class exercise exploring technology choice. *Journal of Management Education, 36,* 777–801.

22. Alge, B. J., Wiethoff, C., & Klein, H. J. (2003). When does the medium matter? Knowledge-building experiences and opportunities in decision-making teams. *Organizational Behavior and Human Decision Processes, 91,* 26–37. See also Hobman, E. V., Bordia, P., Irmer, B., & Chang, A. (2002). The expression of conflict in computer-mediated and face-to-face groups. *Small Group Research, 33,* 439–465.

23. Capdeferro, N., & Romero, M. (2012). Are online learners frustrated with collaborative learning experiences? *International Review of Research in Open & Distance Learning, 13,* 26–44.

24. Nunamaker, J. F., Jr., Reinig, B. A., & Briggs, R. O. (2009). Principles for effective virtual teamwork. *Communications of the ACM, 52*(4), 113–117.

25. Steinzor, B. (1950). The spatial factor in face-to-face discussion groups. *Journal of Abnormal and Social Psychology, 45,* 522–555.

26. Strodtbeck, P. L., & Hook, L. H. (1961). The social dimensions of a twelve-man jury table. *Sociometry, 24,* 397–415.

27. Russo, N. F. (1967). Connotations of seating arrangements. *Cornell Journal of Social Relations, 2,* 37–44.

28. Gouran, D. S., Hirokawa, R. Y., Julian, K. M., & Leatham, G. B. (1992). The evolution and current status of the functional perspective on communication in decision-making and problem-solving groups. In S. A. Deetz (Ed.), *Communication yearbook 16* (pp. 573–600). Newbury Park, CA: Sage. See also Wittenbaum, G. M., Hollingshead, A. B., Paulus, P. B., Hirokawa, R. Y., Ancona, D. G., Peterson, R. S., Jehn, K. A., & Yoon, K. (2004). The functional perspective as a lens for understanding groups. *Small Group Research, 35,* 17–43.

29. Mayer, M. E. (1998). Behaviors leading to more effective decisions in small groups embedded in organizations. *Communication Reports, 11,* 123–132.

30. Bales, R. F., & Strodtbeck, P. L. (1951). Phases in group problem solving. *Journal of Abnormal and Social Psychology, 46,* 485–495.

31. Bormann, E. (1990). *Small group communication: Theory and practice.* New York: Harper & Row.

32. Postman, N. (1976). *Crazy talk, stupid talk.* New York: Dell.

33. Aristotle. (1958). *Politics.* New York: Oxford University Press, Book 7.

34. See Kelsey, B. L. (1998). The dynamics of multicultural groups. *Small Group Research, 29,* 602–623.

35. Bennis, W., & Nanus, B. (1985). *Leaders: The strategies for taking charge.* New York: Harper & Row.

36. Lewin, K., Lippitt, R., & White, R. K. (1939). Patterns of aggressive behavior in experimentally created social climates. *Journal of Social Psychology, 10,* 271–299.

37. Cheney, G. (1995). Democracy in the workplace: Theory and practice from the perspective of communication. *Journal of Applied Communication Research, 23,* 167–200.

38. Rosenbaum, L. L., & Rosenbaum, W. B. (1971). Morale and productivity consequences of group leadership style, stress, and type of task. *Journal of Applied Psychology, 55,* 343–358.

39. Hall, J., & Donnell, S. (1979). Managerial achievement: The personal side of behavioral theory. *Human Relations, 32,* 77–101.

40. Blake, R. R., & McCanse, A. A. (1991). *Leadership dilemmas grid solutions.* Houston, TX: Gulf.

41. For a discussion of situational theories, see Wilson, G. L. (2002). *Groups in context* (6th ed.). New York: McGraw-Hill, pp. 190–194.

42. Fiedler, F. E. (1967). *A theory of leadership effectiveness.* New York: McGraw-Hill.

43. Hersey, P., & Blanchard, K. (2001). *Management of organizational behavior: Utilizing human resources* (8th ed.). Upper Saddle River, NJ: Prentice Hall.

44. Kuhnert, K. W., & Lewis, P. (1987). Transactional and transformational leadership: A constructive/developmental analysis. *Academy of Management Review, 12,* 648–657.

45. Collins, J. (2001). *Good to great: Why some companies make the leap . . . and others don't.* New York: HarperCollins.

46. Ibid., p. 72

47. Kelleher, H. (1997, Spring). A culture of commitment. *Leader to leader.* New York: Leader to Leader Institute, paragraph 5.

48. Senge, P. M. (2006). *The fifth discipline: The art and practice of the learning organization.* New York: Doubleday/Currency.

49. For a detailed discussion of leadership emergence, see Bormann, E. G. G., & Bormann, N. C. (1997). *Effective small group communication* (6th ed.). New York: Pearson Custom.

50. Hackman, M. Z., & Johnson, C. E. (2004). *Leadership: A communication perspective.* Long Grove, IL: Waveland. See also Anderson, C., & Kilduff, G. J. (2009). Why do dominant personalities attain influence in face-to-face groups? The competence-signaling effects of trait dominance. *Journal of Personality and Social Psychology, 96,* 491–503.

51. See note 31, Bormann (1990). For a succinct description of Bormann's findings, see note 12, Rothwell (2004, p. 165).

52. Kelley, R. E. (2008). Rethinking followership. In R. E. Riggio, I. Chaleff, & J. Lipman-Blumen (Eds.), *The art of followership: How great followers create great leaders and organizations* (pp. 5–16). San Francisco: Jossey-Bass; Ibid., p. 8.

53. Agho, A. O. (2009). Perspectives of senior-level executives on effective followership and leadership. *Journal of Leadership & Organizational Studies, 16,* 159–166.

54. Kelley, R. E. (1992). *The power of followership.* New York: Doubleday Business.

55. Kellerman, B. (2008). *Followership: How followers are creating change and changing leaders.* Boston, MA: Harvard Business Press.

56. Ibid., p. 179.

57. The following types of power are based on the categories developed by French, J. R., & Raven, B. (1968). The basis of social power. In D. Cartright & A. Zander (Eds.), *Group dynamics* (pp. 259–269). New York: Harper & Row, p. 265.

58. Rothwell, J. D. (2004). *In mixed company: Small group communication* (5th ed.). Belmont, CA: Wadsworth, pp. 247–282.

59. See note 8, Limb (2008).

# CHAPTER 10

1. HP's Susie Wee named 2010 WITI Hall of Fame inductee. (2010, September 13). *YouTube*. Retrieved from http://www.youtube .com/watch?feature=player_embedded&v=w0BdP8hlHHc.

2. Zieger, M. (2010, September 14). Susie Wee: From hockey rink to hall of fame [Web log post]. Retrieved from http:// h20435.www2.hp.com/t5/367-Addison-Avenue-Blog/ Susie-Wee-From-Hockey-Rink-to-Hall-of-Fame/ba-p/58169.

3. Kowalenko, K. (2008, March 7). Susie Wee: Picture perfect digital images. *The Institute*. Retrieved from http://theinstitute.ieee.org/ people/profiles/susie-wee-picture-perfect-digital-images162.

4. Understanding our differences, celebrating our uniqueness: Cisco [Web log post]. (n.d.). Retrieved from http://diversitywoman.com/ understanding-our-differences-celebrating-our-uniqueness-cisco/.

5. Wee, S. (2007, March 26). The agony of defeat! Reflections by Susie Wee [Web log post]. Retrieved from http://www.susiewee .com/blog/2007/03/26/the-agony-of-defeat/.

6. See note 1, HP's Susie Wee named 2010 WITI Hall of Fame inductee (2010).

7. Robles, M. M. (2012). Executive perceptions of the top 10 soft skills needed in today's workplace. *Business Communication Quarterly, 75,* 453–465.

8. Lutgen-Sandvik, P., Riforgiate, S., & Fletcher, C. (2011). Work as a source of positive emotional experiences and the discourses informing positive assessment. *Western Journal of Communication, 75,* 2–27.

9. See, for example, Pavitt, C. (2003). Do interacting groups perform better than aggregates of individuals? *Human Communication Research, 29,* 592–599, Wittenbaum, G. M. (2004). Putting communication into the study of group memory. *Human Communication Research, 29,* 616–623, and Frank, M. G., Feely, T. H., Paolantonio, N., & Servoss, T. J. (2004). Individual and small group accuracy in judging truthful and deceptive communication. *Group Decision and Negotiation, 13,* 45–54.

10. Rae-Dupree, J. (2008, December 7). Innovation is a team sport. *The New York Times.* Retrieved from http://www.nytimes .com/2008/12/07/business/worldbusiness/07iht-innovate.1 .18456109.html?_r=0.

11. See note 1, HP's Susie Wee named 2010 WITI Hall of Fame inductee (2010).

12. Aritz, J., & Walker, R. C. (2009). Group composition and communication styles: An analysis of multicultural teams in decision-making meetings. *Journal of Intercultural Communication Research, 38*(2), 99–114.

13. Stier, J., & Kjellin, M. (2010). Communicative challenges in multinational project work: Obstacles and tools for reaching common understandings. *Journal of Intercultural Communication, 24,* 1–12.

14. Rivetti, C. (n.d.). My history, my company. *Stone Island.* Retrieved from http://www.stoneisland-corporate.com/en/ persons-and-passions/.

15. Tadmor, C. T., Satterstrom, P., Jang, S., & Polzer, J. T. (2012). Beyond individual creativity: The superadditive benefits of multicultural experience for collective creativity in culturally diverse teams. *Journal of Cross-Cultural Psychology, 43,* 384–392.

16. Information drawn from García, M., & Cañado, M. (2011). Multicultural teamwork as a source of experiential learning and intercultural development. *Journal of English Studies, 9,* 145–163; and van Knippenberg, D., van Ginkel, W. P., & Homan, A. C. (2013, July). Diversity mindsets and the performance of diverse teams. *Organizational Behavior and Human Decision Processes, 121,* 183–193.

17. Ibid., van Knippenberg, van Ginkel, & Homan (2013).

18. Diversity makes us smarter [Web log post]. (2011, July 12). Retrieved from http://freethoughtblogs.com/ crommunist/2011/07/12/diversity-makes-us-smarter/.

19. Adler, R. B., & Elmhorst, J. M. (2010). *Communicating at work: Principles and practices for business and the professions* (10th ed.). New York: McGraw-Hill, pp. 278–279.

20. Wheelan, S. A., Murphy, D., Tsumura, E., & Kline, S. F. (1998). Member perceptions of internal group dynamics and productivity. *Small Group Research, 29,* 371–393.

21. Wee, S. (2007, August 20). Deceit, trickery, encouragement, and teamwork. Reflections by Susie Wee [Web log post]. Retrieved from http://www.susiewee.com/blog/2007/08/.

22. Hülsheger, U. R., Anderson, N., & Salgado, J. F. (2009). Team-level predictors of innovation at work: A comprehensive meta-analysis spanning three decades of research. *Journal of Applied Psychology, 94,* 1128–1145.

23. Fisher, B. A. (1970). Decision emergence: Phases in group decision making. *Speech Monographs, 37,* 53–66.

24. Frantz, C. R., & Jin, K. G. (1995). The structure of group conflict in a collaborative work group during information systems development. *Journal of Applied Communication Research, 23,* 108–127.

25. Poole, M., & Roth, J. (1989). Decision development in small groups IV: A typology of group decision paths. *Human Communication Research, 15,* 323–356. Also, Poole, M., & Roth, J. (1989). Decision development in small groups V: Test of a contingency model. *Human Communication Research, 15,* 549–589.

26. Bohm, D. (1996). *On dialogue* (L. Nichol, Ed.). London: Routledge & Kegan Paul.

27. Isaacs, W. (1999). *Dialogue: The art of thinking together.* New York: Currency.

28. Berry, G. R. (2011). Enhancing effectiveness on virtual teams. *Journal of Business Communication, 48,* 186–206.

29. Altschuller, S., & Benbunan-Fich, R. (2010). Trust, performance, and the communication process in ad hoc decision-making virtual teams. *Journal of Computer-Mediated Communication, 16,* 27–47.

30. Johnson, G. M. (2006). Synchronous and asynchronous text-based CMC in educational contexts: A review of recent research. *Tech Trends, 50,* 46–53.

31. Lin, C., Standing, C., & Liu, Y. (2008). A model to develop effective virtual teams. *Decision Support Systems, 45,* 1031–1045.

32. Baltes, B. B., Dickson, M. W., Sherman, M. P., Bauer, C. C., & LaGanke, J. S. (2002). Computer-mediated communication and group decision making: A meta-analysis. *Organizational Behavior and Human Decision Processes,* 156–179.

33. Nowak, K., Watt, J. H., & Walther, J. B. (2009). Computer mediated teamwork and the efficiency framework: Exploring the influence of synchrony and cues on media satisfaction and outcome success. *Computers in Human Behavior, 25,* 1108–1119.

34. Kraut, R. E., Gergle, D., & Fussell, S. R. (2002). The use of visual information in shared visual spaces: Informing the development of virtual co-presence. *Carnegie Mellon University Research Showcase.*

35. Rico, R., Alcover, C., Sánchez-Manzanares, M., & Gil, F. (2009). The joint relationships of communication behaviors and task interdependence on trust building and change in virtual project teams. *Social Science Information, 48,* 229–255.

36. Altschuller, S., & Benbunan-Fich, R. (2010). Trust, performance, and the communication process in ad hoc decision-making virtual teams. *Journal of Computer-Mediated Communication, 16,* 27–47.

37. Steinel, W., Van Kleef, G. A., & Harinck, F. (2008). Are you talking to *me*?! Separating the people from the problem when expressing

emotions in neogotiation. *Journal of Experimental Social Psychology, 44,* 362–369.

38. Shipman, A. S., & Mumford, M. D. (2011). When confidence is detrimental: Influence of overconfidence on leadership effectiveness. *The Leadership Quarterly, 22,* 649–665.

39. Dewey, J. (1910). *How we think.* New York: Heath.

40. Poole, M. S. (1991). Procedures for managing meetings: Social and technological innovation. In R. A. Swanson & B. O. Knapp (Eds.), *Innovative meeting management* (pp. 53–109). Austin, TX: 3M Meeting Management Institute. See also Poole, M. S., & Holmes, M. E. (1995). Decision development in computer-assisted group decision making. *Human Communication Research, 22,* 90–127.

41. Lewin, K. (1951). *Field theory in social science.* New York: Harper & Row, pp. 30–59.

42. Osborn, A. (1959). *Applied imagination.* New York: Scribner's.

43. See, for example, Diehl, M., & Strobe, W. (1987). Productivity loss in brainstorming groups: Toward the solution of a riddle. *Journal of Personality and Social Psychology, 53,* 497–509, and Brown, V., Tumero, M., Larey, T. S., & Paulus, P. B. (1998). Modeling cognitive interactions during group brainstorming. *Small Group Research, 29,* 495–526.

44. Hastle, R. (1983). *Inside the jury.* Cambridge, MA: Harvard University Press.

45. Ming-Yi, W. (2008). Comparing expected leadership styles in Taiwan and the United States: A study of university employees. *China Media Research, 4,* 36–46.

46. Ibid.

47. Dimitratos, P., Petrou, A., Plakoyiannaki, E., & Johnson, J. E. (2011). Strategic decision-making processes in internationalization: Does national culture of the local firm matter? *Journal of World Business, 46,* 194–204.

48. Adapted from Adler, R. B., & Elmhorst, J. M. (2005). *Communicating at work: Principles and practices for business and the professions* (8th ed.). New York: McGraw-Hill, p. 269.

49. Rothwell, J. D. (2013). *In mixed company* (8th ed.). Boston: Wadsworth-Cengage, pp. 139–142.

50. Carmeli, A., Sheaffer, Z., & Helevi, M. Y. (2009). Does participatory decision-making in top management teams enhance decision effectiveness and firm performance? *Personnel Review, 38,* 696–714.

51. Rains, S. A. (2007). The impact of anonymity on perceptions of source credibility and influence in computer-mediated group communication. *Communication Research, 34,* 100–125.

52. Waller, B. M., Hope, L., Burrowes, M., & Morrison, E. R. (2011). Twelve (not so) angry men: Managing conversational group size increases perceived contribution by decision makers. *Group Processes & Intergroup Relations, 14,* 835–843.

53. Janis, I. (1982). *Groupthink: Psychological studies of policy decisions and fiascoes.* Boston: Houghton Mifflin. See also Baron, R. S. (2005). So right it's wrong: Groupthink and the ubiquitous nature of polarized group decision making. In M. P. Zanna (Ed.), *Advances in experimental social psychology* (vol. 37, pp. 219–253). San Diego, CA: Elsevier Academic Press.

54. Peralta, E., Memmott, M., & Coleman, K. (2012, July 12). Paterno, others slammed in report for failing to protect Sandusky's victims. *National Public Radio.*

55. Adapted from Rothwell (2013, pp. 223–226), see note 49.

56. Zieger, M. (2011, January 19). HP's Susie Wee takes on the Sharks [Web log post]. Retrieved from http://h20435.www2.hp.com/t5/367-Addison-Avenue-Blog/HP-s-Susie-Wee-Takes-on-the-Sharks/ba-p/61123.

## CHAPTER 11

1. Dwyer, K. K., & Davidson, M. M. (2012, April–June). Is public speaking really more feared than death? *Communication Research Reports, 29,* 99–107. This study found that public speaking was selected more often as a common fear than any other fear, including death. However, when students were asked to select a top fear, students selected death most often.

2. For an example of how demographics have been taken into consideration in great speeches, see Stephens, G. (1997, Fall). Frederick Douglass' multiracial abolitionism: "Antagonistic cooperation" and "redeemable ideals" in the July 5 speech. *Communication Studies, 48,* 175–194. On July 5, 1852, Douglass gave a speech titled "What to the Slave Is the 4th of July," attacking the hypocrisy of Independence Day in a slaveholding republic. It was one of the greatest antislavery speeches ever given, and part of its success stemmed from the way Douglass sought common ground with his multiracial audience.

3. Polisetti, S. (2012). The loss of Native American culture. In L. Schnoor (Ed.), *Winning orations, 2012* (pp. 163–165). Mankato, MN: Interstate Oratorical Association, p. 163. Polisetti was coached by Lee Mayfield and Ken Young.

4. For example, see Kopfman, J. E., & Smith, S. (1996, February). Understanding the audiences of a health communication campaign: A discriminant analysis of potential organ donors based on intent to donate. *Journal of Applied Communication Research, 24,* 33–49.

5. Stutman, R. K., & Newell, S. E. (1984, Fall). Beliefs versus values: Silent beliefs in designing a persuasive message. *Western Journal of Speech Communication, 48*(4), 364.

6. Kelley, M. (2012). The new catch-22: Unemployment discrimination. In L. Schnoor (Ed.), *Winning orations, 2006* (pp. 56–58). Mankato, MN: Interstate Oratorical Association, p. 56. Kelley was coached by Craig Brown and Darren Epping.

7. In information science parlance, these are referred to as Boolean terms.

8. Some recent literature specifically refers to public speaking anxiety, or PSA. See, for example, Bodie, G. D. (2010, January). A racing heart, rattling knees, and ruminative thoughts: Defining, explaining, and treating public speaking anxiety. *Communication Education, 59*(1), 70–105.

9. See, for example, Borhis, J., & Allen, M. (1992, January). Meta-analysis of the relationship between communication apprehension and cognitive performance. *Communication Education, 41*(1), 68–76.

10. Daly, J. A., Vangelisti, A. L., & Weber, D. J. (1995, December). Speech anxiety affects how people prepare speeches: A protocol analysis of the preparation process of speakers. *Communication Monographs, 62,* 123–134.

11. Researchers generally agree that communication apprehension has three causes: genetics, social learning, and inadequate skills acquisition. See, for example, Finn, A. N. (2009). Public speaking: What causes some to panic? *Communication Currents, 4*(4), 1–2.

12. See, for example, Sawyer, C. R., & Behnke, R. R. (1997, Summer). Communication apprehension and implicit memories of public speaking state anxiety. *Communication Quarterly, 45*(3), 211–222.

13. Adapted from Ellis, A. (1977). *A new guide to rational living.* North Hollywood, CA: Wilshire Books. G. M. Philips listed a different set of beliefs that he believes contributes to reticence. The beliefs are as follows: (1) an exaggerated sense of self-importance. (Reticent people tend to see themselves as more important to others than others see them.) (2) Effective speakers are born, not made. (3) Skillful speaking is manipulative.

(4) Speaking is not that important. (5) I can speak whenever I want to; I just choose not to. (6) It is better to be quiet and let people think you are a fool than prove it by talking (they assume they will be evaluated negatively). (7) What is wrong with me requires a (quick) cure. See Keaten, J. A., Kelly, L., & Finch, C. (2000, April). Effectiveness of the Penn State program in changing beliefs associated with reticence. *Communication Education, 49*(2), 134.

14. Behnke, R. R., Sawyer, C. R., & King, P. E. (1987, April). The communication of public speaking anxiety. *Communication Education, 36,* 138–141.

15. Honeycutt, J. M., Choi, C. W., & DeBerry, J. R. (2009, July). Communication apprehension and imagined interactions. *Communication Research Reports, 26*(2), 228–236.

16. Behnke, R. R., & Sawyer, C. R. (1999, April). Milestones of anticipatory public speaking anxiety. *Communication Education, 48*(2), 165.

17. Hinton, J. S., & Kramer, M. W. (1998, April). The impact of self-directed videotape feedback on students' self-reported levels of communication competence and apprehension. *Communication Education, 47*(2), 151–161. Significant increases in competency and decreases in apprehension were found using this method.

18. Research has confirmed that speeches practiced in front of other people tend to be more successful. See, for example, Smith, T. E., & Frymier, A. B. (2006, February). Get "real": Does practicing speeches before an audience improve performance? *Communication Quarterly, 54,* 111–125.

19. Adora Svitak, e-mail correspondence with authors, January 2013.

20. See, for example, Rosenfeld, L. R., & Civikly, J. M. (1976). *With words unspoken.* New York: Holt, Rinehart and Winston, p. 62. Also see Chaiken, S. (1979). Communicator physical attractiveness and persuasion. *Journal of Personality and Social Psychology, 37,* 1387–1397.

21. A study demonstrating this stereotype is Street, R. L., Jr., & Brady, R. M. (1982, December). Speech rate acceptance ranges as a function of evaluative domain, listener speech rate, and communication context. *Speech Monographs, 49,* 290–308.

22. See, for example, Mulac, A., & Rudd, M. J. (1977). Effects of selected American regional dialects upon regional audience members. *Communication Monographs, 44,* 184–195. Some research, however, suggests that nonstandard dialects do not have the detrimental effects on listeners that were once believed. See, for example, Johnson, F. L., & Buttny, R. (1982, March). White listeners' responses to "sounding black" and "sounding white": The effect of message content on judgments about language. *Communication Monographs, 49,* 33–39.

23. Smith, V., Siltanen, S. A., & Hosman, L. A. (1998, Fall). The effects of powerful and powerless speech styles and speaker expertise on impression formation and attitude change. *Communication Research Reports, 15*(1), 27–35. In this study, a powerful speech style was defined as one without hedges and hesitations such as *uh* and *anda*.

24. Svitak's comments that are not part of her speech were gathered via e-mail correspondence with the authors during January 2013.

25. A video of Svitak's TED talk is available at www.ted.com/talks/lang/en/adora_svitak.html. More information about Svitak is available at her website: www.adorasvitak.com/Main.html.

## CHAPTER 12

1. See, for example, Stern, L. (1985). *The structures and strategies of human memory.* Homewood, IL: Dorsey Press. See also Turner, C. (1987, June 15). Organizing information: Principles and practices. *Library Journal, 112* (11), 58.

2. Booth, W. C., Colomb, G. C., & Williams, J. M. (2003). *The craft of research.* Chicago: University of Chicago Press.

3. Koehler, C. (1998, June 15). Mending the body by lending an ear: The healing power of listening. *Vital Speeches of the Day,* 543.

4. Hallum, E. (1998). Untitled. In L. Schnoor (Ed.), *Winning orations, 1998* (pp. 4–6). Mankato, MN: Interstate Oratorical Association, p. 4. Hallum was coached by Clark Olson.

5. Monroe, A. (1935). *Principles and types of speech.* Glenview, IL: Scott, Foresman.

6. Adapted from http://vaughnkohler.com/wp-content/uploads/2013/01/Monroe-Motivated-Sequence-Outline-Handout1.pdf, accessed May 23, 2013.

7. Graham, K. (1976, April 15). The press and its responsibilities. *Vital Speeches of the Day,* 42.

8. Hamilton, S. (2000). Cruise ship violence. In L. Schnoor (Ed.), *Winning orations, 2000* (pp. 92–94). Mankato, MN: Interstate Oratorical Association, p. 92. Hamilton was coached by Angela Hatton.

9. Anderson, G. (2009). Don't reject my homoglobin. In L. Schnoor (Ed.), *Winning orations, 2009* (pp. 33–35). Mankato, MN: Interstate Oratorical Association, p. 33. Anderson was coached by Leah White.

10. Eggleston, T.S. The key steps to an effective presentation. Retrieved May 19, 2010 from http://www.the-eggman.com/writings/keystep1.html.

11. Cook, E. Making business presentations work. Retrieved May 19, 2010 from www.businessknowhow.com/manage/presentation101.htm.

12. Kotelnikov, V. Effective presentations. Retrieved May 19, 2010 from http://www.1000ventures.com/business_guide/crosscuttings/presentations_main.html.

13. Toastmasters International, Inc.'s Communication and Leadership Program Retrieved May 19, 2010 from www.toastmasters.org.

14. Cochran, J. (2012). Untitled. In L. Schnoor (Ed.), *Winning orations, 2012* (pp. 40–42). Mankato, MN: Interstate Oratorical Association, p. 40. Cochran was coached by Dan Smith and Michael Chen.

15. Davis, K. C. (2007, July 3). The founding immigrants. *New York Times.* Retrieved from http://www.nytimes.com/2007/07/03/opinion/03davis.html?_r0.

16. Dunn, N. (2012). There's nothing special about restraining and secluding students with disabilities. In L. Schnoor (Ed.), *Winning orations, 2012* (pp. 126–128). Mankato, MN: Interstate Oratorical Association, p. 126. Dunn was coached by Jacob Stutzman and Tai Du.

17. Griesinger, C. (2006). Untitled. In L. Schnoor (Ed.), *Winning orations, 2006* (pp. 37–39). Mankato, MN: Interstate Oratorical Association, p. 37. Griesinger was coached by Ray Quiel.

18. Hobbs, E. (2006). Untitled. In L. Schnoor (Ed.), *Winning orations, 2006* (pp. 45–47). Mankato, MN: Interstate Oratorical Association, p. 45. Hobbs was coached by Kevin Minch and Kris Stroup.

19. Ibid.

20. Wideman, S. (2006). Planning for peak oil: Legislation and conservation. In L. Schnoor (Ed.), *Winning orations, 2006* (pp. 7–9). Mankato, MN: Interstate Oratorical Association, p. 7. Wideman was coached by Brendan Kelly.

21. Herbert, B. (2007, April 26). Hooked on violence. *New York Times.* Retrieved from http://www.nytimes.com/2007/04/26/opinion/26herbert.html.

22. Sherriff, D. (1998, April 1). Bill Gates too rich [Online forum comment]. Retrieved from CRTNET discussion group.

23. Elsesser, K. (2010, March 4). And the gender-neutral Oscar goes to . . . *New York Times*. Retrieved from http://www.nytimes.com/2010/03/04/opinion/04elsesser.html.

24. Reagan, R. (1989, February 1). President's farewell address to the American people. *Vital Speeches of the Day*, 226.

25. Khanna, R. (2000). Distortion of history. In L. Schnoor (Ed.), *Winning orations, 2000* (pp. 46–48). Mankato, MN: Interstate Oratorical Association, p. 46. Khanna was coached by Alexis Hopkins.

26. Notebaert, R. C. (1998, November 1). Leveraging diversity: Adding value to the bottom line. *Vital Speeches of the Day*, 47.

27. McCarley, E. (2009). On the importance of drug courts. In L. Schnoor (Ed.), *Winning orations, 2009* (pp. 36–38). Mankato, MN: Interstate Oratorical Association, p. 36.

28. Teresa Fishman, director of the Center for Academic Integrity at Clemson University, quoted in Gabriel, T. (2010, August 1). Plagiarism lines blur for students in digital age. *New York Times*. Retrieved from http://www.nytimes.com/2010/08/02/education/02cheat.html?pagewanted-all.

29. See note 27, McCarley (2009).

30. Curt Casper, e-mail to George Rodman, March 2013.

31. Casper, C. (2011). Survivor Support. In L. Schnoor (Ed.), *Winning orations, 2011* (pp. 85–87). Mankato, MN: Interstate Oratorical Association.

## CHAPTER 13

1. Ubin, B. (2013, April 25). Learn to read Chinese in eight minutes. *Forbes*. Retrieved from http://www.forbes.com/sites/bruceupbin/2013/04/25/learn-to-read-chinese-in-eight-minutes/.

2. Sigler, M. G. (2010, August 4). Eric Schmidt: Every 2 days we create as much information as we did up to 2003. *Techcrunch*. Retrieved from http://techcrunch.com/2010/08/04/schmidt-data/.

3. See, for example, Wurman, R. S. (2000). *Information anxiety 2*. Indianapolis: Que.

4. Buffett, W. (2012, November 25). A minimum tax for the wealthy. *New York Times*. Retrieved from http://www.nytimes.com/2012/11/26/opinion/buffett-a-minimum-tax-for-the-wealthy.html?_r=0

5. See Fransden, K. D., & Clement, D. A. (1984). The functions of human communication in informing: Communicating and processing information. In C. C. Arnold & J. W. Bowers (Eds.), *Handbook of rhetorical and communication theory* (pp. 338–399). Boston: Allyn and Bacon.

6. Allocca, K. (2001, November). *Why videos go viral*. TEDYouth talk, New York City. Retrieved from http://www.ted.com/talks/kevin_allocca_why_videos_go_viral.html.

7. Konda, K. J. (2006). The war at home. In L. Schnoor (Ed.), *Winning orations, 2006* (pp. 74–76). Mankato, MN: Interstate Oratorical Association, p. 74. Konda was coached by Kevin Sackreiter.

8. Levine, K. (2001). The dentist's dirty little secret. In L. Schnoor (Ed.), *Winning orations, 2001* (pp. 77–79). Mankato, MN: Interstate Oratorical Association, p. 77. Levine was coached by Trischa Goodnow.

9. Cacioppo, J. T., & Petty, R. E. (1979). Effects of message repetition and position on cognitive response, recall, and persuasion. *Journal of Personality and Social Psychology, 37*, 97–109.

10. Schulz, K. (2011, March). *On being wrong*. Speech presented at the TED Conference. Retrieved from http://www.ted.com/talks/kathryn_schulz_on_being_wrong.html.

11. New York Public Interest Research Group, Brooklyn College chapter. (2004). Voter registration project.

12. Parker, I. (2001, May 28) Absolute PowerPoint. *New Yorker*, p. 78.

13. Steven Pinker, a psychology professor at MIT, quoted in Zuckerman, L. (1999, April 17). Words go right to the brain, but can they stir the heart? *New York Times*, p. 9.

14. Tufte, E. (2003, September). PowerPoint is evil: Power corrupts. PowerPoint corrupts absolutely. *Wired*. Retrieved from http://www.wired.com/wired/archive/11.09/ppt2.html.

15. Simons, T. (2004, March). Does PowerPoint make you stupid? *Presentations*, p. 25.

16. Tufte, E. R. (2003). *The cognitive style of PowerPoint*. Cheshire, CT: Graphics Press.

17. See note 12, Parker (2001, p. 86).

18. Don Norman, a design expert cited in Simons (2004), see note 15, p. 26.

19. Hsueh, S. (2013, February). *How to learn Chinese . . . with ease!* Speech presented at the TED Conference, Long Beach, CA. Retrieved from http://www.ted.com/talks/shaolan_learn_to_read_chinese_with_ease.html.

## CHAPTER 14

1. Powell, T. (2012, February 9). I want my son to be a rapper! Tunette's baby steps [Web log post]. Retrieved from http://blog.mysanantonio.com/tunettepowell/2012/02/i-want-my-son-to-be-a-rapper/.

2. Powell, T. (2012, June). Video clip available at Tunette Powell's website. Retrieved from http://www.tunettepowell.com/#!media/c1qpy.

3. Ibid.

4. About Tunette Powell. (n.d.). Retrieved from http://www.tunettepowell.com/#!about/cfvg.

5. See note 2, Powell (2012).

6. For an explanation of social judgment theory, see Griffin, E. (2012). *A first look at communication theory* (8th ed.). New York: McGraw-Hill.

7. Lasch, C. (1990, Spring). Journalism, publicity and the lost art of argument. *Gannett Center Journal*, 1–11, p. 3.

8. See, for example, Jaska, J. A., & Pritchard, M. S. (1994). *Communication ethics: Methods of analysis* (2nd ed.). Boston: Wadsworth.

9. Eugene Nemirovskiy, "Mental Health Care: A Slow-Motion Train Wreck," won first place at the 2009 Arizona Interstate Oratory Contest and placed in multiple final rounds in the Southwest and in California during 2009.

10. Some research suggests that audiences may perceive a direct strategy as a threat to their freedom to form their own opinions. This perception hampers persuasion. See Brehm, J. W. (1966). *A theory of psychological reactance*. New York: Academic Press.

11. Stallings, H. (2009). Prosecution deferred is justice denied. In L. Schnoor (Ed.), *Winning orations 2009* (pp. 46–48). Mankato, MN: Interstate Oratorical Association. Hope was coached by Randy Richardson and Melanie Conrad, p. 47.

12. Monroe, A. (1935). *Principles and types of speech*. Glenview, IL: Scott, Foresman.

13. For an excellent review of the effects of evidence, see Reinard, J. C. (1988, Fall). The empirical study of persuasive effects of evidence: The status after fifty years of research. *Human Communication Research*, 3–59.

14. There are, of course, other classifications of logical fallacies than those presented here. See, for example, Warnick, B., & Inch, E. (1994). *Critical thinking and communication: The use of reason in argument* (2nd ed.). New York: Macmillan, pp. 137–161.

15. Sprague, J., & Stuart, D. (1992). *The speaker's handbook* (3rd ed.). Fort Worth, TX: Harcourt Brace Jovanovich, p. 172.

16. Myers, L. J. (1981). The nature of pluralism and the African American case. *Theory into Practice, 20*, 3–4. Cited in Samovar,

L. A., & Porter, R. E. (1995). *Communication between cultures* (2nd ed.). New York: Wadsworth, p. 251.

17. Ibid., Samovar & Porter (1995, pp. 154–155).

18. For an example of how one politician failed to adapt to his audience's attitudes, see Hostetler, M. J. (1998, Winter). Gov. Al Smith confronts the Catholic question: The rhetorical legacy of the 1928 campaign. *Communication Quarterly, 46*(1), 12–24. Smith was reluctant to discuss religion, attributed bigotry to anyone who brought it up, and was impatient with the whole issue. He lost the election. Many years later, John F. Kennedy dealt with "the Catholic question" more reasonably and won.

19. Mount, A. (1973). Speech before the Southern Baptist Convention. In W. A. Linkugel, R. R. Allen, & R. Johannessen (Eds.), *Contemporary American speeches* (3rd ed., pp. 203–205). Belmont, CA: Wadsworth, p. 204:

20. Rudolf, H. J. (1983, Summer). Robert F. Kennedy at Stellenbosch University. *Communication Quarterly, 31*, 205–211.

21. Preface to Barbara Bush's speech, "Choices and Change," in Peterson, O. (Ed.). (1991). *Representative American speeches, 1990–1991.* New York: H. W. Wilson, p. 162.

22. B. Bush, "Choices and Change," speech presented to the graduating class of Wellesley College in Wellesley, MA, on June 1, 1990. Reprinted in ibid., p. 166.

23. DeVito, J. A. (1986). *The communication handbook: A dictionary.* New York: Harper & Row, pp. 84–86.

24. Rodriguez, G. (DATE). How to develop a winning sales plan. Retrieved July 26, 2010, from www.powerhomebiz.com/062006/salesplan.htm.

25. Sanfilippo, B. (DATE). Winning sales strategies of top performers. Retrieved May 15, 2010, from www.selfgrowth.com/articles/Sanfilippo2.html.

26. Powell, T. (2012). It's not the addict, it's the drug: Redefining America's war on drugs. In L. Schnoor (Ed.), *Winning orations 2012* (pp. 100–102). Mankato, MN: Interstate Oratorical Association.

## APPENDIX

1. Granovetter, M. (1995). *Getting a job: A study of contacts and careers* (2nd ed.). Chicago: University of Chicago Press.

2. Bolles, R. N. (2009). *What color is your parachute? A practical manual for job-hunters and career-changers 2009 edition.* Berkeley, CA: Ten Speed Press, pp. 27–40.

3. Baker, W. (2000). *Achieving success through social capital.* San Francisco: Josey-Bass, p. 10.

4. Crispin, G., & Mehler, M. (2002). Impact of the Internet on source of hires. Retrieved August 28, 2013, from http://www.careerxroads.com/news/impactoftheinternet.doc.

5. Granovetter, M. S. (1973). The strength of weak ties. *American Journal of Sociology, 78*, 1360–1380.

6. The information in this section is based on material in Adler, R. B., & Elmhorst, J. M. (2010). *Communicating at work: Principles and practices for business and the professions* (10th ed.). New York: McGraw-Hill, pp. 19–23.

7. Dodds, P. S., Muhamad, R., & Watts, D. J. (2003). An experimental study of search in global social networks. *Science, 301*, 827–829.

8. Tullier, M. (2002). The art and science of writing cover letters: The best way to make a first impression. Retrieved from http://resume.monster.com/coverletter/coverletters.

9. Rabin, M., & Schrag, J. L. (1999). First impressions matter: A model of confirmatory bias. *The Quarterly Journal of Economics, 14*, 37–82.

10. Rosen, J. (2010, July 25). The end of forgetting. *New York Times Magazine*, pp. 30–35.

11. Habib, M. C. (2007). Managing your identity online. *Net Connect, 132*, 2–4

12. Kang, J. (2010). Ethical conflict and job satisfaction of public relations practitioners. *Public Relations Review, 36*, 152–156.

13. Covey, S. R. (2001). Principled communication. *Executive Excellence.* Retrieved July 14, 2010, from Get Synergized: http://www.getsynergized.com/communication_covey.htm.

14. Ibid.

15. Farley, S., Timme, D., & Hart, J. (2010). On coffee talk and breakroom chatter: Perceptions of women who gossip in the workplace. *Journal of Social Psychology, 150*, 361–368.

16. Zaslow, J. (2010, January 6). Before you gossip, ask yourself this . . . *Moving On.* Retrieved July 10, 2010, from http://online.wsj.com/article/SB10001424052748704160504574640111681307026.html.

17. Ibid.

18. New hires—stand out at work. (2010, May). *OfficePro.* Retrieved July 10, 2010, from http://web.ebscohost.com.libproxy.sbcc.edu:2048/bsi/detail?vid=4&hid=9&sid=079bf30df37c-4ad6-897ec1626aa9bb49%40sessionmgr14&bdata=JnNpdGU9YnNpLWxpdmU%3d#db=buh&AN=50544049.

19. Ibid.

20. Lublin, J. S. (2010, July 6). The keys to unlocking your most successful career: Five simple but crucial lessons culled from many years of offering advice to workers, bosses and job seekers. *Wall Street Journal.* Retrieved July 12, 2010, from http://online.wsj.com/article/SB1000142405274870429360457534332251650841 4.html.

21. Ibid.

# Glossary

**abstract language** Language that lacks specificity or does not refer to observable behavior or other sensory data. See also *Behavioral description*. p. 118

**abstraction ladder** A range of more- to less-abstract terms describing an event or object. p. 117

**actuate** To move members of an audience toward a specific behavior. p. 410

**addition** The articulation error that involves adding extra parts to words. p. 344

**ad hominem fallacy** A fallacious argument that attacks the integrity of a person to weaken his or her position. p. 416

**advising response** Helping response in which the receiver offers suggestions about how the speaker should deal with a problem. p. 155

**affect blend** The combination of two or more expressions, each showing a different emotion. p. 182

**affect displays** Facial expressions, body movements, and vocal traits that reveal emotional states. p. 171

**affinity** The degree to which people like or appreciate one another. As with all relational messages, affinity is usually expressed nonverbally. p. 205

**all-channel network** A communication network pattern in which group members are always together and share all information with one another. p. 275

**altruistic lies** Deception intended to be unmalicious, or even helpful, to the person to whom it is told. p. 228

**ambushing** A style in which the receiver listens carefully to gather information to use in an attack on the speaker. p. 139

**analogy** An extended comparison that can be used as supporting material in a speech. p. 369

**analytical listening** Listening in which the primary goal is to fully understand the message, prior to any evaluation p. 149

**analyzing statement** A helping style in which the listener offers an interpretation of a speaker's message. p. 156

**anchor** The position supported by audience members before a persuasion attempt. p. 405

**androgynous** Combining both masculine and feminine traits. p. 52

**anecdote** A brief, personal story used to illustrate or support a point in a speech. p. 370

**argumentum ad populum fallacy** Fallacious reasoning based on the dubious notion that because many people favor an idea, you should, too. p. 418

**argumentum ad verecundiam fallacy** Fallacious reasoning that tries to support a belief by relying on the testimony of someone who is not an authority on the issue being argued. p. 417

**articulation** The process of pronouncing all the necessary parts of a word. p. 344

**assertive communication** A style of communicating that directly expresses the sender's needs, thoughts, or feelings, delivered in a way that does not attack the receiver's dignity. p. 250

**asynchronous communication** Communication that occurs when there's a time gap between when a message is sent and when it is received. p. 17

**attending** The process of focusing on certain stimuli from the environment. p. 136

**attitude** The predisposition to respond to an idea, person, or thing favorably or unfavorably. p. 331

**attribution** The process of attaching meaning. p. 55

**audience analysis** A consideration of characteristics including the type, goals, demographics, beliefs, attitudes, and values of listeners. p. 329

**audience involvement** The level of commitment and attention that listeners devote to a speech. p. 389

**audience participation** Listener activity during a speech; a technique to increase audience involvement. p. 390

**authoritarian leadership style** A leadership style in which the designated leader uses legitimate, coercive, and reward power to dictate the group's actions. p. 282

**avoidance spiral** A communication spiral in which the parties slowly reduce their dependence on one another, withdraw, and become less invested in the relationship. p. 243

**bar chart** A visual aid that compares two or more values by showing them as elongated horizontal rectangles. p. 393

**basic speech structure** The division of a speech into introduction, body, and conclusion. p. 355

**behavioral description** An account that refers only to observable phenomena. p. 118

**behavioral interview** Session that explores specifics of the applicant's past performance as it relates to the job at hand. p. A-15

**belief** An underlying conviction about the truth of an idea, often based on cultural training. p. 331

**brainstorming** A method for creatively generating ideas in groups by minimizing criticism and encouraging a large quantity of ideas without regard to their workability or ownership by individual members. p. 313

**breadth (of self-disclosure)** The range of topics about which an individual discloses. See also *Depth.* p. 222

**breakout groups** A strategy used when the number of members is too large for effective discussion. Subgroups simultaneously address an issue and then report back to the group at large. p. 307

**cause-effect pattern** An organizing plan for a speech that demonstrates how one or more events result in another event or events. p. 361

**certainty** Messages that dogmatically imply that the speaker's position is correct and that the other person's ideas are not worth considering. These messages are likely to generate a defensive response. p. 245

**chain network** A communication network in which information passes sequentially from one member to another. p. 275

**channel** The medium through which a message passes from sender to receiver. p. 8

**chronemics** The study of how humans use and structure time. p. 189

**citation** A brief statement of supporting material in a speech. p. 372

**climax pattern** An organizing plan for a speech that builds ideas to the point of maximum interest or tension. p. 359

**closed question** Interview question that can be answered in a few words. p. A-6

**coculture** The perception of membership in a group that is part of an encompassing culture. p. 77

**coercive power** The power to influence others by the threat or imposition of unpleasant consequences. p. 290

**cohesiveness** The totality of forces that causes members to feel themselves part of a group and makes them want to remain in that group. p. 302

**collectivistic culture** A culture in which members focus on the welfare of the group as a whole, rather than a concern by individuals for their own success. See also *Individualistic culture.* p. 80

**column chart** A visual aid that compares two or more values by showing them as elongated vertical rectangles. p. 393

**comforting** A response style in which a listener reassures, supports, or distracts the person seeking help. p. 158

**communication** The process of creating meaning through symbolic interaction. p. 5

**communication climate** The emotional tone of a relationship as it is expressed in the messages that the partners send and receive. p. 239

**communication competence** The ability to maintain a relationship on terms acceptable to all parties. p. 25

**compromise** An approach to conflict resolution in which both parties attain at least part of what they seek through self-sacrifice. p. 260

**conclusion (of a speech)** The final structural unit of a speech, in which the main points are reviewed and final remarks are made to motivate the audience to act or help listeners remember key ideas. p. 363

**confirming responses** A message that expresses respect and values the other person. p. 239

**conflict** An expressed struggle between at least two interdependent parties who perceive incompatible goals, scarce rewards, and interference from the other party in achieving their goals. p. 246

**conflict stage** A stage in problem-solving groups when members openly defend their positions and question those of others. p. 304

**connection power** The influence granted by virtue of a member's ability to develop relationships that help the group reach its goal. p. 290

**consensus** Agreement among group members about a decision. p. 315

**content message** A message that communicates information about the subject being discussed. See also *Relational message.* p. 205

**contextually interpersonal communication** Any communication that occurs between two individuals. See also *Qualitatively interpersonal communication.* p. 203

**control** The social need to influence others. p. 205

**controlling communication** Messages in which the sender tries to impose some sort of outcome on the receiver, usually resulting in a defensive reaction. p. 244

**convergence** Accommodating one's speaking style to another person, who usually is desirable or has higher status. p. 112

**convincing** A speech goal that aims at changing audience members' beliefs, values, or attitudes. p. 410

**coordination** Interaction in which participants interact smoothly, with a high degree of satisfaction but without necessarily understanding one another well. p. 32

**counterfeit question** A question that disguises the speaker's true motives, which do not include a genuine desire to understand the other person. p. 145

**credibility** The believability of a speaker or other source of information. p. 420

**critical listening** Listening in which the goal is to evaluate the quality or accuracy of the speaker's remarks. p. 151

**culture** The language, values, beliefs, traditions, and customs people share and learn. p. 77

**database** A computerized collection of information that can be searched in a variety of ways to locate information that the user is seeking. p. 335

**debilitative communication apprehension** An intense level of anxiety about speaking before an audience, resulting in poor performance. p. 337

**decoding** The process in which a receiver attaches meaning to a message. p. 10

**defensive listening** A response style in which the receiver perceives a speaker's comments as an attack. p. 139

**deletion** An articulation error that involves leaving off parts of words. p. 344

**democratic leadership style** A style in which the nominal leader invites the group's participation in decision making. p. 282

**demographics** Audience characteristics that can be analyzed statistically, such as age, gender, education, and group membership. p. 329

**depth (of self-disclosure)** The level of personal information a person reveals on a particular topic. See also *Breadth*. p. 222

**description** A type of speech that uses details to create a "word picture" of the essential factors that make something what it is. p. 382

**descriptive communication** In terms of communication climate, statements in which the speaker describes his or her position. See also *Evaluative communication*. p. 244

**developmental models (of relational maintenance)** These models propose that the nature of communication is different in various stages of interpersonal relationships. p. 207

**diagram** A line drawing that shows the most important components of an object. p. 392

**dialectical model (of relational maintenance)** A model claiming that, throughout their lifetime, people in virtually all interpersonal relationships must deal with equally important, simultaneous, and opposing forces such as connection and autonomy, predictability and novelty, and openness versus privacy. p. 212

**dialectical tensions** Inherent conflicts that arise when two opposing or incompatible forces exist simultaneously. p. 212

**dialogue** A process in which people let go of the notion that their ideas are more correct or superior to others' and instead seek to understand an issue from many different perspectives. p. 308

**direct aggression** An expression of the sender's thoughts or feelings or both that attacks the position and dignity of the receiver. p. 248

**direct persuasion** Persuasion that does not try to hide or disguise the speaker's persuasive purpose. p. 410

**direct question** Interview question that makes a straightforward request for information. p. A-6

**disconfirming response** A message that expresses a lack of caring or respect for another person. p. 240

**disfluency** A nonlinguistic verbalization—for example, um, er, ah. p. 183

**disinhibition** The tendency to transmit messages without considering their consequences. See also *Flaming*. p. 20

**divergence** A linguistic strategy in which speakers emphasize differences between their communicative style and others' in order to create distance. p. 113

**dyad** A two-person unit. p. 11

**dyadic communication** Two-person communication. p. 11

**dysfunctional roles** Individual roles played by group members that inhibit the group's effective operation. p. 278

**either-or fallacy** Fallacious reasoning that sets up false alternatives, suggesting that if the inferior one must be rejected, then the other must be accepted. p. 416

**emblems** Deliberate nonverbal behaviors with precise meanings, known to virtually all members of a cultural group. p. 176

**emergence stage** A stage in problem solving when the group moves from conflict toward a single solution. p. 306

**emergent leader** A member who assumes leadership roles without being appointed by higher-ups. p. 286

**emotional evidence** Evidence that arouses emotional reactions in an audience. p. 415

**emotive language** Language that conveys the sender's attitude rather than simply offering an objective description. p. 121

**empathy** The ability to project oneself into another person's point of view, so as to experience the other's thoughts and feelings. p. 59

**encoding** The process of putting thoughts into symbols, most commonly words. p. 10

**environment** Both the physical setting in which communication occurs and the personal perspectives of the parties involved. p. 9

**equality** When communicators show that they believe others have just as much worth as human beings as they do. p. 245

**equivocal language** Language with more than one likely interpretation. p. 229

**equivocal words** Words that have more than one dictionary definition. p. 114

**equivocation** A vague statement that can be interpreted in more than one way. p. 123

**escalatory spiral** A reciprocal pattern of communication in which messages, either confirming or disconfirming, between two or more communicators reinforce one another. p. 243

**ethical persuasion** Persuasion in an audience's best interest that does not depend on false or misleading information to induce change in that audience. p. 407

**ethnicity** A social construct that refers to the degree to which a person identifies with a particular group, usually on the basis of nationality, culture, religion, or some other unifying perspective. p. 86

**ethnocentrism** The attitude that one's own culture is superior to others'. p. 96

**ethos** A speaker's credibility or ethical appeal. p. 423

**euphemism** A pleasant-sounding term used in place of a more direct but less pleasant one. p. 121

**evaluative communication** Messages in which the sender judges the receiver in some way, usually resulting in a defensive response. See also *"You" language*. p. 243

**evidence** Material used to prove a point, such as testimony, statistics, and examples. p. 415

**example** A specific case that is used to demonstrate a general idea. p. 368

**expert power** The ability to influence others by virtue of one's perceived expertise on the subject in question. p. 290

**explanations** Speeches or presentations that clarify ideas and concepts already known but not understood by an audience. p. 382

**extemporaneous speech** A speech that is planned in advance but presented in a direct, conversational manner. p. 340

**face** The socially approved identity that a communicator tries to present. p. 62

**facework** Verbal and nonverbal behavior designed to create and maintain a communicator's face and the face of others. p. 62

**facilitative communication apprehension** A moderate level of anxiety about speaking before an audience that helps improve the speaker's performance. p. 337

**factual question** Interview question that investigates matters of fact. See also *Opinion question*. p. A-6

**factual statement** A statement that can be verified as being true or false. See also *Inferential statement; Opinion statement*. p. 120

**fallacy** An error in logic. p. 416

**fallacy of approval** The irrational belief that it is vital to win the approval of virtually every person a communicator deals with. p. 338

**fallacy of catastrophic failure** The irrational belief that the worst possible outcome will probably occur. p. 338

**fallacy of overgeneralization** Irrational beliefs in which (1) conclusions (usually negative) are based on limited evidence or (2) communicators exaggerate their shortcomings. p. 338

**fallacy of perfection** The irrational belief that a worthwhile communicator should be able to handle every situation with complete confidence and skill. p. 338

**feedback** The discernible response of a receiver to a sender's message. p. 10

**flaming** Sending angry and/or insulting e-mails, text messages, and website postings. p. 20

**focus group** A procedure used in market research by sponsoring organizations to survey potential users or the public at large regarding a new product or idea. p. 307

**force field analysis** A method of problem analysis that identifies the forces contributing to resolution of the problem and the forces that inhibit its resolution. p. 312

**formal outline** A consistent format and set of symbols used to identify the structure of ideas. p. 355

**formal role** A role assigned to a person by group members or an organization, usually to establish order. p. 276

**forum** A discussion format in which audience members are invited to add their comments to those of the official discussants. p. 308

**gatekeepers** Producers of mass messages who determine what messages will be delivered to consumers, how those messages will be constructed, and when they will be delivered. p. 276

**gender** socially constructed roles, behaviors, activities, and attributes that a society considers appropriate for men and/or women. p. 52

**general purpose** One of three basic ways a speaker seeks to affect an audience: to entertain, inform, or persuade. p. 327

**Gibb categories** Six sets of contrasting styles of verbal and-nonverbal behavior developed by Jack Gibb. Each set describes a communication style that is likely to arouse defensiveness and a contrasting style that is likely to prevent or reduce it. p. 243

**group** A small collection of people whose members interact with one another, usually face-to-face, over time in order to reach goals. p. 269

**group goals** Goals that a group collectively seeks to accomplish. See also *Individual goals*. p. 273

**groupthink** A group's collective striving for unanimity that discourages realistic appraisals of alternatives to its chosen decision. p. 319

**haptics** The study of touch. p. 185

**hearing** The process wherein sound waves strike the eardrum and cause vibrations that are transmitted to the brain. p. 135

**hidden agendas** Individual goals that group members are unwilling to reveal. p. 273

**high-context culture** A culture that relies heavily on subtle, often nonverbal cues to maintain social harmony. p. 81

**hypothetical example** An example that asks an audience to imagine an object or event. p. 369

**hypothetical question** Seeks a response by proposing a "what-if" situation. p. A-7

**"I" language** Language that describes the speaker's position without evaluating others. Synonymous with Description. p. 244

**identity management** Strategies used by communicators to influence the way others view them. p. 62

**illustrators** Nonverbal behaviors that accompany and support verbal messages. p. 176

**immediacy** The degree of interest and attraction we feel toward and communicate to others. As with all relational messages, immediacy is usually expressed nonverbally. p. 205

**impromptu speech** A speech given "off the top of one's head," without preparation. p. 340

**indirect communication** Hinting at a message instead of expressing thoughts and feelings directly. See also Assertive communication; Passive aggression. p. 250

**indirect persuasion** Persuasion that disguises or deemphasizes the speaker's persuasive goal. p. 411

**indirect question** Interview question that does not directly request the information being sought. See also *Direct question*. p. A-7

**individual goals** Individual motives for joining a group. p. 273

**individualistic culture** A culture in which members focus on the value and welfare of individual members, as opposed to a concern for the group as a whole. p. 80

**inferential statement** A conclusion arrived at from an interpretation of evidence. See also *Factual statement*. p. 120

**informal roles** Roles usually not explicitly recognized by a group that describe functions of group members, rather than their positions. These are sometimes called "functional roles." See also *Formal role*. p. 276

**information anxiety** The psychological stress that occurs when dealing with too much information. p. 380

**information hunger** Audience desire, created by a speaker, to learn information. p. 385

**information overload** The decline in efficiency that occurs when the rate of complexity of material is too great to manage. pp. 317 and 380

**information underload** The decline in efficiency that occurs when there is a shortage of the information that is necessary to operate effectively. p. 317

**informational interview** Interview intended to collect facts and opinions from the respondent. p. A-4

**informative purpose statement** A complete statement of the objective of a speech, worded to stress audience knowledge and/or ability. p. 384

**in-groups** Groups with which we identify. See also *Out-groups*. p. 79

**insensitive listening** The failure to recognize the thoughts or feelings that are not directly expressed by a speaker, and instead accepting the speaker's words at face value. p. 139

**instructions** Remarks that teach something to an audience in a logical, step-by-step manner. p. 382

**insulated listening** A style in which the receiver ignores undesirable information. p. 139

**intergroup communication** The interaction between members of different cocultures. p. 77

**interpersonal communication** Communication in which the parties consider one another as unique individuals rather than as objects. It is characterized by minimal use of stereotyped labels; unique, idiosyncratic social rules; and a high degree of information exchange. p. 12

**interpretation** The perceptual process of attaching meaning to stimuli that have previously been selected and organized. p. 49

**intimacy** A state of closeness between two (or sometimes more) people. Intimacy can be manifested in several ways: physically, intellectually, emotionally, and via shared activities. p. 215

**intimate distance** One of Hall's four distance zones, ranging from skin contact to 18 inches. p. 187

**intrapersonal communication** Communication that occurs within a single person. p. 11

**introduction (of a speech)** The first structural unit of a speech, in which the speaker captures the audience's attention and previews the main points to be covered. p. 363

**irrational thinking** Beliefs that have no basis in reality or logic; one source of debilitative communication apprehension. p. 338

**jargon** The specialized vocabulary that is used as a kind of shorthand by people with common backgrounds and experience. p. 116

**Johari Window** A model that describes the relationship between self-disclosure and self-awareness. p. 223

**judging response** A reaction in which the receiver evaluates the sender's message either favorably or unfavorably. p. 156

**kinesics** The study of body movement, gesture, and posture. p. 180

**knowledge** The understanding acquired by making sense of the raw material of information. p. 380

**laissez-faire leadership style** A style in which the designated leader gives up his or her formal role, transforming the group into a loose collection of individuals. p. 282

**language** A collection of symbols, governed by rules and used to convey messages between individuals. p. 103

**latitude of acceptance** In social judgment theory, statements that a receiver would not reject. p. 405

**latitude of noncommitment** In social judgment theory, statements that a receiver would not care strongly about one way or another. p. 405

**latitude of rejection** In social judgment theory, statements that a receiver could not possibly accept. p. 405

**Leadership Grid** A two-dimensional model that identifies leadership styles as a combination of concern for people and for the task at hand. p. 282

**leading question** A question in which the interviewer—either directly or indirectly—signals the desired answer. p. A-7

**legitimate power** The ability to influence a group owing to one's position in a group. See also *Nominal leader*. p. 290

**linear communication model** A characterization of communication as a one-way event in which a message flows from sender to receiver. p. 8

**line chart** A visual aid consisting of a grid that maps out the direction of a trend by plotting a series of points. p. 393

**linguistic intergroup bias** The tendency to label people and behaviors in terms that reflect their in-group or out-group status. p. 113

**linguistic relativism** A moderate form of linguistic determinism that argues that language exerts a strong influence on the perceptions of the people who speak it. p. 112

**listening** The process wherein the brain reconstructs electrochemical impulses generated by hearing into representations of the original sound and gives them meaning. p. 135

**listening fidelity** The degree of congruence between what a listener understands and what the message sender was attempting to communicate. p. 136

**logos** A speaker's use of logical arguments to appeal to an audience's sense of reasoning. p. 423

**lose–lose problem solving** An approach to conflict resolution in which neither party achieves its goals. p. 259

**low-context culture** A culture that uses language primarily to express thoughts, feelings, and ideas as directly as possible. p. 81

**manipulators** Movements in which one part of the body grooms, massages, rubs, holds, fidgets, pinches, picks, or otherwise manipulates another part. p. 181

**manuscript speech** A speech that is read word for word from a prepared text. p. 341

**mass communication** The transmission of messages to large, usually widespread audiences via broadcast means (such as radio and television), print (such as newspapers, magazines, and books), multimedia (such as CD-ROM, DVD, and the World Wide Web), and other forms of media such as recordings and movies. p. 13

**mediated communication** Communication sent via a medium other than face-to-face interaction, e.g., telephone, e-mail, and instant messaging. It can be both mass and personal. p. 8

**memorized speech** A speech learned and delivered by rote without a written text. p. 341

**message** A sender's planned and unplanned words and non-verbal behaviors. p. 8

**metacommunication** Messages (usually relational) that refer to other messages; communication about communication. p. 206

**mindful listening** Active, high-level information processing. p. 138

**mindless listening** Passive, low-level information processing. p. 138

**model (in speeches and presentations)** A replica of an object being discussed. It is usually used when it would be difficult or impossible to use the actual object. p. 392

**monochronic** The use of time that emphasizes punctuality, schedules, and completing one task at a time. p. 189

**Motivated Sequence** A five-step plan used in persuasive speaking; also known as Monroe's Motivated Sequence. p. 415

**narration** The presentation of speech supporting material as a story with a beginning, middle, and end. p. 371

**narrative** The stories people create and use to make sense of their personal worlds. p. 54

**networking** The strategic process of deliberately meeting people and maintaining contacts that results in information, advice, and leads that enhance one's career. p. A-2

**neutrality** A defense-arousing behavior in which the sender expresses indifference toward a receiver. p. 245

**neutral question** A question that gives the interviewee a chance to respond without any influence from the interviewer. p. A-7

**noise** External, physiological, and psychological distractions that interfere with the accurate transmission and reception of a message. p. 9

**nominal leader** The person who is identified by title as the leader of a group. p. 290

**nonassertion** The inability or unwillingness to express one's thoughts or feelings when necessary. p. 247

**nominal group technique** A method for including the ideas of all group members in a problem-solving session. p. 313

**nonverbal communication** Messages expressed by other than linguistic means. p. 169

**norms** Shared values, beliefs, behaviors, and procedures that govern a group's operation. p. 274

**number chart** A visual aid that lists numbers in tabular form in order to clarify information. p. 392

**open question** Interview question that requires the interviewee to respond in detail. See also *Closed question*. p. A-6

**opinion question** Interview question seeking the interviewee's opinion. See also *Factual question*. p. A-6

**opinion statement** A statement based on the speaker's beliefs. See also *Factual statement*. p. 120

**organization** The perceptual process of organizing stimuli into patterns. p. 49

**organizational communication** Communication that occurs among a structured collection of people in order to meet a need or pursue a goal. p. 12

**organizational culture** A relatively stable, shared set of rules about how to behave and a set of values about what is important. p. 93

**orientation stage** A stage in problem-solving groups when members become familiar with one another's position and tentatively volunteer their own. p. 304

**out-groups** Groups of people that we view as different from us. See also *In-groups*. p. 79

**panel discussion** A discussion format in which participants consider a topic more or less conversationally, without formal procedural rules. Panel discussions may be facilitated by a moderator. p. 307

**paralanguage** Nonlinguistic means of vocal expression: rate, pitch, tone, and so on. p. 182

**paraphrasing** Feedback in which the receiver rewords the speaker's thoughts and feelings. Feedback can be used to verify understanding, demonstrate empathy, and help others solve their problems. p. 146

**parliamentary procedure** A problem-solving method in which specific rules govern the way issues may be discussed and decisions made. p. 307

**passive aggression** An indirect expression of aggression, delivered in a way that allows the sender to maintain a facade of kindness. p. 249

**pathos** A speaker's use of emotional appeals to persuade an audience. p. 423

**perceived self** The person we believe ourselves to be in moments of candor. It may be identical to or different from the presenting and ideal selves. p. 62

**perception checking** A three-part method for verifying the accuracy of interpretations, including a description of the sense data, two possible interpretations, and a request for confirmation of the interpretations. p. 61

**personal distance** One of Hall's four distance zones, ranging from 18 inches to 4 feet. p. 187

**personality** The set of enduring characteristics that define a person's temperament, thought processes, and social behavior. p. 42

**persuasion** The act of motivating a listener, through communication, to change a particular belief, attitude, value, or behavior. p. 405

**phonological rules** Linguistic rules governing how sounds are combined to form words. p. 104

**pictogram** A visual aid that conveys its meaning through an image of an actual object. p. 393

**pie chart** A visual aid that divides a circle into wedges, representing percentages of the whole. p. 392

**pitch** The highness or lowness of one's voice. p. 344

**polychronic** The use of time that emphasizes flexible schedules in which multiple tasks are pursued at the same time. p. 189

**post hoc fallacy** Fallacious reasoning that mistakenly assumes that one event causes another because they occur sequentially. p. 417

**power** The ability to influence others' thoughts and/or actions. p. 290

**power distance** The degree to which members of a group are willing to accept a difference in power and status. p. 83

**pragmatic rules** Rules that govern how people use language in veryday interaction. p. 105

**prejudice** An unfairly biased and intolerant attitude toward others who belong to an out-group. p. 96

**presenting self** The image a person presents to others. It may be identical to or different from the perceived and ideal selves. See also *Face*. p. 62

**probe** An interjection, silence, or brief remark designed to open up or direct an interviewee. p. A-7

**problem census** A technique used to equalize participation in groups when the goal is to identify important issues or problems. Members first put ideas on cards, which are then compiled by a leader to generate a comprehensive statement of the issue or problem. p. 307

**problem orientation** A supportive style of communication in which the communicators focus on working together to solve their problems instead of trying to impose their own solutions on one another. p. 244

**problem-solution pattern** An organizing pattern for a speech that describes an unsatisfactory state of affairs and then proposes a plan to remedy the problem. p. 360

**procedural norms** Norms that describe rules for the group's operation. p. 274

**prompting** Using silence and brief statements of encouragement to draw out a speaker. p. 159

**proposition of fact** A claim bearing on issue in which there are two or more sides of conflicting factual evidence. p. 409

**proposition of policy** A claim bearing on issue that involves adopting or rejecting a specific course of action. p. 409

**proposition of value** A claim bearing on issue involving the worth of some idea, person, or object. p. 409

**provisionalism** A supportive style of communication in which the sender expresses a willingness to consider the other person's position. p. 245

**proxemics** The study of how people and animals use space. p. 187

**pseudolistening** An imitation of true listening in which the receiver's mind is elsewhere. p. 138

**public communication** Communication that occurs when a group becomes too large for all members to contribute. It is characterized by an unequal amount of speaking and by limited verbal feedback. p. 13

**public distance** One of Hall's four distance zones, extending outward from 12 feet. p. 187

**purpose statement** A complete sentence that describes precisely what a speaker wants to accomplish. p. 327

**qualitatively interpersonal communication** Interaction in which people treat one another as unique individuals, regardless of the context in which the interaction occurs or the number of people involved. This concept contrasts with impersonal communication. See also *Contextually interpersonal communication*. p. 203

**questioning** A style of helping in which the receiver seeks additional information from the sender. Some questioning responses are really disguised advice. p. 144

**race** A social construct originally created to explain differences between people whose ancestors originated in different regions of the world—Africa, Asia, Europe, and so on. p. 85

**rate** The speed at which a speaker utters words. p. 343

**receiver** One who notices and attends to a message. p. 8

**reductio ad absurdum fallacy** Fallacious reasoning that unfairly attacks an argument by extending it to such extreme lengths that it looks ridiculous. p. 416

**referent power** The ability to influence others by virtue of the degree to which one is liked or respected. p. 291

**reflected appraisal** The influence of others on one's self-concept. p. 43

**reflecting** Listening that helps the person speaking hear and think about the words just spoken. p. 159

**reinforcement stage** A stage in problem-solving groups when members endorse the decision they have made. p. 306

**relational listening** A listening style that is driven primarily by the concern to build emotional closeness with the speaker. p. 148

**relational message** A message that expresses the social relationship between two or more individuals. p. 205

**relative words** Words that gain their meaning by comparison. p. 115

**remembering** The act of recalling previously introduced information. Recall drops off in two phases: short term and long term. p. 137

**residual message** The part of a message a receiver can recall after short- and long-term memory loss. p. 137

**respect** The degree to which we hold others in esteem. p. 205

**responding** Providing observable feedback to another person's behavior or speech. p. 136

**reward power** The ability to influence others by the granting or promising of desirable consequences. p. 290

**richness** A term used to describe the abundance of nonverbal cues that add clarity to a verbal message. p. 17

**roles** The patterns of behavior expected of group members. p. 276

**rule** An explicit, officially stated guideline that governs group functions and member behavior. p. 274

**salience** How much weight we attach to a particular person or phenomenon. p. 78

**selection** The perceptual act of attending to some stimuli in the environment and ignoring others. p. 48

**selection interview** Interview in which a candidate is evaluated for a new position—either initial employment, promotion, or reassignment. p. A-8

**selective listening** A listening style in which the receiver responds only to messages that interest him or her. p. 139

**self-concept** The relatively stable set of perceptions each individual holds of himself or herself. p. 41

**self-disclosure** The process of deliberately revealing information about oneself that is significant and that would not normally be known by others. p. 220

**self-esteem** The part of the self-concept that involves evaluations of self-worth. p. 42

**self-fulfilling prophecy** A prediction or expectation of an event that makes the outcome more likely to occur than would otherwise have been the case. p. 46

**self-serving bias** The tendency to interpret and explain information in a way that casts the perceiver in the most favorable manner. p. 56

**semantic rules** Rules that govern the meaning of language as opposed to its structure. See also *Syntactic rules*. p. 105

**sender** The originator of a message. p. 8

**sex** A biological category such as male, female, or intersexed. p. 52

**sex role** The social orientation that governs behavior, in contrast to a person's biological gender. p. 126

**significant other** A person whose opinion is important enough to affect one's self-concept strongly. p. 43

**signpost** A phrase that emphasizes the importance of upcoming material in a speech. p. 389

**sincere question** A question posed with the genuine desire to learn from another person. See also *Counterfeit question*. p. 145

**situational leadership** A theory that argues that the most effective leadership style varies according to leader-member relations, the nominal leader's power, and the task structure. p. 282

**slang** Language used by a group of people whose members belong to a similar coculture or other group. p. 115

**slurring** The articulation error that involves overlapping the end of one word with the beginning of the next. p. 395

**small group communication** Communication within a group of a size such that every member can participate actively with the other members. p. 12

**social capital** The potential benefits that come from belonging to one or more social networks. p. 231

**social distance** One of Hall's four distance zones, ranging from 4 to 12 feet. p. 187

**social judgment theory** An explanation of attitude change that posits that opinions will change only in small increments and only when the target opinions lie within the receiver's latitudes of acceptance and noncommitment. p. 405

**social media** Digital communication channels used primarily for personal reasons, often to reach small groups of receivers. p. 15

**social norms** Group norms that govern the way members relate to one another. See also *Task norms*. p. 274

**social penetration model** A model describing how intimacy can be achieved via the breadth and depth of self-disclosure. p. 222

**social roles** Emotional roles concerned with maintaining smooth personal relationships among group members. Also termed "maintenance functions." p. 278

**sociogram** A graphic representation of the interaction patterns in a group. p. 275

**space pattern** An organizing plan in a speech that arranges points according to their physical location. p. 359

**specific purpose** The precise effect that the speaker wants to have on an audience. It is expressed in the form of a purpose statement. p. 327

**spiral** A reciprocal communication pattern in which each person's message reinforces the other's. p. 242

**spontaneity** A supportive communication behavior in which the sender expresses a message without any attempt to manipulate the receiver. p. 245

**stage hogging** A listening style in which the receiver is more concerned with making his or her own point than with understanding the speaker. p. 139

**statistic** Numbers arranged or organized to show how a fact or principle is true for a large percentage of cases. p. 369

**stereotyping** The perceptual process of applying exaggerated beliefs associated with a categorizing system. pp. 55 and 97

**strategy** A defense-arousing style of communication in which the sender tries to manipulate or trick a receiver; also, the general term for any type of plan, as in the plan for a persuasive speech. p. 244

**substitution** The articulation error that involves replacing part of a word with an incorrect sound. p. 344

**superiority** A type of communication that suggests one person is better than the other. p. 245

**supportive listening** The reception approach to use when others seek help for personal dilemmas. p. 153

**survey research** Information gathering in which the responses of a sample of a population are collected to disclose information about the larger group. p. 336

**symbol** An arbitrary sign used to represent a thing, person, idea, event, or relationship in ways that make communication possible. p. 7

**symbols** Arbitrary constructions that represent a communicator's thoughts. p. 103

**sympathy** Compassion for another's situation. See also *Empathy.* p. 59

**symposium** A discussion format in which participants divide the topic in a manner that allows each member to deliver in-depth information without interruption. p. 308

**synchronous communication** Communication that occurs in real time. p. 17

**syntactic rules** Rules that govern the ways in which symbols can be arranged as opposed to the meanings of those symbols. See also *Semantic rules.* p. 104

**target audience** That part of an audience that must be influenced in order to achieve a persuasive goal. p. 418

**task norms** Group norms that govern the way members handle the job at hand. See also *Social norms.* p. 274

**task-oriented listening** A listening style that is primarily concerned with accomplishing the task at hand. p. 143

**task roles** Roles group members take on in order to help solve a problem. See also *Social roles.* p. 278

**territory** Fixed space that an individual assumes some right to occupy. p. 188

**testimony** Supporting material that proves or illustrates a point by citing an authoritative source. p. 370

**thesis statement** A complete sentence describing the central idea of a speech. p. 328

**time pattern** An organizing plan for a speech based on chronology. p. 359

**topic pattern** An organizing plan for a speech that arranges points according to logical types or categories. p. 360

**trait theories of leadership** The belief that it is possible to identify leaders by personal traits, such as intelligence, appearance, or sociability. p. 280

**transactional communication model** A characterization of communication as the simultaneous sending and receiving of messages in an ongoing, irreversible process. p. 10

**transition** A phrase that connects ideas in a speech by showing how one relates to the other. p. 362

**uncertainty avoidance** The cultural tendency to seek stability and honor tradition instead of welcoming risk, uncertainty, and change. p. 83

**understanding** The act of interpreting a message by following syntactic, semantic, and pragmatic rules. p. 136

**value** A deeply rooted belief about a concept's inherent worth. p. 331

**virtual groups** People who interact with one another via mediated channels, without meeting face-to-face. p. 272

**visual aids** Graphic devices used in a speech to illustrate or support ideas. p. 392

**visualization** A technique for behavior rehearsal (e.g., for a speech) that involves imagining the successful completion of the task. p. 340

**vocal citation** A simple, concise, spoken statement of the source of your evidence. p. 388

**Web 2.0** A term used to describe how the Internet has evolved from a one-way medium into a "masspersonal" phenomenon. p. 15

**wheel network** A communication network in which a gatekeeper regulates the flow of information from all other members. p. 276

**win–lose problem solving** An approach to conflict resolution in which one party reaches its goal at the expense of the other. p. 259

**win–win problem solving** An approach to conflict resolution in which the parties work together to satisfy all their goals. p. 260

**word chart** A visual aid that lists words or terms in tabular form in order to clarify information. p. 392

**working outline** A constantly changing organizational aid used in planning a speech. p. 355

**"you" language** Language that judges another person, increasing the likelihood of a defensive reaction. See also *Evaluative communication.* p. 244

# Credits

## PHOTOGRAPHS

**Page 2** Jody Horton; **4** Used with permission, Pensacola News Journal / pnj.com, Copyright 2012; **7** Alberto E. Rodriguez/Getty Images; **9** (AP Photo/Tsering Topgyal); **11** Tanya Davis; **12** Mel Yates/Getty Images; **13** (AP Photo/Daily Progress, Kaylin Bowers); **14** iStockphoto; **17** Four Teenagers Sitting in a Line/Masterfile; **18** (AP Photo/Marcio Jose Sanchez, File); **20** Photo courtesy of DePoe Barksdale Studios; **25** AllStar; **38** © Richard T. Norbis/Corbis; **40** (Rex Features via AP Images); **44** BEI Images; **46** The Kobal Collection at Art Resource, NY; **48** Shutterstock; **51** The Kobal Collection at Art Resource, NY; **55** AllStar; **58** (Rex Features via AP Images); **62** Jeff Kravitz/AMA2009/Getty Images; **63** Frazer Harrison/Getty Images; **69** © Robbie Cooper; **69** © caLLie cLine; **74** Gary Gay/Getty Images; **76** Robin Luo; **77** AllStar; **79** Peter "Hopper" Stone/©ABC/Getty Images; **82** Michael Buckner/Getty Images; **86** (Photo by Kyle Petrozza / PictureGroup / AP IMAGES), **89** AllStar; **90** AllStar; **92** AllStar; **94** (AP Photo/Warner Bros., Michael Rozman, File); **100** Travelif/Punchstock ; **102** Used with permission from Meiga Loho-Noya and Zac Hughes; **103** The Kobal Collection at Art Resource, NY; **105** Eric McCandless/©ABC/Getty Images; **109** AllStar; **113** AllStar; **114** © Todd Elert; **119** Bravo/Getty Images; **121** iStockphoto; **124** AllStar; **128** AllStar; **132** Shutterstock; **134** © Harvey Wang, used with permission by Dave Isay; **138** AllStar; **143** Bravo/Getty Images; **152** Randy Holmes/©ABC/Getty Images; **153** The Kobal Collection at Art Resource, NY; **156** AllStar; **158** Fotosearch; **166** Nathalie Michel © Abacana / AgenceImages / Getty Images; **168** Thom Gossom Jr.; **170** AllStar; **171** *The Hackensack Record*; **182** AllStar; **185** The Kobal Collection at Art Resource, NY; **187** Veer; **189** Photo by: Caroline Seidel/picture-alliance/dpa/AP Images; **189** Photo by: Caroline Seidel/picture-alliance/dpa/AP Images; **196** Ernst Haas/ Getty Images; **198** (AP Photo/Matt Sayles); **199** Ethan Miller/Staff/Getty Images; **201** CBS / Getty Images; **202** (Photo by Evan Agostini/Invision/AP); **211** Fox/Getty Images; **215** AllStar; **116** AllStar; **230** Andrew Eccles/©ABC/Getty Images; **236** Shutterstock; **238** © Steve Niedorf 2012, Used with permission of Kevin Curwick; **242** (Photo by Todd Williamson/Invision/AP); **246** Rex USA; **253** AllStar; **256** (AP Photo/Matt Sayles); **257** (AP Photo/Matt Sayles); **266** suedhang/Punchstock; **268** (AP Photo/Denis Farrell); **271** CBS/Getty Images; **273** CBS Photo Archive/Getty Images; **276** AllStar; **285** Fox/Getty Images; **288** Hannes Magerstaedt/Getty Images; **296** Sharon Green/Getty Images; **298** Susie Wee; **299** AllStar; **302** AllStar; **307** NBC/Getty Images; **311** The Kobal Collection at Art Resource, NY; **316** NBC/Getty Images; **324** Shutterstock; **326** Used with permission from Adora Svitak; **329** AllStar; **332** (AP Photo/Rich Pedroncelli); **333** The Kobal Collection at Art Resource, NY; **337** Gregg DeGuire/Getty Images; **341** The Kobal Collection at Art Resource, NY; **347** Anne Frank Fonds-Basel/ Anne Frank House/Getty Images; **347** Austin Winters, Bacon Boy; **352** Shutterstock; **354** ©Mark R. Wegener, used with permission of Curt Casper; **360** (Copyright Bettmann/Corbis / AP Images); **365** AllStar; **371** AllStar; **378** Frederick M. Brown/Stringer/Getty Images; **380** Used with permission of ShaoLan Hsueh; **383** (Kyodo via AP Images); **387** (AP Photo/Keystone/Jean-Christophe Bott); **395** Fiona Hanson/AP Images for SapientNitro; **402** Kevork Djansezian/Getty Images; **404** Used with permission of Tunette Powell; **410** (Rex Features via AP Images); **414** Adam Taylor/©ABC/Getty Images; **418** (AP Photo/United Nations, Rick Bajornas); **430** iStockphoto.

## CARTOONS

**Page 5** © The New Yorker Collection 1984 Warren Miller from cartoonbank.com. All Rights Reserved. **15** © Tribune Media Services, Inc. All Rights Reserved. Reprinted with permission. **16** © Alex Gregory / The New Yorker Collection / www.cartoonbank.com. **21** Mick Stevens / www.cartoonbank.com. **21** CALVIN and HOBBES © 1994 Watterson. Distributed by UNIVERSAL PRESS SYNDICATE. Reprinted with permission. All Rights Reserved. **47** © The New Yorker Collection 1991 Ed Frascino from cartoonbank.com. All Rights Reserved. **52** © Edward Koren / The New Yorker Collection / www.cartoonbank.com. **59** © Peter Steiner/The New Yorker Collection / www.cartoonbank.com. **60** © The New Yorker Collection 1997 William Steig from cartoonbank .com. All Rights Reserved. **87** © Paul Noth / The New Yorker Collection / www.cartoonbank.com. **112** © Drew Dernavich / The New Yorker Collection / www.cartoonbank.com. **121** © 2000 Leo Cullum from cartoon bank.com. All Rights Reserved. **127** ©ZITS ©2013 Zits Partnership, Dist. By King Features. **136** ZITS © 2003 Zits Partnership, Dist. By King Features. **139** © Scott Adams / Dist. by United Feature Syndicate, Inc. **141** CALVIN and HOBBES © Watterson. Reprinted with permission of UNIVERSAL PRESS SYNDICATE. All Rights Reserved. **147** © 1997 Ted Goff www.tedgoff.com. **173** DILBERT © Scott Adams/Dist. By United Feature Syndicate, Inc. **178** DILBERT © Scott Adams/Dist. By United Feature Syndicate, Inc. **183** © Alex Gregory / The New Yorker Collection / www.cartoonbank.com. **207** © Cartoonbank.com. **213** ZITS ©2006 Zits Partnership, Dist. By King Features. **244** © Reprinted by special permission of North America Syndicate. **259** © Leo Cullum/The New Yorker Collection / www.cartoonbank.com. **270** THE FAR SIDE © 1987 FARWORKS, INC. Used by permission. All Rights Reserved. **318** © Original Artist. Reproduction rights obtainable from www.Cartoon Stock.com. **331** © Robert Weber/The New Yorker Collection /www .cartoonbank.com. **370** DILBERT © Scott Adams, Inc./Dist. By United Feature Syndicate, Inc. **384** © The New Yorker Collection 1987 James Stevenson from cartoonbank.com. All Rights Reserved. **391** By permission of Leigh Rubin and Creators Syndicate, Inc. **397** DILBERT © Scott Adams, Inc./Dist. By United Feature Syndicate, Inc.

## TEXT, TABLES, AND FIGURES

**Page 17** "Satisfaction Scores for Selected Communication Media." Adapted from A. J. Flanagan, "IM Online: Instant Messaging Use Among College Students." *Communication Research Reports* 22 (2005): 173–187. **19** "Choosing a Communication Channel." Adapted from R. B. Adler and J. M. Elmhorst, Communicating at Work: Principles and Practices for Business and the Professions, 10th ed. (New York: McGraw-Hill, 2010), p. 29. **63** "Self-Selected Adjectives Describing Perceived and Presenting Selves of College Students." Adapted from C. M. Shaw and R. Edwards, "Self-Concepts and Self-Presentations of Males and Females: Similarities and Differences," Communication Reports 10 (1997): 55–62. **84** "Managing Identity and Coming Out" by J. C. Rivas. **79** Adapted from F. Trompenaars. (2012). *Riding the Waves of Culture*, 3rd ed. New York: McGraw-Hill, p. 67. **80** "The Self in Individualistic and Collectivistic Cultures." Adapted by Sandra Sudweeks from Triandis, H. C. (1990). Cross-cultural studies of individualism and collectivism. In J. Berman (Ed.), Nebraska symposiumon motivation (pp. 41–133). Lincoln: University of Nebraska Press; and Hall, E. T. (1959). Beyond culture. New York: Doubleday. **91** J. Harwood. (2007). *Understanding communication and aging: Developing knowledge and awareness.* Newbury Park, CA: Sage, p. 76. **95** Permission to use courtesy of Guo-Ming Chen. Chen, G.M., & Sarosta, W.J. (2000). The development and validation of the intercultural sensitivity scale. *Human Communication*, 3, 1–14. **141** Four Thought Patterns. Source: A. D. Wolvin and C. G. Coakley, Perspectives on Listening (Norwood, NJ: Ablex, 1993), p. 115. **145** Adapted with the author's permission from Bodie, G.D., Worthington, D.L., & Gearhart, C.G. (2013). The Revised Listening Styles Profile (LSP-R): Development and validation. *Communication Quarterly*, 61, 72–90. **169** Adapted from John Stewart and Gary D'Angelo, Together: Communicating Interpersonally, 2nd ed. (Reading, MA: Addison-Wesley, 1980), p. 22. Copyright © 1993 by McGraw-Hill. Reprinted/adapted by permission. **179** "Leakage of Nonverbal Clues to Deception." Based on material from Ekman, P. (1981). Mistakes When Deceiving. In Thomas A. Sebok and Robert Rosenthal (Eds.), *The Clever Hans Phenomenon: Communication with Horses, Whales, Apes and People* (pp. 269–278). New York: New York Academy of Sciences. **221** Adapted from V. J. Derlega and J. Grezlak, "Appropriateness of Self-Disclosure," in G. J. Chelune, ed., Self-Disclosure (San Francisco, CA: Jossey-Bass, 1979). **227** Adapted from A. L. Vangelisti, J. P. Caughlin, and L. Timmerman, "Criteria for Revealing Family Secrets." Communication Monographs 68 (2001): 1–27. **229** "Some Reasons for Lying." Adapted from categories originally presented in C. Camden, M. T. Motley, and A. Wilson, "White Lies in Interpersonal Communication: A Taxonomy and Preliminary Investigation of Social Motivations." Western Journal of Speech Communication 48 (1984): 315. **241** "Distancing Tactics." Adapted from J. A. Hess, "Distance Regulation in Personal Relationships: The Development of a Conceptual Model and a Test of Representational Validity." Journal of Social and Personal Relationships 19 (2002): 663–683. **245** Adapted with permission from The Assertive Woman © 1970, 1987, 1997, and 2000, by Stanlee Phelps and Nancy Austin, San Luis Obispo, CA: Impact, 1975, p. 11; and Gerald Piaget, American Orthopsychiatric Association, 1975. Further reproduction prohibited. **279** "Dysfunctional Roles of Group Members." From "Functional Roles of Group Members" and "Dysfunctional Roles of Group Members," adapted from Groups in Context: Leadership and Participation in Decision-Making Groups by Gerald Wilson and Michael Hanna, pp. 144–146. © 1986. Reprinted by permission of McGraw-Hill Companies, Inc. **281** Reprinted with permission of The Free Press, a division of Macmillan, Inc., from Stodgill's Handbook of Leadership, rev. ed., by Bernard M. Bass. Copyright © 1974, 1981 by The Free Press. **284** The Leadership Grid® Source: The Leadership Grid® Figure from Leadership Dilemmas–Grid Solutions, by Robert R. Blake and Anne Adams McCanse (Houston: Gulf Publishing Co.), p. 29. Copyright © 1991 by Scientific Methods, Inc. Reproduced by permission of the owners. **285** "Situational Leadership Behavior." From Management of Organizational Behavior, 8th edition, © 2001. Adapted/reprinted with permission of Center for Leadership Studies, Escondido, CA 92025. All Rights Reserved. **291** "Methods for Acquiring Power in Small Groups." Adapted from J. Dan Rothwell, In Mixed Company: Small Group Communication, 3rd ed. (Fort Worth, TX: Harcourt Brace, 1998), pp. 252–272. Reprinted with permission of Wadsworth, an imprint of the Wadsworth Group, a division of Thomson Learning. Fax 800-730-2215. **304** Adapted from research summarized in S. A. Wheelan, D. Murphy, E. Tsumaura, and S. F. Kline, "Member Perceptions of Internal Group Dynamics and Productivity." Small Group Research 29 (1998): 371–393. **306** "Cyclical Stages in an Ongoing Problem-Solving Group." From John K. Brilhart, Gloria J. Galanes, and Katherine Adams, Effective Group Discussion, 10th ed. (New York: McGraw-Hill, 2001), p. 289. **315** Adapted from "Adapting Problem-Solving Methods," Effective Group Discussion, 10th ed., John Brilhart and Gloria Galanes, p. 291. Copyright © 2001. Reprinted by permission of McGraw-Hill Companies, Inc. **347** Adora Svitak, "What Adults Can Learn from Kids." used with permission of Adora Svitak. **361** Jaffe, C. (2007. *Public Speaking: Concepts and skills for a diverse society* (5th ed.). Boston: Wadsworth, © 2007. Reprinted with the permission of Wadsworth, an imprint of the Wadsworth Group, a division of Thomson Learning. **374** Curt Casper, "Survivor Support." Used with permission of Curt Casper. **393** Adapted from graphjam.com. **394** IDC report" Extracting Value from Chaos" 6/11. **398** ShaoLan Hsueh, "Learn to Read Chinese . . . with Ease!" Used with permission of ShaoLan Hsueh. **408** "Unethical Communication Behaviors." Adapted from Mary Klaaren Andersen, "An Analysis of the Treatment of Ethos in Selected Speech Communication Textbooks" (unpublished dissertation, University of Michigan, 1979), pp. 244–247. **423** Used with permission of Tunette Powell. **A-13** Based on research reported by Einhorn, L.J. (1981, July). An inner view of the job interview: An investigation of successful communicative behaviors. *Communication Education, 30*, 217–228.

# Index